A
Glossary
to the
Delaware Publications
of
Ira D. Blanchard

by
Miles Beckwith
and
Ives Goddard

Mundart Press

2021

Copyright © 2021 by Joshua Jacob Snider
Mundart Press, 807 Howard Street, Petoskey MI 49770

All rights reserved. No part of this book may be reproduced or
transmitted in any form or by any means, electronic or mechanical,
including photocopying, recording, or by any information storage
and retrieval system, without permission in writing from the publisher.

The publisher hereby grants such permission to the Delaware Tribe of
Indians and the Delaware Nation of Western Oklahoma for any tribal
educational or cultural purpose.

A publication of the Recovering Voices Program of the Smithsonian
Institution, supported in part by a gift from the Shoniya Fund.

Publisher's Cataloguing-in-Publication Data

Names: Beckwith, Miles, 1959- compiler. | Goddard, Ives, 1941- compiler

Title: A glossary to the Delaware publications of Ira D. Blanchard / by Miles Beckwith and Ives Goddard.

Description: Petoskey MI : Mundart Press, 2021. | Includes bibliographical references

Identifiers: ISBN: 9780990334477 (paperback) | LCCN: 2021911781

Subjects: LCSH: Blanchard, Ira D., 1808-1872. | Delaware language--Glossaries, vocabularies, etc. | Algonquian languages--Glossaries, vocabularies, etc. | Delaware Tribe of Indians--Language-- Glossaries, vocabularies, etc. | Delaware Nation, Oklahoma--Language--Glossaries, vocabularies, etc.

Classification: LCC: PM1033 .B43 2021 | DDC: 497/.345--dc23

Contents

Preface	v
Introduction	vii
References	xi
Abbreviations	xiii
Glossary	1
Table of Gospel Locations	245

Preface

I began working with Ives as he was in the final stages of his work on Ira Blanchard's *A Harmony of the Four Gospels in Delaware* (now published as Blanchard and Conner 2021). Ives supplied me with several word lists which served as the foundation for this glossary. As I read through the *Harmony*, I recorded each instance of each word and then checked those words against those lists and against my own Unami word list (compiled from published sources during my 2011-2012 sabbatical). I later expanded the glossary to include words from Blanchard's three primers and words from the grammar that Ives was writing concurrently (now published as Goddard 2021; noted as "Gr." below). Eventually, I included words from other sources and speakers to fill out entries; however, this book is not intended as a comprehensive lexicon of the language.

Ives read through drafts of the glossary and made many corrections and additions. He added most of the comparative data as well as most of the discussions of Blanchard's orthography and spelling. He rewrote many entries especially those on particles and preverbs, and he added the bulk of the comments on usage and idiom. No doubt much of the value in this work comes from his insights and observations, both those I added from his published and unpublished works, and those that he added in his own hand. Nevertheless, although Ives corrected many of my errors and misunderstandings, it is likely that some remain, and I take responsibility for those (as well as other typos and omissions).

Many individuals have helped me over the years in my studies of Algonquian languages. I would like to express my deepest thanks to my late mother, Lois Jean Messenger Wright (1934-2020), who passed away during this most difficult year. She was a historian of New England culture who first introduced me to the study of those languages when she handed me a copy of William Jones' "Algonquian [Fox]" and asked me if I could "make any sense of this." I would also like to thank the members of the Ojibwe community who allowed me to follow through on my study of Algonquian during my stay in Northern Michigan from 1998-2001.

A number of scholars have helped me in my study of language, and it would not be possible to thank them all, but I would like to express my appreciation to Brent Vine, who not only advised my thesis, but also gave me all of his notes on Meskwaki and first introduced me to Ives. I should also thank the late Floyd Lounsbury for his help and encouragement and the many scholars who have responded to my many queries and questions with patience, with special thanks to David Costa, Raymond Whritenour, and the late Emmon Bach.

Many others have contributed to this project. I would like thank those who have given me support while I worked on this project with special thanks to my colleagues at Iona College, especially for the financial support during my 2011-2012 sabbatical. I would like to thank the members of the English Department and especially Dorothy Brophy for her help and encouragement, and I would further like to thank the very helpful staff of the Iona College Library, with special thanks to Ed Helmrich in Inter-Library Loan.

Finally, and most importantly, I would like to thank my wife, Mary McCune, for her unending support while I worked on this project.

Miles Beckwith
New York City, 2021

Introduction

The following is a glossary of the Unami dialect of the Delaware (Lenape) language as preserved in the publications of Ira D. Blanchard (prepared with James Conner, Charles Journeycake and possibly others) as printed in several volumes between 1834 and 1842: the *Harmony of Gospels* (Blanchard [and Conner] 1837, now re-edited as Blanchard and Conner 2021), and the three Delaware primers (1834a, 1834b, and 1842, now re-edited in Blanchard 2021). Blanchard's edtion of *Delaware Hymns* (Blanchard 1836 and later reprints) has not been re-edited, and its vocabulary has not been included in this volume.

We have tried to make this book as user-friendly as possible, but it has been a difficult challenge. A glossary of Unami faces a number of special difficulties because the language is unusually ill-suited to alphabetic listing. In Unami Delaware, as in other Algonquian languages, pronominal elements are prefixed to nouns and verbs (and even occasionally particles), but while in most Algonquian languages, this process is more or less transparent, in Unami, changes in the stress pattern of words often produce doublets that are quite different in surface appearance. For example, hít·ukw 'tree' (anim.), 'stick' (inan.) and the possessed nəmí·tkəm 'my stick' come from the same underlying form |məhtəkw|, but because of a number of phonological and morphological processes, the resulting surface forms differ in appearance. These variations are further compounded by initial change (IC; Gr. §4.6) and the pervasive use of reduplication in the language; e.g., pəmə́ske· 'he walks'; ahpá·mske·p 'he had walked around' (Ra+; see Gr. §5.4); pep·a·mská·č·i·k 'those that passed by' (Ra+; IC). The general principle of this glossary has been to combine multiple stems into a single entry whenever possible, as here under hít·ukw and pəməska·-, and then to arrange those stems in an alphabetic list with definitions, grammatical information, and text locations. Extensive cross-references direct the reader from divergent surface forms to the main entry for each set of stems.

For an overview of the phonemic system of the language and the representation of those sounds, see Gr. §2.1 and following. Those interested in further details should consult the audio files available in both the "Lenape Talking Dictionary" <https://www.talk-lenape.org/> and in sound files on the Smithsonian website <https://repository.si.edu/handle/10088/17269>. Forms from Blanchard's texts are cited in phonemic orthography throughout (see Gr. §2.2 for the conventions), but in some cases, Blanchard's original spelling is also noted in angled brackets, e.g., ahkwí·an ⟨aqeun⟩ 'blanket'. Delaware forms in Unami and Munsee from other sources have generally been standardized, e.g., /ya·k·á·ɔn/ for Voegelin's ⟨ya·ḱá·ᴜn⟩ "shade house" (1946:135) or Munsee /ta·xkše·nkwe·n-/ 'hold open the eye of' for O'Meara's ⟨taaxkshéengwéeneew⟩ (dict.), but forms from older lexicographic sources (which contain forms from different Delaware dialects) have not been phonemicized and are printed as they appear, again in angled brackets, e.g. ⟨chowasquall⟩ 'old dried grass' (Z.), and occasionally the same convention is used for more modern sources as well, e.g., ⟨amàxke⟩ "he sops up (food; eating)" (LTD). When the phonetics of Blanchard's spellings are unclear, the word is listed with an initial obelus "†": this is especially common in non-Delaware words whose phonetic realities are to some extent unrecoverable, especially in Biblical proper and place names, e.g., †e·pəlíham 'Abraham' ⟨Rplivam(-)⟩ 'Abraham' or †í·čipt ⟨Ehipt⟩ 'Egypt', but occasional also for Unami words when we lack sufficient evidence to confirm the exact phonetic shape, e.g., †thakaé·t·u ⟨tvakartw⟩ 'in a short time'.

The alphabetical order of the glossary is as follows:

a, a·, č, č·, e, e·, ə, h, i, i·, k, k·, l, m, n, o, o·, ɔ, ɔ·, p, p·, s, s·, š, š·, t, t·, u, w, x, x·, y.

The glossary includes virtually all the words from Blanchard's texts although not every instance of every word is listed, and the glossary is not a concordance in scope. Still, for each word, a representative sample of forms is given, and we have tried to include examples that were most typical both in formation and usage as well as forms that were unusual or idiomatic. For many forms with unusual morphology, the grammar (Goddard 2021) offers more detailed discussions. Although we have tried to make the glossary as detailed as possible, there has been no attempt to make this a complete record of the language, and the nature of the texts included naturally circumscribes the vocabulary under review. Further, the glossary is primarily a dictionary of words and does not attempt to catalogue the complexity of stem forming morphemes. Nevertheless, some initial elements do have separate entries, especially when their presence explains morphological alternation in multiple forms, e.g., čhɔ·pᵒ (-čɔhɔ·pᵒ) 'into water, dip', and many entries contain information on word formation with cross-references to derivational discussions in the grammar.

Each entry lists multiple examples of each word organized according to the variant stems as noted above: 1) variant metrical forms after prefixation—these are marked with an initial hyphen (e.g., -t-ač·inkxe·taw-); 2) forms with initial change; and 3) reduplicated forms (indicated by a formula for the reduplication beginning with [R]; see Gr. §5.4). In some cases, an underlying form (in |..|) is listed last. Many citations show no variant forms, but some show all of the above, and some stems show multiple types of reduplication, e.g., ahpi·- 'be, stay in a place' (-t-ap·i·-, e·p·i·-, i·ahpi·- [Rī+], -ihahpi·- [Rih+], ehahpi·- [Rih+; IC], a·yahpi·- [Rā+], |apī-|). Note, however, that some variations (especially those in the length of the final vowel, see Gr. §2.10a) are not treated as separate stems, and some atypical variations are noted with "~", e.g., the -nihəl- ~ -nil- from nhil- 'kill' or the extremely irregular variations in wum- 'come from' (wum- ~ um-, we·m- ~ wen-, etc.).

Dependent stems (Gr. §4.2b) are generally listed with the first person singular prefix, e.g., nté· 'my heart' (alphabetized just before †nté·pit 'David'), but those with no first person form attested are listed with the third person prefix, e.g., wəlúnkwink 'under his arm'. All other possessed forms are listed with their unpossessed counterparts without pronominal prefixes (e.g., nči·čánkəm 'my spirit' is listed under čí·čankw 'spirit, soul').

For nouns and pronouns, the most unmarked form (e.g. the singular or proximate) heads the entry. The order of the remaining forms is as follows: proximate before obviative, singular before plural, older before more innovated, locative forms last. Possessed forms follow unpossessed and use the same general order but with the forms divided by possessors in person order (1st, 2nd, 3rd, followed by the plurals). In general, semi-colons separate individual examples, but commas divide forms that are grammatically identical (e.g. ahpó·nal, ahpó·na "loaves").

Particles are cited in their simplest form with reduplicated particles listed under their unreduplicated counterparts, e.g., mé·či (mi·mé·či) 'now, already'. Particles which only occur in enclitic position are listed with a double hyphen (equal sign) which is ignored in alphabetization, e.g., =k (listed as the first entry under **k**).

Verbs are in general cited by an endingless form with no accent and the shape of the unprefixed stem (the simple indicative or imperative for intransitive verbs and the absolute or imperative for transitive verbs). However, we have not invented forms without evidence, and so there are a very small number of forms listed under the prefixed stem (e.g., -kəphikamaw- 'shut

O2 off from') or listed under a given changed conjunct form (e.g., pe·mhakamí·k·e·k 'the world, the earth'). In the listing of verb forms, the unprefixed forms (including imperatives and unchanged conjuncts) precede prefixed forms; indicative forms precede subordinative. When multiple examples from the same mode are given, forms mostly follow the same person order as the nouns above, but a third singular often begins the listing, and sometimes forms were reordered for other reasons.

Verb forms beginning with an underlying |wə°|, are noted as having a prefixed form with an -o·° (e.g., wəlahəl- 'have', -o·lhat-: ko·lhátu 'you have it') which technically misdivides the morphemes (i.e., ko·lhátu is not from |*k-o·laht-|, but from |kə-wəlaht-|). Still, other notations would require more abstract representations which would depart from the surface forms; see the full discussion in the grammar (Gr. §2.10c with examples).

Whenever possible forms are collected under a single entry: reduplicated stems and derived stems are listed under the simplest stem; however, again, we have not invented unreduplicated forms, and so some orphaned forms are listed as they appear, e.g., kək·amo·kant- 'gnash (teeth)'. In a very small number of cases, reduplicated and non-reduplicated forms are separated (e.g., ahke·p·inkɔ·- 'be blind' and the isolated non-reduplicated form ke·p·inkɔ́·č·i·k 'the blind'). In the case of the words beginning with ahse° 'scatter', most are listed under **a** because they occur only with the reduplicated stem, but sehəla·- ~ ahsehəla·- (with non-reduplicated and reduplicated forms) is listed under **s**.

Verbs occurring in pairs are in most cases listed together (TA and TI; AI and II) although a few very divergent forms have separate listings, e.g., hwil- TA 'get from {smwh}' is listed under **h**, while wənt- TI(3) 'get from {smwh}' is listed under **w** (but even these two forms come from the same root |wəm-|; see Gr. 2.50a, 5.4f. for the phonological origins of this paradigm split). Derived stems (including diminutives and collectives) are generally joined to the simple stem. In the lemma, the switch between stem pairs is marked with an *m*-dash (—); in the following text, the section for each stem type is marked with a square bullet (▪). Three other bullets are used: a round bullet (•) indicates a change of stem shape; a diamond bullet (♦) indicates a comment on usage or idiom; an arrow bullet (▶) directs readers to a cross reference or other note.

For each listed stem, examples from Blanchard's texts follow with translations and citation locations. Whenever possible, we have tried to give at least two examples of each variant stem, and again, whenever possible, we have tried to give at least two or more instances of each form cited. Although we have frequently added "etc." to indicate that there are many additional examples of a given form, the lack of "etc." should not be taken as indicating that a given listing is complete.

Translations in general conform to those in the text itself or in the grammar although we have in some cases simplified the capitalization and punctuation, and some translations needed to be reworded to reflect forms cited in isolation outside of their broader context. Enclitics in examples are generally left untranslated if their scope is or includes parts of a sentence that are not included. For all sources other than Blanchard, the glossing follows the original in content, but we have standardized the format and punctuation (e.g., ⟨Atenkpatton⟩ 'to quench fire' for B&A's "**Atenkpatton** to quench fire").

The glossary provides only minimal parsing of forms: we have occasionally added "IC" ("initial change"), "obv." (obviative) or other parsing, but these are used sparingly and mostly only to avoid confusion. The translations provided should disambiguate most forms, and many citations are accompanied by a further reference to the relevant section in the grammar. Still, readers should be familiar with the basic morphemes of Delaware, especially the person prefixes and the obviative and locative endings with their various allomorphs. Frequent cross-references will help steer readers to correct entries, but these cross-references assume a degree of sophistication. For instance, tɔ́p·i·n 'he is here (sbd.)' is glossed under the verb ahpi·-: a cross-reference redirects the reader from -apº to ahpº, but the reader must be aware of 1) the third person prefix |wə-|, 2) the rule governing the insertion of -t- before forms with a vowel, and 3) change of -a- > -ɔ- after the w- and the frequent subsequent loss of w- (see especially Gr. §2.13f.).

Passages and translations are followed by a citation to the source text in parentheses mostly to one of Blanchard's texts, but sometimes also to the grammar and frequently to later speakers as recorded in one of several sources (most frequently in Goddard's or Voegelin's published and unpublished works, or in the "Lenape Talking Dictionary"). These speakers are identified whenever possible and noted by initials (see the abbreviations below). For Blanchard's texts, Bible passages in the *Harmony* are cited by chapter and verse. For passages that have multiple sources (e.g., Mk 2.12, Lk 5.25), only the first source is listed and an ampersand is added in the entry (e.g., Mk 2.12&). Locations are generally noted in text order—not in standard *New Testament* order (e.g., Jn 1.4 [Blanchard, Chapter 1] precedes Mt 4.18 [Blanchard, Chapter 24], etc.). The Table of Locations at the end of the Glossary gives Blanchard's page and chapter numbers which correspond to the Bible chapter and verse locations. References to Blanchard's primers are listed by date without other attribution (i.e., 1834a, 1834b, 1842) followed by the page number. In the 1834a text, some paragraphs are numbered, and those numbers are included after the page number separated by a period; for the latter two primers, paragraph numbers have been added; these are editorial and not part of the printed text, but they are included in the text of the primers as printed in Blanchard (2021).

References

For full bibliographical information on Blanchard's publications, see the Bibliography in the Introduction to the edition of his translation of the *Harmony* [Blanchard and Conner 2021].

Alford, Thomas Wildcat. 1929. *The Four Gospels of Our Lord Jesus Christ in Shawnee Indian Language*. Xenia, Ohio: W.A. Galloway. (Normalized text prepared by Carl Schaefer, mss. version 12-13-2020).

Blanchard, Ira D. 1834a. *Linapi'e Lrkvekun*. Shawnee Mission: J. Meeker.

Blanchard, Ira D. 1834b. *Linapie Lrkvekun, Ave Apwatuk*. Shawannoe Mission: J. Meeker.

Blanchard, Ira D. 1836. [*Delaware Hymns*. McMurtrie and Allen 1930: 147, no. 45]. Reprinted as *Hymns in the Delaware Language*: [1] Herald Steam Printing House, Wyandott, Kansas, 1875; [2] Journal Steam Printing House, Coffeyville, Kansas, 1894.

Blanchard, Ira D. [and James Conner]. 1837 [completed in 1839]. *The history of our Lord and Saviour Jesus Christ, by the Rev. Samuel Lieberkuhn.* Translated by I.D. Blanchard. Shawanoe Baptist Mission: J. Meeker [and John G. Pratt].

Blanchard, Ira D., [and Charles Journeycake]. 1842. *The Delaware First Book*. Second Edition. Shawanoe Baptist Mission: John G. Pratt.

Blanchard, Ira D. 2021. *The Delaware Primers of Ira D. Blanchard*, ed. by Ives Goddard and Miles Beckwith. Petoskey, Mich.: Mundart Press.

Blanchard, Ira D., and James Conner. 2021. *A Harmony of the Four Gospels in Delaware: The Translation by Ira D. Blanchard and James Conner (1837-1839)*, ed. by Ives Goddard. Petoskey, Mich.: Mundart Press.

Brinton, Daniel G., and Albert S. Anthony, eds. 1889. *A Lenâpé-English Dictionary*. Philadelphia: The Historical Society of Pennsylvania. [Second title page has "1888."].

Campanius, Johan. 1696. *Lutheri Catechismus Öfwersatt på American-Virginiske Språket*. Stockholm. [Facsimile reprint: *Martin Luther's Little Catechism translated into Algonquian Indian by Johannes Campanius.* With some notes by Isak Collijn. Stockholm–Uppsala, 1937.]

Cuoq, J.-A. 1886. *Lexique de la langue algonquine*. Montreal: J. Chapleau & Fils.

Denke, Christian Frederick. 2014. *The Gospel of John in Delaware*. Translated by Christian Frederick Denke, ed. by Raymond Whritenour. Butler, N.J.: Lenape Texts & Studies.

Goddard, Ives. 1974 [1975]. The Dutch Loan Words in Delaware. *A Delaware Indian Symposium*, ed. by Herbert C. Kraft, pp. 153-160. Pennsylvania Historical and Museum Commission, Anthropological Series 4.

Goddard, Ives. 1979. *Delaware Verbal Morphology: A Descriptive and Comparative Study*. New York and London: Garland Publishing, Inc.

Goddard, Ives. 1982. The Historical Phonology of Munsee. *International Journal of American Linguistics* 48.1: 16-48.

Goddard, Ives. 2013 [2014]. The Munsee of Charles Halfmoon's Translations. *Papers of the 41st Algonquian Conference*, ed. by Karl S. Hele and J. Randolph Valentine, pp. 81-119. Albany: SUNY Press.

Goddard, Ives. 2015. Three Nineteenth-Century Munsee Texts: Archaisms, Dialect Variation, and Problems of Textual Criticism, in *New Voices for Old Words*, ed. by David J. Costa, pp. 198-314. University of Nebraska Press.

Goddard, Ives. 2019. The Kansas Unami Writings of Ira D. Blanchard, Pioneering Algonquian Linguist. *Papers of the 48th Algonquian Conference*, ed. by Monica Macaulay and Margaret Noodin, pp. 87-106. East Lansing: Michigan State University Press.

Goddard, Ives. 2021. *A Grammar of Southern Unami Delaware (Lenape)*. Petoskey, Mich.: Mundart Press.

Goddard, Ives, and Kathleen J. Bragdon. 1988 [1989]. *Native Writings in Massachusett*. 2 vols. Memoirs of the American Philosophical Society 185. Philadelphia: The American Philosophical Society.

Lieberkühn, Samuel. 1823. *A Harmony of the Four Gospels, or the History of Our Lord and Saviour Jesus Christ.* Second edition revised. London: W. M'Dowall.

[Halfmoon, Charles.] 1852. *A series of catechisms.* Toronto: Thomas Hugh Bentley.

Heckewelder, John. 1819. An Account of the History, Manners, and Customs of the Indian Nations, Who Once Inhabited Pennsylvania and the Neighbouring States. *Transactions of the Historical & Literary Committee of the American Philosophical Society* 1:1-348.

Hewitt, J.N.B. 1896. [J.N.B. Hewitt vocabulary of Munsee obtained from John Armstrong at Cattaraugus, 1896.]. National Anthropological Archives ms. no. 15.

Hewson, John. 1993. *A Computer-Generated Dictionary of Proto-Algonquian.* Hull, Que.: Canadian Museum of Civilization.

Myers, Albert Cook. 1937. *William Penn: His Own Account of The Lenni Lenape or Delaware Indians*, 1682. Moylan, Pa.

Nelson, William. 1894. *The Indians of New Jersey.* Paterson, N.J.: Press Printing and Publishing Company.

O'Meara, John. 1996. *Delaware-English / English-Delaware Dictionary.* Toronto: University of Toronto Press.

Speck, Frank G. 1937. *Oklahoma Delaware Ceremonies, Feasts and Dances.* Memoirs of the American Philosophical Society, vol. 7. Philadelphia.

Voegelin, Carl F. 1946. Delaware, an Eastern Algonquian Language. *Linguistic Structures of Native America*, by Harry Hoijer et al., pp. 130–157. Viking Fund Publications in Anthropology 6. New York.

[Wampum, John B., and H.C. Hogg.] 1847. *Morning and Evening Prayers.* London: SPCK.

Williams, Roger. 1936. *A Key into the Language of America. With an introduction by Howard M. Chapin.* Fifth edition. Providence: The Rhode Island and Providence Plantations Tercentenary Committee, Inc.

Wolley, Charles. 1902. *A Two Years' Journal in New York (1701).* Cleveland: The Burrows Brothers Company.

Zeisberger, David. 1776. *Essay of a Delaware-Indian and English Spelling-Book.* Philadelphia. Facsimile reprint by Arthur W. McGraw (1991).

Zeisberger, David. 1806. *Delaware Indian and English Spelling Book* [2nd edition]. Philadelphia.

Zeisberger, David. 1821. *The History of our Lord and Saviour Jesus Christ. ... By the Rev. Samuel Lieberkuhn, M.A. Translated into the Delaware Indian Language by the Rev. David Zeisberger.*

Zeisberger, David. 2014. *Zeisberger's Delaware Vocabulary of 1772.* Ed. by Raymond Whritenour. Butler, N.J.: Lenape Texts & Studies.

Zeisberger, David. 2016. *Delaware Glossary.* Ed. by Ray Whritenour. Butler, N.J.: Lenape Texts & Studies.

Abbreviations

Abbreviations (grammatical terms and references)

A.	Albert Anthony
Acts	Acts of the Apostles
AGTV	agentive (see Gr. §5.6.l)
AI	animate intransitive (see Gr. §3.7e)
AI+O	AI stem taking a secondary object (transitivized AI; see Gr. §3.7f)
AN, AN, anim.	animate (see Gr. §3.2)
B	Blanchard (esp. Blanchard 1837[-1839])
B&A	Brinton and Anthony (1889)
CC	changed conjunct (see Gr. §4.6)
cf.	compare
CNJ	the conjunct indicative or PLAIN conjunct (see Gr. §4.6)
COLL, coll.	collective (see Gr. §5.8c)
CONT	continuative (continuative-attenuative) (see Gr. §5.4)
Cor	Corinthians
CS	changed subjunctive (see Gr. §4.6)
DIM, dim.	diminutive (see Gr. §5.5b, §5.8a)
dict.	O'Meara (1996), a Munsee dictionary
/e	emended text
EAb	Eastern Abenaki (esp. Penobscot dialect)
em.	emended, emendation, to be emended
EMPH	emphatic (see Gr. §3.6; §6.5d)
exc.	exclusive (see Gr. §3.6)
EXT	extended (see Gr. §5.4)
FI	future imperative (see Gr. §4.12d)
FOC	focus (see Gr. 5.24o)
FUT	future (see Gr. 5.24b)
Gr.	Grammar (Goddard 2021)
HAB	habitual (see Gr. §5.4)
Heb	Hebrews
HRSY	(evidential for hearsay account) (see Gr. 5.24g)
IC	initial change (see Gr. §4.6)
II	inanimate intransitive (see Gr. §3.7e)
Ill	Illinois
IMP, imp.	(ordinary) imperative (see Gr. §4.12a)
IN, IN, inan.	inanimate (see Gr. §3.2)
inc.	inclusive (see Gr. §3.6)
IND, ind.	independent indicative (see Gr. §4.4a)
indef.	indefinite (see Gr. §3.6)
INJ	injunctive (see Gr. §4.12c)
ital.	italics
Jn	John

KJV	King James Bible
L.	Lieberkühn
Lk	Luke
LOC	locative (see Gr. §4.2d)
Mah	Mahican
Mass	Massachusett
MEP	*Morning and Evening Prayers* (Wampum and Hogg 1847)
Mes	Meskwaki
MH	*A Collection of Hymns in Muncey and English* (Halfmoon 1874)
Mk	Mark
Mt	Matthew
ms.	manuscript
Mun	Munsee
Narr	Narragansett
NEG	negative (see Gr. §4.4c)
NF	noun final (see Gr. §5.1)
O1	primary object (see Gr. §3.7a)
O2	secondary object (see Gr. §3.7a)
OBL	oblique (see Gr. §3.7b)
obv., OBV	obviative (see Gr. §3.4)
OBV.POSS	obviative possessor (see Gr. §4.2a)
Oj	Ojibwe
om.	omitted
p	plural
P	particle (see Gr. §3.1a)
PA	Proto-Algonquian
PC	plain conjunct (see Gr. §4.6)
PEA	Proto–Eastern Algonquian
PERF	perfective
PL	plural reduplication (see Gr. §5.4)
pl.	plural
PN	prenoun (see Gr. §5.9)
PF	particle final (see Gr. §5.1)
poM	postmedial (see Gr. §5.2)
poR	postradical (= postinitial) (see Gr. §5.2)
POSS.TH	possessed theme (see Gr. §4.2)
PP	preparticle (see Gr. §5.9)
PPL, ppl.	participle (see Gr. §4.6)
PRES	presentational (see Gr. §6.5b; 6.10h-q)
PRET, pret.	preterite (see Gr. §4.4b)
prF	prefinal (see Gr. §5.2)
prM	premedial (§5.2)
PROH, proh.	prohibitive (negative imperative) (see Gr. §4.12b)
prox.	proximate (see Gr. §3.4)
PRST	present (see Gr. §4.8)
PST	past (see Gr. 5.24m)

Abbreviations

PV	preverb (see Gr. **§5.9**)
Q	question (see Gr. 5.24eh)
R	(abstract marker of reduplication formula; see Gr. **§5.4**)
redup.	reduplication (see Gr. **§5.4**)
REP	repetitive (repetitive-intensive) (see Gr. **§5.4**)
RSV	Revised Standard Version
s	singular
SB1	Spelling-Book, first edition (Zeisberger 1776)
SB2	Spelling Book, second edition (Zeisberger 1806)
s.b.	should be
SBD, sbd.	subordinative (see Gr. **§4.4a**)
SBJ	subjunctive (see Gr. **§4.6**)
sg	singular
Sh	Shawnee
smthg	something (place-holder for the complement of a relative root)
smwh	somewhere (place-holder for the complement of a relative root)
s.o.	someone (third person animate; 'him', 'her', or animate 'it')
/t	translation of line "/p"
TA	transitive animate (see Gr. **§3.7e**)
TA+O	TA taking a secondary object (double-object stem; see Gr. **§3.7f**)
TH	theme (see Gr. **§4.2a**, **§4.4d**)
TI	transitive inanimate (see Gr. **§3.7e**)
TI-O	TI stem not taking an object (see Gr. **§3.7f**)
VOC, voc.	vocative (see Gr. **§4.2f**)
Z.	Zeisberger (1887)
Z. 2014	Zeisberger (2014)

Abbreviations (speakers and other sources)

AD	Anna Davis
AP	Anna (pronounced "Annie") Parks
APh	Anderson Pheasant (Munsee)
B	Ira D. Blanchard
BF	Blanche French
BS	Bessie Snake (in LTD)
CH	Charles Halfmoon (Munsee)
CS	Cephas Snake (Munsee)
CW	James C. (Charlie) Webber
EJ	Enoch Jacobs (Munsee)
EJo	Emily Johnson (Munsee)
ER	Elijah Reynolds
FE	Frank Exendine
FF	Fred Fallleaf (in LTD)
FW	Freddie Washington
JA	John Armstrong (Munsee)
JH	John Huff (Munsee)
JM	Josephine Martinez (in LTD)
JN	Joe Noah (Munsee)
JP	Josephine Plake (Munsee)
LB	Lucy Blalock (in LTD)
LHW	Lillie Hoag Whitehorn (in LTD)
LTD	Lenape Talking Dictionary (http://www.talk-lenape.org)
ME	Martha Ellis
MR	Mary Riley (Munsee)
ND	Nora Dean (fieldnotes; "LTD ND" if in the LTD)
NP	Nicodemus Peters (Munsee)
OA	Ollie Anderson
RH	Rosanna Hopkins (Munsee)
RS	Rebecca Snake (Munsee)
SP	Stella Parton
V	C.F. Voegelin
VJ	Vester Jacobs (Munsee)
WL	Willie Longbone
WP	Winnie Poolaw
WS	Willie Snake (in LTD)
WT	Willard Thomas (LTD)

Symbols

*	(before a stem or word) Reconstructed for a protolanguage but not attested; conjectured correct spelling of a misprinted word.
*	(after a stem or word) Unattested shape or form (supported by other forms).
†	Phonemic shape conjectured.
º	Indicates part of word omitted (not necessarily at a morpheme boundary)
|..|	enclose the underlying form (§2.1)
/../	enclose a phonemic transcription (§2.1)
[..]	enclose a (more detailed or specific) phonetic transcription (§2.1 end); in lines /k, /kl, or /l these enclose untranslated words
⟨..⟩	enclose the exact spelling of the source
{..}	enclose the conventional gloss of an oblique complement (§3.7b)
(..)	enclose the pronominal gloss of the indefinite object (or inverse subject) of an absolute form

>	becomes (becoming), develops to, changes to, making the derivative
<	coming from
←	the realization of, the recategorized use of
-	separates the parts of a compound stem, or flags parts that are not contiguous
=	marks the following word as an enclitic (§5.3a)

Bullets

- ■ (square bullet)   marks the section for a stem type or the like
- • (round bullet)   indicates a change of stem shape
- ♦ (diamond bullet) indicates a comment on usage or related words
- ▶ (arrow bullet)   directs readers to a cross reference or other note

Person-marking

Persons: 1 first person; 1s first singular; 1p first plural exclusive; 12 first plural inclusive; 2 second person; 2s second singular; 2p second plural; 3 third person animate; 3s third person animate singular; 3p third person animate plural; 3´ third person animate obviative; 0 third person inanimate; 0s third person inanimate singular; 0p third person inanimate plural; X indefinite person.

Inflection for arguments: 3s third singular subject or possessor; 1s–2s first singular subject acting on second singular primary object; 3s–(0) third singular animate subject acting on inanimate object (absolute); 3s–0s third singular animate subject acting on third singular inanimate (objective); 3p–3´+0 third plural animate subject acting on third obviative primary object plus inanimate secondary object (objective).

a

aéhəle AN 'bird'; aehəlé·ɔk 'birds' (1842:6.7). ▸ Cf. ⟨Awehhelleu⟩ 'bird, fowl' (B&A 24 [A. "applied to large fowls, etc."]).

aésəs AN 'wild animal' (1842:8.1, 14.4; Gr. 2.77a); aesə́s·ak 'animals' (1834a:16, 1842:7.1, 9.2); aesə́s·a 'wild animals (obv.)' (Mk 1.13); aesəs·í·na 'animals (obv. pl.)' (ME; Gr. 4.12a); aesə́s·ink 'an animal (loc.)' (1834b:9.11).

aesəs·i·ke·- II 'be an abundance of animals': wiáki-aesəs·í·ke·p 'there was a great abundance of animals' (1834b:42.11); mé·či máta aesəs·i·ké·i 'there are no longer many game animals' (1834b:46.5); sé·ki-áləmi- máta yúkwe -aesəs·í·ke·k 'while there continues to be now no abundance of animals' (1834a:23.59).

ae·ke·- (e·e·ke·-, i·ae·ke·- [Rī+], |awēkē-|) AI(+O) 'use, ride': aé·ke· 'he is riding' (Mt 21.5); maxkahsə́na ae·ké·ɔk 'they used bricks' (1834b:19.3, 1842:9.8); ki·skəní·k·anak ae·ké·t·amo·kw 'let's cast lots' (*lit.*, 'use broken-off (sticks)'; Jn 19.24); ae·kénke 'when it (anim.) is ridden' (⟨yakifi⟩ 1834a:14); mwí·laxk tɔé·ke·n '(and) she used her hair' (Lk 7.38, Jn 12.3); ná tɔe·ké·li·n 'then he (obv.) rode it (animal)' (Mt 21.7&); tɔləwí·i-ləs·əwa·k·anúwa tɔe·ke·né·ɔ 'they use their power (ind. or sbd.)' (Mt 20.25); tɔe·ke·né·ɔ linnuwahkəs·əwá·k·an 'they exercise authority (sbd.)' (Mt 20.25).

• e·e·ke·-: e·e·ké·an 'that you use' (Mt 7.2).

• i·ae·ke·-: né·ləma i·ae·ké·yunk 'which has never yet been ridden' (Lk 19.30&; Gr. 4.95r).

ae·t·əl- TA+O 'use O2 on': xinkɔnší·k·an=č=háč ntae·t·əla·wəná·nak 'shall we use a sword on them?' (Lk 22.49). ▸ Cf. Mun awé·he·w 'he uses (it)'; Mes ayo·ten- (~ ayo·teš-) TA 'use (it) on' (< ayo·- TI(3) 'use'; cf. Sh hawo·t- TI(1) 'wear' < haw- TA, TI(3) 'use').

ahaləwí·i: see aləwí·i.

ahas·é·i: see ahsé·i.

aha·nhúkwi: see a·nhúkwi.

aha·pto·na·l-: see a·pto·na·l-.

ahčínki P (with ind.) 'have a hard time, it is difficult' (Lk 11.46; Gr. 5.25a); kéhəla ahčínki=č 'it will be really difficult' (Mt 19.23).

ahčinkxa·- (-t-ač·inkxa·-, e·č·inkxa·- |ačīnkaxā-|; Gr. 5.79b) AI 'be disobedient, be ill-behaved': ahčínkxe·w 'he is hard-headed, disobeys' (ME); máta=á· maxínkwi-ahčinkxá·t·e 'if he were not disobedient in major ways' (Jn 18.30); ahčinkxa·lí·č·i 'the disobedient (obv.)' (Lk 1.17).

• -t-ač·inkxa·-: ntač·ínkxa 'I'm hard-headed' (ME).

• e·č·inkxa·-: e·č·inkxá·či·k 'the disobedient' (Lk 12.46).

ahčinkxe·taw- (-t-ač·inkxe·taw-) TA 'disobey': tɔč·inkxe·taɔ́·ɔ 'he disobeys him' (Lk 16.13); máta ktač·inkxe·to·ló·wi 'I did not disobey you' (Lk 15.29; Gr. 4.89j).

ahčinkxe·whe·- (|ačīnkaxēwəhē-|; Gr. 5.79b) AI+O 'make O2 disobedient': tə́li-ahčinkxé·whe·n 'he was making them disobedient' (Lk 23.2).

ahči·čkɔlanihi·- AI+O 'throw O2 down head first': tə́li-=á· -ahči·čkɔlanihi·né·ɔ 'so that they would throw him down headfirst' (Lk 4.29).

ahči·čkɔlihəla·- AI 'fall headfirst': ahči·čkɔlíhəle· 'he fell headfirst' (Acts 1.18).

-ahempᵒ: see hempsi·nó·t·ay.

ahe·ləm- TA — ahe·lənt- TI(1a) 'honor, have high regard for'.

■ ahe·ləm- (TA): ahe·ləmó·me kó·x ɔ́·k kkáhe·s 'honor your (sg.) father and your mother' (1834b:21.3); e·li-ahé·ləma·t 'in that he has honored them' (Lk 1.48).

▪ aheˑlənt- (TI): wə́nči- wéˑmi awéˑn -aheˑlə́ntank 'so that everyone honors it' (Mt 8.4).
aheˑləmukwsiˑ- AI 'be honored': máta=č -aheˑləmukwsíˑwən 'he would not be honored' (Jn 4.44).
aheˑləmuwahkəniˑm- TA 'praise': tə́ləmi-aheˑləmuwahkəniˑmawwáˑɔ 'they began praising him' (Lk 2.20; KJV "glorifying and praising").
aheˑlənsiˑ-* (eheˑlənsiˑ- [IC]) AI 'be proud': eheˑlənsiˑlíˑčˑi (obv.) 'the proud' (Lk 1.51).
  ▸ Cf. xinkweˑlənsiˑ- AI 'think oneself great'.
aheˑlənt- (TI(1a)) TI-O 'suffer, have pain': áhi-=hánkw -aheˑlə́ntam 'she feels a lot of pain' (Jn 16.21; KJV "hath sorrow," i.e., physical pain); ntaheˑlə́ntam=č 'I will be in distress' (Lk 12.50); ktaheˑləntamúhəmɔ 'you (pl.) feel anguish' (Jn 16.22); tə́li-aheˑlə́ntamən 'that she felt pain' (Jn 16.21). ♦ This TI-O has a special lexicalized usage of aheˑlənt-, but both aheˑləm- and aheˑlənt- have diverged from the etymological sense of 'think much about'.
-ahəl-: see hal- TA 'put'.
ahhaphik°: see haphik°.
áhi (aˑyáhi; Gr. 5.28a, 5.129a) PV 'very, very much' (Jn 1.14, Lk1.18, 2.5, etc.); 'a lot' (Jn 6.10; KJV "much"). • aˑyáhi: ntaˑyáhi-líˑnam 'bad things happen to me' (Lk 22.28).
  ♦ áhi (with verbs of saying 'implore, plead'): tə́hi-láˑɔl 'they implored him' (Jn 4.40).
  ♦ áhi with liˑn- (in a negative sense): ktáhi-líˑnam 'you are suffering severely' (Lk 16.25), etc.
  ▪ áhi P 'very much' (Mt 15.22, Mt 21.15), 'very' (Mt 26.7& [2x]), 'intently' (Lk 15.4), etc. ♦ áhi (possibly in a particle phrase; Gr. 6.9c): áhi xéˑli 'a great many'; but this is better taken as a particle compound (see next).
  ▪ áhi PP (Gr. 5.133a) áhi-alapˑaˑíˑi 'very early in the morning' (Jn 8.2); áhi-hwə́ska 'extremely' (Mk 5.42); áhi-kwə́la 'I greatly wish' (Lk 9.38); áhi-nihəláči 'completely on his own' (Mk 1.27); áhi-wə́li 'in a very good way' (Mt 6.16); áhi-xéˑli 'a great many' (Lk 12.1, Mt 19.2, Mt 21.8).
ahiˑh- TA 'make angry': ntahíˑha 'I made him mad' (LTD LB); ntahíˑhukw 'he made me mad' (LTD ND); ktahihəlúhəmɔ=háč 'do I make you (pl.) angry?' (Jn 7.23); ná tə́ləmi-ahihkoˑnéˑɔ 'they began to be angered by them' (Mk 10.41; KJV "they began to be much displeased"); nána tɔhiˑhaˑnéˑɔ 'then they made him angry' (1834b:19.4).
ahkahamaw- (-t-akhamaw-) TA+O 'distribute to': télən púntink tɔkhamaɔ́ˑɔ 'he distributed ten pounds to them' (Lk 19.13); ktakhamáɔˑn=č keˑtˑəmaˑksíˑčˑiˑk 'you must distribute it to the poor' (Mt 19.21).
  ▪ ahkahamaˑohtiˑ- (-t-akhamaˑohtiˑ-) AI+O (recip.; Gr. 5.110j) 'share O2 with each other': ahkahəmáˑohtiˑkw 'share it among yourselves (you pl.)' (Lk 22.17).
  • -t-akhamaˑohtiˑ-: tɔkhamaˑohtiˑnéˑɔ 'they distributed it to each other' (Jn 19.24).
ahkanšaehɔˑsˑiˑ-: see kanšaehɔˑsˑiˑ-.
ahkánši: see kánši.
ahkeˑkəntəwáˑkˑan (Gr. 5.60a, 5.114a) IN 'teaching' (Mk 1.27, Mt 13.11).
ahkeˑkhamaˑ- (-t-akˑeˑkhama-) AI 'judge': ntakˑeˑkháma 'I judge' (Jn 5.30).
ahkeˑkhamweˑɔ́ˑkˑan (-t-akˑeˑkhamweˑɔ́ˑkˑan) IN 'judgment': ntakˑeˑkhamweˑɔ́ˑkˑan 'my judgment' (Jn 5.30).
ahkeˑkhəweˑ- AI 'judge (people)': takóˑ ahkeˑkhəwéˑi 'he does not judge' (Jn 5.22).
ahkeˑkhoˑtˑəwáˑkˑan IN 'judgment' (Jn 9.39).
ahkeˑkhoˑtˑəwíˑi (Gr. 5.132b) PN '(of) judgment'; eˑlkíˑkwi-ahkeˑkhoˑtˑəwíˑi-kíˑškwiˑk 'at the time of the day of judgment' (Mt 10.15, 11.22, 11.24).
ahkeˑkhoˑtˑiˑ- AI (recip.; Gr. §5.8m) 'be judged': íka .. énta-ahkeˑkhóˑtˑink '(to) court' (Mt 5.25).

ahke·khw- (-t-ak·e·khw-, e·k·e·khw-, |akēhkahw-|; Gr. 5.132b) TA — ahke·kh- (-t-ak·e·kh-) TI(1a) 'select, judge'.
- ahke·khw- (TA): máta awé·n ahke·khɔ·ót·e 'if you do not judge anyone' (Lk 6.37); ktə́li-=č máta ké·pe -ahke·kho·k·é·wən 'so that you (sg.), too, will not be judged' (Mt 7.1); é·li-=č .. a·šíte -ahké·khunt 'he will be instead judged' (Mt 5.25).
  - -t-ak·e·khw-: ntak·é·khɔ 'I picked him out' (OA); tɔk·e·khɔ́·ɔ 'he selected them' (Lk 6.13), tɔk·e·khɔ́·ɔ=č 'he shall separate and select them' (Mt 25.32; KJV "separate them one from another"); ntak·e·kho·kw 'he selected me' (Lk 4.18).
  - e·k·e·khw-: e·k·e·khɔ́·č·i 'those he chose' (Mt 24.22).
- -t-ak·e·kh- (TI): ntak·e·khámən 'I picked it out' (OA); ɔ́·k=č tɔk·e·khámən lač·e·s·əwá·k·an 'and he will select some of his possessions' (Lk 11.22).

ahke·kinke·- (-t-ak·e·kinke·-, ihahke·kinke·- [Rih+], ehahke·kinke·- [Rih+; IC], |akēhkīnkē-|; Gr. 5.59a) AI 'teach': ahke·kínke·p 'he taught' (Mt 9.35, 11.1, Lk 6.6, etc.); énta-ahke·kinke·á·ne 'when I was teaching' (Mk 14.49; Gr. 5.128e); énta-ahke·kínke·t 'when he was teaching' (Mt 22.41-42&; Gr. 4.61e, 5.128e); énta-ahke·kinké·t·e 'when he taught' (Jn 6.59, 8.20; Gr. 4.62h); é·li-ahke·kinkéhti·t 'how they taught' (Mk 6.30).
- -t-ak·e·kinke·-: ktak·e·kinké·həmp 'you have taught' (Lk 13.26; Gr. §2.12k).
- ihahke·kinke·-: ktə́li-ihahke·kínke·n 'that you (sg.) are a teacher' (Jn 3.2).
- ehahke·kinke·-: ehahke·kínke·t 'teacher' (Lk 3.12, 6.40).

ahke·kinke·ɔ́·k·an (-t-ak·e·kinke·ɔ́·k·an; Gr. 5.59a) IN 'teaching, doctrine' (Mk 1.22); †pa·lasi·í·i-ɔ́·k †helat·í·i-ahke·kinke·ɔ́·k·ana 'the teachings of the Pharisees and Herod' (Mt 16.12).
- -t-ak·e·kinke·ɔ·k·an-: ntak·e·kinke·ɔ́·k·an 'my doctrine' (Jn 7.16).

ahke·ki·m- (-t-ak·e·ki·m-, e·k·e·ki·m, |akēhkīm-|-; Gr. 5.60a) TA 'teach': ahke·kí·mo· 'teach them (you pl.)' (Mt 28.19); mɔ́i-ahke·ki·má·p·ani 'he went to teach them' (Mk 1.21); kkát·a-=háč -ahke·ki·míhəna 'do you wish to teach us?' (Jn 9.34).
- -t-ak·e·ki·m-: tɔk·e·ki·má·ɔ 'he teaches them' (Jn 7.35).
- e·k·e·ki·m- (with TH.1): e·k·e·ki·mák·i·k 'my disciples' (*lit.*, 'the ones I teach') (Jn 8.31, Mk 14.14, Jn 15.8); é·li e·k·e·kí·mat 'as one you teach' (Mt 10.42); e·k·e·ki·máč·i·k 'your disciples' (Mt 12.2, Jn 7.3); e·k·e·ki·ma·tpáni 'his disciples' (*lit.*, 'the ones he had taught') (Jn 1.35, 1.37, 2.1, 2.22, etc.); e·k·e·ki·má·č·i·l 'his disciples' (Jn 2.17, 3.22, 3.25, etc. [Lk 6.40 'teacher' is an error]); e·k·e·ki·má·č·i 'his disciples' (Jn 2.11, 2.12, 4.33, Mk 3.7, etc.); e·k·e·ki·mahtí·č·i 'their disciples' (Mt 22.16&; Gr. 4.65e); e·k·e·kí·mənt 'disciple, the one instructed' (Lk 11.1, Jn 12.4, Mk 13.1, etc.); e·k·e·ki·mə́nči·k 'disciples' (Mt 15.12, Lk 18.15&, Mt 26.8, etc.).
- e·k·e·ki·m- (with TH.2): e·k·e·kí·mkɔn 'your teacher' (Mk 5.35, Mt 17.24); e·k·e·kí·mkúk·i 'his teacher' (Mt 10.25); e·k·e·kí·mkwenk 'teacher' (*lit.*, 'he who teaches us') (Jn 1.38); e·k·e·kí·mkwe·kw 'your (pl.) teacher' (Mt 23.8, Jn 13.14).
- e·k·e·ki·m- (with TH.3): e·k·e·kí·mian 'my teacher' (Lk 5.5); e·k·e·kí·mienk 'our teacher' (Jn 1.49, Mt 23.7 [2x], etc.).
- e·k·e·ki·m- (with TH.4): e·k·e·kí·mələn 'student' (*lit.*, 'you whom I teach') (Jn 3.26); e·k·e·kí·məle·kw 'my disciples' (Jn 4.31).

ahke·p(·)º (|(k)akēp-| < |Ra+kəp-|) 'close, block' (Gr. §5.2a, 5.13a,e.1).

ahke·pxa·- (-kak·e·pxa·-, ke·k·e·pxa·-, |(k)akēpaxā-|) AI 'be deaf': ahké·pxe· 'he is deaf' (LB; Gr. 5.13a).
- -kak·e·pxa·-: nkak·é·pxa 'I am deaf' (OA, BS; Gr. 5.13a).

- ke·k·e·pxa·-: ke·k·é·pxa·t 'who is deaf' (Mk 9.25; as 2s voc.); ke·k·e·pxá·č·i·k 'ones who are deaf' (Lk 7.22); ke·k·e·pxa·lí·č·i (obv.) (Mk 7.32).

ahke·p·inkɔ·- (-kak·e·p·inkɔ·-, ke·k·e·p·inkɔ·-, |(k)akēpīnkwā-|; Gr. 4.49p, 5.13e.1, 5.34s) AI 'be blind': ahke·p·ínkwe· 'he was blind' (Mt 12.22); wənči- wá lə́nu -ahke·p·ínkɔ·t 'because of which this man is blind' (Jn 9.2); ahke·p·inkɔ·é·k·we=á· 'if you (pl.) were blind' (Jn 9.41); tə́li- khičí·i -ahke·p·inkɔ́·ne·p 'that he had truly been blind' (Jn 9.18).
- -kak·e·p·inkɔ-: nkak·e·p·inkɔ́·həmp 'I was blind' (Jn 9.25); kkak·e·p·ínkɔ 'you (sg.) are blind' (Mt 23.26); kkak·e·p·inkɔ́həmɔ 'you (pl.) are blind' (Mt 23.17, 23.19); nɔxpí·k·i·n kɔk·e·p·ínkɔ·n 'he was born blind (sbd.)' (Jn 9.19, 9.20; Gr. 4.49p).
- ke·k·e·p·inkɔ·- (⟨krk-⟩ throughout; ⟨kck-⟩ 1x): ke·k·e·p·ínkɔ·t 'a blind person' (Lk 6.39, Mt 15.14, 15.31); ke·k·e·p·inkɔ́·e·kw 'you (pl.) blind [guides]' (Mt 23.16); ke·k·e·p·inkɔ́·č·i·k 'who were blind' (Jn 5.3, Mt 9.27. 9.28, etc.; ⟨kck-⟩ Mt 21.14); ke·k·e·p·inkɔ·lí·č·i 'a blind person (obv.)' (Lk 6.39, Mt 15.14, etc.), 'blind people' (Lk 7.21, Mt 15.14, 15.30, Jn 11.37); ke·k·e·p·inkɔ·lí·t·əp 'who had been blind' (Jn 9.13, 9.17, 9.24; Gr. 4.75p).
- ▶ Cf. also ke·p·inkɔ́·č·i·k 'the blind'.

ahke·p·inkwe·ha·l- (-kak·e·p·inkwe·ha·l-, |(k)akwēpīnkwēhāl-|; Gr. 5.83b) TA 'blind': kɔk·e·p·inkwe·ha·lkəwá·ɔ 'he (obv.) blinded them' (Jn 12.40).

ahké·xkami P 'immediately' (⟨avkrxkumi⟩ Mt 13.20 [KJV "anon," RSV "immediately"], ⟨avkrxkami⟩ Lk 11.53; ⟨avkrxami⟩ 1842:16.1 [context supports 'immediately']).

ahkəni·m- (-t-ak·əni·m-, e·k·əni·m-, |akənīm-|) TA 'talk about, accuse, judge' — ahkəno·t́- (-t-ak·əno·t́-, e·k·əno·t́-, a·yahkəno·t́- [Rā-]) TI(1b) 'talk about' (Gr. 5.12m).
- ▪ ahkəni·m- (TA): káči ahkəni·mié·k·ač 'do not pronounce judgment on them (you sg.)' (Mt 7.1; Gr. 2.47d); xe·lennáɔhki kéku kkát·a-ahkəni·məlúhəmɔ 'I want to say many things about you (pl.)' (Jn 8.26); tə́li-ahkəní·ma·n 'that he was talking about him' (Mt 17.13); ahkəní·mko·wan 'who pronounces judgment on you' (Lk 6.37; no IC).
- -t-ak·əni·m-: máta awé·n tɔk·əni·ma·í·ɔ 'no one spoke of him' (Jn 7.13); ntak·əní·mukw 'he tells of me' (Jn 8.18, 15.26); ktak·əni·míhəmɔ 'you (pl.) tell about me' (Jn 15.27).
- e·k·əni·m-: e·k·əni·mák·əp 'who I was talking about' (Jn 1.15; Gr. 4.76a); e·k·əní·me·kw 'who you (pl.) are talking about' (Lk 22.59-60&); e·k·əní·mkwe·kw 'who accuses you' (Jn 5.45).
- ▪ ahkəno·t́- (TI): ahkənót·əmo· wé·lhik a·pto·ná·k·an 'tell about the gospel (you pl.)' (Mk 16.15); ahkəno·t·əmá·ne=á· 'if I do tell it' (Jn 8.14).
- -t-ak·əno·t́-: ntak·ənó·t·əmən=č 'I tell it' (Mt 13.35, Jn 8.18); tɔk·əno·t·amə́ne·p manət·uwwá·k·an 'he was speaking about the spiritual power' (Jn 7.39); tɔk·əno·t·əməné·ɔ·p 'they had talked about it' (Jn 12.10).
- e·k·əno·t́-: e·k·əno·t·əmihtí·t·e 'after they talked about it' (Mt 27.7).
- a·yahkəno·t́-: kéku=háč kta·yahkəno·t·əmúhəmɔ 'what are you (pl.) talking about?' (Lk 24.17).

ahkəno·t·a·s·i- (e·k·əno·t·a·s·i·-; Gr. 5.105z) II 'be told about': ahkəno·t·á·s·u 'it is told about' (Mk 14.9); ahkəno·t·a·s·í·k·e yó·l nta·pto·ná·k·ana 'when these words are told about' (Mk 14.9).
- e·k·əno·t·a·s·i-: e·k·əno·t·á·s·i·k 'whatever is spoken of' (Lk 12.3).

ahkəno·t·əmaw- (-t-ak·əno·t·əmaw-, |akənōtəmaw-|; Gr. 5.94f) TA+O 'speak about O2 to, accuse': mé·či .. ahkəno·t·əmaɔ́·t·e 'after he told them about it' (Acts 1.3 [ch. sbj.]); ná=nə tə́nta-ahkəno·t·əmáɔ·n 'there he explained to him' (1842:17.1); ktə́li-=á· -ahkəno·t·əmo·lə́né·ɔ

'that I would accuse you (pl.)' (Jn 5.45; Gr. 4.50d); ktəli- máta -ahkəno·t·əmo·lo·wəné·ɔ ahpɔ́·n pá·ste·k 'that I was not speaking to you about the yeast of bread' (Mt 16.11).
   • -t-ak·əno·t·əmaw-: ntak·əno·t·əmaɔ·né·ɔ·p 'I have talked to them about it' (Jn 17.26); tɔk·əno·t·əmaɔ́·ne·p né·l mi·məntə́t·al 'she spoke about the baby to them' (Lk 2.38; Gr. 4.71e).
ahkənta·s·i- II 'be counted': wé·mi ahkəntá·s·u 'all are counted' (Mt 10.30).
ahki·m- (ehahki·m- [Rih+; IC]) TA — ahkənt- (-t-ak·ənt-) TI(1a) 'count, read' (Gr. 5.12n).
   ▪ ahki·m- (TA): é·li-káhta-ahkí·ma·t le·khí·k·ana 'as he wanted to read scriptures (anim.)' (Lk 4.16); kkáski-=háč -ahkí·ma? 'Can you read it (anim.)?' (1834a:12).
   • ehahki·m-: ehahkí·mat 'you (sg.) who read it (anim.)' (1834b:7.2).
   ▪ ahkənt- (TI): ahkəntánke 'if he reads' (Mt 24.15), káhta-ahkəntánke 'when he wanted to count up' (Mt 18.23), mé·či é·ləmi-ahkəntánke 'after he had begun counting it' (Mt 18.24).
   • -t-ak·ənt-: tɔk·əntaməné·ɔ 'they read it' (Jn 19.20).
ahki·mkwəs·i- AI 'be counted' (Gr. 5.107a): takó· ahki·mkwəs·i·í·ɔk 'they were not counted' (Mt 15.38).
ahkɔ·n- TA 'fish with a net for': pé·-ahkɔ·ná·č·i·k namé·s·a '(ones) who were fishing with a net' (Mt 4.18). ▸ Cf. Mun ăkwá·nŏme·w 'fishes with a net' (dict.).
ahkɔn- (-t-ak·ɔn-) TA — TI(1b) 'dress, clothe'.
   ▪ ahkɔn- (TA): ahkɔ́no· 'dress him in it (you pl.)' (Lk 15.22); ktəli- .. -ahkɔnələ́ne·n 'we clothed you' (Mt 25.38).
   • -t-ak·ɔn-: máxke·k xinkɔ·khuk·wí·ɔn tɔk·ɔnawwá·ɔ 'they dressed him in a large red coat' (Mt 27.28); ktak·ɔníhəmɔ·p 'you (pl.) clothed me' (Mt 25.36); takó· ktak·ɔni·húmɔ·p 'you (pl.) did not clothe me' (Mt 25.43).
   ▪ ahkɔn- (TI): ke·tanət·ó·wi·t=á· ahkɔnínke skí·kɔ 'if God clothes the grass' (Lk 12.28).
ahkɔne·kha·si- II 'cover': énta-ahkɔne·khá·s·i·k 'the roof covering' (Mk 2.4).
ahkɔ́·ni: see kwə́ni.
ahkɔ·ní·k·an (-t-akɔ·ni·k·an-) IN 'fishing net' (Mt 4.21, Mt 13.47, Jn 21.8).
   • -t-akɔ·ni·k·an-: ntakɔ·ní·k·an 'my net' (Lk 5.5); ktak·ɔ·ní·k·an 'your net' (Lk 5.4); tɔk·ɔ·ní·k·an 'his net' (Lk 5.6). ▸ Cf. Mun ăkwa·ní·kan AN 'fishnet'; ⟨achgonican⟩ "fish Dam" (Z. 75; see Goddard 2019: 101).
ahkwe·č·ihtəwá·k·an (Gr. 5.115a.) IN 'temptation' (Mt 26.41); ahkwe·č·ihtəwá·k·anink 'into temptation' (Mt 6.13, Lk 11.4).
ahkwe·č·i·h- (-kɔk·we·č·i·h-, kwe·k·we·č·i·h-, |(kw)akwēčīh-|; Gr. 5.115a) TA 'tempt, test': káči ahkwe·č·i·hié·k·ač 'do not tempt him (you sg.)' (Mt 4.7); ná mahtánt·u kíši-ahkwe·č·i·há·t·e 'then after the devil finished tempting him' (Lk 4.13); kéku=háč wénči-ahkwe·č·í·hie·kw 'why do you (pl.) test me?' (Mt 22.18); é·li-ahkwe·č·i·háhti·t 'because they were testing him' (Jn 8.6); é·li-=č -ahkwe·č·íhkwək 'to tempt him' (*lit.*, 'that he (obv.) tempt him') (Mt 4.1); ná=nə só·ki- mahtant·ówal -ahkwe·č·íhkɔ·n 'for that long the devil (obv.) tempted him (prox.)' (Mk 1.13; Gr. 4.43d); kót·a-ahkwe·č·i·há·ɔ 'desiring to test him' (Mt 22.35).
   • -kɔk·we·č·i·h-: kɔk·we·č·i·há·ɔ 'he tested him' (Lk 10.25); kɔk·we·č·i·hawwá·p·ani 'they tested him' (Mt 16.1, 19.3).
   • kwe·k·we·č·i·h-: kwe·k·we·č·ihkuk·i 'the one (obv.) who tempted him (prox.)' (Mt 4.3).
   ♦ A lexicalized reduplicated form; cf. kwčº; for the formation, see Gr. §5.4a.
ahkwi·- (-t-ak·wi·-, e·k·wi·-, ehahkwi·- [Rih+; IC], |akwī-|; Gr. 4.40i) AI(+O) 'wear': xé·s·a ahkɔ́·p 'he wore skins' (1834a:19.12); či·t·anahémpəs yá·e·k šúkw ahkú 'he wore only a piece of thick cloth' (Mk 14.51); né·li- máta tahkɔp·o·ha·ltəwí·i-lač·e·s·əwá·k·an -ahkwían (or possibly -ahkwí·ɔn) 'when you're not wearing wedding garments' (Mt 22.12).

• -t-ak·wi·-: máxke·k xinkɔ·khuk·wí·ɔn tók·wi·n 'he wore the large red coat' (Jn 19.5).
• e·k·wi·-: é·k·wia 'my clothes' (Mk 5.30); é·k·wian 'what you wear' (Mt 6.31); é·k·wit 'his clothing' (Mk 5.28, Mt 26.65, 28.3); e·k·wí·li·t 'his (obv.) garment' (Mt 14.36, Lk 10.30); e·k·wí·č·i 'his clothes' (Mt 17.2, Lk 24.4, 1834b:37.1); é·k·wiankw 'what we wear' (1834b:3.3); é·k·wie·kw 'what you (pl.) wear' (Lk 12.22); e·k·wíhti·t 'their garments' (Mk 10.50). • ehahkwi·-: ehahkwiá·ni 'my garments' (*lit.*, 'what I customarily wear') (Jn 19.24; Gr. 4.66j); ehahkwí·č·i 'his clothing' (Mk 13.15, Jn 13.12, Lk 22.36); ehahkwí·li·t 'his (obv.) clothing' (Jn 19.23), 'their clothing' (Mt 21.7&, Mt 21.8&; Gr. 4.40i); éhahkwink 'clothing' (*lit.*, 'what someone wears') (⟨rvaqif⟩ Mt 6.25, Lk 12.23).

ahkwí·an (-t-ak·wi·an-) 'blanket' (WS), (⟨aqeun⟩ 1834a:19.12), ahkwí·yan (LTD FW), "robe" (⟨avqeun⟩ Lk 15.22); ahkwí·anal 'blankets' (1834a:19.14).
• -t-ak·wi·an-: ntak·wí·an 'my blanket' (⟨ntaqeun⟩ 1834a:13).

-aho·s·-: see hó·s 'pot'.

ahɔn- (|ahwan-|; Gr. 4.81g) II 'be strong': wáin ó·k kéku áhɔnk 'wine and anything strong' (Lk 1.15).

ahɔt- (ehɔht- [Rih+; IC]) II 'be trouble': áhɔt 'it is difficult' (Mt 18.7), áhɔt=č 'it will be difficult' (Lk 6.26, Mt 11.21 [2x]), ləkhíkwi-áhɔt 'how hard is it..' (Mk 10.24); áhɔhtək=č 'it will be trouble' (Lk 6.24, 6.25 [2x], Lk 10.13).
• ehɔht-: ehɔhtók·i 'that are difficult' (Mt 24.29).

ahɔ·l- (ehɔ·l-, |àhwāl-|) TA — ahɔ·t- (ehɔ·t·-) TI(1a) 'love'.
■ ahɔ·l- (TA): ahó·lo· 'love them (you pl.)' (Lk 6.35; Gr. 4.104r); ahɔ·lo·mɔ́·e 'love them (you pl.)' (Mt 5.44; Gr. 4.116g); é·li-ahólle·kw 'because I love you' (1834b:48.5, 1842:18.4); ahɔ́·la·n 'for one to love (them) (sbd.)' (Mk 12.33); tɔhɔ·lá·ɔ 'he loves him' (Jn 5.20, Lk 7.42, Mk 12.33); ktahɔ·lkó·na 'he loves us (inc.)' (Lk 7.5; Gr. 4.27n); ni·núči ktahɔ·lí·həmp 'you (sg.) loved me long ago' (Jn 17.24; Gr. 2.53d, 4.69w).
• ahɔ·l- (participle without IC): ahó·li·t 'one who loves me' (Lk 7.47; perhaps influenced by preceding é·li-áhi-ahó·li·t); ahɔ·lá·č·i·k 'those who loved him' (1834b:27.4).
• ehɔ·l-: ehó·lak 'who I love' (Mt 3.17, 12.18, Lk 9.35; Gr. 4.64j); ehó·lat 'who you love' (Jn 11.3); ehó·lkɔn 'one who loves you' (Mt 5.46); ehó·lkwihtí·č·i 'those (obv.) that love them' (Lk 6.32; Gr. 4.65g); awé·n máta ehó·li·t 'anyone who does not love me' (Jn 14.24); ehɔ·lá·č·i·k 'who loved him' (1834b:36.9, 38.2, etc.); ehɔ·lkúk·i 'those (obv.) who loved him' (1834b:25.7, 34.2, etc.).
■ ahɔ·t- (TI): éntxi-ahɔ·t·ánki·k 'all those that love it' (1834b:8.8).
• ehɔ·t·-: ehó·t·ank 'who loves [his life]' (Mt 16.25; Gr. 4.64m), 'what he loves' (Lk 16.15; Gr. 4.66g); ehɔ·t·ánki·k 'the ones that love it' (1842:21.5).
■ ahɔ·lti·- AI (pl.) 'love each other': ahɔ·ltúwak=á· 'they would love each other' (1834b:43.7); ahó·lti·kw 'love each other (you pl.)' (Jn 13.34); ahɔ·ltié·k·we 'if you (pl.) love each other' (Jn 13.35); ktáli-=á· -ahɔ·lti·né·ɔ 'that you love each other' (Jn 15.17).

ahɔ·ltəwá·k·an (Gr. 5.60b) IN 'love' (Jn 15.13, 12.25); ktahɔ·ltəwá·k·an 'your love' (Jn 17.26); tɔhɔ·ltəwá·k·an 'his love' (Mt 24.12, Jn 15.10; Gr. 5.116d); tɔhɔ·ltəwá·k·an ke·tanət·ó·wi·t 'God's love' (Lk 11.42); ntahɔ·ltəwá·k·anink 'in my love' (Jn 15.9, 15.10).

ahɔ·ɔhti·- (ehɔ·ɔhti·-, |àhwāwatī-|) II 'be valuable': ahó·ɔhtu 'it's expensive' (OA, ND, LB).
• ehɔ·ɔhti·-: áhi ehó·ɔhti·k 'which was very expensive' (Mt 26.7&); ehɔ·ɔhtí·k·i 'ones of great value' (Mt 13.45, 25.15; Gr. 4.66h).

ahó·p·e AN 'rich man' (1834a:20.29).

ahɔ·p·e·ínnu AN 'rich man' (Lk 16.19, 16.22, Mt 27.57&); ahɔ·p·e·innúwa (Lk 16.21).

ahɔ·p·e·i·- (ehɔ·p·e·i·-, |àhwāpēwī-|; Gr. 5.58q, 5.67a) AI 'be wealthy': ahɔ·p·é·yu 'he is rich' (1842:23.1); áhi-ahɔ·p·é·yo·p 'he was very rich' (Lk 19.2); é·li-áhi-ahɔ·p·e·í·t·əp 'for he was very rich' (Mt 19.22&); ahɔ·p·é·ie·kw 'you (pl.) who are rich' (Lk 6.24).
- ehɔ·p·e·i·-: ehɔ·p·é·i·t '(who is) rich' (Lk 12.16, 12.21 [2x], Mt 19.24); ehɔ·p·e·í·t·əp 'a rich [man]' (Lk 16.1); ehɔ·p·e·í·č·i·k 'rich people' (Lk 14.12, Mk 12.41); ehɔ·p·e·i·lí·č·i 'the rich (obv.)' (Lk 1.53).

ahɔ·p·e·ɔ́·k·an (Gr. 5.58q) IN 'wealth' (Mt 6.24, Mt 13.22, etc.); ktahɔ·p·e·ɔ·k·anúwa 'your (pl.) wealth' (Lk 16.9); tɔhɔ·p·e·ɔ́·k·an 'his wealth' (1834b:31.8); tɔhɔ·p·e·ɔ·k·anəwá·ink .. wə́nči 'out of their riches' (Lk 21.4).

ahpa·m° (|(p)apām-| < |Ra+pəm-|; Gr. 5.88d).

ahpá·mi P 'about, around'.
  ♦ with respect to time (Lk 1.56, Lk 3.23).
  ♦ with respect to place: (Mt 2.16, Lk 3.1, Mt 3.5, Mt 4.23, Mt 4.24, etc.).
  ♦ with respect to quantity: (Lk 16.6, 16.7).
  ♦ with a demonstrative, 'hereabouts': yú ahpá·mi 'what's around here' (1842:15.2).
  ■ ahpá·mi* (-pəp·á·mi; Gr. 5.129b) PV 'around, about'.
  - -pəp·á·mi: pup·á·mi-ahke·kínke·n '(by him) going around teaching' (Lk 23.5).

ahpa·mi·t·e·ha·- AI 'be preoccupied': wénči-=č .. máta ná=yú -ahpa·mi·t·e·há·e·kw 'so that you (pl.) are not preoccupied with the here and now' (Lk 21.34; KJV "lest .. your hearts be overcharged with .. cares of this life").

ahpa·mska·-: see pəməska·-.

ahpíči*(?) (-t-apíči): tɔpíči-lá·ɔl(?) 'he put him off' (⟨topihi lawl⟩ Mt 3.14; KJV "forbad").
  ▶ Zeisberger (1821:16) has ⟨achpitschiechemap⟩ (a passive form); cf. ⟨achpitschiechen⟩ "to stop, to prevent" (B&A 12).

ahpi·- (-t-ap·i·-, e·p·i·-, i·ahpi·- [Rī+], ihahpi·- [Rih+], ehahpi·- [Rih+; IC], a·yahpi·- [Rā+], |apī-|; Gr. 5.3c) AI 'be, stay in a place': ahpú 'he is here' (Lk 7.16; Gr. 2.10g), 'he exists' (Mk 12.32), íka ahpú 'he was there' (Jn 6.9; Gr. 3.13(4)a); ahpihtí·t·eč ki·s·ó·x·ɔk ɔ́·k alánkɔk 'Let there be the sun, the moon, and the stars' (1842:6.6), ahpihtí·t·eč aehəlé·ɔk 'Let there be birds' (1842:6.7); ahpianpáne=á· 'if you had been there' (Jn 11.21, 11.32; Gr. 4.74a).
- -t-ap·i·-: takó· čí·č yú entalá·wsink ntap·í·wən 'I am no longer in the world' (Jn 17.11); á·pči=č nə́ tóp·i·n 'he will stay there always' (Jn 8.35; Gr. 4.42m); takó·=tá yú tɔp·í·wən 'he is not here' (Mt 28.6).
- e·p·i·-: é·p·ia 'where I am' (1842:21.2; Gr. 2.25a, 3.13(4)b); é·p·ian 'you (sg.) who are [in heaven]' (Mt 6.9, Lk 11.2; Gr. 2.31d); e·p·iánəp 'where you were' (Lk 11.27; Gr. 4.75c); é·p·i·t 'who is [in heaven]' (Mt 5.16, 5.45, 6.1, etc.); né·skɔ e·p·í·k·we 'before he was' (Jn 8.58; Gr. 4.95m); e·p·í·t·əp 'where he was, had been' (Mt 2.9, Jn 7.42, 12.1; Gr. 4.75g); é·p·iankw 'where we are' (Jn 11.48); e·p·í·č·i·k 'who were (there)' (Lk 2.38, Mt 2.3, Jn 4.53, etc.).
- i·ahpi·-: takó· .. i·ahpí·i 'he never stays [in one place]' (Jn 8.35).
- ihahpi·-: ná=máh=nə tíhahpi·n 'he used to stay there' (OA; Gr. 4.42n, 5.41p).
- ehahpi·- ehahpi·lí·č·i '[moss, obv.] that is (habitually) there' (Mt 27.48).
- a·yahpi·-: íka ntá·yahpi 'I am staying there' (Lk 19.5); ná=nə́ tɔ·yahpí·ne·p 'that is where he stayed' (Jn 11.54).

ahpi·k·we·- (e·p·i·k·we·-) AI 'play music': ahpí·k·we· 'he's playing a "flute," a musical instrument' (ME), '(cat) purrs' (BS [-ɛi]).
- e·p·i·k·we·-: e·p·i·k·we·lí·č·i 'musicians (obv.)' (Mt. 9.23).

ahpi·k·ɔw- (-t-ap·i·k·ɔw-, |apīkwaw-|; Gr. 5.90a) TA 'play music for': ktap·i·k·o·lhúmǝna 'we played music for you' (Lk 7.32; Gr. 4.33).

ahpí·nay (-t-ap·i·nay-, |apīnay-|; Gr. 5.52a) IN 'bed'; ahpí·nenk 'on a bed' (Mk 7.30).
- -t-ap·i·nay-: ktap·í·nay 'your bed' (Jn 5.10, 5.11, 5.12, Mk 2.11); tɔp·í·nay 'his bed' (Jn 5.8 [!; error for 'your bed'], Jn 5.9, Mk 2.12&).

ahpi·taw- (-t-ap·i·taw-, e·p·i·taw-, |apīhtaw-|) TA — ahpi·t- TI(1a) 'be in' (Gr. 5.91a).
- ▪ ahpi·taw- (TA): ahpí·tai·kw 'be in me (you pl.)' (Jn 15.4); ahpi·taɔ́k·e 'if I am in them' (Jn 15.5); ahpi·taié·k·we 'if you (pl.) are in me' (Jn 15.7); máta ahpi·taié·k·we 'if you (pl.) are not in me' (Jn 15.4; or -i·é·k·we, if the negative was distinct); manǝt·uwwá·k·an ahpí·ta·kw 'a power is in him' (Mk 9.17; Gr. 4.27d); ahpi·ta·k·wé·k·we 'if they (inan.) are in you' (Jn 15.7); ntǝli- né·pe -ahpí·taɔ·n 'that I, too, am in him' (Jn 10.38).
- -t-ap·i·taw-: ntap·í·taɔ 'I am in him' (Jn 6.56); ntap·i·taɔ́·ɔk 'I am in them' (Jn 17.23); ntap·í·ta·kw 'he is in me' (Jn 6.56); wǝlankuntǝwá·k·an ktap·í·ta·kw 'peace is in you' (Lk 7.50; Gr. 4.27b); mɔnt·uwwá·k·an ntap·i·tá·k·o·n 'his spiritual power is in me' (Lk 4.18; Gr. 4.27v); máta ktap·i·ta·k·o·wǝné·ɔ 'it is not in you (pl.)' (Jn 5.38; Gr. 4.85u).
- e·p·i·taw-: e·p·i·tá·kwkǝp 'the one that [the devils] had been in' (Lk 8.34&, Mk 5.15, 5.18; Gr. 4.76w); e·p·i·tá·kwki·k 'who had [devils] in them' (Mt 8.28); e·p·í·tai·t 'who is in me' (Jn 14.10); e·p·i·taí·k·ǝp '(inan.) that was in me' (Jn 17.26; Gr. 4.77e).
- ▪ ahpi·t- (TI): e·lkí·kwi- .. -ahpí·tama 'as much as I am in [his love]' (Jn 15.10).

ahpɔ́·n (-t-ap·ɔ·n-, -t-ap·ɔ·nǝm- |apwān|; Gr. 5.51g) IN 'bread' (Mt 4.4, 7.9, 12.4, Jn 6.5, etc.); ahpɔ́·nal 'loaves of bread' (Mk 8.6), ahpɔ́·na (Mk 6.38, Jn 6.9, 6.11, 6.13, etc.).
- -t-ap·ɔ·n-: tɔp·ɔ́·nǝwa 'their bread' (Mt 15.26).
- -t-ap·ɔ·nǝm-: tɔp·ɔ́·nǝm 'his bread' (Jn 6.33).
- ▪ ahpɔ́·nt·ǝt (dim.; Gr. 5.46d) 'piece of bread' (Jn 13.26, 13.30).
- ▪ ahpɔ·ní·i (Gr. 5.122a) PN '(of) bread' (Jn 7.42).

ahpɔ·ni·- II 'be bread': ahpɔ·ní·k·eč yó·l ahsǝnal 'let these stones be bread' (Mt 4.3).

ahse° (|asē°|) 'scatter' ("fossilized plural or repetitive reduplication" Gr. 5.39). ▸ Cf. se° below.

ahsehǝla·-: see sehǝla·-.

ahselaht- (-t-as·elaht-) TI(2) 'scatter': tɔs·élahto·n 'he scatters it' (Mt 12.30).

ahse·skaw- (-t-as·e·skaw-) TA 'scatter': tɔs·e·skaɔ́·ɔl 'he scattered them' (⟨tusrskaol⟩ Lk 1.51).

ahsé·i P 'to scattered places' (Lk 21.24 [⟨vusri⟩ for ⟨uvs-⟩]).
- ahas·é·i P 'in more scattered places' (⟨avasri⟩ 1834b:43.6).

ahse·n- (-t-as·e·n-, |asēn-|; Gr. 5.39a) TI(1b) 'scatter': ntas·é·nǝmǝn 'I scattered it' (Gr. 5.39a).

ahse·x·we·-: see se·x·we·-.

ahsǝn (-t-as·ǝnǝm-; Gr. 5.5f) IN 'stone, rock' (Jn 1.42, Mt 7.9, Lk 6.47&, etc.); xínkwi-ahsǝ́n 'a large stone' (Lk 17.2, Jn 19.42&); ahsǝ́nak 'stones (anim.)' (Lk 19.40); ahsǝ́nal 'stones' (Mt 3.9, Jn 8.59; Gr. 3.6c); ahsǝ́na (Jn 10.31, Lk 13.34; Gr. 2.9b); ahsǝ́nink 'on a stone' (Mt 4.6, Lk 6.48, etc.; Gr. 2.28f).
- -t-as·ǝnǝm-: ktás·ǝnǝm 'a stone of yours' (Lk 19.44).
- ▸ For the occasional animate forms, see Goddard (2019: 98).
- ▪ ahsǝni·ké·i 'among rocks': énta ahsǝni·ké·i P+P 'where it was stony' (Mt 13.5); see énta P below and Gr. 4.10i (and following).

ahsǝnha·s·i·- II 'be made like rock': énta-ahsǝnhá·s·i·k 'the Pavement' (Jn 19.13).

ahsǝní·i PN '(of) stone': ahsǝní·i-tǝmahí·k·an 'a stone axe' (1834a:18.12).
- ▪ P like a PN with a participial phrase (Jn 19.41).

ahsəni·ke·- II 'be (an abundance of) rocks': ahsəní·ke· 'there are many rocks, it is a rocky place' (OA, LB; Gr. §4.2e); énta-ahsəní·ke·k 'where there are stones' (Mt 13.20).

ahša·kčehəla·- AI 'fall over backwards': ahša·kčehəlé·ɔk 'they went over backwards' (Jn 18.6).

ahša·sk-* (-t-aš·a·sk-) TI(1a) 'drive away': wə́ški=hánkw †toš·á·skamən 'whiskey always drives it away' (1834b:11.7). ▸ Cf. Mun |aša·n-| 'drive away, cast away'.

ahtanke·t·i·-: see tankti·t·i·-.

ahtuhé·p·i IN 'body, flesh, one's body' (Lk 23.52&, Mk 15.45&, Lk 24.23); nahtuhé·p·i 'my body' (Lk 22.19; Gr. 2.67i); wahtuhé·p·i 'body' (Mt 6.25, Mt 10.28, Lk 12.23), wahtuhé·p·i 'his body' (Lk 24.3); wahtuhé·p·i šawəs·ó·u 'the body is weak' (Mt 26.41); či·čánkɔ ɔ́·k wahtuhé·p·i 'both soul and body' (Mt10.28); wahtuhé·p·ink 'from flesh' (Jn 3.6).

†aisák·a (obv.) (Mt 8.11 [with /k/]), †aisák·a (abs.) (Lk 13.28 [with /k/], Mk 12.26).

†aitó·liink 'in Ituraraea' (Lk 3.1).

-ak°: see ahk°.

†akástəs †sí·sal 'Augustus Caesar' (Lk 2.1).

ála (é·la, i·ála [Rī+]; Gr. 2.74a, 5.23a, 5.128a) PV 'stop, cease, no longer': éši-ála- énta-xé·link -ahpíhti·t 'whenever they were no longer in a crowd' (Lk 22.6); énta- tá·á· háši -ála-wəlamalsíhti·t 'where they will never cease to be blissful' (Mt 25.46); káhta-áləmi-ála-hat·é·k·e hák·i 'when the world is about to (begin to) cease to exist' (Mt 24.3).
- é·la: é·la-ne·ɔ́·t·e 'when he no longer saw him' (1842:17.1).
- i·ála: énta- máta -i·ála-pəmá·wsink 'where one never stops living' (Jn 12.25; Gr. 5.44l).
- ♦ (with gapped verb) ála 'he is no longer'(1834b:27.7).

alai·- (e·lai·-, |alawī-|) AI 'hunt': alái· 'he hunts' (ME, ND; Gr. 2.38h); énta-alaíhti·t 'when they went hunting' (LB).
- e·lai·-: e·laínke 'when someone hunts' (1834a:19.12).

alai·ɔ́·k·an(?) IN 'hunting' (cf. Gr. 5.58): alai·ɔ́·k·anink 'hunting (loc.)' (⟨rlyeo-|kunif⟩ 1834b:46.4); interpretation uncertain.

alánkw (-t-alankəm-; Gr. 2.16f, 3.1e) AN 'star' (Mt 2.7, 2.9); alánkɔk (pl.) (Lk 21.25, Mt 24.29, 1842:6.6); ; alánkɔl 'stars (obv.)' (1834b:15.10), télən ɔ́·k kwə́t·i alánkɔ 'eleven stars (obv.)' (1842:13.3).
- -t-alankəm-: tɔlánkəmal 'his star' (Mt 2.2).

aláp·a P 'tomorrow' (Mt 6.30, 6.34 [2x], Lk 12.28, 13.32).

alap·a·e·- (e·lahpa·e·-, |alapāyē-|) II 'be the next day': ə́nta-alap·á·e·k 'when it was morning' (OA).
- e·lahpa·e·-: e·lahpá·e·k 'the next morning' (Jn 19.31); e·lahpa·é·k·e 'the next moring, the next day' (Jn 1.35, 1.43, Lk 7.11, 9.37, etc.).

alap·a·í·i P 'in the morning' (Mt 16.3, 20.1, Lk 21.38, Mk 13.35, etc.); áhi-alap·a·í·i 'very early in the morning' (Jn 8.2).

alaskwe·k-* (-t-alskwe·k-) TI(1a) 'smother (and make rot) (?)': ná .. tɔlskwe·kaməné·ɔ 'then they (brambles) smothered(?) them (plants)' (⟨tolsqrkamunro⟩ Mt 13.7; KJV "choked them").
- ♦ Apparently with |al-| 'rotten' + |-askwē-| 'plant'.

alax·at- II 'be empty': lí-aláx·at 'that it is empty' (Mt 12.44).

aláx·i* (-t-álxi-; Gr. 5.129c) PV 'empty': tɔ́lxi- palí·i -ləskaɔ́·ɔl 'he sent them away empty' (Lk 1.53).

alá·ho·n IN 'cane' (Mt 10.10); ala·hó·na 'canes' (Mk 14.43&, Mt 26.55-56&).

ala·x·i·məwe·í·i (~ ala·x·i·məwí·i; Gr. 5.125a) PN, PV 'of rest': ala·x·i·məwe·í·i-kí·šku 'it is the day of rest' (Jn 19.31). ala·x·i·məwe·í·i-kí·škwi·k 'the day of rest' (Mk 2.27, Mt 12.8), '(when it was) the day of rest' (Jn 5.16, Jn 5.18, Lk 6.7, 6.9, Mt 12.12).

• ala·x·i·məwí·i: ala·x·i·məwí·i-kí·šku 'it is the day of rest' (Jn 5.9, 7.22); ala·x·i·məwí·i-kwi·škó·yəm 'his day of rest' (1842:11.4).
▪ P (Gr. 5.126e): ala·x·i·məwí·i=tá yúkwe kí·šku 'today is the day of rest' (Jn 5.10).

ala·x·i·mo·ha·l- TA 'give rest' (Gr. 5.81g): ní·=č ktala·x·i·mo·hallúhəmɔ '*I* will give you rest' (Mt 11.28).

ala·x·i·mwi·- AI 'rest': ala·x·í·mo·p 'he rested' (1834b:16.6, 1842:7.2); təli-=á· -ala·x·í·mwi·n 'in order to rest' (*lit.*, 'that he might rest') (Mt 12.43); é·li- nčí·sas tihtəmí·ki nə́ -táli-ala·x·í·mwi·t 'as Jesus often used to rest there' (Jn 18.2); énta-=č xó·ha -ala·x·í·mwie·kw 'where you (pl.) will be alone and rest' (Mk 6.31); ala·x·í·mwi 'rest (you sg.)' (Lk 12.19).

ale·p·ɔ·m- (|alēpwā·m-|; Gr. 5.39b) TA 'give advice to': ale·p·ɔ́·mi 'give me advice' (FF); wé·mi=č .. ktale·p·ɔ·mkúwa 'he will give all of you advice' (Jn 6.45; KJV "teach"); énta-ale·p·ɔ·má·t·e 'when [the Holy Ghost] inspired his words' (Mk 12.36&); é·li- lə́nəwa tɔ·pto·na·k·aní·li·t -ale·p·ɔ·mkwíhti·t 'as they are taught by men the laws of men' (Mt 15.9); wwə́nči-=á· .. -ale·p·ɔ́·mko·n 'thereby they (obv.) would give him (ill) advice' (⟨alrmpomkwn⟩ 1834b:44.2).

aləl- AI — alət·- II 'be, become rotten' (Gr. 5.10h).
▪ aləl- (AI): alə́l 'it (anim.) rots' (Gr. 5.10h).
▪ alət·- (II): alə́t·ək=á· 'that would rot' (Jn 6.27); šúkw=á· alə́tke 'but if it decays' (Jn 12.24); máta .. alə́tke 'if it does not decay' (Jn 12.24).

aləm° (|aləm-|, |àləm-|) 'away, off' (Gr. §5.2a). ▸ Cf. álǝmi.

†aləmatía 'Arimathaea' (Mt 27.57&).

aləma·mali·ke·- AI 'start taking steps': á·p·əwat tɔləma·malí·ke·n 'it's easy for him to start taking steps' (1842:21.4).

aləma·mehəla·- AI 'begin to run, run away': ⟨alëmamehële⟩ 'he is beginning to run' (LTD); ná .. tɔləma·méhəla·n 'then she ran from there' (Jn 20.2).

aləmhake·x·ən- (e·ləma·ke·x·ən-) II 'be a road extending': e·ləma·ké·x·ink 'along the road' (1834b:26.12, 41.7).

álǝmi (é·ləmi [IC]; Gr. §2.4, 5.128b) PV 'begin, start to, become' (Lk 1.24, 1.80, 3.23, Jn 4.6, 4.35, etc.), 'away' (Mk 14.52, Mt 19.22).
• é·ləmi (Jn 4.51, Mt 13.21, 13.26, etc.).
▪ álǝmi P: †nči·lo·sələmink=č wə́nči álǝmi 'starting from Jerusalem' (Lk 24.47).
▪ é·ləmi PN 'beginning': é·ləmi-le·khí·k·an 'Beginning Book' (1842:6.1).

aləmihəla·- II 'go forth': aləmíhəle·p 'it went forth' (Lk 2.1).

aləmilahta· (e·ləmilahta·-) AI 'go away in a boat': aləmílahta·l 'move the boat out (you sg.)' (Lk 5.4); ná tɔləmilahta·né·ɔ·p 'then they started out in the boat' (Lk 8.22).
• e·ləmilahta·-: e·ləmilahtahtí·t·e 'when they departed in the boat' (Mk 6.33).

aləmi·k·i·- (e·ləmi·k·i·-) AI — aləmi·k·ən- II 'grow, grow up, begin or continue to grow'.
▪ aləmi·k·i·- (AI): aləmí·k·u 'he begins to grow' (LTD); ná=nə́ tə́nta-aləmí·k·i·n 'that's where she began to grow' (WL); ntaləmi·k·íhəna 'we (exc.) grow' (V).
• e·ləmi·k·i·-: e·ləmi·k·ihtí·t·e 'when they grew' (Mt 13.7).
▪ aləmi·k·ən- (II): aləmí·k·ən 'it grew, grew up' (Mt 13.8); aləmí·k·ənu 'they continue to grow' (Mt 13.30; Gr. 2.17a, 4.49e).

aləmi·x·ən- II 'begin': nanáli yó·l wə́nči-aləmí·x·ən ši·e·ləntaməwá·k·an 'from these does sorrow begin' (Mt 24.8).

aləmo·x·ɔl- (|aləmōxwal-|; Gr. 5.78b) TA — aləmuxɔht- (|aləmōxwat-|) TI(2) 'take away, lead'.

▪ aləmo·x·ɔl- (TA): aləmóx·ɔl 'take him away (you sg.)' (Mt 2.13, Lk 23.18, Jn 19.15 [2x]); kíˑ aləmox·ɔlatsháne 'if *you* have taken him from here' (Jn 20.15; Gr. 4.79a); tɔləmo·x·ɔláˑɔ 'he lead them out' (Mt 26.37, Lk 24.50); ke·k·e·p·inkóˑč·i·k tɔləmo·x·ɔla·néˑɔ ke·k·e·p·inkɔ·líˑč·i 'Let the blind lead the blind (obv.)' (Mt 15.14; Gr. 4.52f).

▪ aləmuxɔht- (TI): aləmúxɔhto·kw kəmi·č·əwa·k·anúwa 'take your food with you (you pl.)' (1842:16.2); kóč=háč aləmuxɔhtáe·kw 'why are you (pl.) taking it?' (1842:16.2).

aləmskaw- TA 'send away': yúkwe=áˑ aləmskaók·e 'if I send them away now' (Mk 8.3); tɔləmskaɔwwáˑɔ 'they drove him away' (Mk 12.4&); ná tɔləmskáɔ·n 'then he sent him away' (Mk 8.26).

aləmska·- (e·ləmska·-; Gr. 5.11f) AI 'depart': aləmske·w 'he left' (Jn 5.15; Gr. 4.21c); aləmskép·ani·k 'they headed out' (Mt 2.14, Mk 16.20; Gr. 4.68h); aləmska·l 'go (you sg.)' (Mt 8.4, Lk 7.50, Jn 7.3, etc.; Gr. 4.103d), aləmska (Jn 8.11; Gr. 4.103c); aləmska·kw 'go (you pl.)' (Mt 20.14, Lk 18.42&, Mt 28.7); aləmska·á·ne 'if I depart' (Jn 16.7); máta aləmska·á·ne 'if I do not depart' (Jn 16.7); lahápa níˑ hítami ntaləmska·n 'let me first go (sbd.)' (Mt 8.21; Gr. 4.52g); ná tóli-aləmska·n 'and so departed' (Jn 5.9; Gr. 4.51c), ná tɔləmska·n 'then he departed' (Mt 25.15; Gr. 4.49i); ná tɔləmska·néˑɔ·p 'then they left' (Mt 2.9; Gr. 4.72b).

• e·ləmska·-: e·ləmská·t·e 'when he left' (Mk 1.45); mé·či e·ləmskahtí·t·e 'after they left' (Mt 2.13, Mk 1.29, etc.; Gr. 4.62b); e·ləmská·č·i·k '(pl.) that went' (Mk 6.31).

alən- (-t-ann-) TA — TI(1b) 'touch, take hold of'; (TA, TI both require íka).

▪ alən- (TA): alən-: íka aləni·kw 'touch me (you pl.)' (Lk 24.39); pa·lsi·líˑč·i=č íka alənahtí·t·e 'if they will put their hands on sick people' (Mk 16.18).

• -t-ann-: íka tɔnnáˑɔ 'he put his hand on him' (Mt 14.31, Mk 8.23 [2x], etc.); takóˑ awé·n íka tɔnna·íˑɔ 'no one laid a hand on him' (Jn 7.30); ná íka tónna·n 'then he touched her, took hold of her' (Mk 1.31, 5.41, Lk 13.13).

▪ alən- (TI): káski- šúkw íka -alənmá·ne 'if I could just touch [his clothes]' (Mk 5.28); né·li- talaxhakiá·k·an íka -alənink 'with his hand on the plow' (Lk 9.62); wé·mi éntxi- íka -alənínki·k 'all those that touched it' (Mt 14.36); awé·n tóli- íka -alənəmən 'who was it that touched my clothes?' (Mk 5.30).

alənəmaw- TA+O 'touch the O2 of': tóli-=áˑ íka -alənəmaɔ·néˑɔ e·k·wí·li·t 'if they could touch his garment' (Mt 14.36).

alət-: see aləl- — alət·-.

aləw° (|àləw-|) 'more' (Gr. §2.10h, §5.2a).

aləwa·p·ensi·- (e·ləwa·p·ensi·-, |àləwāpēnsī-|) AI(+O) 'be more blessed than': ktaləwa·p·ensí·nak 'you are more blessed than them' (Lk 1.42; Gr. 4.45a).

• e·ləwa·p·ensi·-: e·ləwa·p·énsian 'you are the most blessed' (Lk 1.28; Gr. 4.66a).

aləwe·ləmukwsi·- (e·ləwe·ləmukwsi·-) AI 'be most thought of': aləwe·ləmúkwsu 'he is thought the most of' (Jn 1.16).

• e·ləwe·ləmukwsi·-: e·ləwe·ləmúkwsi·t 'the one most highly regarded' (Lk 1.32, 1.35, 6.35).

aləwe·lənt- TI(1a) 'prefer': wénči-=č máta -aləwe·ləntamó·we·kw 'so that you (pl.) do not have too high a regard [for food and drink]' (Lk 21.34); é·li-aləwe·ləntamíhti·t 'as they prize most of all [being praised]' (Jn 12.43); tɔləwe·lóntamən 'they preferred it' (Jn 3.19).

aləwíči P 'a little, a little more' (⟨alwehi⟩ Jn 4.52) ~ aləwi·íči 'a little later' (⟨alweihi⟩ Lk 12.38).

aləwihəla·- (e·ləwihəla·-, |àləwīhlā-|) II 'be left over': aləwíhəle· 'there is some left over' (Lk 15.17, 1834b:28.11).

• e·ləwihəla·-: e·ləwihəláˑk·i 'the ones (inan.) that were left over' (Jn 6.13; Gr. 4.66i).

aləwí·i (ahaləwí·i; Gr. 5.1g, 5.28b, 5.129d) P 'more, greater' (Jn 5.20, 5.36, Mt 9.13, Mk 2.21, Lk 11.22, etc.).
- • ahaləwí·i (Gr. 5.38s) P 'all the more' (Mt 20.31&, Mk 15.14, Mt 27.24).
- ♦ aləwí·i (in particle phrase): aləwí·i txí 'more, a greater amount' (Lk 10.35; Gr. 6.9e).
- ▪ PV (Lk 3.16, Jn 2.11, Jn 3.31 [2x], etc.); ktaləwí·i (Jn 4.12, Jn 8.53, etc.), tɔləwí·i (Lk 1.35, 6.40, 5.17, etc.), etc.
- ▪ PN (< PV): aləwí·i-ləs·əwá·k·an 'power' (Jn 5.2, Mt 10.1, Lk 10.19, etc.); wtaləwí·i-ləs·əwá·k·an 'his power, his "glory"' (Jn 2.11, Mt 6.29), tɔləwí·i-ləs·əwá·k·an (Lk 1.35, Lk 5.17, etc.). ♦ Derived from aləwí·i-lə́s·u 'he is greater' (see lə́s·i·-).
- ♦ aləwí·i P, PV: occurs with an adjunct as a standard of comparison (Mt 10.31 [Gr. 3.15f], Jn 5.36, Lk 12.24, etc.).

aləwi·khá·ɔn IN 'porch'; aləwi·khá·ɔnink 'on the porch' (LB); tɔləwi·khá·ɔnink 'on his porch' (Jn 10.23).

aləwi·kha·ɔni·- II 'be a porch': énta-aləwi·khá·ɔni·k 'where there was a porch' (Jn 10.23).

aləwi·k·a·p·ai·-* (e·ləwi·k·a·p·ai·-) AI 'stand further (away)': e·ləwi·k·a·p·ái·t(?) (⟨rlbekapet⟩ 1834a:22.42). Form and context unclear.

aləwi·na·k·ɔt- (e·ləwi·na·k·ɔ) II 'appear better, be better': e·ləwi·ná·k·ɔ 'a better one' (Lk 14.10).

álike P 'anyway' (Mt 19.10), 'nevertheless' (1842:15.5); álike íka ntá·n 'well, I'll go anyway' (ME); 'even so, nevertheless' (LTD); ⟨Alike⟩ "yet, still, nevertheless, however; for; already" (B&A 16).

ali·ke·- (e·lhike·-, |aləhkē-|) AI 'step', AI+O 'step on': é·li- nə́ni né·k·a -alí·ke·t 'as he himself steps on it' (Mt 5.35).
- • e·lhike·-: e·lhíke·t 'his tracks' (ME; Gr. 5.38u).

ali·tehw- (-t-alhitehw-, e·lhitehw-, ehalhitehw- [Rih+; IC]; |-əhtehw-| Gr. 5.18h) TA 'wound' ('hit' WL).
- • e·lhitehw-: məkó·s·ak e·lhitehúntəp 'where the nails were hammered' (Jn 20.25).
- • ehalhitehw-: ehalhitehó·link 'his (obv.) wounds' (Lk 10.34; with |àl-| generalized).

allət·o·nhe·-: see lət·o·nhe·-.

alo·ká·k·an AN 'servant' (Lk 7.10, Mt 10.24, 10.25, etc.); alo·ká·k·anak 'servants' (Jn 2.9, Lk 7.10, 12.37, etc.); alo·ká·k·ana 'servant (obv.)' (Lk 4.20, 15.26), 'servants (obv.)' (Jn 2.5), wíči-alo·ká·k·ana 'his fellow servants' (Mt 24.49); ntalo·ká·k·ana 'my messenger (obv.)' (Jn 13.20); ntalo·ká·k·anak 'my servants' (Jn 18.36); ktalo·ká·k·an 'your (sg.) servant' (1842:11.4); tɔlo·ká·k·anal 'his servant' (⟨tal-⟩ Lk 1.54), tɔlo·ká·k·ana 'his servant or servants' (Mt 22.3, 22.8, 22.13, etc.).

alo·ka·l- (e·lo·ka·l-, ihalo·ka·l- [Rih+], ehalo·ka·l- [Rih+; IC]) TA 'order (to do something), send (to do something)': alo·ka·lép·ani·k wehi·hunke·lí·č·i 'they sent priests' (Jn 1.19); é·li-alo·ká·lənt 'because he is a hired hand' (Jn 10.13); kí· e·lkí·kwi-alo·ká·lian 'in the same way that *you* sent *me*' (Jn 17.18); é·li-=k máta awé·n -alo·ka·lkó·wenk 'because no one hired us' (Mt 20.7; Gr. 4.97p); ktalo·kallúhəmɔ·p 'I sent you (pl.)' (Jn 4.38; Gr. 4.69cc, cf. Gr. 2.14a); ná .. tɔlo·ka·la·né·ɔ 'then they sent them' (Jn 7.32).
- • e·lo·ka·l-: e·lo·ka·lá·t·əp 'one who employed him' (Lk 16.8); e·lo·ka·lá·č·i '(the ones) he sent' (Mt 21.6), 'his apostles' (Acts 1.3); e·lo·ká·li·t 'my employer' (*lit.*, 'the one who orders me') (Lk 16.3, 16.5); néke e·lo·kallé·k·we 'when I sent you (pl.) forth' (Lk 22.35); e·lo·ká·lənt 'the hired hand, the one sent' (Jn 10.12, 10.13, 13.16); e·lo·ka·lə́nči·k 'the ones sent, apostles, angels'; (Mt 10.2, Lk 15.17, 17.5, 22.14); e·lo·ka·ləntpáni·k 'those that were sent' (Jn 1.24; Gr. 4.76r).

- ihalo·ka·l-: mái-ihalo·ka·lá·ɔk 'they went to be servants (*lit.*, to be given tasks)' (Mt 4.11).
- ehalo·ka·l-: ehalo·ka·lá·č·i 'his angel(s)' (obv.) (*lit.*, 'who he used to send') (Mt 1.20, 1.24, Lk 2.9, Mt 2.19, etc.), 'the messengers he had sent' (Lk 7.24), 'his servants' (Mt 14.2); ehalo·ká·lənt 'angel' (Lk 1.13, 1.19, 1.26 [as obv.; cf. Gr. 4.65.lmn], etc.); ehalo·ka·lə̆nči·k 'angels' (Lk 2.15, 6.13, Mt 13.39, etc.).
  ▪ ehalo·ká·lənt 'angel, messenger' (lexicalized participle, *lit.*, 'the one sent'): ehalo·ka·lə́ntink 'by the angel' (Lk 2.12).
  ▪ Derivative: ehalo·ka·ləntí·i (Gr. 5.123b) PN 'of the messenger' (Jn 9.7, 9.11, Lk 13.4).

alo·ke·mwi·- (e·lo·ke·mwi·-) AI 'order, send a message': ná tɔlo·ke·mwi·né·ɔ 'then they sent (someone with) a message' (Lk 19.14).
- e·lo·ke·mwi·-: e·lo·ke·mwí·t·əp 'who had ordered' (Mk 6.17).

aló·t P 'actually (often untranslated)' (Jn 4.2, 4.27, Lk 7.47, 11.28, Mk 6.5, Jn 6.9, etc.).

alo·ta·- AI 'fight back': káči alo·t·á·he·kw 'do not fight back (you pl.)' (Mt 5.39).
  ► Cf. EAb /álote/ AI 3s 'fights back, resists attack, retaliates', /élotɑt/ 3s ppl., etc.

aluhəmaw- TA(+O) 'show': ktaluhəmó·lən 'let me show you' (⟨ktalwvwmwlin⟩ Lk 6.47).
  ► Cf. Mun alo·hə̆máwi·l 'show me!'.

aluhikaw- TA 'be greater than, overpower, overcome' — aluhik- TI(1a) 'overcome'.
  ▪ aluhikaw- (TA): ntaluhikaɔ·wəná·nak 'we overpowered them' (Lk 10.17); ntaluhíka·kw 'he is greater than me' (⟨ntalovekaoq⟩ Jn 1.27, 1.30); ktaluhikaíhəna=č=háč 'are you greater than us?' (1842:13.5); é·li- manət·ó·wak -aluhíkae·kw 'because you (pl.) are greater than spirits' (Lk 10.20); wə́nči-=č máta -aluhika·k·ó·we·kw ahkwe·č·ihtəwá·k·an 'so that temptation will not overcome you (pl.)' (Mt 26.41).
  ▪ aluhik- (TI): ntaluhíkamən 'I overcame it' (Jn 16.33; KJV "have overcome"); awé·n máta aluhikánke 'if someone does not overcome [inconvenience]' (Mt 10.38).
  ♦ The stem (underlying |aləwəhk(aw)-|) may have /-uwh-/, and the LTD has ⟨uhw⟩; Mun aləwihkaw- 'overcome, dominate'.

alúns IN 'arrow' (1834a:12), aló·ns (ME; Gr. §2.1c, 3.5a).

-álxi-: see aláx·i-.

amač·º (|Ra+mat-|) 'bad (pl.)'; cf. also mahč°.

amač·əwihəl-* TA (amač·əwil-) TA 'call bad names': amač·əwilkwé·k·we 'if they call you (pl.) bad names' (Lk 6.22).

amam- (e·mam-) TA — amant- TI(1a) 'feel, be aware of'.
  ▪ amam- (TA): ntamáma 'I feel his presence' (LTD ND).
  - e·mam-: e·mamahtí·t·e 'when they became aware of them' (Lk 18.36).
  ► Cf. Mun amáme·w 'feels (s.o.'s) presence' (dict.), ntámama·w 'I feel his presence' (APh).
  ▪ amant- (TI): mé·či amantánke 'after he became aware of it' (1834b:30.6); ntamántamən 'I felt it' (⟨ntamutamun⟩ Lk 8.46; em.); máta ktamantamó·wən 'you (sg.) do not feel it' (Lk 6.41; Gr. 4.93c).

amank° (-məmmank°, memmank°) 'big (pl.)' (Gr. 5.35).

amankahtən- II 'be large hills': wé·mi énta-amánkahtink 'all the large hills' (1842:9.4).
  ♦ The singular has the stem maxat·ən- (see below).

amankala·mwi·- AI 'shout with loud voices': amankalá·məwak 'they shouted with loud voices' (Mt 21.9, Mk 15.14, Jn 19.6).

amankanší·k·ana: see xinkɔnší·k·an 'sword'.

amanká·kɔk AN (pl.) 'big trees' (LTD FW), obv. amanká·kɔl 'big trees (obv.)' (1834b:44.3).

amanke·wt- (TI(1b)) TI-O 'sob loudly': áləmi-amanké·wtəm 'he began sobbing loudly' (1842:17.1).

amankəwe·- (memmankəwe·-; Gr. 5.35f) II 'make a loud sound': memmánkəwe·k po·t·a·č·í·k·an 'trumpet' (*lit.*, 'loud-sounding whistle') (⟨mcmufwrk⟩ Mt 24.31).

amánki PN 'great, large (pl.)' (Mk 13.2, Jn 21.11).

amanki·thwəne·e·- II 'have large branches': amanki·thwəné·e· 'it has large branches' (Lk 13.19).

amanki·xsi·- AI 'shout, speak in a loud voice': amankí·xsu 'he spoke with a loud voice' (Jn 11.43, 12.44, Mk 15.34, etc.), táli-amankí·xsu (Jn 7.28; Gr. 3.13(3)c); amankí·xso·p 'he spoke in a loud voice' (Jn 1.15, Mk 5.7, Jn 7.37), 'she raised her voice' (Lk 11.27; KJV "lifted up her voice"); amanki·xsúwak 'they raised their voices' (Lk 17.13, Jn 19.12, 19.15); né·li-amankí·xsi·t 'while crying out with a loud voice' (Mt 27.54&).

amankpehəla·- II 'fall in large drops': tɔ·pti·ksəwá·k·an amankpéhəle· 'his sweat fell in large drops' (Lk 22.44).

amant-: see amam- — amant-.

amatsəs·i·- II 'be rough (ground)': amatsə́s·u 'it's rough (ground)' (OA); énta-amatsə́s·i·k 'rough ground' (Lk 3.5; KJV "the rough ways").

amat(·)ᵒ (|Ra+mat-|) 'bad (pl.)'; cf. also mahčᵒ ~ mahtᵒ.

amat·alo·ka·s·i·- AI 'do bad deeds': amat·alo·ká·s·ie·kw 'you (pl.) who do bad deeds' (Mt 7.23).

amat·a·pto·nᵒ: see also mahta·pto·na·l-.

amat·a·pto·ne·ɔ́·k·an IN 'blasphemy' (*lit.*, 'saying evil things') (Mt 15.19).

amat·a·p·e·i·taw-: see mahta·p·e·i·taw-*.

amaxke·- AI 'sop up food': ⟨amàxke⟩ "he sops up (food; eating)" (LTD). See next.

amaxke·m- TA (with wíči- PV) 'sop up food (eating from a dish) along with': wíči-amaxké·mi·t 'who sops up food with me' (Mk 14.20; KJV "that dippeth with me").

amax·ahᵒ (|Ra+maxàh(w)-|) 'a great deal'.

amax·ahe·lənt- (-məmxahe·lənt-, |amaxàhēlənt-| TI(1a); Gr. 5.34b) TI-O 'suffer torments': é·li-amax·ahe·ló́ntank 'as he was suffering torments' (Lk 16.23; KJV "being in torments"); né·ləma-amax·ahe·ləntamó·wa 'before my great suffering' (Lk 22.15); xahe·lennáɔhki=č kéku núnči-amax·ahe·lɔ́ntam 'I shall suffer greatly from many things' (Mt 16.21).

• -məmxahe·lən̨tam-: nəməmxahe·lɔ́ntam 'I am suffering torments' (Lk 16.24).

amax·ahi·laeh- TA 'torment': kəmái-amax·ahi·laéhi '(that) you come to torment me' (Mt 8.29); ktə́li-=á· máta -amax·ahi·laehí·wən 'that you not torment me' (Mk 5.7).

amax·ahi·laehkwəs·i·- AI 'be in torment': kəwíči-amax·ahi·laehkwə́s·i 'you (sg.) are in torment with him' (Lk 23.40).

amax·ahɔla·mwi·-: see maxahɔla·mwi·-.

amayahki·t- (-məmayak·i·t-) TI(2) 'waste': amayahkí·to· 'he is wasteful' (LB); ná=nə́ wé·mi tə́nta-amayahkí·to·n 'that is where he wasted everything' (Lk 15.13); amayahkí·to·n 'it is wasted' (Mt 26.8).

• -məmayak·i·t-: mumayak·i·tó·na 'he wastes them' (Lk 16.1).

♦ Only reduplicated, but cf. Mun mayakíhto·w 'he wastes (it)' (Gr. 5.34c).

amayaksi·- (memmayaksi·-) AI 'be reckless': amayáksu 'he is reckless' (LB).

• memmayaksi·-: memmayáksi·t(?) 'who is wasteful' (⟨Mumyukset⟩ 1834b:28.1; "prodigal").

ame·manthiteha·s·i·- II 'be marvelously hewn' (presumably): †e·lkí·kwi-ame·manthitehá·s·i·k ahsə́na 'how marvelously hewn the stones are' (Lk 21.5; KJV "how it was adorned with goodly stones").

▸ Cf. ⟨amemansásu⟩ 'it is dyed' (Z. 56); ⟨amemanschelinam⟩ 'he sees wonderful, extraordinary things' (Z. SB1:84).

amənči·h- TA 'force, force to do something': tá=á· awé·n kóski-amənči·ha·í·ɔ 'no one would be able to force him' (Jn 10.29); tɔmənči·hawwá·ɔ 'they compelled him [to help Jesus]' (Mt 27.32&); máta=á· háši awé·n ntamənčihkówəna 'no one would ever force them away from me' (Jn 10.28; KJV "pluck them out of my hand").

amənči·həwe·- (ehamənčihəwe·- [Rih+; IC]) AI 'force people (to do things)': ehamənčihəwé·č·i·k 'ones who force people to do things' (Lk 18.11; KJV "extortioners").

amənčí·i P 'by force, insisting, persisting; regardless, anyway': amənčí·i təmi·k·é·ɔk 'they forced their way in' (Mt 11.12); 'insistently' (Jn 8.7), 'persistently' (Lk 13.27); amənčí·i lápi pí·li íka lalo·ká·le· 'he persisted and sent yet another' (Lk 20.12); amənčí·i kəwitahpi·míhəmɔ 'you (pl.) persevere with me' (Lk 22.28); amənčí·i 'regardless' (Mk 7.36, Jn 16.32), 'despite that' (Mt 16.24, Mt 21.32), 'anyway' (Mt 18.8, 18.9, 1842:16.1), 'nevertheless' (Jn 12.42, Mt 26.33), 'being forced to' (1834b:45.10).

amənči·ihəla·- AI 'go forcefully': amənči·íhəle· 'he went "boldly"' (Lk 23.52&).

amənči·m- TA 'coerce': awé·n amənči·mkóne 'if someone coerces you (sg.)' (Mt 5.41).

aməní·i (Gr. 5.29a) P 'nevertheless, despite that, regardless' (Jn 16.32, Mt 26.33, Mk 14.59).

aməntahkənənti·- AI (recip.; Gr. 5.111a) 'betray each other': xé·li=č awé·n .. aməntahkənə́ntu 'many will betray each other' (Mt 24.10; KJV, RSV "betray").

♦ Reciprocal of aməntahkəni·m-* TA 'betray'.

amənta·p·e·i·- (e·mənta·p·e·i·-) AI 'be high-handed': ntóli-amənta·p·é·i·n 'that I am a high-handed man' (Lk 19.22); któli-amənta·p·é·i·n 'that you (sg.) are a high-handed man' (Mt 25.24; KJV "an hard man").

• e·mənta·p·e·i·-: e·mənta·p·é·i·t lənu 'a high-handed man' (Lk 19.21; KJV "austere," RSV "severe").

amí·ka (Gr. 5.23b) P 'much later' (Mt 25.19, 1842:19.1), 'for a long time' (1834b:3.7), 'late' (OA). ▸ Cf. amiga 'late' (Z 110), 'long, a long time' (B&A 20).

-ami·mənsᵒ: see mí·məns.

ami·mənshe·- AI+O 'make O2 a child': ná ní·š·ən ktánči-ami·mənshe·né·ɔ 'then you (pl.) make him two times more the child' (Mt 23.15).

amí·mi AN 'pigeon' (FW, ND), originally 'passenger pigeon'; pl. ami·mí·ɔk (FW).

▪ ami·mi·t·ət·ak AN (dim. pl.) 'young pigeons' (Lk 2.24).

anansi·- (younger ana·nsi·-; e·nansi·- [IC]; Gr. §2.1c) AI(+O) 'lie on (as) bedding (as a mat or blankets)': (í)ka .. ənta-aná·nsi·t '(to) where he lay' (OA).

• e·nansi·-: e·nánsian 'your bed (or bedding)' (Mk 2.9); e·nánsi·t 'his bed' (Mk 2.12&).

▸ Cf. aná·nso·n IN 'mattress' (V, ME, LB), Mun aná·nso·n.

ánči (Gr. 5.129e) PV 'greater, longer, bigger, etc.' (Mt 6.27, Lk 17.5, 12.25); ánči-é· 'he went on further' (Mt 26.39); ntánči=č -ləkhikwí·to·n 'I'll build it bigger' (Lk 12.18); tónči- e·nunthake·ó·k·an -lá·ɔ 'he told them a parable in addition' (Lk 19.11).

anči·t- TI(2) 'mend': ó·k=č wé·mi kéku tɔnčí·to·n 'and he shall restore everything' (Mk 9.12); tɔnči·to·né·ɔ 'they were mending them' (Mt 4.21).

†ani 'Anna' (⟨Ani⟩ Lk 2.36). The spelling may reflect a dialectal English pronunciation with /-iy/ for "-a"; compare má·si 'Martha' and †nčɔ·é·ni 'Joanna'.

ankəl- (enkəl-, i·ankəl- [Rī+], ehankəl- [Rih+; IC]; Gr. 5.10f, 5.17b) AI 'die': ánkəl 'he died' (Lk 20.30), káhti-ánkəl 'he was almost dead' (Jn 4.47, Lk 7.2, Lk 10.30); ánkəlo·p 'she died' (Mk 12.22; Gr. 4.68d); †e·pəliháma ánkəla 'Abraham (abs.) is dead' (Jn 8.52; Gr. 3.9c);

tá=á· ankəlo·wí·ɔk 'they will not die' (Mt 16.28; Gr. 4.81r); ankəlúnka 'they (abs.) are dead' (⟨wfulwfu⟩ Mt 2.20 [em.], ⟨ufulwfu⟩ Jn 8.52; Gr. 3.9d); né·skɔ-ankəló·wa 'before I die' (1842:18.2; Gr. 4.95d); é·li-ánkələk 'how he died' (Mt 27.54&).
  • enkəl-: enkələk·i·k 'the dead (pl.)' (Jn 5.25, Lk 7.22, Mt 22.30&); enkələlí·č·i 'the dead (obv.)' (Mt 8.22, Lk 20.38&, etc.; Gr. 5.65b); enkələlít·əp 'one who had died' (Lk 16.30, 16.31; Gr. 4.75q); enkələk·əp 'one who had been dead' (Lk 7.15, 15.24, 15.32; Gr. 4.75l); enkələkpáni·k 'who had died (pl.)' (1834b:35.4).
  • i·ankəl-: táli-=č máta -i·ankəló·wən 'that he would never die' (Lk 2.26); énta-=č máta -i·ankələli·kw 'where they will never die' (Mk 9.44, 9.48; Gr. 4.95p).
  • ehankəl-: ehankələk·i·k 'the dead (pl.)' (Mt 8.22; Gr. 5.65); ehánkəlink 'what people die from' (Mk 16.18; Gr. 3.17a).
  ▪ énkələk 'one who is dead' > lí enkələk·i·ké·i P+P 'among the dead' (Lk 24.5; Gr. 4.10f, 5.65b); enkələk·í·i PN 'of the dead' (Mt 23.27; Gr. 5.123c).
ankələwá·k·an (Gr. 5.58l) IN 'death' (Lk 1.79, Jn 2.22, 5.24, etc.); ankələwá·k·anink 'death (loc.)' (Jn 5.24), 'to death' (Mt 7.13); wə́nči ankələwá·k·anink 'from the dead' (Jn 2.22), 'from death' (Mt 14.2, Mk 9.9, etc.); wə́nči ankələwá·k·an 'from death' (Mk 6.16).
ankhil- TA — ankhit- (enkhit-) TI(2) 'lose'.
  ▪ ankhil- (TA): takó· kwət·i ntankhilá·i 'I have not lost one' (Jn 18.9).
  ▪ ankhit- (TI): wə́nči=č máta kéku -ankhitó·wa 'so that I do not lose anything' (Jn 6.39); tə́ta=č éntxi- aləwí·i txí -ankhítaɔn 'whatever amount more it costs you (sg.)' (lit., 'that you lose') (Lk 10.35); awé·n ankhitá·k·we 'if someone loses it' (Mt 10.39, Lk 17.33; Gr. 4.63a); tá=á· tɔnkhitó·wən 'he will not lose [his reward]' (Mt 10.42; Gr. 4.93g).
  • enkhit-: enkhitaɔ́·nəp 'what I had lost' (Lk 15.9; Gr. 4.78b).
-ann-: see alən-.
ansh- TI(1a) 'dip up': anshámo·kw 'dip some up' (Jn 2.8; KJV "Draw out"); anshamihtí·t·əp 'the ones that had dipped it up' (Jn 2.9; Gr. 4.78n).
anshí·k·an IN 'fishing net' (Jn 21.11 [2x]); ktanshi·k·anúwa 'your (pl.) net' (Jn 21.6).
  ♦ From ansh- TI(1a) 'dip up' (Goddard 2019:101).
anshi·k·e·- AI 'scoop up (water)': kéku .. anshi·k·é·an 'something to scoop up water with' (lit., 'that you scoop up water') (⟨unsekreun⟩ Jn 4.11; Gr. 3.14d).
†ántəlu 'Andrew' (Jn 1.40, 1.44, Mt 4.18, Lk 6.14); †ántəlo·s (Mt 4.18-19&, Mk 1.29, Jn 6.8, 12.22, Mk 13.3); †antəló·s·a (obv.) (Mt 10.2, Jn 12.22).
aɔn- II 'be foggy': aɔ́n 'there is fog, mist' (LB; Gr. 5.10o); é·li- .. -aɔ́nk 'as it's foggy' (Mt 16.3).
aɔs·i·- (-t-aɔhsi·-, e·ɔhsi·-, |awasī-|) AI 'warm oneself': wíči-aɔ́s·u 'he warmed himself with the others' (Jn 18.18&; Gr. 2.24d, 5.99a); pé·-aɔs·í·li·t 'as he (obv.) warmed himself' (Lk 22.56-57&).
  • -t-aɔhsi·-: kwí·la .. ntáɔhsi 'I am unable to warm myself' (1834a:12).
  • e·ɔhsi·-: e·ɔhsihtí·t·e 'when they warmed themselves' (Jn 18.18&).
-ap°: see ahp°.
apahtai·x·i·n- AI 'lie against': apahtai·x·í·no·p 'he lies against' (Jn 13.23; KJV "leaning on"); é·li-apahtai·x·ínkəp 'the one who lay against him' (Jn 13.25).
apahtaɔhpi·- AI 'sit leaning on {smwh}': a·yáhi- .. íkali -apahtáɔhpi·t 'who previously sat leaning on him' (Jn 21.20).
ápi PV 'come from, have done, have been' (Gr. 5.128c): ápi-mi·kəmɔ·s·i·lí·t·e 'when he (obv.) comes from his work' (Lk 17.7); e·lkí·kwi- we·k·wí·s·ink lə́nu -ápi-ne·ykwə́s·i·t 'when the man who is the Son has appeared' (Lk 17.30).

askᵒ (1) (|ask-|) 'raw' (Gr. §5.2a).
askᵒ (2) (|ask-|) 'tired' (Gr. §5.2a).
askaskwe·- II 'be green' (Gr. 2.4): askáskwe· 'it is green' (OA; Gr. 5.7e); né·li-askáskwe·k 'while it is green' (1834a:16).
askaskwi·x·ən- II 'be green': lí-askaskwí·x·ən skí·kɔl 'that the grass is green' (1834a:14).
aská·kɔ (obv.) 'green': aská·kɔ hítkɔ 'a green tree' (Lk 23.31).
aske·lənt- (TI(1a)) TI-O 'be impatient': nni·núči- .. -aske·lə́ntam kəwi·po·mələné·ɔ yúkwe yó·ni 'I am impatient to eat this with you (pl.)' (Lk 22.15).
 ▸ Cf. ⟨Asgelendam⟩ "to wait with impatience" (B&A 23).
áski P 'must' (⟨Uskc⟩ Jn 4.4, Lk 9.44).
aspᵒ (|asp-|) 'up' (Gr. §5.2a).
aspa·k·ən- TI(1b) 'raise (a building)': ktaspa·k·ənə́mən 'you raise it up' (Jn 2.20; Gr. 5.13c.2).
aspən- TA 'raise': áspəna· 'he will be lifted up' (Jn 12.34); aspəná·t·əp 'who lifted up [the snake]' (Jn 3.14); mé·či=č lə́nu .. aspəné·k·we 'after you (pl.) have lifted up the man' (Jn 8.28); aspənínke 'when I am lifted up' (Jn 12.32); tɔspəná·ɔl 'he raised them up' (Lk 1.52), tɔspəná·ɔ 'he lifted him' (Mk 9.27), tɔspəná·ɔ wánkɔna 'he raised his heel' (Jn 13.18 [Bible idiom]); wwə́nči-aspənúk·u 'they (obv.) (shall) lift him by (+ loc.)' (Mt 4.6); lí-áspəna·n '(that is) how he (shall) be lifted up' (Jn 3.14).
asphukwe·- AI 'lift one's head' (|-əhkw-| 'head, hair'; Gr. 5.13f): asphúkwe· 'he looked up' (Lk 19.5, Jn 17.1); takó· náxpəne asphukwé·i·p 'he did not even lift up his head' (Lk 18.13); é·li-asphukwé·t·e '(as he was) looking up' (Mk 7.34).
aspinkwe·x·i·n- AI 'look up, lift one's eyes': kéku=háč wénči- .. -aspinkwe·x·í·ne·kw 'why are you looking up?' (Acts 1.11); íka táli-aspinkwe·x·í·no·p 'he looked up' (Lk 16.23); ná nčí·sas tɔspinkwe·x·í·nən 'then Jesus lifted up his eyes' (Jn 11.41).
aspi·- AI 'go up': álami-áspi· 'he began rising upwards' (Acts 1.9); ntáspi 'I am going up' (Jn 20.17); tə́li-áspi·n 'that he ascends' (Jn 6.62).
aspi·nxke·- AI 'raise one's hand(s)' (Gr. 5.21b): tə́nta-aspí·nxke·n 'he raised his hands (there)' (Lk 24.50).
aspi·t- TI(2) 'raise': ntaspí·to·n 'I raise it up' (Jn 2.19).
aspo·x·we·- AI 'walk up' — aspo·x·we·yo·wi·- II 'rise' (Gr. 5.76f).
 ▪ aspo·x·we·- (AI): aspó·x·we· 'he's walking up [a hill]' (OA; Gr. 5.11d).
 ▪ aspo·x·we·yo·wi·- (II): lí- éhəli-wsí·ka·k -lí-péči-aspo·x·we·yó·u '(to) come rising up in the west' (Lk 12.54).
átax P 'ten (plus)': átax ní·š·a 'twelve' (Mt 10.2, 10.5, Lk 22.3, etc.), ó·k né·l átax ní·š·a 'and (with him) the twelve (obv.)' (Mt 21.17&); átax kwə́t·i 'eleven' (Lk 24.9-10, Lk 24.33, Jn 20.19&, Mt 28.16).
awé·n 'someone, anyone, people' (often sg. with collective sense; Gr. 4.18) (Jn 1.13, Lk 2.24, etc.); awé·ni (obv.) (Lk 1.17, 1.22, 2.34, etc.); awé·ni·k 'people' (Mt 7.12); wə́nči awé·nink 'out of someone' (Mt 12.43); ki·ló·wa awé·n 'anyone of you' (Mk 23.11); takó· ki·ló·wa awé·n 'none of you' (Jn 7.19).
 ♦ awé·ni 'who (obv., with relative clause): é·li- .. -wwá·ha·t awé·ni máta we·lsət·amalí·k·wi 'for he knew who did not believe' (Jn 6.64).
 ▪ awé·n (interrogative) 'who?': awé·n=háč khák·ay 'who are you?' (Jn 1.19, 1.22); awé·n=ksí=láh 'who then?' (Jn 1.21); awé·n=háč (+ sbd.) 'awé·n=háč tə́li-ahpá·mska·n 'who is it going about ..?' (Jn 7.20), awé·n=háč tə́li-mahtá·wsi·n 'who was the sinner?' (Jn 9.2).

- awé·n 'who' (in an indirect question): awé·n=č=tá '(as to) who will or would be (the one)' (Lk 22.23, Jn 19.24); awé·n=š=tá 'as to who' (1834b:47.14).

awe·nháke AN 'foreigner'; awe·nháke '(Indian of) another tribe; Indian', pl. awe·nhaké·ɔk (OA).
- awe·nhake·i·ké·i P 'among foreigners' (Mt 10.5).

awe·ni·- AI 'be who, be the one that': awə́·nia ní· 'who I am' (⟨awmia ne⟩ Mt 16.13, misprint for ⟨awrnia ne⟩); awé·nian 'who you are' (Mk 1.24).

-axko·k·i·-. see xko·k·i·- AI 'be a snake'.

-ax·am-: see xam-.

-ax·e·s·-: see xé·s.

ay- TI(1b) 'take, pick out, buy': ayə́mo·kw 'obtain them (you pl.)' (Lk 12.33); ntáyəmən 'I picked it out' (ME); tɔyəməné·ɔ 'they (would) take them (inan.)' (Jn 11.48), 'they picked them (inan.) out' (Jn 19.23).

ayá·skami P 'must' (⟨yaskamih⟩ Mt 16.21, with =č). ▸ Cf. Mun ayá·ska 'must, is necessary'.

a·

a·- (e·a·-, i·a·- [Rī+], i·ha·- [Rih+]; Gr. 2.31a, 5.3a, §5.4d) AI 'go {to smwh}': íka é·w 'he went there' (Lk 7.8; Gr. 2.24a), íka é· (Mk 11.13&, Lk 22.39); íka é·ɔk 'they went there' (Jn 4.30, Mk 3.21, Jn 11.55, etc.); íka é·p·ani·k 'they went there' (Lk 2.41, 2.42, Mk 1.29, etc.); á·l 'go (you sg.)' (Jn 4.50, 7.3, Mt 17.27, Jn 20.17); á·t·amo·kw 'let's all go to (+ loc.)' (Lk 2.15, Mk 1.38, etc.; Gr. 4.103o); á·kw 'go (you pl.)' (Mt 2.8, Mk 6.31, etc.); káči á·han 'don't go (sg.)' (Mk 8.26); káči íka á·he·kw 'do not go (you pl.)' (Mt 10.5 [2x], Mt 24.26); íka á·me 'go there (you sg.)' (Mt 6.6; Gr. 4.116a); íka a·mɔ́·e 'go (you pl.)' (Lk 10.10); wə́ntax á·t·eč 'let him come' (Jn 4.16; Gr. 4.114a); íka(=č) ntá 'I (will) go there' (⟨nta⟩ Jn 7.33, Mt 16.21, ⟨ntu⟩ Jn 9.11; Gr. 3.13(2)a); palí·i=č ntá 'I shall go away' (⟨natav⟩ for ⟨ntav⟩ Jn 8.21; ⟨ntav⟩ also Jn 14.12, 14.28, etc.); tá·=č=háč ktá? 'Where will you go?' (⟨ktav⟩ Jn 13.36; form also Jn 11.8); ktáhəna 'we (inc.) go' (Lk 18.31; Gr. 2.43b); ná íka tɔ́·n 'then he went there' (Jn 4.47, Mk 5.27, Mk 6.27, etc.); ná təli- palí·i -a·né·ɔ 'and with that they went away' (Jn 19.42&, Gr. 4.51a).

• e·a·-: e·á·a (also e·yá·a?) 'where I go, the way I am going' (⟨rau⟩ Mt 16.23; ⟨reau⟩ Jn 13.33, 13.36, 14.4); e·á·an (also e·yá·an?) 'where you go' (⟨raun⟩ Mt 8.19, Lk 7.27, Jn 21.18; ⟨ran⟩ Mk 1.2; ⟨reaan⟩ Jn 14.5); e·á·t (also é·ya·t?) 'where he goes' (⟨reat⟩ Jn 12.35); e·á·t=č 'the way he will go' (⟨rat⟩ Mt 3.3, Jn 1.23; Gr. 3.13(2)b); e·á·č·i·k 'the ones that go' (⟨rathek⟩ Mt 7.13); é·ank 'the way' (*lit.*, 'where one goes') (⟨reuf⟩ Jn 14.6; Gr. 2.14c).

• i·a·-: ló·məwe nə́ tí·a·n 'he went there long ago' (OA; Gr. 4.42l, 5.43g).

• i·ha·-: ná=nə tí·ha·n 'he always goes over there' (OA; Gr. 4.42k, 5.41t).

=á· P POT (enclitic particle of potentiality; Gr. 5.24a) 'would, should, etc.' (Lk 1.60, Mt 3.14, Jn 1.46, etc.); máta=á· 'it shouldn't be' (Lk 1.60).

♦ With a subjunctive indicates a general truth (Mk 2.21, Lk 5.37, Mt 18.14).

♦ tá=á· 'would not, will not' (see tá (2)): któli-=č tá=á· -ne·mó·wən 'so that you cannot see them' (Lk 19.42).

♦ May be repeated redundantly in a subordinate clause (e.g., Mk 3.26, Jn 3.12, Jn 5.31, Jn 5.46, Jn 6.44).

♦ May have scope over a following main clause (e.g., Jn 8.39, Lk 12.28).

†a·či·lé·yas 'Archelaus' (Mt 2.22).

a·č·i·mo·lsi·- (iha·č·i·mo·lsi·- [Rih+], eha·č·i·mo·lsi·- [Rih+; IC]) AI 'deliberate, hold a council': máta=háč=á· lahápa a·č·i·mo·lsí·i 'would he not take the time to hold a council?' (Lk 14.31); mái-wíči-a·č·i·mo·lsúwak 'they went to hold a council' (Mt 12.14); ehənta-a·č·i·mo·lsihtí·t 'where they had their councils' (Lk 22.66); mé·či kíši-a·č·i·mo·lsihtí·t·e 'after they had deliberated' (Mt 28.12); énta-a·č·i·mó·lsink 'to the councils' (Mt 10.17, Mk 13.9&); ná .. mɔ́i-a·č·i·mo·lsi·né·ɔ 'then they went to hold a council' (Mt 22.15).
 • iha·č·i·mo·lsi·-: nihəláči=č iha·č·i·mo·lsúwak 'they will hold their own councils' (1834b:45.9).
 • eha·č·i·mo·lsi·-: eha·č·i·mo·lsí·č·i·k 'the council members, councillors' (Mt 26.59, Lk 22.66, Mk 15.3, Mt 28.12); eha·č·i·mo·lsi·lí·č·i (obv.) (Jn 11.47, Mt 27.3).

a·č·i·mo·lx- (|āčīmōlax-|; Gr. 5.98) TA 'report to', TA+O 'tell about O2, recount O2 to': a·č·i·mó·lxi·kw 'tell me (you pl.)' (Mk 11.30); mé·či a·č·i·mo·lxúkwke né·l i·lá·ɔ 'after the captain (obv.) had reported to him' (Mk 15.45&); a·č·i·mo·lxié·k·we=č 'if you (pl.) tell me' (Mt 21.24); tɔ·č·i·mo·lxawwá·ɔ wé·mi é·le·k 'they recounted to them everything that happened' (Mk 5.16); kta·č·i·mo·lxálən 'I'm telling you about it' (1842:22.5).
 ▸ Cf. ⟨Atschimolehan⟩ (error for ⟨°chan⟩) "to relate to somebody" (B&A 24).

a·č·i·mwi·- AI 'tell' (Gr. 5.104e): a·č·í·mwi·l ntəli-mahta·ptó·ne·n 'report my evil sayings (you sg.)' (Jn 18.23); təli-=č -a·č·í·mwi·n 'to tell about [that light]' (*lit.*, 'that he would tell about') (Jn 1.7); xkwi·t·á·k·e=č táli-a·č·í·mwi·n 'it shall be announced on the rooftops' (Lk 12.3).

-a·ki·- 'land': see hák·i.

á·ksən (-a·ksənəm-) AN 'ox' (BS); a·ksə́nak 'oxen' (Lk 14.19; LTD); a·ksə́nal 'oxen (obv.)' (Jn 2.14), a·ksə́na (Jn 2.15).
 • -a·ksənəm-: nta·ksənómak 'my oxen' (Mt 22.4).
 ▸ From the English plural *oxen*.

a·k·ɔntpé·p·i IN 'head scarf' (1834a:13).

á·lai PV (Gr. 5.27a, 5.23c, 5.128d) 'be unable to' (Mk 2.4&, Lk 14.30, 18.27); tɔ́·lai 'they failed to' (Jn 10.39, Mk 9.18, Lk 18.27 [gapped main verb; Gr 6.32a]); tɔ́·lai-káski 'he cannot do it' (1834b:23.3).
 ▸ See Gr. 2.74a and 5.23c; and contrast ála above.

a·ləmi·- AI 'be afraid': á·ləmu 'he or she is afraid' (Gr. 5.10e); a·ləmó·p·ani·k 'they became afraid' (Lk 1.65); káči a·ləmí·he·kw 'don't be afraid (you pl.)' (Lk 12.32, Jn 14.27).

a·lə́nte P 'some' (used of anim. and inan.) (Jn 3.25, Lk 8.2, Mt 12.2, 12.38, etc.).

a·ləntemi·- AI 'be some': a·lənté·mie·kw 'some of you (pl.)' (Lk 21.16, 1834b:46.2).

a·lo·kwé·p·i IN 'headdress'; ka·wənší·i-a·lo·kwé·p·i 'a headdress of thorns' (Mt 27.29).

a·lo·kwe·p·i·s·i·- AI 'wear as headdress': tɔ·lo·kwe·p·i·s·í·na ka·wə́nša 'he was wearing the thorns as a headdress' (Jn 19.5).

a·lo·kwi·- AI 'be thin': a·ló·ku 'he's thin, in poor shape' (OA), 'skinny' (LTD); áhi-a·ló·ku 'he's doing very poorly' (Mk 9.18).

a·lo·lahtehəla·- AI 'throw oneself face-down': a·lo·lahtéhəle· 'he threw himself face-down' (Lk 17.16; KJV "fell down on his face"); hák·ink lí-a·lo·lahtehəlé·ɔk 'they threw themselves face-down on the ground' (Mk 16.5&; Gr. 6.7b).

†á·lɔ·s IN 'aloe': †məl ó·k †á·lɔ·s 'myrrh and aloes' (Jn 19.39).

†a·lpías 'Alphaeus' (Lk 6.15, Mk 2.14, Mt 10.3).

á·man IN 'fishhook' (Mt 17.27).

a·manihi·- AI+O 'knock over': tɔ·manihí·na 'he knocked them (inan.) over' (Mk 11.15).

á·məwe AN 'bee' (FW, 1834a:12).
- a·məwe·í·i (Gr. 5.122b) PN '(of) bee(s)' (Mt 3.4).

a·mwi·- AI 'arise (from sleep or death)': á·mwi·p 'he has risen' (Mt 28.6); á·mwi·l 'get up (you sg.)' (Mt 2.13, 2.20, Mk 2.9, etc.); a·mwi·lí·t·əp 'who (obv.) had risen' (Jn 12.9; Gr. 4.75s); ntá·mwi 'I shall rise' (Mt 27.63); ntə́li-=č naxo·k·wənakháke lápi -á·mwi·n 'for me to rise up again after three days' (Mt 16.21); ná tó·mwi·n 'then he got up' (Mk 9.27).
- a·mo·lti·- AI (coll.; Gr. 5.75c): a·mo·ltínke 'when people all rise up' (Jn 11.24).

a·mwi·kən- TA 'raise (from a lying position or death)': a·mwí·kəno· 'raise up [the dead] (you pl.)' (Mt 10.8); é·li- we·t·ó·x·ink -a·mwí·kəna·t 'as the father raises [the dead]' (Jn 5.21); a·yáhi-a·mwi·kənə́ntəp 'who had earlier been raised up' (Jn 12.1); énta-a·mwi·kəná·t·e 'when he raised him up' (Jn 12.17; Gr. 4.62i); tɔ·mwi·kəná·ɔ 'he raised her up' (Mk 1.31).
▶ /k/ in a·mwí·kəna 'lift him up!' (prefixless form used as an imperative; LTD ND); cf. Mun a·mwihkən- (dict.).

a·mwi·kihəla·- II 'rise up': a·mwi·kíhəle· nihəláči '[his bundle] rose up by itself' (1842:13.2).

a·mwi·m- TA (with wíči- PV) 'rise with' : kəwíči-=č -a·mwi·mkúwa 'she will rise up along with you (pl.)' (Mt 12.42).

a·mwi·ɔ́·k·an IN 'resurrection' (Jn 11.25).

†á·nas 'Annas' (Lk 3.2, Jn 18.13).

a·nhuk° (|ānəhkw-|) 'in succession' (Gr. §5.2a).

a·nhukɔ·č·i·mwi·- AI 'interpret, translate' (cf. Gr. 5.63a): énta-a·nhukɔ·č·í·mwink 'when interpreted' (Mt 1.23).

a·nhukwənte·- II 'be an added-on room, a porch': ná é·li-a·nhukwə́nte·k tɔ́·n 'then he went into the porch' (Lk 22.56-57&); né·li- nə́ é·li-a·nhukwə́nte·k -ahpí·t 'while he was sitting on the porch' (Lk 22.58&); é·li-a·nhukwə́nte·k '(to) an adjoining room' (1842:16.1).

a·nhúkwi (aha·nhúkwi) P 'succeeding, in addition, in turn' (Lk 1.50, 1.55, Lk 3.19-20, etc.); a·nhúkwi .. o·x·wi·s·əwá·ɔl 'great-grandchildren' (1834b:20.10).
• aha·nhúkwi P 'succeeding': aha·nhúkwi nni·č·a·nəná·nak 'the succeeding generations of our children' (Mt 27.25); aha·nhúkwi kəni·č·a·nəwa·i·ké·i e·ləmo·k·wənák·a 'through the succeeding generations of your and their descendants forever' (1842:8.1); né·wən aha·nhúkwi 'four generations' (1842:11.1).

†a·pailə́nink 'in Abilene' (Lk 3.1; misprinted ⟨Apyliuif⟩, presumably for ⟨Apylinif⟩).

á·pči (i·á·pči; Gr. 5.43h) P: 'always' (Lk 1.80, 2.37, 2.41, Mt 7.17, etc.); 'still' (Jn 4.35, 8.14).
• ihá·pči 'always' (1834b:32.9 2x, back cover 10); also in a hymn in LTD.
• i·á·pči P 'still' (1834b:11.3; Jn 8.14, 9.30, Mt 17.27, Lk 12.38). Cf. ⟨ábtschi⟩ "alway" (Z. 10), ⟨ihìabtschi⟩ 'still, yet' (Z. 183), ⟨Ijabtschi⟩ 'still' (Z. 236, s.v. "yet").

-a·phik°: see haphik°.

a·phishikaw- TA 'go to meet (one who is coming)' (Gr. 2.49b): a·phishíko· 'go to meet him (you pl.)' (Mt 25.6); a·phishikaɔhtí·t·e 'they went to meet one' (Mt 25.1); tɔ·phishikaɔ́·ɔ 'she went to meet him' (Jn 11.20); ná tɔ·phishíkaɔ·n 'then he went to meet him' (Lk 15.20).

á·phit P 'on the way, before reaching one's destination' (1834b:37.7; V, OA).

a·phita·ɔ́nkwe (Gr. 5.31i.1) P 'halfway up the hill' (Lk 4.29).

a·phitxənehəla·- AI 'row into the wind': é·li-a·phitxənehəláhti·t 'as they were rowing into the wind' (Mk 6.48).

a·phukwe·- AI 'look up': a·phúkwe· 'he lifted his gaze' (Lk 6.20); a·phúkwe·kw 'lift your (pl.) gaze' (Jn 4.35); a·phukwé·t·e 'when he looked up' (Mk 8.24, Mk 8.25, Lk 21.1); kta·phukwéhəmɔ=č 'you (pl.) must look up' (Lk 21.28).

-á·pi: see hápi.

a·pkən- TA 'open': mé·či a·pkəná·t·e le·khí·k·ana 'after he had opened the book' (Lk 4.17).

a·pt° (|āpət-|) 'to death' (Gr. §5.2a).

a·ptəpe·- (aha·ptəp·e·- [Rvh+]) AI 'drown': wé·mi awé·n a·ptəp·e· 'everyone drowned' (1842:9.5); wé·mi a·ptəp·é·p·ani·k 'they all were drowned' (Mt 24.39); ə́nta-a·ptəp·éhti·t 'where they drowned in the sea' (Mk 5.13).
  • aha·ptəp·e·-: aha·ptəp·é·ɔk 'they drown' (OA; Gr. 5.38w).

a·pti·ksəwá·k·an* IN 'sweat'; tɔ·pti·ksəwá·k·an 'his sweat' (Lk 22.44).

a·pto·ná·k·an IN (Gr. 5.55b) 'word' (Jn 1.14, Lk 4.18, Mt 4.23, 9.35, 13.19), 'words' (Mk 5.36), 'commandment' (Mt 22.36), 'voice' (Mt 3.3, 3.17), 'vow' (Mt 5.28); wé·lhik a·pto·ná·k·an 'good word' (Lk 4.18, Mt 4.23, 9.35, Mk 16.15; KJV "gospel"); a·pto·ná·k·anal 'laws' (Mt 5.19; KJV "commandments"); xúwi-a·pto·ná·k·anal 'ancient laws' (Mt 5.17; KJV "the law"); 'words' (Jn 14.10); nta·pto·ná·k·an 'my word(s)' (Jn 5.24, 5.47, Mt 7.24, 7.26, Jn 8.37, Jn 8.43 [2x], etc.); nta·pto·ná·k·ana 'my words' (Mk 14.9); kta·pto·ná·k·an 'your (sg.) word' (Jn 17.6, 17.14, 17.17); kta·pto·ná·k·ana 'your (sg.) words' (Mt 12.37); nta·pto·na·k·anə́na 'our report' (Jn 12.38); kta·pto·na·k·anúwa 'your (pl.) words' (Mt 10.14, Jn 15.20); wta·pto·ná·k·an 'his order' (Lk 2.1; Gr. 2.56a); tɔ·pto·ná·k·an 'his word(s)' (Lk 1.6, 3.2, Jn 3.34, etc.); tɔ·pto·ná·k·ana 'his words' (Mt 13.35); tɔ·pto·na·k·anúwa 'their law' (Mt 7.12, Lk 16.29), 'their word(s)' (Mt 11.13, Jn 8.17, etc.; ⟨tapt-⟩ Lk 24.11); tɔ·pto·na·k·aní·li·t 'their (obv.) laws' (Mt 15.9); nta·pto·ná·k·anink 'in my word' (Jn 8.31); kta·pto·na·k·anəwá·ink 'by your (pl.) traditions' (Mt 15.3, 15.6); wta·pto·ná·k·anink 'in his law' (Lk 2.39); tɔ·pto·ná·k·ana 'his words' (⟨toptwnaknu⟩ Mt 13.35 [em.]); tɔ·pto·na·k·anəwá·ink 'within their laws' (Mk 7.5); yó·l xúwi-a·pto·ná·k·anal 'the old laws' (Mt 5.17).

a·pto·na·l- (aha·pto·na·l- [Rvh+]; Gr. 5.38v) TA 'say about' — a·pto·na·t- TI(1a) 'speak'.
  ▪ a·pto·na·l- (TA): wé·mi .. ə́ntxi- awé·n nó·čkwe -a·pto·ná·li·t 'every frivolous thing anyone says about me' (Mt 12.36).
  • aha·pto·na·l-: aha·pto·ná·lkɔn 'the one speaking to you' (Jn 4.26).
  ▪ a·pto·na·t- (TI): é·li- .. -a·pto·ná·t·ank 'for he speaks [God's word]' (Jn 3.34).

a·pto·ne·- AI 'speak': é·li- máta nihəláči -a·pto·né·a 'because I do not speak on my own' (⟨aptwnru⟩ Jn 12.49); nta·ptó·ne 'I speak' (Jn 5.34, Mt 13.35); máta=á· ki·ló·wa nihəláči kta·pto·ne·húmɔ 'it would not be *you* (pl.) speaking yourselves' (Mk 13.11); ná tɔ·ptó·ne·n 'then he spoke' (Lk 1.64).

a·pto·ne·t- TI(2) 'speak, utter': a·pto·né·ta·kw 'who speaks [the word of God]' (Mk 2.6); a·pto·né·tae·kw 'what you (pl.) speak' (Mt 10.20); a·pto·ne·tuhtí·t·əp 'which they reported' (Mt 1.22; Gr. 4.78s).

a·p·á·č·i PV 'returning, in return' (Gr. 5.129f): ə́nta-a·p·a·č·i-alaíhti·t 'when they got back from their hunt' (ME); tá·á· kta·p·á·č·i- kéku -li·húmɔ 'you (pl.) won't speak to me in return' (Lk 22.68; KJV "ye will not answer me").

a·p·á·č·i- AI 'return home, come back': a·p·a·č·iá·ne·č 'when I return' (Lk 10.35); a·p·a·č·í·t·e 'when he got back' (Lk 14.21, 15.25, Mk 14.40); a·p·a·č·ihtí·t·e 'when they returned home' (Lk 7.10).

a·p·a·kwi·- AI 'rise up (from stooping)': a·p·á·kwi·p 'he rose up' (Jn 8.7); takó· kí·kski-a·p·a·kwí·i·p 'she was never able to straighten up' (Lk 13.11); a·p·a·kwí·t·e 'when he raised himself up' (Jn 8.10); tɔ·p·á·kwi·n 'she straightened up' (Lk 13.13).

a·p·ensi·- AI(+O) 'inherit': ə́ntxi-=á· -a·p·énsia 'everything I would inherit' (Lk 15.12).

áp·ələš AN 'apple'; a·p·ələš·ak 'apples' (Mk 11.13&). ▸ A loanword (< Mun á·pə̆ləš < Dutch; Gr. 3.1h, 5.9d; Goddard 1974:157).

a·p·əwat·- II 'be easy': á·p·əwat 'it is easy' (Mt 11.30, 1842:20.2, 21.4), tá=háč nə́ aləwí·i á·p·əwat 'which is easier?' (Mk 2.9); a·p·əwát·u 'they are easy' (1834a:13); e·lkí·kwi-a·p·əwát·ək 'how easy it is' (Mt 19.24; Gr. 5.128m).

a·p·əwe·lənt- TI(1a) 'think easy': wə́nči-a·p·əwe·ləntamíhti·t 'because they think it's easy' (1834a:16); kta·p·əwe·lə́ntamən=č 'you (sg.) will think it's easy' (1842:19.7, 20.2).

á·p·əwi (Gr. 5.129g) PV 'easily' (Mt 13.5, Mk 9.23, Mt 19.24, Lk 22.6).

a·p·əwihəla·- II 'become easy': a·p·əwíhəle· 'it becomes easy' (1834a: Cover, 1).

a·s·o·wi·- AI 'sing': a·s·ó·u 'he sings' (Gr. 2.14d); lí-a·s·ó·wi·n 'that there was singing' (Lk 15.25); ná tɔ·s·o·wi·né·ɔ 'then they sang' (Mt 26.30).

a·s·uwwá·k·an IN 'song' (LB; Gr. 2.14d, 5.58o).

a·s·uwwe·khí·k·an IN 'psalm (*lit.*, written song)'; a·s·uwwe·khí·k·anink 'in the psalms' (Mk 12.36, Lk 24.44).

†á·šəl 'Aser (tribe)' (Lk 2.36).

a·šíte P 'instead, on the other hand' (Lk 1.52, 1.53, Mt 4.8, Jn 4.20, etc.; Gr. 2.73a).

a·š·əwº (|āšəw-|) 'across' (Gr. 5.7f).

a·š·əwa·khwitehá·s·i·k (cf. Gr. 5.7f) 'cross' (Jn 19.17, Mt 27.32&), énta-a·š·əwa·khwitehá·s·i·k (Mt 27.42, Jn 19.25). ▸ Cf. a·š·əwa·kwhitehá·s·ian 'Christ (voc.)' (ME; *lit.* 'you who were crucified' < |āšəwāhkwəhtehāsī-|).

a·š·əwi·teha·s·i·-* II, as if 'be struck across': (lexicalized participle) a·š·əwi·tehá·s·i·k*, as if 'what is struck across', used to mean 'what is paid back' (perhaps a gambling term).

• -t-a·š·əwi·teha·s·i·k·əm-: kta·š·əwi·teha·s·í·k·əm 'your recompense(?)' (⟨ktajwetrvasekum⟩ Mt 19.21; KJV "treasure in heaven").

a·š·unté·i P: a·š·unté·i khak·ayəwá·ink wə́nči 'from each other (of you)' (Jn 5.44).

a·š·unte·n- (eha·š·unte·n- [Rih+; IC]) TA, TI(1b) 'trade': wə́nči-=á· -a·š·unté·na·t 'which they (indef.) would trade (it [anim.]) for' (Mt 16.26); kí·xki tə́nta-a·š·unté·na·n 'he traded (them) near there' (Jn 5.2).

• eha·š·unte·n-: eha·š·unte·nínki·k móni 'changers of money' (Jn 2.14); eha·š·unte·nəməlí·č·i (obv.) (Jn 2.15).

a·š·unte·na·si·- II 'be traded, exchanged' (Gr. 5.105x): ehə́nta-a·š·unte·ná·s·i·k 'where it is exchanged' (Lk 19.23, Mk 11.15).

-a·tahəl-: see hatahəl-.

-a·taw-: see hataw-.

a·tenkpe·- (i·a·tenkpe·- [Rī+]) II 'be extinguished': máta i·a·ténkpe·kw 'that is never extinguished' (Lk 3.17). ▸ Cf. ⟨Atenkpatton⟩ [TI(2)] 'to quench fire' (B&A 23).

a·te·- (i·a·te·- [Rī+]) II (also AI) 'go out (of fire, etc.)': a·té·ɔk '[our lamps (anim.)] have gone out' (Mt 25.8).

• i·a·te·-: nə́ tə́ntay máta=á· i·a·té·i 'the fire would never go out' (Mk 9.44, 9.48; Gr. 5.44p); máta=á· i·á·te·k 'that will never go out' (Mt 25.41).

†á·təm 'Adam' (1834b:17.9).

á·wəlink P 'hour(s)'; kwə́t·i á·wəlink 'for one hour' (Mt 20.12, Mk 14.37, Lk 22.59-60&); télən ɔ́·k ní·š·a á·wəlink 'for twelve hours' (Jn 11.9); naxá á·wəlink 'for three hours' (1834b:35.5; LB).

a·yáhi (1): see áhi.

a·yáhi (2) (Gr. 5.27b) PV 'previously, formerly, earlier, already' (⟨aeavi⟩ Jn 11.37, Jn 12.1, Mt 26.6, Mt 10.10, ⟨yerve⟩ Mt 23.37, ⟨yeave⟩ Lk 13.34, ⟨yavi⟩ Jn 19.39, Mk 16.9, Jn 21.20)

a·yahkən°: see ahkən°.

a·yahpi-: see ahpi·-.

a·yant- TI(a) 'desire, want' (Gr. §2.11b): nni·núči- nté·hink -táli-a·yántamən 'I have long desired it in my heart' (Lk 22.15).

č

=č P FUT (indicating future time, etc.; Gr. 5.24b) (Jn 1.7 [2x], 1.8, 1.9, Lk 1.13 [2x], etc.); =š before /t/: awé·n=š=tá 'as to who' (1834b:47.14); kéku=š=tá 'what (fut.)' (Jn 6.6; LTD FW).
 ♦ May be placed (or anticipated redundantly) outside its own clause: (e.g.) tá·ɔni=č i·ánkəlo·p, šúkw=č lápi lehəlé·x·e· 'even though he died some time ago, still he shall live again' (Jn 11.25); occurs three times in Lk 18.31.
 ♦ May be gapped in a following clause: Jn 7.35.

čan° (|čan-|) 'bad, wrong' (Gr. §5.2a); čəčan- (with [Rə̀+]), the short /-č-/ conjectured.

čanaehɔ·s·i- AI 'do wrong': nčanaehɔ́·s·i 'I did wrong' (⟨hairvosi⟩ 1834b:29.8 [em.] if correct so; LTD WS); mé·či=tá kčanaehɔ́·s·i 'you (sg.) have done something wrong' (WL).

čana·pto·na·l- TA 'speak ill of': awé·n čana·pto·na·lá·t·e 'if anyone speaks ill of him' (Mt 12.32 [2x]).

čana·wsəwá·k·an IN 'misdeed(s), sin' (Jn 7.18, Mt 18.7); kčana·wsəwá·k·an 'your misdeeds' (Mt 6.14, 6.15); čɔna·wsəwá·k·an 'his misdeeds' (Mt 6.14, 6.15, Mt 26.28); nčana·wsəwa·k·anə́na 'our misdeeds' (Mt 6.12, Lk 11.4); kčana·wsəwa·k·anúwa 'your (pl.) sins' (Mk 11.25, 11.26); čɔna·wsəwa·k·anúwa 'their misdeeds' (Mt 18.35).

čana·wsi·- (čəčana·wsi·- [Rə̀+]) AI 'do wrong': čaná·wsu 'he does wrong' (Lk 12.48).
 • čəčana·wsi·-: čəčana·wsúwak 'they keep doing wrong' (Mt 18.7).

†čanesalití·i PN '(of) Gennesaret': †čanesalití·i-hák·ink 'to the land of Gennesaret' (Mt 14.34).

čane·ləm- TA 'be disappointed in' — čane·lənt- (TI(1a)) TI-O 'be reluctant, be disappointed'
 ■ čane·ləm- (TA): máta=háč=á· kúnči-čane·ləmí·wən 'wouldn't you be disappointed with me because of it' (1834b:9.7).
 ■ čane·lənt- (TI-O): káči čane·ləntánkhan 'do not be reluctant (to)' (Mt 1.20; KJV "fear not (to)"; Gr. 4.50h); wénči-=č máta -čane·ləntamó·we·kw 'so that you (pl.) will not be reluctant' (Jn 16.1; KJV "be offended"); šáxahki=á· kčane·lə́ntam 'you (sg.) would certainly be disappointed' (1842:22.3).

čane·ləntaməwá·k·an 'disappointment' (1834b:25.2).

čane·ləntamo·ha·ləwe·- (če·ne·ləntamo·ha·ləwe·-) AI 'make people dissatisfied, spread discontent': če·ne·ləntamo·há·ləwe·t 'one who spreads discontent' (Lk 23.14; KJV "one that perverteth the people").

čane·ləntamo·he·- AI+O 'make dissatisfied': čɔne·ləntamo·hé·na 'he makes them discontented' (Lk 23.5; KJV "stirreth up").

čanəstaw- (-čans·ət·aw-) TA — čanəst- (-čans·ət·-) TI(1a) 'take amiss'.
 ■ čanəstaw- (TA): káči=tá čanəstaí·he·kw 'do not take what I say amiss' (Jn 6.43; KJV "murmur not among yourselves").
 • -čans·ət·aw-: čɔns·ət·aɔwwá·ɔ 'they took what he said amiss' (Jn 6.41; KJV "murmur at").

▪ čanəst- (TI): kəmax·ínkwi-čanəstamúhəmɔ 'you (pl.) greatly misunderstand' (Mk 12.27; KJV "err"); kúnči-čanəstamənéʼɔ 'you (pl.) take it amiss' (Jn 6.61; KJV "offend you").

čáni (with ləsi·-; Gr. 5.129h) PV 'wrong' (Mt 12.5, 18.15 [2x], Lk 16.10 [2x], etc.); máta=háč nə́ kúnči-čáni-ləs·i·wənéʼɔ 'are you not going wrong because of it?' (Mk 12.24).

čani·laenke·- AI 'urge bad things on people': éntxi-čani·laénke·t 'as many as tempt people to sin' (Mt 18.7; RSV "for temptations to sin"); čani·laenkéʼtʻe 'if he tempts people to sin' (Lk 17.1).

čani·laentəwá·k·an (Gr. 5.114b) IN 'temptations to sin' (Lk 17.1; RSV [KJV "offences"]).

čani·lae·h- (če·ni·lae·h-, čəčani·lae·h- [R$\grave{\partial}$+]) TA 'offend, mistreat': čani·laehkóne 'if it offends you' (Mt 5.29, 5.30, 18.8, 18.9); čani·lae·híʼtʻe 'if he mistreats me' (Mt 18.21); nčani·laéʻha·p 'I have offended him' (Lk 15.18, 15.21; Gr. 4.69d); ná lápi čɔni·lae·ha·néʼɔ 'then they again offended [God]' (1842:9.9).

• če·ni·lae·h-: če·ni·laéhkweʻkw 'who has wronged you (pl.)' (Mk 11.25).

• čəč·ani·lae·h-: čəčani·laehkwénki·k 'those that mistreat us' (Mt 6.12, Lk 11.4).

čani·lae·m- (čəčani·lae·m- [R$\grave{\partial}$+]) TA 'provoke, urge to do wrong': čani·lae·máʼtʻe 'if he causes (one) to do wrong' (Mk 9.42, Lk 17.2; RSV "cause .. to sin" [KJV "offend"]); tóləmi-káhta-čani·lae·ma·néʼɔ 'they began to seek to provoke him' (Lk 11.53; KJV "to urge him vehemently"; RSV "provoke").

• čəčani·lae·m-: tá=č=háč ksá·ki-čəčani·lae·míʼneʼn 'how long will you keep us in doubt?' (Jn 10.24; KJV "make us to doubt"; RSV "keep us in suspense").

čani·m- TA 'accuse, criticize': lí-=áʻ -čaníʼmaʻ 'that he would be accused' (1834b:25.3); kéku=áʻ éʻli-čani·máhtiʼt 'some way they could accuse him' (Lk 6.7; Gr. 4.67(1)b); tá=áʻ kčani·maʻíʼɔk 'you would not criticize them' (Mt 12.7; KJV "condemn"; Gr. 4.83k); čɔni·mawwáʼɔ 'they criticized him, her' (Mk 14.5, Mt 20.11 [KJV "murmured against"]), 'they admonished her' (Mk 14.5).

čani·neho·t·i·- (čəčani·neho·t·i·- [R$\grave{\partial}$+]) AI (recip.; Gr. 5.110g) 'dispute with each other': čani·nehóʻtʻəwak 'they dispute among themselves' (Jn 10.19).

• čəčani·neho·t·i·-: čəčani·nehóʻtʻiʼn '(that) there are disputes' (⟨hehanenevwten⟩ Lk 2.34); kéku=háč wénči-čəčani·nehóʻtʻieʼkw 'what did you (pl.) argue with each other about?' (⟨hihanencv-⟩ Mk 9.33).

čani·x·ən- II 'be broken': wənči-=áʻ máta -čaníʼx·ink 'so that [the law] would not be broken' (Jn 7.23).

čá·ləs 'Charles' (1842:[p. 2]); i.e. (presumably), Charles Journeycake.

čečhɔ·pwənúweʻt 'Baptist': see čhɔ·pwənawe·-.

čehči·sktəlínkhwink hémpəs 'towel' (⟨hchesktulifqvif vcmpus⟩ Jn 13.4), *lit.*, 'face-wiping cloth'.
  ♦ Cf. čehči·sktəlínkwink (LB).

†čelikóʻwunk (loc.) 'to Jericho' (Lk 10.30). ▸ See also †nčéliku.

†čeli·mayás·a: see †nčeli·máya.

čéʻkəp 'Jacob' (1834b:19.10). ▸ The later texts use †nčéʻkəp.

†čéʻləs 'Jairus' (Mk 5.22).

čəčani·neho·t·i·-: see čani·neho·t·i·-.

čəčpa·ke·i·- AI 'be separate tribes': éʻli-čəčpa·ke·íhtiʼt 'how they were separate tribes' (1834b:42.10).

čəčpe·ləntóʻpʻaniʼk 'there was a difference of opinion among them' (Jn 7.43; KJV "there was a division among").

čə́čpi PV 'separately, distinct from each other' (Gr. 5.129k): čə́čpi-luwé·ɔk 'they gave differing accounts' (Mk 14.56); lí-čə́čpi-lé· wé·mi yú táli 'that things are happening in all different places' (Mk 13.7).

čəčpi·t·e·hé·ɔk 'they have a difference of opinion' (Jn 9.16; KJV "there was a division among them").

čəmi·na P 'on and on' (1842:21.3). ▸ Cf. kwčəmí·na 'on and on' (OA), ⟨Ktschimine⟩ "as soon as" (B&A 58).

čəphik IN 'root'; čəphíkink 'at the root' (Mt 3.10).

čəphiko·wi·- II 'have root(s)': takó· čəphiko·wí·i 'it had no roots' (Mt 13.6), 'it has not yet taken root' (Mt 13.21); é·li máta čəphikó·wi·k 'because it had no roots' (1834b:26.14).

čə́p·wi·- AI 'disappear into the crowd, woods, etc.': čə́p·wi·kw 'disappear [into the fire] (you pl.)' (Mt 25.41); čə́p·wi·p 'he passed through [wheat fields]' (⟨hwpwep⟩ Lk 6.1; KJV "went through"), 'he slipped into [the crowd]' (Jn 8.59); ná tɔ́ləmi-čə́p·wi·n 'then he disappeared off into the crowd' (Lk 4.30; KJV "passing through the midst of them"; Gr. 5.128b).

čhɔ·pº (-čɔhɔ·pº, |čahwāhpw-|) 'into water, dip' (Gr. §5.2a; the peculiar shape of this initial comes from its onomatopoetic quality; cf. English *kersplash, kerplunk*).

čhɔ·pɔnihi·- (-čɔhɔ·pɔnihi·-) AI+O 'cast into water': lí-čhɔ·pɔníhi·kw ktanshi·k·anúwa 'dip your net (you pl.)' (Jn 21.6).
• -čɔhɔ·pɔnihi·-: kčɔhɔ·pɔníhi·n=č ktak·ɔ·ní·k·an 'you must throw in your net' (Lk 5.4).

čhɔ·pɔ·k·ihəl- (-čɔhɔ·pɔ·k·ihəl-; Gr. 5.11a, 5.18b) AI 'jump into water': ná čɔhɔ·pɔ·k·íhələn 'then he jumped into the water' (Jn 21.7).

čhɔ·pwələnče·- AI 'dip fingers in water': máta təmí·ki čhɔ·pwələnčé·k·we 'if he does not dip his fingers in water often' (Mk 7.3 [3s for 3p]; KJV "they wash their hands oft").

čhɔ·pwən- (-čɔhɔ·pwən-, |čahwa·hpwən-|) TA 'baptize' — TI 'dip in water'.
▪ čhɔ·pwən- (TA): čhɔ·pwəná·č·i·l '(ones, obv.) that he baptized' (Jn 4.1); čhɔ·pwənát·əp 'who had baptized them' (Lk 7.29); čhɔ́·pwəna·n 'he is baptized' (Jn 3.26); mái-čhɔ·pwəná·ɔk 'they are coming to be baptized' (Lk 3.12); ktə́li-čhɔ·pwənək·éhəmɔ 'you (pl.) shall be baptized (so)' (Acts 1.5 [em.]); tə́nta-čhɔ́·pwəna·n 'he baptized them (there)' (Jn 3.23).
• -čɔhɔ·pwən-: kčɔhɔ·pwənukw=č 'he will baptize you (sg.)' (Lk 3.16); ɔ́·k=č kčɔhɔ·pwənə́k·e 'and you (sg.) will be baptized' (1834b:23.1); čɔhɔ·pwənuk·əwá·p·ani 'they were baptized by him (obv.)' (Mt 3.6; Gr. 4.69s); kčɔhɔ́·pwəni 'you baptize me' (Mt 3.14; Gr. 5.100c).
▪ čhɔ·pwən- (TI): čhɔ·pwənínkeč 'let him dip it' (Lk 16.24; Gr. 4.114n); kíši-čhɔ·pwənəmá·ne 'after I have dipped it' (Jn 13.26); kíši-čhɔ·pwənínke 'after he dipped it' (Jn 13.26).

čhɔ·pwəna·s·i·- II 'be washed' (Gr. 5.105s): énta-čhɔ·pwəná·s·i·k 'when they (inan.) are washed' (Mk 7.4).

čhɔ·pwənəntəwá·k·an (-čɔhɔ·pwənəntəwa·k·an-; Gr. 5.114c) IN 'baptism' (Lk 3.3, 12.50).
• -čɔhɔ·pwənəntəwa·k·an-: wčɔhɔ·pwənəntəwá·k·an 'his baptism' (Mt 21.25; Gr. 5.116e); wčɔhɔ·pwənəntəwá·k·anink 'in his baptism' (Lk 7.29 [em.]; B ⟨hvop-⟩ /čhɔ·p-/).

čhɔ·pwənəwe·- (čičhɔ·pwənəwe·- [Rih+], čečhɔ·pwənəwe·- [Rih+; IC], |čahwāhpwənəwē-|; Gr. 5.101g) AI 'baptize people': mpínk ntíhəli-čhɔ·pwənúwe 'I baptize people in water' (Jn 1.26); máta čhɔ·pwənəwé·i·p 'he had not baptized people' (Jn 4.2); kɔ́č=háč čhɔ·pwənəwé·an 'why do you baptize people?' (Jn 1.25; Gr. 4.60a); énta-čhɔ·pwənúwe·t 'where he was baptizing people' (Mt 3.7); énta-čhɔ·pwənəwé·t·əp 'where John baptized people' (Jn 1.28); etc.
• čičhɔ·pwənəwe·-: čičhɔ·pwənəwé·p·ani·k 'they baptized people' (Jn 3.22); nčá·na čičhɔ·pwənəwé·t·əp 'John the Baptist' (Mt 16.14); énta- nčá·na -čičhɔ·pwənəwé·t·əp 'where John had baptized people' (Jn 10.40).

• čečhɔ·pwənəwe·-: čečhɔ·pwənúwe·t 'Baptist' (always with nčá·n 'John') (Lk 7.20, 7.28, etc.).

čhɔ·pwəni·k·e·- (čičhɔ·pwəni·k·e·- [Rih+], |čahwāhpwənīkē-|; Gr. 5.100c) AI 'baptize, perform baptism': čhɔ·pwəní·k·e·kw 'baptize (you pl.)' (Mt 28.19); ktəli-čhɔ·pwəni·k·éhəmɔ 'you (pl.) shall baptize (so)' (Acts 1.5 [as written]).

• čičhɔ·pwəni·k·e·-: nčá·na khičí·i čičhɔ·pwəní·k·e·p lí mpínk 'the late John indeed baptized in water' (Acts 1.5).

čhɔ·pwi·nxke·- AI 'wash hand(s)': né·skɔ čhɔ·pwi·nxkéhti·t 'before they dipped their hands in water' (Mk 7.5); tá=á· čhɔ·pwi·nxkehtí·t·e 'if they do not wash their hands' (Mk 7.4).

čínke P 'when?': čínke=ét=tá kpi·p·á·həmp 'when did you come here?' (Jn 6.25); čínke=háč kəne·wəlúhəna·p 'when did we see you?' (Mt 25.44).

♦ čínke néke 'at times before' (Lk 22.53; meaning conjectured, but not a question).

čípahkɔ: see čí·p·akw.

čipahkweho·l- (|čīpakwehōl-|; Gr.5.78i) TA 'put shoes on': čipahkwehó·lo· 'put shoes on his feet (you pl.)' (Lk 15.22).

čípi PN 'dreadful; in an awful way, bad, etc.' (Gr. 2.74c, 5.120a): čípi-aésəs 'a dangerous animal' (1842:22.1); čípi-kéku 'terrible thing' (i.e., whiskey) (1834a:21.32, 1834b:8.9).

▪ čípi (ahčípi [Ra+]) PV: čípi-lé· 'it is dangerous, it is a bad situation, it is powerful' (ME; Gr. 5.129i).

• ahčípi: ə́nta-ahčípi-le·k 'when evil things happened' (OA; Gr. 5.129i).

čí·č (Gr. 5.23d) P 'more, again' (Jn 5.14 [2x], Lk 12.50, etc.).

čí·čankw (-či·čankəm-) AN 'spirit, soul' (Lk 2.27, 4.1, Jn 1.32, 4.24); či·čánkɔ (Jn 1.33, Mt 10.28 [2x]); či·čánkunk 'in the spirit' (⟨Hehufwf⟩ Lk 3.16, Jn 1.33, 4.23; ⟨Hehwfwf⟩ Mt 1.20), mpínk wə́nči ó·k či·čánkunk 'from water and the spirit' (⟨hehwfwf⟩ Jn 3.5; Gr. 6.9l).

• -či·čankəm-: nči·čánkəm 'my spirit' (Lk 1.46); kči·čánkəm 'your soul' (Mt 11.29); wči·čánkəmal 'his spirit' (Lk 1.15, 1.80), wči·čánkəma 'his soul' (Mt 16.26 [2x]).

♦ In latter usage 'mirror' (V, FW, LB; Gr. 3.2c).

či·čankəwá·k·an IN 'spirit' (Lk 1.35); či·čankəwá·k·anink 'from spirit' (Lk 1.35, Jn 3.6, 3.8).

či·čankwi·- AI 'be spirit': či·čánku 'he is a spirit' (Jn 4.24).

či·kh- (|čīkah-|; Gr. 5.100g) TI(1a) 'sweep': máta=háč=á·.. ó·li-či·khamó·wən wí·k·əwam 'would she not sweep the house well?' (Lk 15.8).

či·kha·s·i·- II 'be swept' (Gr. 5.105e): lí- .. -či·khá·s·u 'that it is swept out' (Mt 12.44).

či·k·ən- (či·či·k·ən- |Rvh+| REP) TA+O 'take O2 from, rob of O2': čí·k·əno· 'take it away from him (you pl.)' (Lk 19.24, Mt 25.28); ná né·k wči·k·əna·nć·ɔ 'then they robbed him of it' (Lk 10.30); tá=á· awé·n kči·k·ənuk·o·wəné·ɔ 'no one will take it from you (pl.)' (Jn 16.22).

• či·či·k·ən-: é·li kči·či·k·əna·né·ɔ 'for you (pl.) (repeatedly) take it away from them' (⟨khehequnanro⟩ Mt 23.14, for ⟨khehekunanro⟩).

či·ló·k·e·s IN 'leather strap' (Mt 3.4).

▪ či·lo·k·e·s·í·i PN as P 'of leather strips' (Jn 2.15).

či·ma·kwsi·- AI — či·ma·k·ɔt- II 'smell bad, stink' (Gr. 3.18c, 5.10k).

▪ či·ma·kwsi·- (AI): mé·či=ét či·má·kwsu 'he must already be stinking' (Jn 11.39; OA, LB).

▪ či·ma·k·ɔt- (II): či·má·k·ɔt 'it stinks' (V, OA; Gr. 2.7c).

či·me·- AI 'row': áhi-či·mé·ɔk 'they were rowing hard' (Mk 6.48).

▸ Cf. či·má·k·an 'paddle' (V). ▸ Cf. čí·mhe· 'he is rowing, paddling' (LTD ND).

či·mha·s·i·- II 'be shut up': ná lí-či·mhá·s·u nə́ wí·k·əwam 'and at that the house was shut up tight' (Mt 25.10).

či·mí·i P 'forever' (Mt 10.22, Jn 8.31, 8.35, etc.), 'permanently' (Mt 18.14), 'always' (Jn 14.16).

či·p·akw- (čipahkw-, -mač·ipahkw-, |(ma)čīpakw-|; Gr. 2.7a, 4.2v) IN 'shoe': čí·p·akw 'shoe' (ND, LB), čípahkɔ 'shoes' (V, ND; Mt 10.10, Lk 10.4, 22.35; Gr. 2.17d).
- -mač·ipahkw-: mɔč·ípahkɔl 'his shoes' (Jn 1.27; Gr. 2.17d), mɔč·ípahkɔ (Lk 3.16).

čí·p·ay AN 'ghost' (Mk 6.49, Lk 24.37); čí·p·aya (1834b:32.8).

čí·p·ayankǝlǝk·i·k 'those that had palsy' (Mt 4.24). ▸ Cf. čí·p·ay, ankǝl-.

čí·sas 'Jesus' (⟨Hesus⟩ 1834b:22.7, etc.); či·sás·al (1834b:23.5, etc.), či·sás·a (1834b:23.8, etc.); či·sás·ink 'to Jesus' (1834b:33.3). ▸ Most likely this was /nčí·sas/; see nčí·sas ⟨Nhesus⟩ below.

či·skantamaw- TA+O 'lick O2 of': wči·skantamaɔ·né·ɔ mwǝk·ial 'they licked his sores' (1834b:30.4); wči·skantama·k·ó·ne·p mwǝk·ia 'they (obv.) licked his sores' (Lk 16.21; Gr. 4.71g).

či·skh- TI(1a) 'wipe': wči·skhámǝna 'she wiped them' (Lk 7.44; Gr. 4.39j).

či·skhamaw- TA+O 'wipe O2 of, for' (Gr. 5.94b): wči·skhamáɔ·n 'he wiped them (of, for him) (sbd.)' (Lk 7.38, Jn 12.3, 13.5).

či·skha·s·i·- II 'be wiped away': kǝmat·a·wsǝwa·k·anúwa=č či·skhá·s·u. 'Your sins will be wiped away.' (1834b:40.8).

či·tkwǝs·i·- AI 'be silent': či·tkwǝ́s·u 'he keeps silent' (Mt 13.44); či·tkwǝ́s·ǝwak 'they kept silent' (Mk 9.34, Lk 14.4); či·tkwǝ́s·i·l 'be quiet (you sg.)' (Mk 1.25); či·tkwǝ́s·i·kw 'be quiet (you pl.)' (Mk 10.48&); wénči-či·tkwǝ́s·i·t 'because he remained silent' (Lk 1.22; Gr. 4.67(2)i).

či·t·anᵒ (|čītan-|) 'strong' (Gr. §5.2a).

či·t·anahémpǝs IN 'thick cloth' (Mk 14.51, 14.52); či·t·anahémpsink 'in a thick cloth' (Lk 19.20).

či·t·ana·pto·ne·- AI 'speak strongly': alǝwí·i-či·t·ana·ptó·ne· 'he spoke even more strongly' (Mk 14.31).

či·t·ane·-: see či·t·anǝs·i·- — či·t·ane·-.

či·t·ani·k·i·- AI 'be strong': álǝmi-či·t·ani·k·i·ló·p·ani '(he, obv.) became strong' (Lk 1.80).

či·t·anǝn- TA — TI(Ib) 'hold (on to) firmly'.
- či·t·anǝn- (TA): kči·t·anǝnáwwa=č 'you (pl.) must hold him firmly' (Mk 14.44).
- či·t·anǝn- (TI): čí·t·anǝni 'hold on to it firmly' (1834b:6.5).

či·t·anǝs·ǝwá·k·an IN 'strength'; wči·t·anǝs·ǝwá·k·an 'his strength' (Lk 1.51); kči·t·anǝs·ǝwá·k·anink 'your strength (loc.)' (Lk 10.27, Mk 12.30); mǝsǝč·é·i wǝ́nči wči·t·anǝs·ǝwá·k·anink 'with all his strength' (Mk 12.33).

či·t·anǝs·i·- (ahči·t·anǝs·i·- [Ra+]) AI — či·t·ane·- II 'be strong' (Gr. 5.1d).
- či·t·anǝs·i·- (AI): či·t·anǝ́s·u 'he is strong' (Mk 8.17); či·t·anǝ́s·i·t '(who is) strong' (Mt 12.29 [2x], Lk 11.21); alǝwí·i či·t·anǝs·i·lí·č·i '(who [obv.] is) stronger' (Lk 11.22); é·li-či·t·anǝs·íhti·t ktehǝwá·ok 'because your hearts were hard' (Mt 19.8; KJV "because of the hardness of your hearts"); é·li-či·t·anǝs·í·li·t wtehǝwá·ɔ '(the fact) that their hearts were hard' (Mk 16.14; KJV "hardness of heart," i.e., obtuseness); tǝ́li-či·t·anǝs·i·né·ɔ 'that they (anim.) were strong' (Mt 15.31).
  - ahči·t·anǝs·i·-: alǝwí·i ahči·t·anǝs·óp·ani·k 'they were stronger' (1834b:7.8).
- či·t·ane·- (II): čí·t·ane· 'it is strong, hard' (LB), it (cloth) is thick'; čí·t·ane·k hémpǝs 'a thick cloth' (Jn 11.44; KJV "a napkin"; Gr. 3.14b); hukwé·yunk énta-čí·t·ane·k 'the firmament of heaven (lit., what is strong in heaven)' (Lk 21.26; KJV " the powers of heaven"); čí·t·ane·k wi·k·ǝwáhǝmink 'in a prison' (lit., 'a strong house') (1834b:41.4).

či·t·anəs·i·t- TI(2) 'make strong': tá=háč=á· [wə́nči-]či·t·anəs·í·to·n 'how would it be made strong?' (Mt 12.26).
čí·t·ani P 'firmly, powerfully' (Lk 1.73).
- PV (Mk 3.24, 3.25, 3.26; Gr. 5.129j); é·li- tɔ·pto·ná·k·an -čí·t·ani-lé·k 'as his words had power' (Lk 4.32); yó·ni luwe·ó·k·an čí·t·ani-kəle·lə́ntamo·kw 'hold this statement firmly in your minds (you pl.)' (Lk 9.44); wə́nči-=á· aləwí·i -čí·t·ani-lé·k 'by which it would be more serious' (⟨hetani lri⟩ Mt 27.64 [em.]).
- PN 'powerful' (Jn 7.26).
či·t·ani·lae·m- TA 'strengthen the heart of': či·t·ani·lae·mó·me ki·mahtə́s·ak 'strengthen the hearts of your brothers (you sg.)' (Lk 22.32); wči·t·ani·laé·mku 'he (obv.) gave him inner stength' (Lk 22.43).
či·t·ani·t- TI(2) 'make strong': wči·t·ani·tó·ne·p nə́ a·pto·ná·k·an 'he strengthened the word' (Mk 16.20).
či·t·ani·taw- TA+O '"harden" O2 for': wči·t·ani·ta·k·o·né·ɔ wtehəwá·ɔ 'he hardened their hearts' (Jn 12.40; translated literally).
či·t·ani·t·e·ha- AI 'be strong minded': tá=á· yúkwe ktépi-či·t·ani·t·e·ha·húmɔ 'you (pl.) would not be strong-minded enough now' (Jn 16.12); ná nčɔ́·səp tɔ́·lai- čí·č -či·t·ani·t·é·ha·n 'then Joseph was not able to control his emotions any longer' (1842:17.1).
či·t·ani·xt- TI(2) 'make secure': či·t·aní·xto·kw 'make it secure (you pl.)' (Mt 27.65); wči·t·aní·xto·n 'he fixes it securely' (⟨whetanexun⟩ Jn 3.33 [em.]; RSV: "sets his seal to this, that .."); wči·t·ani·xto·né·ɔ 'they made [the tomb] secure' (Mt 27.66).
či·t·ani·x·ən- II 'be tough': či·t·aní·x·ən 'it is tough' (1834a:16).
či·xhamɔ́·k·an (|čīxahamwākan|) 'comb' (OA, LB; Gr. 5.55h). ♦ Sometimes heard as with [x] for /xh/ (V; Gr. 3.2d), but it is possible that only phonemic /xh/ existed.
čó·ləns AN 'bird', čó·lə·ns (WL; Gr. 5.70b); čo·lə́nsak 'birds' (Mt 6.26, 8.20, etc.).
- čo·ləntə́t·ak (dim. pl.) 'little birds' (Mt 10.29, 10.31, Lk 12.6).
-čohɔ·p°: see čhɔ·p°.
čɔ·mhákie P 'into the ground' (Jn 12.24, Lk 10.15 [KJV "down to hell"]), 'under the earth' (1842:11.1).
- čɔ·mhakamí·k·we 'underground' (1834b:20.5).
čɔ́·səp 'Joseph' (⟨Hoscp⟩ 1834b:36.2). ▸ Cf. nčɔ́·səp (⟨Nhoscp⟩) below.
čpahəl- (če·p·ahəl-, |čəpàhl-|) TA 'separate': če·p·ahəlá·t·e 'when he separates them' (⟨hrpavlatc⟩ Mt 25.32; or perhaps emend to expected ⟨hrpvalatc⟩ /če·phalá·t·e/).
čpe·ləm- (-čəp·e·ləm-) TA 'exclude': čpe·ləmuk·wé·k·we 'if [people] exclude you (pl.)' (Lk 6.22; KJV "when they shall separate you from their company").
• -čəp·e·ləm-: wčəp·e·ləmá·ɔ 'he excludes him' (Lk 12.53 [5x]); wčəp·e·ləmawwá·ɔ 'they exclude them' (Lk 12.52 [2x]; KJV "against").
čpən- (-čəp·ən-) TA — TI(1b) 'separate'.
- -čəp·ən- (TA): wčəp·ənawwá·ɔ=č 'they shall separate them' (Mt 13.49).
- čpən- (TI): káči awé·n čpənínkhi·č 'let no one break it apart' (Mt 19.6; Gr. 4.112h).
čpəs·o·wi·- (-čəpso·wi·-) AI 'be a stranger': ktə́li-čpəs·ó·wi·n 'that you were a stranger' (Mt 25.38, 25.44).
• -čəpso·wi·-: nčəpso·wí·həmp 'I was a stranger' (Mt 25.35; 25.43); kčəpsó·wi 'you are a stranger' (Lk 24.18).
ču° (~ -ɔwč°) (|wəčəw-|) 'fill'.
čuhɔl- TA — čuhɔt- (ɔwčuhɔt-; |(wə)čəwaht-|, |Ra+wəčəwaht-|) TI(2) 'fill'.

- čuhɔl- (TA): čuhɔ́lo· yó·k hó·s·ak mpí 'fill these vessels with water (you pl.)' (⟨Hovalw⟩ Jn 2.7).
- čuhɔt- (TI): čuhɔ́to·kw 'fill [their bags] (you pl.)' (1842:16.1).
  - ɔwčuhɔt-: ɔwčuhɔto·né·ɔ 'they filled [twelve baskets]' (⟨owvhwvotwnro⟩ Jn 6.13).

čuhɔta·s·i·- II 'be filled': čuhɔta·s·í·k·eč 'let it be filled' (⟨hova-⟩ Lk 3.5).

čuhɔte·- II 'fill, be filled, be full': čuhɔ́te· 'it is full' (⟨hovo-⟩ Jn 19.29); čuhɔté·ɔ 'they (inan.) were filled' (⟨hovo-⟩ Lk 5.7, ⟨hwvo-⟩ Mt 23.25); čuhɔ́te·k 'which was full' (⟨hwvo-⟩ Lk 7.37); čuhɔté·k·e 'when it was full' (⟨hova-⟩ Mt 13.48); tákta kéku awé·n čuhɔté·li·k wté·hink 'whatever (obv.) fills someone's heart' (⟨hwva-⟩ Mt 12.34; Gr. 6.26b).

čuwé·yunk P 'in the hills' (Gr. 5.26a), 'onto a hill' (1834b:25.7): e·li·khátink čuwé·yunk †nčo·tí·yunk 'in the hill country of Judaea' (Lk 1.65).

čúwi P 'filling' (Mt 15.37).

čuwi·ma·k·ɔt- II 'its odor fills': čuwi·má·k·ɔt 'its odor filled' (Jn 12.3; with a locative).

čuwi·x·i·n- AI — čuwi·x·ən- II 'fill (a container, etc.)'.
- čuwi·x·i·n- (AI): čuwi·x·í·no·k amánki-namé·s·ak 'it was full of large fish' (Jn 21.11); táli-=č -čuwi·x·i·nəné·ɔ 'so that they may fill up [my house]' (Lk 14.23).
- čuwi·x·ən- (II): wənči- ši·e·ləntaməwá·k·an -čuwí·x·ən ktehəwá·ink 'sorrow fills your hearts because of (it)' (Jn 16.6).

čuwpe·- (-ɔwčuwpe·-; |wəčəwəpē-|, |Ra+wəčəwəpē-|) AI — II 'be full (of water)'.
- -ɔwčuwpe·- (AI): ná ɔwčuwpe·né·ɔ 'then they were filled to the brim' (Jn 2.7; ⟨ovhovprnru⟩; /ɔw-/ is apparently for |wə-wa+wəº|). ▸ Cf. čuwpé·k·at 'it is full of water' (LB).

†čúxkwi(?) P 'completely (?)' (⟨hwxqi⟩ 1842:19.4). Form and meaning uncertain.

e

ehahke·kinke·-: see ahke·kinke·-.

ehahke·kínke·s AN 'teacher' (often as a vocative; Gr. §5.6.1) (Jn 3.2, Mt 8.19, Lk 7.40, etc.); éntxi ehahke·kínke·s 'every teacher' (Mt 13.52); ehahke·kinké·s·a 'teacher (obv.)' (Mt 10.24).

ehahki·hɔke·-: see ki·hɔke·-.

ehahki·m-: see ahki·m-.

ehahkwi·-: see ahkwi·-.

ehahpi·lí·č·i: see ahpi·-.

ehaləmá·kami·k P (with [Rih+; IC]) 'forever; for forever, eternal' (Lk 1.33, 1.55, Jn 4.14, etc.).

ehaləmo·k·wənák·aº: see e·ləmo·k·wənák·a.

ehalhitehº: see ali·tehw-.

ehalo·ka·l-: see alo·ka·l-.

ehalo·ka·ləntí·i PN: see alo·ka·l-.

ehankəlº: see ankəl-.

eha·č·i·mo·lsi·º: see a·č·i·mo·lsi·-.

eha·š·unte·n-: see a·š·unte·n-.

ehe·lənsi·lí·č·i (obv.) 'the proud': see ahe·lənsi·-*.

ehəlaehɔ·s·i·- see laehɔ·s·i·-.

ehəlak·e·ki·m-: see lahke·ki·m-.

ehəlák·wink: see lak·wi·-.

ehəla·pto·na·l-: see la·pto·na·l-.
ehəle·khi·k·á·kwki 'his bookkeeper': see le·khi·k·aw-*.
ehəle·khi·k·e·-: see le·khi·k·e·-.
ehəle·khí·k·e·s AN 'scribe' (Mk 12.32); ehəle·khi·k·é·s·ak 'scribes' (Mk 1.22, Lk 20.39, Mk 12.35, Mt 23.2, Mk 12.38); ehəle·khi·k·e·s·i·ké·i P '(among) the scribes' (Mk 14.43&).
ehələkhíkwi: see ləkhíkwi.
ehəlí·lamank: see li·lama·-.
ehəli·namíhti·t: see li·n-.
ehə́nta: see énta.
ehəntala·č·i·mó·lsink: see tala·č·i·mo·lsi·-.
ehəntalí·p·wink 'table' (*lit.*, 'where one customarily eats'; Gr. 4.9e; ME): ehəntali·p·wínkink 'on the table' (Lk 22.21; ME, ND); tehəntali·p·wínkəmink 'his table (loc.)' (Lk 16.21, Mt 15.27).
ehə́ntxi: see éntxi.
ehhaki·he·-: see haki·he·-.
ehhaki·hé·s·ak 'farmers' (Lk 20.10&); ehhaki·he·s·i·ké·i wə́nči P+P 'from the farmers' (Mt 21.34&).
ehhate·-: see hat·e·-.
ehɔht-: see ahɔt-.
ehɔ·ɔhti·-: see ahɔ·ɔhti·-.
ellí·i P 'both' (Lk 5.7, 6.39, 5.38, Mt 10.28, etc. [for Lk 7.42 see Gr. 3.7]).
-empsi·no·t·ay-: see hempsi·nó·t·ay.
enkəl-: see ankəl-.
enna·s·i·-: see ləna·s·i·-.
énnink: see lən-.
énta PV: see táli.
énta P 'where (it is ..), while being': énta ahsəni·ké·i 'where it was stony' (Mt 13.5); énta wehi·penke·t·i·ké·i, me·t·a·wsi·t·i·ké·i táli 'while among the fornicators and sinners' (Mk 8.38; /-e·t·i·k-/: ⟨-rek-⟩). ♦ A lexicalization of énta PV, the changed form of táli PV.
entala·wsi·-: see tala·wsi·-.
entali·p·wínki 'tables' (Mk 7.4); entali·p·wínkink wə́nči 'from the table' (1834b:30.3).
▶ Usually reduplicated, see ehəntalí·p·wink.
enta·-: see ta·-.
entxa·ke·i·-: see txa·ke·i·-.
entxennáɔhki (1) P '{so many} kinds': wé·mi entxennáɔhki mahta·wsəwá·k·an 'all kinds of sins' (Mt 12.31).
♦ Lexicalized from txennáɔhki (2) PV with IC. ▶ See also txennáɔhki (1) P.
entxennáɔhki (2) PV: see txennáɔhki (2).
éntxən: see txə́n.
éntxi (ehə́ntxi [Rih+; IC]; Gr. 5.25b) P 'every' (Mt 3.10); éntxi ehahke·kínke·s e·k·e·ki·mə́ntəp 'every teacher that is taught' (Mt 13.52).
• ehə́ntxi P: wé·mi ehə́ntxi 'every one of them' (Mt 25.15).
♦ Lexicalizations of forms of txí PV with IC.
entxi·-: see txi·- AI.
entxo·k·wənakháke: see txo·k·wənak·at-.
éši PV 'every (time that), whenever' (in changed conjunct; Gr. 5.128g): éši-ála- .. -ahpíhti·t 'whenever they were no longer (there)' (Lk 22.6); éši-kí·škwi·k 'every day' (Lk 16.19, 19.47,

22.53); éši-tpəskwíhəla·k 'whenever it is the right time' (⟨cji⟩ Lk 12.42); éši-=č nə́ -lə́nəme·kw 'whenever you (pl.) do that' (1 Cor 11.25).

=ét P 'maybe, must, must have', (in questions) 'possibly' (indicates doubt or possibility; Gr. 5.24c) (Lk 1.22, 2.44); 'maybe' (Jn 6.10), 'must be' (Mk 3.21, Lk 11.44), '(I guess)' (Jn 8.57); 'whether (or not)' (Jn 9.25); (in questions) 'I wonder' (Lk 12.49), 'do you think' (Mt 12.27, Lk 12.42), 'can (it be that)' (Mt 13.54), 'don't you think' (Lk 12.28).

e·

é·čənal 'Agent (obv.)' (1834a:24.65).

e·čki·x·əm- TA 'stick on (the end of)': ná tə́li- wi·kənáskunk -e·čkí·x·əma·n 'and he proceeded to stick it ('moss' anim.) on a reed' (Mt 27.48).

é·kəlink 'acre(s)' (1834b:13.4); kwə́t·i é·kəlink 'one acre' (OA).

e·khɔké·i·t AN 'nation' (Lk 1.48, Lk 2.31); wé·mi e·khɔké·i·t 'all nations' (Lk 1.48); e·khɔke·í·č·i·k 'nations' (Mt 12.21, 24.7, Lk 24.47); e·khɔke·i·lí·č·i (obv.) (Mt 12.18).
 ♦ The participle of an otherwise unused e·khɔke·i·- AI.
 ▸ Cf. èkhokéwit "nations" (Z 128); Mun ehkwahké·wi·t 'nation' (Charles Halfmoon).

e·ki·he·-: see haki·he·-.

e·k·e·khᵒ : see ahke·khw-.

e·k·e·kínke·s AN 'teacher' (Mt 8.21, Jn 8.4).

e·k·e·ki·mᵒ: see ahke·ki·m-.

e·k·e·ki·mkwəs·i·t AN 'disciple, student' (Lk 6.40, Mt 10.24, 10.25, etc.); e·k·e·ki·mkwəs·í·č·i·k 'disciples' (Jn 20.10, Mt 28.13, etc.); e·k·e·ki·mkwəs·i·lí·č·i 'the disciples (obv.)' (Mk 7.2, Mk 9.18, etc.), 'a disciple (obv.)' (Jn 20.2). The participle of |akēhkīməkwəsī-| AI 'be taught' (Gr. 5.107b).

e·k·wəlúnkɔne P (Gr. 6.9f): lí e·k·wəlúnkɔne '(to) under her wings' (Lk 13.34, Mt 23.37).
 ♦ Also: e·k·wəlúnkɔye (OA), e·k·wəlúnkwie (ME) 'under the arm'. ▸ Cf. wəlúnkɔn 'wing'.

e·k·wí·i P 'under': e·k·wí·i ksí·t·ink 'under your (sg.) feet' (Mk 12.36). ▸ Cf. Mun é·kwi· 'under'.

é·la: see ála.

e·lahki·- AI(+O) 'paint one's face (with O2)': é·li-=hánkw -e·lahkíhti·t 'for they paint their faces' (Mt 6.16; KJV "they disfigure their faces"); wte·lahkí·na né·l 'he paints himself with that (obv.)' (ME).

e·lahki·hɔké·t·əp 'his previous deception' (Mt 27.64); ▸ Cf. ki·hɔke·- 'cheat people, deceive'.

e·lahkwi·-: see lak·wi·-.

e·lahté·ləmink(?) 'the disapproval of me(?)' (Lk 1.25; KJV "my reproach").

†é·lanink '(from) Aaron's [family]' (Lk 1.5).

e·lankɔ·m-: see lankɔ·m-.

e·la·č·i·məwá·k·ani·k 'history' (B: Title Page). ▸ Participle of a noun formed from la·č·i·mwi·-; see below.

e·lá·me·k: see la·me·-.

e·ləma·kamí·k·e P 'all over this world' (1834a:14).

e·ləma·ké·x·ink: see aləmhake·x·ən-.

e·ləmo·k·wənák·a (ppl.; ehaləmo·k·wənák·a [Rih+; IC]) 'for eternity' (Mk 3.29, 1842:7.2, 8.1).
 • ehaləmo·k·wənák·a 'forever' (Jn 3.15, 3.16, 3.36; Gr. §5.4f).

▪ ehaləmo·k·wənak·aí·i PN 'of eternity, eternal' (Prenoun from lexicalized ppl.; Gr. 5.123a): ehaləmo·k·wənak·aí·i-pəma·wsəwá·k·anink 'in eternal life' (Jn 4.36).
▸ Cf. tətá ehe·ləmo·k·wənák·a 'forever and ever' (ME; as if |IC+Rih+IC+| [Gr. 5.45a]).

e·ləwensí·li·t: see luwensi·-.
e·ləwe·tá·kwsi·t: see luwe·ta·kwsi·-.
e·ləwihəl-: see luwihəl-.
e·lhake·i·-: see la·ke·i·-.
e·lhaké·x·ink: see la·ke·x·ən-.
e·lhiteh°: see ali·tehw-.
e·lhukwe·°: see lo·kwe·°.
é·li (1) P (with a verb) 'as, for': é·li khikayó·p·ani·k 'as they were old' (Lk 1.7; also Lk 1.7, 1.17, 1.20, Jn 2.24, etc.); é·li xinkwe·ləmúkwsu=č 'for he will be well thought of' (Lk 1.15; also Lk 1.13, 1.34, 1.76, etc.).
• é·li P (with a noun) 'because of, for the sake of' (Lk 18.29, Mt 20.24). ♦ Lexicalized from the changed form of lí PV (cf. Gr. 5.128n); gapped where second occurrence would be é·li-PV (Mk 1.22).
é·li (2) P 'how': é·li .. mwe·k·əne·ó·p·ani 'how they handed him over' (Lk 24.20).
e·linkwe·x·i·n°: see linkwe·x·i·n-.
e·linnuwahkəs·í·č·i·k: see linnuwahkəs·i·-.
e·li·khátink: see li·k·e·-.
†e·li·ksántəl 'Alexander' (Mt 27.32&).
e·lí·kte·k: see li·kte·-.
e·li·t·é·ha·t: see li·t·e·ha·-.
e·lkí·kwi: see ləkhíkwi.
e·lo·ka·l°: see alo·ka·l-.
e·lsi·t·e·x·i·n-: see ləs·i·t·e·x·i·n-.
e·mi·mənsi·-: see mi·mənsi·-.
e·nansi·-: see anansi·-.
e·nənthake·ó·k·an: see e·nunthake·ó·k·an.
e·nhaw- (ihe·nhaw- [Rih+], |ēnahaw-|; Gr. 5.90b) TA 'pay, reward': é·nhaw 'pay them (you sg.)' (Mt 20.8); e·nhái·l 'pay me (you sg.)' (Mt 18.28); ná=č .. e·nháɔ·n 'then he shall be paid for it' (Mt 16.27); é·li- .. tihtépi -wə́nči-é·nhunt 'for he is compensated with the appropriate amount each time' (Lk 10.7); tá=á· kte·nha·k·ó·wi 'he will not reward you' (Mt 6.1; Gr. 4.85c).
• ihe·nhaw-: ihe·nhaɔ́·ɔk 'they get paid' (Jn 4.36); énta-ihé·nhunt móni 'where he was (customarily) paid money' (Mk 2.14).
▪ e·nha·ɔhti·- (recip.; Gr. 5.112b) 'pay each other': e·nha·ɔhtúwak 'they're paying each other' (OA; Gr. 5.112).
e·nha·ɔhtəwá·k·an IN 'payment (received)' (when possessed 'reward') (Mt 17.25); kte·nha·ɔhtəwá·k·an 'your reward' (Lk 6.35; Gr. 5.116h); wte·nha·ɔhtəwá·k·an 'his reward' (⟨wt-⟩ Mt 10.41 [2x]; ⟨t-⟩ Mt 10.42).
e·nha·ɔhtəwa·k·ani·- II 'be a reward': é·li xínkwi-e·nha·ɔhtəwá·k·anu 'for there is a great reward' (Mt 5.12).
e·nhe·- (ihe·nhe·- [Rih+]; Gr. 5.90b) AI(+O) 'pay O2': e·nhé·ɔk 'their account is even', *lit.*, 'they have been paid in full' (Mt 6.5, 6.16); wte·nhe·né·ɔ 'their account is even', *lit.*, 'they have been paid in full for it' (Mt 6.2); kéku=á· é·nhe·t 'anything he could pay' (Mt 18.25); mé·či

kwíˑla-eˑnhéˑtˑe 'after he was unable to pay' (Lk 7.42); tə́li-=č -éˑnheˑn 'so that he would pay it' (Mt 18.30).
- iheˑnheˑ-: eˑkˑeˑkímkɔn=háč ɔ́ˑk ihéˑnheˑ 'does your teacher also pay (tribute)?' (Mt 17.24).

eˑniˑxˑiˑn- AI 'stoop to look': íkali eˑníˑxˑiˑn 'he stooped down to look in' (Jn 20.5, 20.11; KJV "stooping down, *and looking in*").

eˑnunthakaw- TA 'tell a parable to': teˑnunthakaɔ́ˑpˑani 'he told them a parable' (Mt 22.1 [em.]).

eˑnunthakeˑ- AI 'tell a parable': takó.. kteˑnunthakéˑi 'you (sg.) do not talk in parables' (Jn 16.29); ná teˑnunthákeˑn 'then he told a parable' (Lk 15.3).

eˑnunthakeˑɔ́ˑkˑan ~ eˑnənthakeˑɔ́ˑkˑan IN 'parable': eˑnunthakeˑɔ́ˑkˑan (⟨rnwntº⟩ Lk 5.36, Mt 13.3, 13.13, etc.), eˑnənthakeˑɔ́ˑkˑan (⟨rnuntº⟩ Lk 6.39, ⟨rncntº⟩ Mk 3.23, Mt 13.34 [adjunct]; misprinted ⟨rnenº⟩ Mt 13.10; etc.); eˑnunthakeˑɔ́ˑkˑana 'parables' (Mt 13.35, 13.51, 13.53).
▸ Cf. ⟨enendhackewágan⟩ 'example' (Z. 69), ⟨enendhakgewoãgan⟩ 'parable' (Z. 139).

†éˑpaya 'Abia' (Lk 1.5).

†éˑpəla 'Abel (abs.)' (Lk 11.51, Mt 23.35).

†eˑpəléˑham 'Abraham' (⟨Aplrvam⟩ 1834b:30.5; ⟨Rplrvam⟩ 1834b:30.8); †eˑpəleˑhámal (⟨Rplrvamul⟩ 1834b:30.6, etc.). ▸ The *Harmony* has ⟨Rplivam(-)⟩ and later ⟨Rplivcm(-)⟩; see next entry.

†eˑpəlíham 'Abraham' (Mt 3.9, Lk 16.22); †eˑpəlihémal (obv.) (Lk 1.55, 1.73), †eˑpəlihéma (abs.) (Lk 13.28); †eˑpəlihéma (obv.) (Lk 16.23, 19.9, Mk 12.26); †eˑpəliháma 'Abraham (abs.)' (Mt 3.9) ~ †eˑpəliháma (Mt 8.11, Jn 8.39, etc.); †eˑpəliháminkˑ 'from Abraham' (Jn 8.37, Lk 13.16).

eˑpˑiˑkˑweˑlíˑčˑi 'musicians (obv.)': see ahpiˑkˑweˑ-.

eˑš(·)º (|ēš-|) 'through' (Gr. §5.2a).

éˑškanš AN 'needle' (Mt 19.24), éˑškaˑnš (ND, LB; Gr. §2.1c).

eˑšˑiˑ- AI 'go through' (Gr. §5.2a): eˑšˑíˑtˑe 'when he went through' (Jn 9.1).

eˑšˑíˑi P 'through': eˑšˑíˑi líˑlóˑwiˑp '(and) he passed through' (Jn 8.59).

eˑteˑ-: see háteˑ-.

ə

-əl-: see l-.

-əlˑweˑ-: see lúweˑ-.

-əlˑweˑɔˑkˑan-: see luweˑɔ́ˑkˑan.

-əlˑwihəl-: see luwihəl-.

-əlhakeˑi-: see laˑkeˑi-.

-əlhukº: see loˑkweˑ-.

-əlskaw-: see ləskaw-.

-ənnaˑhaˑɔn- ~ -ənneˑhaˑɔn-: see lənaˑháˑɔn.

-ənnaˑpº: see lənaˑpº.

-ənnəmº: see lən-.

=ə́nt P 'nevertheless, despite that' (Gr. 5.24d): saˑkˑíˑma=ə́nt khákˑay? 'are you nevertheless a king?' (Jn 18.37; KJV "then"). ▸ Cf. Mun =ə́nt 'on the contrary, nevertheless, rather, then'.

ə́nta: see énta.

-əskɔnteˑyəm-: see skɔ́ntay.

h

=háč P Q (marks questions; Gr. 5.24e) (Lk 1.34, Lk 1.43, 1.62, 1.66, Mt 2.2, etc.).
♦ Also =heč after Blanchard for some speakers.

hákhakw (-ma·khakw-; Gr. 2.6f) IN 'bottle' (Mk 14.3); ɔpahsəní·i-hákhakw 'a white-stone bottle' (Mt 26.7&).
• -ma·khakw-: nəmá·khakw 'my bottle' (V; Gr. 2.6f).

hákink (Gr. 4.15l) P 'down' (Lk 1.52, Mt 2.11, Lk 3.5, etc.; perhaps Jn 18.6). ▸ Cf. hák·ink.

haki·há·k·an (-t-a·ki·ha·k·an-, |ahkīhākan-|; Gr. 5.55d) IN 'field' (Mt 13.38, 13.44); amánki-haki·há·k·anal 'great farms' (1834b:43.9); amánki-haki·há·k·anak 'large fields (anim.)' (1834a:23.60); haki·há·k·anink 'field (loc.)' (Mt 13.36, 13.44, Lk 15.15, etc.); haki·ha·k·ani·ké·i 'the fields (loc.)' (Jn 4.35).
• -t-a·ki·ha·k·an-: tɔ·ki·há·k·an 'his field' (Lk 13.7, Mt 21.33, etc.); nta·ki·há·k·anink 'in my field' (Mt 21.28); kta·ki·há·k·anink 'in your (sg.) field' (Mt 13.27); tɔ·ki·há·k·anink 'in his field' (Mt 13.24, 13.31, etc.), lí tɔ·ki·há·k·anink 'for his field' (Mt 20.1); tɔ·ki·ha·k·anəwá·ink 'to their farms' (Mt 22.5).

haki·he·- (-t-a·ki·he·-, e·ki·he·-, i·haki·he·- [Rī+], ehhaki·he·- [Rih+; IC], |ahkīhē|; Gr. 5.70c) AI 'plant, farm', AI+O 'plant O2': hakí·he· 'he gardens' (OA; Gr. 5.70c); haki·hé·p·ani·k 'they planted' (Lk 17.28); máta haki·he·í·ɔk 'they do not plant' (Mt 6.26; Gr. 4.81p); haki·hé·t·e xkáni·m 'when he plants seed' (Mk 4.26; cf. Mt 13.31).
• -t-a·ki·he·-: tɔ·ki·he·né·ɔ 'that they plant (sbd.)' (1834a:16).
• i·haki·he·-: takó· i·haki·he·í·ɔk 'they never plant' (Lk 12.24; Gr. 5.44q).
• e·ki·he·-: máta .. e·ki·hé·ɔ 'what I never planted' (Lk 19.22, Mt 25.26); máta háši .. e·ki·hé·ɔn 'what you never planted' (Lk 19.21, Mt 25.24); e·kí·he·t 'the grower' (Jn 15.1).
• ehhaki·he·-: ehhakí·he·t 'farmer' (Mt 20.1, 21.33); ehhaki·hé·č·i·k 'farmers' (Lk 20.14); ehhaki·he·lí·č·i 'farmers (obv.)' (Mt 21.33, 21.40, 21.41&, Mk 12.9).

haki·i·- AI 'be of earth': hakí·yu 'he is of earth' (⟨vakew⟩ Jn 3.31; Gr. 2.32a, 5.68o).

hák·i (-t-a·ki, -t-a·ki·y-, |ahkəy|; Gr. 2.8a) IN 'earth, land' (Jn 4.5, Mt 4.15 [2x], 6.30, etc.), AN (as possessor) wáni hák·i 'this earth' (Lk 16.8), hák·i hók·enk wənči 'from the body of the earth' (Mk 4.28 [presumably AN]); mhukwí·i-hák·i 'the land of blood' (Mt 27.8); hák·ink 'earth, land, etc. (loc.)' (Jn 3.31 [2x], Lk 2.14, 4.31, etc.), 'on the ground' (Jn 8.6, Mt 26.39); †isəlɔ́lí·i-hák·ink 'to the land of Israel' (Mt 2.20).
• -t-a·ki: tɔ́·ki 'his land' (Mk 10.29); tɔ·kií·li·t 'his (obv.) land' (1834a:19.15); tɔ́·kink 'his land (loc.)' (Lk 12.16); kta·kí·yəwa 'your (pl.) land' (OA; Gr. 2.34g); kta·ki·yəná·nink 'in our (inc.) land' (⟨ktakenɔnif⟩ Lk 4.23; KJV "in thy country"); tɔ·ki·yəwá·unk 'on their land' (1834b:43.9).

hak·ií·i P 'of earth': hak·ií·i=á· hó·s·ak. 'Pots were only of clay.' (1834a:19.12).

hal- (-t-ahəl-, ehəl-, ehhal- [Rih+; IC], |ahl-|) TA — TI(2) hat·- (-t-a·t-, e·t-, ehhat- [Rih+; IC], |aht-|) 'put, place, set {smwh}' (Gr. 5.4d).
▪ hal- (TA): hál 'put him, them {smwh} (you sg.)!' (Gr. 2.5d); íka ɔ́·k yó·k hálo· 'put these there also (you pl.)' (Mk 8.7); íka halé·ɔk 'they stationed them there' (Mt 27.66); hála· 'he is put {smwh}' (1834b:14.9); tɔ́li- íka -hala·né·ɔ 'they proceeded to set him on it' (Mt 21.7&).
• -t-ahəl-: kpaho·t·əwi·k·á·ɔnink=č ntáhəla 'I will put him in prison' (1842:15.3); tənna·há·ɔnink=č tɔhəlá·ɔ mwekí·s·əma 'he shall put his sheep on his right' (Mt 25.33); ná=nə́ le·lá·i tɔ́həla·n 'he set him in the middle there' (Mt 18.2; Gr. 4.43c).

- ehəl-: tə́ta éhəlat 'where you put him' (Jn 20.15); tə́ta ehəláhti·t 'where they put him' (Jn 20.2, 20.13); awé·n=á· éhələnt 'tomb' (*lit.*, 'where someone would be put') (Jn 19.41); ehəlá·t·əp 'where he put them' (1834b:17.2).
- ehhal-: ehhaláhti·t 'where they always put them' (Mt 13.48).
▪ hat·- ~ hat- (TI): hát·o·l 'set it down (there)' (Mt 5.24); é·li-kwí·la-hát·aɔ 'as I have no place to put them' (Lk 12.17); wénči- .. íka -hataɔ́nəp 'a reason for you (sg.) to put it there' (Mt 25.27; Gr. 4.78e); hat·únke 'if it is put (there)' (Lk 5.38); wwə́nči- íka -hát·o·n 'that she puts it there out of [her poverty]' (Mk 12.44&).
- -t-a·t-: íka ntá·tu 'I'll put (it) there' (Lk 13.8); manák·ɔ·n hókunk tɔ́·to·n 'he put the rainbow in the sky' (1842:9.7); máta íka tɔ·tó·wən hók·ay 'he did not commit himself' (*lit.*, 'put himself there') (Jn 2.24).
- e·t-: máta ní· tə́ta e·tó·wa 'that *I* didn't put down anywhere' (Lk 19.22); máta háši kéku tə́ta e·tó·wan 'things you (sg.) never put down anywhere' (Lk 19.21; Gr. 4.99i); tə́ta=á· é·ta·kw wí·l 'where he could lay his head' (Mt 8.20).
- ehhat-: ehhátunk mɔ́ni 'where money is put' (Jn 8.20); kéku ehhátunk '(one) to put things in' (Lk 22.35).

halpánkəl AN 'barrel, keg' (LB), also inan. (ND); halpánkəlak pl. (LB; 1834b:13.4 ⟨valopufuk⟩ for *⟨valopufuluk⟩).
▪ halpánkəlink P 'barrelful(s), barrel(s) of': kwə́ti-halpánkəlink 'one barrelful' (⟨Koti valopufulif⟩ 1834b:13.4).
♦ A loanword from Dutch *half anker* 'half anker; five gallons', the standard size of a keg (Goddard 1974:154); the spellings with ⟨halop-⟩ may indicate a variant with /haləp-/ from Dutch *half* ([haləf]).

=hánkw P 'always, usually, generally, would, etc.' (Gr. 5.24f) (Jn 2.10, 3.6 [2x], 4.13, etc.).
♦ Indicates a general truth and usually not translated as a separate word.

hapahpi·- (-t-a·pahpi·-) AI+O 'sit on O2': hápahpi 'sit on (it) (you sg.)' (Lk 14.10); káč·i hapahpí·han 'don't sit on (it)' (Lk 14.8); ná tə́li-hápahpi·n 'and with that he sat on it' (Mt 28.2).
- -t-a·pahpi·-: ktá·pahpi·n '(that) you (sg.) sit on it' (Lk 14.9, 14.10; Gr. 2.7f); tɔ·pahpi·né·ɔ †mo·šə́š·a wəlehələmatahpínkəm 'they sit in Moses's seat' (Mt 23.2).

haphikaw- (-t-a·phikaw-) TA — haphik- (-t-a·phik-) TI(1a) 'step on, tread on, tread down, fall bodily or massively on'.
▪ haphikaw- (TA): haphikaí·ne·n 'fall on top of us!' (Lk 23.30 [addressed to mountains]); ktə́li-=č -haphikaɔ·né·ɔ xkó·k·ak '(that you [pl.]) step on snakes' (Lk 10.19).
- -t-a·phikaw-: †nči·ló·sələm=č tɔ·phiká·k·u 'they (obv.) will tread Jerusalem down' (Lk 21.24).
▪ haphik- (TI): é·li-=á· tá·mse -haphikamíhti·t 'for they might trample on it' (Mt 7.6).
▪ haphika·ɔhti·- (ahhaphika·ɔhti·- [ày+]; Gr. 5.37i, 5.112a) AI 'trample each other':
- ahhaphika·ɔhti·-: ahhaphika·ɔhtúwak 'they were stepping on each other' (Lk 12.1).

haphika·s·i·- (ahhaphika·s·i·- [ày+], |-ahpəhkāsī-|; Gr. 5.37h) II 'be trampled on': haphiká·s·u 'it is trampled on' (Gr. 5.105i).
- ahhaphika·s·i·-: énta=č -ahhaphiká·s·i·k 'where it will be trampled on (continually)' (Mt 5.13; KJV "to be trodden under foot of men").

hápi (Gr. 5.28c, 5.129l) P '(along) with, also' (Lk 5.19, Mk 10.30, Mt 25.4; Jn 14.11 [KJV "or else"]); ɔ́·k hápi 'and .. as well' (Lk 1.52).

▪ hápi (-t-á·pi, |ahpī|; Gr. 5.107c) PV 'with, along with, in addition': "together" (OA); ⟨Happi⟩ "with it, in the bargain" (B&A 47).
 • -t-á·pi: ktá·pi-=č yó·l wé·mi -mi·lkwəs·i·né·ɔ 'you (pl.) will be given all these things in the bargain' (Mt 6.33).
háši P 'never' (with negative) (Jn 1.18, 4.14, 5.24, 5.37, Mt 7.23, etc.).
hatahəl- (-t-a·tahəl-, |ahtāhl-|; Gr. 5.87c) TA+O 'turn O2 over to, let have O2': kta·tahəlí·həmp 'you let me have them' (Mt 25.20, Mt 25.22; KJV "deliveredst unto"); tɔ·tahəlá·ne·p 'he turned it over to them' (Mt 25.14; KJV "delivered unto").
hataw- (-t-a·taw-) TA+O 'put, place O2 {smwh} for, on': hata·k·e·é·k·we 'when they are set (there) for you (pl.)' (Lk 10.8); tə́li-=á· íka -hataɔ·né·ɔ 'that they should put them there for them' (Mk 8.6).
 • -t-a·taw-: tɔ·taɔwwá·ɔ 'they put (it) on him' (Lk 23.11); wé·mi kéku nhák·enk nta·tá·k·o·n nó·x 'all things were placed in me by my father' (Lk 10.22); ó·k=č šinka·ltəwá·k·an te·t·aí·i kta·to·ləné·ɔ 'and I shall place hatred between you and them (1842:8.1).
hatá·p·i AN (|ahtāpəy|; Gr. 2.5c, 3.2f) 'bow' (1834a:19.12; V, FE, LTD ND, LB).
hata·s·i·- II 'be put {smwh}': hatá·s·əwa 'they (grass, pl.) are put (there)' (1834a:16).
hatehəla·- AI 'stoop down': hatéhəle·p 'he stooped down' (Jn 8.6).
haté·i·- AI (-t-a·te·i·-, |ahtēwī-|) 'stoops down': haté·yu 'he stooped over' (OA; Gr. 2.13e); ná lápi haté·i·p 'then he stooped down again' (Jn 8.8).
 • -t-a·te·i·-: nta·té·i 'I stooped over' (OA; Gr. 2.13e).
hat·e·- (e·te·-, ahhat·e·- [ày+], ehhate·- [ày+; IC], |ahtē-|; Gr. 2.8b, 5.37g) II 'exist, be, be put ({smwh})': hát·e·w mənəp·é·kwtət 'there was a pool (there)' (Jn 5.2); hát·e· 'it was there' (Jn 4.6); íka hát·e· 'it is there' (Lk 11.39); tá=háč txí ahpó·na hát·e· 'how many loaves of bread are there?' (Mk 6.38; Gr. 4.42y); máta hat·é·i 'it does not exist' (Jn 15.22); hók·enk hat·é·lo·p 'it (obv.) was present in him' (Lk 5.17; /t·/ assumed); hat·é·k·e 'when there is' (Lk 6.42; Gr. 2.8b).
 • e·te·-: é·te·k 'where it is (was)' (Lk 1.39, Mt 6.2, Lk 6.41, Lk 6.47&, etc.); né·skɔ e·té·k·e yú hák·i 'before the earth existed' (Jn 17.5; Gr. 4.62k).
 • ahhat·e·-: wé·mi kéku éntxi- íka -ahháte·k 'everything that is in them' (1834b:21.2); é·ləmi-ahhaté·k·e 'when there begin to be [torments] (ch. subj.)' (Mt 13.21; Gr. 5.37g).
 • ehhate·-: mehəma·e·ná·s·i·k móni ehháte·k 'treasury (*lit.*, where the collected money was always put)' (Mk 12.41), móni ehháte·k 'a purse' (Lk 10.4, Lk 22.35, 22.36); ehháte·k 'granary, barn (*lit.*, where it is (or they are) always put)' (Lk 3.17, Lk 12.18); mpí ehháte·k '(ones) for holding water (*lit.*, where water is always put)' (Jn 2.6).
 ▶ For the corresponding AI stem, see ahpi·-; Gr. 5.3c.
†hélat 'Herod' (Lk 1.5, Mt 2.1, 2.3, 2.7, etc.); †helát·a 'the late Herod' (Mt 14.1); †helát·ink 'to Herod' (Mt 2.12, Mt 12.14); o·x·únka †helat·ínka 'of his late father Herod' (Mt 2.22).
 ▪ †helat·í·i PN 'of Herod' (Mk 8.15, Mt 16.11, Mt 16.12, Mt 22.16&).
†helɔ́·tias 'Herodias' (Mk 6.19, 6.22); †helɔ·tiás·a (Lk 3.19-20, Mk 6.17 [2x]).
hémpəs IN 'cloth' (Jn 11.44, 13.4, Mt 27.51, etc.); wəno·t·amensəwí·i-hémpəs 'his fisherman's shirt' (Jn 21.7); hémpsal 'shirts and dresses' (1834a:19.14); hémpsa 'pieces of cloth' (Jn 20.5, 20.6, 20.7). ▶ A loanword (Gr. 5.14a; Goddard 1974:154).
hempsi·nó·t·ay (-empsi·no·t·ay-, -ahempsi·no·t·ay-) IN 'cloth bag': hempsi·nó·t·aya 'cloth bags' (Lk 12.33); hempsi·no·t·ai·ké·i P 'in the bags' (1842:16.2).
 • -empsi·no·t·ay-: tempsi·no·t·ayəwá·ɔ 'their bags' (1842:16.1); tempsi·nó·t·enk 'in his bag' (1842:16.2).

- -ahempsi·no·t·ay-: tɔhempsi·nó·t·enk 'in his bag' (1842:16.1).
  ▸ Cf. empsi·nó·t·ay 'bag' (V); for hemp° ~ -ahemp° see Gr. 5.5e, 5.14a.
hikahəla·- II 'be water receding': hikáhəle· 'the water is receding' (OA), ná kə́nč pahkánči hikáhəle· 'only then had the waters completely receded' (1842:9.6).
hiló·səs (Gr. 2.77b; -mihəlo·s·əm-: Gr. §2.15, end) AN 'old man' (1842:15.4, 15.5, 17.1 [2x]); hilo·sə́s·ak 'old men' (V, LB).
- -mihəlo·s·əm-: nəmihəló·s·əm 'my husband', *lit.*, 'my old man' (AD, ND).
hilo·s·í·- (|(m)əhlōsī-|; Gr. 5.67f) AI 'be an old man': tá·ɔni mé·či hiló·s·u 'even though he has become old' (1842:19.4); hilo·s·iáne 'when you are old' (Jn 21.18; Gr. §2.15, end); mé·či hilo·s·í·t·e 'if he is already an old man' (1834b:23.13).
hítami (-ní·tami, né·tami, |(n)əhtamī|; Gr. 4.76g, 5.129m) PV 'first' (Mt 6.33, Jn 20.4).
- -ní·tami: wəní·tami-kánši- kéku -laehɔ·s·í·ne·p 'he performed his first miracle' (Jn 2.11).
- né·tami (Lk 2.23, Jn 5.4, etc.); né·tami-mi·kəmɔ·s·í·č·i·k 'the first workers' (Mt 20.8).
- hítami (Gr. 5.28d) P 'first, in the beginning, in the first place' (Jn 1.40, Mt 5.24, 6.2, etc.); né·k hítami mi·kəmɔ·s·í·č·i·k 'the first workers' (Mt 20.10).
hitamí·x·ən- II 'be first' (ne·tami·x·ən-, |nəhtamīxən-|; Gr. 2.6d): hitamí·x·ən '(it is) the first' (Mt 12.29, 12.30); hitamí·x·əno·p '[the word] was the first thing' (Jn 1.1).
- ne·tami·x·ən-: ləna·p·e·í·i-le·khí·k·an ne·tamí·x·ink 'First Delaware Book' (1842:[p. 2]).
híta· (-ni·ta·) PV 'skilled at' (⟨vetu⟩; Mk 12.28), hitá·i (LTD ND, LB).
- -ní·ta·: kəní·ta·-tahpa·lawwá·ɔk 'you're good at taking care of them' (⟨kneta⟩; Lk 11.13).
hita·e·khi·k·e·- AI 'know how to write': wénči·=č -hita·e·khí·k·e·t 'so that he will know how to write' (1834a:24.65).
hita·t·- (-ni·ta·t·-, |(n)əhtā°|; Gr. §5.2a) TI(2) 'learn, know how to': ɔ́·k kəni·ta·t·o·né·ɔ=č 'and you (pl.) shall learn (to bear) it ("my yoke")' (Mt 11.29).
hitkwi·ke·- II 'be (an abundance of) trees': é·li- máta -hitkwí·ke·kw 'as there are no trees' (1834b:44.7).
hít·ukw (-mi·tkəm-, |məhtəkw|; Gr. 2.6e) AN 'tree' (IN 'stick') (⟨vetkwf⟩ Mt 3.10 [miswritten]; Mt 12.33 [3x], Lk 13.7, etc.); hítko·k 'trees' (Mt 7.19, Mk 8.24, Lk 21.29, 1842:6.5; Gr. 2.16c); hítkɔl 'trees (obv.)' (⟨vetqul⟩ 1834b:16.3), hítkɔ 'tree (obv.)' (⟨vetko⟩ Lk 13.6, etc.; ⟨vetkov⟩ Mk 11.13&); hítkunk '(to, next to, under) a tree, bush' (Mt 3.10 [2x, the second time for intended hít·ukw], Jn 1.48, 1.50, etc.); hitkwi·ké·i 'on trees' (1842:7.4 [2x]).
- -mi·tkəm-: nəmí·tkəm 'my stick' (ME; Gr. 2.6e).
- hitkwə́t·ət (dim.) 'a small tree' (Mt 13.32; Gr. 5.46a).
†hi·pəlo·wí·i PV 'Hebrew' (Jn 5.2).
hó·s (-t-aho·s·-; Gr. 3.2g) AN 'a pot' (Jn 19.29); hó·s·ak 'vessels' (Jn 2.7), si·skəwí·i-hó·s·ak 'clay pots' (Mt 27.7); hó·s·ink 'under a pot' (Mt 5.15).
- -t-aho·s·-: tɔhó·s·a 'her pot' (Jn 4.28).
hókw IN 'sky' (⟨voq⟩ 1834b:15.8, 1842:6.4); hókunk 'in heaven' (⟨vokwf⟩ Jn 1.51; 6x; ⟨vokuf⟩ 1834b:39.3), 'in the sky' (1842:9.7), wə́nči hókunk 'from the sky, from on high' (Lk 17.24, Jn 19.11 [KJV "from above"]).
  ▸ Cf. Mun wáhkw 'sky, the heavens' (JA).
hɔk·ai·- (we·hɔk·ai·-, |wəhakayī-|) AI+O 'have O2 as one's body': é·li-hɔ́k·ai·t pa·tamwe·i·k·á·ɔn 'that his body was a temple' (Jn 2.21).
- we·hɔk·ai·-: yó·k we·hɔk·aí·č·i·k mahtantó·wa 'those possessed by devils' (Mt 4.24); we·hɔk·aí·li·t mahtantó·wa 'ones (obv.) possessed by devils' (Mk 1.32); we·hɔk·ai·tpáni·k 'who had been possessed (by it)' (Lk 8.2).

hók·ay: see nhák·ay.
hópəni·s AN 'potato' (V, OA; Gr. 3.1k): hɔpəní·s·ak 'potatoes' (1834a:14; OA, AD).
hɔpí·k·ɔn 'shoulder bone' (ME); mo·s·í·i-hɔpí·k·ɔn 'an elk scapula' (1834a:18.12).
hukwé·yunk (Gr. 5.26b) P 'above' (Lk 2.14, Mt 2.9, Jn 8.23, etc.), '(to) heaven' (1842:9.8), 'on high' (Lk 19.38, Jn 12.28), hukwé·yunk énta-kpát·ək 'an upper room' (Mk 14.15), wə́nči hukwé·yunk 'from the sky' (Mt 24.29), '(live) on high' (Mk 11.10), '(to) the sky' (Lk 21.28), lí hukwé·yunk 'to heaven' (Jn 6.62; cf. Lk 9.51), 'in heaven' (Lk 21.11&, 21.26); as a substantive: 'heaven' (a subject; Lk 16.17), 'the heaven' (an object; 1842:11.4).
=húnt P HRSY (evidential enclitic particle indicating hearsay; Gr. 5.24g).
hupxkɔní·li·t: see nhúpxkɔn.
hwə́ska P 'very' (Jn 2.12, Mk 3.8); hwə́ska + áhi PV 'vehemently' (Lk 23.10), áhi-hwə́ska 'extremely' (Mk 5.42); takó· hwə́ska xé·li-kahtənó·wi 'it was not very many years' (1842:10.6).
hwə́ski: see wə́ški.
hwiká·t·ink: see nhíka·t.
hwil- (-uhəl-, |wəhl-| < |wəm-| + |-l|; Gr. 2.50a, 5.4f) TA 'get from {smwh}': ná=ni hwilát·e 'if you (sg.) get him there' (ME; Gr. 3.13(8)a).
• -uhəl-: ná=ni núhəla·n 'that's where I got him' (ME; Gr. 2.65l); tá=háč .. kúhəla·n 'where did you (sg.) get it (anim.) from?' (1834a:12).
▸ Cf. wənt- below for the corresponding TI(3) stem.
hwitaɔk·a: see nhítaɔk.
hwitaɔk·i·- (we·hitaɔk·i·-; |wəhtawakī-|, with IC as if |wəwəhtawakī-|) AI 'have ears': éntxi- awé·n -hwitaɔk·i·t 'everyone who has ears' (Mt 13.9, Lk 14.35); éntxi-hwitaɔk·ie·kw 'all of you (pl.) who have ears' (Mk 7.16).
• we·hitaɔk·i·-: we·hitaɔk·i·t 'who has ears' (⟨wrvetaoket⟩ Mt 11.15, 13.43, Mk 8.18).
hwí·t IN 'wheat' (Lk 3.17, Jn 4.35, 4.36, 4.38, Lk 6.1, etc.). ▸ From English *wheat*.
hwi·tí·i PN 'of wheat' (Jn 12.24).
hwi·ti·k·á·ɔn IN 'granary'; hwi·ti·k·á·ɔnink 'into the granary' (Mt 13.30).
hwi·thaki·há·k·an IN 'wheat field'; hwi·thaki·há·k·anink 'wheat fields (loc.)' (Lk 6.1).

i

-íči: see wíči (1).
†ihahka·me·í·i P 'back and forth to the other side' (⟨ea-|kaxkamree⟩ 1834b:44.1 [perhaps for this]; cf. ká·mink 'on the other side of the water' < PA *aka·m-).
ihahki·hɔke·-: see ki·hɔke·-.
iha·č·i·mo·lsi·-: see a·č·i·mo·lsi·-.
ihá·pči: see á·pči.
ihələn-: see lən-.
íhəli '{so}' (with habitual reduplication; Gr. §5.4d): see lí.
ihikalíči P 'gradually' (Lk 2.52, 1834b:8.1).
íka (Gr. 2.72g) P 'there' (Lk 2.16, Mt 2.22, Lk 2.42, Jn 1.39, etc.); íka péči 'up to then' (Jn 13.1). ♦ Non-deictic, and thus not treated as a definite oblique.

♦ Precedes the verb, frequently as an empty placeholder for a locative that follows the verb: ná íka pó·ne·p wto·t·é·nink 'then he came to his city' (Mt 2.23); íka é·p·ani·k †nči·ló·sələm 'they went to Jerusalem' (Lk 2.41); íka ntá·ne·n kwəškwəš·i·ké·i '(that) we go among the hogs' (Mk 5.12); íka á·l ni·mahtəs·i·ké·i 'go to my brothers' (Jn 20.17); íka=ét é· mahči·k·amí·k·unk 'she must be going to the grave' (Jn 11.31, 11.38); íka .. wsi·t·í·li·t 'on his (obv.) feet' (Jn 11.2).

♦ Also used redundantly before a locative: íka nči·sás·ink pe·á·t·e 'when she came to where Jesus was' (Jn 11.32).

♦ As the locative of a demonstrative: (anim.) 'to him' (Mt 19.13; KJV "unto him"), íka li·ná·kwsu 'he is like him' (Jn 9.9); (inan.) íka wənčí·ayu 'it comes from it' (Jn 12.24).

íkali P (B ⟨ekali⟩ 56x, pp. 47-219; ⟨eku li⟩ 6x, pp. 50-109, ⟨eka li⟩ p. 86): generally as if íka P 'there, etc.' + lí P, PV 'to {smwh}': 'to there, in there' (Mt 8.32, Mt 13.25, Mk 9.25, Jn 18.1, etc.); 'away' (Jn 6.37, Mk 7.19, Mt 15.23); 'further on, later' (Lk 13.32); 'going there': íkali né·e· 'he saw (someone) go there' (Lk 21.2); (as the locative of a demonstrative) 'to him, to them, etc.': íkali kwələp·i· 'he turned to them' (Lk 9.55); káči čí·č íkali pənčí·han 'don't ever go in him again' (Mk 9.25); †páilat íkali kčí· 'Pilate went out to them' (Jn 18.29); 'to them' (Lk 7.9), 'into them' (Mk 5.13).

♦ Like íka, often with a locative noun or oblique-headed participle, which typically follows a verb or associated noun: íkali kwi·kayo·yəməwá·ink 'against their parents' (Mt 10.21); íkali kí·mahtəs wəškínkunk 'in your brother's eye' (Lk 6.42); íkali təmí·k·e·p wi·k·əwáhəmink 'he entered into a house' (Mk 7.24); íkali po·s·í·t·e mux·ó·link 'when he got into the boat' (Mk 5.18); íkali təmi·k·é·ok xkwé·čəč šenkí·x·ink 'they went in to where the girl lay' (Mk 5.40).

ikalíči P 'further' (Lk 2.52, Mt 4.21); ikalíči ləkhíkwi 'further on, later on' (1834b:45.6).

ikalísi 'more, greater' (Lk 3.13, Jn 1.50, 5.14, Mt 5.35); ikalísi .. šúkw 'more .. than' (Lk 3.13).

• ihikalísi 'more and more' (Jn 3.30); ihikalísi nuntai 'gradually.. fewer' (1834a:19.17).

ille·-: see le·-.

illəkhíkwi: see ləkhíkwi.

ílli (Gr. 5.43j) 'even' (Jn 1.12, Lk 3.16, Mk 5.28); corresponding to "neither" in (Jn 4.21), perhaps a misunderstanding of /(n)íyðər/.

†ime·niyó·wəl 'Emmanuel' (Mt 1.23).

=ínk P Q (also =nínk; used in rhetorical or exclamatory questions to imply unusual uncertainty or doubt; Gr. 5.24h): tá=háč=ínk=láh e·li·ná·kwsi·t 'what shall I say (he) is like?' (Lk 7.31); tá=háč=ínk=láh ləkhíkwi-áhot 'how hard do you imagine it is?' (Mk 10.24).

• =nínk: kekú=nínk=č=háč ntɔ́ləwe li·ná·k·ɔt? 'what shall I say it is like?' (Lk 13.18, 13.20); awé·n=nínk=láh nán? 'who is that?' (OA); kéku=nínk=láh ntɔ́ləwe? "what in the world did I say?" (LB).

†ísələl 'Israel' (Lk 1.16, 1.68, Mt 2.21); †isəlɔ́lak (pl.) 'the Israelites' (Mt 2.6, Jn 1.31, Mt 10.6, 10.23, 19.28, etc.); †isəlɔ́lal (obv.) (Lk 1.32, 1.54, 1.80), †isəlɔ́la (Mt 15.31); †isəlɔ́link 'in Israel' (Lk 2.34, Jn 3.10, Lk 4.25, 4.27, 7.9, Mt 9.33); né·k .. entxa·ke·í·č·i·k †isəlɔ́lak 'the tribes of Israel' (Lk 22.30).

†isələli·- AI 'be an Israelite': †isəlɔ́li·t '(one who is) an Israelite' (Jn 1.47).

†isələlí·i PN 'of Israel': †isələlí·i-sa·k·í·ma 'the king of Israel' (Jn 1.49).

■ PV: †isələlí·i-sa·k·i·má·t·e 'if he is the King of Israel' (Mt 27.42).

†iská·liat 'Iscariot' (⟨Iskrliut⟩ Jn 14.22; ⟨Iskal-⟩ 6x); see †nčó·tas.

-ite (-t-íte): see líte.

i·

i·ae·ke·-: see ae·ke·-.
i·ahki·hɔke·-: see ki·hɔke·-.
i·ankəl-: see ankəl-.
i·á·pči: see á·pči.
i·a·tenkpe·-: see a·tenkpe·-.
i·a·te·-: see a·te·-.
†í·čipt 'Egypt' (Mt 2.13, 2.14); †i·číptink 'in Egypt' (Mt 2.19), 'to Egypt' (1842:13.4 [2x]).
i·haki·he·-: see haki·he·-.
í·la (-t-i·la·yəm-, |īlāw-|) AN 'officer, captain, warrior' (Jn 18.22, Mt 27.54& [2x]); i·lá·ɔk 'officers' (Jn 7.45, 7.46, Jn 18.18&); i·lá·ɔ 'the captain (obv.)' (Mk 15.44, Mk 15.45&), 'officers (obv.)' (Jn 7.32).
 • -t-i·la·yəm-: wti·lá·yəma 'his warriors' (Mt 22.7; Gr. 2.61e), ti·lá·yəma 'his captains' (Lk 23.11; Gr. 2.60g); wti·la·yəmí·na 'his officers' (Mk 6.21; Gr. 4.12b); ti·la·yəməwá·ɔ 'their captains' (Mk 14.43&; Gr. 2.60g).
"†í·lae, í·lae, láma sapaktáne" (from the Greek transliteration of the Aramaic) (Mk 15.34).
†i·láyas 'Elias' (Jn 1.21, Lk 4.26, Mt 11.14, etc.); †i·layás·a 'Elias (abs.)' (Lk 4.25, 4.27, 9.54, Mt 6.15, 17.3, 27.49); †i·layás·a 'Elias (obv.)' (Mt 27.47). ♦ Elias is called Elijah in the Old Testament.
i·layas·i·- AI 'be Elias': máta i·layas·í·ɔne 'if you are not Elias' (Jn 1.25).
†i·lísapat 'Elisabeth' (Lk 1.5, 1.36, 1.41, 1.57); †i·lisapát·al (obv.) (Lk 1.24, 1.40).
†í·nanink 'in Enon' (Jn 3.23).
†í·pələm 'Ephraim' (Jn 11.54).
†i·se·yə́s·a 'Esaias (abs.)' (⟨Esrusu⟩ 8x in pp. 18-103: Mt 3.3, Jn 1.23, Lk 4.17, etc.; ⟨Esrisu⟩ 1x p. 37: Mt 4.14); †i·sayə́s·a (⟨Esyusu⟩ 3x in pp. 153-154: Jn 12.38, 12.39, 12.41). ♦ 'Esaias' is used incorrectlly for 'Elias' in Mt 16.14. ♦ Esaias is called Isaiah in the Old Testament.
-i·t·e·ha·- see li·t·e·ha·- AI 'think'.
i·yəntxíti P 'already a little bit' (1834b:15.3). Cf. ta·txíti.

k

-k (=ké) P (Gr. 5.24i) 'Well' (Mt 17.20, Lk 10.37, Mt 20.7); píši=k ktá 'Yes, indeed, in fact' (Lk 7.26). • =ké: yú=ké=č ntə́lsi·n 'Well, this is what I'll do' (Lk 12.18); nə́=ke=x 'well, in fact it was' (Jn 11.13).
káči P (prohibitive; Gr. 2.73b; §4.12b) 'don't' (Lk 1.13, 1.30, Mt 1.20); (as a refusal) 'no, I won't' (Mt 21.29), 'no, we won't' (Mt 25.9).
káč·i P (contrastive) 'but' (Mt 6.1, Mk 6.47), 'while' (Jn 1.17, 4.9, Lk 7.41, Jn 15.5).
kahəní·i PN 'having a dry river bed': in kahəní·i-sí·p·unk "Dry-River-Bed River [loc.]" (⟨Kavane sepwf⟩ 1834b:45.2), the northern boundary of the proposed Indian state; unidentified, but perhaps the Platte. From ká·han 'dry river bed' (LB).
kahəwé·yunk 'itch weed (loc.)' (⟨kavwruf⟩ Mt 7.16); LTD ⟨kahuwe⟩ "itch weed".
kahpal- TA — kahpat·- (-kapaht-) TI(2) 'haul out of the water'.
 ▪ kahpal- (TA): kahpaló·me 'haul him (a fish) out (you sg.)' (Mt 17.27).

■ -kapaht- (TI): kópahto·n 'he hauled it (a net) out of the water' (Jn 21.11).
kahpa·- (-kap·a·-, ke·p·a·-) AI 'come out of water': kahpé· (OA); péči-kahpé·ɔk 'they came ashore' (OA); tə́li-kahpa·né·ɔ 'they proceeded to disembark' (Mk 6.54).
  • -kap·a·-: ná .. kɔ́p·a·n 'then he got out of the water' (Jn 21.11); ná kɔp·á·ne·p (Mt 3.16).
  • ke·p·a·-: mé·či ke·p·á·t·e 'after he came ashore' (Mk 6.34).
kahpé·s AN 'twin' (as a nickname: Jn 11.16, 20.24, 21.2; KJV "Didymus").
káhta (-kát·a, ké·t·a; Gr. 5.23e, 5.128h) PV 'want to, be about to, intend to' (⟨kavta⟩ 5x, ⟨kavtu⟩ 47x, ⟨kuvtu⟩ 2x, ⟨kutu⟩ 19x): é·li-káhta-ahkí·ma·t le·khí·k·ana 'as he wanted to read the book' (Lk 4.16); lí-káhta-sa·k·i·má·whe·n 'that there was a desire to make him king' (Jn 6.15).
  • • -kát·a: nkát·a- (Mt 12.38, etc.), kkát·a- (Jn 5.35, etc.), kɔ́t·a- (Mt 1.19, etc.).
  • ké·t·a: ké·t·a-pəntaɔ́·č·i·k 'ones who wanted to hear him' (Lk 5.15); ké·t·a-ki·k·e·hə́nči·k 'ones who wanted to be cured' (Lk 6.17, Lk 5.15).
  ♦ 'be about to': lápi káhta-pá·ane 'when you (sg.) are about to come again' (Mt 24.3); káhta-áləmi-ála-hat·é·k·e hák·i 'when the world is about to cease to exist' (Mt 24.3).
  ♦ With imperative: káhta-ki·š·əná·kwsi·kw 'you (pl.) must be keen to be ready' (Mt 24.44); káhta-pé·š·əw 'seek to bring them (you sg.)' (Lk 14.23, KJV "compel them to come in").
kahtao·x·we·- (-kat·ao·x·we·-, ke·t·ao·x·we·-) AI 'want to go': nkat·aó·x·we 'I want to go' (LB).
  • ke·t·ao·x·we·-: máta ke·t·ao·x·wé·an 'where you don't want to go' (⟨krtu wxrun⟩ Jn 21.18; possibly for /-é·ɔn/).
kahtaɔhče·s·əwe·-* (ke·t·aɔč·e·s·əwé·- [IC]) AI 'be covetous': ke·t·aɔč·e·s·əwé·č·i·k 'the covetous ones' (Lk 16.14). ▶ See next.
kahtaɔhče·s·əwe·ɔ́·k·an 'covetousness' (Lk 12.15).
kahta·l- (-kat·a·l-, ke·t·a·l-) TA — kahta·t- (-kat·a·t-, ke·t·a·t-) TI(1a) 'want, need' (Gr. 3.20c).
  ■ kahta·l- (TA): takó· kahta·lé·i nta·ktə́la 'he has no need of a doctor' (Mt 9.12; Gr. 4.83b); é·li-kahtá·la·t 'in a way to desire her' (Mt 5.28; Gr. 4.67(1)a).
  • -kat·a·l-: kɔt·a·lá·ɔ 'he wants it (animal)' (Mk 11.3, Lk 19.34); tá=á· kɔt·a·la·iwwá·ɔ 'they will not want him' (Jn 14.17); mahtánt·u kkat·á·lukw 'the devil desires you (sg.)' (Lk 22.31).
  • ke·t·a·l-: ke·t·a·la·línki 'who (obv.) was desired' (Lk 23.25; Gr. 4.65j).
  ■ kahta·t- (TI): káči kahta·t·ánkhan 'do not desire it (you sg.)' (Jn 6.27); é·li-kahtá·t·aman 'because you (sg.) desired it' (Mt 18.32); é·li-kahtá·t·ank 'that he wanted it' (Lk 1.63); ktə́li-ké·pəwa -kahta·t·aməné·ɔ 'that you (pl.) also desire that' (Lk 12.30).
  • -kat·a·t-: nkat·á·t·amən 'I want it' (Jn 11.15, 13.15, 17.24; Gr. 4.49a); máta nkat·a·t·amó·wən 'I do not desire it' (Jn 5.34; Gr. 4.93a); kkat·a·t·aməné·ɔ 'you (pl.) want it' (Mt 16.4, 27.21); kɔt·a·t·amə́ne·p xáma·n 'he wanted to be fed' (Lk 16.21); kɔt·á·t·amən wwi·pó·mko·n 'he wanted to have him eat with him' (Lk 7.36); takó· kɔt·a·t·amo·wəné·ɔ 'they did not want it' (Jn 19.31; Gr. 4.93n).
  • ke·t·a·t-: ke·t·á·t·aman 'what you (sg.) desire' (Mt 6.8); máta ke·t·a·t·ankpáni·k 'those that don't want it' (Lk 19.27; Gr. 4.78m).
kahta·t·amaw- (-kat·a·t·amaw-) TA+O 'desire O2 of' (Gr. 5.94e): kahta·t·amáɔ·n 'it was desired of him [that he ..]' (Mk 8.22).
  • -kat·a·t·amaw-: kkat·a·t·ama·k·ó·ne·n ktahɔ·lá·ne·n 'he wants us to love him' (1834b:29.13).
kahtən- II (ke·t·ən-, |katən-|; Gr. 5.129bb) 'be {so many} years': takó· hwə́ska xé·li-kahtənó·wi 'it was not very many years' (1842:10.6); éntxən-kahtínk 'every year' (Lk 2.41); mé·či kí·xki ní·š·ən télən txá·pxki kahtínke 'after nearly two thousand years' (1842:8.3 [no IC]); mé·či kéxi-kahtínke 'several years later' (1842:14.4).
  • ke·t·ən-: mé·či xé·li ke·t·ínke 'after many years' (1834b:21.13).

kahtə́n P 'for {so many} tears': mé·či náxi-kahtə́n 'for three years now' (Lk 13.7); kwə́ti-kahtə́n 'one year' (1834a:17); télən ɔ́·k ní·š·a txí-kahtə́n 'for twelve years' (Lk 8.43).

kahtənami·- (ke·t·ənami·-) AI 'be {so many} years old': ahpá·mi=ét télən ɔ́·k ní·š·a kahtənámu 'she must have been about twelve years old' (Lk 8.42); xá·š txí·nxke ɔ́·k né·wa kahtənámo·p 'and she was eighty-four years old' (Lk 2.37); né·skɔ=ét palé·naxk txí·nxke kkat·ənamí·i 'you (sg.) can't yet be fifty years old' (Jn 8.57).
- ke·t·ənami·-: télən ɔ́·k ní·š·a ke·t·ənamí·t·e 'when he was twelve years old' (Lk 2.42).

kahtəné·i P 'for {so many} years' (⟨kavtinri⟩ 6x; Gr. 2.13a): kwə́ti-kahtəné·i 'for one year' (1842:9.6); náxi-kahtəné·i 'for three years' (Lk 4.25); ní·š·a·š txí-kahtəné·i 'for seven years' (⟨kavtenri⟩ Lk 2.36); télən ɔ́·k palé·naxk txí-kahtəné·i 'for fifteen years' (Lk 3.1); télən ɔ́·k xá·š txí-kahtəné·i 'for eighteen years' (Lk 13.11); ne·í·nxke ɔ́·k kwə́t·a·š kahtəné·i 'in forty-six years' (Jn 2.20).

káhti (-káti, kə́kahti [Rə̀+]; Gr. 2.74d, 5.27c, 5.36f) PV 'almost' (Jn 4.47, Mk 5.23, Lk 5.7, etc.), káhti (OA, LTD ND).
- -káti: nkáti-nhíla 'I pretty near killed him' (OA; Gr. 5.129n); nkáti-kaíhəla 'I almost fell down' (BS); nkatí-kawí (as if nkatíkawi) 'I almost went to sleep' (LTD ND).
- kə́kahti: kwə́kahti- né·k·a né·-mi·č·í·na 'he would almost eat them himself' (⟨Qwk-⟩ Lk 15.16).
▶ Cf. ⟨Gachti⟩ "almost, nearly" (B&A 36); kahtí (LB) P 'almost'.

kahto·nal- (-kat·o·nal-, ke·t·o·nal-; Gr. 5.12e) TA 'want to kill, try to kill, persecute': é·li- .. -kahtó·nala·t=č 'for (he) .. will seek to kill him' (Mt 2.13); lí-kahto·nalíe·kw 'wanting to kill me (you pl.)' (Jn 7.19; mode apparently by attraction to the higher verb).
- -kat·o·nal-: kɔt·o·nalawwá·ɔ 'they wanted to kill him' (Jn 5.16; Gr. 4.24k); kkat·o·nalíhəmɔ 'you (pl.) want to kill me' (Jn 8.37, 8.40).
- ke·t·o·nal-: ke·t·o·nala·tpáni·k né·l mi·məntə́t·a 'those that wanted to kill the baby' (Mt 2.20; Gr. 4.76j); ke·t·o·nalúk·ɔn 'the one that persecutes you (sg.)' (Mt 5.44).
▪ **kahto·nalət·i·-** AI (recip.; Gr. 5.110c): ɔ́·k=č sa·k·i·ma·ɔ́·k·anak kahto·nalə́t·əwak 'and kingdoms (anim.) shall attack each other' (Mt 24.7).

kahto·p·wi·- (-kat·o·p·wi·-, ke·t·o·p·wi·-, ka·kahto·p·wi·- [Rā+], |katōpwī-|; Gr. 5.104h) AI 'be hungry': áhi-kahtó·p·u 'he was very hungry' (1834b:28.9); kahtó·p·o·p 'he was hungry' (Mt 21.16&); máta=č háši kahto·p·wí·i 'he will never be hungry' (Jn 6.35); ktəli-kahtó·p·wi·n 'that you (sg.) were hungry' (Mt 25.44).
- -kat·o·p·wi·-: nkat·o·p·wí·həmp 'I was hungry' (Mt 25.35, 25.42); kkat·o·p·wíhəmɔ=č 'you (pl.) will be hungry' (Lk 6.25); ná .. kɔt·o·p·wí·ne·p 'then he was hungry' (Lk 4.2).
- ke·t·o·p·wi·-: ke·t·o·p·wí·t·e 'when he was hungry' (Mt 12.3); ke·t·o·p·wí·č·i·k 'those that are hungry' (Mt 5.6); ke·t·o·p·wi·lí·č·i 'the hungry (obv.)' (Lk 1.53; Gr. 4.65a).
- ka·kahtó·p·wi·-: nka·kahtó·p·wi 'I'm hungry all the time' (1834b:28.11).
▪ **kahto·phɔti·-** (|katōpwahtī-|; Gr. 5.75o) AI 'be hungry (coll.)': kahto·phɔ́ti·n 'there will be famine' (Lk 21.11&); áhi-kahto·phɔtí·ne·p 'there was great famine' (Lk 4.25; Gr. 4.68k).

kahto·s·əmwi·- (-kat·o·s·əmwi·-, ke·t·o·s·əmwi·-) AI 'be thirsty': kahtó·s·əmu 'he is thirsty' (Jn 4.13); máta=č háši kahto·s·əmwí·i 'he will never be thirsty' (Jn 6.35); ktəli-kahtó·s·əmwi·n 'that you (sg.) were thirsty' (Mt 25.44).
- -kat·o·s·əmwi·-: nkat·ó·s·əmwi 'I'm thirsty' (Jn 19.28; Gr. 5.85c); nkat·o·s·əmwí·həmp 'I was thirsty' (Mt 25.35, 25.42).
- ke·t·o·s·əmwi·-: ke·t·ó·s·əmwi·t 'who is thirsty' (Jn 7.37); ke·t·o·s·əmwí·č·i·k 'those that are thirsty' (Mt 5.6).

kahtunkɔ·m- (-kat·unkɔ·m-, |katənkwām-|; Gr. 5.11c) AI 'be sleepy': kahtúnkɔ·m 'he is sleepy' (Gr. 2.3e); áhi-kahtunkɔ́·mo·k 'they were very sleepy' (Lk 9.32); é·li-áhi-kahtunkɔ́·məli·t 'they (obv.) were very sleepy' (Mk 14.40).
- -kat·unkɔ·m-: nkat·únkɔ·m 'I'm sleepy' (Gr. 2.3e).

kaihəla·- (|kawīhlā-|) AI 'fall': kaihəlé·ɔk 'they fell down' (1834b:37.2); hák·ink təli-kaíhəla·n 'he fell to the ground' (Mk 9.20).

kai·- (~ kawi·-, ke·i·-) AI 'sleep': kawí· 'she is sleeping' (Mk 5.39; Gr. 2.9a) ~ kaí· 'he is sleeping' (Jn 11.11; Gr. 2.37c); táli-kaí·p 'he was asleep {smwh}' (Mk 4.38); kaí·kw 'sleep (you pl.)' (Mt 26.45; Gr. 2.37b, 4.103h); énta-kaí·t 'when he was asleep' (Mt 1.20; Gr. 2.37a); né·li-kaíenk 'while we (exc.) slept' (Mt 28.13); təli-kaí·li·n 'that they (obv.) were sleeping' (Mk 14.37, 14.40, Lk 22.45); ná wé·mi kɔi·né·ɔ 'then they all slept' (Mt 25.5).
- ke·i·-: ke·i·tpáni·k 'who (pl.) had been sleeping' (Mt 27.52).

▸ For the loss of intervocalic -w-, see Gr. §2.11a and the extended discussion at §2.37; note that analogical levelling has taken place in both directions.

kai·teho·kw- AI 'be made to fall by a weight or blow': máta kai·teho·k·o·wí·ɔk 'they are not made to fall' (Lk 11.46).
▸ Cf. kɔwhitehɔ́·ɔ (|-kawəhtehw-|) 'he hit him and knocked him down' (LB; Gr. 2.38b).

-kaki·ɔl-: see ki·ɔl-.

-kakši·tehw-: see kši·tehw-.

-kak·e·p·inkwa·-: see ahke·p·inkwa·-.

-kak·e·p·inkwe·ha·l-: see ahke·p·inkwe·ha·l-.

-kak·əlo·ne·-: see kəlo·ne·-.

-kak·i·hɔke·ɔ·k·an-: see ki·hɔke·ɔ́·k·an.

†kaməlí·i: see kémal.

kančº (|kant-|) 'hide' (Gr. §5.2a). ▸ Cf. kantº below.

kanči·x·i·n- AI 'hide, be hidden': kančí·x·i·n 'is hidden' (ME, LB; Gr. 5.11m).

†kánkələs 'congress' (⟨Kaflis⟩ 1834b:46.10); †kankələs·ak 'congressmen' (1834a:21.38, 1834b:42.5, etc.); kankələs·i·ké·i 'to Congress' (1834b:46.11).

kankwi·- (-kihkankwi·- [Rih+]) AI 'be, become jealous': kánku 'he or she is jealous' (LTD ND); kkánkwi 'you are jealous' (BS).
- -kihkankwi·-: kihkánkwi· 'she gets jealous' (LB), nkihkánkwi 'I get jealous' (1834b:20.7, 1842:11.1).

kankwi·l- TA 'be jealous of': kɔnkwi·lá·ɔ 'he is jealous of him' (LB); é·li-kankwi·láhti·t 'because they were jealous of him' (Mk 15.10; Gr. 3.15a).

kanšº (|kanš-|) 'amazing(ly)' (Gr. §5.2a); in later sources ka·nšº (Gr. §2.1c).

kanšaehɔ·s·əwá·k·an IN 'miracle(s)' (Jn 3.2, Mt 11.21, 11.23, etc.); nkanšaehɔ·s·əwá·k·an 'my miracles' (Jn 4.48); nkanšaehɔ·s·əwá·k·ana 'my miracles' (Jn 6.26); kɔnšaehɔ·s·əwá·k·an 'his miracles' (Mk 3.8, Lk 7.17, Mt 13.54).

kanšaehɔ·s·i·- (ahkanšaehɔ·s·i·- [Ra+]) AI 'perform miracles': kanšaehɔ́·s·u 'he does miracles' (Jn 11.47); takó· xé·li lí-kanšaehɔ·s·í·i 'he did not do many miracles' (Mt 13.58); énta-aləwí·i-kanšaehɔ·s·í·t·əp 'where he had done most of his miracles' (Mt 11.20).
- ahkanšaehɔ·s·i·-: e·lkí·kwi-ahkanšaehɔ·s·í·t·əp 'how great were the miracles he performed' (Jn 2.23); é·li-ahkanšaehɔ·s·í·li·t 'the way they (obv.) did miracles' (Mk 16.20).

kanšala·məwá·k·an IN 'screaming' (Mt 2.18).

kanšala·mwi·- AI 'shout': tá=á· kanšala·mwí·i 'he will not shout' (Mt 12.19); kanšala·mó·p·ani·k 'they shouted' (Mk 3.11); kanšalá·mwink 'the sound of [someone] screaming' (Jn 1.23).

kanša·š·i·mwi·- AI 'have an amazing dream': kanša·š·í·mu 'he had an amazing dream' (1842:14.1).

kanše·lənt- TI(-O) 'be amazed, astonished': kanše·ləntam 'he was astonished' (Mk 6.6, Lk 11.38); kanše·ləntamo·p wé·mi awé·n 'everyone was amazed' (Mt 12.23); kanše·ləntamo·k 'they were astonished' (Mk 5.20, 5.42, Mt 9.33, etc.; Gr. 2.16e, 4.38q); kanše·ləntamó·p·ani·k 'they were amazed' (Lk 1.63, 2.47, 2.48, Mk 1.22, etc.); káči kanše·ləntánkhan 'don't be amazed (you sg.)' (Jn 3.7; Gr. 4.112b); káči kanše·ləntamó·he·kw 'do not be astonished (you pl.)' (Jn 5.28; Gr. 4.112f); nəni wwənči-áhi-kanše·ləntamən 'he was greatly astonished by that' (Mt 27.14).

kanšhita·k·ɔt- (kanšhitakɔht-) II 'sound loud': ka·nšhitá·k·ɔt 'it sounds big (loud)' (LB); kanšhitákɔhtu 'they (seas and waves) roar' (Lk 21.25; KJV "roaring").

kánši (ahkánši; Gr. 5.129o) PV, PP 'great, powerful, wonderful' (Lk 1.49, Lk 10.19, 24.19); wəní·tami- kánši-kéku -laehɔ·s·í·ne·p 'he performed his first miracle' (Jn 2.11).
• ahkánši PP (plural): ahkánši-kéku 'miracles, marvelous things' (1834b:26.5, 40.4).

kanši·laeh- TA 'astonish': kkanši·laehkó·na 'he astonished us (inc.)' (Mk 12.11); máta=háč kkanši·laehkó·wən? 'Doesn't this astonish you (sg.)?' (1834b:13.5).

kanši·laem- TA 'astonish by speech': nkanši·lae·mko·ná·nak a·lənte ntuxkwe·yəməná·nak 'we were astonished by the report of some of our women' (Lk 24.22).

kanši·na·kwsi·- AI — kanši·na·k·ɔt- II 'be marvelous to behold' (Gr. 5.108c).
▪ kanši·na·kwsi·- (AI): kanši·na·kwsúwak 'they are marvelous to behold' (Lk 21.25).
▪ kanši·na·k·ɔt- (II): kanši·ná·k·ɔ 'wonders' (Mt 24.23).

kantº, kančº (|kant-|) 'hide' (Gr. §5.2a).

kantahpi·- AI 'stay hidden, in hiding': kántahpu 'he hid' (Jn 8.59); sháki-kántahpo·p 'she stayed in hiding for [so long]' (Lk 1.24); takó· káski-kantahpí·i·p 'he was not able to stay hidden' (Mk 7.24).

kanthal- TA — kanthat- TI(2) 'hide'.
▪ kanthal- (TA): é·li-kanthále·kw 'you (pl.) have hidden [the key (anim.)]' (Lk 11.52).
▪ kanthat- (TI): wé·mi kéku kanthatúhti·t 'everything they hide' (Mt 10.26); kanthatúnke 'when they are hidden' (Mt 13.44); tə́li- máta -káski-kantható·wən '(that) she could not hide it' (Lk 8.47); tá=á· káski-kantható·wən 'it cannot be hidden' (Mt 5.14; Gr. 4.93p).

kanthataw- TA+O 'hide O2 from': é·li-kanthátaɔt yó·l le·p·ɔ́·č·i·k 'as you concealed these things from the wise' (Lk 10.21); é·li kanthataɔ·né·ɔ 'as it was hidden from them' (Lk 9.45).

kanthata·s·i·- II 'be hidden' (Gr. 5.106a): mé·či kanthatá·s·u 'they are hidden' (Lk 19.42).

†kápənal AN 'governor' (⟨Kopunul⟩ 1834b:45.8). ▸ See also †nkápənal.

†kapənali·- AI 'be governor': †kapənáli·t 'who is governor' (⟨Kopunrlet⟩ 1834b:45.6); tə́nta-†kapənáli·n 'he is governor (there)' (⟨tuntu Kopunrlel⟩ 1834b:45.5 [⟨-l⟩ for ⟨-n⟩]); †kapənalí·t·e 'when he was governor' (⟨kupunuletc⟩ Lk 2.2; p. 12).

†kapə́niam 'Capernaum' (⟨Kupunium⟩ Jn 2.12, Lk 4.23, etc.; ⟨Kpunium⟩ Lk 7.1); †kapəniámink 'in Capernaum' (Jn 4.46, Lk 4.31, Mk 1.21, etc.).

-kap·a·-: see kahpa·-.

káski (ké·ski, kí·kski [Rī+]; Gr. 5.27d, 5.128i) PV 'be able to' (Lk 1.74, Jn 3.27, 5.27, etc.); kɔ́ski- |wə- + kaski-| (Lk 1.22, Jn 3.3, Mt 6.24 [2x], 6.27, etc.); šúkw máta káski 'but he could not' (Lk 19.3 [with gapped verb]).
• ké·ski (Mt 11.15, Mk 9.39, Lk 12.4, etc.).
• kí·kski (with negative) 'be never able to' (Mt 9.32, 12.22 [2x], Mk 7.32, etc.; Gr. §2.4).

kaski·khata·s·í·k·e(?) 'if it is tamped down(?)' (⟨kuskekvatasekc⟩ Lk 6.38). ▸ Cf. kaskí·khwi· 'he tucks himself in (as in bed)' (LB), with apparent |-ahwī-| AI 'act on self with something'.

kathake·- (-nəkathake·-) AI 'move residence, move family': íkali katháke· 'he moved there' (1834a:23.54); katháke·l 'move your (sg.) family' (Mt 2.20); sé·ki-núči-katháke·t 'while he began moving' (1834a:19.20); nə́ wwə́nči- †nkelalí·yunk -lí-katháke·n 'for that reason he took his family to Galilee' (Mt 2.22).
- -nəkathake·-: lápi=á· kənəkatháke·n 'you must move again' (1834a:19.16).

-kat·a·l-: see kahta·l-.

-kat·o·p·wi·-: see kahto·p·wi·-.

kawi·-: see kai·-.

káxkat 'it is broken' (V; Gr. 5.10p).

kaxkha·s·i·- II 'be broken': tá=á· .. kaxkha·s·í·i 'it (bone) will not be broken' (Jn 19.36).
▸ Cf. Mun kaxkh- TI(1a) 'break in two (with axe, stick, car)' (APh).

kaxpi·l- TA 'tie, bind' — kaxpt- (ke·xpt-, kəkxpt- [Rə̀+], |kaxpət-|) TI(2) 'tie, tie together' (Gr. 3.20i, 5.12f).
- kaxpi·l- (TA): kaxpí·lo 'tie him (you pl.)' (Mt 22.13); kaxpi·lə́nte 'if he was tied up' (Mt 12.29); nkaxpí·la=č 'I will tie him up' (1842:15.3); kɔxpi·lá·ɔ '[the devil] has bound her' (Lk 13.16); kɔxpi·la·né·ɔ 'they tied him up' (Jn 18.12); lí-kaxpí·la·n 'that he be bound' (Mk 6.17).
- kaxpt- (TI): ní·link nkáxpto·n 'I'll tie it on my head' (1834a:13; Gr. 5.12f).
- ke·xpt-: né·k·a ke·xptá·k·wi 'his bundle' (1842:13.2; KJV "sheaf"); ke·xptó·li·t 'the one they (obv.) tied together' (1842:13.2; for omitted |-ī|, see Gr. 4.59).
- kəkxpt-: kəkxptó·wak 'they were tying it into bundles' (1842:13.2); kkəkxpto·né·ɔ=č 'you must tie them in bundles' (Mt 13.30; Gr. 4.50n).

kaxpi·s·i·- (ke·xpi·s·i·-, |kàxpīsī-|; Gr. §2.4, 5.104k) AI 'be bound' — kaxpi·s·o·wi·- II 'be tied'.
- kaxpi·s·i·- (AI) kaxpí·s·u 'it (animal) was tied' (Mk 11.4&); kaxpí·s·o·p 'he had been bound' (Mk 5.4); wíči-kaxpi·s·ó·p·ani·k 'they were tied up with him' (Mk 15.7).
- ke·xpi·s·i·-: ke·xpí·s·i·t 'tied up' (Lk 19.30&).
- kaxpi·s·o·wi·- (II): kaxpi·s·úwwa 'they (inan.) were tied' (⟨kaxpeswu⟩ Jn 11.44).

kaxpt- : see kaxpi·l- — kaxpt-.

kaxptí·k·an IN 'a tied thing': nkaxptí·k·an "my yoke" (Mt 11.29, 30).

kaxpti·k·e·- AI(+O) 'tie on (things)': kkaxpti·k·e·né·ɔ=á· nkaxptí·k·an 'you (pl.) should tie on my yoke' (Mt 11.29).

ka·kpəč·e·í·i PV 'in a foolish way' (⟨kakpethri⟩ 1834b:11.9). ▸ Cf. kpəč·a·- 'be foolish', etc.

-ka·k·əlinkɔ·m-: see kəlinkɔ·m-.

ka·lo·m- (-kak·a·lo·m- |Ra+|; -kək·a·lo·m- [Rə̀+]; Gr. 5.36t) TA 'berate, scold': nka·ló·ma 'I scold him' (V).
- -kak·a·lo·m-: nkak·a·ló·ma 'I scolded ("got after") him', kɔk·a·lo·má·a 'he berates him'(OA).
- -kək·a·lo·m-: kwək·a·lo·mawwá·ɔ 'they berated them' (⟨kwvkalwmawao⟩ Lk 5.30; /kwək·-/ ME 2x in other words; /kwək(·)-/ in B also ⟨qwk-⟩ 2x and ⟨kwk-⟩ 1x).

ká·mink (Gr. 5.26c) P 'on the other side (of water)' (Mt 8.18, Mk 6.45, Jn 6.22 2x, Mk 8.13); tpə́skwi ká·mink †nčátan 'on the opposite side of the Jordan' (Jn 1.28), †nčátanink ká·mink 'across the Jordan' (Jn 3.26, Mt 4.15, 4.25, Jn 10.40, Mt 19.1); mənəp·é·k·unk táli ká·mink 'on the other side of the sea' (Jn 6.25).

ká·wənš AN 'thorn'; in later sources ká·wə·nš (LB); ka·wə́nšak 'thorns, briars, brambles' (Mt 13.7); ka·wə́nša 'the thorns' (Jn 19.5).
- ka·wənší·i PN 'of thorns' (Mt 27.29).

ka·wənša·kw-: ka·wənšá·kunk 'on a thorn bush' (Mt 7.16).
ka·wənše·i·k·a·ɔn-: ka·wənše·i·k·á·ɔnink 'in booths of brush' (Jn 7.2).
ka·wənši·ke·- II 'be a lot of brambles': énta-ka·wənší·ke·k 'among brambles' (Mt 13.7, 13.22).
ká·xəne (Gr. 2.73c) P 'I wonder if (or whether)' (Lk 13.6, 13.7, Mk 11.13&), '(to see) whether' (⟨kavunc⟩ Lk 6.7), 'Let's see whether' (Mt 27.49), 'Haven't (we) ..?' (⟨kavni⟩ Jn 6.42).
 ▸ Cf. ⟨Gachene⟩ 'if, whether' (B&A 35); ⟨gáchanne⟩ 'whether' (Z. 229).
 ◆ (adding emphasis) 'really' (1834a: Cover, 1; 1834b:3 3x, 6.2, 14.8, 26.6, 28.9, 28.11; 1842:18.4). ▸ Cf. ⟨gachene wullet⟩ 'it is surely good' (Z. 85); ⟨gahenne⟩ 'very' (Z. 205); also ká·xane (OA), ká·xani (ME; Gr. 2.73c).
ka·xkᵒ (|kāxk-|) 'dry' (Gr. §5.2a).
ka·xksa·s·i·- II 'be dried': ka·xksá·s·u 'it is dried' (1834a:16).
ka·xksi·- AI 'be dried up, be parched': mé·či ká·xksu 'it (tree) has dried up' (Mk 11.21); təlkí·kwi- šá·e -ká·xksi·n wá hít·ukw 'how quickly this tree has dried up' (Mt 21.20).
kčᵒ (|kət-|) 'out' (Gr. §5.2a).
kčaxkihəla·- II 'become loose': kčaxkíhəle· '[his tongue] came loose' (Mk 7.35).
kčihəlal- (-kəč·ihəlal-, ke·č·ihəlal-, |kəčīhlal-|) TA 'expose': wənči-=á· máta -kčihəlalúk·o·kw 'so that they would not expose him' (Mk 3.12; Gr. 4.97m).
 • kəč·ihəlal-: kkəč·ihəlalúk·o·n 'it exposes you' (Lk 22.59-60&).
 • ke·č·ihəlal-: ke·č·íhəlala·t 'who exposed him' (Mt 10.4; Gr. 4.64g); ke·č·ihəlalúkwki 'who (obv.) betrayed him' (lit., 'who exposed him') (Lk 6.16).
kčilahsi·- AI 'undress': kčílahsu 'he took his clothes off' (Jn 13.4), 'he is undressing' (LB).
kčilahso·l- (-kəč·ilahso·l-) TA 'strip, undress': kwəč·ilahso·la·né·ɔ 'they stripped him' (Mt 27.28, 27.31&).
kčilaht- (-kəč·ilaht-) TI(2) 'pull out quickly' (gloss: LTD); also metaphorical "confess": kwəč·ílahto·n 'he quickly drew it (a sword)' (Jn 18.10); kwəč·ilahto·né·ɔ mɔt·a·wsəwa·k·anúwa 'they confessed their sins' (Mt 3.6; KJV "confessing their sins").
kčinkwehəla·- (|kəčīnkwēhlā-|) AI 'rise (of the sun)', II 'be sunrise': kčinkwehəle· 'it is sunrise' (Gr. 2.24b); máta háši kčinkwehəl[e·]i 'the sun never comes out' (1834a:15; ⟨-li⟩); wənči-kčinkwéhəla·t 'so that it (anim.) rises' (Mt 5.45).
 ◆ wénči-kčinkwéhəla·k 'the east' (lit., '(in) the direction of the sunrise') (Mt 2.1, 2.2, 8.11; Gr. 3.13(7)d, 4.67(2)h), wehənči-kčinkwéhəla·k (Lk 13.29, Mt 24.27); énta-kčinkwéhəla·k 'in the east' (Mt 2.9); wehənči-kčinkwéhəla·t kí·š·o·x 'on the sun-rise side (anim.)' (1834b:44.10).
kči·- (-kəč·i·-, ke·č·i·-) AI 'come out, emerge': kčí· 'he went out' (Mt 21.17&, Mk 14.72, Jn 18.29, 18.38); kčí·ɔk 'they went out' (Jn 8.9, 19.17, Jn 20.3; Gr. 4.21m); kčí·l 'come out (you sg.)' (Mk 5.8); kčí·t·eč 'let him leave' (Lk 21.21); hɔ́k·enk wənči-kčí·ləwa 'they (obv.) came out of her' (Lk 8.2; cf. Gr. 4.21e); wénči-=č máta -káski-kčí·ɔn 'so that you (sg.) will not be able to get out' (Lk 19.43; Gr. 4.95g).
 • -kəč·i·-: ná .. kwə́č·i·n 'then he went out' (Mt 24.1, Jn 13.30, 18.16); ná mahtant·ó·wak kwəč·i·né·ɔ 'then the devils went out' (Mk 5.13).
 • ke·č·i·-: ke·č·í·t·e 'when he came out' (Lk 1.22, Mt 12.43, 13.1, etc.); mé·či ke·č·ihtí·t·e 'after they had gone out' (1842:9.7).
 ▪ kčo·lti·- AI (coll.; Gr. 5.75d) 'go out (in a group)': kčo·ltúwak 'they all come out' (V, ME); ⟨Ktscholtin⟩ "to come out of church" (B&A 58).
kčo·ha·l- (-kəč·o·ha·l-, ke·č·o·ha·l-, |kəčōhāl-|; Gr. 5.81a) TA 'save, ransom' (lit., 'get Oˡ out'): kčo·há·la·=č 'he shall be saved' (Mt 10.22); wénči-=č -káski-kčo·ha·lké·e·kw 'so that you (p.) shall be saved' (Jn 5.34); tɔ́li-=č xé·li awé·n -kčo·há·lko·n 'so that many will be saved by him'

(Mt 20.28; KJV "[to be] a ransom for"); ktə́li-=č -kčo·ha·lké·ne·n 'that we would be saved' (Lk 1.71).
- -kəč·o·ha·l-: kəna·ka·t·amwe·ɔ́·k·an kkəč·o·há·lko·n 'your faith has saved you' (Lk 7.50; Gr. 4.27w); kkəč·o·ha·lke·né·ɔ 'for you (pl.) to be saved' (Lk 21.28).
- ke·č·o·ha·l-: ke·č·o·há·la·t 'savior' (Jn 4.42); ke·č·o·ha·lkɔnkw 'Our Savior' (B: Title Page); ke·č·o·há·li·t 'my savior' (Lk 1.47).

kčo·há·ləwe·- (ke·č·o·ha·ləwe·-; Gr. 5.101) AI 'save people': ke·č·o·há·ləwe·t 'savior' (*lit.*, '(one) who saves people') (Lk 2.11).

kčo·ha·ltəwá·k·an (-kəč·o·ha·ltəwa·k·an-; Gr. 5.81a, 5.115c) IN 'salvation' (Lk 2.30, Jn 4.22).
- -kəč·o·ha·ltəwa·k·an-: kwəč·o·ha·ltəwá·k·an 'his or her salvation' (Lk 3.6; Gr. 5.116g).

kčo·he·- (ke·č·o·he·-) AI+O 'save O2': é·li=č ke·č·ó·he·t 'as he is one who will rescue (them)' (Mt 1.21).

kehahki·hɔke·-: see ki·hɔke·-.

kehahki·hɔ́ke·s AN 'hypocrite'; kehahki·hɔke·s·i·ké·i P 'to the hypocrites' (Mt 24.51).

kéhəla P 'really' (Lk 4.23, Jn 9.30, Lk 10.41, 11.13, 11.46, etc.).

kehkəlo·hit°: see kəlo·hitaw-.

kehkəmo·tke·-: see kəmo·tke·-.

kehkəmó·tke·s AN 'thief' (Mt 26.55-56&; Gr. 5.66d); kehkəmo·tké·s·a 'thieves (obv.)' (Lk 10.30, 10.36), 'a thief (obv.)' (Mt 24.43).

kehkəmo·tke·s·i·k·a·ɔni·- II 'be a house of thieves': wénči-kehkəmo·tke·s·i·k·á·ɔni·k '(that) by which it is a house of thieves' (Mt 21.13&).

kéku (Gr. 2.72h, 4.18) 'thing, things, something, anything' (Jn 1.3, Lk 1.15, Lk 2.24, Mt 2.11, 3.8, Jn 3.27, etc.); wé·mi kéku 'everything' (Jn 1.3, 3.35, Lk 5.11, etc.); (with negative) 'nothing' (Lk 1.37, Lk 5.5, etc.), 'not anything' (Mt 5.13, etc.); kéku lí 'in any way' (1834b:20.6).
- kéku (interrogative), usually kéku=háč 'what?': kéku=háč nə́ lé·w 'what is that?' (Lk 6.34); kéku=háč kəmái-ne·mhúmɔ 'what did you (pl.) go to see?' (Lk 7.24); kéku=č=ksí ntəlsíhəna? 'What, then, shall we do?' (Lk 3.10); kéku=háč wə́nči 'why?' (*lit.*, 'because of what?') (Lk 2.48, etc.); kéku=ksí wə́nči- 'why?' (Jn 2.4); (without =háč) kéku wénči-kələstáe·kw 'why do you listen to him?' (Jn 10.20).
- kéku 'what' (in an indirect question): kéku=č=tá e·ləwé·e·kw 'what you will say' (Mt 10.19); kéku=š=tá e·ləwéhti·t 'what they would say' (Jn 6.6); kéku=š=tá e·laehɔ́·s·i·t '(let's see) what he will do' (LTD FW).
- Idiom (mirative): kéku=xán 'but here it was' (Mt 2.9); kéku=xán=hánkw yúh mé·či 'why, already always' (Jn 5.7); kéku=láh=wáni 'people were startled to see this one; why, here was this one' (V 3x; "lo and behold").

kelántink ~ nkelántink P 'gallon(s)': kelántink (Jn 2.6), nkelántink (Lk 16.6); nkəlántink (LB).
- L. has a note to Lk 16.6 that 100 measures of oil equals nine gallons and three quarts, but Blanchard assumes that the measure of oil is an ephah (8 gallons).

†keləlí·yunk 'to Galilee' (1834b:37.5). ▶ Cf. †nkélali· 'Galilee' (⟨Fclule⟩) below.

†kelpə́li 'Calvary' (Lk 23.33); †kélpeli (1834b:35.2).

kéməl AN 'camel' (⟨kcmil⟩ Mt 19.24); kéməlak 'camels' (Mt 23.24).
- †kaməlí·i PN '(of) camel' (⟨kamile⟩ Mt 3.4).

képəč AN 'cabbage' (LB; Gr. 2.79d); kepə́č·ak (1834a:17; LTD speaker).

†képtən 'captain' (⟨Kaptin⟩ 1834b:35.5); spelling presumably influenced by English.

kéxi PV 'few': é·li-kéxi-kahtínk 'for a few years' (1842:19.1).

▪ kéxi PP (Gr. 5.133b): mé·či kéxi-kí·škwe 'over the last few days' (Lk 24.18).
†ke·ápas 'Caiaphas' (Lk 3.2, Jn 11.49, Mt 26.3, etc.); †ke·apás·a (Jn 18.24, 18.16); wə́nči †ke·apás·ink 'from Caiaphas' (Mt 27.2&).
ke·č·o·ha·l-: see kčo·ha·l-.
ke·č·o·ha·ləwe·-: see kčo·ha·ləwe·-.
ke·kai·°: see khikai·-.
ke·kayəmhe·-: see khikayəmhe·-.
ke·kayə́mhe·s (-ke·kayəmhe·s·əm-) AN 'ruler'; náka máta wé·li-ləs·í·t·əp ke·kayəmhé·s·a 'that unrighteous ruler (abs.)' (Lk 18.6); táli ke·kayəmhé·s·ink 'before the ruler' (Lk 20.20); ke·kayəmhe·s·i·ké·i P 'among rulers' (Mk 13.9, Lk 22.4, Mk 14.43&).
• -ke·kayəmhe·s·əm-: nke·kayəmhe·s·əməná·nak 'our rulers' (Lk 24.20).
▪ ke·kayəmhé·t·ət (dim.): ke·kayəmhé·t·ət skínnu 'a young man of the ruling class' (Mk 10.17&).
ke·kayə́mhe·t: see khikayəmhe·-.
ke·kayəmhe·t·í·i PN 'of the ruler(s)' (Gr. 5.123d): ke·kayəmhe·t·í·i-a·pto·ná·k·an 'the laws of the rulers' (Mk 7.3).
ke·ke·xíti: see ke·xíti.
ke·k·e·p·inkɔ·-: see ahke·p·inkɔ·-.
ke·k·e·pxa·°: see ahke·pxa·-.
ke·k·i·wsi·°: see ki·wsi·-.
ke·k·o·n- (-ke·k·o·nəm-; Gr. 2.55h) 'thing': ké·k·o·n (in a question) 'what thing?' (1834b:9.12; AD); amánki-ke·k·ó·nal 'large things' (1834a:15); ke·k·ó·na 'things' (LTD ND, LB); wé·mi yó·l ke·k·ó·ni 'all these things' (Mt 24.2); ke·k·ó·nink 'on anything' (1834a:15).
• -ke·k·o·nəm-: kwe·k·ó·nəm 'his thing' (commonly with obscene sense) (ND; Gr. 2.55h).
▪ ke·k·o·ní·i PN 'what kind of?' (LTD ND, LB).
ke·nahkinkɔ·m- TA 'keep an eye on': ke·nahkinkɔ·má·č·i·k 'who were keeping an eye on him' (1834b:37.2); kwe·nahkinkɔ·mawwá·p·ani 'they kept an eye on him' (Lk 14.1; KJV "watched"); ⟨geenachging quamuk⟩ "he look at Thee" (Z. 116 [sic]).
ke·nahki·h- TA — ke·nahki·t- TI(2) 'take care of' (Gr. 5.12a).
▪ ke·nahki·h- (TA): ké·nahki· 'take care of him (you sg.)' (Lk 10.35; Gr. 2.11b); ke·nahkí·ha·t 'who takes care of them' (Jn 10.2); nke·nahki·há·p·ani·k 'I took care of them' (Jn 17.12; Gr. 4.69e); só·čəlak nke·nahkí·ha 'I have soldiers under me' (lit., 'have soldiers in my care') (Lk 7.8; KJV "having under me soldiers"); kke·nahkí·hi 'you (sg.) take care of me' (Lk 17.8); kwe·nahki·há·ɔ 'he watched out for him' (Mk 6.20).
▪ ke·nahki·t- (TI): ke·nahkí·to·kw khak·ayúwa 'watch yourselves!' (Mk 13.35; Gr. 4.15j, 4.106o); máta wəli-ke·nahki·to·wé·k·we 'if you (pl.) do not take good care of it' (Lk 16.12; Gr. 4.99o); kpúntəm nó·li-ke·nahkí·to·n 'I took good care of your pound' (Lk 19.20).
♦ pa·tamwe·ɔ́·k·an ke·nahkí·ta·kw 'the high priest' (lit., 'prayer guardian') (Mt 26.3, Jn 18.10, 18.15, etc.); ke·nahki·tá·k·əp pa·tamwe·ɔ́·k·an néke ləkhíkwi 'the high priest at that time' (Jn 18.13; KJV "the high priest that same year"; cf. Gr. 4.78o); pa·tamwe·ɔ́·k·an ke·nahki·to·lí·č·i (obv.) (Mt 28.11); pa·tamwe·ɔ́·k·an ke·nahki·tá·k·wi·k (Mk 14.43&; KJV "chief priests").
ke·nahki·taw- TA+O 'take care of O2 for': ke·nahki·tá·kwki 'who (obv.) took care of it for him' (Lk 8.3).
ke·na·m- TA 'give thanks to': ké·na·m ke·tanət·ó·wi·t 'give thanks to God (you sg.)' (Jn 9.24); káči ke·na·mié·k·e·kw 'do not give thanks (you pl.) to them' (1834b:20.6; KJV "Thou shalt not bow down thyself to them"); kwe·na·má·ɔ 'he thanked him' (Lk 5.25, Lk 17.16, etc.);

kwe·na·mawwá·p·ani 'they gave thanks to him' (Lk 5.26); kke·ná·məl 'I give thanks to you' (Jn 9.38, Lk 10.21, Jn 11.41).

ke·na·mwi·- AI 'give thanks': ke·ná·mu 'he gave thanks' (Mt 26.27; Gr. 5.58e); mé·či ke·na·mwí·t·e 'after giving thanks' (Jn 6.11, Mk 8.7); ná tə́li-ke·ná·mwi·n 'and he proceeded to give thanks' (Mk 8.6, Lk 22.17; Gr. §4.51).

†ké·ne· 'Cana' (⟨Krnr⟩ Jn 2.11) ~ †ké·ni (⟨Krni⟩ Jn 4.46); †ke·né·ink 'in Cana' (⟨Krnrif⟩ Jn 2.1) ~ ke·ní·yunk 'Cana (loc.)' (⟨Krnebf⟩ Jn 21.2).
- †ké·nanink 'Canaa (loc.)' (Mt 10.4).

†ke·ní·xkwe AN 'Canaanite woman' (Mt 15.22).

ke·pča·-: see kpəč·a·-.

ké·pe (Gr. 4.13) 'you (sg.) too' (Mt 7.1, Lk 6.37, 6.38, etc.).
- ké·pəwa 'you (pl.) also' (Jn 6.67, Mt 11.21, Jn 8.44).

ke·pha·s·i·-: see kpaha·s·i·-.

ke·p·inkɔ́·č·i·k 'the blind' (Lk 4.18); otherwise reduplicated; cf. ahke·p·inkwa·-.

ke·šxin-: see kšax·ən-.

†ke·š·e·t(?) (⟨krjrt⟩ 1834b:24.11); context suggests 'only'.

ke·š·i·la·n- : see kši·la·n-.

ke·tanət·o·wi·-, ke·tanət·o·wi·t·í·i: see khitanət·o·wi·-.

†ke·tsi·mé·ni 'Gethsemane' (Mt 26.36).

ke·t·aɔč·e·s·əwé·č·i·k: see kahtaɔhče·s·əwe·-.

ke·t·əma·k·i·h-: see ktəma·k·i·h-.

ke·x(·)º (‖kēx-‖) 'few' (Gr. §5.2a).

ke·xháke '(for) several tribes' (1834b:43.4).

ke·xíti P (ke·ke·xíti; Gr. 2.76a) 'a little' (Lk 5.3, Lk 12.48, Lk 16.10, Lk 18.12).
- ke·ke·xíti 'a little each time' (Lk 18.12, 1842:21.3).

ké·x·a P 'a few, some' (Lk 4.25, Mk 6.5, 8.7), 'several' (Mt 21.36, 22.4, Mk 16.2&); takó· ké·x·a awé·ni·k 'it was not several people' (Lk 4.26); ké·x·a ki·š·ó·x·ink 'for a few months' (1842:19.1).
- ké·x·a P (interrogative): ké·x·a=háč 'how many?' (Mk 8.5, 8.19); ké·x·a=háč, ké·x·a=hěč 'how much?' (ME).

ke·x·á·pto·n IN 'a few words'; kkát·a- ke·x·á·pto·n kéku -ləlhúmɔ 'I want to tell you a few words about something' (1842:18.6).

ke·x·a·pto·na·l- TA 'say a few words to': nke·x·a·pto·na·lá·ɔk yó·ki·k 'I say a few words to these' (1834b:13.6).

ke·x·á·pxki P 'a few hundred' (1834b:19.12).

ke·x·ennáɔhki P 'several kinds' (Mk 14.43&;1834b:42.13).

ke·x·i·- AI (pl.) 'be several, be few': ké·x·əwak 'there were several' (Jn 2.23); ke·x·í·ləwal 'they (obv.) are few' (1834b:28.11).

ke·x·o·k·wənak·at- (‖kēxōkwənakat-‖) II 'be a few days': máta ke·x·o·k·wənakahtó·wi 'it was not several days' (1834b:28.6; máta kwəní·i 'not long after' in Lk 15.13, translating KJV "not many days after"); é·li-ke·x·o·k·wənák·a 'in a few days' (Acts 1.5; Gr. 2.48c), '(it is) for a few days' (1834b:3.9, 1842:19.1).

ke·x·ó·k·wəni P 'in, for several days' (1834b:10.17; OA, LTD ND).

kəktəmakº: see ktəmakahkwi·-.

kəkxpt-: see kaxpt-.

kək·amo·kant- TI(1a) 'gnash (teeth)': énta-=č -kək·amo·kantamíhti·t wi·p·i·t·əwá·ɔ 'where they will gnash their teeth' (Mt 13.42); kwək·amo·kantamə́na 'he gnashes them' (Mk 9.18); kkək·amo·kantamənέ·ɔ ki·p·i·t·əwá·ɔ 'you (pl.) will gnash your teeth' (Lk 13.28).
 ♦ Only reduplicated in B, but cf. /kamo·k-/ (ME), /kamɔ·k-/ 'crush' (OA).
kək·amo·kanta·s·i- II 'be gnashed': énta-=č .. -kək·amo·kantá·s·i·k wi·p·í·t·a 'where there shall be teeth being gnashed' (Mt 22.13, 25.30).
kək·ələntəl-: see kələntəl-.
-kək·ɔ́·ni-: see kwə́ni.
kəlahaw- (ke·lhaw-, |kəlahw-|) TA 'fall on': kəlahó·k·o·k '(it) falls on them' (Lk 21.35); ɔ́·k=č awé·n yú ahsə́n kəlahó·kwke 'and if this stone falls on anyone' (Lk 20.18).
 • ke·lhaw-: ke·lho·khwití·t·əp 'those that it fell on' (Lk 13.4; Gr. 4.76bb).
kəlahí·k·an IN 'trap' (Lk 21.35).
 ♦ Note: this would refer to a deadfall trap but is used to translate "snare" (KJV).
kəláist (-kəlaistəm-) 'Christ' (Lk 2.11, Mk 1.1, Lk 3.15, etc.); kəláistal (obv.) (Mt 2.5).
 • -kəlaistəm-: nehəlá·ləwe·t kwəláistəmal 'the Lord's Christ' (Lk 2.26).
kəlaisti·- (|kəlaistī-| [accents conjectured]; Gr. 5.67g) AI 'be Christ': é·li-kəlaístia 'as I am Christ' (Mk 9.41); kəlaistiáne 'if you are Christ' (Jn 10.24, Lk 23.39); máta=x=á· kəlaistí·ɔne 'if in fact you are not Christ' (Jn 1.25; Gr. 4.95i); kəlaistí·t·e 'if he is Christ' (Mt 27.42); nkəlaistí·i 'I am not Christ' (Jn 3.28); ktə́li-kəláisti·n 'that you are Christ' (Jn 11.27).
kəlamº (|kəlam-|) 'calm, still' (Gr. §5.2a).
kəlamahpi·- (-kəlamap·i·-, ke·lamahpi·-) AI 'sit still': kəlámahpo·p 'she sat quietly' (Jn 11.20); kəlamahpúwak 'they sat quietly' (Lk 23.56); kəlámahpi "Behave [you sg.]!" (LB); kəlámahpi·kw 'Be still (you pl.).' (Mk 4.39&); né·li-kəlámahpi·t 'while he sat quietly' (Mt 25.5; KJV "tarried").
 • -kəlamap·i·-: nkəlamáp·i 'I sit quietly' (ND).
 • ke·lamahpi·-: ke·lamahpi·lí·t·e 'when they (obv.) sat quietly' (⟨krlumuvpeletc⟩ Mt 27.17).
kəlama·pi·º ~ kəlamampi·º: 'gird'.
kəlama·pi·l- TA 'put a belt on' (takes an instrumental oblique [§3.7c]): kwəlama·pí·la·n hɔ́kaya 'he tied it on around him (i.e., himself)' (Jn 21.7; cf. Gr. §3.7c).
kəlama·pi·s·i·- (with |-āhpīsī|; Gr. 5.53d) AI 'put on a belt, have a belt on': kəlama·pí·s·i·kw 'have your (pl.) belt on' (Lk 12.35).
 ▪ kəlamampi·s·i·- (ke·lamampi·s·i·- [IC]) AI 'put on a belt' (takes an instrumental oblique [§3.7c]): kəlamampí·s·o·p 'he wore [a leather strap] as a belt' (Mt 3.4).
 • ke·lamampi·s·i·-: ke·lamampí·s·i·t 'what he was wearing as a belt' (Jn 13.5).
kəlama·pi·s·o·l- TA 'put a belt on': kwəlama·pi·s·o·lá·ɔ hɔ́kaya 'he puts on his (own) belt' (Lk 12.37).
 ▪ kəlamampi·s·o·l- TA 'put a belt on' (takes an instrumental oblique [§3.7c]): nihəláči=hánkw kkəlamampi·s·ɔ́·la·p khák·ay 'you (sg.) would put on your own belt' (Jn 21.18); pí·li=č awé·n kkəlamampi·s·ɔ́·lukw 'someone else will put your belt on you (sg.)' (Jn 21.18); kwəlamampi·s·ɔ́·la·n hɔ́kaya 'he tied it around himself as a belt' (Jn 13.4).
kəlama·pí·s·o·n IN 'belt' (WT; Gr. 5.53d).
kəlamihəla·- II 'be, become calm': xé·li=č awé·n tɔhɔ·ltəwá·k·an kəlamíhəle· 'many people's love will go still' (Mt 24.12); mənə́p·e·kw kəlamíhəle·p 'the sea became calm' (Mk 4.39).
kəlamo·t·a·s·i·- II 'be heaped up': kəlamo·t·á·s·u 'it is heaped up' (1834a:16).
kəle·lənt- (ke·le·lənt-) TI(1a) 'keep, hold (in the mind), take (to heart)': kəle·lə́ntamo·kw 'keep it in mind (you pl.)' (Jn 15.20); kəle·lə́ntamo·mɔ́·e 'take it to heart (you pl.)' (Mt 23.3);

kəle·ləntank 'what he holds to (ppl.)' (Mt 13.21); kkəle·ləntamən=č 'you must keep [the commandments]' (Mt 19.17 [em.]); kwəle·ləntamən=č nta·pto·ná·k·an 'he will take my words to heart' (Jn 14.23).
- ke·le·lənt-: ke·le·ləntánki·k '(ones) who held to it' (1842:10.3), ke·le·ləntánki·k nta·pto·ná·k·an 'those who take my commandments to heart' (1842:11.1).
▸ Cf. Mun kə̆le·lə́ntam 'keeps (it) in mind' (dict.).

kələksi·- AI 'laugh': kələksu 'he or she laughs' (V, WS; Gr. 5.10i).
- kələksahti·- AI (coll.): kələksahtíe·kw 'you (pl.) who laugh' (Lk 6.25).

kələk·a·wsi- AI 'live joyfully, be joyful': kkələk·a·wsí·ne·n 'let us be joyful' (1834b:29.2).

kələn- (-kənn-, kenn-) TA — TI(1b) 'hold, carry' (Gr. 5.12o).
- kələn- (TA): le·khí·k·ana kələ́ne·p 'he held a book (anim.)' (1834b:41.8); ke·x·ennáɔhki ɔ·s·əle·ní·k·ana kələné·ɔk 'they carried several kinds of portable lights (anim.)' (Mk 14.43&); kələné·p·ani·k 'they carried [lamps (anim.)]' (Mt 25.3, 25.4; Gr. 4.69c); tə́nta-kələnawwá·ɔ 'they carried him on [a litter]' (Lk 5.18&).
- -kənn-: kwənná·p·ani 'he held him' (Lk 2.28); kwənnuk·ó·p·ani kɔhé·s·al 'he was being held by his mother (obv.)' (Mt 2.11; Gr. 4.69q).
- kenn-: kenná·č·i·k 'the ones carrying him' (Lk 7.14; Gr. 4.64u).
- kələn- (TI): kələ́nəmo·k 'they carried [swords and canes]' (Mk 14.43&); káči kələnínkhe·kw 'don't carry it (you pl.)' (Mt 10.9; Gr. 2.44b); kələnínke 'if he carries it' (Lk 11.21; Gr. 2.3b); ktə́li-kələ́nəmən 'for you (sg.) to carry it' (Jn 5.10; Gr. 4.50i).
- -kənn-: takó· kéku kkənnəmó·wi anshi·k·é·an 'you (sg.) don't have anything to scoop up water with' (Jn 4.11; Gr. 3.14d, 4.91b); kwənnə́mən 'he carries it' (Lk 22.36); kwənnəməné·ɔ nə́ mpí·s·o·n 'they carried the medicine' (Mk 16.2&; Gr. 4.39w).
- kenn-: máta kennəmo·wé·k·we 'when you (pl.) didn't have [a purse]' (Lk 22.35; Gr. 4.99f).

kələntəl- (kək·ələntəl- [Rə̀+]; Gr. 5.87d) TA+O 'hand O2 out to': kwələntəlá·ɔ khwitələt·əwá·k·an 'he gave them the law to have' (1842:10.6); ná kwəló́ntəla·n 'then he handed them out to them' (⟨qwlintulan⟩ Jn 6.11); tə́li-=č -kələntəla·né·ɔ 'for them to hand out to them' (⟨tclih kulintulanro⟩ Jn. 6.11).
- kək·ələntəl-: kwək·ələ́ntəla·n 'he handed them out to them (sbd.)' (⟨qwkuluntulan⟩ Jn 21.13); ná tə́li-kək·ələ́ntəla·n 'he then proceeded to hand it out to them' (Lk 24.30).

kələnthike·- (|kələntəhkē-|; Gr. 5.102j) AI+O 'give O2 to people to have, keep': kwələnthiké·ne·p 'he gave it to people to have' (Jn 1.17, Jn 5.33); kwələnthiké·li·n hɔ́k·ay 'he (obv.) handed him (prox.) over' (Mt 18.34).

kələstaw- (-kələsət·aw-) TA — kələst- (-kəlsət·-) TI(1a) 'listen to, heed' (Gr. 5.12bb).
- kələstaw- (TA): kələ́sto· 'listen to him (you pl.)' (Lk 9.35); kələstái·l 'listen to me (you sg.)' (Lk 1.31, 1842:22.5; Gr. 2.36a, 4.105g), kələstái (1834b:10.8; Gr. 4.105h); kələstái·kw 'hear me (you pl.)' (Mt 15.10, 1842:18.6); kéku wénči-kələstáe·kw 'why do you (pl.) listen to him?' (Jn 10.20; Gr. 4.67(2)j); mé·i-kələstá·k·uk ' the one they (obv.) went to hear' (Lk 6.17); máta kələsta·k·ó·wane 'if he doesn't listen to you (sg.)' (Mt 18.16; Gr. 4.97j).
- -kəlsət·aw-: nkəlsə́t·aɔ é·li·t 'I obey what he tells me' (Jn 8.55; Gr. 5.12bb); kwəlsət·aɔ́·ɔ 'he listens to him' (Jn 9.31, ⟨-ao⟩ for ⟨-aoo⟩); kwəlsət·aɔ́·ɔ '(he was) listening to them' (Mk 12.28, ⟨-ao⟩ for ⟨-aoo⟩); ná kwəlsə́t·aɔ·n. 'Then he did what he asked (lit., he listened to him).' (Mt 3.15); né·skɔ kkəlsət·ai·húmɔ 'you (pl.) do not yet believe me' (Jn 6.36; Gr. 4.89f).
- kələst- (TI): lápi kələstámo·kw e·nunthake·ɔ́·k·an 'listen to another parable (you pl.)' (Mt 21.33); káči kələstánkhe·kw 'don't listen to it (you pl.)' (Lk 21.8); šínki-kələstánke 'if he is unwilling to listen to [your words]' (Mt 10.14).

- -kəlsət·-: nkəlsət·amən 'I listen to it' (ME; Gr. 5.12bb); nə́ni=á· kwəlsət·aməné·ɔ 'they should listen to *that*' (Lk 16.29; Gr. 4.39v); kwəlsət·amɔ́li·n tɔ·pto·ná·k·an 'she (obv.) listened to his talk' (Lk 10.39; Gr. 4.39n); máta kkəlsət·amo·wəné·ɔ 'you (pl.) do not believe it' (Jn 6.64).

kəlinkɔ·m- (-ka·k·əlinkɔ·m- [Rā+]) TA 'look closely at': tɔ́hi-kəlinkɔ·má·ɔ 'she looked at him intensely' (Lk 22.56-57&); ná tɔ́ləmi-kəlinkɔ́·ma·n 'then he began to fix his gaze on him' (1842:16.1).
- -ka·k·əlinkɔ·m-: kɔ·k·əlinkɔ·má·ɔ 'he fixed his gaze on them' (Lk 20.17; KJV "beheld", RSV "looked at").

†kəliɔ́·pəs 'Cleophas' (Jn 19.25, Lk 24.18).

kəli·ta·- II 'be attached, come together, be fastened together': kəlí·ta· 'it goes together' (ME); kə́nč wisahki·múnšink lí-kəli·tá·k·e 'unless it remains attached to the vine' (Jn 15.4; KJV "abide in").

kəli·x·a·s·i·- AI, II 'be sewn': kəli·x·á·s·u 'it (anim.) was sewed up' (OA); takó· kəli·x·a·s·í·i 'it (inan.) was not sewn together' (Jn 19.23). ♦ Note: /x·/ (OA) for earlier /xh/, found in the TI(1a) forms: nkəli·xhámən 'I'm sewing it' (OA, LTD ND).

kəlo·hitaw- TA — kəlo·hit- (kehkəlo·hit- [Rih+; IC]) TI(1a) 'disbelieve'.
▪ kəlo·hitaw- (TA): káči .. kəlo·hitawié·k·ač 'don't disbelieve him (you sg.)' (Lk 3.14).
▪ kəlo·hit- (TI): kəlo·hítam 'he was in disbelief' (1842:18.1); é·li-kəlo·hítaman 'since you (sg.) don't believe it' (Lk 1.20); káči kəlo·hitánkhan 'do not disbelieve it (you sg.)' (Jn 20.27).
- kehkəlo·hit-: kehkəlo·hítank 'the unbeliever' (Jn 3.18).

kəlo·l- (-kak·əlo·l- [Ra+]) TA 'curse at': nkəlɔ́·la 'I cussed him' (OA).
- -kak·əlo·l-: kɔk·əlo·lawwá·ɔ 'they cursed at him' (Mk 15.29).
▪ kəlo·lti·- AI (recip.): kəlo·ltúwak 'they're cussing each other' (OA).
▶ Cf. ⟨Gakloltowagan⟩ IN 'quarrel, dispute' (B&A 37).

kəlo·ne·- AI 'lie' (-kak·əlo·ne·- [Ra+], ke·k·əlo·ne·- [Ra+IC]): kəlɔ́·ne· 'he lies, tells a lie' (ME; Gr. 5.34n); káči kəlo·né·han 'do not lie (you sg.)' (Mt 19.18; Gr. 6.6k); šúkw é·li-kəlo·néhti·t 'but they are lying' (Lk 6.22).
- -kak·əlo·ne·-: nkak·əlɔ́·ne·=á· 'I would be a liar' (Jn 8.55); máta nkak·əlo·né·i 'I do not lie' (Lk 1.20; Gr. 4.81a).
- ke·k·əlo·ne·-: ke·k·əlo·né·t·e 'when he lies' (Jn 8.44); é·li ke·k·əlɔ́·ne·t 'as he is a liar' (Jn 8.44); ke·k·əlo·né·č·i·k 'those that lied' (Lk 6.26, Mt 24.11, Mt 26.60 [2x]).

kəlo·ne·ɔ́·k·an IN 'lie'; 'lying (in a list of sins)' (Mt 15.19); kəlo·ne·ɔ́·k·ana 'lies' (Mt 26.59).
- (AN as possessor; Gr. §3.2) kəlo·ne·ɔ́·k·anak o·x·əwá·ɔ 'the father of lies (anim.)' (Jn 8.44); for the animate use, see Goddard 2019: 99.

kə́mhɔkw 'cloud' (Lk 9.34, 12.54, Acts 1.9); kəmhɔ́kunk 'cloud, clouds (loc.)' (Lk 9.35, Mk 14.62; Mt 24.30, Mk 14.62). ▶ Cf. Mun ăkə́mahkw, ăkə́mwahkw (CH).

kəmo·tke·- (kihkəmo·tke·- [Rih+], kehkəmo·tke·- [Rih+; IC]; Gr. 5.41c) AI(+O) 'steal (O2)': káči kəmo·tké·han 'do not steal (you sg.)' (Mt 19.18, 1842:12.5); énta-=á· .. -kəmo·tkéhti·t 'where they would steal them' (Mt 6.19); ɔ́·k·=á· énta- máta .. -kəmo·tkéhti·t 'and where they would not .. steal them' (Mt 6.20); tə́li-=á· -kəmɔ́·tke·n 'that he would steal' (Jn 10.10); kumɔ́·tke·n 'he stole it' (OA; Gr. 2.59c).
- kihkəmo·tke·- 'steal habitually, be a thief' (Gr. 5.42c): káči háši kihkəmo·tké·han. 'Never be a thief (you sg.).' (1834b:21.6); kihkəmɔ́·tke·p ná †mpalápas 'Barabbas had been a thief' (Jn 18.40); é·li-kihkəmɔ́·tke·t 'because he was a thief' (Jn 12.6).
- kehkəmo·tke·-: kehkəmɔ́·tke·t 'thief' (Jn 10.1, 10.10, Lk 12.33, Lk 12.39); kehkəmo·tké·č·i·k 'thieves' (Mt 6.19, 6.20, Jn 10.8).

kəmo·tke·ó·k·an IN 'theft' (Mt 15.19); kəmo·tke·ó·k·anink 'thieving (loc.)' (Lk 11.39).

kəmo·t·əm- TA 'rob', TA+O 'steal O2 from': kəmo·t·əmá·t·e 'if he steals from him' (1834b:45.10); ktə́li-káhta-kəmo·t·əmúk·o·n 'that he intends to rob you (pl.)' (1842:22.2); nkəmo·t·əmuk·o·ne·ná·ni 'they stole him (obv.) from us (exc.)' (Mt 28.13; Gr. 4.41f).

kəmpahkwihəla- II 'grow leaves': ké·t·a-áləmi-kəmpahkwihəlá·k·e 'when they are going to start growing leaves' (Mt 24.32; Gr. 4.62m).

kəmpahkwi·- AI 'have leaves': kə́mpahku ná hít·ukw 'the tree had leaves' (Mk 11.13&).

kə́mpakw AN 'leaf' (AD, LTD ND), kúmpakw (LB); kə́mpahkɔ 'leaves' (Mk 4.28, 11.13&; OA, LTD ND), kúmpahkɔ 'leaves' (V, LB).

kə́nč P (qualifies or limits actions): 'unless' (Jn 6.44, 15.4, Mt 17.21); '(not) until' (Lk 2.26); kə́nč=č lápi pəntaiáne 'until you hear from me again' (Mt 2.13); kə́nč=á· nó·x mi·lá·t·e 'only if my father grants it to them' (Jn 6.65); níši-ki·škwí·k·e kə́nč 'only after two days' (Lk 2.46); kə́nč †nči·lo·səlómink 'except in Jerusalem' (Lk 13.33); kə́nč yúkwe 'here lately' (Jn 11.8; KJV "of late"). ♦ ná kə́nč 'only then' (Lk 1.56, 4.2, Mt 5.24, Jn 11.14, Mt 22.10), '(then) at that point, thereupon' (Mt 12.45, Jn 20.6), 'at that' (Lk 14.4).

kənčč° (|kəntəč-|) 'push' (Gr. 5.7a).

kənčča·khw- (|-āhkw-ah-|; Gr. 5.18g) TI(1a) 'push off (with a pole)': kənččá·khɔ 'push it off (you sg.)' (Lk 5.3).

kənččən- (-kək·ənččən- [Rə̀+]; Gr. 5.7a) TA 'push, force to go, send' — TI(1a) 'push, move'.

▪ kənččən- (TA): nkənččə́na 'I push him' (OA); íka ntə́li-kənččə́na·p 'I sent him to him' (Lk 23.15); péči kwənččəná·ɔl 'he sent him here' (Lk 1.26); ná=č šá·e kwənččə́na·n 'then he will send it (animal) off immediately' (Mk 11.3; KJV "straightway he will send them hither").

• -kək·ənččən-: kuk·ənččənawwá·ɔ 'they drove him off' (Lk 4.29; KJV "thrust him .. and led him unto").

▪ kənččən- (TI): nkənččənə́mən 'I pushed it' (ND).

kənči·mwi·- (kək·ənč·mwi·- [Rə̀+]) AI 'cry out, sing (of birds)' — kənči·mo·wi·- II 'sound (out)'.

▪ kənči·mwi·- (AI): kənčí·mu 'he's singing (as a bird)' (Gr. 5.76a); típa·s tá=á· kənči·mwí·i 'the rooster will not crow' (Jn 13.38, Lk 22.34); ahsə́nak kənčí·məwak 'the stones cry out' (Lk 19.40); né·skɔ=č típa·s ní·š·ən kənčí·mwi·t 'before the rooster crows twice' (Lk 22.61); ná típa·s kwənčí·mwi·n 'then the rooster crowed' (Lk 22.56-57&).

• kək·ənč·mwi·-: kək·ənčí·mu 'he's crowing' (OA; Gr. 5.36p).

▪ kənči·mo·wi·- (II): kənči·mó·u '[trumpet] sounds' (Mt 24.31; Gr. 2.30h, 3.19a, 5.76a).

-kənn-: see kələn-.

kəntahəla·- II 'pierce': kté·hink lí-kəntáhəle· 'it will pierce your (sg.) heart' (Lk 2.35).

kəntahko·s·i·- AI 'climb (a tree)': kəntahkó·s·u 'he climbed up' (Lk 19.4; OA; Gr. 5.11g).

kənte·ləm- TA — kənte·lənt- TI(1a) 'condemn'.

▪ kənte·ləm- (TA): kənte·ləmát·əp 'that you (sg.) condemned' (Mk 11.21; Gr. 4.76e); kwənte·ləmawwá·ɔ 'they condemn him' (Mt 20.18); máta kkənte·ləməló·wi 'I do not condemn you' (Jn 8.11; Gr. 4.89i).

▪ kənte·lənt- (TI): ⟨Gendelendam⟩ "to condemn" (B&A 39).

kənte·ləmukwsəwá·k·an IN 'condemnation, being condemned' (Jn 12.31, 16.8, 16.11; KJV "judgement"), ⟨Gendelemuxowagan⟩ "condemnation, damnation" (B&A 39); kənte·ləmukwsəwá·k·anink 'to damnation' (Jn 5.24, 5.29).

kənte·ləmukwsi·- AI 'be condemned': é·li- .. sa·k·í·ma -kənte·ləmúkwsi·t 'because .. the king is condemned' (Jn 16.11).

kəntəweha·l- TA 'convert' (Gr. 5.83a): ktə́li-=á· kwə́t·i awə́·n -kəntəweha·la·né·ɔ 'in order for you (pl.) to convert one person' (Mt 23.15).
▸ Cf. kəntəwe·- AI 'be a Christian': kə́ntəwe· "he doesn't believe in the Big House" (V); kəntəwe·ɔ́·k·an 'Baptist religion' (V). ▸ Munsee ke·ntə̄wé·sak 'Christian Indians' (JP, APh).

kəntəweí·i PN 'Christian'; kəntəweí·i-ki·škwí·k·e 'on Sunday' (1834b:16.8), éntxi-=č -kəntəweí·i-kí·škwí·k·e 'every Sunday' (1834b:20.1).

kəntka·- (|kəntəkā-|; Gr. 4.63j, 5.11e) AI 'dance': máta kkəntka·húmɔ 'you (pl.) did not dance' (Lk 7.32); ná tə́li-kə́ntka·n '(then) she danced' (Mk 6.22); lí-kə́ntka·n 'that there was dancing' (Lk 15.25); kə́ntke· 'he or she dances' (V, ME, LB).

-kəpha·s·i·-: see kpaha·s·i·-.

-kəphikamaw- TA+O 'shut O2 off from': kkəphikamaɔ·né·ɔ 'you (pl.) shut it off from them' (Mt 23.13).

-kəpto·na·- AI 'be mute': kkəptó·na=č 'you will be mute' (Lk 1.20; Gr. 5.24b).

-kətskᵒ: see ktəskaw-.

khičí·i (kəkhičí·i [Rə̀+]; Gr. 5.29b) P 'truly, really' (Mk 14.30, Lk 22.67, Jn 18.37, etc.; ⟨kehi⟩ Mt 4.3 only: ⟨kehe⟩ 55x; ⟨kvehe⟩ 25x, ⟨kvehei⟩ 42x); khičí·i, khičí·i 'truly, truly' (Jn 3.3, 3.5, 3.11, etc.).
• kəkhičí·i: kəkhičí·i ktəllúhəmɔ 'I tell you (pl.) very truly' (Jn 1.51).
▪ -ki·čí·i PV: kwi·čí·i-lá·ɔ 'he strongly admonished them' (Mt 9.30; KJV "straitly charged them": RSV "sternly charged them").

khikai·- (-ki·kai·-, ke·kai·-, |kəhkayī-|) AI 'be old, be the older (one)': íka péči-khikaiáne 'until you (sg.) are old' (1842:20.1); áhi-khíkayo·p 'she was very old' (Lk 2.36); khikayó·p·ani·k 'they were old' (Lk 1.7); mé·či khikaí·t·e 'when she was already old' (Lk 1.36).
• -ki·kai-: péxu kki·kaíhəna 'we'll be old' (1842:19.2); péxu kki·kaíhəmɔ 'you will be old' (1834b:3.9).
• ke·kai·-: ké·kai·t 'older' (Lk 15.25, Mt 21.31); ke·kai·tpána 'who was the eldest' (Lk 20.29; Gr. 4.75i); ke·kaí·č·i·k 'oldest ones' (Jn 8.9); ke·kai·lí·č·i 'the older one (obv.)' (Mt 21.28).

khikayəmhe·- (-ki·kayəmhe·-, ke·kayəmhe·-) AI 'rule': khikayə́mhe· 'he is a ruler' (1842:17.1); énta-khikayə́mhe·t 'where he ruled' (Lk 23.7); †i·číptink énta-khikayəmhe·lí·č·i 'who (obv.) was a ruler in Egypt' (1842:13.4); ktə́nta-khikayə́mhe 'you rule {smwh}' (Lk 19.17, 19.18).
• -ki·kayəmhe·-: nki·kayə́mhe·n 'that I rule (sbd.)' (Lk 19.27); kwi·kayə́mhe·n 'for him to be the ruler (sbd.)' (Lk 19.14).
• ke·kayəmhe·-: ke·kayə́mhe·t 'ruler' (Jn 3.1, 3.10, Lk 7.3, 7.6, etc.); ke·kayəmhé·t·e 'when he was the ruler' (Lk 3.1 [4x]); ke·kayəmhe·lí·č·i 'rulers (obv.)' (Lk 23.13); ke·kayəmhé·č·i·k 'rulers, authorities' (Mk 7.5, Jn 7.26, Mt 16.21, etc.).
♦ ke·kayəmhe·t 'ruler' (lexicalized participle): nə́ táli-ke·kayəmhe·t 'a ruler there' (Lk 7.2), 'The President' (1834b:43.5, etc.); ke·kayəmhé·t·ink 'to the ruler' (Jn 2.8, Mt 10.18, Lk 12.58). ▸ Cf. ke·kayəmhe·s, ke·kayəmhe·tí·i.

khikayúxkwe AN 'the older woman' (Lk 12.53 [2x]; KJV "the mother," "the mother in law").

khikələná·p·e AN 'older person' (1834b:20.10, 1842:11.1; Gr. 5.14g).

khikələna·p·e·i·- AI 'be an old person' (Gr. 5.67b): mé·či khikələna·p·e·iáne 'after you (sg.) are grown up' (1834b:4.9); mé·či khikələna·p·e·ihtí·t·e 'even after they are old' (1834b:5.1, 6.2).

khikəwəs·i·- AI 'be old': ntáhi-khikəwə́s·i 'I am now much too old' (Lk 1.18).

khikəwínnu AN 'old man' (Lk 12.53; KJV "the father"); khikəwinnúwak 'the elders' (Mk 11.27&, Mk 14.53, 1842:19.2).
▸ Cf. next.

khikəwi·lənəwi·- AI 'be an old man': mé·či khikəwi·lənəwihtí·t·e 'after they become old men' (1834b:5.5). ♦ A Northern Unami form; cf. ⟨kikuwileño⟩ 'elderly man' (Z. 64); Mun kihkə̆wí·lə̆nəw 'adult man' (dict.).

khikh- (|kəhkah-|; Gr. 5.57b) TI(1a) 'mark (to make known)': khikhámo·kw nə́ni hák·i 'mark the bounds of that land (you pl.)' (1834a:22.49). ▸ Cf. Munsee kihkh- TI(1a) 'mark (for identification), mark the perimeter of'; see also khikhá·k·an below.

khikhat-(?) TI(2): é·li- máta .. -khikháta·kw(?) 'as he does not limit(?) it' (⟨kekvataq⟩ Jn 3.34; KJV "giveth not .. by measure"), perhaps literally 'does not measure it out (stintingly)'. (Word unknown; shape and meaning conjectured.)

khikhá·k·an 'landmark; survey line' (1834b:44.9; V), 'state' (LTD CW). ▸ Cf. khikhí·k·an 'boundary marker' (OA "stakes used in measuring"), ⟨kĭkhican⟩ 'boundary' (Z. 27).

khiki·n- TI(1a) 'be aquainted with': kkát·a-=ét šúkw -khiki·naməné·ɔ yú ahpá·mi 'you (pl.) probably only want to become acquainted with what's around here' (1842:15.2).

khiki·no·ləwá·k·an IN 'sign' (Lk 2.12, Jn 2.18, 6.30, Mt 16.1, 16.4 [3x]; Gr. 4.83w); nə́ khiki·no·ləwá·k·an †nčɔ·nás·a 'the sign of Jonas' (Mt 16.4).

khík·ay (-ki·kayo·yəm-, |kəhkay|; Gr. 2.8c) AN 'old person, parent' (Lk 1.18); khíkayak 'parents' (Lk 2.27), 'old people, older folks' (V, ME).
 • -ki·kayo·yəm-: kki·kayo·yəməwá·ok 'your parents' (Lk 21.16); kwi·kayó·yəma 'his parents' (Lk 2.41, Jn 9.2, 9.3, etc.); kwi·kayo·yəməwá·ɔ 'their parents' (Mk 13.12); íkali kwi·kayo·yəməwá·ink 'against their parents' (Mt 10.21).

khitᵒ (-ki·tᵒ, |kəht-|) 'great, greatly' (Gr. §5.2a, 5.17c).

khítahtən (|kəhtatənw-|; Gr. 5.31c; cf. Gr. 5.11i) IN 'mountain' (V); khitahtə́nunk 'to the mountains' (Mt 24.16).

khitanət·o·wi·- (ke·tanət·o·wi·- [IC]; |kəhtanətōwī-|) AI 'be the great spirit, be God'.
 • khitanət·o·wi·-: é·li yú šé·, kí· ktə́nta-khitanət·o·wi·n 'because you are the only powerful spirit here' (ME; translated so).
 • ke·tanət·o·wi·-: ke·tanət·ó·wian 'O God' (lit., 'you (sg.) who are the great spirit') (Lk 18.11, 18.13, Mt 21.9, etc.); ke·tanət·ó·wi·t 'God' (Mk 3.11, Mt 5.33, Mk 1.24, etc.); ke·tanət·o·wi·lí·č·i 'God (obv.)' (Mt 6.24, Lk 5.25, 5.26, etc.; Gr. 4.65d).
 ♦ ke·tanət·ó·wi·t 'God' (as a lexicalized participle; cf. Gr. 5.65): ke·tanət·o·wí·t·ink 'God (loc.)' (Jn 6.46, 8.42, etc.).
 • -ke·tanət·o·wi·t·-əm- (possessed theme [Gr. §4.2a]): nke·tanət·o·wí·t·əmink 'to my God' (Jn 20.17); kke·tanət·o·wí·t·əm 'your (sg.) God' (1842:11.1, etc.); kke·tanət·o·wí·t·əmink 'to your (pl.) God' (Jn 20.17). ▸ See also: kwe·tanət·o·wi·t·əmi·-.
 ▪ ke·tanət·o·wi·t·í·i PN 'of God' (derivative of the lexicalized participle; Gr. 5.123e): ke·tanət·o·wi·t·í·i-awé·n 'someone of God' (Jn 8.47); ke·tanət·o·wi·t·í·i-pa·tamwe·i·k·á·ɔnink 'into the temple of God' (Mt 21.12).
 ▪ ke·tanət·o·wi·t·í·i P (derived from the prenoun; Gr. 5.126c): ná lə́nu takó· ke·tanət·o·wi·t·í·i 'that man is not of God' (Jn 9.16); o·wá·to·n=č lí ke·tanət·o·wi·t·í·i 'he will know that it is God's' (Jn 7.17).

khitá·kɔ 'ears (of wheat?)' (⟨ketakw⟩ Mk 4.28; KJV "the ear").

khita·č·i·mwi·-* (-ki·ta·č·i·mwi·- |kəhtāčīmwī-|, Gr. 5.17c) AI 'testify': nki·ta·č·í·mwi 'I testify' (Jn 1.34).

khita·č·i·mo·lx-* (-ki·ta·č·i·mo·lx-) TA 'testify to': nčá·n kwi·ta·č·i·mo·lxá·p·ani 'John testified to them' (Jn 1.32).

khita·k·i·ma·- (ke·ta·k·i·ma·-) AI 'be an emperor': ke·ta·k·i·má·t·e 'when he was emperor' (Lk 2.1).

khita·pto·na·l- (-ki·ta·pto·na·l-) TA 'promise, swear to': khita·pto·na·lát·e 'if you swear an oath to him' (Mt 5.33); é·li-khita·pto·ná·la·t 'as he had promised her' (Mk 6.26).
- -ki·ta·pto·na·l-: kwi·ta·pto·ná·la·n 'And he swore to her ..' (Mk 6.23).

khita·pto·ne·- (|kəhtāpətōnē-|; Gr. 5.17d) AI 'swear, insist': khita·ptó·ne· 'he insisted' (Lk 22.58&, Lk 22.59-60&); káči khita·pto·né·han 'do not swear (you sg.)' (Mt 5.34); ktəli-=č máta téxi -khita·pto·ne·wəné·ɔ 'that you (pl.) are not to swear at all' (Mt 5.34).

khitá·pxki P 'thousand' (1834a:21.32).

khite·lənt- (|kəhtēlənt-| TI(1a)) TI-O 'be serious': awé·n khite·ləntánke 'if anyone is serious' (Mt 24.13).

khithánunk 'the main river (loc.)' (⟨ketvanwf⟩ 1834b:43.10). ▸ Cf. ⟨kidhánnünk⟩ "in the main River" (Z. 118, 169). Cf. also Pidgin Delaware ⟨Makerick Kitton⟩ "the River Dellaware" (1682; Myers 1937:77), with ⟨Makerick⟩ from me·xkí·lək 'the biggest (anim.)' (see maxak·i·l-); ⟨kethaning⟩, ⟨kitthanning⟩ 'river' (Nelson 1894:137-138).

khupahki·x·ən- (|kəhpakīxən-|) II 'be thick, deep': énta- máta -khupahkí·x·ink hák·i 'where the earth was not deep' (*lit.*, 'thick') (Mt 13.5).

khwil- (-kwihəl-, |kwəhl-|) TA — kwənt- TI(1a) 'swallow' (Gr. 5.4e).
- khwil- (TA): khwíl 'swallow it (anim.) (you sg.)' (OA); kəməmsəč·é·i-khwilawwá·ɔk 'you (pl.) swallow them whole' (Mt 23.24); é·li-khwíta-khwíle·kw 'because you (pl.) are afraid to swallow it (anim.)' (Mt 23.24).
- -kwihəl-: nkwíhəla 'I swallow him' (V; Gr. 5.4e).
- kwənt- (TI(1a)): kwə́nta 'swallow it (you sg.)' (OA, AD, LB); nkwə́ntamən 'I swallowed it' (AD, LB; Gr. 5.4e).

khwit- (-kwi·t-, kwe·t-, |kwəht-|; Gr. §2.5, 5.4l) TI(1a) 'fear': khwíta 'fear it (you sg.)!' (LB); wə́nči é·li-khwítank 'because he fears it' (1834b:25.3).
- -kwi·t-: nkwí·tamən 'I'm afraid of it' (OA; Gr. 2.38e); kkwi·taməne·p 'he was fearful of it' (Mt 2.22, 14.30; Gr. 4.70e); kkwi·taməné·ɔ·p 'they were afraid of it' (Jn 7.13; Gr. 4.70l).
- kwe·t-: aləwí·i=á· kwé·taman 'you (sg.) should fear it more' (1842:22.6). ▸ For the matching TA stem, see kxw- (|kwax-|) below; (Gr. 5.4l).

khwíta (-kwí·ta; Gr. 5.128j) PV 'be afraid to': é·li-khwíta-khwíle·kw 'because you're afraid to swallow it (anim.)' (Mt 23.24).
- -kwí·ta: kkwí·ta-nto·xtaɔ·né·ɔ 'they were afraid to ask him about it' (Mk 9.32).

khwitayal- (-kwi·taya·l-) TA 'fear, avoid': aləwí·i-khwitayá·lo· 'fear him more (you pl.)' (Mt 10.28); káči khwitaya·lié·k·e·kw 'do not be afraid of them (you pl.)' (Mt 10.28); wwə́nči-khwitaya·lawwá·p·ani 'from (then on) they avoided approaching him' (Mt 22.46&).
- -kwi·taya·l-: kkwi·taya·la·né·ɔ nət·o·xtaɔ·né·ɔ 'they were afraid to ask him about it' (Lk 9.45).

khwita·s·i·- II 'be frightful': e·lkí·kwi-khwitá·s·i·k 'which is more frightful' (⟨qetasekr⟩ 1834b:9.11 [em.]).

khwitəl- (-kwi·təl-, kwe·təl-, |kwəhtəl-|; Gr. 4.73d, 5.87a) TA, TA+O — khwi·tələt·- (-kwi·tələt·-) TI(1b) 'admonish, warn, forbid'; TA+O 'forbid O2 to'.
- khwi·təl- (TA): khwítəl 'admonish them (you sg.)' (Lk 19.39); káči khwitəlá·he·kw 'don't tell him not to (you pl.)' (Lk 9.50); é·li-khwitəlá·t·əp 'because he had admonished him' (Lk 3.19-20; Gr. 4.73d); ná tóləmi-khwítəla·n 'then he began to admonish him' (Mt 16.22).

- -kwi·təl-: kkwi·təlá·ɔl 'he admonished him' (Mk 1.27), 'he forbade them' (Mk 7.36), kkwi·təlá·ɔ 'he admonished them' (Mk 9.9, Lk 9.55, etc.); nkwi·təlá·wəna 'we told him not to' (Lk 9.49); kkwi·təlawwá·ɔ 'they admonished them' (Lk 18.39); kkwi·təla·né·ɔ 'you (pl.) forbade him to' (Lk 11.52); ná kkwí·təla·n 'then he told him not to do it' (ME; Gr. 2.58l; Gr. 2.64g).
- kwe·təl-: kwe·təlukhwíti·t ke·tanət·o·wi·lí·č·i 'what God had forbidden to them' (1842:7.6).
▪ -kwi·tələt·- (TI): kkwi·tələt·əmə́ne·p ké·šxink ɔ́·k énta-tkó·wi·k 'he admonished the wind and the waves' (Mk 4.39&).

khwitələt·əwá·k·an (-kwi·tələt·əwa·k·an-; Gr. 5.87a, 5.114d) IN 'law' (Jn 1.17, 7.19, 19.7, etc. [KJV "law"]; Mk 10.19 [KJV "the commandments"]), 'laws' (1834b:45.7, etc.); wé·mi khwitələt·əwá·k·ana 'all the laws' (Mt 22.40; KJV "all the law"; pl. only here and construed as sg.); khwitələt·əwá·k·anink 'in the law' (Mt 22.36).
- -kwi·tələt·əwa·k·an-: nkwi·tələt·əwá·k·an 'my law' (1834b:20.9); kkwi·tələt·əwá·k·an 'his law' (Jn 7.23, Jn 8.5), 'his laws' (1834b:45.7. 46.2); nkwi·tələt·əwa·k·anə́na 'our law' (Jn 7.51, 1834b:46.2); kkwi·tələt·əwa·k·anúwa 'your (pl.) law' (Jn 8.17, 18.31).
♦ Note: derived from khwitələt·i·- AI (recip.) 'be admonished, be forbidden'.

khwithike·- (kwe·thike·-, kwekhwithike·- [Rih+; IC], |kwəhtəhkē-|; Gr. 5.102b) AI 'forbid people', AI+O 'forbid O2 (to people)': káči khwithiké·he·kw 'do not forbid anyone' (Mk 10.14); ɔ́·k=č kéku máta khwithike·é·k·we 'and if you (pl.) do not forbid something' (Mt 18.18).
- kwe·thike·-: kwe·thíke·t 'what he forbids' (1842:12.8).
- kwekhwithike·-: kwekhwithiké·an 'you (who are an) admonisher' (Mt 16.23); kwekhwithiké·č·i·k 'those who admonish others' (1834b:26.2).

kíči: see wíči.
kihahki·hɔke·-: see ki·hɔke·-.
-kihkankwi·-: see kankwi·-.
kihsáh! 'For shame!' (⟨Kevsav⟩ Mk 15.29; KJV "Ah"). ▸ Cf. kəsá· (LTD ND), kəsa·á! (an exclamation) "for something nasty" (LB).
kišahkəni·m- (kihkišahkəni·m- [Rih+]) TA 'judge, pronounce sentence on': kišahkəni·mák·e 'if I did judge them' (Jn 8.16); kišahkəní·me·kw 'you (pl.) judge them' (Jn 8.15); ehə́nta- awé·n -kišahkəní·mənt 'where people were judged and sentenced' (Jn 18.28, 18.33, 9.9).
- kihkišahkəni·m-: kkihkišahkəni·máhəmɔ 'you (pl.) are the judges' (Mt 12.27).
▸ Cf. ⟨Gischachgeniman⟩ "to judge somebody" (B&A 42).

kišahkəni·məwá·k·an IN 'judgment'; nkišahkəni·məwá·k·an 'my judgment' (Jn 8.16).
kíši (marks a completed action; Gr. 2.74e, Gr. 5.128k) PV 'already, after, etc.' (Lk 1.20, Mt 1.18, Mt 3.16, Lk 4.13, etc.).
kí· (Gr. 3.10) 'you (sg.)' (Lk 1.76, Mt 3.14, Jn 1.21, etc.); kí· khák·ay 'you' (Jn 3.10); kí·=tá 'you are' (Jn 1.49 [2x]); kí· †mpetəlíhem 'O (lit., 'you') Bethlehem' (Mt 2.6).
-ki·čí·i: see khičí·i.
ki·hɔke·- AI 'cheat people, deceive' (kihahki·hɔke·- [Rih+], kehahki·hɔke·- [Rih+; IC], ihahki·hɔke·- [Rih+], ehahki·hɔke·- [Rih+; IC]; i·ahki·hɔke·- [Rī+]; see Gr. §5.4d for |Rih+| doublets): káči ki·hɔké·han 'do not cheat people (you sg.)' (Mk 10.19).
- kihahki·hɔke·- 'habitually deceive, be a hypocrite': kkihahki·hɔ́ke 'you are a hypocrite' (Lk 13.15); kkihahki·hɔkéhəmɔ 'you are hypocrites' (Lk 11.44, 12.56, Mt 23.13, 23.14, etc.).

- kehahki·hɔke·-: kehahki·hóke·t 'hypocrite' (Mt 6.5, 6.16; Gr. 5.41u); kehahki·hɔke·č·i·k 'hypocrites' (Mt 6.2).
- ihahki·hɔke·-: e·lkí·kwi-ihahki·hɔké·li·t 'how hypocritical they (obv.) were' (Mt 22.18&; Gr. 5.41u).
- ehahki·hɔke·- (Gr. 5.41u): ehahki·hóke·t 'hypocrite' ([as a vocative] Lk 6.42); ehahki·hɔké·č·i·k 'hypocrites' ([as a vocative] Mt 15.7, 16.3, Mt 22.18); náka ehahki·hɔké·t·əp 'that deceiver' (Mt 27.63).
- i·ahki·hɔke·-: máta i·ahki·hóke·t 'who never cheats' (Jn 1.47; 5.44o).

ki·hɔke·ó·k·an (-kak·i·hɔke·ɔ·k·an-; Gr. 5.59d) IN 'hypocrisy' (*lit.*, 'deception') (Mt 23.28).
- -kak·i·hɔke·ɔ·k·an-: kɔk·i·hɔke·ɔ·k·anúwa 'their hypocrisy' (Lk 12.1).

ki·i·k·am- (|kīwīkam-|; Gr. 5.89a) TA 'visit': nki·í·k·amukw 'he is coming to visit me' (1834a:18.10).

ki·i·k·e- AI 'visit': ki·i·k·é·a 'where I visited' (1834a:12); nki·í·k·e šúkw 'I was just visiting' (1834a:18.12). ▸ Cf. ⟨Kiwiken⟩ "to visit" (B&A 55).

ki·kai- (-nakhikai·-, |(na)kəhkayī-|; Gr. 2.68h) AI(+O) 'borrow (O2)': awé·n káhta-ki·kaí·t·e 'if someone wants to borrow' (Mt 5.42).
- -nakhikai·-: nnakhíkai·n 'I borrowed it' (OA).
- Also restructured as |kīhkayī-|: nkí·kai·n 'I borrowed it' (OA).

ki·kai·h- (-nakhikai·h-, |(na)kəhkayī-|; Gr. 2.68h) TA(+O) 'lend (O2) to': ki·kaí·hi 'lend (them) to me (you sg.)' (Lk 11.5); ki·kaí·ho· 'lend to them (you pl.)' (Lk 6.35); ki·kai·hát·e 'if you lend to them' (Lk 6.34); ki·kai·há·t·e 'if he lends to them' (Lk 6.34).
- -nakhikai·h-: nɔkhikaí·ha·n 'he lends it to them' (Mt 21.33, Mt 21.41&).

-ki·kayəmhe·-: see khikayəmhe·-.
-ki·kayo·yəm-: see khík·ay.
ki·kᵒ (|kīhk-|) 'touch' (Gr. §5.2a).
ki·kən- TA — ki·kən- TI(1b) 'touch'.
- ki·kən- (TA): nkí·kəna 'I touched him' (LB); khiči·i=tá awé·n nkí·kənukw 'truly someone touched me' (Lk 8.46).
- ki·kən- (TI): ki·kəni 'touch it (you sg.)!' (AD).

ki·kənəmaw- TA+O 'touch O2 of': ná kwi·kənəmáɔ·n wəškinkwí·li·t 'then he touched their eyes' (Mt 9.29).

kí·kxkwe (Gr. 5.14f) AN 'unmarried girl, virgin' (Mt 1.23); ki·kxkwé·ɔl (obv.) (Jn 3.29), ki·kxkwé·ɔ (obv.) (Lk 1.27).

ki·kxkwe·n- TA 'touch the neck of': kwi·kxkwe·ná·ɔ 'he touched his neck' (Lk 15.20).

ki·k·a·l- TA 'visit (to bring comfort to), go to see about (as, a sick person)': kki·k·a·líhəmɔ·p 'you (pl.) came to see about me' (Mt 25.36; Gr. 5.78a); takó kki·k·a·li·húmɔ·p 'you did not come to see about me' (Mt 25.43). ♦ This is |kīkāl-| 'visit (to bring comfort to)' < ki·k·e·- AI 'be cured' (Gr. 5.78a); it is not related to ki·i·k·e·- AI 'visit'.

ki·k·e- AI 'be cured': e·lkí·kwi- šá·e -kí·k·e·t 'how immediately she was cured' (Lk 8.47); kkí·k·e 'you are cured' (Jn 5.14); ná (..) kwí·k·e·n 'then he was cured' (Jn 5.4, Lk 7.7).
- (with an adjunct referring to the ailment:) ná kwí·k·e·n kéku e·lankələk·əp '(he) was then cured of whatever his ailment had been' (Jn 5.4); ná .. kwí·k·e·n nə́ wəni·skankələwá·k·an '(then) he was cured of his nasty disease' (Mt 8.3).

ki·k·e·h- (|kīkēh-|; Gr. 5.77a) TA 'cure': mái-ki·k·é·haw 'come and cure her (you sg.)' (Mt 9.18; Gr. §4.12a); lí-=á· -mái-ki·k·e·há·li·n 'so that he (obv.) would be cured (by someone coming)' (Lk 7.3); é·li-ki·k·é·hak 'because I cured him' (Jn 7.23); ki·k·e·hɔ́nči·k 'who were cured' (Lk

8.2; Gr. 2.47c); ké·ta-ki·k·e·hə́nči·k wé·mi pɔ·lsəwa·k·anúwa 'ones who wanted to be cured of all their diseases' (Lk 5.15); kwi·k·e·há·ɔ 'he cured him, them' (Mt 4.24, 12.22, 14.14, etc.; Gr. 4.24g); kwi·k·e·há·p·ani 'he cured them' (Mt 4.23, Mk 1.32, Mk 134, etc.; Gr. 4.24f); nčí·sas=tá ntə́li-ki·k·éhko·n 'it was Jesus that cured me' (Jn 5.15; Gr. 4.50t).

ki·k·ehəwe·- AI 'heal people': ki·k·éhəwe·p 'he healed people' (Mt 19.2); ɔ́·k=č nki·k·éhəwe 'and I shall heal people' (Lk 13.32).

ki·k·ehəwe·ɔ́·k·an (Gr. 5.59f) IN 'curing power' (Mk 5.30, Lk 8.46).

ki·ló·na (Gr. 3.10) 'we (inc.)' (Mt 23.30, Jn 17.11, 17.22, Lk 23.41).

ki·ló·wa (Gr. 3.10) 'you (pl.)' (Mt 3.7, Jn 3.28, 4.20, 4.38, Lk 6.24, etc.); ki·ló·wa ɔ́·k xé·li awé·n 'you and many people' (construed as third person; Mt 26.28).

ki·mᵒ (|kīm-|) 'secretly' (Gr. §5.2a).

ki·mí·i (Gr. 5.127a) P 'secretly, in secret' (Mt 1.19, 2.7, Mk 6.32, Jn 7.4, 7.10, 8.3, 8.4, etc.).
- ki·mí·i PN (Mt 5.32, Jn 8.41, Mt 19.9), with nouns derived from verbs.

ki·nᵒ (|kīn-|) 'sharp' (Gr. §5.2a).

ki·na·ləwa·- AI 'be sharp tailed' (|-āləw-| 'tail' + |-ā|; Gr. 5.1i): kánši-lɔ́s·i·t ki·ná·ləwa·t mó·x·we·s 'powerful sharp-tailed bug' (Lk 10.19; KJV "scorpions").

ki·ɔl- (-kak·i·ɔl- [Ra+]) TA 'fool, cheat, deceive': xé·li=č ki·ɔlé·ɔk 'they will deceive many' (Mt 24.5); tə́li-ki·ɔlúk·o·n 'that he was fooled by them (obv.)' (⟨tcli kealokwl⟩ Mt 2.16 [em.]); káči awé·n ki·ɔlúkhwe·kw 'do not let anyone deceive you (pl.)' (Mt 24.4; Gr.4.111m); é·li-kí·ɔla·t 'for he deceives them' (Jn 7.12); takó·=tá kki·ɔləlo·húmɔ 'I didn't cheat you (pl.)' (Mt 20.13; Gr. 4.89p, 6.6b).
- -kak·i·ɔl-: kkak·í·ɔla=háč 'are you (sg.) deceiving him?' (Lk 22.48); kkak·i·ɔlúk·əwa 'he deceived you (pl.)' (Jn 7.47; Gr. 2.27h).

ki·skᵒ (|kīsk-|) 'cut, sever, separate' (Gr. §5.2a).

ki·ska·lahkat·- II 'be a ditch': xínkwi-ki·ská·lahkat 'there is a large trench' (Lk 16.26; KJV "great gulf"); énta-ki·ská·lahka (Mt 12.11 [KJV "pit"]; Lk 6.39, Mt 15.14 [em.; KJV "ditch"]).

ki·ska·ɔnke·- II 'be a cliff' (|-āwank-| 'hill, hillside'; Gr. 5.31i): íkali énta-ki·ska·ɔ́nke·k 'over a cliff' (Mt 8.32).

ki·skčašw- (|kīskəčašw-|; Gr. 5.22c) TA 'cut up': ná=č kwi·skčaš·ɔ́·k·o·n 'then he (obv.) shall cut him up' (Lk 12.46, Mt 24.51).

ki·skəní·k·an AN, lit., 'broken-off (stick)' ("the root of an Indian medicinal plant used for charms" [LTD ND]); ki·skəní·k·anak "lots" (Jn 19.24). ▸ Cf. Shawnee kiškinikani[-]talwa·ti- AI 'cast lots' in T.W. Alford's translation (also in Lk 23.34), with talwa·ti- AI 'gamble'.

ki·skəni·k·anahe·- AI 'cast lots': ki·skəni·k·anahé·ɔk 'they cast lots' (Jn 19.24); ná kwi·skəni·k·anahe·né·ɔ 'then they cast lots' (Lk 23.34). See the preceding entry.

ki·skhw- TA 'chop down' (usually with hít·ukw 'tree' [anim.]) — TI ki·skh- 'cut (off)'.
- ki·skhw- (TA): kí·skhɔw 'chop it down (you sg.)' (Lk 13.7; Gr. 4.104n); ná=č nkí·skhɔ·n 'then I will chop it down' (Lk 13.9).
- ki·skh- (TI): tuhənət·ɔ́t·a ki·skhámo·k 'they cut branches' (Mt 21.8).

ki·skikɔhšw- TA 'cut the head off': ki·skikɔhšák·əp 'who I beheaded' (Mk 6.16); nə́ni=háč=á· wwə́nči-ki·skíkɔhša·n awé·n hɔ́kaya 'would that be the reason why someone cuts their head off?' (1842:23.7).

ki·ski·k·wehw- TA 'chop off the head of' (Gr. 5.1k): ná tə́li-ki·ski·k·wéhɔ·n 'then he proceeded to chop his head off' (Mk 6.27).

ki·skša·s·i·- II 'be cut': hwí·t ki·skšá·s·u 'wheat is cut' (1834a:16); skí·kɔl ki·skšá·s·əwal 'grass (pl.) is cut' (1834a:16).

ki·skšw- (ki·ki·skšw- [Rvh+], |kīskəsw-|) TA — ki·skš- TI(1b) 'cut'; (Gr. 5.12v).
- ▪ ki·skšw- (TA): kwi·skšó·k·wən 'it cut him' (OA; Gr. 2.23c); kki·skšəwi 'you (sg.) cut me' ~ kki·skšúwi (ME; Gr. 2.26e).
- • ki·ki·skšw-: kwi·ki·skšá·ɔ hókaya 'he (repeatedly) cut himself' (Mk 5.5).
- ▪ ki·skš- TI 'cut': wénči-=á· -ki·skšə́me·kw kkwənta·k·anəwá·ɔl '[the reason..] why you (pl.) would cut your throats' (1834b:12.7).

ki·spo·l- TA 'fill (by feeding)' (Gr. 5.78g): é·li-=č -ki·spó·lənt 'for their hunger shall be satisfied' (Mt 5.6); kwi·spó·la·n 'he filled the hungry with it' (Lk 1.53). ▸ Cf. ki·spo·ha·l- TA (ME).

ki·spwi·- (|ki·səpwi·-|; Gr. 5.78g) AI 'be full, eat one's fill': wé·mi ki·spúwak 'all were filled' (Mk 6.42, Mt 15.37; accent: V); mé·či wé·mi ki·spwihtí·t·e 'after all were filled' (Jn 6.12).
- ▪ ki·spwi·-AI+O: kki·spwi·ne·ó·p·ani 'you (pl.) were filled by them' (Jn 6.26; Gr. 4.71b).

ki·šhakwte·- II 'be a light': ki·šhákwte·k '(which was) a light' (Lk 2.32); ki·šhakwté·k·eč 'let it shine' (Mt 5.16).
- ▪ ki·šhakwte·- (used as AI): nčá·n ki·šhákwte·p 'John was a light' (Jn 5.35).

kí·šku IN (-ki·ško·yəm-) 'day'; kwə́t·ən kí·šku 'one day' (1842:13.4); manunksəwí·i-ki·škúwal 'days of anger' (Lk 21.22), né·l ki·škúwa 'those days' (Mt 24.22 [2x]).
- • -ki·ško·yəm-: nki·škó·yəm 'my day' (⟨fejkweum⟩ Jn 8.56; ⟨fej kw eum⟩ 1842:7.2; ⟨-n kejqeum⟩ 1834b:16.6); yú kki·škó·yəm 'this day of yours' (Lk 19.42); kki·škó·yəmal 'your days' (1842:12.2); kwi·škó·yəm 'his day' (Lk 17.21, 17.24, 1842:11.4 [with a prenoun]).

kí·škwe P 'day'.
- ▪ (with a free particle; cf. Gr. 2.25): kwə́t·i kí·škwe 'in one day' (Lk 13.32, Mt 20.2), 'one day (ago)' (OA, LB).
- ▪ (in a particle compound): kwə́ti-kí·škwe 'for the whole day' (Mt 20.2), 'all day' (Mt 20.12; LB); nkwə́ti-kí·škwe 'all day long' (Lk 2.44); náxi-kí·škwe 'in three days' (Mt 12.40, Mk 8.2, Lk 13.33); ní·š·a·š txi-kí·škwe 'in (the course of) seven days' (Lk 18.12); kwə́t·a·š txí-kí·škwe 'for six days' (Lk 13.14).

ki·škwəní·i P 'by day' (Mk 4.27), 'during the day' (Jn 11.9).

ki·škwi·- II 'be a day': yúkwe kí·šku 'today is the day' (Jn 5.10), ala·x·i·məwí·i-kí·šku 'it is a day of rest' (Jn 5.9, 7.22, etc.); ala·x·i·məwí·i-kí·ško·p 'it had been the day of rest' (Jn 9.14); né·li-kí·škwi·k 'while it is daytime' (Jn 9.4), é·ləmi-kí·škwi·k 'during this day' (Lk 13.32), é·ləmi-=č -kí·škwi·k 'later today' (Lk 23.43); mé·či xá·š éntxi-ki·škwí·k·e 'eight days later' (Lk 1.59); kóna=č máta mi·tsahtinkí·i-ki·škwí·k·e 'let it not be on the feast day' (Mt 26.5).
- ♦ kí·škwi·k 'day' (Lk 1.20, 1.25, 1.80, etc); ki·škwí·k·i 'days' (Lk 1.23, 17.22, etc.): yúkwe kí·škwi·k 'today' (Lk 4.21, Mt 6.11, 6.30, etc.).

ki·š·alo·ka·s·i·- 'finish work': ntə́li-=č -ki·š·alo·ká·s·i·n 'for me to finish' (lit., 'that I finish the work') (Jn 4.34, 5.36).

ki·š·a·pto·ne·- AI 'finish speaking' (Gr. 5.17d): mé·či ki·š·a·pto·né·t·e 'after he had finished speaking' (⟨-twn-⟩ Mt 7.28, ⟨-tun-⟩ Mt 19.1).

ki·š·e·ləm- TA — ki·š·e·lənt- TI(1a) 'create (by [divine] thought)' (Gr. 5.12i).
- ▪ ki·š·e·ləm- (TA with TH.1): lə́nəwa .. ki·š·é·ləme·p 'he created a man' (1842:7.1); ki·š·e·ləmá·t·əp 'he who made them' (Mt 19.4); é·li-ki·š·e·ləmá·tsa 'because he had created them' (1842:8.4; Gr. 4.79b).
- ♦ ki·š·e·ləm° (with TH.2; only found in ppl. and lexicalized ppl.): ki·š·e·ləmúkwki †ísələl 'the God (obv.) of Israel' (lit., 'who (obv.) created Israel (sg.)') (Lk 1.68); ki·š·e·ləmúk·ɔn 'your (sg.) God' (lit., 'who created you') (Mt 4.7, 4.10); ki·š·e·ləmúk·wenk 'our (exc.) creator' (Jn 8.54); ki·š·e·ləmúk·ɔnkw 'our (inc.) creator' (Jn 1.13, Lk 1.6, 1834b:3.3, etc.);

ki·š·e·ləmuk·ónkwi 'God (obv.)' (Jn 1.12, Lk 2.37, 2.52, 6.12); ki·š·e·ləmuk·ónkunk 'to our creator' (1834b:23.14, 24.11, etc.).
- ♦ ki·š·e·ləmukhwití·č·ink 'to their God' (Lk 1.16), locative of ki·š·e·ləmukhwití·č·i 'the one (obv.) who created them' (1834b:17.3 [em.]).
- ▪ ki·š·e·lənt- (TI): wé·mi kéku ki·š·e·lə́ntam 'he created everything' (1834a:14, 1834b:15.6); ki·š·e·ləntánke 'when he made them' (1842:11.4); né·k·a tə́li-ki·š·e·ləntamə́ne·p 'he himself was the one who had created it' (Jn 1.10; Gr. 4.72i); ki·š·e·ləntánki 'the things created' (1834b:16.7).

ki·š·e·ləmuk·ɔnkwi·- AI 'be God' (Gr. 5.65f): ki·š·e·ləmuk·ɔ́nko·p 'it was God' (Jn 1.1). Derived from ki·š·e·ləmúk·ɔnkw 'our (inc.) creator' (see above) taken as a lexicalized participle.

ki·š·e·ləmuwe·- AI 'create things, people': ki·š·e·ləmúwe·t 'God' (Jn 1.1, 1.2, Lk 1.26, etc.); ki·š·e·ləməwe·lí·č·i 'God (obv.)' (Lk 2.13, Mt 3.16, Jn 3.2, Mt 5.8, Lk 7.29), ki·š·e·ləməwé·č·i 'God (obv.)' (Jn 1.18, Lk 1.64, 2.28); ki·š·e·ləməwé·t·ink 'to God' (Jn 1.6, 3.2, 5.18, 5.44).

ki·š·e·lənta·s·i·- II 'be created': éntxi-ki·š·e·lənta·s·í·k·əp kéku 'as many things that were made' (Jn 1.3); kéku ki·š·e·lənta·s·í·k·e 'when things were created' (Lk 1.70).

ki·š·e·nhe·- AI 'be able to pay': wə́nči-=č -ki·š·é·nhe·t 'so that he shall be able to pay' (Mt 18.25).

ki·š·əna·kwsi·- AI 'be ready, be prepared': káhta-ki·š·əná·kwsi·kw 'be keen to be ready (you pl.)' (Mt 24.44); wə́nči-=č -káski-ki·š·əna·kwsíe·kw 'so that you (pl.) can be ready' (1834b:4.1); éntxi-ki·š·əna·kwsi·tpáni·k 'all those that were ready' (Mt 25.10); ná=č nki·š·əná·kwsi·n 'then I shall have finished my work and be ready' (Lk 13.32; KJV "I shall be perfected"; RSV "I finish my course").

ki·š·əna·kwso·ke·taw- (|kīšənāhkwəsōhkēhtaw-|; Gr. 5.91d) TA+O 'prepare O2 for': wénči-=č -ki·š·əna·kwso·ké·tunt 'so that (they) will be made ready for him (prox.)' (Lk 1.17).

ki·š·i·h- TA — ki·š·i·t- TI(2) 'make, finish (making)'.
- ▪ ki·š·i·h- (TA): ki·š·e·ləmúwe·t wtépi-=á· yó·l ahsə́nal -wə́nči-ki·š·i·há·ɔl mi·mə́nsa 'God would be able to make children from these stones' (Mt 3.9).
- ▪ ki·š·i·t- (TI2): ki·š·í·to·p sía·kw 'he made a whip' (Jn 2.15); ki·š·í·tuhtí·t·e 'after they made it' (Mt 27.29); ki·š·í·tunk 'that was made' (Mk 14.58); ná kə́nč kwi·š·í·to·n 'until he finished it' (1842:9.1); mé·či ki·š·í·to·n 'now it is finished' (Jn 19.30; Gr. 4.39z).

ki·š·i·kha·- AI 'finish building a house for oneself': ki·š·i·khá·t·e 'after he finished building his house' (Mt 7.25&). ▸ Cf. wi·kha·- AI 'build one's house'.

ki·š·i·khe·- AI 'finish building a house': á·lai-ki·š·í·khe· 'he couldn't finish the building' (Lk 14.30). ▸ Cf. wi·khe·- AI 'build (a house)'.

ki·š·i·k·ən- TA — ki·š·i·k·ən- TI(1b) 'raise (a child, a crop)'.
- ▪ ki·š·i·k·ən- (TA): nki·š·i·k·ənuk·ó·na 'she raised us' (ME); nki·š·í·k·əna hɔpəní·s·ak 'I have grown some potatoes' (OA).
- ▪ ki·š·i·k·ən- (TI): é·li- mé·či -ki·š·í·k·ənink 'as he has now raised it' (Lk 1.69); ki·š·i·k·ənə́me·kw 'what you (pl.) raised' (Jn 15.16); ktə́li-=č -mái-ki·š·i·k·ənəməné·ɔ 'for you (pl.) to go and raise crops' (Jn 15.16).

ki·š·i·k·əwá·k·an IN 'birth'; wə́ski-ki·š·i·k·əwá·k·anink 'the new birth (loc.)' (Mt 19.28).

ki·š·i·k·i·- AI 'be born, grow (up), mature; turn into' — ki·š·i·k·ən- II 'grow, ripen'.
- ▪ ki·š·i·k·i·- (AI): ki·š·í·k·u 'he has been born' (Lk 2.11); ki·š·í·k·i·t 'the one born' (Lk 1.35), né·tami-ki·š·í·k·i·t 'first-born' (Lk 2.23); awé·n máta lápi wə́ski-ki·š·í·k·i·t·e 'if someone is not born again anew' (Jn 3.3); máta ki·š·i·k·í·k·we 'if he is not born' (Jn 3.5; Gr. 2.46b, 4.95k); šé· yú núnči- yú -táli-ki·š·í·k·i·n 'this is why I was born here' (Jn 18.37);

tóli- mi·mə́ntət lápi -ki·š·í·k·i·n 'that another baby has been born' (Jn 16.21); xú ki·š·i·k·iáne 'when you grow up' (OA).
- ki·š·i·k·ən- (II): ki·š·í·k·ən 'it ripens' (Mk 4.28, Mt 13.8), kéku ki·š·í·k·ən 'that things ripen (sbd.)' (Mt 21.41&); tá=á· nihəláči kéku íka wə́nči-ki·š·i·k·ənó·wi 'nothing will grow from it by itself' (Jn 15.4); ála- kéku -ki·š·i·k·ínkeč 'let fruit (*lit.*, things) cease to grow' (Mt 21.19&); énta-ki·š·í·k·ink kéku 'a place where things grow' (1842:7.4); é·ləmi-ki·š·i·k·ínke 'when it began to get ripe' (Mt 13.26).

ki·š·i·k·i·taw- TA+O 'give birth to O2 for' (Gr. 5.95b): kki·š·i·k·í·ta·kw=č we·k·wí·s·ian 'she will bear you a son, *lit.*, she will cause to be born for you one you (will) have as a son' (Lk 1.13).

ki·š·i·k·o·ha·t·amaw- TA+O 'raise, rear O2 for' (Gr. 5.81i): mi·mə́nsa=č kwi·š·i·k·o·ha·t·amaó·ɔ 'he must raise children for him' (Mt 22.24&).

ki·š·i·k·o·he·- (‖kīšīkōhē-‖; Gr. 5.79a) AI+O 'give birth to, raise': ki·š·i·k·ó·he·=č pi·laečə́č·a 'she will give birth to a boy' (Mt 1.21); énta-ki·š·i·k·o·hénkəp 'where he had been raised' (Jn 4.44, Lk 4.16; Gr. 4.75w).

ki·š·i·m- TA 'assign, appoint, declare a plan to (a plan of action, a duty with a commitment)' ('agree with to do' [OA]): ki·š·i·mé·ɔk=č lə́nəwal 'they will designate some men' (1834b:45.10); é·li- nə́ni -ki·š·í·ma·t 'what he assigned him to do' (Jn 6.27); ki·š·í·mkuk 'who he (obv.) assigned (to ..)' (Mt 24.45); kwi·š·í·mku=č 'he (obv.) will assign him' (Mt 24.47); kki·š·i·məlúhəmɔ 'I assigned you (pl.)' (Jn 15.16); ná kə́nč .. kwi·š·í·ma·n lə́nəwa 'after that he appointed men' (Lk 10.1).
  ▶ Cf. Meskwaki kîshimêwa 'settles on a plan for s.o., promises s.o.'.

ki·š·i·t-: see ki·š·i·h- — ki·š·i·t-.

ki·š·i·t·e·ha·- AI 'make up one's mind': kkát·a-ki·š·i·t·é·ha 'try to make up your mind' (1834b:13.8); kki·š·i·t·e·ha·né·ɔ 'that you make up your minds' (1834b:47.14).

ki·š·i·xt-: see ki·š·i·x·əm- — ki·š·i·xt-.

ki·š·i·xtaw- TA+O 'prepare O2 for': ki·š·i·xta·k·e·é·k·əp 'that was prepared for you (pl.)' (Mt 25.34; Gr. 4.76cc); ki·š·i·xtaɔ́·p·ani·k '(it) was prepared for them' (Jn 12.2); ki·š·i·xto·lé·k·we 'when I prepare it for you (pl.)' (Jn 14.3); éntxi-ki·š·i·xtáɔ·t 'as many as he prepares it for' (Mt 20.23); ktə́li-ki·š·i·xtáɔ·n 'that you prepare it for them' (Lk 2.31).

ki·š·i·xta·s·i·- II 'be arranged': kéku e·lkí·kwi-ki·š·i·xtá·s·i·k 'to what extent things are arranged' (1834a:18.4).

ki·š·i·x·əm- TA — ki·š·i·xt- TI(2) 'prepare, make ready' (Gr. 5.12g).
- ki·š·i·x·əm- (TA): ní .. ntə́li-ki·š·i·x·əmúk·o·n 'I am the one he made ready (for his purpose)' (Jn 10.36; KJV "sanctified").
- ki·š·i·xt- (TI): ki·š·í·xto·p 'he arranged (it)' (Lk 14.16); ki·š·í·xto·kw 'prepare it (you pl.)' (Mt 3.3); mé·či nki·š·í·xto·n 'I have prepared it' (Mt 22.4); ki·š·i·xtaɔ́ne 'if you arrange it' (Lk 14.12, 14.13); kwi·š·i·xto·né·ɔ 'they prepared it' (Mk 14.16).

ki·š·i·x·ən- II 'be ready': ki·š·í·x·ən 'it is ready' (Lk 14.17, Mt 22.4, 22.8; KJV "ready"), ki·š·í·x·ən 'it's already fixed' (OA); ⟨Gischiechen⟩ "ready, .. done, .. finished" (B&A 43).

kí·š·o·x (-ki·š·o·x·əm-; Gr. 3.1f) AN 'sun, moon, month' (Mt 13.43, 1834a:15); ki·š·ó·x·ɔl (obv.) (1834a:15); ki·š·ó·x·ɔk 'the sun and the moon' (Lk 21.25, Mt 24.29); ellí·i ki·š·ó·x·ɔ 'the sun and the moon (obv.)' (1842:13.3); ki·š·ó·x·ink (loc.) (Gr. 2.41f), 'as the sun' (Mt 17.2).
- -ki·š·o·x·əm-: kwi·š·ó·x·əma 'his sun' (Mt 5.45). ▶ See next.

ki·š·ó·x·ink, ki·š·ó·x·unk P 'for {so many} months': naxá ki·š·ó·x·ink 'for three months' (Lk 1.56); né·wa ki·š·ó·x·ink 'four months' (Jn 4.35); palé·naxk txí-ki·š·ó·x·unk 'for five months'

(Lk 1.24), palə́·naxk ki·š·ó·x·unk 'for five months' (OA); kwə́t·a·š ki·š·ó·x·ink '(in, for) six months' (Lk 1.26, Lk 1.36, Lk 4.25). ▸ Cf. kí·š·o·x AN.

kí·š·ukw P '(by) day': kwə́ni-kí·š·ukw ɔ́·k kwə́ni-tpó·kw 'day and night' (Lk 2.37, Mk 5.5, Lk 18.7; KJV "night and day," "day and night"). ▸ Cf. ⟨Gunigischuk⟩ "daily" (B&A 46).

-ki·ta·č·i·mwi·-: see khita·č·i·mwi·-*.

-ki·ta·č·i·mo·lx-: see khita·č·i·mo·lx-*.

†ki·təlan 'Cedron' (Jn 18.1).

ki·thaké·ɔk: see ni·tháke.

ki·wsəwá·k·an 'drunkenness'; ki·wsəwá·k·anink lí 'to drunkenness' (1834b:11.2).

ki·wsi·- (-kak·i·wsi·-, ke·k·i·wsi·-, |(ka)kīwəsī-|; Gr. 5.34p) AI 'be drunk': ki·wsúwak=ét 'they must be drunk' (1834b:40.2); áləmi-ki·wsiáne 'if you (sg.) begin getting drunk ..' (1842:20.2); ná tə́li- .. -kí·wsi·n 'then he proceeds to be drunk' (Lk 12.45).
• -kak·i·wsi·-: nkak·í·wsi 'I am drunk' (Gr. 5.34p); tá=á· čí·č kkak·i·wsí·i 'you'd no longer get drunk' (1834b:13.8).
• ke·k·i·wsi·-: ke·k·i·wsi·lí·č·i 'drunks (obv.)' (Mt 24.49).

kí·xki P 'near' (Jn 1.39, 3.23, 3.29, 4.5, 5.2, etc.); 'nearly' (1834b:36.8).
• ki·xkíti 'closer' (Lk 24.4; Gr. 2.76b).

kkwí·s·al, kkwí·s·a 'his or her son, sons': see nkwí·s.

kkwi·s·əm- (-o·k·wi·s·əm-, we·k·wi·s·əm-; Gr. 5.72b) TA 'have as a son': kkwi·s·əmúk·ɔne ke·tanət·ó·wi·t 'if you (sg.) are the son of God' (lit., 'if God has you as a son') (Mt 27.40).
• -o·k·wi·s·əm-: †e·pəlihéma o·k·wi·s·əmúk·u̥ 'he is a son of Abraham (obv.)' (Lk 19.9).
• we·k·wi·s·əm-: †nte·pít·a we·k·wi·s·əmúk·ɔn 'you son of David (lit., you who David (abs.) has as his son)' (Mt 20.30, Lk 18.38, Mt 20.31&); we·k·wi·s·əmúk·wək 'the one who is the son of him (obv.)' (Jn 3.13, 3.14, Jn 6.42, etc.; Gr. 2.27c); we·k·wí·s·əmənt '(the one who is) the Son' (Jn 6.53, 6.62).

kkwi·s·i·- (-o·k·wi·s·i·-, we·k·wi·s·i·-, |wəkwīsī-|; Gr. 5.71c) AI+O 'have O2 as a son': kkwi·s·ít·e 'if he has a son' (Lk 11.11); tá=háč wwə́nči-kkwí·s·i·n 'why is he his son?' (Mt 22.45).
• -o·k·wi·s·i·-: náni=č ko·k·wí·s·i·n 'he will be your son' (Jn 19.26).
• we·k·wi·s·i·-: we·k·wí·s·ian 'a son' (lit., 'one you have as a son') (Lk 1.13); we·k·wí·s·i·t 'his (obv.) father' (Lk 15.20, 15.22); we·k·wi·s·í·li·t 'the one (obv.) whose son he was' (Mk 9.24); we·k·wí·s·ink 'the son' (Jn 1.18, 5.19 [2x], etc.; used for obv. Jn 5.26); we·k·wi·s·ínki 'the son (obv.)' (14x; Jn 3.36 [2x], 5.23 [2x], etc.), we·k·wi·s·i·línki (Mk 14.21).
♦ lə́nu we·k·wí·s·ink 'the man who is the Son' (Mk 2.10, Mt 12.8, etc.), we·k·wi·s·ínki lə́nəwa (obv.) (Lk 12.10, Mt 24.30, etc.), and variants; this was apparently an alternative interpretation of "the Son of man" (KJV), the standard literal translation of the Greek, which was itself ultimately from an Aramaic expression that was misunderstood. A more literal misunderstanding is yó·ni entalá·wsi·t kkwí·s·a 'the son of mankind' (Jn 5.27).

ko·lá·k·ens, ko·la·k·ensəwá·ɔ: see lɔ́·k·ens.

kó·n (-ko·nəm-; Gr. 3.3a) AN 'snow' (1834b:37.1; V, ME, FW), 'ice' (OA, ME, FW); kó·na 'snow (abs.)' (Gr. 3.9f); kó·nink 'as snow' (Mt 28.3).
• -ko·nəm-: kkó·nəma 'his ice' (ME; Gr. 2.58j).

kó·pəne P 'at least': kó·pəne kí· 'you, at least' (Lk 19.42; KJV "even thou").
▸ Cf. ⟨gópene⟩ "thereabouts," i.e., 'approximately' (Z. 195).

†kó·si 'Chuza' (Lk 8.3).

kɔ́č ~ kwáč P (question particle; Gr. 4.60): kɔ́č=háč 'why?' followed by plain conjunct (Jn 1.25, 7.19, 8.43, etc.); kɔ́č (one-word question) "Why?" (Lk 23.22); kwáč=háč (Mt 3.14, Jn 4.27).
▶ Cf. ⟨quatsch?⟩ 'why' (Z. 230; cf. B&A 121). An explanation of this word is in Gr. §4.6b.
kɔ́čəmink (Gr. 2.73d, 5.26d; AD, ME, LB) P 'outside' (Lk 1.10, Mt 5.13, 8.12, Mk 5.40, etc.).
kɔhán P 'yes, indeed' (particle of affirmation): 'yes' (Mt 9.28, Mt 13.51, 17.25, etc.); 'indeed' (Lk 2.35); kɔhán 'It is so!' (Mt 5.37 [2x]); kɔhán, mé·či yúkwe 'indeed, it is already now' (Jn 16.32; Gr. 6.10a). ▶ Cf, kɔhán (listener's response) (ME); kɔhán=láh! 'See there!' (LTD LB); ⟨gohan⟩ 'yes' (Z. 236); Mun i·kó·han.
kɔhó·k·an (-takhɔ·k·an-, |(ta)kwahākan|; Gr. 5.51e) IN 'mortar (for grinding dried corn)'; "mill" (1834a:15); kɔhó·k·anink '(to) the mill' (1834a:15).
• -takhɔ·k·an-: ntakhó·k·an 'my corn mortar' (OA; Gr. 2.6c).
▶ Cf. tahkɔh- TI(1a) 'grind (corn in a mortar)' (ME).
kɔhɔ·k·e- AI 'grind corn in a mortar' (Gr. 2.6c, 5.51e): ɔ́·k=č ní·š·a kɔhɔ·k·é·ɔk 'and two will be pounding corn' (Mt 24.40), níši-kɔhɔ·k·é·ɔk 'they (two) pound corn in a mortar together' (Lk 17.35).
kɔk·i·hɔke·ɔ·k·anúwa: see ki·hɔke·ɔ́·k·an.
-kɔk·we·č·i·h-: see ahkwe·č·i·h-.
†kɔlé·sən 'Chorazin' (Mt 11.21, Lk 10.13).
kɔ́na P (Gr. 4.49e, 5.12z) 'free to; let it (be); even though': kɔ́na pɔk·i·lá·ɔ 'he is free to divorce her' (Mt 19.7); kɔ́na=á· nahkɔ́·i kúnči-mi·tsíhəmɔ 'you are free to eat from any' (1842:7.4); kɔ́na=háč=á· nəmái-pəphwənəmáne·n? 'Would it be alright if we went and pulled them up?' (Mt 13.28); kɔ́na tə́li-ktəmá·ksi·n 'even though he was poor' (1834b:31.10); kɔ́na yúkwe nə́ni lé·k·eč 'let that be done now' (Mt 3.15).
♦ Idiom with |əlīnaw-| TA, |əlīn-| TI(1a), |əlīnāsī-| AI (literally 'see, experience {so}') 'leave alone, let go, allow' (note: the particle is sometimes written in B without a following space; Mk 1.24, 5.12, 5.13, 10.14, Mt 13.30, 15.14): ná .. kɔ́na təli·naɔ·n 'then .. he released them' (Mk 5.13); kɔ́na lí·naw 'let him go (you sg.)' (Mt 5.25); kɔ́na li·naí·ne·n 'let us alone' (Mk 1.24), 'release us (to ..)' (Mk 5.12); tákta kéku kɔ́na e·li·ná·s·ian 'whatever you .. allow' (Mt 16.19); ná=č kɔ́na ktəli·naɔ·né·ɔ 'then you must leave him (to ..)' (Mt 18.17).
♦ kɔ́na (with negative): kɔ́na=č máta .. 'Let it not be ..' (Mt 26.5; KJV "Not .."); kɔ́na=č máta 'I guess I won't be able to' (Lk 14.18, declining an invitation).
▶ Cf. ⟨quonna⟩ and ⟨quónna⟩ "althò" (Z. 10), "however" (Z. 98), "nevertheless" (Z. 129), "it is all one" (Z. 134).
kɔnánunk: see nánanu.
kɔnši·ph- TA 'hide from' (later /kɔ·nši·ph-/; Gr. §2.1c): nkɔ·nší·pha 'I'm hiding from him' (ME); kɔnši·phá·p·ani 'he hid from them' (Jn 12.36).
-kɔxkahka·-: see xkɔhka·-.
-kɔx·-: see kxw-.
kɔ·thɔ·wi·- AI 'be a widow': kɔ·thó·u 'she was a widow' (Lk 7.12); kɔ·thɔ·wí·t·əp xkwé· 'a widowed woman' (Lk 18.3); kɔ·thɔ·wí·č·i·k 'widows' (Lk 4.25).
kɔ·thó·xkwe AN 'widow' (Lk 18.5, Mk 12.43); kɔ·thɔ·xkwé·ɔk 'widows' (Mt 23.14); kɔ·thɔ·xkwé·ɔ 'widow (obv.)' (Lk 21.2); kɔ·thɔ·xkwé·yunk 'to a widow' (Lk 4.26).
kpº (|kəp-|) 'close, block' (Gr. §5.2a).
kpaha·s·i·- (-kəpha·s·i·-, ke·pha·s·i·-) AI 'be imprisoned' — II 'be shut, be closed' (Gr. 5.105a).
▪ kpaha·s·i·- (AI): kpahá·s·o·p 'he had been imprisoned' (Mt 27.16; Gr. 4.68c);

né·li-kpahá·s·ian 'when you were in prison' (Mt 25.39); é·li- né·ləma nčá·n -kpahá·s·i·kw 'for John had not yet been imprisoned' (Jn 3.24; Gr. 4.95j); ktə́li-kpahá·s·i·n 'that you were in prison' (Mt 25.44); tə́li- nčá·n -kpahá·s·i·n 'that John was put in prison' (Mt 4.12).

• -kəpha·s·i·-: nkəpha·s·í·həmp 'I was in prison' (Mt 25.36, 25.43); ná kuphá·s·i·n 'then he was put in prison' (1842:13.5).

• ke·pha·s·i·-: néke ke·pha·s·iá·ne 'when I was in prison' (1842:14.2); ke·phá·s·i·t 'prisoner' (Jn 18.39); kwə́t·i ke·pha·s·i·lí·č·i 'one prisoner (obv.)' (Mt 27.15).

▪ kpaha·s·i·- (II): kpahá·s·u 'it was closed' (Jn 20.26); é·li-kpahá·s·i·k 'as it is shut' (Lk 11.7); mé·či kíši-kpaha·s·í·k·e 'after it had been shut' (Jn 20.19).

kpahəmaw- TA+O 'shut O2 on' (= 'shut out of O2'): é·li-kpahəmáe·kw 'as you (pl.) shut them out of it' (Mt 23.13; KJV "shut [it] up .. against [them]').

kpáho·n (Gr. 5.53e) IN 'door' (Lk 13.25).

kpaho·t·əwi·k·á·ɔn IN 'prison'; kpaho·t·əwi·k·á·ɔnink 'in prison' (1842:14.2, 15.3).

kpaho·t·i·- AI (recip.; Gr. §5.8m) 'be imprisoned': íka .. énta-kpahó·t·ink 'to the prison' (Mk 6.27), ehə́nta-kpahó·t·ink 'into prison, in prisons' (Mt 18.30, Lk 21.12&); lí ehə́nta-kpahó·t·ink 'to (the) prison' (Mt 18.34, Lk 22.33).

kpahw- (-kəphw-, |kəpahw-|) TA 'imprison' — kpah- (-kəph-, |kəpah-|) TI(1a) 'shut, close (up)' (Gr. 3.20e, 5.12r; for the TI theme sign /-əm-/ from |-am-|, see Gr. 2.29a).

▪ kpahw- (TA): lí-kpáhɔ·n 'that he be imprisoned' (Mk 6.17); é·li-=á· tá·mse -kpaho·k·é·an 'for you could perhaps be imprisoned' (Lk 12.58).

• -kəphw-: kuphó·p·ani 'he put him in prison' (Lk 3.19-20); kuphɔwwá·ɔ 'they shut them in' (OA; Gr. 2.59b); kkəphó·k·o·n 'and (then) he puts you (sg.) in prison (sbd.)' (Mt 5.25).

▪ kpah- (TI): kpahəmáne 'when you shut the door' (Mt 6.6); kpahánke 'when he closes it' (Lk 13.25; Gr. 2.3f).

• -kəph-: nkəphámən 'I closed it' (Gr. 2.29a); ná ke·tanət·ó·wi·t kuphámən nə́ múx·o·l 'then God shut the boat up' (1842:9.3).

kpat·- II 'be closed, separated off': hukwé·yunk énta-kpát·ək 'an upper room' (Mk 14.15; Gr. 5.10p).

kpa·p·ehəla·- II 'be curtained off': énta-kpa·p·éhəla·k 'where it was curtained off' (Mt 27.51).

kpəč·a·- (-kəpča·-, ke·pča·-, |kəpəčā-|; Gr. 5.13d) AI 'be foolish': kpə́č·e·w 'he is foolish' (1834a:13); é·li-=k -kpə́č·a·t. 'Well, because he's foolish.' (1842:23.5); é·li- .. -kpəč·áhti·t 'because they are foolish' (1842:23.6).

• -kəpča·-: kkə́pča 'you (sg.) are foolish' (⟨Kwphav⟩ Lk 12.20); kkəpčáhəmɔ 'you (pl.) are foolish' (Lk 11.40, Mt 23.17, etc.; Gr. 4.21i).

• ke·pča·-: ké·pča·t lə́nu 'a foolish man' (Mt 7.26; Gr. 4.64a); ké·pča·t khák·ay 'you're an idiot' (Mt 5.22); ke·pčá·č·i·k 'fools' (1842:21.7).

kpəč·a·ne·- AI 'be stupid(?)': áhi-kpəč·a·né·ɔk 'they are very stupid' (1834b:6.3).

kpəč·e·hɔ·l-* (-kəpče·hɔ·l-, ke·pče·hɔ·l-) TA 'make crazy': yó·ni kupče·hó·lko·n 'this makes him crazy' (1834a:20.26).

• ke·pče·hɔ·l-: ke·pče·hó·lkɔn 'what makes you foolish' (1834b:6.5); ke·pče·hó·lkuk 'what made him foolish' (⟨krp hr vwk⟩ 1834b:5.10 [em.]).

kpəč·e·hɔ·s·i·- AI 'do foolish things': kpəč·e·hó·s·u 'he acts foolish, he acts crazy' (LTD LB; Gr. 2.38j); é·li-kpəč·e·hó·s·i·t 'because he did foolish things' (Lk 15.13).

kpəč·e·ɔnkəl- (ke·pče·ɔnkəl-) AI 'be crazy': kpəč·e·ɔ́nkəl=ét 'he must be out of his mind' (Mk 3.21).

- ke·pče·ɔnkəl-: ke·pče·ɔ́nkələk 'crazy person' (as a lexicalized participle) mahtant·o·wí·i-ke·pče·ɔ́nkələk 'someone with devil madness' (Jn 10.20); ke·pče·ɔnkələk·i·k 'the insane' (1834b:23.4).

kpəč·e·ɔ́·k·an 'foolishness'; kpəč·e·ɔ·k·anink lí 'to foolishness' (1834b:5.3).

kpəč·e·wən-* (-kəpče·wən-, |kəpəčēwən-|) TA 'drive mad': kupče·wənúk·u 'she was driven mad by him (obv.)' (Mt 15.22; KJV "vexed").

kpi·k·a·p·ai-* (-kəp·i·k·a·p·ai-, |kəpīkāpawī-|; Gr. 5.11b) TA 'stand blocking': íka kkəp·i·k·á·p·ai e·á·a 'you (sg.) stand blocking my way' (Mt 16.23).

kpi·xkwe·n- TA 'choke': tɔ́ləmi-kpi·xkwé·na·n 'he began choking him' (Mt 18.28).

=ksí P 'then, So, well (if you're saying THAT), are you saying' (with a question or imperative, but often not translated; Gr. 5.24j): ktaləwí·i-=ksí -lə́s·i·n 'are you greater?' (Jn 4.12); kéku=ksí 'what?' (responding to a question) (Lk 10.26); máta=ksí 'ought (he) not to?' (Mt 6.30); =ksí=láh 'then, in that case' (in a question) (⟨kselav⟩ Jn 1.21; ⟨ksela⟩ Mt 18.1); kéku=ksí=á· awé·n təla·p·éntamən 'what benefit would it be to someone?' (Mt 16.26); máta=ksí li·x·ənó·wi 'wasn't it laid down (or set) that ..' (Lk 24.26); kələstái·kw=ksí 'So, listen to me' (1842:18.6).
▸ Cf. Mun ksí 'you say'.

ksinkwe·- (-kəs·inkwe·-, |kəsīnkwē-|) AI 'wash one's face': ksínkwe· 'he washed his face' (Jn 9.7, 1842:16.1); mái-ksínkwe·l 'go wash your face (you sg.)' (Jn 9.7), mái-ksínkwe (Jn 9.11).
- -kəs·inkwe·-: nkəs·ínkwe 'I washed my face' (Jn 9.11); ná nkəs·ínkwe·n 'then I washed my face' (Jn 9.15; Gr. 4.49h).

ksi·nhake·-* (-ka·ksi·nhake·- [Rā+]) AI 'be indifferent': ⟨Ksünháckge⟩ "careless" (Z. 33).
- -ka·ksi·nhake·-: kka·ksi·nhakéhəmɔ 'you (pl.) were indifferent [to our grieving for you]' (⟨kaksenvakrvwmw⟩ Lk 7.32; KJV "ye have not wept").

ksí·ni (†ka·ksí·ni; Gr. 5.25c) P 'unconcernedly' (Jn 7.26, Jn 8.6, Mt 22.5).
- †ka·ksí·ni 'unconcernedly' (⟨kaksini⟩ LTD).

kšᵒ (|kəš-|) 'fast, hot, etc.' (Gr. §5.2a).

kšax·ən- (ke·šxən-; Gr. 5.11o) II 'blow (of wind)': áhi-kšáx·ən 'the wind blew very hard' (Mt 7.25&, 14.30); kšáx·əno·p 'there was wind' (Mt 7.27&); énta-kšáx·ink 'in the wind' (Lk 7.24).
- ke·šxən-: ké·šxink 'the wind' (Jn 3.8; KJV "winds": Mk 4.39&, Lk 8.25&).

kša·mehəla·- AI 'run fast': kša·méhəle· 'runs fast' (LB, LTD ME); é·li- .. -kša·mehəláhti·t 'as .. they were running fast' (Mt 28.8&).

kša·pto·na·l- TA 'scold': tɔ́ləmi-kša·pto·ná·la·n 'he began to scold the people' (Mt 11.20).

kšəlante·- (ke·š·əlante·-) II 'be hot (weather)': kšəlánte· 'it is a hot day' (LB); káhta-kšəlánte· 'it's going to be hot' (Lk 12.55); énta-kšəlánte·k 'in the heat' (Mt 20.12).
- ke·š·əlante·-: mé·či ke·š·əlanté·k·e 'after it was hot weather' (1834b:26.14).

kšəle·x·i·n- AI 'have a fever': áhi-kšəlé·x·i·n 'she had a high fever' (Mk 1.30).

kšəp·ehəla·- II 'be fast-flowing water' (Gr. 5.19h): kšəp·éhəle·w 'it (will) flow' (Jn 4.14; KJV "springing up"; Gr. 4.21d), kšəp·éhəle· 'the water flowed fast' (Mt 7.25&); kšəp·éhəle·p 'the water flowed fast' (Mt 7.27&).

kšəs·i·- AI 'be warm': máta=háč ktehəná·nak kšəs·i·í·ɔk 'weren't our hearts warm?' (Lk 24.32).

kší (-kə́ši; Gr. 5.129p) PV 'fast, hard': kší-wí·ne· 'it's snowing hard' (OA).
- -kə́ši: nkə́ši-pahkántamən 'I hit it hard' (OA); kwə́ši-lí·x·i·n 'he quickly came down' (Lk 19.6).

kšihəla·- AI 'run, rush, fall' (Gr. 5.11n): áhi-kšihəlé·ɔk 'they ran rapidly' (Mt 8.32); təlkí·kwi-kšíhəla·n 'he was falling (that) fast' (Lk 10.18).

kší·k·an (-paxkši·k·an-, |paxkəsīkan-|; Gr. 2.6a, 3.5c) IN 'knife' (1834a:18.12); xínkwi-kší·k·an 'sword' (Lk 21.24); kší·k·anal 'knives' (1842:23.7), kší·k·ana (1842:23.7).
- -paxkši·k·an-: kpaxkší·k·an 'your knife' (Mt 26.52&).
▸ Cf. also xinkɔnší·k·an IN 'sword'.

kši·la·n- (ke·š·i·la·n-, ahkəš·i·la·n- [Ra+]; Gr. 5.11h) II 'rain hard': ná áləmi-kší·la·n 'then it started in to rain hard' (1842:9.4).
- ke·š·i·la·n-: ke·š·i·lánke 'when it rained heavily' (Mt 7.25&, Mt 7.27&).
- ahkəš·i·la·n-: ə́nta-ahkəš·í·lank 'when there was a heavy rain' (OA).

kši·lənče·- (-kəš·i·lənče·-, ke·š·i·lənče·-, |kəšīlənčē-|; Gr. 5.1l) AI 'wash one's hands': kši·lə́nče· 'he washed his hands' (Mt 27.24); é·li- máta -kši·lənčé·li·t 'because he (obv.) did not wash his hands' (Lk 11.38).
- -kəš·i·lənče·-: nána .. kwəš·i·lə́nče·n 'then he washed his hands' (1834b:34.9).
- ke·š·i·lənče·-: né·skɔ ke·š·i·lənčé·li·t 'before they (obv.) washed their hands' (Mk 7.2; Gr. 4.61l).

kši·nal- (-kəš·i·nal-) TA 'hurt': kéku li-kši·nalúk·ɔne 'if it hurts you (sg.) in some way' (1834a:16).
- -kəš·i·nal-: nkəš·í·nala 'I hurt him' (LB).

kši·tehw-* (-kakši·tehw- [Ra+]; |-əhtehw-| Gr. 5.18h) TA 'wound': kɔkši·tehɔwwá·ɔ 'they wounded him' (Mk 12.4&, Lk 20.12).

kši·te·x·ən- II 'be hurt by falling or colliding' (Gr. 5.18c): wə́nči- máta -kši·té·x·ink ksí·t·al ahsə́nink 'so that your (sg.) feet are not hurt on a stone' (Mt 4.6).

kši·x(·)° (|kəšīx-|) 'wash' (Gr. §5.2a).

kši·xtaw- (-kəš·i·xtaw-; Gr. 5.95a) TA+O 'wash O2 for': mé·či kíši-kši·xtaɔ́·t·e 'after he finished washing [their feet]' (Jn 13.12); máta-č kši·xto·ló·wane 'if I don't wash them for you (sg.)' (Jn 13.8; Gr. 4.97x); tɔ́ləmi-kši·xtáɔ·n wsí·t·a 'he began to wash his feet (sbd.)' (Lk 7.38).
- -kəš·i·xtaw-: tá·á· háši kkəš·i·xtaí·wəna nsí·t·a 'you (sg.) shall never wash my feet' (Jn 13.8).
▪ kši·xta·ɔhti·-* (-kəš·i·xta·ɔhti·-; Gr. 5.110k) AI+O (recip.) 'wash O2 for each other': kkəš·i·xta·ɔhti·ne·ɔ́·i 'you wash them for each other' (Jn 13.14; Gr. 4.40g).

kši·x·a·č·i·mwi·- AI 'make clear' (gloss assumes kši·x·- 'wash, clean'): kši·x·a·č·í·mo·p 'she made clear' (Lk 8.47; KJV "declare").

kši·x·əm- (-kəš·i·x·əm-, ke·š·i·x·əm-, |kəšīxəm-|) TA — kši·xt- (-kəš·i·xt-, |kəšīxət-|) TI(2) 'wash' (Gr. 5.12g).
▪ kši·x·əm- (TA): kší·x·əm 'wash him (you sg.)!' (LB).
- -kəš·i·x·əm-: nkəš·í·x·əma 'I wash him' (OA; Gr. 5.12g).
- ke·š·i·x·əm-: awé·n ke·š·i·x·əmə́ntəp 'someone that has been washed' (Jn 13.10).
▪ kši·xt- (TI): wə́nči-á· -kši·xtáɔ nsí·t·al 'for me to wash my feet' (Lk 7.44); kši·xtaɔ́·ne 'if I washed them' (Jn 13.14); kkát·a-=háč -kši·xtó·na 'are you (sg.) intending to wash them?' (Jn 13.6).
- -kəš·i·xt-: ɔ́·k=č kkəš·í·xto·n kə́škinkw 'you must wash your face' (Mt 6.17); kwəš·i·xtó·na nsí·t·a 'she washed my feet' (Lk 7.44; Gr. 4.39k).

=ktá P 'instead, rather, indeed' (Gr. 5.24k): šúkw=ktá 'but rather' (Mt 5.15); náni=ktá wə́nči 'that, rather, is why' (Mt 14.2); lehəle·x·e·lí·č·i=ktá 'but living ones (obv.)' (Lk 20.38); ktə́ləl=ktá 'Alright then, I'll tell you' (1834b:9.12 etc.).
- P (not enclitic): píši=k ktá 'Yes, indeed' (⟨kta⟩ Lk 7.26).

ktahw- TA 'dig up': ktahɔ́·ɔk 'they are dug' (1834a:17).

ktanihi·- (-kət·anihi·-) AI+O 'throw out': ktaníhi·n 'it is discarded' (LTD; "replaced"): kkət·aníhi·n=č 'you must tear it out' (Mt 5.29, 18.9; KJV "pluck it out").

kta·me·x·í·no·k 'they streamed out' (⟨ktamruxenwk⟩ Lk 4.29).
▶ Cf. Mun kta·mane·xí·no·k 'they came trooping out' (JA).

ktəmakahkwi·- (kəktəmakahkwi·- [Rə̀+]) AI 'wear pitiful clothing': kəktəmakahkó·p·ani·k=á· 'they would have put on pitiful clothing' (Lk 10.13).

ktəmáki (OA; Gr. 2.74f, 5.28e, 5.129q) PV 'miserably' (⟨ktumuk-⟩ 2x, ⟨ktumak-⟩ 2x; Lk 13.11 [no IC], Mt 21.41&); ktəmáki-=č -wi·š·a·sháti·n 'there will be the torment of terror' (Lk 21.25; KJV "perplexity" = 'torment'); ktəmáki-lí·nam 'he suffers a miserable fate' (Mk 14.21).

ktəma·k(·)°(|kətəmāk-|) 'poor, pitiful' (Gr. §5.2a).

ktəma·ksəwá·k·an (-kət·əma·ksəwa·k·an-, |kətəmākəsəwākan|; Gr. 2.26d) IN 'misery, poverty, pitiful thing' (Jn 3.19, Mt 23.14), 'pitiful state' (LB); (AN as possessor; Gr. §3.2) ktəma·ksəwá·k·an kkwí·s·a 'the son of wretchedness' (Jn 17.12; KJV "perdition").
• -kət·əma·ksəwa·k·an-: kwət·əma·ksəwá·k·anink 'her poverty (loc.)' (Mk 12.44&).

ktəma·ksi·- (ke·t·əma·ksi·-) AI 'be poor, miserable, pitiful, in a bad way' — ktəma·k·at- II 'be miserable'.
▪ ktəma·ksi·-: ktəmá·ksu 'he is pitiful' (Lk 17.1, 1834a:15); ká·xəne ktəmá·kso·p 'he was really poor' (1834b:26.6); ktəma·ksúwak 'they are pitiful' (Jn 7.49); kí·=č kənax·ó·ha-ktəmá·ksi·n 'it is you alone that will be miserable' (1842:8.1).
• ke·t·əma·ksi·-: ke·t·əmá·ksi·t 'one who is poor' (Lk 11.41, 1834b:30.1, etc.); ke·t·əma·ksí·č·i·k 'the poor' (Lk 7.22, 12.33, etc.); ke·t·əma·ksi·lí·č·i (obv.) (Jn 12.6, Lk 21.2, Jn 13.29).
▪ ktəma·ksahti·- AI (coll.; Gr. 5.75s): só·mi=č áhi-ktəma·ksáhti·n 'there will be very great misery' (Lk 21.23).
▪ ktəma·k·at- (II): ktəmá·k·at=č yú entalá·wsink 'this world will be miserable' (1842:7.6).

ktəma·kto·nha·l- TA 'speak pitifully to': kíši-ktəma·kto·nha·lá·t·e 'after he had spoken pitifully to him' (1842:17.1).

ktəma·k·amalsəwá·k·an 'torment(s)' (1834b:31.1).

ktəma·k·at-: see ktəma·ksi·- — ktəma·k·at-.

ktəma·k·a·wsi·- (-kət·əma·k·a·wsi·-) AI 'be pitiful, live pitifully': kkət·əma·k·a·wsíhəmɔ 'you are miserable wretches' (Lk 11.42, 11.43, Mt 23.13, 23.14, 23.16, etc.).

ktəma·k·e·ləm- (-kət·əma·k·e·ləm-, ke·t·əma·k·e·ləm-) TA — ktəma·k·e·lənt- (-kət·əma·k·e·lənt-) TI(1a) 'take pity on, have mercy on' (Gr. 5.12i).
▪ ktəma·k·e·ləm- (TA): ktəma·k·é·ləm 'have mercy on him (you sg.)' (1842:17.1); ktəma·k·é·ləmi·l 'have mercy on me (you sg.)' (Mt 15.22. 18.26, 18.29, Lk 16.24; Gr. 4.105c), ktəma·k·é·ləmi 'take pity on me' (Mt 14.30, Lk 18.13; Gr. 4.105d); ktəma·k·e·ləmí·ne·n 'have mercy on us' (Mt 9.27, Mk 9.22, Mt 20.30, etc.); ke·tanət·ó·wi·t ktəma·k·e·ləmúk·oneč 'may God have take pity on you' (1842:16.1; Gr. 4.114i); é·li- né·k·əma -ktəma·k·é·ləma·t 'for *he* takes pity on those' (Lk 6.35).
• -kət·əma·k·e·ləm-: nkət·əma·k·e·ləmá·ok 'I pity them' (Mk 8.2); kwət·əma·k·e·ləmá·ɔ 'he pitied them' (Mt 9.36); kkət·əma·k·e·ləmuk·ó·na 'he has mercy on us' (1842:18.5); ná nčí·sas kwət·əma·k·é·ləma·n 'then Jesus had pity on them' (Mt 20.34).
• ke·t·əma·k·e·ləm-: ke·t·əma·k·e·ləmúk·ɔne '(when) he took pity on you' (Mk 5.19); ke·t·əma·k·e·ləmúkwki '[the one (obv.)] who took pity on him' (Lk 10.37).
▪ -kət·əma·k·e·lənt- (TI): nkət·əma·k·e·léntamən 'I take pity on it' (V; Gr. 5.12i).

ktəma·k·e·ləmukwsi·- AI 'be shown pity': ktəma·k·e·ləmukwsúwak=č 'they shall be shown pity' (1834b:25.9, etc.; KJV "blessed are").

ktəma·k·e·lənsi·- (ke·t·əma·k·e·lənsi·-) AI 'be humble': ktəma·k·e·lənsí·č·i·k 'the humble' (Mt 5.3; no IC).
- ke·t·əma·k·e·lənsi·-: ke·t·əma·k·e·lə́nsi·t 'who is humble' (1834b:25.8); né·ki·k ke·t·əma·k·e·lənsí·č·i·k 'those who are humble' (1834b:25.10).

ktəma·k·e·ləntəwá·k·an (-kət·əma·k·e·ləntəwa·k·an-; Gr. 5.60c, 5.115d) IN 'mercy' (Mt 9.13).
- -kət·əma·k·e·ləntəwa·k·an-: kwət·əma·k·e·ləntəwá·k·an 'his mercy' (Lk 1.54, 1.58, 1.72, etc.; Gr. 5.116b).

ktəma·k·e·ləwá·k·an IN 'mercy' (Mt 23.23).
▶ Cf. ⟨Gettemagelowagan⟩ 'mercy' (B&A 41), ⟨Gektemagelowoágan⟩ 'mercy' (Z. 122).

ktəma·k·e·li·- (ke·t·əma·k·e·li·-) AI 'show mercy, be merciful': ke·t·əma·k·e·lí·č·ik (or kektəma·k·e·lí·č·ik) 'those who are merciful' (⟨krvtumakrlethek⟩ 1834b:25.12).
▶ Cf. ⟨gettemagélo⟩ 'he is merciful' (Z. 122), ⟨[gettemagé]lian⟩ 'you who are merciful' (Z 122: "he who shews Mercy unto me"), ⟨Gettemagelin⟩ 'to be merciful' (B&A 41).

ktəma·k·əwe·yo·wi·- II 'cry out pitifully(?)': ktəma·k·əwe·yó·u 'it [seems to] cry out pitifully' (⟨ktumakewrbw⟩ 1834b:12.1). Passage and form uncertain.

ktəma·k·ihkwəs·i·-* (ke·t·əma·k·ihkwəs·i·-) AI 'be persecuted': awé·ni ke·t·əma·k·ihkwəs·i·lí·č·i 'anyone (obv.) who is persecuted' (1834b:26.3).

ktəma·k·i·h- (-kət·əma·k·i·h-, ke·t·əma·k·i·h-) TA 'condemn, persecute' ("abuse, treat badly, do wrong to" [LTD]): ktəma·k·i·hónči·k 'the persecuted' (Lk 4.18); táli-=á· -ktəma·k·í·ha·n 'that he might condemn them' (Jn 3.17; 'condemn' 2x in Jn 3.18).
- -kət·əma·k·i·h-: tá=á· ní· nkət·əma·k·i·há·i 'I will not condemn them' (Jn 12.47); kkət·əma·k·íhko·n 'it makes you (sg.) miserable' (1842:20.3); nánal=č nə́ni kwət·əma·k·íhko·n 'that is what will condemn them' (Jn 12.48).
- ke·t·əma·k·i·h-: ke·t·əma·k·í·ha·t=č 'who will condemn them' (Jn 12.48); ke·t·əma·k·i·hə́nči·k 'those that are persecuted' (Mt 5.10).

ktəma·k·i·na·k·ot- (ktəma·k·i·nákoht-) II 'look pitiful' (Gr. 5.108d): ktəma·k·i·ná·k·ot 'it looks pitiful' (Lk 2.12); ktəma·k·i·nákohto·p 'it looked pitiful' (Lk 2.7).

ktəma·k·i·x·i·n- AI 'be poor': ktəma·k·i·x·i·nəlálu wtehəwá·o 'their hearts falter' (Lk 21.26; KJV "failing them"). ♦ Note: /-əlálu/ 3´ (on a consonant-final stem) is for expected (but unattested) /-əlu/ or /-əlúwa/, but this may be a correct variant when the first /ə/ is weak.

ktən- (-kət·ən-) TA — TI1(b) 'take out'.
▪ -kət·ən- (TA): máta=háč=á· kwət·əna·í·ɔ 'would he not take it (anim.) out? (Lk 14.5).
▪ ktən- (TI): ní·š·a moni·t·ə́t·a ktə́nəm 'he took out two coins' (Lk 10.35); ktə́nəmo·kw 'bring it out (you pl.)' (Mt 3.8).
- -kət·ən-: lahápa pəlali·k·á·xkwtət nkət·ənə́mən 'let me pull out the little splinter' (Lk 6.42; Gr. 2.55i).

ktəp·ehəla·- II 'flow out': mhúkw ɔ́·k mpí íka wə́nči ktəp·éhəle·w. 'Blood and water flowed out of there.' (1834b:35.3); hók·enk=č wə́nči-ktəp·ehəlé·ɔ 'they shall flow out of him' (Jn 7.38).

ktəskamaw- TA+O 'drive O2 out of': a·yáhi- ní·š·a·š mahtant·ó·wa -ktəskamaɔ́·t·əp 'who he had previously driven seven devils out of' (Mk 16.9).

ktəskaw- (-kətskaw-, ke·tskaw-, |kətəskaw-|) TA — ktəsk- TI(1a), 'drive out'.
▪ ktəskaw- (TA): ntəlsəwá·k·an=č wə́nči-ktəskaé·ok mahtant·ó·wa 'they shall drive out devils by my power' (Mk 16.17); ktə́sko· 'drive them out (you pl.)' (Mt 10.8); ktəskaók·e 'if I cast out [devils]' (Mt 12.27, Lk 11.20; Gr. 2.15a); ktəskaɔ·=č 'he shall be driven out' (Jn 9.22).

- -kətskaw-: nkətskaó·ɔk=č 'I shall drive them out' (Lk 13.32); kwətskaó·ɔ 'he drives them out' (Mt 9.34); kwətskaó·p·ani 'he drove them out' (Jn 2.15, Mk 1.34).
- ke·tskaw-: mé·ci ke·tskúnte 'after they had been driven out' (1834b:17.6).
▪ ktəsk- (TI): wənči-káski-ktəskamíhti·t 'by which they could drive it out' (Mt 10.1).

ktíte 'you think': see líte.

kti·te·x·ən- II 'fall out on impact': wəlakšía kti·té·x·ənu 'the intestines fell out on impact' (Acts 1.18; KJV "gushed out").

kto·x·ɔl- (-kət·o·x·ɔl-, ke·t·o·x·ɔl-, |kətōxwal-|; Gr. 5.78d) TA 'lead out, take out': pwéči-kto·x·ɔlawwá·ɔ 'they were bringing [a dead body] out' (Lk 7.12; Gr. 2.55c).
- -kət·o·x·ɔl-: kwət·o·x·ɔlá·ɔ 'he leads them out' (Jn 10.3); máta=háč=hánkw .. awé·n kwət·o·x·ɔla·í·ɔ 'doesn't someone take them out?' (Lk 13.15).
- ke·t·o·x·ɔl-: mé·či ke·t·o·x·ɔlá·t·e mwekí·s·əma 'after he has led his sheep out' (Jn 10.4).

kúhəla·n: see hwil-.

kuk·wəluk·wihəla·- AI 'be lame': kuk·wəluk·wíhəle· 'he is lame' (OA, LB); kuk·wəluk·wihəlá·č·i·k 'the crippled, lame people' (Lk 7.22, 14.13, etc.).
 ▶ Cf. ⟨Quekulukquihilleu⟩ 'lame' (B&A 121).

kwáč: see kóč.

kwč° (|kwəč-|) 'try'.

kwčí (-kwə́či; Gr. 2.74g, 5.128l) PV 'try' (Lk 13.24, 1834a:13, 1842:19.5).
- -kwə́či: kkwə́či- íka -lo·x·ɔlawwá·ɔ 'they tried to bring him to him' (Lk 5.18); nkwə́či (with |nə-|) (OA, ME).

kwčihəlal- TA 'try out': nkát·a-mái-kwčihəlalá·ɔk 'I want to go and try them (oxen) out' (Lk 14.19).

kwčuk(w)° (|kwəčəkw-|) 'move' (Gr. §5.2a).

kwčukhɔkehəla·- II 'be an earthquake' (Gr. 5.19b.2): kwčukhɔkéhəle· 'there was an earthquake' (Mt 27.51); lí-kwčukhɔkéhəle· 'that there was an earthquake' (Mt 27.54&).

kwčukwpe·k·ihəla·- II 'tremble (of water)' (Gr. 5.19i): kwčukwpe·k·íhəle· nə́ mpí 'the water trembles' (Jn 5.3).

kwčuk·ɔnihi·- AI+O 'shake': kwčuk·ɔnihínke 'if it is shaken' (Lk 6.38).

kwčuk·wihəla·- II 'be shaken, be moved': áhi-kwčuk·wíhəle· hák·i 'there will be great earthquakes" (Lk 21.11); máta káski-kwčuk·wihəlé·i 'it could not be shaken' (Lk 6.48; Gr. 4.81w); mé·či kwčuk·wihəlá·k·e mpí 'after the water moved' (Jn 5.4); é·li-kwčuk·wíhəla·k 'as it shook' (Lk 7.24).

kwčuk·wilaht- TI(2) 'cause to tremble': mɔ́i-kwčuk·wílahto·n nə́ mpí 'he went and made the water move' (Jn 5.4). ♦ Causative of kwčuk·wihəla·- II (cf. Gr. 5.78).

kwek·ɔ́·nxa·s AN 'donkey' (Gr. 5.34r; FF); kwek·ɔ·nxá·s·ak 'donkeys' (OA).
▪ kwek·ɔ·nxá·t·ət AN (dim.) 'a little donkey' (Lk 19.30&); kwek·ɔ·nxa·t·ət·a (obv.) (Mt 21.5).

kwe·k·we·č·ihkuk·i: see ahkwe·č·i·h-.

kwe·na·k·a°: see kwəná·k·at-.

kwe·ni·tó·naya·t: see kwəni·to·naya·-.

kwe·šate·i·-: see kwša·te·i·-.

kwe·t- 'fear': see khwit-.

kwe·tanət·o·wi·t·əmi·- AI+O 'have O2 as God': káči pí·li kwe·tanət·o·wi·t·əmí·han 'don't have any other God (you sg.)' (1842:10.9). ♦ From the possessed theme of ke·tanət·ó·wi·t 'God', a lexicalized participle of khitanət·o·wi·-.

kwe·xkahka·-: see xkɔhka·-.

kwe·xsi·- AI 'be on guard' (‖kwēxəsī-‖; Gr. 5.8c): kwé·xsi·kw 'be on guard (you pl.)' (Lk 21.36, Mk 13.35, 13.37, Mt 25.13).

kwə́la (Gr. 5.23f) P 'I wish' (Mt 7.12, Lk 9.38); kwə́la íka ktəlalo·ká·la·n 'I wish you would send him there' (Lk 16.27); kwə́la yú lé·k 'let it happen' (*lit.*, 'I wish this would happen') (Mt 8.13); kwə́la tə́la·n 'I wish he would tell them' (1834b:31.4); kwə́la awé·n íka á·t 'I wish someone would go to them.' (1834b:32.6); ⟨qwlu⟩ (Lk 17.22, Mk 10.36; 7x in B; 1842:20.3), ⟨qulu⟩ (Lk 16.27).

• kwə́lah: kwə́lah (1843:21.20 ⟨qwlav⟩); kwə́lah álike 'I wish, however' (1834b:31.3 ⟨qwla valeki⟩); /kwə́lah=á·/ 'I wish, I hope (it would be that)' (OA, ME, AD; LTD ND "to wish; to hope").

kwələpáči P 'even' (⟨qwlupuhi⟩ Mt 28.8&).

▸ Cf. Mun kwə̆lə́p 'even; in turn; turn around and; doing the opposite'.

kwələp·ən- TA 'turn': kkwəlpə́nk·u 'he (obv.) turns them [treated as prox. sg.] (to ..)' (Lk 1.16).

kwələp·i·- (-kwəlpi·-, kwe·lpi·-) AI 'turn around, repent, convert': kwələ́p·i· 'he turned' (Lk 9.55); íkali kwələ́p·i·p 'he turned to them' (Lk 7.9); kwələp·í·ɔk=á· 'they would repent' (Lk 16.30); máta kkwəlpi·húmɔ·p 'you (pl.) did not repent' (Mt 21.32); kwələ́p·i·l 'repent (you sg.)' (Mt 3.2); kwələ́p·i·kw 'repent (you pl.)' (Mt 4.17); kwələp·iáne 'after you (sg.) are converted' (Lk 22.32); kwələp·í·p·ani·k=á· 'they would have repented' (Lk 10.13); tə́li- máta -kwələp·i·wəné·ɔ 'so that they would not be converted' (Jn 12.40).

• -kwəlpi·-: li·ló·məwe=á· kkwəlpi·né·ɔ·p 'it would have been long that they repented (sbd.)' (⟨qlpwp-⟩ Mt 11.21).

• kwe·lpi·-: kwe·lpí·t·e 'when (one sinner) repents' (Lk 15.10).

kwənᵒ (‖kwən-‖) 'long, tall, deep' (Gr. §5.2a).

kwənaéke P 'in the end' (1842:21.5; OA).

kwəna·k·at- II 'be high (a house or the like)': kwəná·k·at wí·k·əwam 'the house is tall' (OA); kwe·ná·k·a 'which is high (seat), tall (house)' (Lk 11.43, 14.28).

kwəna·ke·- (-kwənhake·-, ‖kwənahkē-‖) AI 'be gone a long while': káhta-kwəná·ke· 'he was intending to stay away a long time' (Lk 20.9); é·li-kwəná·ke·t 'because he was gone a long time' (Lk 1.21).

• -kwənhake·-: nkwənháke 'I was gone a long time' (OA).

kwəná·lahkat II 'it is a deep hole' (⟨qwnaluvkwt⟩ Jn 4.11; Gr. 5.1i).

kwə́ni (ahkó·ni [Ra+], -kək·ó·ni; Gr. 5.21g, cf. 5.34r, 5.129r) PV 'long': kwə́ni-pí·ske· 'it's been dark for some time' (ME; Gr. 5.129r).

• ahkó·ni: ahkó·ni-lehəle·x·é·p·ani·k 'they lived long' (1842:20.4).

• -kək·ó·ni: kkək·ó·ni=hánkw -pa·tamáhəmɔ 'you (pl.) always say long prayers' (Mt 23.14).

▪ kwə́ni PP 'throughout' (Gr. 5.133c): kwə́ni-kí·š·ukw ɔ́·k kwə́ni-tpó·kw 'day and night' (Lk 2.37, 18.7; cf. Mk 5.5); kwə́ni-tpó·kw 'all night long' (Lk 2.37, 5.5, 6.12).

kwənihəla·- II 'become long; extend way down (of clothing)': kwe·níhəla·k 'long (garment)' (Mk 16.5); kwe·nihəlá·k·i 'long clothing (pl.)' (Mk 12.38&).

kwəní·i P '(not) long after': máta kwəní·i 'not long after (that)' (⟨Mutu qune⟩ Lk 15.13; ⟨Mutu qwnei⟩ Jn 21.1; ⟨mu tu qu ne⟩ 1842:7.6).

▪ Without máta: kwəní·i P 'long' (1834a:22.43; unclear).

kwəni·to·naya·- (kwe·ni·to·naya·-, ‖kwənīhtōnayā-‖) AI 'have a long beard': kwəni·tó·naye· 'he has a long beard' (LB; Gr. 5.21a).

• kwe·ni·to·naya·-: kwe·ni·tó·naya·t mekí·t·ət 'kid' (*lit.*, 'little long-bearded sheep') (Lk 15.29).

kwənt-: see khwil- — kwənt-.

kwə́škwəš AN 'hog' (OA, ND, LB); kwəškwə́š·ak 'hogs' (Mt 7.6, Mk 5.11, Mt 8.32, Mk 5.16); kwəškwə́š·a 'hogs (obv.)' (Lk 8.34&, Lk 15.15, 15.16); kwəškwəš·i·ké·i P 'into the swine' (Mk 5.12, 5.13; Gr. 4.10a). ▸ Cf. Munsee kó·ško·š < Dutch dialect hog-call.

kwət- ~ -nukwt- (|nəkwət-|) 'one': see kwət·ennaɔhkəs·i·-.

kwətháke IN 'one tribe' (1834b:43.6, 46.11, 1842:10.6).

kwə́ti PP 'the whole (period of time)' (Gr. 2.75a, 5.133d): kwə́ti-kí·škwe 'for the whole day' (Mt 20.2), 'all day' (Mt 20.12; LB); kwə́ti-tpó·kwe 'all night' (Jn 21.3). ▸ Cf. kwə́t·i, nkwə́ti.

kwət·a·pto·na·l- TA 'say one word to': ké·ski- ílli -kwət·a·pto·ná·la·t 'who was able to say even one word to him' (Mt 22.46).

kwət·á·pxki (Gr. 5.31h) P 'one hundred' (Mt 13.8, 13.23, 18.12, etc.).

kwə́t·a·š P 'six' (Lk 1.26, 1.36, Jn 2.6, etc.); kwə́t·a·š txí·nxke 'sixty' (Mt 13.8, 13.23).

-kwət·a·ti·k·e·-: see kwta·ti·k·e·-.

kwət·ennaɔhkəs·i·- (-nukwtennaɔhkəs·i·-) AI 'be one kind': wénči-=á· -kwət·ennaɔhkə́s·i·t 'by which [all] would become a single kind' (1834b:43.7).

• -nukwtennaɔhkəs·i·-: wé·mi kənukwtennaɔhkə́s·i·n 'for you all to be of one kind' (1834b:47.1).

kwət·ennáɔhki (Gr. 5.31j.1) P 'one thing, one kind' (⟨kwtrnaoki⟩ Lk 6.9, ⟨Kotrnaoki⟩ Jn 7.21, ⟨kwtrnaoki⟩ Lk 10.42, etc.), 'in one place' (⟨kotrnaovki⟩ Jn 6.13; ⟨kwtrnaovki⟩ Jn 8.35, 10.16, 20.26, 21.2), 'as one group' (1834b:42.14); kwət·ennáɔhki txí 'the same amount' (Mt 20.10, 20.14).

kwət·énni(?) P 'as a unit' (⟨kotcni⟩1834a:15).

kwə́t·ən P 'once, one time' (1834b:5.1, 8.3, etc.; V, OA, ME, LB).

♦ Idiom with álɔmi PV 'all at the same time': kwə́t·ən=č ktáləmi-a·mwi·né·ɔ 'you shall rise up all at the same time' (Mt 12.41); kwə́t·ən áləmi-luwé·ɔk 'all at the same time they said {so}' (Lk 23.18; KJV "they cried out all at once").

kwə́t·i P 'one' (Lk 3.11, 4.26, 4.27, Mt 5.29, 6.27, 12.11, etc.; Gr. 2.75a); kwə́t·i kí·škwe '(in) one day' (Lk 13.32, Mt 20.2; OA, LB); kwə́t·i máilink 'one mile' (Mt 5.41); kwə́t·i .., kwə́t·i 'one .., another' (Lk 7.8). ▸ Cf. kwə́ti.

kwət·unše·- AI 'give birth to one child': nə́ tə́li-kwət·unše·lí·ne·p 'she (obv.) had had only that one child' (Lk 7.12).

kwiá·kwi P 'still, more, yet' (Mt 6.25, 9.38, 11.23, etc.); kwiá·kwi 'more' (Jn 11.6; KJV "still"); wé·mi kéku kwiá·kwi 'everything else' (1834a:19.14).

kwihəl-(?) AI 'jump abruptly(?)': tóləmi-kwihələné·ɔ 'they began to jump up (sbd.)' (Mt 8.32; no word in KJV). ▸ Perhaps equivalent to Mes kokw- 'suddenly, abruptly' + |-īhl| AI 'jump'.

kwihəlo·t·aw- TA — kwihəlót·- TI(1a) 'chase, run after'.

▪ kwihəlo·t·aw- (TA): məsi táli kwihəlo·t·aɔ́·p·ani·k 'they were chased all over' (Mt 23.34); kkwihəlo·t·aɔwwá·ɔ 'they chased them' (Lk 20.10&; KJV "caught"); ná kkwihəlo·t·aɔ·né·ɔ 'then they chased him' (Mt 21.39&).

▪ kwihəlót·- (TI): kwihəlót·a 'run after it (you sg.)' (V; Gr. 4.106b); kwihəlót·amo·kw 'run after it (you pl.)' (V; Gr. 4.106f); nkwihəlót·amən 'I ran after it' (OA).

kwi·kayo·yəm-: see khík·ay.

kwi·kwínkəm AN 'duck' (V, FW, LTD ND); kwi·kwínkəmo·k 'ducks' (FW, LB; 1834a:14).

kwí·la (Gr. 5.129s) PV 'at a loss, in a quandary, be unable, etc.' (Lk 2.7, 7.42, 14.28, Mt 22.12, etc.); kwí·la-lé· 'there's no avoiding (that ..)' (with ind. complement; Mt 18.7, Lk 17.1); kwí·la- kéku -mi·č·ó·p·ani·k 'they had nothing to eat' (Mk 8.1); é·li-kwí·la-le·ləntamíhti·t 'as they couldn't imagine' (i.e., 'were puzzled') (Jn 13.22).

♦ kwí·la-ləs·i·- AI 'be hopeless, be unable to do anything, be no longer able to help oneself, be no more; die (LTD LB)': kéhəla kkwí·la-ləs·íhəna 'there's really nothing we can do' (Jn 12.19); kwí·la-ləs·ie·kw 'you hopeless ones' (Mt 25.41); tá·mse kwí·la-ləs·ié·k·we 'when at some point you are no more' (Lk 16.9).

kwi·law- TA — kwi·l- TI(1a), 'be unable to find'.
- kwi·law- (TA): kwi·laɔhtí·t·e 'when they could not find him' (Lk 2.45).
- kwi·l- (TI): šúkw kkwi·laməné·ɔ 'but they didn't find one' (Lk 19.48).

kwi·lo·t·aw- TA 'attack': kwi·lo·t·á·kwke 'if he is attacked by him (obv.)' (⟨qelwtaqkc⟩ Lk 11.22; KJV "come upon .. and overcome"). ▸ Cf. ⟨Quilutamen⟩ TI(1) 'fall upon, attack' (B&A 122). But cf. kwihəlo·t·aw- TA 'chase, run after'.

kwí·n P 'for a long time' (as a predicate takes sbd. compliment): kwí·n kpəmto·nhá·lke·n 'long have you been preached to' (Mt 11.23); kwí·n kpənuntələláne·p 'long have I shown them to you' (Lk 10.15). ▸ Cf. kwí·n kwət·əmá·ksi·n 'for a long time he was poorly' (ME); má·e=húnt kwí·n pó·lsi·n. 'she'd been sick a really long time' (ME).

kwi·p·əlánay (Gr. 5.52b) IN 'hoe' (1834a:18.12; ME); kwi·p·əlánayal 'hoes' (1834a:19.14; ME). ▸ Cf. Mun ăkwi·pŏlá·wan 'hoe' (VJ, MR, RS).

kwi·škamúwe AN 'copperhead' (LTD ND); kwi·škaməwé·ɔk 'copperheads' (Mt 3.7, Mt 12.34; KJV "vipers"); kwi·škaməwé·yunk 'copperhead(s) (loc.)' (⟨qejkomwrbf⟩ Mt 23.33).
♦ Despite ⟨Quischgumowe⟩ 'viper, snake' (B&A 122 < Zeisberger 1806:62), the spelling variation in B (⟨kum⟩ ~ ⟨kom⟩) points to /kam/, matching ND's pronunciation.

-kwi·təlº: see khwitəl-.

kwsi·- AI 'move (to a new place)': kwsí· 'he moved (his place of residence)' (LB); kwsí·ɔk 'they are mowing [sic, for moving] in a group' (Voegelin 1946:131); kwsí·l yú wə́nči íkali lí 'move from here over to there (you sg.)' (Mt 17.20).

kwsuk(·)º (|kwəsəkw-|) 'heavy' (Gr. §5.2a).

kwsukhwik-* (-kwəskwi·k-) TI(1a) 'burden, weigh down on': kwəskwí·kamən 'he (tree) burdens [the ground]' (Lk 13.7; KJV "cumbereth").

kwsukwsi·- (kwe·skwəs·i·-, |kwəsəkwəsī-|) AI — kwsuk·ɔn- II 'be heavy' (Gr. 5.10j).
- kwsukwsi·- (AI): kwsúkwsu 'he is heavy' (ME, LB; Gr. 5.10j).
• kwe·skwəs·i·-: kwe·skwə́s·ie·kw 'you (pl.) who are heavy' (Mt 11.28; a misunderanding of "heavy laden").
- kwsuk·ɔn- (II): kwsúk·ɔn 'it is heavy' (OA, LB; Gr. 5.10j).

kwsuk·əwale·whe·-* (-kwəskəwale·whe·-, |kwəsəkəwalēwahē-|; Gr. 5.79c) AI+O 'make O2 carry a heavy load on the back': é·li kkwəskəwale·whe·ne·ɔ́·i 'for they put heavy loads on their (obv.) backs' (Mt 23.4; Gr. 4.40k).

kwsuk·ɔmalsi·- AI 'feel heavy': áləmi- .. -kwsuk·ɔmálsu 'he began to feel heavy' (Mt 26.37). ▸ Cf. ⟨Ksukquamallsin⟩ 'to be perplexed' (B&A 58).

kwša·te·i·- (kwe·šhate·i·- , |kwəšahtēwī-|) II 'smoke': kwe·šhaté·i·k '(which is) smoking' (Mt 12.20). ▸ Cf. kwe·šháte·k 'smoke' (V, OA, ME, LTD ND).

kwtaihəla·- (|kwətawīhlā-|) AI 'sink': ná tóləmi-kwtaíhəla·n 'then he began to sink' (Mt 14.30).

kwtam-* (-kwət·am-) TA — kwtant- (-kwət·ant-, kwe·t·ant-) TI(1) 'taste, try the taste of' (Gr. 3.20a, 5.12j).
- -kwət·am- (TA): nkwə́t·ama TA 'I taste it (anim.)' (OA; Gr. 3.20a).
- kwtant- (TI): kwtánta 'taste it!' (LB).
• -kwət·ant-: takó· náxpəne kwə́t·i kwət·antamó·wən 'let not even one taste it' (Lk 14.24).

- kwe·t·ant-: kwe·t·antánke 'after he had tasted it' (⟨qrtantufc⟩ Jn 2.9, ⟨qrtuntufc⟩ Mt 27.34; ⟨qtufi⟩¦ 1834b:35.6).

kwtawən- TA 'bury': ehə́nta-=č -kwtáwənənt 'a place where they will be buried' (Mt 27.7).
▸ Cf. Mun kwtawŏná·səw 'is buried' (dict.).

kwtawhite·x·ən- II 'sink from the impact': káhti-kwtawhité·x·ənu 'they (the boats) almost sank from it (being loaded with fish)' (Lk 5.7).

kwta·tí·k·an IN 'measure' (⟨ktatekun⟩ Mt 7.2, with ⟨kt-⟩ for /kwt-/; KJV "measure"), 'measure for content' (V).

kwta·ti·k·e·- (-kwət·a·ti·k·e·-) AI 'measure': wə́li-kwta·ti·k·é·ane 'if you measure well' (⟨qt-⟩ Lk 6.38).
- -kwət·a·ti·k·e·-: kkwət·a·tí·k·e·n 'you measure with it' (Mt 7.2; KJV "it shall be measured to you again," perhaps with "you're measured" misunderstood as "you measure").

kwtək(·)ᵒ (‖kwətək-‖) 'back' (Gr. §5.2a).

kwtə́k·i (-kwə́tki) PV 'back': máta=á· kwə́tki-wwa·tó·wən 'he would not go back and know it' (1842:19.5, with ⟨kotki⟩, copying ⟨kot ki⟩ 1834b:4.3). ▸ Cf. ktə́k·i: ktə́k·i-pe·š·əwát·e 'when you (sg.) bring her back' (LHW), but this presumably has dialectal /kt-/ for earlier /kwt-/.

kwtək·inkwe·x·i·n- (kwe·tkinkwe·x·i·n-; Gr. 5.18d) AI 'look back': kwtək·inkwé·x·i·n 'he looked back' (Lk 23.28); awé·n=á· .. kwtək·inkwe·x·ínke 'if someone .. looks back' (Lk 9.62).
- kwe·tkinkwe·x·i·n-: †pí·təl kwe·tkinkwe·x·ínke 'when Peter looked back' (Jn 21.20).

kwtə́k·i·- (-kwə́tki·-, kwe·tki·-) AI 'return, turn back': kwtə́k·i·w 'he went back' (V; Gr. 2.3a); íka ntə́li-kwtə́k·i 'I'm going back there' (⟨ktuke⟩ Mt 12.44, presumably with ⟨kt-⟩ for /kwt-/ [cf. kwta·tí·k·an]); kwtə́k·í·ok 'they returned' (Lk 24.33, 24.52; V); kwtə́k·í·p·ani·k 'they turned back' (Lk 2.45); tə́li-kwtə́k·i·né·ɔ 'that they came ' (Lk 17.18).
- -kwə́tki·-: á·phit ná kkwə́tki·n 'he went so far and came back' (ME; Gr. 2.58m; cf. Gr. 2.64g); nána kkwə́tki·né·ɔ 'then they returned' (Lk 2.20).
- kwe·tki·-: kwe·tkí·t·e 'when he returned' (Mt 21.16&).
▸ Cf. ktə́k·i· 'he went back' (ND); but ⟨kt-⟩ in B (1x) is most likely for /kwt-/.

kxántki (~ xántki; also kxánk·i?; Gr. 5.25d) P 'until, finally, eventually, in the end' (⟨kxuntki⟩ Lk 1.20, Mt 5.18, Jn 9.18; ⟨kxuntkc⟩ Lk 1.80; ⟨kxunki⟩ Jn 8.5, etc., 14x, 1842:16.2, 17.1; ⟨kxutki⟩ 1834a:23.54 [misprint]); tə́li-=á· kxántki -máxkaɔn 'until he finds him' (Lk 15.4); tə́li-=á· kxántki -máxkamən 'until she finds it' (Lk 15.8); kxántki kí·škwi·k 'until the day (when)' (Lk 1.80).
- xántki (⟨xuntki⟩ Mt 13.8; 1834a:19.17, 1834b:8.11; V, OA, ME, ER).

kxuwe·- AI 'fear people, be in fear': kxuwé·p·ani·k 'they were in fear of the people' (Lk 22.2); wə́nči-=č máta -kxuwé·ɔnkw 'so that we would not fear' (Lk 1.74; Gr. 4.95n).
♦ Note: perhaps better written with /kxəw-/.

kxw- (-kɔx·-, kwe·x·-, ‖kwax-‖; Gr. 2.15d, 5.4l) TA 'fear': kxɔ́· 'he is feared' (LB); kxɔ́· 'fear him (you pl.)' (Lk 12.5 [2x]); káči kxwié·k·e·kw 'do not fear them (you pl.)' (⟨qxw⟩ Mt 10.26); káči kxwí·he·kw 'don't be afraid of me' (⟨kwx⟩ Mk 6.50); é·li- †hélat -kxɔ́·t·əp 'as Herod had feared him' (Mk 6.20); é·li-kxɔ́hti·t 'because they feared him, them' (Jn 9.22, Mt 28.4, Jn 20.19; Gr. 2.39f).
- -kɔx·-: kɔx·á·ɔ nčó·wa 'he feared the Jews' (Mt 27.57&; cf. Gr. 2.15d); kɔx·awwá·ɔ 'they feared them' (Mt 21.46&); kɔx·awwá·p·ani 'they feared him' (Mk 11.18); kkɔ́x·əl 'I was afraid of you (sg.)' (Lk 19.21); kkɔx·əlúhump 'I was afraid of you (pl.)' (Mt 25.25).
- kwe·x·-: awé·n=á· kwé·x·e·kw 'who you (pl.) should fear' (Lk 12.5).
▸ For the matching TI stem, see khwit- (‖kwəht-‖) above (Gr. 5.4l).

l

l- (-t-əl-, e·l-, -ihəl- [Rih+], all- [Rā+], |əl-|; Gr. 5.4a) TA 'say {so} to, about': takó· awé·ni kéku le·í·ɔk 'they did not speak to anyone' (Mt 28.8&; Gr. 4.83d); lə́l 'tell her' (Lk 10.40; Gr. 4.104o), 'tell them' (Jn 20.17; with indirect discourse complement); ló· 'tell them (you pl.)' (Mt 21.5; Gr. 4.104s); lí·l 'tell me (you sg.)' (Lk 7.42, Mt 14.28, Jn 20.15; Gr. 4.105a); máta kɔ́ski- kéku -luk·o·wiwwá·ɔ 'he (obv.) was unable to speak to them' (Lk 1.22; Gr. 4.85t); kéku=háč wə́nči-lát 'why do you (sg.) tell them [a parable]?' (Mt 13.10; Gr. 4.67(2)m); é·li-lák e·lsíhti·t 'because I say (*lit.*, tell them) what they do' (Jn 7.7); é·li- wió·s ɔ́·k mhúkw máta háši -luk·ó·wan 'for flesh and blood never told you' (Mt 16.17; Gr. 4.97l); lúk·ɔne 'if he tells you' (Lk 17.4; Gr. 2.16g); máta lǝló·wane 'I don't tell you (sg.)' (1842:22.1; Gr. 4.97w); wə́nči-lə́le·kw 'why I say to you (pl.)' (Mt 6.25, Jn 8.24, Lk 12.22; Gr. 4.67(2)n); né·tami-lǝlé·k·ǝp 'what I first said to you (pl.)' (Jn 8.25; Gr. 4.77g); ná lá·ne·p 'then he was told' (Lk 16.1; Gr. 4.72e).

• -t-əl-: tǝlá·ɔl 'he told him' (Mt 3.14, etc.; pp. 19-94), tǝlá·ɔ 'he said to him' (Lk 5.4, etc.; pp. 37-221); tǝlá·ɔ e·nǝnthake·ɔ́·k·an 'he told them a parable' (Lk 6.39), e·nunthake·ɔ́·k·an tǝlá·ɔ (Lk 21.29); tǝlawwá·ɔ 'they said to him' (⟨tulaoao⟩ Jn 20.25, ⟨Tulaowao⟩ Jn 21.5); wtǝlá·p·ani·l 'he said to them' (Mt 3.7; Gr. 2.61b), tǝlá·p·ani 'he said to him, her, or them' (Jn 1.18, 1.47, 2.7, 2.10, 4.7, Mt 9.12, Lk 5.36, Mk 3.23, etc.; Gr. 2.60b); tə́lko·l 'he (obv.) said to him' (Mt 4.3; Gr. 2.18a), tə́lku (Lk 2.48, Mt 8.19, etc.; Gr. 2.18b); máta=háč kéku ktǝlí·i 'aren't you speaking to me?' (Jn 19.10; Gr. 4.89a); ktǝllúhǝmɔ 'I tell you (pl.)' (Mt 3.9, Jn 1.51, 4.35, etc.; Gr. 2.5n); takó· ktǝllo·húmɔ 'I'm not telling you (pl.)' (Jn 16.26; Gr. 4.89o); ntǝla·né·ɔ 'I tell it to them' (Jn 8.26; Gr. 4.41c); ntə́lko·n 'he told me' (Jn 5.11 [sbd.]); ktə́lko·n 'he says to you (sbd.)' (Lk 14.9); tə́lko·n 'he, she, or they (obv.) told him or her (sbd.)' (Jn 2.25, Jn 4.39, Lk 19.19, etc.); ntǝlkó·ne·n 'it tells us' (Jn 8.5; Gr. 4.27aa); awé·n=háč ktǝlko·né·ɔ 'who told you?' (⟨tclkwnru⟩ Mt 3.7); ná tǝlá·ne·p 'then he said to them' (Mt 2.8, Jn 6.61, Lk 16.1, etc.; Gr. 4.72c); ná tǝla·né·ɔ·p 'then they said to him' (Jn 6.34; Gr. 4.72d).

• e·l-: e·lák·ǝp nčó·wak 'as I told the Jews' (Jn 13.33; Gr. 4.76b); e·lá·t·ǝp 'as he had said to him, them (obv.)' (Lk 1.55, 1.72, etc.; Gr. 4.76i), 'who had told them' (Jn 18.14 [em.]); e·lkúk·ǝp 'what he (obv.) had said to him' (Lk 22.61 [2x]; Gr. 4.76v); e·lkwé·k·ǝp 'what he said to you (pl.)' (Lk 24.6, Acts 1.4; Gr. 4.76y); e·lkwihtí·t·ǝp 'what they (obv.) said to them' (Mt 5.21; Gr. 4.76x); e·liáne 'when you told me' (Lk 15.29; Gr. 2.25c, 2.31e); kéku é·la·t 'what he was saying to them' (Jn 10.6); é·li·t 'he who told me {so}, says to me {so}' (Jn 4.29, Mt 7.21); ellé·k·ǝp 'what I said to you (pl.)' (Jn 15.20; Gr. 4.77f); élle·kw 'what I said to you (pl.)' (Jn 14.25).

• ihǝl-: ntihǝluk·ó·na 'he, she used to tell us (exc.)' (OA, ME; Gr. 2.27e).

• all-: allúk·ɔn 'the one speaking to you' (Jn 9.37).

▪ lǝt·i·- (-t-ǝlti·- e·lti·-) AI (recip.; Gr. 5.112c) 'say {so} to each other': lǝ́t·ǝwak 'they said {so} to each other' (Jn 11.56, Mt 21.25, etc.); lǝt·ó·p·ani·k 'they said {so} to each other' (Lk 2.15, Jn 4.33, Mk 9.10, etc.); énta- kéku -lǝt·íhti·t 'when they spoke to each other' (1834a:18.11).

• -t-ǝlti·-: ná .. tǝlti·né·ɔ 'then they said {so} to each other' (Jn 16.17).

• e·lti·-: kéku ki·mí·i e·ltíe·kw 'something you (pl.) said secretly to each other' (Lk 12.3); e·ltíhti·t 'what they say to each other' (Lk 7.32).

lač·e·s·əwá·k·an (-t-əlahče·s·əwa·k·an- ~ -t-əlàč·e·s·əwa·k·an-) IN 'possessions' (Mt 6.19, 6.20, Lk 11.22, Mt 13.44), tahkɔp·o·ha·ltəwí·i-lač·e·s·əwá·k·an 'wedding garments' (Mt 22.12); lač·e·s·əwá·k·ana (pl.) (Lk 12.20, 12.33); lač·e·s·əwá·k·anink 'in goods' (Lk 8.3).
  • -t-əlahče·s·əwa·k·an-: ktəlahče·s·əwá·k·an 'your property' (1842:22.3); ktəlahče·s·əwá·k·ana 'your possessions' (Lk 16.1); təlahče·s·əwá·k·an 'his possessions' (Lk 12.15, 1834b:21.8); təlahče·s·əwá·k·ana (Lk 17.31); təlahče·s·əwa·k·aní·li·t 'his (obv.) possessions' (Mt 24.47); ktəlahče·s·əwa·k·anəwá·ɔ 'your (pl.) possessions' (1842:17.1).
  • -t-əlàč·e·s·əwa·k·an-: ntəlač·e·s·əwá·k·an 'my clothes' (ME); ktəlač·e·s·əwá·k·an 'your possessions' (Mt 6.21; KJV "your treasure"); təlač·e·s·əwá·k·an 'his possessions' (Mt 12.29, Lk 11.21); təlač·e·s·əwá·k·ana 'his possessions' (Mt 13.52); wtəlač·e·s·əwa·k·anəwá·ɔl 'their goods' (⟨wtclathrswakunwal⟩ Mt 2.11).
  ▸ Cf. ⟨Latschessowagan⟩ "goods, merchandise" (B&A 61).
laehɔ·s·əwá·k·an (-t-əlaehɔ·s·əwa·k·an-) IN 'deed(s)' (Jn 5.20, 5.36, 10.38); laehɔ·s·əwá·k·ana 'deeds' (Jn 10.32).
  • -t-əlaehɔ·s·əwa·k·an-: ntəlaehɔ·s·əwá·k·ana 'my deeds' (Jn 10.25); nə́ni ntəlaehɔ·s·əwá·k·an '(by) those very deeds of mine' (Jn 5.36 [instrumental oblique (§3.7c)]); ktəlaehɔ·s·əwá·k·an 'your deeds' (Jn 7.3); təlaehɔ·s·əwá·k·an 'his deeds' (Jn 10.37).
laehɔ·s·i·- (-t-əlaehɔ·s·i·-, e·laehɔ·s·i·-, ehəlaehɔ·s·i·- [Rih+; IC], |əlaehwāsī-|; Gr. 4.42h) AI 'do {so}, act {so}, behave {so}': pí·li laehɔ́·s·u '(and) he adopted another form' (Mk 16.12); xkó·k·ink laehɔ́·s·u 'he adopted the form of a snake' (1842:7.6); wénči- yú -laehɔ́·s·ian 'by which you (sg.) do this' (Mk 11.28 [2x]).
  • -t-əlaehɔ·s·i·-: kéku=háč ktəlaehɔ́·s·i 'what did you do?' (Jn 18.35); ná təlaehɔ́·s·i·n 'then he acted [as if ..]' (Lk 24.28).
  • e·laehɔ·s·i·-: né·l ntəlaehɔ·s·əwá·k·ana e·laehɔ́·s·ia 'the deeds I have done' (Jn 10.25); e·laehɔ·s·í·t·əp 'what he had done' (Lk 9.43); e·laehɔ·s·íhti·t 'what they all did' (Mt 27.57&; 'all' = prox. + obv.).
  • ehəlaehɔ·s·i·-: wé·mi ehəlaehɔ́·s·ink 'all the acts one performs' (Mk 12.33).
=láh P (used in rhetorical questions and mirative statements; Gr. 5.24l): awé·n=ksí=láh 'who then?' (Jn 1.21); tá=háč=ínk=láh e·li·ná·kwsi·t yú e·lhaké·i·t 'what is this tribe like?' (Lk 7.31); tá=háč=ínk=láh ləkhíkwi-áhɔt 'how hard do you imagine it is?' (Mk 10.24); kéku=láh=wáni '(people were startled to see that) here was this one ..' (V; "lo and behold"). ▸ See also šé·=láh.
lahápa P 'for a while, for now, take the time to, instead, in turn, let *me*' (Gr. 5.23g; Lk 4.13, 6.42, Mt 8.21, Lk 14.31, etc.).
lahəlápi: see lápi.
láhpi P 'quickly' (Lk 19.5; ND).
lai·k·e·- (-t-əlai·k·e·-) AI 'settle {smwh, so}': máta=á· čí·č nalahí·i laí·k·e· 'he will not settle any further upstream' (1834a:22.48; with ⟨lyekc⟩ for expected /lai·k·é·i/).
  • -t-əlai·k·e·-: nə́ni ɔ·ká·i təlaí·k·e·n '(he) settled around there' (1834b:43.10).
  ▸ Cf. mai·k·e·- 'spend the night, camp'.
lak·e·kinke·- (-t-əlahke·kinke·-, e·lahke·kinke·-) AI 'teach {so}': ná=nə́ lak·e·kinké·t·e 'if he teaches that way' (Mt 5.19 [2x]).
  • -t-əlahke·kinke·-: ktəlahke·kínke·n 'you (sg.) teach (that way)' (Mt 22.16).
  • e·lahke·kinke·-: e·lahke·kínke·t 'the way he taught' (Mk 1.22); e·lahke·kinké·t·əp 'what he had taught' (Mt 7.28), 'his teachings' (Mk 11.18).

laküe·ki·m- (-t-əlahke·ki·m-, ehəlak·e·ki·m- [Rih+; IC], |əlakēkīm-|) TA 'teach {so}': lak·e·kí·mo· 'teach them (you pl.)' (Mt 28.20).
- -t-əlahke·ki·m-: təlahke·ki·má·p·ani 'he taught them' (Lk 3.18, Mk 6.34 [em.]).
- ehəlak·e·ki·m-: ehəlak·e·kí·mi·t 'as he taught me' (Jn 8.28).

lak·əni·m- (-t-əlahkəni·m-, e·lahkəni·m-) TA 'tell about {so}, accuse of doing {so}', TA+O 'tell O2 about': káči kəlo·ne·ó·k·an lak·əni·mié·k·ač wi·t·a·wsó·mat 'do not tell a lie about your neighbor (you sg.)' (1842:12.6).
- -t-əlahkəni·m-: kéku=háč ktəlahkəní·ma khák·ay 'what do you (sg.) say about yourself?' (Jn 1.22; Gr. 4.15h).
- e·lahkəni·m-: e·lahkəní·me·kw 'what you accuse him of' (Lk 23.14); e·lahkəni·mké·an 'the testimony against you' (Mk 14.60).

lak·əni·mkwəs·i- (e·lahkəni·mkwəs·i·-) AI 'be accused {so}': e·lahkəni·mkwəs·í·li·t 'what the accusation against him (obv.) was' (Jn 19.19).

lak·əno·t·a·s·i·- II 'be told about {so}': wənči- xe·lennáɔhki -lak·əno·t·á·s·i·k 'the reason for many kinds of things being told' (1834a:23.56).

lak·o·s·i·- (|əlakōsī-|; Gr. 5.11g) AI 'climb {so}': palí·i lak·o·s·í·t·e 'if he climbs up another way' (Jn 10.1).
▸ Cf. hitá·i-ahkó·s·u 'he is a skilled climber' (LB). ▸ Cf. kəntahko·s·i·-.

lak·wi·- (e·lahkwi·-, ehəlak·wi·- [Rih+; IC], |əlakwī-|) AI 'wear {so}': máta e·lahkwí·li·t 'who (obv.) was not wearing {such} clothes' (Mt 22.11; cf. Gr. 4.65.l).
- ehəlak·wi·-: ehəlák·wink 'what one customarily wears' (Mt 22.11).

lale·p·ɔ·m- (-t-əlale·p·ɔ·m-; cf. Gr. 5.39b) TA 'teach to do {so}': wé·mi kéku ktəlale·p·ɔ·mkúwa 'he teaches you (pl.) to do everything' (Jn 14.26).

lalo·ka·l- (-t-əlalo·ka·l-, e·lalo·ka·l-, |əlalōhkāl-|) TA 'send to {smwh}': pí·li íka lalo·ká·le· 'he sent another there' (Lk 20.12); íka lalo·ká·le·p 'he sent (some) to him' (Lk 7.3), lə́nəwa ni·k·a·ní·i lalo·ká·le·p 'he sent men ahead' (Lk 9.52); tə́li-=á· kwiá·kwi pí·li íka -lalo·ká·la·n 'that he should send still more there' (Lk 10.2); takó· pí·li ntəlalo·ka·lké·i 'I was not sent to anywhere else' (Mt 15.24; Gr. 4.87a).
- -t-əlalo·ka·l-: ni·k·a·ní·i təlalo·ka·lá·ɔ 'he sent them ahead' (Lk 10.10), íka təlalo·ka·lá·ɔ 'he sent them there' (Mt 21.34&, Mt 22.7); ná šá·e təlalo·ká·la·n 'then he immediately ordered them' (Mk 6.45).
- e·lalo·ka·l-: e·lalo·ka·lə́ntəp 'where he was sent' (Lk 4.26; Gr. 4.76s); e·lalo·ká·lian 'what you (sg.) sent me [to do]' (Jn 17.4; Gr. 4.67(1)d).

lalo·ka·s·i·- (e·lalo·ka·s·i·-) AI 'do (things) {so}': e·lalo·ká·s·i·t 'the things he does' (Jn 5.19, 5.20).

lalo·ke·mwi·- AI 'send a message to {smwh}': nči·sás·ink lalo·ke·mwí·lu 'they (obv.) sent a message to Jesus' (Jn 11.3).

lamalsi·- (-t-əlamalsi·-) AI 'feel {so}': aləwí·i-lamálsu 'she was worse' (Mk 5.26).
- -t-əlamalsi·-: tá=háč ktəlamálsi·n 'how do you feel?' (LB).

lami·kəmɔ·s·i·- (e·lami·kəmɔ·s·i·-, |əlamīhkəmwāsī-|; Gr. 5.17f) AI 'work {so}': kəwi·šíki-lami·kəmɔ́·s·i 'you (sg.) work hard' (Lk 10.41).
- e·lami·kəmɔ·s·i·-: e·lami·kəmɔ·s·í·li·t=č 'the tasks they (obv.) were to perform' (Mk 13.34).

lami·kənt- (-t-əlami·kənt-, e·lami·kənt-) TI(1a) 'do {so} as work or deed'.
- -t-əlami·kənt-: né·k·a=č nə́ təlami·kə́ntamən '*he* shall do the deeds' (Jn 14.12).

• e·lami·kənt-: e·lami·kə́ntama 'what work I do' (Jn 13.7); e·lami·kəntamə́li·t 'what he (obv.) does' (Jn 15.15); e·lami·kə́ntame·kw 'what you (pl.) accomplished' (Mt 23.23; KJV "have done").

lanehəma·l- (-t-əlanehəma·l-, |əlanēhəmāl-|; Gr. 5.93a) TA 'throw to {smwh}':
é·li-=á· .. tənté·yunk -lanehəma·lké·an 'as you (sg.) would be cast into the fire' (Mt 18.9).
• -t-əlanehəma·l-: hákink=č ktəlanehəmá·lke 'you will be thrown down' (Mt 11.23); íka=č təlanehəmá·lku 'he (obv.) shall throw him there' (Lk 12.46).

lanihəmaw- TA+O 'throw O2 {so} to': káči (..) íka lanihəmawié·k·ač 'do not throw it to them (you sg.)' (Mt 7.6 2x, with pleonastic 'there').

lanihi·- (-t-əlanihi·-, e·lanihi·-, |əlanihī-|) AI+O 'throw{so}, {smwh}': aləwí·i txí íka laníhi· 'she tossed in more' (Mk 12.43); mənəp·é·k·unk .. lanihinkpáne 'if he had then been thrown into the sea' (Mk 9.42; Gr. 4.74c); mənəp·é·k·unk lanihínke 'if he were thrown into the sea' (Lk 17.2; Gr. 4.63d); móni lí- íka -laníhi·n 'that people tossed money into it' (Mk 12.41; Gr. 3.11a); hákink=č laníhí·nak 'they (anim.) will be thrown down' (Lk 21.24; Gr. 4.40q); wə́nči-=č máta .. mahtánt·unk -laníhink 'so that it will not be thrown into the devil's place' (Mt 5.29, 5.30).
• -t-əlanihi·-: tənté·yunk təlanihí·na 'it (anim.) throws him into the fire' (Mk 9.22); hákink təlaníhi·n hɔ́k·ay 'he threw himself down' (Mk 5.22; Gr. 4.15l); hákink təlanihi·né·ɔ·p hɔk·ayúwa 'they threw themselves down' (Mt 2.11).
• e·lanihi·-: e·laníhink mənəp·é·k·unk 'that is thrown into the sea' (Mt 13.47).

lánkan: see lanksi·- — lankan-.

lankəl- (e·lankəl-, |əlankəl-|; 5.17b) AI 'die {so}, be diseased {so}': entxennáɔhki-lankələlí·č·i 'ones (obv.) with all kinds of afflictions' (Mt 4.24); wé·mi entxennáɔhki-lankələ́k·i·k 'people with all sorts of diseases' (Mk 1.32).
• e·lankəl-: e·lánkələk=č 'how he would die' (Jn 18.32); kéku e·lankələ́k·əp 'whatever his ailment had been' (Jn 5.4); tákta kéku e·lankələ́li·t 'any diseases and conditions they (obv.) had' (Mt 4.23); wé·mi kéku e·lankələlí·č·i 'who (obv.) suffered from every disease' (Mt 9.35).

lanko·m- (-t-əlanko·m-, e·lanko·m-, |əlankōm-|; Gr. 2.47b) TA 'be related to, have or treat as a relative' — lankunt- (TI(1a)) TI-O 'have relatives'.
  ▪ lánko·m (TA): lánko·m šinká·lkɔn 'agree with your adversary (you sg.)!' (Mt 5.25; KJV "agree with"); é·li-lanko·má·t·əp nte·pit·ínka 'as he was related to David' (Lk 2.4).
  • e·lanko·m-: e·lanko·mák·i·k 'my friends and neighbors' (Lk 15.29; KJV "my friends"); e·lankó·mat 'your (sg.) relative' (Lk 1.36, 10.27, etc.; Gr. 2.47b); e·lanko·má·č·i·k 'your (sg.) relatives' (Lk 1.61, 14.12; Gr. 2.47b); e·lankó·ma·t 'one who had him (obv.) as a relative' (Lk 22.59-60&); e·lanko·má·č·i 'her relatives (obv.)' (Lk 1.58), 'her friends (obv.)' (Lk 15.9); e·lanko·ma·tpáni 'his relative (obv.)' (Lk 1.27; Gr. 4.76m); e·lanko·má·č·i·k 'his (obv.) neighbors and relatives' (Mk 3.21; KJV "his friends"); e·lanko·ma·liáni 'your (sg.) relative(s) (obv.)' (1834b:8.13, 1842:22.1); e·lanko·ma·liénki 'our (exc.) people (obv.), lit., relatives' (Lk 23.2; KJV "the nation"; Gr. 4.65k); e·lanko·mánkwi·k 'our (inc.) own people' (Mt 21.26; KJV "the people"); e·lanko·mé·k·wi·k 'your (pl.) kinsmen' (Lk 11.46, 21.16); e·lanko·mahtí·č·i 'their own people (obv.)' (Mt 21.46&).
  • ahalankó·m-(?): tə́li-[aha]lankó·mko·n 'that are related to him' (1834a:21.33).
  ▸ Cf. ntəlankó·ma.
  ▪ lankunt- (TI-O) 'have relatives': énta-lankúntank 'in his own country' (lit., 'where he has relatives') (Mt 13.54, 13.57), 'among his relatives' (Lk 2.44).

lanksi·- AI — lankan- II 'be light (in weight)' (Gr. §5.2a, 5.10j).

- lanksi·- (AI): lánksu 'he is light' (Gr. 5.10j; ME).
- lankan- (II): nəwí·ɔhšo·n lánkan 'my pack is light' (Mt 11.30; V, ME).

lankunt-: see lanko·m- — lankunt-.

lapahpi·- AI+O 'take the place of': é·li-lápahpi·t 'as he took the place of (his father)' (Mt 2.22); wénči-=á· -káski-lapahpíe·kw ko·x·əwá·ɔk 'so that you (pl.) would be able to take the place of your fathers' (1842:19.3).
  ▸ Cf. Mun lá·păpəw AI+O 'takes (s.o.)'s place' (dict.).

lápi (lahəlápi; Gr. 2.73e, 5.25e) P 'again, back, more, next' (Lk 1.26, Mt 1.20, Lk 2.39, Mt 2.9, etc.); lápi ɔ·p·ánke 'the next day' (Jn 1.29), énta- lápi -ɔ́·p·ank 'the next day' (V); lápi e·lahpa·é·k·e 'the next morning' (Jn 1.35); lápi xé·li 'many more' (Jn 4.41); lápi mwí·la·n '(then) he gave it back to him' (Lk 4.20).
  • lahəlápi 'again and again' (Jn 1.16; Gr. 5.45f).

lap·i·- (e·lahpi·-) AI 'be {so}': nəwínki- le·lá·i -láp·i lápi 'I would like to sit in the center again' (ND).
  • e·lahpi·-: e·lahpí·li·t wté·ha 'the way his heart is' (Lk 6.45; KJV "of the abundance of the heart").
  • ne·lahpi·- (nə́ + e·l- lexicalized as ne·l- 'while'; cf. Gr. 4.61ab): ne·lahpí·t·əp 'while she was there' (Lk 2.6; Gr. 4.73a).

lat·o·n- TI(1a) 'search for': ná tɔ́ləmi- .. -lat·ó·namən 'then he set about searching for it (in ..)' (1842:16.2).
  ▸ Cf. lat·o·ni·k·e·- (-əlahto·ni·k·e·-) AI 'search (for things)': lat·o·ní·k·e· 'he's searching', ntəlahto·ní·k·e 'I'm searching' (OA, accepting ⟨Lattoniken⟩ 'to search' [B&A 61]).

laxae·ləm- TA 'worry about': kɔ́č=háč=á· laxaé·ləmat 'why would you (sg.) worry about him?' (Jn 21.22, 21.23).
  ▸ Cf. Mun lxawé·lŏme·w 'takes care of (s.o.), looks after (s.o.)' (dict.).

laxaihtəwá·k·an IN 'hindrance(s)'; awé·n máta aluhikánke laxaihtəwá·k·an 'if someone does not overcome hindrances' (Mt 10.38; KJV "taketh not his cross"). ♦ Noun derived from a reciprocal stem (|laxawīh-ətī-| AI; see next) with a passive meaning (Gr. 5.115).

laxai·h- (laxaih-, -lax·ai·h-, |laxawīh-|) TA 'annoy, hinder': máta laxai·hí·t·e awé·n 'if someone does not hinder me' (Lk 9.50; KJV "he that is not against us"); tá=háč ksá·ki-laxaihələné·ɔ 'how long will I annoy you (pl.)?' (Mk 9.19; KJV "suffer you" [RSV "bear with you"], evidently misunderstood).
  • -lax·ai·h-: llax·aí·hukw 'she annoys me' (Lk 18.5; KJV "troubleth me"); llax·aí·ha 'I'm bothering him' (OA); kəlax·aí·ha 'you're bothering him' (ME).

laxak·wihəla·- II 'loosen, become loose': wí·lanu laxak·wíhəle·p 'his tongue loosened' (Lk 1.64).

laxən- (-lax·ən-, le·x·ən-) TA 'untie, untangle, release' — TI(1b) 'untie, unwrap'.
- laxən- (TA): laxə́no· 'untangle him (you pl.)' (Jn 11.44); é·li- †páilat -wínki-=á· -laxə́na·t nči·sás·a 'as Pilate would be willing to release Jesus' (Lk 23.20; Gr. 5.128y).
  • -lax·ən-: lɔx·əná·ɔ 'he released him' (Mk 15.15; Gr. 2.55q); yúkwe=á· lɔx·ənúk·u 'he (obv.) would release him now' (Mt 27.43; Gr. 2.27g); máta=háč wəli·x·ənó·wi laxəna·n 'is it not right for her to be unbound?' (Lk 13.16; Gr. 4.49f).
- -lax·ən- (TI): llax·ənə́mən 'that I untie them (sbd.)' (Jn 1.27).
  • le·x·ən-: le·x·ənəmihtí·t·e 'when they unwrapped them' (⟨lrxwrnº⟩ Mt 2.11 [the wrong word; em.]; KJV 'opened').

laxənəmaw- (-lax·ən-) TA+O 'unwrap, untie O2 for': llax·ənəmáɔ·n 'that I untie them for him (sbd.)' (Lk 3.16).

laxi·- (-lax·i·-) AI 'be set free, be set loose': kəláx·i 'you (sg.) are set free' (Lk 13.12; KJV "loosed").

laxka·m- TA 'scold': lɔxka·má·ɔ 'he yells (angrily) at him' (LTD); ó·x·ɔ lɔxká·mku 'his father scolded him' (1842:13.4).
  ▸ Cf. Mun laxká·me·w 'scolds (s.o.)' (dict.).

laxwe·keha·s·i·- II 'be harrowed': hák·i á·pči laxwe·kehá·s·u 'the ground is always harrowed' (1834a:16). ▸ Cf. lelxwe·kehí·k·an 'harrow' (V ⟨le·l-⟩).

laxwe·skaw- TA 'scatter (acting on by foot or body)' (cf. Gr. 5.12y): ná=á· .. laxwé·skaɔ·n 'then they would be scattered' (Jn 10.12).

laxwe·x·we·- (le·x·we·x·we·-) AI 'disperse': laxwé·x·we·kw 'disperse (you pl.)!' (Mt 13.36, Mk 6.45); laxwe·x·wehtí·t·eč ma·ehəlá·č·i·k 'let the crowd disperse' (Mt 14.15).
  • le·x·we·x·we·-: mé·či le·x·we·x·wehtí·t·e ma·ehəlá·č·i·k 'after the crowd had dispersed' (Mt 15.39).

la·(w)° (|lāw-|) 'in the middle' (Gr. §5.2a).

la·č·i·mo·lx- (-t-əla·č·i·mo·lx-) TA 'report {so} to': šúkw=á· kóski- nə́ -la·č·i·mo·lxúk·o·n 'they (obv.) could only tell him about it' (1834a:18.7).
  • -t-əla·č·i·mo·lx-: máta kkáski- xé·li kéku ktəla·č·i·mo·lxuk·o·wi·wəná·nak 'they are not able to tell us about many things' (1834a:18.8; with prefix |kə-| repeated); wé·mi təla·č·i·mo·lxuk·ó·ne·p 'they (obv.) told him about all of that' (Lk 7.18; Gr. 4.71f).

la·č·i·mwi·- (-t-əla·č·i·mwi·-, e·la·č·i·mwi·-) AI 'tell, report {so}'.
  • -t-əla·č·i·mwi·-: təla·č·í·mwi·n 'he reported it' (Jn 19.35); ktəla·č·i·mwi·né·ɔ 'you all must tell about it' (Mt 18.17); təla·č·i·mwi·né·ɔ·p 'they told about it' (Lk 8.34& [2x], Jn 12.17).
  • e·la·č·i·mwi·-: e·la·č·í·mwi·t 'what he reported' (Jn 19.35), 'his testimony' (Jn 3.32, 3.33); wé·mi éntxi-la·č·i·mwí·t·əp 'everything he told about' (Jn 10.41); e·la·č·i·mwíhti·t 'the way they described it' (Lk 24.24).

la·é·nae P 'in the middle of the crowd' (⟨larnac⟩ Mk 5.27; KJV "in the press").
  ♦ Shape conjectured but certain.

lá·i (Gr. 5.129t) PV 'middle': lá·i-tpo·kwi·- II 'be midnight' (Lk 11.5, 12.38, Mt 25.6).
  ▪ PP: lá·i-tpo·kwəní·i 'at midnight' (Mk 13.35).

la·í·tane (|-īhtanē| 'stream, body of water'; Gr. 5.31o) P 'in mid-stream' (V, ME), 'in the middle of the lake ("sea")' (Mk 6.47, Jn 21.8).

la·ke·i·- (-t-əlhake·i·-, e·lhake·i·-) AI 'be of, from a tribe': ke·x·ennáɔhki la·ké·yu 'they [representative singular] are from many different tribes' (1834b:42.9);
†pa·lasi·í·i-la·ke·yó·p·ani·k 'they were of the tribe of the Pharisees' (Jn 1.24).
  • -t-əlhake·i·-: kwi·škaməwé·ɔk ktəlhake·íhəmɔ 'you (pl.) are of the tribe of copperheads' (Mt 12.34).
  • e·lhake·i·-: e·lhaké·i·t 'division' (Lk 1.5), 'tribe' (Lk 7.31, Mt 12.45); e·lhaké·i·t·əp 'tribe' (in the past) (Lk 2.36); e·lhaké·iankw 'we (inc.) that are of our tribe' (Lk 7.5); e·lhaké·í·č·i·k 'tribes' (Jn 11.50).

la·ke·x·ən- (e·lhake·x·ən- [IC], |əlahkēxən-|) II 'be a road (to {smwh})': la·ké·x·ən 'there is a road' (ME).
  • e·lhaké·x·ink '(road) that leads to (loc.)' (Mt 7.14; 1834b:48.2).
  ▸ Cf. aləmhake·x·ən-, ɔ·khake·x·ən-, tankhake·x·ənti·-.

la·m° (|lām-|) 'inside, under' (Gr. 5.31b).

lá·mahte P (|-atē| 'belly' Gr. 5.31b) 'in the womb' (Lk 1.41, Jn 3.4); xínkwi-namé·s·ink lá·mahte 'in the belly of the whale' (Mt 12.40).

- lá·mahte IN 'the womb' (as a noun: Lk 11.27); llá·mahtenk 'in my womb' (Lk 1.44).

la·mali·ke·- (-t-əla·mali·ke·-) AI 'step {so}': íka wə́ntahkwi la·mali·ké·t·e 'if he takes a step in that direction' (1834b:8.4).
- -t-əla·mali·ke·-: á·p·əwat lápi təla·malí·ke·n 'it's easy for him to take another step' (1834b:8.4).

la·mamé·nxke (Gr. 5.32c) P 'inside the fence' (Mt 21.33, Jn 19.41).

la·me·- (e·la·me·-, |əlāmē-|) II 'extend along {so}, to {smwh}': ká·mink lá·me· 'it extends across to the other side' (ME).
- e·la·me·-: e·lá·me·k P 'the length of it, along it' (Mt 4.15, Mt 9.26).

la·mhákie (Gr. 5.32a) P 'inside the earth' (Mt 12.40).
- la·mhakamí·k·we (Gr. 5.31a) P 'inside the earth' (1834b:36.8).

la·mi·k·əwáhəme (Gr. 5.32e) P 'inside the house' (⟨lamekwavmc⟩ Jn 4.53, Lk 11.7, 17.31, etc. [5x], ⟨lumekwavmc⟩ Lk 17.31).

la·múnkwe (Gr. 5.31k) P 'inside' (Mt 7.15, Lk 9.34, 11.39, Mt 23.26, Jn 20.11); 'under [a pot]' (Mt 5.15); la·múnkwe enkələk·í·i·xkána 'inside are the bones of the dead' (Mt 23.27); nə́ la·múnkwe 'the inside' (Lk 11.40).

la·ɔhti·- (-t-əla·ɔhti·-, e·la·ɔhti·-) AI — II 'be worth {so}, be valued {so}, cost {so}', 'amount to {so}'.
- la·ɔhti·- (AI): máta=háč .. la·ɔhti·í·ɔk 'are they (anim.) not worth [one cent]?' (Mt 10.29).
- -t-əla·ɔhti·-: é·li aləwí·i ktəla·ɔhtíhəmɔ 'as you (pl.) are worth more' (Mt 10.31; Gr. 3.15f); aləwí·i ktəla·ɔhti·ne·ɔ́·i·k čo·ləntət·ak 'you (pl.) are more highly valued than the little birds' (Lk 12.7; Gr. 4.45b).
- e·la·ɔhti·-: e·lá·ɔhti·t ná lə́nu 'the price ('value') of the man' (Mt 27.9).
- la·ɔhti·- (II): ná=nə lá·ɔhtu 'that's what it cost' (OA, checking ⟨Lawachto⟩ "worth, value" [B&A 61]); é·li- xí·nxke -lá·ɔhti·k 'for thirty dollars' (Jn 12.5).
- e·la·ɔhti·-: e·lá·ɔhti·k 'the amount or value of (so much)' (Lk 7.41, Jn 6.7, Mt 18.24, etc.), xé·li e·lá·ɔhti·k 'a large amount' (Mt 26.9); máta náxpəne kwə́t·i séns e·la·ɔhtí·k·i '(ones) that were not even worth one cent' (Mk 12.42).

la·phataw- TA+O 'restore O2 to' (Gr. 5.95c): é·li-la·phata·k·é·an 'because you (sg.) are paid back' (*lit.*, 'it will be restored to you') (Lk 14.14; KJV "recompensed").

la·pto·nahkat·- II 'be spoken {so}': la·pto·nahkát·o·p 'it has been said (that ..)' (Mt 5.31).

la·pto·na·l- (e·la·pto·na·l-, ehəla·pto·na·l- [Rih+; IC]) TA(+O) 'tell {so}'.
- e·la·pto·na·l-: e·la·pto·ná·lkuk 'what he (obv.) said to her' (Mk 16.10&); e·la·pto·ná·lian 'as you tell me to' (Lk 5.5); e·la·pto·na·liánəp 'what you told me' (Lk 2.29; Gr. 4.77c).
- ehəla·pto·na·l-: né·l a·pto·ná·k·anal ehəla·pto·nálle·kw 'the words I speak to you (pl.)' (Jn 14.10); nta·pto·ná·k·ana e·la·pto·nálle·kw 'my words that I have spoken to you' (Jn 15.3).

la·pto·ne·- (-t-əla·pto·ne·-, e·la·pto·ne·-, illa·pto·ne·- [Rī+]; cf. Gr. §5.4e) AI 'say, speak {so}': la·ptó·ne·p 'he said words' (Lk 1.24, 1.67, 2.28, 5.8).
- -t-əla·pto·ne·-: ntəla·pto·néhəna kéku 'we report things' (Jn 3.11).
- e·la·pto·ne·-: e·la·pto·né·a 'that I have spoken' (⟨rlaptwnreu⟩ Jn 12.48); e·la·pto·né·t·əp 'as he said' (Lk 1.70); e·la·ptó·nenk 'that was spoken' (Mk 1.1, Mk 5.36); e·la·pto·nénkəp 'what has been said' (Mt 5.27, 5.38, 5.43).
- illa·pto·ne·-: takó· háši awé·n tilla·pto·né·wən 'no one has ever spoken (that way)' (Jn 7.46).

la·p·ent- (-t-əla·p·ent-, e·la·p·ent-) TI(1a) 'benefit from': tə́li-=á· -káhta-la·p·entaməné·ɔ 'that they would want to make good use of it' (Mt 21.43).

- -tə·la·p·ent-: kéku=ksí=á· awé·n təla·p·éntamən 'what benefit would it then be to someone?' (Mt 16.26).
- e·la·p·ent-: e·la·p·éntaman 'that you (sg.) can make good use of' (1842:20.3).

la·p·e·mkwəs·i·- (-t-əla·p·e·mkwəs·i·-, e·la·p·e·mkwəs·i·-) AI — la·p·e·mkɔt- (e·la·p·e·mkɔt·-) II 'be useful {so}'.
- la·p·e·mkwəsi·- (AI): kéku=háč la·p·e·mkwə́s·u? 'What is it (a cat) useful for?' (1834a:14); takó·=á· kéku la·p·e·mkwəs·í·i 'he wouldn't be fit to do anything' (1842:19.5); kkát·a·=č kéku -la·p·e·mkwə́s·i 'you must have some useful ability ("be fit for something")' (OA).
- -tə·la·p·e·mkwəs·i·-: tá=á· kéku ktəla·p·e·mkwəs·í·i 'you (sg.) won't be fit to do anything' (1842:20.2).
- e·la·p·e·mkwəs·i·-: máta kéku e·la·p·e·mkwə́s·i·t '(who is) worthless' (Mt 25.30); takó· kéku e·la·p·e·mkwəs·í·č·i·k 'who are not good for anything' (Lk 17.10).
- la·p·e·mkɔt·- (II): la·p·é·mkɔt nə́ sí·khay 'salt is useful' (Mk 9.50, Lk 14.34); tá=á· la·p·e·mkɔt·ó·wi 'it would not be useful' (Lk 14.35).
- e·la·p·e·mkɔt-: e·la·p·é·mkɔ '(which is) useful' (1842:23.4).

la·s·o·wi·- AI 'sing {so}': la·s·ó·wi 'sing (you sg.)!' (1834b: back cover 1).

†lá·sələs 'Lazarus' (Lk 16.20, 16.24, etc.); †la·səlás·al (1834b:30.6), †la·səlás·a (Lk 16.23, Jn 11.5, 11.14, etc.).

la·š·í·mwi·- (-t-əla·š·í·mwi·-, e·la·š·í·mwi·-) AI 'dream {so}': lápi la·š·í·mu 'he has another dream (that ..)' (1842:13.3); nčó·səp la·š·í·mo·p 'Joseph dreamt (that ..)' (1842:13.2).
- -tə·la·š·í·mwi·-: šé· yú ntəla·š·í·mwi·n 'this is what I dreamt' (1842:13.4).
- e·la·š·í·mwi·-: e·la·š·í·mwia 'in my dream' (Mt 27.19); e·la·š·í·mwian 'your dream' (1842:14.2); é·li- nə́ -la·š·í·mwi·t 'because he dreamt that' (1842:13.5).

†lá·ta 'Lot (abs.)' (Lk 17.28, 17.29, 17.32).

la·wənəp·é·k·we (|-ənəpēkwē| 'lake'; Gr. 5.32d) P 'in the middle of the sea' (Lk 17.6; KJV "in the sea").

la·wə́nte (|-əntē| 'room, inside space of house'; Gr. 5.31l) P 'in the middle of the floor' (Jn 8.3, 8.9; KJV "in the midst"), 'in the middle of the room' (Jn 18.18& [L. "in the midst of the hall"], Mk 14.60).

la·wo·t·é·naye (|-ōtēnayē| 'town'; Gr. 5.32f) P 'in the middle of town' (⟨lawotrnyc⟩ Mt 6.2).

la·wsəwá·k·an (-t-əla·wsəwá·k·an) IN 'life'; wtəla·wsəwá·k·an 'his life' (B: Title Page).

la·wsi·- (e·la·wsi·-) AI 'live {so}': e·la·wsían 'how you live' (1834a:18.3).

lehəle·x·e·- AI 'be alive, live' (Gr. 5.38k): lehəlé·x·e· 'he is alive' (Jn 4.51, 1842:17.1, 18.2, etc.); é·li-lehəle·x·é·a 'because I live' (Jn 14.19); ki·ló·nə=á· lchəlc·x·e·ankwpáne 'if we (incl.) had been alive' (Mt 23.30; Gr. 4.74d); wə́nči-=č -lehəle·x·éhti·t aləwí·i 'so that they might have more life (*lit.*, live more)' (Jn 10.10); tɔ́li-lehəlé·x·e·n 'that he was alive' (Mk 16.11).
♦ Note: lehəle·x·e·- is a lexicalized reduplicated stem < |lēxē-| 'breathe', cf. ə́nta-léx·e·t 'when he would inhale' (OA; Gr. 5.38k).

lehəle·x·e·mha·l- TA 'bring back to life, save' (Gr. 5.84b): lehəle·x·e·mhá·la·=č 'he shall be restored to life' (Jn 10.9); lehəle·x·é·mha·l khák·ay 'save yourself (you sg.)' (Lk 23.37, 23.39); é·li- ki·š·e·ləmúk·ɔnkw -lehəle·x·e·mhá·lkɔnkw 'because Our Creator made us live' (1842:18.4); máta kóski-lehəle·x·e·mha·la·í·ɔ hókaya 'he cannot save himself' (Mt 27.42).

lehəle·x·e·mha·ltəwá·k·an (Gr. 5.114f) IN 'salvation' (Lk 19.9).

lehəle·x·e·mhe·- AI+O 'save, let live': awé·ni lehəle·x·é·mhe· 'he saves people' (Mt 27.42); lehəle·x·é·mhe·l 'let him live (you sg.)' (Mt 21.9 [2x], Mk 11.10, Mt 21.15), lehəle·x·é·mhe·l khák·ay 'save yourself' (Mk 15.30).

lehəle·x·e·ɔ́·k·an (Gr. 5.58a) IN 'life' (Jn 1.4, Mt 6.25, 10.39 [2x], etc.); lehəle·x·e·ɔ́·k·ana 'lives' (1834b:24.9); llehəle·x·e·ɔ́·k·an 'my life' (Jn 10.18); kəlehəle·x·e·ɔ́·k·an 'your (sg.) life' (1842:20.2); wəlehəle·x·e·ɔ́·k·an 'his life' (Jn 1.4, Mt 10.39, Jn 10.11, Mt 16.25 [2x], etc.); kəmáči-lehəle·x·e·ɔ·k·anúwa 'your (pl.) evil life (1834b:23.2).

lehələmatahpi·ᵒ: see ləmatahpi·-.

lelpi·-: see lhilpi·-.

le·- (e·le·-, ille·- [Rī+], |əlē-|) II 'be {so}, happen {so}, be done {so}': lé·w 'it happens {so}, comes to be {so}, is {so}, etc.' (Lk 1.38, 1.43, 1.45, Mt 7.17, etc.; 39x in B, V, OA; Gr. 4.21d), lé·w 'the truth is (that)' (Mt 23.20), lé· 'it happens {so}, etc.' (⟨lr⟩ 47x, ⟨lri⟩ Mt 6.3 [sbd.], Mt 12.45, Jn 9.30, Lk 18.31; V, OA, ME, LB); mé·či lé· 'it has already happened' (Jn 5.25), tá=háč lé· 'what happened?' (Jn 9.15), kéku=háč nə́ lé·w? 'what is that?' (perhaps 'what happens with that?') (Lk 6.34); aləwí·i-lé· 'it is more (than)' (Lk 12.23 2x), mé·či kíši-lé· 'it has been done' (Lk 14.22); lé·p 'it happened' (Mt 1.21, Lk 2.2); takó· háši lé·i·p 'it never happened' (Mt 9.33); énta=č wé·mi yó·ni -kíši-lé·k 'when all this shall have happened' (Lk 1.20); lé·k·eč 'let it be' (Mt 3.15, Lk 4.23, Mt 6.10, etc.; Gr. 4.114c).
• e·le·-: é·le·k 'that happened, what happened, etc.' (Lk 1.65, 2.15, Jn 1.28, etc.); e·lé·k·əp 'what happened' (Mk 6.52; Gr. 4.75x), '(how) it had been' (Mt 12.45), 'as it was' (Lk 17.28); e·lé·ksa 'what has happened' (1834a:18.7; Gr. §4.8).
• ille·-: máta ílle·k 'which has never been' (Mt 24.21; Gr. 5.44s).
♦ le·- with palí·i PV 'be destroyed': áhi-palí·i lé·w 'it was utterly destroyed' (Mt 7.27&).
♦ le·- with wəli PV 'be good, well, safe': wəli-=č -lé· 'it will be good' (Jn 11.12); ná ellí·i=á· wəli-lé·ɔ 'then both would be in good shape' (⟨lreo⟩ Lk 5.38; KJV "are preserved"); wəli-=á· -lé·lu 'it (obv.) would be safe' (Lk 11.21; Gr. 4.21f).

†lé·čəl 'Rachel' (Mt 2.18).

le·khamaw- (-t-əle·khamaw-, e·le·khamaw-) TA 'be owed money by, have a loan outstanding to (in Lk 7); owe money to, have a debt to (in Mt 18)'.
• -t-əle·khamaw-: təle·khamaɔ́·p·ani 'he was owed by him (obv.)' (Lk 7.41); təle·khamá·k·u 'he (obv.) owed him' (Mt 18.28).
• e·le·khamaw-: e·le·khamaɔ́·č·i 'his debtors (obv.)' (Lk 7.41); e·le·khamá·k·uk 'what he (obv.) owed him' (Mt 18.24); e·le·khamaían 'what you owe me' (Mt 18.28).
♦ Note: the meaning in Luke is the original one, literally 'write (it) down for', from the practice of fur-traders who would write down the price of the items supplied to hunters on credit.

le·khama·- AI 'owe money, have a debt': éntxi-le·khama·lí·č·i 'as many (obv.) as had debts' (Lk 16.5).

le·khamwe·ɔ́·k·an (-t-əle·khamwe·ɔ·k·an-, |əlēkahamwēwākan-|) IN 'debt'; LTD: "written matter; debt; indebtedness": ktəle·khamwe·ɔ́·k·an 'your debt' (Mt 18.32; Gr. 5.59i); təle·khamwe·ɔ́·k·an 'his debt' (Mt 18.30).

le·kha·s·i·- (e·le·kha·s·i·-) AI — II 'be written {so}'.
▪ le·kha·s·i·- (AI): e·le·kha·s·i·-: e·le·khá·s·i·t 'what is written in it (anim.)', *lit.*, 'how it (anim.) is written' (Jn 13.18). ► Cf. (in modern use) le·khá·s·u 'takes a picture' (V).
▪ le·kha·s·i·- (II): le·khá·s·u 'it is written' (Mt 4.4, 4.6, 4.10, Jn 8.17, etc.; Gr. 5.105d), ná=nə le·khá·s·u 'that is how it is written' (Jn 8.17); lí-núči-le·khá·s·o·p 'that it had been written before' (Jn 2.17 [/lí/ em.]); é·li- nəni -le·kha·sí·k·əp 'as that is what was written' (Jn 6.31).
• e·le·kha·s·i·-: e·le·khá·s·i·k 'that was written' (Lk 21.22, 22.37), 'as was written' (Mk 14.21), 'scripture' (Lk 4.21).

le·khí·k·an (-t-əle·khí·k·an-; Gr. 5.51c) AN 'book, scripture, paper, law, letter, etc.' (Jn 7.38, 7.42, 19.24; ME, FW, LB), ná xúwi-le·khí·k·an 'the ancient scripture' (Jn 10.35); xúwi-le·khí·k·anak 'the old writings' (Mk 12.24); le·khí·k·anal 'the book (obv.)' (Jn 2.22), le·khí·k·ana 'scriptures, writings' (Lk 4.16, Jn 7.15), 'a written document' (Mt 5.31), 'books' (Lk 10.25); le·khí·k·anink 'in the scriptures' (Jn 5.39), 'in the law' (Lk 10.26).
• -t-əle·khí·k·an-: ní· ná ntəle·khí·k·an 'that is my book' (LB); ktəle·khí·k·anink 'on your paper' (Lk 16.6, 16.7); ktəle·khi·k·anəwá·ink 'in your (pl.) law' (Jn 10.34; Gr. 3.13(3)d); təle·khí·k·anink 'in his writings' (Mk 12.26); təle·khi·k·anəwá·ink 'in their writings' (Jn 15.25).
♦ Also inan.: yú le·khí·k·an 'this book' (LTD ND 4x).
▪ le·khi·k·anət·ət (dim.) 'little book' (1834b:47.8); le·khi·k·anət·ət·a 'a document (obv.)' (Mt 19.7).
le·khi·k·aw-* (ehəle·khi·k·aw- [Rih+; IC]) TA 'write (things) for': ehəle·khi·k·á·kwki 'his bookkeeper' (*lit.*, 'the one [obv.] who wrote for him') (Mt 20.8; KJV "his steward").
le·khi·k·a·s·i·- (-t-əle·khi·k·a·s·i·-) AI 'write {so}': šé· yú təle·khi·k·a·s·i·né·ɔ·p 'this is what they have written' (Jn 6.45).
le·khi·k·e·- (-t-əle·khi·k·e·-, e·le·khi·k·e·-, ehəle·khi·k·e·- [Rih+; IC], |əlēkahīkē-|; Gr. 3.15h, 5.100e) AI 'write (things) {so}' (in one passage 'read'): le·khí·k·e·p 'he wrote' (Jn 8.6, 8.8, Mt 22.24&); énta-le·khí·k·e·t 'a place (for him) to write' (Lk 1.63); ikalíči le·khi·k·é·ane 'if you read further..' (1834a:16).
• -t-əle·khi·k·e·-: nəni e·le·khi·k·é·a ní· ntəle·khí·k·e·n '*I* wrote what *I* wrote' (Jn 19.22).
• e·le·khi·k·e·-: e·le·khi·k·é·t·əp 'what he wrote' (Jn 5.47, Lk 24.44); e·le·khi·k·ehtí·t·əp 'what they have written' (Lk 18.31, Mt 26.56).
• ehəle·khi·k·e·-: ehəle·khi·k·é·č·i·k 'scribes' (*lit.*, 'ones who write things habitually') (⟨rl-⟩ Mt 2.4, Lk 6.7, Mk 7.5, ⟨rvrl-⟩ Mt 5.20, Jn 8.3, ⟨rvl-⟩ Mt 7.29, Mk 7.1, etc.); ehəle·khi·k·e·lí·č·i 'scribe (obv.)' (Mt 8.19); ehəle·khi·k·e·tpanínka 'scribes (pret., abs.)' (Lk 15.2; cf. Gr. 4.75o).
le·khw- (-t-əle·khw-, e·le·khw-, |əlēkahw-|) TA — le·kh- (-t-əle·kh-) TI(1a) 'write, write about, write on'.
▪ le·khw- (TA): wénči-=č -lé·khunt wé·mi entxa·ké·i·t 'by which all nations were to be enrolled' (Lk 2.1).
• -t-əle·khw-: təle·khɔ·né·ɔ 'they wrote it ('the book' anim.) (sbd.)' (1842:[p. 2]).
• e·le·khw-: e·le·khɔ·tpáni 'which (obv.) he had written' (Lk 4.17); e·le·khɔhtí·t·əp 'the one that they wrote about' (Jn 1.45).
▪ le·kh- (TI): ní·š·a pakahsə́na lé·kham 'he wrote on two flat stones' (1842:10.6); táli-lé·kha 'write on (it, loc.) (you sg.)' (Lk 16.6, 16.7).
• -t-əle·kh-: ná wtəle·khámən 'then he wrote: ..' (Lk 1.63).
lé·k·aw 'sand' (ND); lé·k·unk (loc.) (OA; Gr. 2.22f).
le·k·o·wi·- II 'be sandy': énta-le·k·ó·wi·k 'in a sandy place' (Mt 7.26).
le·lá·i (Gr. 5.25f; ME) P 'in the middle' (⟨lrlyi⟩ Lk 5.19, Lk 6.8; ⟨lrlai⟩ Mt 18.2, 20.3, 20.5, Lk 21.21, 23.33&, Jn 20.26; KJV "in the midst" of them, of it); ahpá·mi le·lá·i lí·spíhəle· '(the sun) went about halfway up' (Mt 20.3); le·lá·i tə́nta·n sháki 'until it stood halfway (down)' (Mk 15.33&). ▶ Also le·lá·i and le·la·í·i (LB).
le·la·ihəla·- II 'be midway through': é·ləmi-le·la·ihəlá·k·e 'when [the feast] was midway through' (Jn 7.14).
le·ləm- (-t-əle·ləm-, e·le·ləm-) TA 'think of {so}, allow (to)' — le·lənt- TI(1a) 'think {so}'.

- le·lǝm- (TA): lé·lǝm 'let them (you sg.)' (Mt 8.22); lé·lǝmo· 'consider him (you pl.)' (Lk 22.26); lé·lǝmi·l 'think of me (you sg.)' (Lk 15.19), lé·lǝmi·l 'let me' (Lk 2.29; Gr. 4.105e); kšínki-lé·lǝmi 'you refused to let me' (Lk 13.34, Mt 23.37); ktǝ́li-=č -le·lǝmǝk·e·né·ɔ 'so that you (pl.) will be allowed' (Lk 21.36).
  - -t-ǝle·lǝm-: máta kéku ntǝle·lǝmá·i nahkɔ́·i lǝ́nu 'I have no special regard for (*lit.*, have no thought for) any man' (Lk 18.4); máta awé·n kéku ktǝle·lǝmá·i 'you have no special regard for anyone' (Mt 22.16); é·li máta kéku tǝle·lǝma·í·ɔ mekí·s·a 'as he has no thought for the sheep' (Jn 10.13); tǝle·lǝmawwá·p·ani 'they wondered about him' (Lk 3.15).
  - e·le·lǝm-: e·lé·lǝmat 'the way you (sg.) think of them' (Lk 15.19); e·le·lǝmíenk '(as) you think of us' (Mt 20.12).
- le·lǝnt- (TI): é·li-kwí·la-le·lǝntamíhti·t 'as they couldn't imagine' (Jn 13.22); né·li-kwí·la-le·lǝntamíhti·t 'while they were wondering what was going on' (Lk 24.4).
  - -t-ǝle·lǝnt-: tɔ·pto·na·k·anúwa tǝle·lǝntamǝ́li·n 'they (obv.) thought their account to be {so}' (Lk 24.11).
- le·lǝnti·- AI (recip.) 'think {so} of each other': kxántki=á· kwǝt·ennáɔhki wé·mi le·lǝ́ntu 'eventually they (representative singular) would all think of each other as of one kind' (1834b:44.11).

le·lǝmukwsi·- (-t-ǝle·lǝmukwsi·-, e·le·lǝmukwsi·-, |ǝlēlǝmǝkwǝsī-|) AI 'be regarded {so}': le·lǝmúkwsu=č 'he shall be honored' (Lk 2.23).
  - -t-ǝle·lǝmukwsi·-: ná=tá=nǝ́ ntǝle·lǝmúkwsi·n ní· 'that's how *I* was created to be' (Gr. 4.42d).
  - e·le·lǝmukwsi·-: e·le·lǝmúkwsi·t 'how he was regarded' (Mt 14.1), "what his status was" (LTD ND).

le·lǝnta·s·i·- II 'be thought {so}': khwíta-le·lǝntá·s·u 'there is concern (*lit.*, "fear")' (1834a:16).

le·linke·- (-t-ǝle·linke·-) AI 'allow, permit (people)': ktǝle·línke·n=č tɔ́nkǝlǝn 'you (pl.) shall let him die' (Mt 15.4).

le·nhaw- (e·le·nhaw-) TA 'pay {so}': e·le·nha·k·é·e·kw 'what you are paid' (Lk 3.14).

le·p·ɔ·-: see lǝpɔ·-.

le·x·a·l- TA 'breathe on' (Gr. 5.88c): wǝle·x·a·lá·ɔ 'he breathed on them' (Jn 20.22).

le·x·e·-: see lehǝle·x·e·-.

lǝč·e·n-* (-t-ǝlčen-) TI(1b) 'roll {so}': palí·i tǝlčé·nǝmǝn nǝ́ni xínkɔhsǝn 'He rolled the large stone away' (1834b:37.1).

lǝč·e·nihi·- (-t-ǝlče·nihi·-) AI+O 'roll O2 {so}': palí·i tǝlče·níhi·n nǝ́ ahsǝ́n 'he rolled the stone away' (Mt 28.2).

lǝkhik(w)- 'to {such} an extent, {so} much' (-ǝlki·k(w)-, |ǝlǝkihkw-|; Gr. 2.42a).

lǝkhikhɔkami·k·e·- (e·lki·khɔkami·k·e·-, |ǝlǝkihkwahkamīkē-|; Gr. 5.7b) II 'be earth extending {so far}': wé·mi .. e·lki·khɔkamí·k·e·k 'the whole wide world' (Mk 13.27, Mk 15.33&, Mt 28.19& [em.]).

lǝkhikɔ·lahkihǝla·- II 'become a hole extending {so far}': alǝwí·i=á· lǝkhikɔ·lahkíhǝle· 'the hole might become bigger' (Mk 2.21).

lǝkhíkwi (-t-ǝlkí·kwi, e·lkí·kwi, ehǝlǝkhíkwi [Rih+; IC], illǝkhíkwi [Rī+]; Gr. 2.42a, 5.28f, 5.43i, 5.128m) PV '{so} much, to {such} extent, at {such} time' (Lk 1.58, 2.52, 3.23, 4.5, etc.).
  - -t-ǝlkí·kwi: ktǝlkí·kwi-ahɔllǝné·ɔ 'I love you (pl.) (that) much' (Jn 15.9); ná=hánkw ɔ́·k nǝ́ .. tǝlkí·kwi-wǝle·lǝntamǝné·ɔ 'that is also how much they rejoice' (Lk 15.10); pǝnó· tǝlkí·kwi-ahɔ́·la·n 'see how much he loved him' (Jn 11.36); tǝlkí·kwi- šá·e -ká·xksi·n 'how quickly it (anim.) has dried up' (Mt 21.20; PV modifies P).

• e·lkí·kwi: e·lkí·kwi-ahó·li·t 'as much as he loves me' (Jn 15.9); e·lkí·kwi-ləs·íhti·t 'how much they do' (Lk 22.25); e·lkí·kwi-ma·ehá·s·i·k 'in the same way that they are gathered' (Mt 13.40; KJV "As .."); e·lkí·kwi- .. e·ləwé·t·əp (s.b. e·lkí·kwi- .. -ləwé·t·əp) 'the time when he had said ..' (Jn 4.53).
• ne·lkí·kwi- (nə + e·lkí·kwi-; Gr. 4.60) 'as much as' (1834a:18.1).
• ehələkhíkwi: 'at the times when' (Jn 5.4), 'whenever' (Mk 9.49), 'as much as' (Lk 17.24).
• illəkhíkwi: illəkhíkwi-ahɔ·lá·t·əp 'as much as he had loved them' (Jn 13.1); máta tilləkhíkwi-ɔwəlahkɔnk·ó·wəne·p 'he was never clothed as beautifully (as ..)' (Mt 6.29); takó· tilləkhíkwi-ɔwəlahkwí·wəne·p 'he was never dressed so well' (Lk 12.27).
▪ ləkhíkwi P: néke ləkhíkwi 'at that time' (Lk 1.5, Mt 2.1, etc.); pe·č·íhəle·=č ləkhíkwi 'the time will come (that ..)' (Jn 4.23).
▪ e·lkí·kwi P (with IC): '(than) the extent of (that of)' (Mt 5.20; an adjunct phrase); e·lkí·kwi mé·k·əni-kí·škwi·k 'at the time of the last day' (Mt 12.36).

ləkhikwi·t- TI(2) 'make {so} big': ntánči-=č -ləkhikwí·to·n 'I'll build it bigger' (Lk 12.18).

ləkhikwi·xə·n- (e·lki·kwi·x·ən-) II 'be {so much}': nə e·lki·kwí·x·ink nəni mi·kəmɔ·s·əwá·k·an 'the extent of that work' (1834a:17).

lək·i·l- (e·lki·l-) AI 'have a body {so} big' (Gr. 5.11l): ihikalíči ləkhíkwi- .. -lək·i·l 'he gradually became taller' (Lk 2.52): aləwí·i e·lkí·lək '(who is) greater' (Mt 12.6); məsəč·é·i e·lkí·lək 'all over his body' (Lk 16.20).

ləmatahpi·- (-ləmahtap·i·- ~ -ləmatahpi·-, le·mahtap·i·- ~ le·matahpi·-, -lihələmatahpi·- [Rih+], lehələmatahpi·- [Rih+; IC], |ləmatapī-|; Gr. 4.67u) AI 'sit down': ləmátahpu 'he sits down'; íka=č wíči-ləmatahpúwak 'they shall sit down together there' (Lk 13.29); ləmatahpó·p·ani·k 'they were sitting' (Lk 10.13, Mt 20.30&, etc.; Gr. 4.68i); šá·e ləmátahpi 'sit down quickly (you sg.)' (Lk 16.6, 16.7).
• -ləmahtap·i·- (⟨-lumuvtupen(-)⟩ 6x): ná nčí·sas wələmahtáp·i·n 'then Jesus sat down' (Lk 5.3; Gr. 4.42s); nə=č wələmahtáp·i·n 'he shall sit there' (⟨wulumutupen⟩ Mt 25.31); wələmahtáp·i·n (⟨wlumuvtupen⟩ Jn 20.12) 'he sat (where ..)'; wələmahtap·i·né·ɔ 'they sat down (sbd.)' (Jn 6.10).
• -ləmatahpi·-: nləmátahpi 'I sat down' (Gr. 2.69b).
• le·mahtap·i·-: le·mahtap·iáne 'when you were sitting' (Jn 1.48); le·mahtáp·i·t 'who was sitting there' (Mk 5.15, 14.62, Mk 16.5).
• le·matahpi·-: le·mátahpi·t '(who was) sitting' (Lk 2.46); le·matahpí·t·e 'when he sat down' (Jn 8.2); le·matahpihtí·t·e 'when they sat down' (Lk 22.55; KJV "And when they .. were set down together").
• -lihələmatahpi·-: náni wəlihəlmátahpi·n 'that's where he always sat' (ME).
• lehələmatahpi·-: wá lehələmátahpi·t 'the one that used to sit' (Jn 9.8); lehələmatahpí·li·t 'their (obv.) accustomed seats' (Lk 1.52).
▶ For the paradigmatic leveling in the internal syllables, see Gr. §2.14 and examples in Gr. 2.69ab; also Goddard (2019: 93, ex. 6a).
▪ lehələmátahpink 'seat' (lit., 'where one customarily sits'; Gr. 4.67(3)u; Lk 11.43, 14.8, etc.), a lexicalized participle: sa·k·i·ma·í·i-lehələmatahpínkink 'on thrones' (Lk 22.30); wəlehələmatahpínkəm 'his seat, throne' (Mt 5.34, 23.2, 23.22); wəlehələmatahpinkəməwá·ɔ 'their seats' (Mk 11.15).

lən- (-t-ənn-, enn-, ihələn- [Rih+], ehələn- [Rih+; IC], |ələn-|; Gr. 4.50o, 5.41) TA — TI(1b) 'do {so}'; with palí·i PV 'away': 'remove'.

- lən- (TA): palí·i ləní·l 'remove me' (Jn 12.27; KJV "save me"); palí·i ləní·ne·n 'remove us' (Mt 6.13, Lk 11.4; KJV "deliver us").
- lən- (TI): palí·i ləni 'remove it (you sg.)' (Lk 6.42); palí·i lənəmo·kw yú ahsən 'take away this stone (you pl.)' (Jn 11.39); éši=č nə́ -lənəme·kw 'whenever you (pl.) do that' (1 Cor 11.25).
  • -t-ənn-: tənnə́mən 'he did it' (Jn 9.26; Gr. 2.60d), tá=háč tənnə́mən 'what did he do?' (Jn 9.26; Gr. 4.44c); tá=háč=á· ktənnəməné·ɔ 'what would you (pl.) do?' (Mt 23.33; Gr. 4.44e);.
  • enn-: ennə́ma=č 'what I shall do' (Lk 16.4); énnink=á· 'what he could do' (Lk 22.6; Gr. 2.14b); ennínkəp 'what he did' (Lk 9.54; Gr. 4.78j); palí·i ennínke 'when it was removed' (Lk 1.25); ennəmíhti·t=č 'what they would do' (Jn 6.6; Gr. 4.67(1)f).
  • ihələn-: ná=ni tihəlнəmən we·ɔ́·psi·t 'that is what the whiteman does' (1834b:45.4); nə́ni=č ktihələnəməné·ɔ 'that's what you must always do' (Lk 22.19, 1 Cor 11.25).
  • ehələn-: ehələnəmíhti·t 'what they do' (⟨rlunumevtet⟩ Jn 19.40); ehələnəmihtí·t·əp 'the way they used to do it' (⟨rvrlinumevtetup⟩ Jn 2.6; Gr. 4.78r).

lənaha·ɔn-* (-t-ənna·ha·ɔn-) IN 'right hand': cf. ⟨Leñahawan⟩, loc. ⟨lennaháwanünk⟩ (Z. 89).
  • -t-ənna·ha·ɔn-: ntənna·há·ɔnink 'on my right hand' (Mk 10.40, 12.36, 14.62); ktənna·há·ɔnink 'on your (sg.) right hand' (Mk 10.37); wtənna·há·ɔnink 'on the right side' (Lk 1.11; Gr. 2.61c), tənna·há·ɔnink 'on his right' (Mt 25.33, 25.34, Mk 16.19&; Gr. 2.60e); wtənna·ha·ɔní·li·t 'on his (obv.) right side' (Jn 18.10, Lk 23.33&; Gr. 2.61c); ktənna·ha·ɔnəwá·ink 'on your (pl.) right side' (Jn 21.6).
  - ləne·ha·ɔn-* (-t-ənne·ha·ɔn-) 'right hand': ktənne·há·ɔn 'your right hand' (Mt 5.30, Mt 6.3); wtənne·há·ɔn 'his right hand' (Lk 6.6); wtənne·ha·ɔnəwá·ink 'to their right' (Mk 16.5).
  ▶ Cf. Mun ntəlne·há·wan 'my right hand' (APh, RS, JN (/lə̃n/)]; MH, MEP).

ləná·p·e (-t-ənna·p·e·yəm-; Gr. 5.9f) AN 'Delaware, person': 'a Delaware' (1834a:20.30), 'the Delaware (people)' (1834a:19.17); ləna·p·é·ɔk 'The Delawares' (1834a:18.13); lena·p·é·ɔ 'people (obv.)' (Jn 7.12).
  • -t-ənna·p·e·yəm-: ntənna·p·é·yəmak 'my people' (Mt 2.6; Gr. 2.61d); wtənna·p·é·yəmal 'his people' (Mt 1.21, Lk 1.68, etc.; Gr. 2.61d), wtənna·p·é·yəma (Lk 7.16, Jn 11.50).
  - lena·p·e·í·i PN '(of) Delaware': lena·p·e·í·i-lekhí·k·an 'a Delaware book' (1834a: Cover; 1834b:1.1).

lena·p·e·ɔ́·k·an (-t-ənna·p·e·ɔ·k·an-; Gr. 5.58r) AN 'soul, spirit' (Mt 26.41).
  • -t-ənna·p·e·ɔ·k·an-: ntənna·p·e·ɔ́·k·an 'my soul' (Lk 12.19, Mt 26.38); ktənna·p·e·ɔ́·k·an 'your soul' (Lk 12.20); ktənna·p·e·ɔ́·k·anink 'your soul (loc.)' (Lk 10.27, Mk 12.30); tənna·p·e·ɔ́·k·anink 'his soul (loc.)' (Mk 12.33; Gr. 2.60f); ktənna·p·e·ɔ·k·anúwa 'your (pl.) soul (sg.)' (Lk 21.19; KJV "your souls"), for 'your souls'.

ləna·s·i·- (enna·s·i·-) II 'be done': ennás·i·k=á· 'what would be done' (1834b:14.11).

ləne·ha·ɔn-*: see ləna·ha·ɔn-*.

lənəmaw- (-t-ənnəmaw-) TA+O 'move, hand, put, offer O2 to or for': palí·i lənəmái·l yú páint 'remove this cup from me (you sg.)' (*lit.*, 'move this cup away for me') (Mk 14.36).
  • -t-ənnəmaw-: íka tənnəmaɔ́·ɔ 'he reached some (up) to him' (Mt 27.48); sí·sku íka ntənnəmá·k·əp nəškínkunk 'he put clay on my eyes' (Jn 9.15); íka tənnəmaɔ·né·ɔ 'they reached it (up) to him' (Lk 23.36); awé·n=č=háč .. palí·i ktənnəma·k·ó·ne·n 'who will move it away for us?' (Mk 16.3).

lənəwi·- AI 'be a man': énta- mé·či -lənəwi·t 'after he had become a man' (WL; V /uw/); wínki- amánki-lənəwíhti·t '(that) they like to be big men' (1834a:18.5). ▶ Cf. lə́nu.

ləní·i (Gr. 5.121a) P 'ordinarily' (Jn 8.15), 'in the ordinary way' (Jn 11.13).

- ləní·i PN 'ordinary': ləní·i-o·t·é·nink 'an ordinary town (loc.)' (Mt 10.11); ləní·i-lə́nu 'an ordinary man' (Jn 10.33).

ləni·xsəwá·k·an IN 'Delaware' (*lit.*, 'ordinary language'); áləmi-ləni·xsəwá·k·an 'Beginning Delaware' (1834a:3; not idiomatic for what was presumably this intended meaning).

ləni·xsi·- (alləni·xsi·- [ày+], |ələnīxəsī-|) AI 'speak Delaware' (*lit.*, 'speak normally'): énta-ləní·xsink 'in(to) the Delaware language' (B: Title Page, Mk 15.34).
- alləni·xsi·-: alləní·xsu 'he or she speaks Delaware' (V, AD, OA; Gr. 5.37d).

lə́nu (Gr. 2.10g, 2.26a, 3.1a, 3.6a, 5.5i) AN 'man' (Lk 1.34, 2.25, Jn 1.51, etc.), 'men (object, indefinite)' (Lk 5.10); lə́nəwak 'men' (Lk 5.18&, Mk 5.35, Mt 9.27, etc.; Gr. 3.6a); lə́nəwal 'men (obv.)' (Lk 1.27, Mk 14.43&), lə́nəwa 'man (obv.)' (Jn 2.9, Lk 8.35, etc.), 'men (obv.)' (Mk 5.1&, Mt 15.9); lə́nəwa 'a man of old' (Mk 13.34); ní·š·a lənúnka 'two departed men' (Mt 17.3, Lk 9.32; Gr. 2.19i); wə́nči lənunk 'out of the man' (Mk 5.13).

ləpak- AI 'weep' (Gr. 5.1b): ləpákw 'he wept' (Lk 7.38, Jn 11.35, Lk 19.41); kələpahkúhəmɔ=č 'you (pl.) shall weep' (Lk 6.25, Jn 16.20; Gr. 4.21j); áhi-ləpák·o·k 'they wept loudly' (Mk 5.38; Gr. 4.21q); káči ləpákhan 'do not weep (you sg.)' (Lk 7.13; Gr. 4.110b); kéku=háč wénči-ləpák·an 'why are you (sg.) weeping?' (Jn 20.13), kɔ́č=háč ləpák·an (Jn 20.15; Gr. 4.60b); né·li-ləpák·ək 'as she wept' (Jn 20.11); tə́li-ləpák·əli·n 'that she (obv.) was weeping' (Jn 11.33).
- ləpakhati·- AI (coll.; Gr. 5.75f): énta=č -ləpakhátink 'where there shall be much weeping' (Mt 25.30); ná tə́ləmi-ləpakhati·né·ɔ 'then they all began weeping' (1842:17.1).

ləpak·i·taw- (-ləpahkí·taw-) TA 'weep in addressing oneself to': é·li- .. -mái-ləpak·i·taɔ́·t·əp 'as she came and wept before him' (Mt 15.22); é·li-ləpak·i·tá·k·uk 'for she (obv.) was weeping before him' (Mk 15.23).
- -ləpahkí·taw-: ná wələpahkí·taɔ·n 'then he wept (to him)' (Lk 16.24); ná .. wələpahki·tá·k·o·n 'then he (obv.) wept before him' (Mk 9.24).

ləpɔ·- (le·p·ɔ·-) AI 'be wise': ləpwé· 'he is a wise (one), is smart' (Mt 24.45, 1842:23.1); ihikalíči ləkhíkwi-ləpwé·p 'he gradually became wiser' (Lk 2.52); ləpɔ́·kw 'be wise (you pl.)' (Mt 10.16); é·li-ləpɔ́·t 'because he was wise' (Mt 22.33).
- le·p·ɔ·-: le·p·ɔ́·e·kw 'you (pl.) wise ones' (Lk 11.44, Mt 23.13, etc.; Gr. 4.66c); éntxi-ləpɔ́·č·i·k 'all who are wise' (Lk 7.35; Gr. 4.67(4)w).

†ləpohəla·- AI 'become smart': mé·či=hánkw †ləpohəlá·t·e 'if he was already becoming smart' (⟨lipolati⟩ 1834b:10.16). A conjecture; no other example.

ləpwe·-: see ləpɔ·-.

ləpwe·e·lənsi·- AI 'think oneself wise': ləpwe·e·lənsí·č·i·k 'those that think they are wise' (Mt 11.25; KJV "prudent").

ləpwe·innəwi·- AI 'be a wise man': ləpwe·innəwí·t·e=hánkw awé·n 'if someone is a wise man' (1834b:11.10); wénči-ləpwe·innəwíhti·t 'because they are wise men' (1834b:5.6).

ləpwe·ínnu AN 'wise man' (Lk 11.45), áhi-ləpwe·ínnu 'a very wise man' (Mt 22.35); ləpwe·innúwak 'wise men' (Mt 2.1, Lk 11.46 [voc.], 11.52 [voc.], etc.); ləpwe·innúwal 'wise men (obv.)' (Mt 2.7, 2.16 [2x]), ləpwe·innúwa 'the learned men (obv.)' (Lk 14.3).

ləpwe·ɔ́·k·an IN 'wisdom' (Lk 7.35, Mt 13.56, Lk 21.15, 1842:19.3); wələp·we·ɔ́·k·an 'his wisdom' (Mt 12.42, 13.54); wələp·we·ɔ·k·anəwá·unk 'to their wisdom' (Lk 1.17).
- ləpwe·ɔ·k·aní·i (Gr. 5.122c) PN 'of wisdom' (Lk 11.52: KJV "of knowledge").

ləskamaw- TA+O 'drive O2 {so} from': mé·či palí·i ləskamúnte 'after he had been driven away from him' (Mt 9.33). See next.

ləskaw- (-t-əlskaw-, e·lskaw-, |ələskaw-|) TA 'send {so}, drive {so}': íkali lə́skaw 'send her away (you sg.)' (Mt 15.23); tɔ́lxi- palí·i -ləskaɔ́·ɔl 'he sent them away empty' (Lk 1.53).
  • -t-əlskaw-: palí·i təlskaɔwwá·ɔ 'they drove him away' (Lk 20.10&; Gr. 2.22c); palí·i=č ktəlska·k·əwá·ɔk 'they will drive you away' (Jn 16.2; Gr. 4.27q); palí·i ktəlska·k·éhəmɔ 'you (pl.) are driven away' (Lk 13.28; Gr. 2.22c, 4.29f).
  • e·lskaw-: mé·či wé·mi kɔ́čəmink e·lskaɔ́·t·e 'after he had shown them all out' (Mk 5.40).
ləstaw- (e·lsət·aw-, ehələstaw- [Rih+; IC], |ələsətaw-|) TA 'hear to say {so}' — ləst- (e·lsət·-, ihələst- [Rih+], |ələsət-|) TI(1a) 'hear {so}' (Gr. 5.12bb).
  ▪ ləstaw- (TA): wé·mi éntxi-ləstáɔk nó·x 'everything I heard from my father' (Jn 15.15); né·li- nə́ -ləstaɔ́hti·t 'as they listened to him' (Lk 19.11).
  • e·lsət·aw-: †páilat nə́ e·lsət·aɔ́·t·e 'when Pilate heard that from him' (Jn 19.13); nə́ e·lsət·aɔhtí·t·e 'when they heard him say that' (Lk 22.5).
  • ehələstaw-: ehələstáɔ·t 'what he always hears them say' (1834a:18.7).
  ▪ ləst- (TI): wénči- nə́ -ləstáma 'the reason I hear that' (Lk 16.2).
  • e·lsət·-: nə́ e·lsət·ánke 'when he heard that' (Mt 19.22&, Jn 19.8, 21.7).
  • ihələst-: xe·lennáɔhki kéku tihələstəməné·p·ani 'he had been hearing many different things' (Lk 23.8).
ləs·əwá·k·an (-t-əlsəwa·k·an-) IN 'power' (Lk 4.6, Jn 2.11); xínkwi-ləs·əwá·k·an 'the great power' (Mk 14.62).
  • -t-əlsəwa·k·an-: ntəlsəwá·k·an 'my doing' (Mt 10.22), 'my deeds' (Mk 9.41), 'my power' (Jn 15.16, Mk 16.17), wə́nči ntəlsəwá·k·an 'on my behalf, acting for me' (Mt 18.5, 18, 20, Mk 9.39); ktəlsəwá·k·an 'your power' (Mt 6.13, Mt 7.22 [3x], Jn 17.6, etc.); wtəlsəwá·k·an 'his power(s)' (Jn 2.23, Lk 5.17, Mt 12.21); wə́nči təlsəwá·k·an 'acting for him' (Mt 21.9&; KJV "in the name of"); təlsəwa·k·aní·li·t 'his (obv.) power' (Mt 16.27); ntəlsəwá·k·anink 'acting for me' *lit.*, 'in my power' (Mt 24.5, Jn 14.26); ktəlsəwá·k·anink 'acting for you' (Jn 17.12; KJV "in thy name"); təlsəwá·k·anink 'acting for him', *lit.*, 'in his power' (Lk 1.17, KJV "in the spirit and power of"; Mt 28.19, KJV "in the name of").
ləsi·- (-t-əlsi·-, e·lsi·-, ehələs·i·- [Rih+; IC]) AI 'do {so}, be {so}': máta=č ləs·i·ɔ́·ne 'if I don't do (it)' (Jn 10.37; Gr. 4.95c); máta ləs·i·ɔ́·p·ane 'if I had not done (it)' (Jn 15.24; Gr. 4.95f); ɔ́·k ná=nə́ ləs·í·t·e 'and if that is what he does' (Jn 14.21; Gr. 3.13(1)d, 4.63g); máta nə́ ləs·í·t·e '(if he) does not act accordingly', *lit.*, 'if he does not do that' (Mt 7.26); šúkw máta nə́ni ləs·í·t·e 'but (he) does not do it', *lit.*, 'but if he doesn't do that' (Lk 12.47); mé·či ná=nə ləs·í·t·e 'after he had done that' (Lk 5.6; no IC); é·li .. máta nə́ -lə́s·i·t 'as he did not do that' (Mk 1.22); nə́ni=á·=máh ləs·ie·kwpáne 'if you (pl.) had done that' (Mt 23.23; Gr. 4.74e); yú ləs·í·l 'do this (you sg.)' (Lk 7.8); pehpa·tamáɔ·t .. ɔ́·k lə́s·i·t e·li·t·é·ha·t 'who prays to him and does what he wants done' (Jn 9.31; with IC gapped).
  • -t-əlsi·-: ná=nə́ ntə́lsi·n 'that's what I am' (Jn 13.13; Gr. 4.42c), 'I'll do that.' (Mt 21.30), ná=č nə́ ntə́lsi·n. 'That's what I will do.' (Jn 14.14), tá=č=háč=ét ntə́lsi·n? 'What shall I do?' (Lk 16.3; cf. Mk 12.6&); čí·č kwət·ennáɔhki né·ləma ktəlsí·i 'there is still one thing you have not yet done' (Lk.18.22); tá=háč wtə́lsi·n=č 'what will he do?' (Lk 1.66; Gr. 4.42o).
  • e·lsi·-: wé·mi kéku e·lsía 'everything I have done' (Jn 4.29); nə́ni e·lsí·t·e 'when he did that' (Mk 1.27), 'when he does that' (Mt 23.15); yó·k e·lsí·č·i·k 'those that do (it)' (Mt 7.21); nə́ni e·lsí·č·i·k 'ones like that' (Mk 10.14; Gr. 3.13(1)e).
  • ehələs·i·-: ehələs·í·li·t 'what he (obv.) does' (Jn 5.19); lə́nəwak ehələs·íhti·t 'as men do' (Lk 12.36).

♦ AI (with a preverb or particle as a complement; Gr. §5.9b, 5.129h) 'be': pahkánči-lə́s·i·kw 'be perfect (you pl.)' (Mt 5.48); aləwí·i-lə́s·u 'he is greater' (Lk 3.16, Jn 3.31 [2x], Lk 7.27, Mt 12.12, Lk 22.27); takó· tɔləwí·i-ləs·í·wəna 'he is not more than him' (Mt 10.24; also the same with -ləs·í·wən); máta=háč ktaləwí·i-ləs·i·wəne·ó·i·k čo·lə́nsak? 'Are you not superior to the birds?' (Lk 12.24; cf. Gr. 3.15); kwí·la-lə́s·əwak 'they were at a loss' (Lk 14.6, Mt 19.12 [3x]); máta mayá·i-ləs·ié·k·we 'if you do not do right' (Lk 16.11; or -ləs·i·é·k·we if the negative inflection was distinct); tá=á· nəmax·ínkwi-ləs·í·i 'I would not be great' (Jn 8.54); é·li-wə́li-ləs·i·lí·t·əp 'as he (obv.) was a kind man' (Mt 1.19); me·x·ínkwi-lə́s·i·t 'the mighty one' (Lk 1.49, 1.76); nuntá·i e·lsí·li·t 'who is lowly (obv.)' (Lk 1.48; obv. ppl. [cf. Gr. 4.65l]); méči-lə́s·i·t 'an evil man' (Mt 12.35); etc.

ləs·i·t·e·x·i·n-* (e·lsi·t·e·x·i·n-, |ələsītēxīn-|; Gr. 5.21c) AI 'have feet {so}': e·lsi·t·é·x·ink 'at his feet' (Lk 10.39); e·lsi·t·e·x·i·nəlí·t·əp 'where his (obv.) feet had been' (Jn 20.12).

ləš·i·mwi·- (|ələšīmwī-|) AI 'flee to {smwh}': o·t·é·nink ləš·í·məwak 'they fled to the town' (Lk 8.34&); ləš·í·mwi·kw 'flee to {smwh} (you pl.)' (Mt 2.13); palí·i ləš·í·mwi·mɔ́·e '(then) flee away (you pl.)' (Mt 10.23); ləš·i·mwí·t·eč 'let him flee to {smwh}' (Mt 24.16).

lə́t·əwak etc.: see lət·i·- under l- TA 'say {so} to'.

lət·o·nhe·- (e·lto·nhe·-, ehələt·o·nhe·- [Rih+; IC], allət·o·nhe·- [ày+], |ələtōnahē-|) AI 'talk {so}': ə́nta- nə́ -lət·ó·nhe·t 'when he talks that way' (LTD ND).
  • e·lto·nhe·-: e·lto·nhé·a· 'what I'm talking about' (OA).
  • ehələt·o·nhe·-: ehələt·o·nhé·t·əp 'how he used to talk' (1834a:23.54).
  • allət·o·nhe·-: allət·ó·nhe·t 'his preaching' (Jn 18.19: KJV "his doctrine").

lhilpi·- (-lilpi·-, lelpi·-, |ləhləpī-|) AI 'be willing': lhílpu 'he's active, industrious, (horse) is frisky' (OA, ME), 1s nlílpi, llílpi.
  • lelpi·-: lelpía 'what I please' (Mt 20.15; KJV "what I will" [idiomatic?]); yó·ki lelpí·č·i·k 'these industrious ones' (1834a:17).
  ▶ Cf. Mun líhlpəw 'he's willing' (APh, MR).

lí (1) PV (-əli, é·li, íhəli [Rih+], éhəli [Rih+; IC]; Gr. 3.13(1), 5.43j, Gr. 5.128n) 'to, into, on {smwh}', '{so}'.
  • lí: ɔhčúnk pe·mi·khátink lí-pəntákɔhto·p 'in the hill country (it) was heard' (Mt 2.18); hók·enk lí-naóhəle·p 'he landed on him' (Jn 1.32); mux·ó·link lí-po·s·ó·p·ani·k 'they got aboard a boat' (Mk 4.36); é·li- nčí·sas -lí-lúk·wenk. 'Because Jesus told us to.' (Mk 11.6); kót·a- nə́ -lí-lehəlé·x·e·n 'he wants to live that way' (Lk 16.16); nə́ táli takó· xé·li lí-kanšaehɔ·s·í·i 'he did not do many miracles' (Mt 13.58);
  • -əli (with pronominal prefixes): †i·číptink ntəli-wenčí·ma·p 'I have called him out of Egypt' (Mt 2.15); ná nčí·sas íka təli-təmí·k·e·n †nči·lo·sələ́mink 'then Jesus entered Jerusalem' (Mk 11.11); mpínk ktəli-čhɔ́·pwənəl 'I baptize you (sg.) in water' (Lk 3.16); nə́ni=č ktəli-mí·lke·n. 'That is how it will be given to you.' (Lk 6.38); ná nčí·sas mux·ó·link təli-pó·s·i·n 'then Jesus got into a boat' (Lk 5.3); kí·xki wsí·t·ink təli-ní·p·ai·n 'and she went and stood near his feet' (Lk 7.38).
  ♦ In the subordinative complement of a question word: awé·n təli- íka -alə́namən é·k·wia? 'Who was it that touched my clothes?' (Mk 5.30); čínke=háč ktəli-kahto·p·wí·ne·p ..? 'When was it that you were you hungry?' (Mt 25.37); additional examples in Mt 25.37, 25.38, 25.44, 27.17.
  • é·li-: é·li-li·x·əmúkwsi·t 'according to his appointment' (Lk 1.9); é·li-pə́ntama·t 'how he understood' (Lk 2.47); é·li-lə́lan '(the fact) that I tell you' (Jn 3.7). ♦ May be gapped: Mt 2.13, Mt 5.17, Mt 7.13, Mk 14.40, etc. ♦ Repeated redundantly in Lk 12.54.

- íhəli: mpínk ntíhəli-čhɔ·pwənúwe 'I baptize people in water' (Jn 1.26).
- ehəli: íka ehəli-šuhəmaɔ́·t·əp wsi·t·í·li·t 'that she had been rubbing on his (obv.) feet' (Jn 11.2); éhəli-wsí·ka·k 'west' (*lit.*, 'whither the sun sets') (Lk 12.54, 13.29, Mt 24.27).
- ♦ (idiom) é·lí- PV (in changed conjunct verb; Gr. 5.128n; selected examples) 'since, as, because, for': é·li-ni·nutahpí·t·əp 'since he existed from the beginning' (Jn 1.15); é·li-pɔ́·i·t 'because she is pregnant' (Mt 1.20); é·li- takó·-wi·wəni·č·a·ní·t·əp 'as she had never had a child' (Lk 1.7); é·li-kwəná·ke·t 'because he was gone a long time' (Lk 1.21); é·li-wəle·lə́ntank 'because he was happy' (Lk 1.44); é·li- ki·š·e·ləmúwe·t máta -pɔ́·i- kéku -lə́s·i·t 'since nothing is impossible for God to do' (Lk 1.37); é·li-wə́li-ləs·i·lí·t·əp 'as he (obv.) was a kind (man)' (Mt 1.19); ko·x·əwa·únka é·li-nhilahtí·t·əp '(and) as it was your forefathers that killed them' (Lk 11.47).
- ♦ (idiom) nɔ́ 'that (inan.)' + lí- PV (with a number word) 'only': nɔ́ ší·kanč tə́li-má·wsi·n 'he is the only one' (Jn 1.18); nɔ́ tə́li-ma·wsí·li·n 'she (obv.) was the only one he had' (Lk 8.42; the obv. gives the meaning 'he (prox.) had'); nɔ́ tə́li-kwət·unše·lí·ne·p 'she (obv.) had had only that one child' (Lk 7.12); é·li- nɔ́ -lí-má·wsi·t nní·č·a·n 'for he is my only child' (Lk 9.38).
- ♦ (idiom) ná 'then' + lí- PV (only tə́li-) 'and with that; and proceeded to': ná tə́li-alə́mska·n. 'And with that he departed.' (Jn 5.9; '.. and so departed.'); ná tə́li-tpáhɔ·n 'And with that he pointed to them ..' (Mt 12.49); ná tə́li- palí·i -a·né·ɔ. 'And with that they went away.' (Jn 19.42); ná tə́li-hápahpi·n. 'And with that he sat on it.' (Mt 28.2); ná tə́li- palí·i -á·n. '... and then he went away.' (Mt 13.25); ná tə́li-kə́ntka·n. '.. she (then) danced.' (Mk 6.22); ná tə́li-ki·ski·k·wéhɔ·n 'and (he) proceeded to chop his head off' (Mk 6.27).
- ♦ lí (-ə́li) PV 'that' (with subordinative complement; Gr. §4.5b, 5.128n; selected examples): e·lo·ke·mwí·t·əp lí- nčá·n -thwə́na·n 'he ordered that John be arrested' (Mk 6.17); nénke lí-káhta-sa·k·i·má·whe·n 'when he saw that there was a desire to make him king' (Jn 6.15); wəné·mən lí-alá́x·at 'he sees it that it is empty' (Mt 12.44); ktə́li·namə́né·ɔ lí-taɔ́·lahkat lí hɔ́kunk 'you shall see a hole open in (*lit.*, to) heaven' (Jn 1.51); é·p lí-=č -lé·khɔ·n 'he went to be enrolled' (Lk 2.3); tɔlo·ke·mwí·ne·p lí-nhíla·n 'he sent orders for them to be killed' (Mt 2.16).
- -ə́li: mpənunthíke·n, ntə́li- nó·x -pe·t·alo·ka·lkó·ne·p 'I give evidence that my father sent me here' (Jn. 5.36); mé·či ktə́llə́né·ɔ·p ktə́li-ne·i·né·ɔ 'I have told you that you see me' (Jn 6.36; Gr. 4.50b); káči li·t·e·há·he·kw, ktə́li-=á· -ahkəno·t·əmo·ləné·ɔ 'do not think that I would accuse you' (Jn 5.45; Gr. 4.50d); káči čane·ləntánkhan ktə́li-wé·t·əna·n 'do not be reluctant to take her' (Mt 1.20); é·li-lə́lan, ktə́li-=á· lápi -ki·š·í·k·i·n 'that I tell you that you should be born again' (Jn 3.7); takó· wəli·x·ənó·u ktə́li-kələ́nəmən ktap·í·nay 'It is not right for you to carry your bed.' (Jn 5.10); ná=nə ntə́lsi·n, ktə́li-=č -pí·lsi·n 'That's what I do for you to be clean.' (Mt 8.3); ne·ɔhtí·t·e tə́li-nahko·x·wé·li·n 'when they saw it (obv.) stop' (Mt 2.10); ná wtəpskwilahtá·ne·p .., wtə́li-=č -núnše·n, kkwí·s·al -ki·š·i·k·i·lí·ne·p 'Then her time had come, for her to give birth and for her son to be born.' (Lk 1.57; cf. Lk 2.6); ktə́li-=č -kčo·ha·lké·ne·n 'that we would be saved' (Lk 1.71); wtə́li-=č -pənunthíke·n 'that he would show it' (Lk 1.72); ntə́li-=č nó·x -mi·kəntamáɔ·n 'that I would be working for my father' (Lk 2.49); ntə́li-=č ɔ́·k nə́ táli -pəmət·ónhe·n 'so that I may preach there also' (Mk 1.38); tə́li-=č -a·č·í·mwi·n '(for him) to tell about it' (Jn 1.7); ntə́li-=č -ki·š·alo·ká·s·i·n 'for me to finish it' (Jn 4.34).
- ♦ (idiom; without an oblique complement) 'be the one who': nčí·sas=tá ntə́li-ki·k·éhko·n. 'It was Jesus that cured me.' (Jn 5.15); tə́li-=č -maya·ɔ·č·í·mwi·n 'he was (to be the one) to testify' (Jn 1.8); tə́li-ki·š·e·ləntamə́ne·p 'he was the one to create (all things)' (Jn 1.3);

lí-=č -nto·t·əmaɔ·né·ɔ 'that is what they will be asked about' (Lk 11.50).

lí (2) P (like lí PV but not part of a verb) '(going) to {smwh}', '{so}', 'for' (Lk 1.16, 1.17, 2.3, 2.15, 13.28, Mt 2.14): lí tɔ·ki·há·k·anink 'for his field' (Mt 20.1, 20.2); lí hɔk·ayəwá·unk 'for them' (Lk 7.30); lí mahči·k·amí·k·unk '(call) from the grave' (Jn 12.17); ná=nə lí kí·xki 'near that place' (Jn 19.42&); lí é·li·á·li·t 'in their (obv.) way' (Mt 21.8&); lí e·le·khá·s·i·k wənči hɔ́k·ay 'in the way that was written about him' (Mk 14.21); éntxi-=lí awé·n -wəlá·ta·kw ' to everyone who has some' (Mt 25.29).

♦ lí P 'that' (complementizer, without a verb): ší=tá lí ní· nihəláči 'or that it is my own' (Jn 7.17); lí kéhəla ní· 'that it is really me' (Lk 24.39); o·wa·hawwá·ɔ lí nánal nehəlá·ləwe·t 'they knew that he was the Lord' (Jn 21.12; Gr. 6.19o).

• -óli P (with a prefix but no inflected verb) 'that' (with complement clause): tóli né·k·əma nčí·sas 'that he was Jesus' (Mt 16.20); tóli náka ehahki·hɔké·t·əp 'that he was a deceiver' (Mt 27.63); tóli=á· nál wá khičí·i kəláist 'that this is truly Christ' (Jn 7.26); ntóli ní· né·k·əma 'that I am him' (Jn 13.19); tóli nál nóni e·lkí·kwi- nčí·sas -ləwé·t·əp 'that that was the time when Jesus said ..' (Jn 4.53 [em.; see text]); tóli-=č .. -káski-=č -wəla·to·né·ɔ 'that they will be able to have it' (Jn 6.40 [em.]).

lihəla·- (e·lihəla·-, |əlīhlā-|) AI, II 'go rapidly to {smwh}, fall {smwh}'.

▪ lihəla·- (AI): hákink líhəle· 'she fell down' (Jn 11.32); íka lihəlé·ɔk 'they fall into it' (Mt 15.14); hák·ink lihəlé·ɔk 'they fell to the ground' (Jn 18.6), íka lihəlé·ɔk 'they rush to it' (1842:21.7); máta=háč=á· .. lihəle·í·ɔk 'wouldn't they fall (there)?' (Lk 6.39); mənəp·é·k·unk líhəla 'jump into the sea (you sg.)' (Mt 21.21); lihəla·lí·t·e 'if he (obv.) fell (there)' (Mt 12.11).

▪ lihəla·- (II): íkali líhəle· 'it goes away' (Mk 7.19).

• e·lihəla·-: e·líhəla·k 'where it goes' (Jn 3.8, 1834b:24.3).

lilaht- (|əlīhlat-|) 'move to be towards {smwh}' TI(2): lápi tákɔ·k íka lilahtó·me 'turn the other one to him also (you sg.)' (Mt 5.39).

lilahta·- (|əlīhlatā-|) AI 'go {smwh} (in a boat)': íka lílahta·p 'he went there in a boat' (Mt 15.39); íka lilahtá·ɔk 'they went there in the boat' (Jn 21.8; Gr. 3.13(1)c, 4.21p); ká·mink lilahtá·p·ani·k 'they were crossing in the boat' (Jn 6.22).

-lilpi·-: see lhilpi·-.

linkhakehəla·- II 'be thawing ground': linkhakéhəle· 'the ground is thawing' (1834a:14).

linkwe·x·i·n- (-t-əlinkwe·x·i·n-, e·linkwe·x·i·n-) AI 'look towards {smwh}': íka linkwé·x·i·n 'he turned his gaze to it' (Lk 19.41); linkwe·x·í·no·kw 'look towards (them) (you pl.)' (Jn 4.35); né·li-áhi- íka -linkwe·x·i·nhíti·t 'while they were looking there intently' (Acts 1.10).

• -t-əlinkwe·x·i·n-: ktəlinkwe·x·i·nhúmɔ 'you lift your gaze to (it)' (Lk 21.28); ná ɔ·ká·i təlinkwe·x·í·nən 'then he looked around' (Mk 10.23).

• e·linkwe·x·i·n- (in participle): e·linkwé·x·ink 'before him, in his presence, in his eyes' (Lk 1.6, 1.8, 1.15, 1.19, etc.); e·linkwe·x·í·na 'in front of me' (Lk 19.27); e·linkwe·x·í·nan 'in front of you (sg.), in your presence' (Mk 1.2, Lk 7.27, 13.26); e·linkwe·x·í·nəli·t 'before him, them (obv.)' (Mk 3.11, Mt 8.2, Mk 8.6, etc.); e·linkwe·x·í·ne·kw 'before you (pl.)' (Lk 10.8); e·linkwe·x·i·nhíti·t 'before their eyes, before them' (Mt 17.2, Lk 12.8, Lk 16.15, etc.); (in changed conjunct) íka e·linkwe·x·i·nhíti·t·e 'when they looked there' (Mk 16.4).

linnuwahkəs·əwá·k·an (-t-əlinnuwahkəs·əwa·k·an-) IN 'official function, authority': 'official function' (⟨lenuwavqwswakun⟩ Lk 1.8), 'authority' (⟨lenwavkuswakun⟩ Mk 11.28 [2x]).

• -t-əlinnuwahkəs·əwa·k·an-: təlinnuwahkəs·əwá·k·an 'his official duty' (⟨tclenawaqwswakun⟩ Lk 1.5). ▶ See next.

linnuwahkəs·i·- (e·linnuwahkəs·i·-, |əlīlənəwakəsī| AI ; Gr. 5.19f) 'be one in authority, have an official duty or function'.
- e·linnuwahkəs·i·- (in a participle): e·linnuwahkəs·í·č·i·k 'officials' (Lk 12.58).
▪ linnuwahkə́s·i·t 'one of authority' (a lexicalized participle without IC): linnuwahkə́s·i·t 'one of authority' (Lk 7.8); linnuwahkəs·í·č·i·k 'officers' (Jn 18.12); linnuwahkəs·í·t·ink 'to authorities' (Lk 12.11).

†lisánias 'Lysanias' (Lk 3.1).

líte P 'he thinks' (OA; Gr. 2.73f).
- ntíte 'I think': ntíte, tá=á·. 'I don't think he would.' (Lk 17.9).
- ktíte 'you think': kéku=háč ktíte? 'What do you think?' (Mt 22.17); ktíte. 'That's what *you* think.' (OA).
▸ Cf. li·t·e·ha·- AI 'think {so}'.

li·h- (-t-əli·h-, e·li·h-, ihəli·h- [Rih+], ehəli·h- [Rih+; IC]) TA 'do {so} to, for, or with; treat {so}' — li·t- (-t-əli·t-) TI(2) 'treat so, make it so'.
▪ li·h- (TA): lí·ho 'treat him {so} (you pl.)' (Jn 18.31); li·hí·ne·n 'do for us {so}' (Mk 15.8); é·li- nék·əma -lí·ha·t 'for *he* makes it (anim.) do {so}' (Mt 5.45); é·li- .. -kánši-lí·hi·t 'for he has done a great thing to me' (Lk 1.49).
- -t-əli·h-: kéku=č=háč ntəlí·ha nčí·sas 'what shall I do with Jesus?' (Mt 27.22); kwə́la ntəlihkó·ne·n 'I wish he would do it to us' (Mk 10.36, Mt 20.32 [in direct-discourse complements]); máta=ksí ki·ló·wa aləwí·i ktəlihko·wíwwa 'ought he not then to treat *you* (pl.) better?' (Mt 6.30; Gr. 4.85p).
- e·li·h-: e·lí·hak wá hít·ukw 'what I did to this tree' (Mt 21.21); e·lí·hənt ná lə́nu 'what had been done to the man' (Lk 8.34&); e·lihkúk·əp 'what he (obv.) had done to her' (Mk 5.33).
- ihəli·h-: ná=húnt=nə́ ihəlí·ha·n 'that's how they used to be treated' (OA; Gr. 5.41r).
- ehəli·h-: ehəlí·hienk 'what you always do for us' (Mk 15.8).
▪ li·t- (TI): lí·to·kw 'treat it so (you pl.)' (Mt 5.16).
- -t-əli·t-: təlí·to·n 'he caused (how that happened)' (Mk 12.11); ktəli·to·né·ɔ 'you (pl.) have caused (how it is)' (Mt 21.13&).
▪ lihti·- AI (recip.; Gr. 5.110d) 'do {so} for each other': nə́ni ktəlihti·né·ɔ 'that you (pl.) do that for each other (sbd.)' (Jn 13.15).

li·i·lae·m- TA 'comfort with words': máta káski-li·i·lae·má·i·p 'she could not be comforted' (⟨leelymaep⟩ Mt 2.18).
▸ Cf. Mun li·wi·lawé·ma·w 'I made him feel better (by talking)' (APh).

li·khe·- AI 'build a house {so}': hukwé·yunk li·khé·t·amo·kw 'let's build a building to heaven' (1842:9.8); tə́li-=á· hɔ́kunk -li·khe·né·ɔ 'that they would build a house to heaven' (1834b:19.3).

li·kte·- (e·li·kte·-) II 'be colored {so}': kéku=héč lí·kte·? 'what color is it?' (LB).
- e·li·kte·-: xe·lennáɔhki e·lí·kte·k ša·khuk·wí·ɔn 'a coat of many colors' (1842:13.1).

li·k·a·p·ai·- (-t-əli·k·a·p·ai·-) AI 'stand {so}' (often for 'come and stand next to'): ná pí·təl íka təli·k·á·p·ai·n 'then Peter came up to him' (Mt 18.21; KJV "Then came Peter to him"), ná íka təli·k·á·p·ai·n 'then she came up to him' (Jn 20.16; KJV "She turned herself," but she had already turned).

li·k·e·- (e·li·k·e·-) AI 'dwell {so}': yúh ahpa·mi, e·li·k·éhti·t 'around here, where they live' (OA).
▪ li·khati·- (e·li·khati·-) AI (|-ahtī| coll.; Gr. §5.8c) 'settle (collectively) {so}': pe·x·o·č·i·=á· -li·khatihtí·t·e 'when they all settle near each other' (1834b:43.7)

e·li·khati·-: e·li·khátink (oblique ppl. of indef. form), *lit.* 'where people are settled', used for '(from) the country' (Mt 27.32&); e·li·khátink čuwé·yunk 'in the hill country' (Lk 1.65), *lit.*, '(to) where many people dwell on the hills'; wé·mi ɔ·ká·i e·li·khátink 'in all the surrounding settlements' (Lk 7.17).

li·lae·m- (-t-əli·lae·m-) TA 'persuade to go {smwh}'; (with inan.subj. [as, a flute]) 'affect {so} by being blown': íka təli·lae·má·ɔ 'he persuaded them to go there' (1842:7.6); təli·lae·má·p·ani '(the spirit) persuaded him to go {smwh}' (Lk 2.27; KJV "he came by the Spirit into"); kéku təli·laé·mkwən 'it (a flute being blown) affected her' (ME).

li·lama·- (-t-əli·lama·-, ihəli·lama·- [Rih+], ehəli·lama·- [Rih+; IC]) AI 'get water {smwh}'.
  • -t-əli·lama·-: [ná=nə] təlí·lama·n 'that is where he got his water from' (LB).
  • -t-ihəli·lama·-: ná=náni ntihəlí·lama·n 'that's where I (customarily) get my water' (OA).
  • ehəli·lama·-: ehəlí·lamank=č 'what will be a source of water' (Jn 4.14).

li·m- TA 'speak about {so}': énta- kéku -li·máhti·t 'when they said things about him' (1834b:34.4).
  ▶ Cf. Mes išim- 'speak {so} to'.

li·naw- (-t-əli·naw-, e·li·naw-, |əlīnaw-|) TA 'see, experience ({so})' — li·n- (-t-əli·n-, e·li·n-, ehəli·n- [Rih+; IC]) TI(1a) 'see, experience ({so}); do {so}'.
  ▪ -t-əlinaw- (TA): təli·naɔ́·ɔ 'he saw them' (1834b:30.6); ntəlí·naɔ '(as I watched) she seemed to me (as if ..)' (ME; Gr. 5.12z).
  • e·li·naw-: e·lí·naɔ·t 'what he saw him do' (1834b:26.8), kéku e·lí·naɔ·t ó·x·ɔl ehələs·í·li·t 'what he sees his father do' (Jn 5.19).
  ▪ li·n- (TI): takó· kɔ́ski-li·namo·wəné·ɔ 'they were unable to see them' (Mt 13.17); mái-li·namó·t·amo·kw 'let's all go and see it' (Lk 2.15; Gr. 4.106l); takó· .. wəlankuntəwá·k·an nəmái-li·namó·wi 'I did not come to experience peace' (Mt 10.34); li·namihti·tpáne kanšaehɔ·s·əwá·k·an 'if they had seen miracles' (Mt 11.21; Gr. 4.74i); wénči- nə́ -lí·namankw 'why that is happening to us' (Lk 23.41); é·li- kanšaehɔ·s·əwá·k·an -li·namánəp 'for you (sg.) have seen the miracles' (Mt 11.23; Gr. 4.73h); é·li- .. wé·mi kéku -á·p·əwi-lí·nank 'for he easily does everything' (Mk 9.23).
  • e·li·n-: kéku e·li·namá·k·əp 'things I have seen' (Jn 8.38; Gr. 4.78c); e·li·namihtí·t·əp 'what they had witnessed' (Lk 9.36; Gr. 4.78q).
  • ne·li·n- (nə́ + e·li·n-; cf. Gr. §4.6b): ne·li·nánke 'as he watched' (Lk 7.39). • ehəli·n-: ehəli·namíhti·t 'as they do' (⟨rvlinumivtet⟩ Mt 6.2); kéku ki·ló·wa ehəlí·name·kw 'the things that *you* (pl.) see' (⟨rlenamrq⟩ Mt 13.17).
  • -t-əli·n-: ná nɔ́ təli·naməné·ɔ 'then they saw that (or found that)' (Mk 14.16,).
  ♦ (idiom) kɔ́na P + li·naw- TA — li·n- TI(1a) 'allow, leave alone, let go' (Gr. 5.12z). ▪ kɔ́na lí·naw- (TA): kɔ́na lí·no· 'leave them alone (you pl.)' (Mt 15.14, Jn 18.8); kɔ́na li·naí·ne·n 'let us alone' (Mk 1.24); kɔ́na=á· li·naɔ́nkwe 'if we (inc.) leave him alone' (Jn 11.48). ▪ kɔ́na lí·n- (TI): kɔ́na lí·namo·kw ellí·i aləmí·k·ənu 'let both (inan.) continue growing (you pl.)' (Mt 13.30; Gr. 4.49e [ind. with sbd. function]).
  ♦ PV + li·n- (TI-O) 'experience —, have — fortune': nkanši-li·namúhəna 'we (exc.) had a miraculous experience' (Lk 24.23; Gr. 4.38k); kó·li-li·namúhump 'you (sg.) had good fortune' (Lk 16.25; Gr. 4.70b); wəli-lí·nam 'he has good fortune' (Lk 16.25); kúnči-wə́li-lí·namən 'good things happen to you because of (it)' (Mt 12.37). With ahi PV 'very much' (see also above) 'suffer, experience bad fortune': áhi-=č -lí·nam 'bad things will happen to him' (Mk 3.29; Gr. 4.38h); nta·yáhi-lí·nam 'bad things happen to me' (Lk 22.28; KJV "in my

temptations"); ktáhi-lí·nam 'you are suffering severely' (Lk 16.25); kúnči-áhi-lí·namən 'bad things (would) happen to you because of it' (Mt 12.37).

li·na·kwsi·- (-t-əli·na·kwsi·-, e·li·na·kwsi·-) AI — li·na·k·ɔt- (e·li·na·k·ɔt-) II 'appear {so}, be {so}, be like {so}, be {such} kind' (Gr. 5.108a).

▪ li·na·kwsi·- (TA): me·me·thaké·munk li·ná·kwsu '(he) looked like a dove' (Jn 1.32).

• -t-əli·na·kwsi·-: ná wi·xkaóči pí·li təli·ná·kwsi·n 'then suddenly his appearance became different' (Mt 17.2).

• e·li·na·kwsi·-: ní· e·li·na·kwsía 'the way *I* look' (Lk 24.39); e·li·ná·kwsi·t 'what he looks like' (Jn 5.37), 'the likeness of (anim.)' (1834b:20.5); e·li·na·kwsí·li·t 'how he (obv.) looked' (Lk 9.32; KJV "his glory"); tákta e·li·na·kwsi·lí·č·i 'whichever one (obv.)' (Mt 27.15).

▪ li·na·k·ɔt- (TI): nəni li·ná·k·ɔt 'it is what it is like' (Mt 13.49), tá=háč málahši li·ná·k·ɔt 'what is it like?' (Lk 13.18), kéku=nínk=č=háč ntələwe li·ná·k·ɔt? 'What shall I say it is like?' (Lk 13.18).

• e·li·na·k·ɔt-: e·li·ná·k·ɔ 'how it is, the way it is, what it is like' (Mk 4.26, Lk 12.56), 'what kind it is; what kinds of things they are' (Mt 16.3 2x, Mk 11.28), 'what kind they are' (Mk 13.1); xe·lennáɔhki e·li·ná·k·ɔ 'many kinds' (Mk 7.13); nəni e·li·ná·k·ɔ 'that kind' (Jn 6.58); tá=háč e·li·ná·k·ɔ? 'Which one(s)?' (Mt 19.18; KJV "Which?"); tá=háč né·l e·li·ná·k·ɔ laehɔ·s·əwá·k·ana 'those deeds of which kind?' (Jn 10.32).

li·na·s·i·- (e·li·na·s·i·-) AI (with kóna P) 'allow {so}': ó·k=č tákta kéku kóna e·li·ná·s·ian 'and whatever you (sg.) shall allow' (Mt 16.19).

li·ne·ó·k·an* (-t-əli·ne·ɔ·k·an-) IN 'disease': wé·mi təli·ne·ɔ·k·aní·li·t 'all their (obv.) diseases' (Mt 10.1).

li·nxke·- (-t-əli·nxke·-) AI 'reach out the hand to {smwh}': íka lí·nxke· 'he reached out his hand to them' (Mk 6.5); takó· háši wəntax ktəli·nxkéhəmɔ 'you (pl.) never reached out your hands to me' (Lk 22.53; KJV "ye stretched forth no hands against me"); wəntax lí·nxke 'reach out your hand this way' (Jn 20.27).

• -t-əli·nxke·-: ná nčí·sas íka təlí·nxke·n 'then Jesus stretched out his his hand to him' (Mt 8.3).

†lí·pay 'Levi' (Mk 2.14, Lk 5.29); †li·paí·ɔk 'Levites' (Jn 1.19).

▪ †li·paí·i PN 'Levite': †li·paí·i-lənu 'a Levite man' (Lk 10.32).

li·t-: see li·h- — li·t-.

li·ta·s·i·- II 'be made {so}': nəni li·tá·s·u 'it was made that way' (1834b:31.2).

li·t·e·ha·- (-t-i·t·e·ha·- [~ -t-əli·t·e·ha·-], e·li·t·e·ha·-, |əlītēhā-|) AI 'think {so}': li·t·é·hew 'he thought ..' (Jn 7.39), li·t·é·he·w=č 'he will think ..' (Jn 16.2), li·t·é·he· (Lk 12.17, 12.18, 13.6, etc.); li·t·e·hé·ɔk 'they thought ..' (Lk 5.21, Mk 3.21, 6.49, etc.); li·t·e·hé·p·ani·k 'they thought ..' (Lk 2.44); li·t·e·há·t·e 'if he wants to' (Jn 5.21, Mt 6.27); é·li-li·t·e·há·a 'because I thought (so)' (Lk 13.7).

• -t-i·t·e·ha·- (unique reduction of |əl-|; Gr. §4.5a, Goddard 1979:77): šúkw nti·t·é·he 'but I think' (1834b:9.4); kti·t·é·ha 'you (sg.) think' (Gr. 3.6j), 'your (sg.) wish' (Mt 11.26; should be sbd.?); máta=háč kéku kti·t·e·há·i 'don't you (sg.) care?' (Lk 10.40); nti·t·e·háhəna·p 'we thought (so)' (Lk 24.21); ná ti·t·é·ha·n 'then he thought ..' (1842:8.6); kti·t·e·háhəmɔ 'you (pl.) think' (Jn 5.39 [parenthetical quotative]; Gr. 3.6j), kéku=háč=á· kti·t·e·háhəmɔ? 'What would you (pl.) think?' (Mt 18.12).

• -t-əli·t·e·ha·-: nána wtəli·t·e·ha·né·ɔ 'then they thought ..' (1834b:43.7; unique regular form).

• e·li·t·e·ha·-: e·li·t·e·há·a 'what I want' (Jn 6.38), 'my will' (Jn 5.30), e·li·t·é·ha·t 'his will, what he wants done' (Jn 5.30, Mt 7.21; Gr. 4.67(1)c); e·li·t·e·ha·lí·t·əp 'ones (obv.) who had thought ..' (Lk 18.9; Gr. 4.75r).

♦ Unprefixed ti·t·é·he· 'he thought' (1834a:19.20) is presumably an early error for li·t·é·he·.

li·xsəwá·k·an IN 'language'; lənə·p·e·í·i-li·xsəwá·k·an 'language of the Lenape (Indian)' (Gr. §1.2). ▸ Cf. ləni·xsəwá·k·an.

li·xsi·- (e·li·xsi·-, ehəli·xsi·- [Rih+; IC]) AI 'speak (a language) {so}': káski-li·xsúwak 'they will be able to speak [languages]' (Mk 16.17).

• e·li·xsi·-: e·li·xsían 'your speech' (Lk 22.59-60&); e·li·xsíhti·t 'their language' (1834b:19.4, 39.13, 1842:9.9).

• ehəli·xsi·-: pí·li ehəlí·xsink 'other languages' (Mk 16.17; KJV "new tongues").

▪ li·xsi·ta·ɔhti·- AI 'speak languages {so} to each another': pi·pí·li li·xsi·ta·ɔhtí·na. 'And different languages were spoken to each other.' (1834b:19.4).

li·xt-: see li·x·əm- — li·xt-.

li·xtaw- (-t-əli·xtaw-, e·li·xtaw-; Gr. 5.95d) TA+O 'set O2 for, establish O2 for', 'put it {smwh} for': máta li·xta·k·é·ɔne 'if it were not established for you' (Jn 19.11; KJV "given thee"; Gr. 4.97s); éntxi-li·xta·k·é·e·kw 'the amount set for you' (Lk 3.13).

• -t-əli·xtaw-: ná mahtánt·u təli·xtáɔ·n pwəna·eləntaməwa·k·aní·li·t 'then the devil put it into his thoughts' (Jn 13.2).

li·x·əm- (e·li·x·əm-) TA — li·xt- (-t-əli·xt-, e·li·xt-) TI(2) 'set {so}, lay (down) {so}'. (For |-īxəm| TA, |-īxət| TI(2), see Gr. 5.12g.).

▪ e·li·x·əm- (TA): e·li·x·əmá·link 'how he (obv.) was laid' (Lk 23.55&; Gr. 4.67(1)e).

▪ -t-əli·xt- (TI): ná ke·tanət·ó·wi·t təlí·xto·n 'then God made the rule' (1842:9.2); énta-ləní·xsink təli·xto·né·ɔ 'they set it into Delaware' (B: Title Page).

• e·li·xt-: ki·š·e·ləmúwe·t e·lí·xta·kw 'what God had set' (Lk 7.30); e·li·xtá·k·əp mo·šə́š·a 'as Moses (had) laid it down (in law)' (Lk 2.22, Mt 8.4; Gr. 4.78p); kéku=č ki·ló·wa e·li·xtáe·kw 'anything you (pl.) shall lay down as law' (Mt 18.18).

li·x·əmukwsi·- AI 'be appointed': é·li-li·x·əmúkwsi·t 'according to his appointment' (Lk 1.9).

li·x·ən- (II): see li·x·i·n- — li·x·ən-.

li·x·ən- (|līxən-|) TA 'take down': wəli·x·əná·ɔ 'he took him down' (Mk 15.46); tóli-=á· .. -li·x·əna·né·ɔ 'for them to take them (obv.) down' (Jn 19.31).

li·x·i·- AI 'come down': lí·x·i·l 'get down (you sg.)' (Lk 19.5); káči li·x·í·hi·č 'he must not come down' (Lk 17.31; Gr. 2.47e); ná kwə́ši-lí·x·i·n 'then he quickly came down' (Lk 19.6); li·x·í·t·e·á· íka wə́nči énta-a·š·əwa·khwitehá·s·i·k 'if he comes down from the cross' (Mt 27.42).

li·x·i·n- (-t-əli·x·i·n-) AI — li·x·ən- (e·li·x·ən-, |əlīxən-|) II 'be {so}, be set to be {so}'.

▪ li·x·i·n- (AI): təli·x·í·nən 'he is destined to do {so}' (Lk 2.34 [2x]); é·li- ná=ní -li·x·í·nankw 'for that is what is set for us' (Mt 3.15).

▪ li·x·ən- (II): lí·x·ən 'it is {so}' (Jn 2.18), 'there is a custom (that)' (Jn 18.39); máta=ksí li·x·ənó·wi 'wasn't it laid down (that)?' (Lk 24.26); máta nə́ni li·x·ənó·wi·p 'that was not the law' (Mt 19.8); li·x·ínkeč 'let it be {so}' (Mt 5.37; Gr. 4.114e); é·li- nə́ni -li·x·ínkəp 'for that has been the rule' (Mt 7.12; Gr. 4.73c).

• e·li·x·ən-: e·lí·x·ink 'the way it is set' (Lk 1.8); é·li- nə́ -lí·x·ink khwitələt·əwá·k·an 'because that accords with the law' (Lk 23.56).

lo·hɔm- TI(1a) 'passes by': ná wəlo·hə́mən 'then he passes by (it)' (⟨lovwmun⟩ Mt 12.43).

▸ Cf. Mun ló·wham 'passes by (it, one's destination)' (dict.).

lo·kᵒ (with short /k/) 'collapse, in pieces'; cf. Mes no·hk- 'soft', Mun lohk- in lohkhámən 'flour'.
lo·kahəla·- AI 'give up, fall away (from faith)': lo·kahəle· 'he gave up, is discouraged' (OA); kəlo·káhəla 'you give up' (LTD ND); xé·li=č awé·n lo·káhəle· 'many will fall away' (Mt 24.10; KJV "be offended," RSV "fall away"); ílli=č wé·mi awé·n lo·kahəlá·t·e 'even if everyone (else) loses their will' (Mt 26.33); é·li-=á·.. máta -lo·kahəlá·ink 'how one should not give up' (Lk 18.1); tá·=á· háši llo·kahəlá·i 'I will never lose my will' (Mt 26.33).
ló·kat '(wheat) flour' (1834b:13.4, Mt 13.33; KJV "meal"); 'flour' (OA, ME, LTD ND), 'corn or wheat flour' (AP); ló·kahtink 'in flour' (Lk 13.21).
lo·kən- TI(1b) 'break up, destroy': ntáli-=á· -lo·kənəmən 'that I would destroy it (the law)' (Mt 5.17; KJV "destroy" 2x); llo·kənəmən=č 'I'll take it down (a barn)' (Lk 12.18; KJV "pull down"): llo·kənəmən 'I gradually break it up' (OA); ⟨lokenumen⟩, ⟨lokenúmmen⟩ 'to demolish, to destroy' (Z. 54; "tear in pieces. pull apart" [B&A 66]).
  ▸ Cf. lo·k·ən- 'break'.
lo·kihəla·- II 'break apart, collapse': lo·kíhəle· 'it collapsed' (OA), ⟨Logihilleu⟩ "it falls in" (B&A 65); lo·kíhəle·p 'it (house) broke apart' (Mt 7.27&; KJV "it fell").
lo·kwe·- (-t-əlhukwe·-, e·lhukwe·-, |ələhkwē-|) AI 'look toward {smwh}, turn to {smwh}': íka ló·kwe· 'he looked there' (Mk 5.30; Gr. 2.5m).
  • -t-əlhukwe·-: ná íka təlhúkwe·n 'then he looked there' (Lk 22.61; Gr. 2.5m).
  • e·lhukwe·-: íka e·lhukwé·t·e 'when he turned to them' (Mk 10.27; KJV "looking upon them").
lo·kwe·p·i·- (-t-əlhukwe·p·i·-, |ələhkwēpī-|) 'sit {so}, sit facing toward {smwh}': lo·kwé·p·u 'he sits {so}' (OA).
  • -t-əlhukwe·p·i·-: ntəlhukwé·p·i 'I sit {so}' (OA); yúkwə=yu=šé· ntəlhukwé·p·i·n 'as I sit here now' (ME).
  • e·lhukwe·p·i·-: e·lhukwé·p·i·t 'in front of where he sat' (Mk 12.41, 1834b:30.5); (táli) e·lhukwe·p·í·li·t 'before them (obv.), in front of them (obv.)' (Jn 20.19, Lk 24.43).
lo·kwe·x·i·n- (e·lhukwe·x·i·n-, |ələhkwēxīn-|) AI 'lie with head {so}': e·lhukwe·x·i·nəlí·t·əp 'where his (obv.) head had lain' (Jn 20.12; Gr. 4.42s).
  ▸ Cf. ⟨Elhokquechink⟩ 'at his head' (B&A 33).
lo·k·ᵒ (with long /k·/; |lōk-|) 'break'.
lo·k·ən- TI(1b) 'break': awé·n lo·k·ənínke 'if anyone breaks it (a law)' (Mt 5.19; KJV "break").
  ▸ Cf. Mun lo·kən- TA, TI(1b) 'break'. ▸ Cf. lo·kən- (above).
lo·mánsak 'the Romans' (⟨Lomunsuk⟩ Jn 11.48, Mt 20.19); lo·mánsa (obv.) (⟨Lomunsu⟩ Lk 21.24). Presumably ⟨o⟩ was due to the English spelling, and the later ⟨w⟩ (see next) is correct.
lo·mansi·xsi·- AI 'speak Latin': lo·mansí·xsi·n 'it was in the Romans' language' (⟨Lwmunsexsen⟩ Jn 19.20).
lo·o·x·we·í·- II 'go past' (|lōwōxwēwī-|; Gr. 2.30i): mé·či lo·o·x·we·í·k·e ala·x·i·məwí·i-kí·škwi·k 'after the day of rest had past' (⟨lwwxrekc⟩ Mk 16.1); mé·či ná luwe·ó·k·an lo·o·x·we·í·k·e 'after the voice had gone past' (Lk 9.36; with ⟨lw-⟩ for ⟨lww-⟩).
†ló·pəs 'Rufus' (Mt 27.32&).
lo·s·a·s·i·- II 'be burned' (Gr. 5.105p): tá·mse=á· alápa lo·s·á·s·əwa 'and perhaps tomorrow it (grass, pl.) will be burned up' (Lk 12.28); e·lkí·kwi-.. -lo·s·á·s·i·k 'in the same way that (they) are burned' (Mt 13.40); lo·s·a·s·í·k·i '(grass, pl.) which is burned up' (Mt 6.30).
lo·s·i·- (|lōsī-|) AI — lo·t·e·- (|lōtē-|) II 'burn, be burned' (Gr. 5.104n).
  ▪ lo·s·i·- (AI): énta=č -lo·s·íhti·t 'where they (anim.) will be burned' (Jn 15.6).
  ▪ ló·t·e· (II) 'it burned' (V, LB).

lo·s·w- (‖lōsw-|) TA — lo·s·- (‖lōs-|) TI(1b) 'burn' (Gr. 5.104n).
- lo·s·w- (TA): wəlo·s·o·k·u 'he (obv.) burned him' (ME; Gr. 2.23b).
- lo·s·- (TI): wəló·s·əmən=č 'he will burn it' (⟨sum⟩ Lk 3.17; Gr. 2.57g); ktáli-=č -lo·s·əməné·ɔ 'in order to burn them' (*lit.*, 'so that you (pl.) will burn them') (⟨sam⟩ Mt 13.30 [em.]; Gr. 4.50n); wəlo·s·əməné·ɔ wto·t·e·naí·li·t 'they burned their (obv.) town' (⟨sum⟩ Mt 22.7).

lo·t·e·nai·- (e·lo·t·e·nai·-) II 'be town(s) {so}': wé·mi e·lo·t·é·nai·k 'through all the towns' (Lk 4.14); wé·mi=yú=tá .. e·lo·t·é·nai·k 'to all the towns' (Mt 9.35).

lo·wan- II 'be winter': áləmi-ló·wan 'winter has begun' (1834a:17); ló·wano·p 'it had been winter' (Jn 10.22); áləmi-=č -lo·wánke 'when it begins to be winter' (⟨1wuf⟩ 1834a:16 [em.]).

lo·wané·yunk (Gr. 5.26e) P 'in, to the north' (Lk 13.29, 1834b:44.9).

lo·waní·i P 'in winter' (Mt 24.20, 1834a:16).

ló·wi PV (only with le·- II; Gr. 5.129u) 'past, over': mé·či ló·wi-lé· 'it is over' (Mt 26.45); ló·wi-=č -lé· 'they (inan.) will pass away (sbd.)' (Lk 21.33); ló·wi-lé·k·e 'when it was (they were) over, past' (⟨Lwilrkc⟩ Lk 1.23, ⟨lwclrkc⟩ Lk 2.43, ⟨Lwev lrkc⟩ Jn 2.12, ⟨lwi lrkc⟩ Mt 13.53); káhti-ló·wi-lé·k·e 'when it was almost over' (Jn 7.27).

lo·wi·- AI 'pass by, through': e·š·í·i lí-ló·wi·p 'he was passing through' (Jn 8.59); ná táli-ló·wi·n 'and he proceeded to pass by' (Lk 10.32); lo·wí·t·e 'after he passed through' (Mk 7.31).
- lo·wi·- AI+O 'go past': kóti-lo·wí·na 'he almost went past them' (Mk 6.48).
- ló·wi·n 'people (indef.) pass through' (lexicalized): nčo·wí·i-ló·wi·n 'the Jews' Passover' (Jn 11.55); ló·wink 'when people (indef.) passed through' (lexicalized): ló·wink 'Passover' (Lk 2.41, Jn 2.13, Mt 26.2); wənči ló·wink 'for Passover' (Jn 2.23).
- lo·winkí·i (Gr. 5.123f) PN 'of Passover' (Mk 14.12 [2x]); lo·winkí·i 'the Passover meal' (with gapped noun) (Mk 14.16, Jn 18.28).
- lo·winkí·i PV 'of Passover': nkát·a- .. -lo·winkí·i-mí·tsi 'I want to eat the Passover meal' (Mk 14.14).

lo·x·ɔl- (-t-əlo·x·ɔl-, e·lo·x·ɔl-, |əlōxwal-|) TA — luxɔht- (-t-əluxɔht-, e·luxɔht-, |əlōxwat-|) TI(2) 'take (to) {smwh}, 'bring (to) {smwh}' (Gr. 5.78c).
- lo·x·ɔl- (TA): wəntax ló·x·ɔlo· 'bring them here (you pl.)' (Lk 18.40); ahsé·i lo·x·ɔlá·ɔk 'they are led away to scattered places' (Lk 21.24); mé·či á·lai- íka -lo·x·ɔlahtí·t·e 'after they had been unable to bring him (there)' (Mk 2.4&; Gr. 5.128d).
- -t-əlo·x·ɔl-: palí·i=č ntəló·x·ɔla 'I shall take him away' (Jn 20.15); təlo·x·ɔlá·ɔl 'he took him to (there)' (Mt 4.8); ktəlo·x·ɔlək·éhəmɔ 'you (pl.) are taken to (there)' (Mk 13.9&).
- e·lo·x·ɔl-: e·lo·x·ɔlá·t·e 'wherever he (the spirit) takes him' (Mk 9.18); e·lo·x·ɔlənči·k 'who are taken to (there)' (Lk 13.23).
- ne·lo·x·ɔl- (nə + e·lo·x·ɔl-; cf. Gr. §4.6b): ne·lo·x·ɔláhti·t 'as they were leading him there' (Mt 27.32&).
- luxɔht- (TI): palí·i lúxɔhto·l 'take it elsewhere (you sg.)' (Jn 2.16); lúxɔhto·kw 'take it (there) (you pl.)' (Jn 2.8); kéku=háč wənči- máta íka -luxɔhtó·wan 'why didn't you take it there' (Lk 19.23); táli-=á· palí·i -lúxɔhto·n 'so that he could take it away' (Lk 23.52&).
- -t-əluxɔht-: kəhó·k·anink ntəluxɔhtó·həmp xáskwi·m 'I took corn to the mill' (1834a:15); ná íka təluxɔhto·né·ɔ 'then they took it to him' (Jn 2.8).
- e·luxɔht-: palí·i e·lúxɔhta·kw 'who takes them (inan.) away' (Jn 1.29).

lo·x·we·- (-t-əlo·x·we·-, e·lo·x·we·-, illo·x·we·- [Rī+]) AI — lo·x·we·i·- II (|əlōxwēwī-|; Gr. 5.76j) 'walk, go {so}, to {smwh}'.
- -t-əlo·x·we·- (AI): áski nə təló·x·we·n 'he had to go through it' (⟨tclwxrn⟩ Jn 4.4).
- illo·x·we·-: nəni illo·x·wehtí·t·əp 'the way they have been going' (1834b:8.11).

- ne·lo·x·we·- (nə́ + e·lo·x·we·-; cf. Gr. §4.6b): ne·ló·x·we·t 'as he was walking' (⟨nrlwxrt⟩ Lk 10.33, ⟨Nrlwxwrt⟩ Lk 17.11); ne·lo·x·wé·t·e 'as he journeyed' (⟨Nrlwxwrtc⟩ Lk 13.22); ne·lo·x·wéhti·t 'as they walked' (Lk 9.57, Mt 21.8&, etc.; Gr. 4.61b).
  ▪ lo·x·we·i·- (II): wé·mi lo·x·wé·yo·p 'it went all around' (Mt 4.24); lí·=á· palí·i -lo·x·wé·yu 'that it might pass away' (Mt 26.39).
lɔ́·k·ens IN (-o·la·k·ens-, |wəlākēns-|) 'dish, plate' (Mk 11.16); lɔ·k·énsink 'on a plate' (Mk 6.25, 6.28), 'in a dish' (Jn 13.5, Mk 14.20).
  • -o·la·k·ens-: ko·lá·k·ens 'your dish' (Mt 23.26); ko·la·k·ensəwá·ɔ 'your dishes' (Lk 11.39, Mt 23.25).
lɔ́·k·əwe P 'yesterday' (Jn 4.52, 1834a:15; OA, ME, LB).
lɔ·k·əwe·- (we·la·k·əwe·-) II 'be evening': we·la·k·əwé·k·e 'that evening' (⟨Wrlakorkc⟩ Mk 1.32).
  ▸ Cf. lɔ·k·wi·-.
lɔ·k·wəní·i P 'in the evening' (Mt 16.2, 20.9, Jn 12.2, Mk 13.35).
lɔ·k·wəni·p·wi·- AI 'have supper, eat the evening meal': énta-məkə́ni-lɔ·k·wəni·p·wihtí·t·əp 'when they had the last supper' (⟨cntu mukuni lokvwenetetu⟩ 1834b:40.11 [with ⟨-pwe-⟩ and ⟨-p⟩ omitted, and perhaps incorrectly repaired]). Cf. ⟨lòkwĕnipu⟩ 3s, etc. (LTD).
lɔ·k·wi·- (we·la·k·wi·-, |wəlākwī-| [but without IC except in 'last night']; Gr. 5.10e) II 'be evening': mé·či lɔ́·k·u 'it is already evening' (Lk 24.29); mé·či lɔ·k·wí·k·e 'after evening had come' (Mt 14.15, etc.); lɔ·k·wí·k·e 'in the evening' (Jn 13.2); é·li- mé·či kí·xki -lɔ·k·wí·k·əp 'as it was already nearly evening' (Jn 1.39).
  • we·la·k·wi·-: we·la·k·wí·k·e 'last night' (OA, LB, LTD ND).
  ▸ Cf. lɔ·k·əwe·-.
  ▪ lɔ·k·wi·t·i·- II 'be early evening' (dim.): mé·či áhi-lɔ·k·wi·t·í·k·e 'after it was late in the early evening' (Mt 20.6).
lɔ́·məwe (li·lɔ́·məwe [Rī+]; Gr. 5.23h) P 'long ago' (Mt 5.21, 5.27, Lk 8.27, etc.); lɔ́·məwe núči 'since long ago' (Mt 7.12, 1834a:18.1).
  • li·lɔ́·məwe P 'long ago' (Lk 10.13); li·lɔ́·məwe=á· 'it would have been long ago (that ..)' (Mt 11.21).
-lunkɔn-: see wəlúnkɔn.
luwensəwá·k·an (-t-əlawensəwa·k·an-) IN 'name': luwe·nsəwá·k·an (V; LTD ND, LB; Gr 5.58g).
  • -t-əlawensəwa·k·an-: ktəlawensəwá·k·an 'your (sg.) name' (Mt 6.9, Lk 11.2, Jn 12.28); təlawensəwá·k·an 'his name' (Jn 3.18); ktəlawensəwa·k·anúwa 'your names' (Lk 10.20); təlawensəwa·k·anəwá·ɔ 'their names' (1834b:45.8).
luwensi·- (-t-əlawensi·-, e·ləwensi·-) AI — II 'be named {so}'.
  ▪ luwensi·- (AI): luwénsu 'he was named {so}' (Jn 18.10, Mt 27.32&, etc.); luwénso·p '(and) he or she was named {so}' (the equivalent of 'named {so}, whose name was {so}')' (Jn 1.6, Lk 1.5, 10.38, etc.); máta=háč.. luwensi·lí·i 'is not her (obv.) name [Mary]?' (Mt 13.55; Gr. 4.81s).
  • -t-əlawensi·-: ntəlawénsi 'my name is [Five-Thousand]' (Mk 5.9); kéku=háč ktəlawénsi 'what is your name?' (Mk 5.9).
  • e·ləwensi·-: nə́ni e·ləwénsi·t 'one with that name' (Lk 1.61), e·ləwénsi·t 'who was named {so}' (Jn 4.25, etc.), 'the name' (1834b:38.8); e·ləwensí·t·əp 'whose name was {so}' (Jn 12.4, Mt 26.3); e·ləwensi·lí·t·əp 'his (obv.) name' (Lk 1.59); e·ləwensí·li·t 'their (obv.) names' (Jn 10.3).
  ▪ luwensi·- (II): luwénsu 'it is called {so}' (1834b:46.10); luwénso·p '(it was) called {so}' (Lk 2.4, Jn 2.13).

- e·ləwensi·-: e·ləwénsi·k 'which was called {so}' (Lk 1.26).

luwent-: see luwihəl- — luwent-.

luwentamaw- TA+O 'say O2 for': máta čí·č kkáski-tépi-luwentamaí·i "ní· nní·č·a·n." 'You can no longer rightly use the name "my child" for me.' (1834b:28.14).

luwenta·s·i·- (e·ləwenta·s·i·-) II 'be called {so}': luwentá·s·u '(it was) named {so}' (Jn 11.54), †hi·pəlo·wí·i-luwentá·s·u '(it was) named in Hebrew {so}' (Jn 5.2); luwentá·s·o·p '(it was) called {so}' (Lk 2.41, Jn 4.5, Jn 5.2, etc.); énta-luwentá·s·i·k 'a place called {so}' (Mt 26.36, Jn 19.13, etc.).

- e·ləwenta·s·i·-: e·ləwentá·s·i·k 'which was called {so}' (Mt 2.23, Lk 21.37, Mt 26.2, Jn 19.39).

lúwe·° (-t-ələwe·-, e·ləwe·-, ihəluwe·- [Rih+], ehəluwe·- [Rih+; IC], |ələwē-|; 2.26c) AI — luwe·yo·wi·- II 'say {so}' (Gr. 5.76g, 5.101a). Takes a direct discourse complement.

- lúwe° (AI): lúwe·w 'he said' (Mk 3.23), lúwe· 'he says' (Mt 3.2, Mk 5.9, 2.23, etc.; Gr. 2.5g, 2.26c; ⟨lwri⟩ Mk 5.30, Mt 12.24, 12.49, 13.24, Mk 4.26, 13.33); ó·k=č tá=á· luwé·wən 'and people will not say' (Lk 17.21; Gr. 4.81t); luwé·ok 'they said' (Lk 1.66, 3.10, 7.33, etc.; Gr. 4.21n); lúwe·n 'a voice (indef.) said' (Mt 25.6); káči luwé·he·kw 'do not say (you pl.)' (Mt 3.9); káči awé·n luwé·he·kw 'do not say of anyone (you pl.)' (Mt 23.9; Gr. 3.15g); kéku=háč wénči-luwé·an 'why do you say ..?' (Lk 6.46; Gr. 4.67(2)l); wénči- nə́ -lúwe·t 'why he said that' (Jn 16.18; Gr. 4.67(2)o); nə́ni wwə́nči-luwe·né·ɔ 'because of that they said ..' (Jn 21.23; Gr. 2.66a, 5.128x); máta kí·kski- kéku -lúwe·t 'one who never says anything' (Mk 9.25; as 2s voc.); é·li- .. tahkwí·i -luwéhti·t 'as they had agreed among themselves (*lit.*, said together)' (Jn 9.22).

- -t-ələwe·-: takó· ntələwé·i 'I don't say' (Mt 18.22; wrongly translated as ⟨ktclwri⟩); ntələwé·həmp 'I said' (Jn 10.34; Gr. 2.53a); ktələwéhəmɔ 'you (pl.) say' (Jn 4.20, Mt 16.2, 16.3, etc.; Gr. 2.5g); ná tə́ləwe·n 'then he said' (Jn 1.29, Lk 19.15, 23.46).

- e·ləwe·-: e·ləwé·a 'what I say' (⟨rlwru⟩ Lk 6.46, Jn 14.24, ⟨rlwreu⟩ Jn 12.49; etc.); e·ləwé·an 'what you're saying' (⟨rlwreun⟩ Lk 22.59-60&); e·ləwe·á·nəp 'the one of whom I said' (Jn 1.30; Gr. 3.17b, 4.75a); e·ləwé·anəp 'as you have said' (Lk 1.38; Gr. 4.75b); é·ləwe·t 'what he says' (Jn 3.21, 3.29, 15.10; Gr. 2.26c); e·ləwé·t·əp 'as he said, what he said' (Mt 1.22, Jn 1.23, Mt 8.17, etc.; Gr. 4.75f), 'when he said' (Mt 21.5, Jn 12.38); e·ləwe·lí·t·əp 'what he (obv.) had said' (Lk 24.8; Gr. 4.75t).

- ihəlwe·-: ihəlúwe· 'he's always saying' (Lk 23.2); kéku=háč wénči- .. -ihələwéhti·t 'why do they always say' (Mk 9.11).

- ehələwe·-: ehələwe·tpáni·k 'ones who used to say' (Mt 22.23&); ehələwénkəp 'who has always been said' (Jn 11.27: cf. Gr 3.17b).

- luwe·yo·wi·- (II): luwe·yó·u 'it said' (Mt 3.17).

luwe·ó·k·an (-t-ələwe·ɔ·k·an-; Gr. 5.59e) IN 'word, etc.': luwe·ó·k·an 'word(s), saying' (Jn 4.37, 7.36; LTD ND), 'a voice' (Lk 9.36, Jn 12.28), 'statement' (Mk 9.10, Lk 9.44), 'tale' (Mt 28.15); luwe·ó·k·ana 'sayings' (Mt 13.34; LTD ND).

- -t-ələwe·ɔ·k·an-: ktələwe·ó·k·an 'your (sg.) word' (Mt 5.37).

luwe·ta·kwsi·- (e·ləwe·ta·kwsi·-) — luwe·ta·k·ɔt- II 'be heard to say' (Gr. 5.109b).

- e·ləwe·ta·kwsi·- (AI): e·ləwe·ta·kwsía 'my voice' (Jn 10.16, 10.27); e·ləwe·tá·kwsi·t 'his voice' (Jn 5.28, Mt 12.19, Jn 10.4 [all for 'his (obv.)']); e·ləwe·ta·kwsí·li·t 'his (obv.) voice' (Jn 10.3, 10.5).

- luwe·ta·k·ɔt- (II): luwe·tá·k·ɔt 'it is heard to say' (Mt 3.3), 'being heard to say' (Lk 9.35, Jn 12.28).

luwihəl- (-t-ələwihəl-, e·ləwihəl-, |ələwīhl-|) TA — luwent- (-t-ələwent-; e·ləwent-) TI(1a) 'name {so}, call {so}'.
- ▪ luwihəl- (TA): luwíhəla·=č 'he will be called {so}' (Lk 1.32, Mt 5.19); luwíhəla·p '(she was) called {so}' (Lk 8.2); luwihəlá·ɔk 'they are called {so}' (Lk 22.25); káči luwihəlá·he·kw nehəlá·ləwe·t 'don't call them master (you pl.)' (Mt 23.10); ktəli-=á· -luwíhəli·n '(so) that you would call me {so}' (Lk 15.19); é·li-=č -luwíhələnt ki·š·e·ləmúwe·t tɔmi·mə́nsəmal 'for they shall be called God's children' (Mt 5.9).
- • -t-ələwihəl-: ktələwíhəla=č 'you shall name him {so}' (Lk 1.13, 1.31, 1.35, Mt 1.21); né·li·l wtələwihəlá·ɔ 'ehalo·ka·lə́nči·k' 'those he named "apostles"' (Lk 6.13); tələwihəlawwá·p·ani 'they called him {so}' (Lk 1.59); ntələwíhəlukw=č 'we·la·p·énsi·t' 'they will call me "blessed"' (Lk 1.48); ktələwihəlíhəmɔ 'you (pl.) address me {so}' (Jn 13.13, Mt 16.15); ktələwillúhəmɔ 'I call you (pl.) (so)' (⟨ktulwevlwvmw⟩ Jn 15.15 [apparently with the ⟨evl⟩ of other forms for /ill/]); tá=á· .. ktələwillo·húmɔ 'I won't call you (so)' (⟨ktulwevlwvmw⟩ Jn 15.15 [see the preceding form]); ktələwílke=č 'you (sg.) will be called {so}' (Lk 1.76; Gr. 4.29d).
- • e·ləwihəl-: e·ləwíhəle·kw nčo·wí·i-sa·k·í·ma 'who you (pl.) call the king of the Jews' (Mk 15.12); e·ləwíhələnt kəláist 'who is called Christ' (Mt 27.17, 27.22).
- ▪ luwent- (TI): luwéntamən 'it is called {so}' (OA).
- • -t-ələwent-: tələwéntamən 'he calls it {so}' (LB); tələwéntamən=č 'he shall call it {so}' (Mt 21.13&); tələwentaməné·ɔ 'they call it {so}' (Jn 19.13; OA).
- • e·ləwent-: e·ləwéntamankw 'what we (inc.) call {so}' (OA).

luxɔht-: see lo·x·ɔl- — luxɔht-.
luxɔhtaw- (-t-əluxɔhtaw-, |əlōxwataw-|) TA+O 'bring O2 {smwh} to': wə́ntax luxɔhtái·l kkwí·s 'bring your son to me' (Mk 9.19).
- • -t-əluxɔhtaw-: ná íka təluxɔhtáɔ·n 'then he brought him there to him' (Mk 9.20).

luxɔhta·s·i·- II 'be made to go {so}': nalahí·i luxɔhtá·s·u múx·o·l 'for a boat to be made to go upstream (with II sbd.)' (1834b:44.8).

m

-mač·ipahkw-: see čí·p·akw.
=máh P PST (indicates past tense; Gr. 5.24m) (Lk 2.5, 2.36, 14.16, etc.); lə́nu=máh 'there was a man (who ..)' (Lk 15.11, Jn 11.1, Lk 19.12, etc.).
mahčamalsi·- (me·č·amalsi·-) AI 'be sick, be in bad condition': wwə́nči-mahčamálsi·n 'they have bad health because of it' (1842:21.1); wə́nči-=č máta .. ikalísi -mahčamalsí·ɔn 'so you (sg.) will not be in worse condition' (Jn 5.14).
- • me·č·amalsi·-: me·č·amalsí·č·i·k 'those in bad condition' (Lk 14.21; KJV "the maimed").

máhči (-máči, méči [IC], amáči [Ra+]; Gr. 2.74b, 5.120b, 5.129v) PV 'bad, evil, etc.' (Mt 6.23, 12.34, Mk 6.19, etc.). ♦ (in a verbless clause): máhči=č 'it will be bad' (Mt 16.3).
- • -máči: kəmáči (Mt 7.11, Lk 11.13, Mt 20.15; /č/ assumed from meči, amáči).
- • méči (⟨mrhi⟩ Lk 6.35, 6.45, 7.34, 7.37, Mt 12.35 [pp. 43-70]; ⟨mchi⟩ Lk 16.8 [p. 130]).
- • amáči: amáči-luk·wé·k·we 'if they say bad things to you' (Lk 6.22); amáči-ləni·xsúwak 'they speak Delaware brokenly' (LB).

♦ máhči (-máči) PN 'bad': kəmáči-lehəle·x·e·ɔ·k·anúwa 'your (pl.) evil life' (1834b:23.2).
mahčihəwe·- AI 'treat people badly, do violence to people' (mehəmahčihəwe·- [Rih+; IC]): mehəmahčihəwé·č·i·k 'doers of violence' (Jn 10.8; KJV "robbers").
mahči·h- (-mač·i·h-, me·č·i·h-) TA 'mistreat badly' — mahči·t- TI(2) 'act badly on, defile' ('make "badly," "poorly," "improperly"' [LTD]).
  ▪ mahči·h- (TA): káči awé·n mahči·há·he·kw 'don't treat anyone badly (you pl.)' (Lk 3.14; Gr. 4.111j); ná=č .. mahčí·ha·n 'then he shall be .. badly mistreated' (Lk 18.32; KJV "spitefully entreated," RSV "shamefully treated").
  • -mač·i·h-: kəmač·íhko·n 'it defiles you' (1834b:7.6).
  • me·č·i·h-: me·č·ihkwé·k·wi·k 'those that treat you (pl.) badly' (Jn 15.20); me·č·i·hí·č·i·k 'those that treat me badly' (Jn 15.20).
  ▪ mahči·t- (TI): tá=á· kəwíči-mahči·to·wəné·na·p 'we would not have joined in defiling it' (Mt 23.30; KJV "we would not have been partakers with them in the blood of the prophets").
mahčí·kwi P 'bad' (Gr. 5.7d, 5.120c).
  ♦ (as predicate): ší=tá mahčí·kwi hít·ukw 'or (if) a tree is bad' (Mt 12.33); mahčí·kwi íka wenčí·k·ink 'what grows from it is bad' (Mt 12.33); mahčí·kwi pwəna·eləntaməwá·k·an 'his thoughts are evil' (Jn 8.44).
  ▪ mahčí·kwi PN: mahčí·kwi-skí·kw 'weeds' (Mt 13.36; KJV "tares"); mahčí·kwi-skí·kɔ 'weeds' (Mt 13.27, Mt 13.29, Mt 13.30, etc.); mahčí·kwi-pəna·eləntaməwá·k·an 'evil thinking' (Mt 15.19); mahčí·kwi-hítkunk 'a bad tree (loc.)' (Mt 7.17).
  ♦ mahčí·kwi kéku 'bad things' (1834a:13).
mahčí·k·ami·kw IN 'grave' (Lk 11.44 [2x], Mt 27.64, 27.66); mahči·k·amí·k·ɔ 'graves' (Lk 11.47, 11.48, etc.); mahči·k·amí·k·unk 'the grave (loc.)' (Lk 11.44, Jn 11.31, etc.); mahči·k·ami·k·wi·ké·i P 'among the graves' (Mt 8.28, Mk 5.5, etc.; Gr. 4.10b).
  ♦ Note: The literal meaning 'bad house' may allude to the fencing erected around a traditional grave: "[and they] enclose the grave with a fence of poles" (Heckewelder 1819: 275).
mahči·m- (-mač·i·m-, me·č·i·m-) TA 'speak ill of, malign': kəmač·i·míhəna 'you malign us' (Lk 11.45; KJV "thou reproachest us").
  • me·č·i·m-: me·č·í·mi·t 'who maligns me' (Mk 9.39; KJV "that can lightly speak evil of me").
mahči·po·k·ɔt- II 'taste bad': mahči·pó·k·ɔ 'that tastes bad' (Mt 7.17, 7.18 [2x]).
mahči·t-: see mahči·h- — mahči·t-.
mahči·t·e·ha·- AI 'have wicked thoughts': é·li-mahči·t·e·háhti·t 'because they had wicked thoughts' (⟨mavhi trvetet⟩ 1834b:22.6).
  ▸ Cf. mahči·t·e·he·ɔ́·k·an 'wickedness' (LTD); ⟨machtschitehewoàgan⟩ 'böse gedanken [wicked thoughts]' (Z 230).
mahčo·t·əmaw- (-mač·o·t·əmaw-) TA+O 'criticize for O2': mɔč·o·t·əmaɔ·né·ɔ 'they criticized them for it' (lit., 'spoke ill of it to them') (Mk 7.2). ▸ Cf. mahči·m- TA.
máhələs (Gr. 3.3b) AN 'flint' (1834a:18.12; V, FW, ND).
máhəmai: see mái.
mahtač·a·h- TA 'treat badly': mahtač·áhkɔn 'one that treats you (sg.) badly' (Mt 5.44; no IC); ⟨Machtatschahen⟩ "to use somebody ill, to treat some one badly" (B&A 70; ⟨-en⟩ s.b. ⟨-an⟩).
mahtaehɔ·s·i·- (-mat·aehɔ·s·i·-) AI 'do evil': kéku=háč lí-mahtaehɔ́·s·u 'what evil has he done?' (Lk 23.22); wé·mi é·li-mahtaehɔ·s·í·t·əp 'for all the evil he had done' (Lk 3.19-20).
  • -mat·aehɔ·s·i·-: kəmat·aehɔ·s·íhəmɔ 'you (pl.) do evil' (1842:16.2).
mahtáhəlay AN 'moss'; mahtáhəlaya .. mpínk ehahpi·lí·č·i 'sponge (obv.)' (lit., 'moss that is characteristically in water') (Mt 27.48).

▶ Cf. Mun mătáhlay 'green moss (on log, not in water), used for beds' (MR).

mahtak·əni·m- (-matahkəni·m-, metahkəni·m-, |matakənīm-|) TA 'say bad things about, accuse, denounce': é·li-mahtak·əní·mat ke·tanət·ó·wi·t 'because you (sg.) say bad things about God' (Jn 10.33); hwəska tóhi-mahtak·əni·mawwá·ɔ 'they vehemently accused him' (Lk 23.10).
• -matahkəni·m-: mɔtahkəni·má·ɔ 'he denounces him' (Mk 13.12; KJV "betray", RSV "deliver up"); mɔtahkəni·mawwá·ɔ=č 'they will denounce them' (Mt 10.21).
• metahkəni·m-: metahkəni·má·č·i·k 'ones who accuse him' (Mt 26.65; Gr. 4.64v); metahkəni·mkóni·k 'your accusers' (Jn 8.10).
▶ Cf. ⟨Machtakeniman⟩ "to accuse somebody, to speak ill of some one" (B&A 69); "talk bad about" (OA).

mahtal- (me·t·al-) TA 'catch up to': mahtále·p 'he came upon (them)' (Lk 10.30); mahtalát·e 'when you (sg.) catch up to them' (1842:16.2).
• me·t·al-: me·t·alá·t·əp 'the one who had come upon them' (Lk 10.36); me·t·alá·t·e 'when he caught up to them' (1842:16.2).

mahtamalsəwá·k·an 'ill health' (1834b:7.9).

mahtamalsi·- (me·t·amalsi·-) AI 'be sick': mahtamálsu 'he's feeling bad' (OA); ⟨Machtamallsin⟩ "be sick" (B&A 69).
• me·t·amalsi·-: me·t·amalsí·č·i·k 'those in bad condition' (Lk 14.13; KJV "the maimed").

mahtanko·m- (-mat·anko·m-) TA 'reject' ("be mean to" [LTD]): mahtanko·mí·t·e 'if he rejects me' (Lk 12.9; KJV "denieth").
• -mat·anko·m-: né·pe=č nəmat·ankó·ma 'I, too, will reject him' (Lk 12.9).

mahtant·o·wami·mənsi·- AI 'be a child of the devil': e·lkí·kwi- .. -mahtant·o·wami·mənsie·kw 'the degree to which you (pl.) are children of the devil' (Mt 23.15).

mahtant·o·wi·- AI 'be a devil' (Gr. 5.67d): mahtant·ó·wi·t 'who is a devil' (Jn 10.21); mahtant·o·wí·č·i·k 'ones possessed by devils' (Mk 1.32); takó·=tá ní· nəmahtant·o·wí·i '*I* am not a devil' (Jn 8.49; Gr. 2.69c); ktəli- kí· -mahtant·ó·wi·n 'that *you* are a devil' (Jn 8.52).

mahtant·o·wí·i PN 'of devil(s)' (Gr. 5.122d): mahtant·o·wí·i-sa·k·í·ma 'Chief of Devils' (Mt 10.25); mahtant·o·wí·i-pəna·eləntaməwá·k·an 'the devil's schemes' (Mt 16.18); (with a lexicalized participle) mahtant·o·wí·i-ke·pče·ónkələk 'someone with devil madness' (Jn 10.20).

mahtánt·u AN 'devil' (Mt 4.5, Lk 4.6, Mt 4.10, etc.); mahtant·ó·wak 'devils' (Mk 5.10, 5.12, 5.13, etc.); mahtant·ó·wal 'devil (obv.)' (Mt 4.1, Mk 1.13, 4.10), 'devils (obv.)' (Mk 1.34, Mt 9.34), mahtant·ó·wa 'devils (obv.)' (Mt 4.24, 1.32, etc.); mahtánt·unk 'in hell,' *lit.*, 'in the devil's (or devils') place' (Mt 5.29, 5.30, Mt 10.28, etc.; KJV "hell").

mahtant·uwwá·k·an IN 'evil spirits' (Mt 10.1; KJV "unclean spirits"), 'evil power' (Lk 8.2).

mahta·ka·l- TA 'fight': mahta·ka·lá·t·e 'if he fought him' (Mk 3.26).
▪ mahta·ka·lti·- AI (recip.) 'fight each other': máta=á· čí·č nihəláči mahta·ka·ltí·i. 'They would no longer fight against themselves.' (1834b:44.11); mahta·ká·lti·n 'people fight each other' (1842:10.1).

mahta·ke·- (-mathake·-, |matahkē-|) AI — mahta·ke·yo·wi·- II 'fight'.
▪ mahta·ke·- (AI): mahtá·ke·w 'he fights' (V; Gr. 2.5b), mahtá·ke· (V, OA); mahta·ké·ɔk 'they fight' (Jn 18.36; V); lí·mahtá·ke·n 'that there is war' (Mt 24.6).
• -mathake·-: nəmatháke 'I fight, I am fighting' (V, OA, AD); tá=á· háši ó·k nəmathaké·e 'I will also never fight' (⟨mutvaki⟩ [em.]; 1834a:13).

▪ mahta·ke·yo·wi·- (II): éntxi- nihəláči -mahta·ke·yó·wi·k 'any that fights by itself' (Mk 3.24); ó·k=á· wí·k·əwam nihəláči mahta·ke·yo·wí·k·e 'and if a house fights by itself' (⟨muvtavkrbekc⟩ Mk 3.25).
♦ Note: these appear to have a misunderstanding of KJV "be divided against itself."
mahta·ke·ínnu AN 'soldier'; mahta·ke·innúwak 'soldiers' (Lk 21.20).
mahta·ke·ó·k·an IN 'war' (1834a:20.23; Gr. 5.58b); mahta·ke·ó·k·ana 'wars' (Mk 13.7).
mahta·pto·na·l- (-mat·a·pto·na·l-, amat·a·pto·na·l- [Ra+]) TA — mahta·pto·na·t·- (-mat·a·pto·na·t·-) TI (1a) 'say bad things about, speak evilly about' (Gr. 5.88b).
▪ mahta·pto·na·l- (TA): awé·n mahta·pto·na·lá·t·e 'if anyone speaks evilly about him' (Mt 15.4, Lk 12.10 [2x]).
• -mat·a·pto·na·l-: kəmat·a·pto·ná·la ke·tanət·ó·wi·t 'you speak evilly about God' (Jn 10.36); mɔt·a·pto·na·lá·ɔ 'he said bad things about him' (Mt 26.65; KJV "hath spoken blasphemy").
• amat·a·pto·na·l-: amat·a·pto·ná·lkɔn 'the one that says bad things about you (sg.)' (Mt 5.44; no IC).
▪ mahta·pto·na·t·- (TI): awé·n mahta·pto·na·t·ánke 'if someone says bad things about it' (Mt 23.16 [2x], 23.18 [2x], 23.20 [2x], etc.; KJV "swear by").
• -mat·a·pto·na·t·-: takó· kéku lé·i awé·n mɔt·a·pto·ná·t·amən 'it is no problem for someone to say bad things about it' (Mt 23.16; KJV "swear by"); takó· nə́ šúkw mɔt·a·pto·na·t·amó·wən 'he does not say bad things about only that' (Mt 23.20, 23.21; KJV "sweareth by"). ♦ KJV "swear by" was misunderstood as 'swear at' in Mt 23.16-22 and translated with the TI verb.
mahta·pto·ne·- AI 'swear, speak evilly': áləmi-mahta·pto·ne· 'he began to swear' (Lk 22.59-60&; Gr. 5.128b); mahta·pto·ne·á·ne 'if I have said bad things' (Jn 18.23); ntə́li-mahta·pto·ne·n 'my evil sayings' (*lit.*, 'that I speak evilly') (Jn 18.23).
mahta·pto·ne·ó·k·ana 'evil utterances' (Mt 12.31).
mahta·p·e·i·- (-mat·a·p·e·i·-, me·t·a·p·e·i·-) AI 'be wicked': kó· mahta·p·e·í·i 'he is not mean' (LB).
• -mat·a·p·e·i·-: kəmat·a·p·é·i 'you (sg.) are wicked' (Mt 25.26).
• me·t·a·p·e·i·-: me·t·a·p·é·i·t 'wicked' (Mt 12.45, 18.32, Lk 19.22); me·t·a·p·e·í·č·i·k 'evil people' (Mt 12.39).
mahta·p·e·i·taw-* (amat·a·p·e·i·taw- [Ra+]) 'be wicked towards O2 of': káči háši amat·a·p·e·i·tawié·k·ač awé·n təlahče·s·əwá·k·an 'never be mean (you sg.) about anyone else's possessions' (1834b:21.8).
mahta·wsəwá·k·an (-mat·a·wsəwa·k·an-) IN 'sin, sins' (Mk 2.7, 2.10, Lk 7.49, Mt 12.31, etc.); mahta·wsəwá·k·anink 'in sin' (Jn 9.34).
• -mat·a·wsəwa·k·an-: kəmat·a·wsəwá·k·an 'your (sg.) sins' (Lk 5.20, Mk 2.9, Lk 7.48); mɔt·a·wsəwá·k·an 'his, her sin' (Lk 7.47, Jn 8.34, etc.); kəmat·a·wsəwa·k·anúwa 'your (pl.) sins' (Jn 8.21, 8.24 [2x], 9.41); mɔt·a·wsəwa·k·anúwa 'their sins' (Lk 1.77, Mt 3.6, etc.); mɔt·a·wsəwa·k·anəwá·unk 'their sins (loc.)' (Mt 1.21).
mahta·wsi·- (-mat·a·wsi·-, me·t·a·wsi·-, |matāwsī-|) AI 'sin, be bad': aləwí·i mahtá·wsu 'he commits more of a sin' (Jn 19.11); mahta·wsúwak 'they were bad' (1842:9.8); káči čí·č mahta·wsí·han 'don't sin again (you sg.)!' (Jn 5.14); tə́li-mahtá·wsi·n 'that he is a sinner' (Jn 9.2; Gr. 2.60b); énta-mahtá·wsink 'where the evil are', *lit.*, 'where people (indef.) are evil' (Mt 5.45).
• -mat·a·wsi·-: tá=á· kəmat·a·wsi·húmɔ 'you (pl.) would not be sinners' (Jn 9.41).
• me·t·a·wsi·-: me·t·a·wsía 'me, a sinner' (Lk 18.13); me·t·á·wsi·t 'a sinner' (Lk 5.8, 6.34, Jn 8.7, etc.); me·t·a·wsí·č·i·k 'sinners' (Lk 6.32, 5.30, etc.); me·t·a·wsi·tpáni·k 'those that led bad lives' (Jn 5.29).

▪ me·t·á·wsi·t 'a sinner' (as a lexicalized participle): me·t·a·wsí·t·ink 'like a sinner' (Mt 5.46, 5.47); me·t·a·wsi·t·i·ké·i P 'among the sinners' (Mk 8.38, Lk 22.37).

mahte·ləm- (-mat·e·ləm-, me·t·e·ləm-) TA — mahte·lənt- (-mat·e·lənt-) TI(1a) 'think little or poorly of, have contempt for, despise, reject, scorn', (TI-O) 'be offended'.

▪ mahte·ləm- (TA): káči mahte·ləmié·k·ač 'do not scorn him (you sg.)' (Mt 5.42; KJV "turn .. away" [from him]); káči mahte·ləmié·k·e·kw 'don't scorn them (you pl.)' (Mt 18.10); mahte·ləmá·t·e 'if he scorns him' (Mt 6.24; KJV "despise"); é·li-mahte·ləmáhti·t 'as they had contempt for him' (Mk 5.40).

• -mat·e·ləm-: mɔt·e·ləmawwá·ɔl 'they felt contempt for him' (Mt 13.57), mɔt·e·ləmawwá·ɔ 'they felt contempt for him' (Lk 23.11); nəmat·é·ləmukw 'he scorns me' (Lk 10.16); kəmat·e·ləmíhəmɔ 'you (pl.) think little of me' (Jn 8.49).

• me·t·e·ləm-: me·t·e·ləma·lí·t·əp 'who (obv.) had thought badly of them (obv.)' (Lk 18.9; Gr. 4.76p); me·t·é·ləmi·t 'who thinks little of me' (Jn 12.48; KJV "that rejecteth me").

▪ mahte·lənt- (TI) (TI-O) takó· nhák·enk wə́nči-mahte·ləntamó·wi 'he is not offended because of me' (Lk 7.23; KJV "offended").

• -mat·e·lənt-: ná šá·e mɔt·e·ləntamən 'then he suddenly has a negative opinion of it' (Mt 13.21); mɔt·e·ləntaməné·ɔ 'they scorned it' (Lk 7.30).

▸ Cf. ⟨Mattelendam⟩ "to be uneasy, to be troubled in mind; to despise" (B&A 75); Mun mătéˑlŏmeˑw 'thinks poorly of, insults, abuses (s.o.)' (dict.).

mahte·ləntaməwo·x·we·- AI 'go feeling bad': áləmi-mahte·ləntaməwó·x·we· 'he went away feeling bad' (Mt 19.22&).

mahte·x·i·n- (-mat·e·x·i·n-) AI — mahte·x·ən- (me·t·e·x·ən-) II '(fall and) land, hit the ground'.

▪ mahte·x·i·n- (AI): mahte·x·ínke 'if he falls' (Lk 20.18).

• -mat·e·x·i·n-: ná .. mɔt·e·x·í·nən 'then he (baby in womb) kicked' (Lk 1.44, *lit.*, 'landed'; KJV "leaped [in my womb]"); nána mi·məntə́t·al lá·mahte mɔt·e·x·í·nəli·n 'the baby then kicked (*lit.*, landed) in the womb' (Lk 1.41); nána .. hɔ́k·enk mɔt·e·x·í·nəli·n 'then she (obv.) landed in his body' (Lk 1.41 [the reverse of the intended meaning, as if KJV "was filled with" was understood as 'filled']).

▪ mahte·x·ən- (II): mahté·x·ən 'it falls, fell' (Mt 13.4, 13.5, 13.7, 13.8, 1834b:27.2 etc.); lí- hɔk·ayəwá·ink -mahté·x·ən 'that it pertained squarely to them' (Mt 21.45&); é·li- máta wtehəwá·ink -mahté·x·ink 'for it does not end up in their hearts' (Mk 7.19).

• me·t·e·x·ən-: me·t·é·x·ink 'what falls (to the ground), lands' (Mt 13.19 [2x], 13.20, etc.; Gr. 2.28g). ▸ Cf. ⟨machteéchen⟩, ⟨machtéchen⟩ II 'to concern; hit against' (Z. 42, 94).

mahtə́t II 'it is bad' (Gr. 5.7d): see mé·thik below.

mahtíti (Gr. 2.76d) P 'little' (Lk 7.47 [2x]).

mái (mé·i, máhəmai [Rvh+ REP]; Gr. 5.128o) PV 'go and, go (in order) to' (Lk 2.15, 3.12, Mt 4.11, etc.); nəmái- (Mt 2.2, 8.7, etc.); kəmái- (Jn 4.38, Mt 7.6, Mk 1.24, etc.); mɔ́i- (Lk 1.59, 2.27, Mt 3.5, etc.).

• mé·i (Mk 3.8, Lk 6.17, Mt 22.11, etc.).

♦ (referring to indefinite subject) lí·=á· -mái-ki·k·e·há·li·n 'so that he (obv.) would be cured (by someone coming)' (Lk 7.3).

• máhəmai: nnúči-máhəmai-pənáɔ 'I have been coming to look at it since then' (Lk 13.7).

máilink P 'mile, miles': kwə́t·i máilink 'a mile' (Mt 5.41), ní·š·a máilink 'two miles' (Jn 11.18), ní·š·a·š máilink 'seven miles' (Lk 24.13).

mai·m- (|mawīm-|; Gr. 5.60d) TA 'weep for, mourn' — mawənt- TI(1a) 'weep for'.

- mai·m- (TA): káči mai·mí·he·kw 'don't weep for me (you pl.)!' (Lk 23.28; Gr. 4.111t); mɔi·má·ɔl 'she weeps for them' (Mt 2.18; Gr. 4.24h); mɔi·mawwá·ɔ 'they wept over him' (Lk 23.27).
  - mawənt- (TI): mawəntamo·kw khak·ayúwa 'weep for yourselves' (Lk 23.28).

mai·k·e·- AI 'spend the night, stay overnight': maí·k·e·l 'stay (you sg.)' (Jn 4.40); ehənta-maí·k·e·t 'where he used to spend the night' (Lk 22.39); é·li-kwí·la-mai·k·ehtí·t·əp 'because they had not been able to spend the night' (Lk 2.7); ná=nə mɔí·k·e·n 'and there he spent the night' (Lk 21.37; Gr. 4.42p); ná=nə mɔi·k·e·né·ɔ 'and there they spent the night' (Mt 21.17).

mai·k·e·i·k·á·ɔn IN 'inn' (Gr. 5.54f); mai·k·e·i·k·á·ɔnink 'an inn (loc.)' (Lk 2.7, 10.34).

mai·k·e·taw- TA 'stay with': awé·n mai·k·e·tá·k·ɔne 'if someone is visiting you' (1834b:21.1); mai·k·e·taí·ne·n 'stay with us' (Lk 24.29); tə́li-=á· -mai·k·étaɔ·n 'that he would stay with them' (Lk 24.29); mɔi·k·e·tá·k·o·n 'that he (obv.) stay with her' (Lk 10.38).

málahši P 'like, as' (Jn 3.14, Mt 6.7, Lk 6.47&, Mt 7.26, 9.36, etc.). ♦ Accent follows álahši (OA, LB), but there is also aláhši (WL).

manák·ɔ·n IN 'rainbow' (⟨manukon⟩ 1834b:19.1, 1842:9.7; LB as AN). Also mənúk·ɔ·n, loc. mənúk·ɔnink (LTD ND); manúk·ɔnk (V; inflected as an II). ► Cf. Mun manákwa·n AN (APh).

manax·e·- AI 'gather (fire)wood': manáx·e· 'he goes after wood, cuts wood' (OA, FW, LB); káhta-=č xé·li -manax·ét·am 'let's try to get a lot of wood' (1834a:13).

manət·o·wi·- (-mant·o·wi·-): AI 'be a spirit, have (such a) spirit': ní·ski-manət·ó·wi·t 'one who had an unclean spirit' (Mk 1.23; KJV "a man with an unclean spirit"); ní·ski-manət·o·wí·č·i·k 'those with unclean spirits' (Mk 3.11; KJV "unclean spirits"); ní·ski-manət·o·wi·lí·č·i 'ones (obv.) with unclean spirits' (Lk 7.21 [em.]; KJV "evil spirits").
  - -mant·o·wi·-: kəmant·o·wíhəmɔ 'you (pl.) are gods' (Jn 10.34).

manə́t·u (Gr. 3.1d) AN 'spirit' (Mt 12.31, Mk 9.20, 9.28, etc.), 'God' (Mt 27.54&); pí·lsi·t manə́t·u 'the holy spirit' (Jn 14.26, 20.22); (ná) wəla·məwe·ɔ·k·aní·i-manə́t·u 'the truth spirit' (Jn 15.26, 16.13; KJV "the Spirit of truth"); ní·ski-manə́t·u 'unclean spirit' (Mk 5.8, Mt 12.43); manət·ó·wak 'spirits' (Mt 12.45 and Jn 10.35 [prox. for obv.]; Lk 10.20); ní·ski-manət·ó·wal 'the unclean spirit (obv.)' (Mk 1.27); manə́t·unk wə́nči 'from spirit' (1834b:24.1).

manət·uwwá·k·an (-mant·uwwa·k·an-; Gr. 5.58p) IN 'spiritual power' (Jn 7.39, Mk 9.17); pí·lhik manət·uwwá·k·anink 'in the power of the holy spirit' (Acts 1.5; *lit.*, 'in holy spiritual-power'; KJV "with the Holy Ghost").
  - -mant·uwwa·k·an-: nɔmant·uwwá·k·an 'my spiritual power' (Mt 12.18), 'my spirit' (Lk 23.46); kəmant·uwwá·k·an 'your (spiritual) power' (ME); mɔnt·uwwá·k·an 'his (spiritual) power' (Lk 4.14, 4.18, Mt 10.20, Lk 11.20, Jn 6.63); mɔnt·uwwá·k·anink 'his (spiritual) power (loc.)' (1834b:22.11).

manni·h- TA — manni·t- (mi·manni·t- [Rī+], mihəmanni·t- [Rih+]) TI(2) 'make'.
  - manni·h- (TA): a·lə́nte manní·he·w awé·ni·l 'some made some creature' (1834b:19.8); ehənta-manni·hə́ntəp si·skəwí·i-hó·s·ak 'where clay pots used to be made' (Mt 27.7); wé·mi awé·n máta nə́ wə́nči-manni·há·wən 'everyone was not made for that' (Mk 2.27).
  - manni·t- (TI): wí·k·əwam íka táli-manní·to· 'he built a house there' (Mt 21.33); xinkó·ltay manní·to·l 'make a large boat (you sg.)' (1842:8.7); manni·tó·t·amo·kw 'let's all make them' (Lk 9.33; Gr. 4.106p); káči manni·tó·he·kw 'don't make it (you pl.)' (1842:10.10; Gr. 4.112j); nəmanni·tó·na 'I made them (inan.)' (ME; Gr. 3.6i); mɔnní·to·n hókw 'he made the sky' (1842:6.4).

• mi·manni·t-: máta=á· we·ɔ́·psi·t mi·manni·tá·k·we 'if the Whiteman didn't make it' (1842:23.6).

• mihəmanni·t-: kší·k·anal ɔ́·k mihəmanní·to· we·ɔ́·psi·t 'The Whiteman also makes knives' (1842:23.7); é·li-mihəmanní·ta·kw kší·k·ana 'because he makes knives' (1842:23.7).

manni·taw- (menni·taw-) TA+O 'make O2 for': kəmanni·ta·k·ó·na pa·tamwe·i·k·á·ɔn 'he built us a house of worship' (Lk 7.5).

• menni·taw-: ná mahtánt·u menni·túntəp 'which was made for the devil' (Mt 25.41).

manni·ta·s·i·- II 'be made' (Gr. 5.106b): táli-=č -manni·tá·s·u xínkwi-wí·k·əwam 'a large house will be built there' (1834b:45.3); manni·tá·s·o·p 'it was made' (Jn 2.20, Mk 2.27); wé·mi kéku náni wə́nči-manni·tá·s·o·p 'everything was made by him' (Jn 1.3).

manunkᵒ (|manōnk-|) 'angry' (Gr. 5.125b).

manunkhita·kwsi·- AI 'shout angrily' (Gr. 5.109c): aləwí·i manunkhita·kwsúwak 'their shouts grew angrier' (Lk 23.5).

manunksəwá·k·an IN 'anger' (Mt 3.7, Lk 21.23).

manunksəwí·i (Gr. 5.125b) PN 'of anger' (Lk 21.22).

manunksi·- AI 'be angry': áhi-manúnksu 'he was very angry' (Mt 22.7); áhi-manunksúwak 'they were very angry' (Lk 4.28, Mt 8.28, Lk 6.11); ná mɔnúnksi·n 'then he was angry' (Lk 15.28).

manunksi·taw- TA 'be angry at': awé·n manunksi·taɔ́·t·e wí·mahta 'if anyone is angry at his brother' (Mt 5.22); mɔnunksi·taɔ́·p·ani 'he was angry at them' (1834b:17.4).

manuxkwe·e·- AI(+O) 'take another's wife as one's wife': káči manuxkwe·é·han 'do not take another man's wife (you sg.)' (Mt 19.18; misprinted ⟨maoxqrrvun⟩ 1834b:21.5); é·li- .. -manuxkwe·é·t·əp 'as he had taken her (his brother's wife) as his wife' (Mk 6.17).

maɔt·a·k·ani·- II 'be a famine': áhi-maɔt·á·k·ano·p 'there was a great famine' (1842:14.4). ▶ Cf. ⟨Mawottakan⟩ 'famine' (B&A 76); Mun mawatá·kanəw 'there is a scarcity of food, a famine'.

maɔ·č·i·mo·lx- (me·ɔ·č·i·mo·lx-) TA 'go to inform': me·ɔ·č·i·mo·lxá·č·i·k 'the ones going to inform them' (Mt 28.9).

máta P 'not' (Gr. 2.73g, 5.23i) (Jn 1.5, 1.12, 1.20, etc.); máta=háč=ét 'don't you think .. ?' (Lk 12.28). ♦ The future negative in Blanchard usually has tá·á· (with tá (2), apparently a reduced form of máta), but máta is sometimes used with =č FUT: ɔ́·k=č wsa·k·i·ma·ɔ́·k·an máta wi·i·kwé·i 'and his kingdom shall never end' (Lk 1.33); máta=č háši kahto·p·wí·i 'they (indef.) will never be hungry' (Jn 6.35); ná=č máta kéku lé·i 'then there will be no problem' (Mt 15.6).

♦ /máta/ may be gapped with a second negative verb (Gr. 6.31bc; Mt 6.25, 18.12).

♦ /máta/ may have scope over a head verb, not including a preverb that precedes it (Mk 9.41).

-mat·a·wsəwa·k·an: see mahta·wsəwá·k·an.

mawənt-: see mai·m- — mawənt-.

mawəntəwá·k·an (Gr. 5.60d, 5.114h) IN 'mourning' (Mt 2.18).

mawo·s·əmo·ke·- (|mawōsəmōhkē-|; Gr. 5.85c) AI+O 'take (animal) to water' (*lit.*, 'make go and drink'): máta=háč=hánkw .. mɔwo·s·əmo·ké·wəna 'doesn't he take them to water?' (Lk 13.15).

maxahɔla·mwi·- (amax·ahɔla·mwi·-, -məmxahɔla·mwi·- [Ra+]; cf. Gr. 5.34b) AI 'scream, shout': énta-=č -maxahɔla·mwíhti·t 'where they will scream loudly' (Mt 13.42, 13.50).

• amax·ahɔla·mwi·-: amax·ahɔlá·mu 'he screamed' (Mk 1.26, 5.5, 9.18); amax·ahɔlá·məwak 'they shouted' (Mt 20.30, Mt 20.31&); énta-=č -amax·ahɔla·mwíhti·t 'where they will scream loudly' (Mt 8.12).

• -məmxahɔla·mwi·-: ná mumxahɔlá·mwi·n 'then he cried out loudly' (Mk 9.26); ná mumxahɔla·mwi·né·ɔ 'then they cried out loudly' (Mk 6.49).

maxak·i·l- (-maxki·l-, me·xki·l-) AI 'be big, be great': maxák·i·l 'he is big, getting big, got big' (OA, AD, V).
- -maxki·l-: nəmáxki·l 'I'm big' (OA); nál=č náni mɔxkí·lən '*he* shall be great' (Mt 5.19).
- me·xki·l-: me·xkí·lək 'the biggest (anim.)' (LB); me·xkí·lək xé·s 'a big hide' (ME).
♦ The II is suppletive; see maxe·-.

maxat·ən- II 'be a high hill or mountain' (Gr. 5.11i): énta-maxát·ink 'a high mountain' (Mt 4.8, 5.1, Mt 17.1). ♦ The plural has the stem amankahtən-.

maxe·- (me·x·e·-, |maxē-|) II 'be large, great': maxé· 'it is big' (V); áhi-maxé·p 'it was very large' (Mk 16.4; Gr. 4.68l).
- me·x·e·-: mé·x·e·k '(which is) great' (Mt 5.22; Gr. 4.66e).

maxe·ləmukwsəwa·k·ani·- II 'be glory': maxe·ləmukwsəwa·k·aní·k·eč ki·š·e·ləmúwe·t lí 'Let there be glory to God' (Lk 2.14).

maxinkɔhkəni·m-: see xinkɔhkəni·m-.

maxinkɔhkəni·mkwəs·i·-: see xinkɔhkəni·mkwəs·i·-.

maxínkwi: see xínkwi.

máxkahsən IN 'red stone', "copper" (Mt 10.9); maxkahsəna "bricks" (1834b:19.3, 1842:9.8).

maxkalət- II 'rust': máxkalət 'it is rusty' (LB); ɔ́·k=á· énta-maxkalə́t·ək 'and where they would rust' (⟨muxalituk⟩ Mt 6.19); énta-=á· máta .. -maxkalə́t·ək 'where they would not rust' (⟨muxalituk⟩ Mt 6.20).

maxkamaw- TA+O 'find O2 with': entxíe·kw=ké=č awé·n maxkamaɔ́k·e 'if I find that any of you has it' (1842:16.2); entxíenk awé·n maxkamaɔ́t·e 'if you (sg.) find that any of us has it' (1842:16.2).

maxkaw- (me·xkaw-) TA — maxk- (me·xk-) TI(1a) 'find'.
■ maxkaw- (TA): nəmáxkaɔ 'I found him, her' (V, OA, ME); é·li-máxkaɔk 'as I've found them' (Lk 15.6); wə́nči-=č máta -káski-maxkaɔ́·ankw 'so that we (inc.) won't be able to find him' (Jn 7.35; Gr. 4.97d); tá=á· kəmaxkai·húmɔ 'you (pl.) shall not find me' (Jn 7.34, 7.36; Gr. 4.89d); kəmaxko·lhúməna 'we found you (sg., pl.)' (OA; Gr. 3.7d, 4.32); tə́li-=á· kxántki -máxkaɔ·n 'until he finds it (anim.)', *lit.*, 'so that he would finally find it (anim.)' (Lk 15.4).
- me·xkaw-: mé·či me·xkaɔ́t·e 'after he had found him' (Jn 9.35); me·xkaɔhtí·t·e 'when they found him' (Mk 1.37, Jn 6.25).
■ maxk- (TI): máxkam kéku 'he finds something' (1834a:14); kəmaxkamúhəmɔ=č. 'You (pl.) will find some [food (inan.), *i.e.* fish].' (Jn 21.6); takó· nəmaxkamó·wi 'I did not find any (of it)' (Lk 23.14; Gr. 4.91a); takó· ní· nəmaxkamó·wi wə́nči-=á· -nhílənt 'I have not found any reason why he should be killed' (Lk 23.22); máta kéku maxkamó·wi 'he found nothing' (Lk 13.6, Mk 11.13&, Lk 23.15; Gr. 4.91c); máta maxkamo·wí·ɔk 'they did not find any' (Mt 26.60; Gr. 4.91k); mé·či nəmáxkamən 'I have now found it' (Lk 16.4; Gr. 4.39a); kəmáxkamən=č 'you shall find it' (Mt 7.7, 11.29; Gr. 4.39f); mɔ́xkamən=č 'he will find it' (Mt 7.8, 10.39; Gr. 4.39g); kəmaxkaməné·ɔ=č 'you (pl.) shall find it' (Lk 11.9; Gr. 4.39t); tə́li-=á· kxántki -máxkamən 'until she finds it', *lit.*, 'so that he would finally find it' (Lk 15.8).
- me·xk-: me·xkánke 'when he found (has found) it' (Mt 13.44, Mt 13.46).

maxka·s·i·- II 'be found' (Gr. 5.105h): é·li- .. -táli-maxká·s·i·k 'for it is found there' (Jn 5.39).

maxke·-: see maxksi·- — maxke·-.

máxki PN 'red' (Gr. 5.120d); máxki-sí·p·unk wə́nči 'from the Red River' (1834b:45.2).

-maxki·l-: see maxak·i·l-.

maxksi·- AI — maxke·- II 'be red' (Gr. 5.10l).

- maxksi·- (AI): máxksu 'he is red' (V; Gr. 3.18b); máxksi·t '(which is) red' (ME, FW).
- maxke·- (II): máxke· 'it is red' (V, ME); é·li- mó·šhakw -máxke·k 'for the sky is red' (Mt 16.2, 16.3); máxke·k '(which was) red' (Mt 27.28, Jn 19.5, Mt 27.31&; Gr. 4.66f).

-max·inkɔhkəni·m-: see xinkɔhkəni·m-.
-max·inkɔhkəni·mkwəs·i·-: see xinkɔhkəni·mkwəs·i·-.
-max·inkɔhkəni·mkwəs·o·ha·l-: see xinkɔhkəni·mkwəs·o·ha·l-.
-max·inkɔ·khuk·wí·ɔn: see xinkɔ·khuk·wí·ɔn.
-max·ínkwi: see xínkwi.

maya·e·lənt- (TI(1a)) TI-O 'be certain' (Zeisberger 2016:44); 'be fixed in purpose, be settled in mind' (B&A 72): máta káski-maya·e·ləntamó·u 'he was unable to be at ease in his mind' (1834a:20.20); wə́nči-=č -maya·e·ləntamenk 'by which we (exc.) will be certain' (Mt 12.38).

maya·e·ləntamawá·k·an IN 'confirmation, assurance' (Mt 12.39 [2x]; KJV "sign").

mayá·i (me·á·i) P 'true, truly' (Gr. 2.13c, 5.120e, 5.129w): 'truly' (Jn 4.53, Mt 9.13), 'plainly' (Jn 16.25), 'exactly' (Jn 12.50, Mt 22.16), 'simply' (Mk 5.4); etc.
- ♦ (idiomatic uses): né·ləma mayá·i íka pé·a·t 'before he had gotten all the way there' (Lk 15.20); †nté·pit mayá·i e·lanko·ma·tpáni 'a direct descendant of David' (Lk 1.27).
- mayá·i PV (me·á·i) 'true': kəmayá·i-ləs·i 'you did just what you were supposed to' (Mt 25.21, 25.23; KJV "hast been faithful"); mayá·i-nalóx·ən 'it is the perfect time' (Lk 21.13&).
- me·á·i: me·á·i-ɔ·x·é·e·k 'the true light' (Jn 1.9).
- mayá·i PN: mayá·i-sa·k·í·ma 'king' (Mt 21.9& [KJV "the King" in Lk 19.38 and Jn 12.13], 1842:14.1).
- maya·í·i PN 'true' (Gr. 5.121b): maya·í·i-ahɔ·p·e·ɔ́·k·an 'true wealth' (Lk 16.11).

maya·i·xt- TI(2) 'set right': yúkwe=háč lápi kkát·a-maya·í·xto·n 'are you (sg.) now going to set it right again?' (Acts 1.6).

maya·i·xtaw- TA+O 'set O2 right for, guide O2 for': kəmaya·i·xta·k·ó·ne·n ksi·t·əná·nal 'it guides our (inc.) feet' (⟨myaextakwnrn nsetunanul⟩ Lk 1.79 [em.]).

maya·ɔ·č·i·m- TA 'testify about': mɔya·ɔ·č·i·má·p·ani 'he testified about him' (Jn 1.15; ⟨myoth-⟩ for ⟨myaoth-⟩).

maya·ɔ·č·i·mo·lx- (me·a·ɔ·č·i·mo·lx-) TA 'be a witness for': kəmaya·ɔ·č·i·mo·lxíhəna 'you yourselves were witnesses for me' (⟨kumy athem-⟩ for ⟨kumyaothem-⟩ Jn 3.28).
- me·a·ɔ·č·i·mo·lx-: me·a·ɔ·č·i·mo·lxát·əp 'the one you (sg.) bore witness for' (⟨mro-⟩ Jn 3.26; Gr. 4.76d).

maya·ɔ·č·i·mwi·- (me·a·ɔ·č·i·mwi·-) AI 'testify': awé·n=háč=á· káski-maya·ɔ·č·í·mu 'who would be able to testify (that ..)?' (⟨myaoh-⟩ Jn 8.46; KJV "convinceth", RSV "convicts"); maya·ɔ·č·í·mo·p 'he made a declaration' (Jn 13.21; KJV "testified" [to a future event]); tə́li-=č -maya·ɔ·č·í·mwi·n 'he was to testify about it' (⟨myath-⟩ Jn 1.8; KJV "was sent to bear witness of").
- me·a·ɔ·č·i·mwi·-: me·a·ɔ·č·i·mwi·t 'who was a witness' (⟨mrothemwet⟩; Jn 1.7).
- ▸ Cf. maya·ɔ·č·i·m- TA.

maya·ɔ·p·e·i·- (me·ya·ɔ·p·e·i·-) AI 'be sensible, proper, etc.': me·ya·ɔ·p·é·ian 'you who are sensible' (Mt 25.21, 25.23; KJV "good and faithful"); me·ya·ɔ·p·é·i·t '(who was) upstanding' (Mt 27.57&; KJV "honourable").

maya·ɔ·p·e·i·taw- TA 'be faithful to': maya·ɔ·p·e·í·taw 'be faithful towards them (you sg.)' (1842:12.2).

ma·č·i·- (|māčī-|; Gr. 5.78j) AI 'go home': má·č·i·l 'go home (you sg.)' (Mt 8.13, Mk 5.19, 2.11); káči káhta-ma·č·í·hi·č 'let him not seek to go home' (Lk 17.31; Gr. 4.110f); mé·či ma·č·í·ɔ 'he (abs.) has already gone' (1834b:40.5); ma·č·í·p·ani·k 'they returned home' (Lk 2.39, 2.43, Jn 7.53); é·ləmi-ma·č·í·t·e 'when he went home' (Jn 4.51, Lk 18.13); ma·č·ihtí·t·e 'when they went home' (Lk 2.15, Mt 2.12); ná mɔ·č·í·ne·p 'then he went home' (Lk 1.23; Gr. 4.72a); ná mɔ·č·i·né·ɔ 'then they left' (1842:15.4).

ma·eha·s·i·- II 'be gathered' (Gr. 5.105f): ɔ́·k xáskwi·m ma·ehá·s·u 'and corn is gathered in' (1834a:17); e·lkí·kwi-ma·ehá·s·i·k 'in the same way (*lit.*, to the same extent) that they (inan.) are gathered' (Mt 13.40).

ma·ehəla·- AI 'gather': xé·li awé·n ma·éhəle·p 'many people gathered' (Mk 2.2, Mt 13.2); ma·ehəlé·ɔk 'they gathered' (Mk 6.33, Jn 12.12, Lk 22.66); ma·ehəlé·p·ani·k 'they gathered' (Mk 1.33, Mt 26.3, Mk 14.53, Acts 1.4); énta-ma·ehəláhti·t 'where they gathered' (Jn 20.19); ma·ehəlá·č·i·k 'the crowd' (Mt 14.15, Mk 15.8), 'those assembled' (Lk 12.13); ma·ehəla·tpáni·k 'the crowd' (Mt 22.33); ma·ehəla·lí·č·i 'the ones (obv.) gathered together' (Mt 9.36, 13.36); tə́li- íkali -ma·ehəlá·li·n '(that they [obv.] were) running together there' (Mk 9.25; KJV "came running together").

♦ énta-ma·éhəlank 'synagogue(s)' (*lit.*, 'where people (indef.) gather'; a calque of the Greek word, meaning literally '(place of) assembly') (Lk 4.15 [2x], Mt 4.23, etc.), ehə́nta-ma·éhəlank (Mk 13.9, Jn 16.2). ▶ See also mehəma·éhəla·s*.

ma·ehw- TA — ma·eh- TI(1a) 'gather' (Gr. 5.12r).

■ ma·ehw- (TA): wé·mi=č entxa·ké·i·t awé·n ma·éhɔ· 'all nations shall be gathered' (Mt 25.32); ma·ehɔ́·ɔk=č 'they will be gathered up' (Jn 15.6); ehələkhíkwi-ma·éhɔ·t 'at the times she gathers them' (Lk 13.34, Mt 23.37; Gr. 5.128m); mɔ·ehɔ́·ɔ=č 'he will gather them' (Jn 11.52); nkát·a-ma·ehɔ́·ɔk 'I have wanted to gather them together' (Lk 13.34).

■ ma·eh- (TI): ma·éhəmo·kw 'gather them (you pl.)' (Mt 13.30); ntə́li-ma·éhəmən 'that I gather it' (Mt 25.26); mɔ·éhəmən=č hwí·t 'he will gather the wheat' (Lk 3.17).

ma·enke·- AI 'gather people together': mɔ·énke·n 'he called people together' (1834b:38.1).

ma·e·i·- AI 'gather': énta- ní·š·a ší=tá naxá -ma·e·ihtí·t·e 'when two or three gather together' (Mt 18.20); énta-ma·é·ink 'in a synagogue' (*lit.*, 'where one gathers') (Mt 23.6; KJV "in the synagogues"), táli ehə́nta-ma·é·ink 'in the synagogues' (Mt 23.34).

ma·e·m- TA 'call together': mé·či ma·e·má·t·e 'after he called them together' (Mt 2.4); mɔ·e·má·p·ani 'he called them together' (Lk 23.13).

ma·e·n- (mehəma·e·n- [Rih+; IC]) TI(1b) 'gather': ma·é·nəmo·kw 'gather them (you pl.)' (⟨marnumwq⟩ Mt 6.20; ⟨macvnumwq⟩ Mt 13.30 [em.; influenced by ⟨Macvmwq⟩ /ma·éhəmo·kw/ two sentences before]; Gr. 4.106h); káči ma·e·nəmó·he·kw 'do not gather it (you pl.)' (Mt 6.19; Gr. 4.112g); awé·n máta wíči-ma·e·nínke 'if anyone does not join in the harvest of them' (Mt 12.30).

• mehəma·e·n-: móni mehəma·é·nink 'tax (*lit.*, money) collector' (Lk 18.11, 18.13); móni mehəma·e·nínkəp 'a tax-collector (of that time)' (Lk 18.10); mehəma·e·nínki·k móni 'tax collectors' (Lk 3.12, Lk 5.29, 5.30); móni mehəma·e·ninkpáni·k 'the tax-collectors (of that time)' (Lk 15.1).

ma·e·na·s·i·- (mehəma·e·na·s·i·- [Rih+; IC]; Gr. 5.105y) II 'be gathered, harvested, collected': ma·e·na·s·i·k·i 'what is harvested (pl.)' (Mt 12.30).

• mehəma·e·na·s·i·-: mehəma·e·ná·s·i·k móni 'the money that was collected' (Mk 12.41).

ma·e·nəmaw- (mihəma·e·nəmaw- [Rih+], |māwēnəmaw-|) TA+O 'to collect O2 for': tə́li- .. -khwithíke·n mihəma·e·nəmáɔ·n móni †sí·sal 'for him to forbid people to collect money for Caesar' (Lk 23.2; Gr. 3.11b).

ma·e·x·we- AI 'gather': ma·e·x·wé·ɔk 'they gathered' (Mt 27.62); ma·e·x·wé·p·ani·k 'they gathered' (Lk 1.59); ma·e·x·we·é·k·we 'when you (pl.) gather' (Mt 18.17 [2x]).

†má·ktali·n 'Magdalene' (Lk 8.2, Jn 19.25); mé·li·s-†má·ktali·n 'Mary Magdalene' (Jn 19.25, Lk 23.55&); mé·li-†ma·ktalí·na (Jn 20.3, Mk 16.9).
- †ma·kté·la 'Magdala' (Mt 15.39).

†má·lkəs 'Malchus' (Jn 18.10).

ma·mahče·é·s·a IN pl. 'property' (⟨mamahrrsu⟩ 1834b:28.4); mɔ·mahče·e·s·əwá·ɔl 'their goods' (⟨omahrswal⟩ 1834a:19.14, for ⟨mom-⟩). ▸ Cf. ⟨Mámachtschees⟩ "ware" (Z 220), ⟨Mamachtschewĩs⟩ "effects, merchandise, ware" (Z 64, 122, 220), ⟨u'Mamachtschewesum⟩ "his ware" (Z 220). See also lač·e·s·əwá·k·an 'goods, merchandise'.

ma·ɔt-: see ma·wsi·- — ma·ɔt-.

má·si 'Martha' (Lk 10.38, 10.40 [2x], etc.); ma·sí·s·a 'Martha (obv.)' (Jn 11.1, 11.19).
▸ For final /i/, cf. †ani above.

†má·to·s 'Matthew' (Lk 6.15, Mt 9.9&, 10.3).

ma·wənap·i·- AI 'sit together': né·li-ma·wənap·íhti·t 'while they were sitting together' (Acts 1.6; KJV "were come together"). ▸ The initial ma·wən- 'together' in this word and the next is derived from the stem ma·wən- TI(1b) 'gather all of': má·wəni 'gather it all up' (LB).

má·wəni PV 'collectively, all together' (Gr. 5.27e): ⟨Mawuni⟩ 'assembled, collectively' (B&A 76); kəmá·wəni-=č -tɔlo·ka·k·ani·né·ɔ 'you must all have him as your servant' (Mk 10.44).

ma·wsi·- (me·a·wsi·-, |m(ay)āwəsī-|) AI — ma·ɔt- II 'be one'.
- ma·wsi·- (AI): má·wsu 'there was one' (Jn 5.5); é·li- nə́ -lí-má·wsi·t nní·č·a·n 'for he is my only child' (Lk 9.38); nə́ ší·kanč tə́li-má·wsi·n we·k·wí·s·ink 'the only one is the Son (lit., the Son is the only one)' (Jn 1.18); é·li- máta -ma·wsí·ɔ 'for I am not one' (Jn 8.16; Gr. 4.95a); nəmá·wsi 'I am one' (Jn 8.18); ná·=nə ntə́li-má·wsi·n 'I'm the only one (living)' (OA); nó·e šúkw tə́li-ma·wsí·ne·p 'Noah was the only one' (1842:8.5); †nó·wa šúkw tə́li-ma·wsi·né·s·a 'Noah was the only person ..' (1834b:18; cf. Gr. §4.8, Goddard 1979: 148-151]).
• me·a·wsi·-: me·á·wsi·t 'one (anim.)' (Mt 25.45), me·á·wsi·t ki·ló·wa 'one of you' (Mk 14.18, Lk 11.11; cf. Mk 14.20); me·á·wsi·t entxíe·kw 'one from among you' (Jn 13.21).
♦ Participles (without IC): ma·wsí·li·t 'one (obv.)' (Jn 3.18); ma·wsi·lí·č·i kkwí·s·al 'his only son' (Jn 3.16).
- ma·ɔt- (II): má·ɔt 'it is (only) one' (Mt 18.9); má·ɔt=č hɔk·ayúwa 'their bodies (sg.) will be one' (Mt 19.6); á·pči=á· má·ɔt 'it would always be (only) one' (Jn 12.24).

má·wsu AN 'one, a certain one' (agent noun [§5.6j] from ma·wsi·- AI 'be one'); má·wsu 'one' (Jn 4.37, 55; Lk 4.41, Lk 8.29, Lk 8.2; Mt 10.42, Lk 7.36, 11.27; Mk 6.15); má·wsu né·k 'one of those' (Jn 1.40); né·k má·wsu télən ɔ́·k ní·š·a entxí·č·i·k 'one of those twelve' (Jn 6.71); má·wsu .. ó·x·ɔ 'the father of one of them' (Mk 10.46; cf. Gr. 6.26); má·wsu .. má·wsu 'one .. the other' (Lk 23.33, Jn 20.12, etc.); ma·wsúwa .. ma·wsúwa 'one (abs.) .. the other (abs.)' (Lk 18.10 [2x]); ma·wsí·lu .., káči ma·wsí·lu 'one (obv.) .., and the other (obv.) ..' (Lk 7.41).

ma·wso·wi·- AI 'be one, be as one': wénči-=č -pahkánči-ma·wso·wíhti·t 'so that they will perfectly be one' (Jn 17.23); tə́li-=č -ma·wso·wí·li·n 'for them (obv.) to be one' (Jn 11.52); ktə́li-=á· ɔ́·k ne·k·əmá·ɔ tahkwí·i -ma·wso·wí·ne·n 'so that we and they would be one together' (Jn 17.21); ní· ɔ́·k nó·x nəma·wso·wíhəna 'I and my father are one' (Jn 10.30).

méči: see máhči.

mehəlamɔ·s·i·lí·č·i: see mhalamɔ·s·i·-.

mehəmahčihəwé·č·i·k: see mahčihəwe·-.

mehəma·éhəla·s* 'congregation' (-mehəma·ehəla·s·əm-; mehəma·ehəla·- [Rih+; IC] < ma·ehəla·- AI 'gather'; Gr. §5.6.l): nəmehəma·ehəlá·s·əmak 'my congregation' (Mt 16.18; KJV "my church").

mehəma·e·na·s·i·-: see ma·e·na·s·i·-.

mehəma·é·nink: see ma·e·n-.

méhəmane·t 'drinker': see məne·-.

mehəmí·č·ink 'food': see mi·č·i·-.

mehəmi·kəmɔ́·s·i·t 'worker': see mi·kəmɔ·s·i·-.

mekisahkwi·- AI 'wear sheep clothes, be costumed as a sheep': mekisahkwí·č·i·k 'those who are in sheep clothes' (Mt 7.15; KJV "in sheep's clothing").

méki·s (-meki·s·əm-; Gr. 5.48a) AN 'sheep' (Mt 12.12); mekí·s·ak (Mt 9.36, 10.6, 10.16, etc.); mekí·s·al (obv.) (Jn 2.14); mekí·s·a (obv.) (Lk 2.8, Jn 2.15, etc.); nehənó·t·əma·t mekí·s·a 'watcher of sheep' (Jn 10.11, Mk 14.27).
- -meki·s·əm-: nəmekí·s·əm 'my sheep (sg.)' (Lk 15.6); nəmekí·s·əmak 'my sheep (pl.)' (Jn 10.14, 10.16, etc.); mwekí·s·əma 'his sheep' (Jn 10.3 [2x], 10.4, Mt 25.33).
- mekí·t·ət (-meki·t·ət·əm-) AN (dim.) 'little sheep or goat, lamb' (Jn 1.29, 1.36, Mk 14.12 [2x]); meki·t·ə́t·ak 'lambs' (Lk 10.3); kwe·ni·tó·naya·t mekí·t·ət 'kid' (Lk 15.29).
- -meki·t·ət·əm-: nəmeki·t·ə́t·əmak 'my lambs' (Jn 21.15).
- meki·s·í·i P 'of sheep': ní·=tá skóntay meki·s·í·i 'I am the door of the sheep' (Jn 10.7).

memhalam°: see mhalamaw-.

memhalamunt- 'merchant': a lexicalized participle (of mhalamaw-), inflected as a noun (memhálamunt 'merchant', memhalamúntak 'merchants' [OA]) and in the folowing words.
- memhalamunti·- AI 'be a merchant' (Gr. 5.42h, 5.65d): énta-memhalamuntíhti·t 'where they were merchants' (Mt 22.5); íka énta-memhalamunti·lí·č·i 'those (obv.) that were merchants there' (Mk 11.15); énta-memhalamúntink 'in the market' (*lit.*, 'where people (indef.) are merchants') (Lk 7.32).
- memhalamunti·k·á·ɔn IN 'a merchant's store' (Jn 2.16).

memmankəwe·-: see amankəwe·-.

memmayaksi·-(?): see amayaksi·-.

me·a·ɔ·č·i·mwi·°: see maya·ɔ·č·i·mwi·-.

me·á·wsi·t: see ma·wsi·-.

me·a·wxwé·e·kw 'you who are guides' (*lit.*, 'warparty leaders') (⟨mrawxwrrq⟩ Mt 23.16; ⟨mreawxwrrq⟩ Mt 23.24).
▶ Cf. Mun me·yá·wŏxe·t 'leader' (Charles Halfmoon; see Goddard 2013:112-113, 2019: 102).

mé·či (mi·mé·či; Gr. 5.25g) P (with changed subjunctive, and often without IC as if subjunctive) 'now, after, already, when, as soon as': 'now' (Lk 1.18, 1.36, 13.12, etc.); 'after' (Lk 2.15, 2.17, 2.21, Mt 2.3, 2.4, 2.9, etc.), 'already' (Lk 1.18, Lk 1.36 2x, Mk 9.13, Lk 12.49, etc.), 'when' (Lk 1.41, Jn 11.20), 'as soon as' (Mt 9.33), etc.
- mi·mé·či 'in the past' (Jn 12.28).

me·čihəla·- II 'pass away' ('be worn out' [OA]): aləwí·i=č yú hák·i ɔ́·k hukwé·yunk a·p·əwi-me·číhəle· 'more easily will the earth and heaven pass away' (Lk 16.17); tá=á· ílli kwə́t·i háši me·čihəlé·i 'not even one (law) will ever pass away' (Lk 16.17; KJV "fail").

me·č·i·h-: see mahči·h-.

me·k·- (mehəme·k·- [Rih+; IC]; Gr. 5.2a) AI+O 'give O2 away': mé·kw 'he gives (it) out' (Jn 2.10); nó·čkwe-mé·k·o·kw 'give it freely (you pl.)' (Mt 10.8; cf. Gr. 4.103k); mé·k·ək 'who gives it' (Jn 15.13), é·li- .. a·nhúkwi -mé·k·ək 'for he in turn gives' (Lk 12.48); nəmé·k·ən=č 'I

shall give it' (Jn 6.51), takó· nnihəla·t·amó·wən ntəli-=á· -mé·k·ən 'I would not have the authority to give it' (Mk 10.40); mwé·k·ən 'he gives [his life]' (Jn 10.11, Mt 20.28; Gr. 2.55k); mwe·k·əné·ɔ 'they gave them' (Mt 27.10); mwe·k·əne·ɔ́·i=č 'they shall hand him over' (Mt 20.19; Gr. 4.40j); mwe·k·əne·ɔ́·p·ani 'they handed him over' (Lk 24.20; Gr. 4.71c).
• mehəme·k·-: e·li·ná·k·ɔ mehəmé·k·e·kw 'the kind of thing you (pl.) give' (Mt 22.19).

me·lhukwehi·-: see məlo·kwehi·-*.

mé·li 'Mary' (Lk 1.27, 1.30, 1.34, etc.); †mé·lial 'Mary (obv.)' (Lk 2.16, 2.34).

mé·li·s 'Mary' (Lk 10.39, 10.42, Jn 11.2, etc.); me·lí·s·a 'Mary (obv.)' (Jn 11.1, 11.19, etc.).

me·me·mántsi·t 'a prophet' (1834b:41.8); me·me·mantsí·č·i·k 'soothsayers, (phony) fortune-tellers' (Mt 7.15); ke·k·əlo·né·č·i·k me·me·mantsí·č·i·k 'lying soothsayers' (⟨mrmrmunsethek⟩ Lk 6.26, ⟨mrmrmuntsehek⟩ Mt 24.11); me·me·mantsi·lí·č·i 'prophet (obv.)' (1834b:31.4).
▸ Cf. ⟨amemantsin⟩ "to divine, tell fortunes, soothsay" (C.F. Denke, cited by Raymond Whritenour [p.c. 8/23/2015]).

me·me·thaké·mu AN 'dove' (Mt 10.16); me·me·thaké·məwal 'doves (obv.)' (Jn 2.14, 2.16); me·me·thaké·munk 'like a dove' (Mt 3.16, Jn 1.32).
▪ mehəme·thake·mó·wa 'doves (obv.)' (⟨mcvmrtvakrmwu⟩ Mk 11.15).
▪ ma·me·thake·mó·wak (⟨mamrtvakrmwwk⟩ Lk 2.24; ME).
▸ For the variant forms, cf. mehəme·thaké·mo·s (OA); ma·me·thaké·mu (ND, ME); ma·me·thaké·mo·s (FW). ♦ Note: the dove in the gospels was a turtledove, while the Delaware word refers to the mourning dove.

mé·naxk IN 'fence' (1834a:16); mé·nxka (pl.) (OA).

me·nxkha·s·i·- II 'be fenced in': táli-me·nxkhá·s·u 'there was a garden {smwh}' (*lit.*, 'it was fenced') (Jn 19.41); énta-me·nxkhá·s·i·k 'where there was an enclosed garden' (*lit.*, 'where it was fenced in') (Jn 18.1).

mé·thik (cf. Gr. 2.48a) 'evil' (Jn 3.19, 3.20, Lk 6.45, etc.); me·thíkink 'evil (loc.)' (Mt 5.34, 5.37, etc.). ♦ Lexicalized participle of mahtət II 'it is bad'.

me·tsí·si·t 'bad one(?)': awé·n wí·mahtal lá·t·e, "me·tsí·si·t" 'if anyone calls his brother a bad one' (⟨mrtseset⟩ Mt 5.22; KJV gloss: "Vain fellow," meaning 'worthless'; RSV "insults [him]").
♦ Participle of mahtəs·í·su 'he is homely' (LTD ND); ⟨Machtississu⟩ "bad, ugly; dirty looking" (B&A 70); cf. me·tsísi "Homely" (nickname of Minnie Fouts).

me·txáki P 'soon after, almost immediately' (V, OA, ME; Gr. 2.73h).

me·t·a·p·e·i·-: see mahta·p·e·i·-.

me·xke·ɔhkə́s·i·t 'Indian(s)' (1834a:21.36, 22.49, etc.); me·xke·ɔhkəs·i·lí·č·i (1834a:21.38).
▸ Participle |mēxkēwakəsīt| 'one who has red flesh'; cf. we·ɔ́·psi·t 'white person'.

me·xkpé·k·a 'wine' (*lit.*, 'red liquid') (Lk 10.34), 'Red River' (OA). ▸ Participle of maxkpé·k·at (|maxkəpēkat-|; Gr. 2.48d) 'it's a stream that runs red' (ME).

me·x·alé·t·ia·t 'glutton': see xale·t·ia·-.

me·x·askwčá·č·i·k: see xaskwča·-.

me·x·é·lki·k: see xe·l-.

me·x·inkó·ɔhti·k: see xinkɔ·ɔhti·-.

me·x·inkwᵒ: see xinkwᵒ.

məkək·e·- II 'be open country': énta-məkák·e·k 'in the open country' (Lk 2.8).

məkənh- (-mək·ənh-) TI(1a) 'gather up, pick up all (multiple small things)': məkənhámo·kw 'gather them up (you pl.)' (Jn 6.12, of uneaten scraps; Gr. 2.70h).
• -mək·ənh-: mwək·ənhamané·ɔ 'they picked them all up' (Mt 13.4, 1834b:26.13; of seeds).

məkə́ni (perhaps /mə́kəni/) PP 'last': məkə́ni-wténk 'last of all' (Mk 12.6, Mk 12.22).

- ▪ PV məkə́ni (mék·əni) 'last'; also makes a superlative: məkə́ni-ki·škwí·k·e 'on the last day' (Mt 12.41, 12.42, Jn 6.39, etc.); e·lkí·kwi-məkə́ni-kí·škwi·k 'at the time of the last day' (Mt 12.36; with ⟨mrk⟩, as if /mék·/ with IC, for /mək/).
- • mé·k·əni: mé·k·əni-tanké·t·i·k 'the smallest' (Mt 13.32; KJV "least").

məkəni·x·ən- II 'be the last one': péči-məkəní·x·ink 'the next one (ahead)' (*lit.*, 'the one at the near end (of the sequence)') (Mk 1.38).

məkí IN 'sore' (LB; Gr. 2.40a), 'scab' (OA); məkía (pl.) (OA); mwə́k·ial 'his sores' (1834b:30.4), mwə́k·ia (⟨mwukeu⟩ Lk 16.21).

məki·i·- AI 'have sores': wé·mi məkí·yu hók·enk 'he had sores all over his body' (1834b:30.3); məkí·yo·p 'he had sores' (Lk 16.20). ♦ There is also: məkíhsu 'he is scabby' (OA; Gr. 2.40c).
- ▶ Cf. Mun mə̆kə́yəw 'have scabs' (dict.).

məkó·s AN 'nail' (⟨mukws⟩ 1834a:12; OA, LB), 'awl' (V) (Gr. 3.2m); məkó·s·ak 'nails' (Jn 20.25; LB).

†mə́l IN 'myrrh' (Jn 19.39).

məlo·kwehi·-* (-məlhukwehi·-*, me·lhukwehi·-) AI+O 'use O2 as a pillow for the head': me·lhukwéhia 'what I use as a pillow for my head' (⟨mrvwlqcvea⟩ [presumably for ⟨mrlvwqcvea⟩] 1834b:26.7).
- ♦ Note: since the medial must be |-əhkwē-| 'head', ⟨lq⟩ cannot be correct.
- ▶ Cf. the derived noun: məlo·kwého·n 'pillow' (OA, LB).

-məmayak·i·t-: see amayahki·t-.

məmhalama·ɔhtó·p·ani·k: see mhalama·ɔhti·- under mhalamaw- TA+O 'buy O2 from'.

məmhalamuntəwá·k·an (cf. mhalamaw-); amánki-məmhalamuntəwá·k·an 'large commercial business(es)' (1834a:24.65).

məmšaluhəla·- II '(waves) to have crests repeatedly reach (?)': aləwí·i †məmšalúhəle·p tkú 'increasingly the crests of the waves were breaking [into the boat]' (⟨mumjalwvlrp⟩ Mk 4.37&; KJV "the waves beat into the ship"). ♦ Both form and sense are uncertain: the interpretation assumes |məš-| 'get, attain, touch' and |-alo·-| 'blade, edge' (for crests of waves).

məmši·x·i·n-: see məši·x·i·n-.

-məmxahe·lənt-: see amax·ahe·lənt-.

məmxé·li: see xé·li.

mənančí·ɔn IN 'left hand, arm' (OA); kəmənančí·ɔn 'your left hand' (Mt 6.3); nəmənančí·ɔnink 'on my left' (Mk 10.40); kəmənančí·ɔnink 'on your left' (Mk 10.37); mwənančí·ɔnink 'on his left' (Mt 25.33, 25.41); mwənanči·ɔní·li·t 'on his (obv.) left' (Lk 23.33&).

məná·tay IN 'island, continent' (ME, LB); yú táli məná·tenk 'on this island' (⟨muna rif⟩ 1834a:18.10; loc. also LTD ND); məna·té·yunk 'to this continent' (1834b:42.13; ME).

məne·- (me·ne·-, mihəməne·- [Rih+], mehəməne·- [Rih+; IC], mi·məne·- [Rī+]; Gr. 5.10c, 5.44g) AI(+O) 'drink O2': məné·w 'he drinks' (Jn 7.37, 1834b:8.1); məné·p·ani·k 'they drank' (Lk 17.27, 17.28); məné·kw 'drink (you pl.)' (Mt 26.27); məne·mó·e 'drink it (you pl.)' (Lk 10.7; Gr. 4.116c); ntəli-=č .. -məne·n 'so that I shall drink' (Lk 17.8; cf. Gr. 2.55l).
- • me·ne·-: ní·=č me·né·a 'what *I* shall drink' (Mk 10.38, cf. Mk 10.39); me·né·an 'what you (sg.) drink' (Mt 6.31); me·né·e·kw 'what you (pl.) drink' (Mt 6.25; Gr. 2.31c).
- • mihəməne·-: míhəməne 'drink (you sg.)' (Lk 12.19); míhəməne· 'he drinks' (Lk 7.34); kəmihəmənéhəmɔ 'you (pl.) drink (customarily)' (Lk 5.33).
- • mehəməne·-: wáin méhəməne·t 'wine-drinker' (Lk 7.34); méhəmənenk 'beverage, a drink' (LTD FF).

• mi·məne·-: máta=č mi·məné·i 'he will never drink' (Lk 1.15; Gr. 4.81g); takó· .. mi·məné·i 'he never drank' (Lk 7.33); takó· mi·məne·í·p·ani·k 'they never never used to drink' (1842:20.4); kəmíhəməne=háč 'do you (sg.) drink?' (1842:20.3); tá=á· awé·n mwi·məné·wən 'no one would ever drink it' (1842:23.6).

▪ mənahti·- AI (coll.; Gr. 5.75q): mənahtó·p·ani·k 'they were all drinking' (Mt 24.38).

məne·ó·k·an IN 'drink' (Jn 6.55, Lk 21.34, 22.17).

mənəp·e·kw (Gr. 5.16b) IN 'lake; sea' (Mt 4.15, Mk 4.39, etc.); mənəp·é·k·ɔ 'seas' (Lk 21.25, 1842:11.4); mənəp·é·k·unk 'to the sea' (Mt 17.27, etc.), 'to the pool' (Jn 5.4).

▪ mənəp·é·kwtət (dim.) 'pool' (Jn 5.2; Gr. 5.46b); ehalo·ka·lənti·i-mənəp·e·kwtət·ink 'the pool of the messenger (loc.)' (Jn 9.7, 9.11).

mənih- (-mənh-, me·nh-, |mənəh-|) TA 'give a drink to': məníhaw 'give him a drink (you sg.)' (LTD LB); məníhi·l 'give me a drink (you sg.)' (Jn 4.7, 4.9, 4.10, 4.15), mənihi (LTD FF); awé·n=č mənihkóne íIli šúkw mpí 'if anyone shall merely give you water to drink' (⟨muncvkonc⟩ Mk 9.41; Gr. 5.77b); čínke=háč .. ktəli-mənihələné·na·p 'when was it that we gave you to drink?' (Mt 25.37).

• -mənh-: kəmənhíhəmɔ·p 'you (pl.) gave me to drink' (Mt 25.35); takó· kəmənhi·húmɔ·p 'you (pl.) did not give me to drink' (Mt 25.42).

• me·nh-: me·nhó·k·ɔn 'who gives you (sg.) it to drink' (Mt 10.42).

mənó·t·e·s IN 'bag, sack' (Lk 22.35, 22.36; V, BF, LB); ⟨Menotees⟩ "Knap Sack" (Z. 108).

▸ Cf. nó·t·e·s, mɔnií·i-nó·t·e·s.

mənt- (TI(1a)) TI-O 'sigh, moan': nəmə́ntam 'I groan, I moan' (LTD LB); mə́ntam 'he sighed, moaned' (Mk 7.34, Jn 11.33); nə́ wwə́nči- nčí·sas lápi -mə́ntamən táli wté·hink 'hearing that, Jesus again moaned in his heart' (Jn 11.38; KJV "groaning in himself").

məsát II 'it is whole, in one piece' (⟨musut⟩ Jn 19.23; KJV "without seam").

məsəč·é·i (Gr. 2.13b) P 'completely, whole' (Mt 5.29, 5.30, 6.22, etc.; 18x); məsəč·é·i 'all over' (Mk 5.29); məsəč·é·e 'whole' (⟨msithr⟩ Lk 6.10; OA); wə́nči məsəč·é·i X 'with all X' (Lk 10.27 [2x], Mk 12.30 [3x], 12.33 [3x]), məsəč·é·i wə́nči X 'with all X' (Lk 10.27, Mk 12.30, 12.33). ▸ Cf. ⟨Mesittschewi⟩ 'quite, whole, entirely' (B&A 82).

▪ PV -məmsəč·é·i ([Rə̀+]): kəməmsəč·é·i-khwilawwá·ɔk 'you swallow them whole' (Mt 23.24; Gr. 5.131a).

mə́si PV 'all (over)' (Gr. 2.74h, 5.129x): mə́si-é·p 'he went all over' (Mt 4.23); mə́si-é·ɔk 'they went all different ways' (Mt 22.5).

▪ P mə́si 'all': mə́si táli 'all over' (Mt 23.34), 'in places' (OA); mə́si kéku 'all things' (Lk 11.53), 'everything' (Lk 12.26).

məšak·a·-* (mešahka·-) AI 'go to shore, land (in a boat)': mešahkahtí·t·e 'when they landed, came to shore' (Jn 21.9).

♦ Cognate with Ojibwe /mišaka·-/ (3s /mišake·/) 'come ashore in a boat, land' (Nipissing dialect [Cuoq 1886:218]; Southwestern Ojibwe mizhagaa).

məšant- (-məš·ant-, me·š·ant-) TI(1a) 'taste, take a taste of': nəməš·ántamən 'I had a taste of it' (OA, checking ⟨Meschandamen⟩ 'to taste' [B&A 82]).

• me·š·ant-: nčí·sas méči me·š·antánke nə́ šəwá·p·u 'after Jesus had taken a taste of the vinegar' (Jn 19.30).

məša·ke·- (-məshake·-, me·šhake·-, |məšahkē-|) AI 'sit down': məšá·ke· 'he sat down' (Lk 7.36, 11.37, Jn 18.18&, 19.13); íkali məšá·ke·p 'he sat down there' (Lk 22.14); hák·ink lí-məšá·ke·kw 'sit down on the ground (you pl.)' (Mk 8.6).

• -məshake·-: ná mwəsháke·n 'then he sat down' (Lk 4.20, Mk 9.35).

• me·šhake·-: me·šhakehtí·t·e 'after they sat down' (Mt 13.48, Lk 24.30).

məša·kwsi·- AI 'attain a height': káski-ánči-məšá·kwsu 'he could attain a greater height' (Lk 12.25).

məša·l- (-məš·a·l-) TA — məša·t- (-məš·a·t·-, me·š·a·t·-) TI(1a) 'remember' (Gr. 5.12d).

    ■ məša·l- (TA): məšá·lo· 'remember her (you pl.)' (Lk 17.32); məša·lí·me 'remember me (you sg.)' (Lk 23.42; Gr. 4.116i); wənči-=č -məšá·la·n 'for her to be remembered' (Mk 14.9); ktə́li-=č -məša·li·né·ɔ 'for you (pl.) to remember me' (Lk 22.19; Gr. 4.50o).

    • -məš·a·l-: mwəš·a·lá·ɔ ke·tanət·o·wi·lí·č·i 'he remembered God' (1842:10.1); kəməš·a·líhəmɔ 'you (pl.) remember me' (1 Cor 11.25).

    ■ məša·t- (TI): məša·t·ánke 'when he remembered it' (Lk 1.54; ch. conj. with no IC); məšá·t·a 'remember it (you sg.)' (Lk 16.25); məšá·t·amo·kw 'remember it (you pl.)' (Lk 17.3, Mk 13.9, Lk 24.6); məša·t·amó·me 'remember it (you sg.)' (1842:11.4; Gr. 4.116k); wé·mi awé·n məša·t·ánkeč 'let everyone remember it' (1842:7.2); wénči-=č -məšá·t·ame·kw 'so that you (pl.) will remember it' (Jn 16.4; Gr. 4.67(2)q).

    • -məš·a·t·-: mwəš·á·t·amən 'he remembered it' (⟨mijatumin⟩ Jn 2.17, ⟨mwjatumun⟩ Lk 22.61); takó·=háč kəməš·a·t·amo·wəné·ɔ 'do you (pl.) not remember it?' (Mk 8.18); mwəš·a·t·aməné·ɔ·p 'they remembered it' (Jn 2.22).

    • me·š·a·t·-: me·š·a·t·ánke 'when he remembered it' (Mk 14.72).

məša·t·a·s·i·- II 'be remembered': ta·txíti káski-məša·t·á·s·i·k 'little can be remembered' (1834a:19.18).

məšən- (-məš·ən-, me·š·ən-) TA 'touch' (as if 'take hold of') — TI(1b) 'obtain, receive'.

    ■ məšən- (TA): káči məšəní·han 'don't touch me (you sg.)' (Jn 20.17; KJV "Touch me not"; Gr. 4.111n).

    ■ məšən- (TI): məšə́nəm=č 'he will receive (unspecified things)' (Jn 16.14); tá=á· káski- máta -məšənəmó·wi 'he would not fail to get (it)' (Mk 10.30); aləwí·i=č ntə́ntxi-məšənəmúhəna 'we will get more' (Mt 20.10; Gr. 6.7g); məšənəmo·k 'they got (them, inan.)' (Mt 20.9, 20.10); məšənəmá·ne nəmoní·yəm 'when I got my money ..' (⟨mujinamanc⟩ Mt 25.27; Gr. 4.63n).

    • -məš·ən-: šúkw=č kəməš·ənəmhúmɔ aləwí·i-ləs·əwá·k·an 'but you (pl.) shall receive power' (Acts 1.8; Gr. 4.38o); wé·mi=č yó·l kəməš·ənəməné·ɔ 'you (pl.) shall obtain all these things' (Lk 12.31; Gr. 4.39u).

    • me·š·ən-: me·š·əní́nkəp 'the one who got it' (Mt 25.16, 25.17, etc.; Gr. 4.78i); mé·či me·š·ənəmhití·t·e 'after they received it' (Mt 20.11; Gr. 4.62c); me·š·əní́nki·k 'ones who have received it' (Lk 6.24; equated to a 2p; Gr. 4.64y).

məši·kaw- (-məšhikaw-, |məšəhkaw-|) TA 'come over, infect': manunksəwá·k·an=č məši·ká·k·o·k 'anger will fall upon those' (Lk 21.23); kəwé·mi-məši·ka·k·ó·ne·n 'it came over all of us' (Jn 1.16).

    • -məšhikaw-: mwəšhiká·k·o·n 'it comes upon them' (Jn 3.36); kəməšhika·k·o·né·ɔ ktehəwá·ink ləpwe·ɔ́·k·an 'for wisdom to infuse your (pl.) hearts' (1842:19.3).

məši·x·i·n- (məmši·x·i·n- [Rə̀+]) AI 'stumble': tá=á· məši·x·i·nó·wi 'he won't stumble' (Jn 11.9).

    • məmši·x·i·n- : məmší·x·i·n=á· 'he would stumble' (Jn 11.10; KJV "stumbleth").

    ▶ Cf. ⟨n'mischichĩn⟩ 'I am fallen' (Z. 71); ⟨mischichĩn⟩ "glide" (Z. 84; German "glitschen" [also 'slide, slip'], fallen ['fall']); ⟨mēschiéchēn⟩ 'stumble' (Z. 186 [for ⟨-chĩn⟩]; cf. B&A 82 "to slip, to fall").

mətak(·)wº (|mətakw-|) 'cover' (Gr. §5.2a).

mətakhɔ·s·i·-* (me·t·akhɔ·s·i·-; cf. Gr. 2.70) II 'be covered': me·t·akhɔ́·s·i·k '(something) that is covered' (⟨mrtukvosek⟩ Lk 12.2).

mətakhw- (|mətakwahw-|) TA — mətakhw- (metahkɔh-, |mətakwah-|) TI(1a) 'cover, conceal'.
- mətakhw- (TA): nkwə́či-mətákhɔ 'I try to cover it (anim.)' (OA); mətákhɔw 'cover him (you sg.)' (LB); kwíši-mətakhɔwwɔ́·ɔ 'they had already covered him up' (WL; Gr. 2.55f).
- mətakhw- (TI): wénči-=á· -mətakhɔmíhti·t mɔt·a·wsəwa·k·anúwa 'so that they might conceal their sin' (Jn 15.22).
- metahkɔh-: wé·mi kéku metahkɔhəmíhti·t 'everything that they cover over' (Mt 10.26).

mətak·winkwehw-* (-mətahkwinkwehw-) TA 'cover the face of': mwətahkwinkwehɔwwá·ɔ 'they covered his face' (Mk 14.65).

mətəme·- (-mət·əme·-, me·t·əme·-) AI 'take a road': mətəme· 'he takes the road' (OA; Gr. 5.55f); kəmət·əmá·k·anink é·ləmi-mətəmé·an 'on your path where you (sg.) go' (1834b:8.13).
- -mət·əme·-: 1s nəmə́t·əme (OA; Gr. 2.68d).
- me·t·əme·-: me·t·əmé·an '(the road) where you (sg.) go' (1842:22.1).

-mət·əma·k·an-: see təmá·k·an.

-mət·əmi·k·am-: see təmi·k·am-.

mhakahte·p·o·s·i- AI+O 'roast, broil on coals': mhakahte·p·o·s·ínki 'roasted (obv.)' (Lk 24.42).
▶ Cf. hákahtay 'red-hot coal' (Mun máhkăte·w); final derived from ahpo·s·i- AI+O 'roast'.

mhalamaw- (-mahəlamaw-, mehəlamaw-, məmhalamaw- [Rə̀+], memhalamaw- [Rih+; IC], |mahlamaw-|) TA+O 'buy O2 from' (passive forms: 'sell O2'; Gr. 4.41n,o): mhalamái 'buy it from me (you sg.)' (1842:24.1 [2x]); mhalamá·k·e·kw kéku 'sell the things (you pl.)' (Lk 12.33); mhalamúnteč ehahkwí·č·i 'let him sell his clothing' (Lk 22.36; Gr. 4.114g); ná we·i·mahtí·č·i·k mhalamaɔ·né·ɔ 'then his brothers sold him' (1842:13.4).
- -mahəlamaw-: mɔhəlama·k·o·né·ɔ 'they sold him to him (obv.)' (1842:13.4).
- mehəlamaw- (Gr. 5.42h): méhəlamunt 'who sold (him) out' (Jn 18.2), méhəlamunt=č nhák·ay 'the one who will sell me out' (Lk 22.21); mehəlamúntəp 'the one who had sold (him) out' (Mt 27.3); nčó·wak mehəlamúnči '(obv.) that the Jews sold' (Mt 27.9).
- məmhalamaw-: entxennáɔhki-məmhálamunt 'as many as they sold' (1834a:19.14).
- memhalamaw- (Gr. 5.65d): memhálamunt 'one that sells, merchant' (V, OA; Gr. 5.42h); memhalamúnči·k 'those that sold (them)' (Mk 11.15); memhalamúnči 'those (obv.) selling (them)' (Jn 2.14, 2.16). Also lexicalized as a noun and an initial (see memhalamunt- above).
- mhalama·ɔhti·- (məmhalama·ɔhti·- [Rə̀+]) AI (recip.; Gr. 5.113b) 'buy from each other': énta-mhalamá·ɔhtink 'the market' (lit., 'where people bought from each other') (Mk 7.4, Mt 25.9), táli ehə́nta-mhalamá·ɔhtink 'in the market' (Lk 11.43).
- məmhalama·ɔhti·-: məmhalama·ɔhtó·p·ani·k 'they bought and sold' (lit., 'bought from each other') (Lk 17.28).

mhalamɔ·s·i- (mehəlamɔ·s·i·- [IC]) AI 'buy': wé·t·ami-mái-mhalamɔ·s·íhti·t 'while they were occupied with going to buy' (Mt 25.10; Gr. 4.61c).
- mehəlamɔ·s·i·-: mehəlamɔ·s·i·lí·č·i 'those buying (obv.)' (Mk 11.15).

mhalaw- (-mahəlaw-, məmhalaw- [Rə̀+]) TA — mhal- (-mahəl-) TI(1a) 'buy' (Gr. 5.4h).
- -mahəlaw- (TA): nəmáhəlaɔ 'I have bought (them)' (Lk 14.19).
- məmhalaw-: nána .. tɔ́ləmi-məmhalaɔ·né·ɔ tɔx·e·s·əwá·ɔ 'then they began to buy their skins' (1834a:19.14; ⟨Nuni⟩).
- mhal- (TI): mhála 'buy it (you sg.)' (1842:24.1); kəwínki=á· kéku -mhálam 'you (sg.) would want to buy something' (1842:24.1); mái-mhálamo·k mi·č·əwá·k·an 'they went to buy food' (Jn 4.8; Gr. 4.38p); mhalamó·p·ani·k mpí·s·o·n 'they had bought medicine' (Mk 16.1; Gr. 4.70d); wə́nči-=č -káski-mhalamíhti·t 'so that they will be able to buy it' (Mt 14.15).

• -mahəl-: nəmáhəlam hák·i 'I bought some land' (Lk 14.18); ná móhəlamən 'then he bought it' (Mt 13.46).
mhala·s·i- II 'be bought, sold' (Gr. 5.105k): kóč=háč máta mhalá·s·i·k 'why wasn't it sold?' (Jn 12.5; Gr. 4.60e), é·li- mhúkw -wənči-mhalá·s·i·k 'as they were bought with blood' (Mt 27.6).
mhič° ~ mhit° (|məht|-) 'plain, normal' (Gr. §5.2a).
mhičí·i 'out in the open' (Mt 24.40, Lk 17.31, Lk 19.44; LB).
mhita·mehəla·- AI 'run along the ground': mhita·méhəle· 'it (bird) ran along the ground' (OA); ná tóləmi-mhita·mehəla·né·ɔ 'then they began to run along on land' (Mk 6.33).
mhito·x·we·- (-mi·to·x·we·-, |məhtōxwē-|) AI 'go on foot': é·li mhitó·x·we·p 'as he had been walking' (Jn 4.6).
• -mi·to·x·we·-: nəmi·tó·x·we 'I'm going on foot' (V, OA; Gr. 2.5l).
mhúkw (-mo·kəm-) IN 'blood' (Mt 16.17, Lk 22.44, etc.); mhúkunk 'blood (loc.)' (Jn 1.13).
• -mo·kəm-: nəmó·kəm 'my blood' (Jn 6.54, 6.55, etc.); mmó·kəm 'his blood' (Jn 6.53, Lk 11.51, etc.); mmo·kəmúwa 'their blood' (Mt 23.30, 23.35).
▪ mhukwí·i PN of blood' (Gr. 5.122e): mhukwí·i-hák·i 'the land of blood' (Mt 27.8).
mhuk·wi·- (|məhkwī-|) AI 'bleed': mhúk·u 'bleeds' (Gr. 2.8d, 5.68l); núči-mhukwí·ne·p 'she had had the bloody flux for (twelve years)' (Lk 8.43).
mhw- (-muhw- [~ -mɔhw-?]; mehw-; |məhw-|; Gr. 3.20.l) TA 'eat, consume': mhók·e 'if I eat it (anim.)' (ME; Gr. 2.16h), énta-=á· -mhót 'where you would eat it (anim.)' (Mk 14.12).
• -muhw-: nəmúhɔ 'I ate him' (ME, AD), nəmuhó·ok 'I ate them (anim.)' (OA); hú kəmúho·l 'I'll eat you' (ME; ⟨kəmóhu·l⟩ V); kəmuhó·ne·n 'let us eat it (anim.)' (⟨kmovonrn⟩ Lk 15.23; ⟨konuvonrn⟩ 1834b:29.2); nəmuhó·k·o·n 'it consumed me' (⟨nmovwkwn⟩ Jn 2.17).
• mehw-: méhɔk 'which (anim.) I ate'; mehó·c·i 'which (obv.) he ate' (ME; Gr. 2.16h).
♦ Note: Blanchard's two prefixed forms with ⟨mov⟩ favor /-mɔh-/, agreeing with V, but the evidence from speakers points to /-muh-/ (with the underlying |məhw-| that the forms with IC also point to). ▸ For the matching TI, see mi·č·i·-.
mihəma·e·nəmaw-: see ma·e·nəmaw-.
mihəməne·-: see məne·-.
mihəmi·tsi·-: see mi·tsi·-.
minkahsé·i P 'better' (Mt 6.26, Mt 11.22, 11.24, Lk 10.12).
▪ mínkahse 'better' (Mt 10.15; OA).
▸ Cf. Mun mí·nkăsa 'better', ⟨Mingachsa⟩ 'better, a little better' (B&A 85).
mínkw IN 'seed, grain'; hwi·tí·i-mínkw 'a grain of wheat' (Jn 12.24); mínkunk 'seed (loc.)': mɔstatí·i-mínkunk 'like a mustard seed' (Mt 17.20).
▪ †mɔstatí·i-mínkwtət (dim.) 'mustard seed' (Mt 13.31, Lk 13.19, 17.6; Gr. 5.46c).
†misáyas 'Messiah' (Jn 1.41, 4.25).
mi·č·əwá·k·an (Gr. 5.58t) IN 'food' (Jn 4.8, Mt 6.25, 10.10, etc.), 'a meal' (Jn 12.2); nəmi·č·əwá·k·an 'my food (metaphorical)' (Jn 4.32, 4.34, etc.), 'my feast' (Mt 22.8); kəmi·č·əwa·k·anúwa 'your (pl.) food' (1842:16.2).
mi·č·i- (mihəmi·č·i·- [Rih+], mehəmi·č·i·- [Rih+; IC]) TI(3) 'eat': ahpó·n mí·č·əwak 'they ate bread' (Mk 7.5; Gr. 4.38r); mí·č·i·kw 'eat it (you pl.)' (Mt 26.26; Gr. 4.106s); káči ná wənči mi·č·í·he·kw 'don't eat it from that' (1842:7.4); mi·č·i·mó·e 'eat it (you pl.)' (Lk 10.7; Gr. 4.116o); máta=č mi·č·ié·k·we (or -i·é·k·we) 'if you (pl.) don't eat it' (Jn 6.53); é·li-mi·č·ié·k·əp 'because you (pl.) ate them' (Jn 6.26; Gr. 4.73i); mi·č·ihtí·t·əp 'which they ate' (Jn 6.58; Gr. 4.78t); mwí·č·i·n 'he ate it' (⟨mwehen⟩ Lk 24.43; Gr. 4.39l); mwi·č·i·né·ɔ 'they ate it' (⟨methenro⟩ Mt 14.21).

- mihəmi·č·i·-: ɔ́·k=č púnkw kəmihəmí·č·i 'and you (sg.) shall (repeatedly) be eating dust' (1842:8.1).
- mehəmi·č·i·-: mehəmí·č·ink 'food' (Lk 17.8, Mt 24.45). ▸ For the TA, see mhw-.

mi·kəmɔ·s·əntamaw- TA 'work for' (Gr. 5.97a): é·li- .. tá=á· -káski-mi·kəmɔ·s·əntamaɔ́·ɔk 'for I will not be able to work for him' (Lk 16.3; Gr. 4.97a); awé·n=č mi·kəmɔ·s·əntamaí·t·e 'if anyone serves me' (Jn 12.26 [2x]); tá=á· awé·n káski-mi·kəmɔ·s·əntamaé·i ní·š·a awé·ni 'no one can work for two people' (Lk 16.13); tá=á· awé·n kɔ́ski-mi·kəmɔ·s·əntamaɔ·í·ɔ ní·š·a nehəla·lkúk·i 'no one can work for two masters (*lit*., who (obv.) own him)' (Mt 6.24); kəmi·kəmɔ·s·əntamo·l 'I worked for you' (Lk 15.29; Gr. 4.33); ná mɔ́i-mi·kəmɔ·s·əntamáɔ·n 'then he went to work for him' (Lk 15.15).

mi·kəmɔ·s·əwá·k·an 'work': nə́ mi·kəmɔ·s·əwá·k·an 'those deeds' (Jn 14.13; KJV "works"); mwi·kəmɔ·s·əwá·k·an 'his work, his deed' (Jn 4.34, 6.28, etc.); mwi·kəmɔ·s·əwa·k·anəwá·ink 'into their work' (Jn 4.38).

mi·kəmɔ·s·i·- (mihəmi·kəmɔ·s·i·- [Rih+], mehəmi·kəmɔ·s·i·- [Rih+; IC], ma·mi·kəmɔ·s·i·- [Rā+], |mīhkəmwāsī-|) AI —mi·kəmɔ·s·o·wi·- II 'work'; (cf. Gr. 5.76a,b, etc.).
- mi·kəmɔ·s·i·- (AI): xé·li kahtəné·i mi·kəmɔ́·s·u 'he worked for many years' (1842:9.1); mi·kəmɔ́·s·o·p 'he worked' (1834b:15.5, 1842:6.2); nəmi·kəmɔ·s·íhəna 'we worked' (Lk 5.5; Gr. 2.43a); íka énta-mi·kəmɔ́·s·i·t 'one who works there' (Lk 22.27); mi·kəmɔ·s·í·č·i·k 'the workers' (Mt 9.37, 20.8 [3x]); ná tɔ́ləmi-mi·kəmɔ́·s·i·n 'then he began to work' (1842:8.7).
- mihəmi·kəmɔ·s·i·-: mihəmi·kəmɔ́·s·u 'he works, is a worker' (ME: Gr. 5.41g).
- mehəmi·kəmɔ·s·i·-: mehəmi·kəmɔ́·s·i·t 'worker' (Mt 10.10, Lk 10.7); mehəmi·kəmɔ·s·i·lí·č·i 'workers (obv.)' (Mt 20.1).
- ma·mi·kəmɔ·s·i·-: ma·mi·kəmɔ·s·ié·k·we 'if you (pl.) spend your time working' (1834b:17.5).
- mi·kəmɔ·s·o·wi·- (II): takó· mi·kəmɔ·s·o·wi·í·ɔ 'they (flowers [inan.]) do not work' (Lk 12.27).

mi·kəmɔ·s·o·ke·- (|mīhkəmwāsōhkē-|; Gr. §5.8e, 5.85d) AI+O 'trouble, cause to have to do something': káči mi·kəmɔ·s·o·ké·han khák·ay 'don't trouble yourself' (Lk 7.6).

mi·kənt- TI(1a) 'do, perform, work on, work for': mi·kəntánkəp 'what he has done' (Jn 5.17, Mt 16.27; Gr. 4.78f); mi·kəntamé·k·we ləní·i-ahɔ·p·e·ɔ́·k·an 'when you work for ordinary wealth' (Lk 16.11); é·li- mé·thik -mi·kəntamíhti·t 'because they do evil' (Jn 3.19); šúkw máta kəmi·kəntamo·wəné·ɔ·p 'but you (pl.) did no work on it' (Jn 4.38).

mi·kəntamaw- TA 'do work for, serve' (Gr. 5.97b): tá=á· kɔ́ski-mi·kəntamaɔ·í·ɔ 'he would not be able to work for him' (Mt 6.24); né·li-mi·kəntamaɔ́·t·əp 'while he was working for him' (Lk 1.8; Gr. 4.73e); má·si tɔ́li-mi·kəntamaɔ́·ne·p 'Martha was the one that served them' (Jn 12.2).

mi·kənta·s·i·- II 'be done as work': áləmi-mi·kəntá·s·u 'work begins' (1834a:16).

mi·ko·m- TA(+O) 'remind (of)': nəmi·kó·ma 'I reminded him' (OA); kəmi·kó·mi 'you reminded me' (LB); ɔ́·k=č .. kəmi·ko·mko·né·ɔ 'and he will remind you of it' (Jn 14.26).

mi·l- (mihəmi·l- [Rih+], |mīl-|; Gr. 5.4b) TA+O 'give O2 to': mí·lo· 'give it to him (you pl.)' (Lk 12.33, 19.24, Mt 22.21, etc.; Gr. 4.104p); mí·li·l 'give it to me' (Lk 15.12; Gr. 4.105i); mí·li·kw 'give it to me (you pl.)' (1834a:13; Gr. 4.105n); mi·lí·ne·n 'give it to us' (Mt 6.11, Lk 11.3, 17.5, etc.; Gr. 4.105o); mi·lá·t·əp 'what he had given to him (obv.)' (Jn 4.5, 1842:10.7; Gr. 4.76h); é·li- pi·lsí·li·t či·čánkɔ né·skɔ -mi·lá·wənt 'for he had not yet been given the Holy Spirit' (Jn 7.39; Gr. 4.97g); mi·lkɔ́·nəp yó·ni 'who gave me this' (Jn 4.12; Gr. 4.77b); mi·lkwé·k·əp 'who gave it to you (pl.)' (Jn 6.32; Gr. 4.76x); mi·lianpáni 'the ones (inan.) you (sg.) gave me' (Jn 17.8; Gr. 4.77d); mi·lianpáni·k 'those (anim.) that you (sg.) gave me' (Jn 17.11, 17.12, etc.; Gr. 4.64aa); mi·lí·t·əp 'that he has given me' (Jn 18.11; Gr. 4.77b); tá=á·

khiki·no·ləwá·k·an mi·la·í·ɔk 'they will not be given a sign' (Mt 16.4; Gr. 4.83w); mi·la·né·ɔ=č pəma·wsəwá·k·an 'life shall be given to them' (Jn 6.33; Gr. 4.41o); lí-=á· -mi·la·né·ɔ·p 'for it to have been given to them' (Mt 26.9); nəmí·la·n 'I give it to him, them' (Lk 19.8; Gr. 3,12b, 4.41a); nəmi·la·né·ɔ né·l a·pto·ná·k·anal 'I gave them the words' (Jn 17.8; Gr. 4.41d); nəmí·lko·p a·pto·ná·k·an 'he gave me words' (Jn 12.49; Gr. 4.69p); kəmí·la·p 'you (sg.) have given it to him' (Jn 17.2; Gr. 4.69f); takó· kəmi·lí·i mpí 'you (sg.) did not give me water' (Lk 7.44; Gr. 3.21d); kəmi·li·né·p·ani·k 'you (sg.) gave them (anim.) to me' (Jn 17.6; Gr. 4.71h); kəmíllən=č 'I will give to you (sg.)' (Mk 6.23; Gr. 4.41i); kəmillané·ɔ '(that) I give it to you, turn him over to you' (Mt 27.17, Mk 15.9, Mt 27.21; Gr. 4.41j); tá=á· nkáski- .. -milló·wi 'I won't be able to .. give you any' (⟨melulwi⟩ Lk 11.7; possibly this is /-mi·ləló·wi/, as written); kéku=č .. mwi·lá·ɔl 'he shall give something to him' (⟨melawl⟩ Lk 2.24); mwi·lá·ɔ 'he gives to him' (Lk 3.11, Mt 7.9, etc.); takó· kéku mwi·la·iwwá·ɔ 'they did not give him anything' (Lk 20.10&, Mk 12.4&; Gr. 4.83s); mwi·la·né·ɔ 'they give him (obv. [unmarked]) to them (obv.)' (Mt 20.19); ó·k mwí·la·n 'and (then he) gave them to them (sbd.)' (Mk 8.6).

• mihəmi·l-: nəmihəmi·lá·ne·n 'for us to be giving it to him' (*lit.*, 'that we give it to him') (Lk 20.22).

▪ mi·lti·- (|mīlətī-|) AI+O (with indefinite subject; Gr. 4.40mno, 5.113c) 'O2 to be given, etc.': nəni=č ləkhíkwi .. mí·lti·n 'at that time he will be delivered' (Mt 26.2); ó·k=č .. lí-mí·lti·n 'and he will be turned over to ..' (Mt 24.51); mí·ltink 'which is given' (Lk 22.19).

mí·laxk (-mi·lx-; Gr. 3.5f) IN 'hair(s) (of the human head)' (Mt 5.36, Lk 12.7); kwət·i mí·laxk 'one hair' (Lk 21.18); mwí·laxk 'her hair' (Lk 7.38, 7.44, Jn 12.3; Gr. 2.55j).

• -mi·lx-: kəmi·lxəwá·ɔ 'your hairs' (Mt 10.30);

mi·lkwəs·i·- AI+O 'be given O2 by a higher power' (Gr. 5.107c): é·li-=č -mi·lkwə́s·ie·kw 'the way it will be given to you (pl.)' (Mk 13.11); kta·pi-=č yó·l wé·mi -mi·lkwəs·i·né·ɔ 'you (pl.) will be given all these things in the bargain' (Mt 6.33).

mi·ltəwá·k·an IN 'gift': kəmi·ltəwá·k·an 'your gift' (Mt 5.23, 5.24 [2x]; Gr. 5.116a).

mí·məns (-t-ami·mənsəm-, -t-ami·məns-; Gr. 5.14c) AN 'child' (Lk 1.80); mi·mə́nsak 'children' (Mt 10.21, Lk 7.32, Mt 14.21, etc.); mi·mə́nsal 'children (obv.)' (Mt. 2.16), mi·mə́nsa 'children (obv.)' (Mt 3.9, 22.24&); mi·mə́nsto·kw 'children (voc.)' (Mk 10.24, Jn 21.5; Gr. 4.11l). ▸ Also mí·mə·ns (V, OA; Gr. §2.1c).

• -t-ami·mənsəm-: ntami·mə́nsəmak 'my children' (Lk 11.7); ktami·mə́nsəmak 'your children' (Lk 13.34, Mt 23.37, 1842:8.7); tɔmi·mə́nsəmal 'his child' (Jn 4.12), '(his) children' (Lk 1.16, Jn 4.12, Mt 5.9), tɔmi·mə́nsəma 'his offspring' (1842:11.1).

• -t-ami·məns-: tɔmi·mənsəwá·ɔ '(their) children' (1834b:20.10).

▪ mi·mə́ntət AN (dim.; Gr. 5.46n) 'baby, little child' (Lk 1.44, 1.66, etc.); mi·məntə́t·ak pl. (Mt 19.13, Mk 10.14); mi·məntə́t·al (obv.) (Lk 1.41, 1.59, etc.), mi·məntə́t·a (obv.) (Mt 2.20, 18.2; Lk 10.21 [for expected prox. pl.]); mi·məntə́t·ink 'as a little child' (Mt 18.4).

mi·mənsi·- (e·mi·mənsi·-) AI 'be a child': ə́nta-mi·mə́·nsienk 'when we (exc.) were children' (OA), ə́nta-mi·mə·nsihti·t 'when they were children' (ME).

• e·mi·mənsi·-: e·mi·mənsí·t·e 'when he was a child' (Mk 9.21).

mi·naɔ́či(?) 'also, as well(?)': †mi·naɔ́či aləwíhəle· 'and there is some left over as well' (⟨menaohi⟩ Lk 15.17).

▸ Perhaps a cognate of Cree mi·na, Ojibwe mi·nawa· 'also, again', with -áči PF.

mi·tsi·- (ma·mi·tsi·- [Rā+], mihəmi·tsi·- [Rih+]) AI 'eat': wə́li-mi·tsúwak 'they eat well' (1834a:17); wíči-mi·tsó·p·ani·k 'they ate along with the others' (Lk 5.29; Gr. 5.99b); mí·tsi 'eat (you sg.)' (Lk 17.7; Gr. 4.103a); mí·tsi·kw 'eat (you pl.)' (Lk 12.37, Jn 21.12);

énta-mi·tsí·t·əp 'where he had eaten' (Jn 13.4; Gr. 4.75h); ehə́nta-mí·tsink 'in the (customary) eating area' (Lk 22.14); máta mi·tsié·k·we (-ié·k·we) 'if you (pl.) do not eat' (Mt 17.21; Gr. 4.95o); nəmi·tsíhəna·p 'we have eaten' (Lk 13.26; Gr. 4.68g); məšá·ke· tə́li=á· -mí·tsi·n 'he sat down to eat' (Lk 7.36; Gr. 4.50m).
- ma·mi·tsi-: ma·mí·tsi·kw 'have something to eat (you pl.)' (Jn 4.31; Gr. 4.103g, 5.40l).
- mihəmi·tsi-: mihəmí·tsi 'eat (you sg.)' (Lk 12.19); mihəmí·tsu 'he eats' (Lk 7.34); kəmihəmi·tsíhəmɔ 'you eat (customarily)' (⟨kmem-⟩ Lk 5.33).
♦ In a phrase with wə́li P + (negative) + káhta PV: 'fast' (lit., 'in a good way not want to eat'): wə́li máta káhta-mi·tsí·i 'he is fasting' (Mt 6.16); áhi-wə́li máta káhta-mi·tsí·ɔne 'when you (sg.) fast' (Mt 6.16, 6.17).
■ mi·tsahti·- AI (coll.; Gr. 5.75r) 'all eat, feast': lápi xínkwi-mi·tsahtúwak 'they had another great feast' (Jn 5.1); mi·tsahtó·p·ani·k 'they were all eating' (Mt 24.38); lí-mi·tsáhti·n 'for there to be a feast' (Jn 10.22), lí-(=á·)-xínkwi-mi·tsáhti·n 'for there to be a great feast' (Lk 5.29, 14.12, etc.); mi·tsáhtink 'the feast' (Mt 26.2), énta-mi·tsáhtink '(where there is) a feast' (Lk 12.36, Jn 11.56); énta-xínkwi-mi·tsahtínkəp 'at the great feast' (Jn 4.45); né·skɔ xínkwi-mi·tsahtí·yunk 'before the big feast' (Jn 12.1; Gr. 2.28e, 4.95q).
■ mi·tsáhtink 'feast' (lexicalized): 'feast' (Mt 26.2); xínkwi-mi·tsáhtink 'great feast' (Jn 2.23); mi·tsahtinkí·i PV '(of) feast' (Mt 26.5).

mi·x·ana·l- TA — mi·x·anat·- TI(1a) 'be ashamed of'.
■ mi·x·ana·l- (TA): awé·n=č mi·x·ana·lí·t·e 'if anyone is ashamed of me' (Mk 8.38); mwi·x·ana·lá·ɔ=č 'he will be ashamed of him' (Mk 8.38).
♦ Note: takó· kɔ́t·a-mi·x·ana·la·í·ɔl (Mt 1.19), which would mean 'he did not want to be ashamed of her', is used to translate "not willing to make her a publick example" (KJV); this is perhaps a misunderstanding of "not want to shame her" provided as a gloss.
▶ Cf. Mun mi·xana·l- TA 'to be ashamed of'.
■ mi·x·ana·t·- kəmi·x·aná·t·amən 'for you to be ashamed of it' (1834b:14.3).

mi·x·anəsi·- AI 'be ashamed': áləmi-mi·x·anə́s·əwak 'they became ashamed' (Jn 8.9); mi·x·anəs·ó·p·ani·k 'they were ashamed' (Lk 13.17); ɔ́·k·á· nəmi·x·anə́s·i·n 'and I would (then) be ashamed' (Lk 16.3; Gr. 4.40s, 4.49q); ná=á· kəmi·x·anə́s·i·n 'then you would be ashamed' (Lk 14.9).

mi·x·aní·i PV 'shamefully' (Mk 12.4&).

mi·x·ani·m- TA 'shame by speaking': kəmi·x·ani·mkúwa=č 'she will shame you (pl.)' (Mt 12.42; KJV "condemn it"); kəmi·x·ani·mkəwá·ɔk=č 'they shall shame you (pl.) by what they say' (Mt 12.41).

mi·x·é·k·ən IN 'hair (not of the human head)'; †kaməlí·i-mi·x·é·k·ana 'camel hair (pl.)' (Mt 3.4).

mmə́n, mmó·k: see wum-.

-mo·kəm-: see mhúkw.

-mo·khɔ·t·- TI(1a) 'put blood on': mmo·khɔ·t·aməné·ɔ nə́ ša·khuk·wí·ɔn 'they put blood on that coat' (1842:14.4). ♦ Note: the unprefixed form (presumably mhukhɔ·t·-) is unattested.

mo·nhake·- AI 'dig a trench': é·li-=č .. ɔ·ká·i -lí-mo·nhakéhti·t 'for they shall dig a trench around' (Lk 19.43).

mo·nhw- TA — mo·nh- TI(1a) 'dig (to, near)'.
■ mo·nhw- (TA): ɔ·ká·i=č ntə́li-mó·nhɔ 'I'll dig around it (anim.)' (Lk 13.8).
■ mo·nh- (TI): mmo·nhámən ahsə́n 'he digs down to rock' (Lk 6.47&).

mo·nihəla·- AI 'become uprooted': mo·níhəla 'uproot (you sg.)' (Lk 17.6; KJV "Be thou plucked up by the root").

mó·s AN 'elk' (ND); mó·s·ak 'elk (pl.)' (LTD LB). ▸ Cf. Mun mó·s 'elk' (JA in Hewitt 1896).
▪ mo·s·í·i PN '(of an) elk': mo·s·í·i-hɔpí·k·ɔn 'an elk scapula' (1834a:18.12).

†mo·sə́s·al 'Moses (obv.)' (⟨Moscsul⟩ 1834b:31.1.4, 31.6). ▸ Spelling influenced by English; cf. mó·šəš (below).

mo·sto·na·m- TA 'kiss': awé·n=č mo·sto·ná·mak 'the one who I shall kiss' (Mk 14.44); é·li-mo·sto·ná·mat 'as you (sg.) are kissing him' (Lk 22.48); mmo·sto·na·má·ɔ 'he kissed him' (Lk 15.20, Mt 26.49); nána tə́li-mo·sto·na·má·ɔl. 'And then he kissed him.' (⟨nwstwnamal⟩ 1834b:28.15b [em.]); máta ntála-mo·sto·na·mkó·wi 'she has not stopped kissing me' (Lk 7.45); takó· kəmo·sto·na·mí·i 'you did not kiss me' (Lk 7.45).
  ▸ Cf. ⟨mosktoname⟩ 'kiss me' (Z. 108).

mó·šəš 'Moses' (⟨mwjij⟩ Jn 1.17, Lk 9.33); mo·šə́š·a (abs.) (⟨Mojiju⟩ Lk 2.22, Jn 1.45; ⟨Mwjiju⟩ Jn 3.14, etc.); †mo·šəš·ínka 'Moses (abs., obv.)' (Jn 9.29).
  ♦ Note: Charles Halfmoon has "Mozez" in his Munsee hymns (with English /z/), but there was a Moraviantown Delaware named (in Munsee) /mó·šəš/: this is the form that B would have heard from a Unami speaker. ▸ Cf. †mo·sə́s·al.

mó·šhakw IN 'sky' (Mt 16.2, 16.3 [2x]).

mo·xkihəla·- AI 'emerge, appear, arrive ({smwh})': hítami íka mo·xkíhəle· 'he was the first to arrive there' (Jn 20.4); mo·xkíhəle·p 'he emerged (from the crowd)' (Mk 5.22); mo·xkihəlé·p·ani·k 'they appeared (emerging from a house)' (Mk 5.35); ná .. íka mmo·xkíhəla·n 'then he arrived there' (Jn 20.6).
  ▸ Cf. EAb móskihle 'he emerges', Mes mo·hkise·wa 'runs into view'.

mó·x·we·s (-mo·x·we·s·əm-) AN 'insect, (larval) worm'; kánši-lə́s·i·t ki·ná·ləwa·t mó·x·we·s 'a powerful sharp-tailed bug' (Lk 10.19; KJV "scorpions"); mo·x·wé·s·ak 'insects' (Mt 6.19, 6.20, Lk 12.33); kánši-ləs·i·lí·č·i mo·x·wé·s·a 'a powerful bug (obv.)' (Lk 11.12; KJV "scorpion").
  • -mo·x·we·s·əm-: mmo·x·we·s·əməwá·ɔ 'their worms' (Mk 9.44, 9.48).
  ▪ mo·x·wé·t·ət AN (dim.) 'little insect' (⟨mwxrtut⟩ Mt 23.24; LB).

mɔ́ni (-mɔni·yəm-) IN 'money' (Jn 2.14, Mk 2.14), 'silver' (Mt 10.9); 'coin' (Mt 25.28); mɔ́nia 'coins' (Mk 11.15, Mt 25.15, etc.), 'money' (Mt 28.15; KJV "the money").
  • -mɔni·yəm-: nəmɔní·yəm 'my money' (Lk 19.23, Mt 25.27 [2x]; Gr. 2.33d); kəmɔní·yəm 'your coin' (Mt 25.25; KJV "thy talent"); mmɔní·yəm 'his money' (Mt 25.18); mmɔni·yəmúwa 'their money' (Jn 2.15); mmɔni·yəməwá·ɔ 'their money' (1842:16.1).
  ▪ mɔní·t·ət IN (dim.) 'coin' (Mt 17.27, 20.13, 22.19); mɔni·t·ə́t·a 'small coins' (Mt 20.9, 20.10; KJV "every man a penny"); ní·š·a mɔni·t·ə́t·a 'two coins' (Lk 10.35); télən mɔni·t·ə́t·a 'ten coins' (Lk 15.8).

mɔnií·i PN '(of) silver': mɔnií·i-mpaíntəm 'my silver cup' (⟨monei mpaentum⟩ 1842:16.1). And see next. ♦ Note: /-ií·i/ is assumed on the basis of the variation in B and apparent ma·nša·p·ií·i PN 'beaded' and ši·mə·nšii·i PN 'of hickory'.

mɔnií·i-nó·t·e·s 'money bag' (⟨monie nwtrs⟩ Jn 13.29; Gr. 5.122f); mmɔnií·i-no·t·é·s·əwa 'their money bag' (⟨monee nwtrswu⟩ Jn 12.6). ♦ Possibly this is one word: mɔnii·nó·t·e·s; and cf. mɔni·nó·t·e·s(?) 'wallet' (BS).

mɔstatí·i-(?) PN '(of) mustard' (Lk 13.19, Mt 13.31, 17.20, Lk 17.6). ♦ With various spellings: ⟨mustute⟩ (Lk 13.19, Mt 13.31) ~ ⟨mostute⟩ (Mt 13.31).

†mpalápas 'Barabbas' (Mt 27.16, 27.17, 27.20, etc.); †mpalapás·a (obv.) (Mk 15.15).

†mpa·tá·lamu 'Bartholemew' (Mt 10.3).

mpénčəman 'Benjamin' (1842:16.1, 16.2, 17.1 2x); †mpenčəmána (obv.) (1842:16.1).

†mpetəlíhem 'Bethlehem' (Lk 2.4, Mt 2.6); †mpetəlihémink (loc.) (Lk 2.15, Mt 2.1, 2.5, 2.16).

†mpétpe·č 'Bethphage' (Lk 19.29&).

†mpetsáite 'Bethsaida' (Mk 6.45) ~ †mpetse·áiti (Jn 12.21) ~ †mpi·tsé·ite· (Mk 8.22) ~ †mpetsaé·te (Lk 10.13).

• †petsé·iti (Mt 11.21); †pi·tse·ité·ink 'from Bethsaida' (Jn 1.44).

mpəlénči·s 'Blanchard' (⟨Mplcnhes⟩ B: Title Page), or possibly mpəlénč·i·s.

mpí IN 'water' (Jn 2.6, 4.7, 4.14 [2x], etc.); mpínk 'in the water' (Lk 3.16, Jn 1.26, etc.; Gr. 2.21a).

▪ mpí·t·ət 'a little water (1834b:31.11).

mpí·s·o·n (Gr. 5.53g) IN 'medicine' (Lk 7.37, 7.38, 7.46, Jn 11.2, etc.); mpi·s·ó·na 'medicines' (Lk 23.56); mpi·s·ó·nink 'as medicine' (1834b:7.10).

†mpúšəlink P 'bushel(s)' (⟨mpwjilif⟩ Lk 16.7); also †púšəlink (⟨pwjilif⟩ 1834b:13.4).

♦ L. has a note to Lk 16.7 that 100 measures of wheat equals 14 bushels and two quarts, but Blanchard assumes that the measure of wheat equals 10 bushels.

-muh-: see mhw-.

munšskho·s·i·- II 'be harvested': munšskhó·s·i·k 'the harvest' (⟨mwnjskosek⟩ Mt 9.38, Lk 10.2 [2x]).

munšskwe·- AI 'harvest (the grain crop)': énta-múnšskwenk 'where people are harvesting' (Lk 10.2), énta-=á· -múnšskwenk '(when there would be) a harvest' (⟨cntu a mwnjsqif⟩ Mt 9.37).

múx·o·l (-amxo·l-; Gr. 2.68b) IN 'boat' (Lk 5.7, Mk 6.47, Jn 6.22); mux·ó·lal 'boats' (1834b:43.9), mux·ó·la (Jn 6.23); mux·ó·link 'boat (loc.)' (Mt 4.21, Lk 5.3, 5.7 [em.], etc.; Gr. 3.13(1)a, 5.128n, 6.7a), nə́ wə́nči mux·ó·link 'from the boat' (Lk 5.3; Gr. 6.9k).

• -amxo·l-: ntámxo·l 'my boat' (V; Gr. 2.68b); tɔmxo·ləwá·ɔ 'their boats' (Lk 5.11); tɔmxó·link 'into his boat' (Lk 5.3).

▪ mux·ó·ltət (dim.) 'a small boat' (Mk 3.9).

mweki·s·əmi·- AI(+O) 'have (as) sheep': é·li- máta ní· -mweki·s·əmí·ɔ khak·ayúwa 'because you are not my sheep' (lit., 'I do not have you as sheep') (Jn 10.26). ▸ See méki·s.

mwé·k·ane AN 'dog' (Gr. 5.5b); mwe·k·ané·ɔk 'dogs' (Mt 7.6, 15.26, 15.27); mwe·k·ané·ɔ 'dogs (obv.)' (Lk 16.21).

mwi·č·əwa·k·ani·- AI 'have food', AI+O 'have O2 as food': pa·kanké·[ɔ] ɔ́·k a·məwe·í·i-šó·k·əl mwi·č·əwá·k·ano·p 'his food was locusts and honey' (⟨me-⟩ Mt 3.4); ɔ́·k=č awé·n mwi·č·əwa·k·aní·t·e 'and if someone has food' (⟨mwe-⟩ Lk 3.11). ▸ Cf. mi·č·əwá·k·an.

n

ná (1) P 'then; And' (with SBD, very frequent; Gr. 4.49h-o, 4.72a-j, 6.17): ná mɔ·č·í·ne·p 'then he went home' (Lk 1.23; Gr. 4.72a); ná tɔ·ptó·ne·n 'then he spoke' (Lk 1.64); ná wtəmi·k·é·ne·p 'then she came in' (Lk 2.38); ná tɔləmska·né·ɔ·p 'then they left' (Mt 2.9; Gr. 4.72b); etc.

♦ ná (with other modes) (with IND) ná kanše·ləntamó·p·ani·k 'and they were amazed' (Lk 1.63); ná wé·mi .. áhi-manunksúwak '(then) everyone was very angry' (Lk 4.28); ná nčí·sas təlá·ɔ 'then Jesus said to them' (Mt 26.38); (with é·li and CNJ) 'as soon as': ná é·li-pá·t 'as soon as he arrived' (Lk 15.30); ná é·li-lá·t 'as soon as he said to them' (Jn 18.6).

♦ See also nána (1).

ná (2) (né·kº, né·lº, náka, nəkáhke; Gr. 4.16b) 'that, the (anim.)': ná mi·məntət 'that child' (Lk 1.66, 2.12, 2.21, etc.); ná alánkw 'the star' (Mt 2.7); ná mahtánt·u 'the devil' (Lk 4.6, 4.13); ná lə́nu 'the man' (Jn 5.15, Lk 6.10, etc.; Gr. 6.2d); ná †mpalápas 'this Barabbas (being referred to)' (Jn 18.40); etc.

• né·k 'those (anim.)' (Mt 13.39 2x; Lk 1.79, 2.38, 3.10, etc.); né·k 'The others ..' (Jn 20.25; new prox.); né·k átax ní·š·a 'Those twelve, ..' (Mt 10.5; new prox.); né·k xkwé·ɔk .. 'Meanwhile, those women ..' (Mk 16.3; new prox., focus as a scene-shifter).

• né·l 'the, that (obv.)' (Lk 1.62, Lk 2.17, 2.38, etc.), né·l 'the, those (obv.)' (Mt 2.16, Mt 4.11, Mt 13.3, etc.).

♦ Also: náni (né·kiº, né·liº) (weakly emphatic or more definite) 'that (anim.)': náni skí·xkwe 'that young woman' (Lk 1.27); náni mahtánt·u 'the devil' (Lk 10.18); náni nó·x 'it is my father that ..' (Jn 6.32); náni pá·t·e 'when *he* comes' (Jn 16.8); náni=á· 'that would be the one' (Mt 27.15).

• né·kiº 'those (anim.)' (Gr. 2.72d): né·ki (Mt 25.46); né·ki·k (Mk 5.16, Mt 15.38).

• né·liº 'that, those (obv.)': né·li 'that (obv.)' (Mt 13.39), 'those (obv.)' (Mt 2.16); né·li·l 'those (obv.)' (Jn 1.12, Mt 2.7, Jn 2.16, etc.).

♦ náka (Gr. 2.72b) 'that (abs. sg.)' (Lk 16.20, 18.6, Jn 11.37, etc.).

• nəkáhke 'those (abs. pl.)' (⟨nukavkc⟩ Mt 12.3, Jn 10.35, Lk 9.33, etc.; ⟨nrkaki⟩, ⟨nrkakc⟩ 1834b:43.3); nəkáhke pé·škunk 'the other nine' (Lk 17.17).

ná (3) P PRES (empty support particle or focus peg used to emphasize a following demonstrative in various ways; Gr. §6.5b): ná=ní tó·n 'that's where he went' (⟨nuni⟩ Lk 4.30; also Jn 8.20; ⟨nani⟩ Jn 3.32, Mk 6.20); ná=nə tə́nta-aspí·nxke·n 'there he raised his hands' (⟨nunc⟩ Lk 24.50); né·k·a=č né· ná=nə́ tóp·i·n 'that's where he, too, shall be' (⟨nanc⟩ Jn 12.26; Gr. 6.17a); é·li- ktéhəwa ná=nə -ahpí·t. 'For that is where your (pl.) heart is.' (⟨nanc⟩ Lk 12.34).

♦ ná=yú 'here' (Mt 12.41, 12.42, Mt 26.38, Lk 9.33, 16.26, 16.28, Jn 21.22, etc.); 'then' (Lk 1.26); (apparently as a substantive) 'the here and now' (Lk 21.34; KJV "cares of this life").

♦ Discontinuous: ná=č yú 'here (fut.)' (Mt 26.36); ná=č nə́ 'that is (fut.), that will be' (Mt 2.13, 7.12, 10.11, 17.27, 18.19, Mk 11.24, etc.); ná ɔ́·k nə́ lé·k·eč 'may that also be (what is) done' (Lk 4.23); ná=č ɔ́·k nə́ 'that is also (fut.)' (Jn 3.14, Mt 6.21, 12.45); ná=á· nə́ lé· (*or* lé·w) 'that's what would happen' (⟨na nc lr⟩ Lk 17.6, ⟨nu a nc lrw⟩ Mt 21.21); ná=nə́ni le·khá·s·o·p 'that is what is written' (Mk 9.13).

♦ Sometimes gives the meaning 'the same' or 'that very (one)': ná=nə 'the same thing' (Lk 13.3, Lk 13.5, Mt 20.5, etc.); ná=nə tə́la·n 'he said the same thing to him' (Mt 21.30); ná=nə txə́n 'the same number of times' (Lk 17.4); ná=nə táli 'in that very place' (Mt 21.14); ná=č ɔ́·k nə́ 'in that same (way) also shall ..' (Mt 12.40).

• ná-néke 'at that time' (Jn 9.14 2x, Jn 10.22, Jn 11.49, Jn 13.23, 30; Mt 16.21, Lk 9.37, Lk 10.21, Lk 13.1); ná-néke wə́nči 'from then' (Lk 16.16); ná-néke kí·škwi·k 'that same day' (Mt 13.1, Mk 8.1, Lk 13.31, Lk 17.29, Mk 22.23&, Mk 22.46&, etc.); ná- ɔ́·k -néke kí·škwi·k 'that same day also (w. sbd.)' (Mk 16.12); ná-néke ləkhíkwi 'at that time' (Lk 13.1, Jn 11.51, Mt 26.3); ná=yúkwe néke 'That was now (three times that ..)' (Jn 21.14).

♦ See also nána (2).

nahəlí·i P 'as well as' (Lk 2.7, 2.16, Mt 2.13, 2.20, Lk 2.43, Jn 2.12, etc.), 'along with' (Lk 19.44, Mk 14.14). ♦ (with negative) 'in any case' (Lk 12.59, Jn 14.18).

nahkihəla·- AI 'stop (going)': nahkihəlé·ɔk 'they stopped' (Lk 7.14); ná .. nɔk·íhəla·n 'then he stopped' (Mt 20.32&); nɔk·ihəlá·li·n 'they (obv.) stopped (sbd.)' (Lk 17.12).

nahko·x·we·- AI 'stop (walking)': tə́li-nahko·x·wé·li·n 'that he (obv.) stopped' (Mt. 2.10).

nahkó·i P 'any (whatever), ordinary, plain, etc.' (used with awé·n, kéku, etc.; Gr. 2.13d): nahkó·i awé·n 'ordinary people' (Lk 6.17, Lk 7.11, Mt 12.4), 'just anyone' (Mt 12.4); nahkó·i lə́nu 'any (mere) man' (Lk 18.2, Lk 18.4); nahkó·i awé·ni 'ordinary people (obv.)' (Lk 23.13; KJV "the people"); nahkó·i kéku 'ordinary things (for food)' (Lk 7.33; KJV "bread"), 'anything at all' (Mt 19.3); nahkó·i .. ləkhíkwi 'anytime' (Mk 14.7).

nahkɔ·ihəla·- AI 'go anyplace' (form and meaning conjectured): káči .. nahkɔ·ihəlá·he·kw 'do not go aimlessly' (⟨Kahi .. nuxkyelevrq⟩ Lk 10.7; KJV "Go not from house to house").

nahkɔ·nalə́t·i·n (⟨navkonaluten⟩ form and meaning conjectured): kpəntəməné·ɔ=č lí-mahtá·ke·n, ɔ́·k lí-nahkɔ·nalə́t·i·n 'you (pl.) will hear that there is war and random conflict' (Mt 24.6: KJV "wars and rumours of wars"; Luke 21.9: KJV "wars and commotions"); lí-nahkɔ·nalə́t·i·n could mean something like 'that there is random fighting', which would make sense for an impersonal reciprocal form.

náka (anim. abs. sg. pronoun): see ná (2).

-nakhikayi·h-: see ki·kai·h-.

nál (náli·k, náli, nál; shortened form of nánal; Gr. §6.5c, 6.18) (presentational deictic):
- nál (anim. sg.): nál=tá wá 'this is him' (Jn 9.9), nál=tá wá nčá·n 'this is John' (Mt 14.2), nál=tá wá nkwí·s·əna 'this is our son' (Jn 9.20); nál=háč wá kkwí·s·əwa 'is this your son?' (Jn 9.19); nál=tá wáni †i·láyas 'this is Elias' (Mt 11.14); nál=tá šúkw tɔs·élahto·n 'he (is one who) just scatters it' (Mt 12.30); nál ná mí·lak=č 'he is the one I will give it to' (Jn 13.26); nál ná (+ noun) 'he is the ..' (Jn 14.17, Jn 14.26); etc.
- náli·k (anim. pl.): náli·k=č né·k 'those are the ones who will' (Jn 6.45); náli·k né·k o·txawwá·ɔ 'it was they who came to him' (Jn 12.21; Gr. 6.19c).
- náli (obv.): náli né·l kwəlsə́t·aɔ 'he (obv.) is one he listens to' (Jn 9.31).
- nál (inan. sg.): nə́ni haki·há·k·an, nál nə́ni pe·mhakamí·k·e·k 'the field, *that* is the world ..' (Mt 13.37; Gr. 6.19a).

nalahí·i P 'upstream' (1834a:22.48; Gr. 5.29d).

nalái PV 'peacefully' (Gr. 5.129y): nnálai-ánkələn '(that) I die peacefully' (Lk 2.29).

nalo·wa·wsi·- (ne·lo·wa·wsi·-) AI 'be a heathen': nɔlo·wá·wsi·n '(him) to be a heathen' (Mt 18.17).
- ne·lo·wa·wsi·-: ne·lo·wá·wsi·t 'pagan' (Mt 6.7); ne·lo·wa·wsí·č·i·k 'the heathen (pl.)' (Mt 4.15, 6.32, 10.18; KJV "Gentiles").
▶ Cf. Mun ne·lo·wá·wsi·t 'a heathen' (APh), ⟨Nelowáuchsīt⟩ 'heathen (sg.)' (Z. 92); Mun nalawá·wsəw 'be an unbeliever' (dict.) appears to be influenced by naláwi· 'peacefully, quietly, contentedly, safely'.

nalo·x·ən- II 'be a time or an opportunity (for)': é·li-naló·x·ink 'how it is the time (for)' (⟨nalwxif⟩ Lk 4.19; KJV and RSV "acceptable year"); mayá·i-naló·x·ən 'it is a perfect time' (⟨nulwxun⟩ Lk 21.13&; KJV "'it shall turn to you for'", RSV "This will be a time for you to").

namé·s AN 'fish' (V, OA, LTD ND, LB); namé·s·ak 'fish (pl.)' (Mt 13.47, Jn 21.9, 21.10, etc.); namé·s·a 'fish (obv.)' (Mt 4.18, Mt 7.10, Lk 5.6, 5.9, 11.11, etc.); namé·s·ink 'fish (loc.)': xínkwi-namé·s·ink 'in the whale' (Mt 12.40).
- namé·t·ət (dim.), pl. name·t·ə́t·ak 'little fish (pl.)' (LB): name·t·ə́t·al 'small fish (obv.)' (Mk 8.7); ní·š·a name·t·ə́t·a 'two little fish (obv.)' (Jn 6.9).

nána (1) P 'then, and then' (the equivalent of ná (1)): nána (Lk 1.41 2x, 2.20, Jn 4,53, Mk 4.36, Mt 13.44; ⟨Nuni⟩ 1834a:19.14); nána=č ná 'then that (fut.)' (Mt 25.34).

♦ Note: other cases of ⟨nunu⟩ are /ná ná/ 'then that (anim.)' (Lk 2.27, Mt 4.5, Lk 7.1 [pp. 14, 20, 63]), which is later most commonly written ⟨na nu⟩ (Lk 15.13, Lk 16.3) or ⟨nu nu⟩ (Jn 13.25, Mt 26.25). ▸ See next.

nána (2) P PRES (the equivalent of ná (3)): nána nɔ́ 'the same' (Lk 10.7 [p. 112, the last ex. of nána]). ♦ Apparent nána with néke '(at) that time' seems best taken as: ná ná-néke (ná 'then' + ná-néke '(at) the same time'): ná ná-néke 'at that time then' (⟨Nunu ncki⟩ Jn 1.2, Lk 1.39, ⟨Nunu nckc⟩ Lk 9.36 [p. 105]).

▸ Cf. ná néke 'then .. that time' (Mt 4.17).

nánal (nanáli·k, nanáli; Gr. §6.5c, 6.18) presentational deictic.

• nánal (anim. sg.): nánal=tá wáni 'this is (the one), this is who he is' (Mt 3.3, Lk 7.27, Jn 6.14); nánal ná mahtánt·u 'that is the devil' (Mt 13.39; Gr. 6.19e); nánal ná kxó· 'fear this one (you pl.)' (Lk 12.5).

• nanáli·k (anim. pl.): nanáli·k né·k ni·mahtɔ́s·ak 'they are my brothers' (Mt 12.50; Gr. 6.19h); nanáli·k né·k wé·li·ləs·í·č·i·k 'those are the righteous' (Mt 13.38); nanáli·k né·k me·t·a·wsí·č·i·k 'those are the sinners' (Mt 13.38; Gr. 6.19i).

• nanáli (obv.): nanáli=á· né·l awé·n tɔhɔ·lá·ɔ 'he is who a person should love' (Mk 12.33; Gr. 6.18k); nanáli ehɔ·la·tpáni. 'He was the one he loved.' (Jn 13.23); nanáli né·l .. pa·tamá·k·uk=č 'the one (obv.) who is the one who will pray to him (prox.)' (Jn 4.23; Gr. 6.19p); nanáli né·l ke·yápas wənənaɔ́·ɔ 'he was one that Caiaphas knew' (Jn 18.15; Gr. 6.19j).

• nánal (inan. sg.): nánal yó·ni nahtuhé·p·i 'this is my body' (Lk 22.19; Gr. 6.19f); etc.

• nanáli (inan. pl.): nanáli né·l wəni·skha·lkó·na awé·n. 'Those are the things that defile a person.' (Mt 15.20); é·li- .. nanáli né·l -ntó·nank 'for those things are what he seeks' (Lk 12.30).

▸ Cf. nál.

nánanu 'my cheek' (V; Gr. 4.7g); ɔnánəwak 'cheeks' (V, ME; Gr. 3.4o); kɔnánunk 'on your cheek' (Mt 5.39). ▸ For other forms and variants, see Gr. 4.7g.

nana·t·o·xtamaw- TA 'ask questions of' (Ra+): wənana·t·o·xtama·k·ó·p·ani 'others (obv.) were asking him questions' (Lk 2.46). ▸ Cf. nto·x·əm- TA — nto·xt- TI(2) 'ask for'.

náni: see ná.

nankihəla·- AI 'tremble' (Gr. 5.11n): áləmi- .. -nankíhəle· 'he began to tremble' (Mt 26.37); nankíhəle·p 'she was trembling' (Lk 8.47); nankihəlé·ɔk 'they trembled' (Mt 28.4, Mt 28.8&).

nánkɔn AN 'my heel' (OA), wánkɔn 'heel' (WS), wánkɔnak 'heels' (OA); wánkɔna 'his heel' (Jn 13.18), 'his heel, his heels' (OA); wánkɔnink 'on his heel' (1842:8.1).

▸ Cf. ⟨Nanquon⟩ "[my] heel" (B&Λ 91).

nao·kwehəla·- AI 'hang one's head': nána nɔo·kwéhəla·n 'then he bowed his head' (⟨nowqcvulan⟩ 1834b:35.8). Cf. nao·kwé·x·i·n 'he has (or puts) his head down' (OA, ME).

naɔ́č·i P 'on the way' (⟨naohi⟩ Mk 9.34).

• naɔč·í·i P (Jn 9.11, Mk 9.33, Lk 12.58, Mt 28.8&, etc.).

▸ Cf. Mes, Mun nawat- 'on the way', Men nawa·t- (-na·wat-).

naɔhəla·- AI 'land, alight' (of birds): naɔ́həle· 'it alit' (FW); wənči-káski- čo·lɔ́nsak -naɔhəláhti·t 'so that birds can alight' (Mt 13.32); hók·enk lí-naɔ́həle·p 'it (bird) landed on him' (Jn 1.32).

naɔm- TA 'act before, anticipate, get there ahead of': nɔɔmá·ɔ 'he anticipated him' (⟨nomao⟩ Mt 17.25; KJV "prevented him," RSV "spoke to him first"); nɔɔmawwá·ɔ 'they outran them' (⟨naomawao⟩ Mk 6.33); nnaɔmə́k·e 'I am outrun, beaten to it' (⟨naomukc⟩; Jn 5.7); kənaɔmuk·əwá·ɔk=č 'they will get ahead of you (pl.)' (Mt 21.31).

♦ The /a/ is assumed to be short; cf. ⟨naom-⟩ 'run ahead of' (LTD).

†násəlat 'Nazareth' (⟨Nasulut⟩ Lk 2.39); †nasəlát·ink 'Nazareth (loc.)' (Lk 2.51, Jn 1.45, 1.46, etc.).
- †nésəlat 'Nazareth' (⟨Ncsulut⟩ Lk 1.26, Mt 2.23).
- †nasəlat·í·i PN '(of) Nazareth' (⟨Nasulute⟩ Lk 2.4, Mt 3.13, 21.11).
- †nesəlat·í·i P (⟨Ncsulutee⟩ Mt 2.23).

†nasəlát·i·t '(who is) of Nazareth' (⟨Nasulutet⟩ Mk 1.24).

-nat·o·naw-: see nto·naw-.

-nat·o·xtº-: see nto·xtº.

naxá P 'three' (Lk 1.56, Jn 2.6, Lk 9.33, etc.; OA, ME, LB); ní·š·a ší=tá naxá awé·ni·k 'with two or three people' (Mt 18.16; Gr. 3.15e); naxá ki·š·ó·x·ink ahpá·mi 'for about three months' (Lk 1.56; Gr. 6.9b).

naxáns 'my older brother' (Lk 12.13); naxánsa 'my older brother (abs.)' (Jn 11.21, 11.32); kxáns 'your older brother' (Jn 11.23; Gr. §2.1c); kxánsak 'your (older) brothers' (1842:13.4); xɔ́nsa 'his older brother' (Jn 11.2), 'his older brothers' (1842:13.4); xɔnsəwá·ɔ 'their older brother' (Jn 11.19). ▸ Cf. naxá·ns (V, OA). ▸ See also xɔnsi·-*.

naxa·l- TA — naxa·t·- TI(1a) 'beware of, watch out for'.
- naxa·l- (TA): naxá·lo 'watch out for them (you pl.)' (Mk 12.38); naxa·ló·me 'watch out for them (you sg.)' (Mt 7.15, Mt 10.17).
- naxa·t·- (TI): naxá·t·amo·kw 'beware of it (you pl.)' (Lk 12.1, 12.15); naxa·t·amo·mɔ́·e 'beware of it (you pl.)' (Mk 8.15, 16.11, 16.12; Gr. 4.116.l).

naxá·pxki P 'three hundred' (1834a:18.9).

naxennáɔhki P 'three kinds, sets, batches, etc.': énta- naxennáɔhki -hát·e·k 'in three batches of it' (Mt 13.33).

naxə́m 'my daughter-in-law' (V, OA, ME); xúṃa (|wə-xəm-a|) 'her daughter-in-law' (⟨xwmav⟩ Lk 12.53, apparently indicating /xúma[h]/).

naxə́n P 'three times, thrice' (Jn 13.38, Lk 22.34, Jn 21.14).

náxi (Gr. 2.75c, 5.129z) PV 'three' (Jn 2.20, Lk 24.7, Lk 24.46).
- náxi PP (Gr. 5.133e): náxi-kí·škwe 'for three days' (Mt 12.40 [2x]); náxi-tpó·kəwe 'for three nights' (Mt 12.40 [2x]).

naxi·- AI 'be three': †nó·wa naxi·ló·p·ani kkwí·s·al 'Noah had three sons' (lit., 'his sons were three') (1834b:18.10).

naxí·s·əməs (|-xīsəməs|; Gr. 2.62g) 'my younger sibling'; naxi·s·əmə́s·ak 'my younger brothers' (Mt 12.48, 12.49); kwə́t·i naxi·s·əmə́s·əna 'one of our younger brothers' (1842:15.2); kxí·s·əməs 'your younger brother' (Lk 15.27, 15.32; Gr. 2.63g); kxi·s·əmə́s·ak 'your younger brothers' (Mt 12.47); xwi·s·əmə́s·al 'his younger brother' (1834b:17.7), xwi·s·əmə́s·a 'his or her younger sibling or siblings' (Jn 2.12, 7.3, Mt 13.55, etc.; Gr. 2.39d); xwi·s·əməs·í·li·t 'her (obv.) younger sister' (Jn 11.5); kxi·s·əmə́s·əwa 'your (pl.) younger brother' (1842:15.3, 15.5).

naxko·m- (ne·xko·m-) TA — naxko·t·- TI(1b) 'answer, agree to'.
- naxko·m- (TA): kó·li-naxkó·məl 'I answered you right[!; error for kó·li-naxkó·mi 'you answered me right']' (Lk 10.28; KJV "Thou hast answered right"); nɔxko·má·ɔ 'he answered him, them' (Lk 7.22, Mt 12.48, 13.11, etc.; Gr. 2.55r); máta nɔxko·ma·í·ɔ 'he did not assent to what the other asked' (Mt 18.30); ná nɔxkó·ma·n 'then he gave them his agreement' (Lk 22.6).
- ne·xko·m-: awé·n ne·xko·mkúk·e 'when someone has the consent of [an unmarried girl (obv.)]' (lit., 'when she (obv.) has said yes to someone') (Jn 3.29).

▪ naxko·t- (TI): naxkó·t·i 'answer it (you. sg.)' (OA; Gr. 4.106c); é·li-naxkó·t·ink 'how he answered' (Lk 2.47).

▪ naxkunti·- (ne·xkunti·-, |naxkōntī-|) AI (recip.; Gr. 5.110n) 'agree with each other; be engaged to marry': naxkúntəwak 'they answered 'yes' to each other' (OA; Gr. 2.45b); naxkúntəwak lənəwal 'she was engaged to a man' (Lk 1.27); kíši-naxkuntó·p·ani·k 'they were already engaged' (Mt 1.18).

• ne·xkunti·-: ne·xkuntíhti·t 'who was engaged to him' (Lk 2.5; Gr. 4.64p); mé·či kíši-naxkuntihtí·t·e 'after he has agreed with them' (Mt 20.2).

naxkuhəma·- AI 'sing': kíši-naxkúhəmahtí·t·e 'after they had sung' (Mt 26.30; KJV "sung an hymn"). ♦ Note: a middle reflexive (5.104abcd) from naxkuhəmaw- TA 'sing for': xkwé·ɔk ə́nta-naxkúhəmunt 'the woman dance (*lit.*, when women are sung for)' (JM).

naxkuntəwá·k·an IN 'agreement, bargain, covenant' (Gr. 5.60e; cf. B&A 88); wə́ski-naxkuntəwá·k·an 'new covenant' (Mt 26.28; KJV "the new testament").

naxkunti·-: see naxko·m- — naxko·t-.

naxkws- (|naxkwəsw-|) TA 'light (fire to)': máta=háč=á· ɔ·s·əle·ní·k·ana naxkwsé·i 'would she not light a candle?' (Lk 15.8); awé·n naxkwsá·t·e ɔ·s·əle·ní·k·ana 'if someone lights a candle' (Mt 5.15).

naxkwsi·- (|naxkwəsī-|) AI — naxkwte·- (|naxkwətē-|) II 'be lit, catch fire'.

▪ naxkwsi·- (AI): kɔ·s·əle·ni·k·anúwa .. naxkwsí·t·eč 'let your (pl.) lantern (anim.) be lit' (Lk 12.35).

▪ naxkwte·- (II): wə́nči-náxkwte· entalá·wsink 'in order that the world catch fire' (Lk 12.49).

naxo·k·wənak·at- (ne·x·o·k·wənak·at-, with |-ōkwən-| 'day'; cf. Gr. 5.31s) II 'be three days': yúkwe mé·či naxo·k·wənák·at 'it has now been three days' (Lk 24.21); naxo·k·wənakháke 'in, after three days (from now)' (Jn 2.19, Mt 16.21, etc.; Gr. 2.48b).

• ne·x·o·k·wənak·at-: ne·x·o·k·wənakháke 'three days later' (Jn 2.1).

naxpankəl- AI+O 'die with O2, die having O2': naxpankəlé·k·we=č kəmat·a·wsəwa·k·anúwa 'when you (pl.) die with your sins' (Jn 8.21, 8.24); kənaxpankələné·ɔ kəmat·a·wsəwa·k·anúwa 'you (pl.) die with your sins' (Jn 8.24).

naxpanko·m- (ne·xpanko·m-) TA(+O) 'give (O2 as) an outright gift to': nnaxpankó·ma 'I give him something in greeting and making friends' (OA); nnaxpankó·ma·n=tá 'I make a gift of it to him' (Mt 15.5); nɔxpankó·mko·n 'he (obv.) made a gift of it to him' (Lk 7.42; KJV "forgave them"); káhta- awé·n -naxpanko·mát·e 'if you (sg.) want to give a present to someone' (Mt 6.1); sháki hókunk wə́nči-naxpanko·mke·é·k·we aləwí·i-ləs·əwá·k·an 'until you (pl.) are granted power from heaven' (Lk 24.49); e·ləwí·i-txí-naxpanko·mkúk·i 'the one (obv.) that gave him the most' (Lk 7.43; KJV "to whom he forgave most," misunderstood).

• ne·xpanko·m-: ne·xpankó·mənt 'what is offered to him' (Lk 21.4).

▪ naxpankunti·- AI 'give presents (to each another)': takó· wə́nči wehə́nči-naxpankúnti·t yú entalá·wsi·t 'not because of the reasons why people (sg.) give presents to each other' (Jn 14.27).

▶ Cf. ⟨Nachpangoman⟩ 'to salute somebody with a present' (B&A 89).

naxpankunke·- AI+O 'give O2 as a present to people': káhta- kéku -naxpankunké·ane 'when you (sg.) want to give a present to someone' (Mt 6.2).

naxpankunsi·- AI 'give presents': naxpankunsiáne 'when you (sg.) give presents' (Mt 6.3, 6.5); ke·ke·xíti=hánkw íka núnči-naxpankúnsi 'I always give a little as gifts from there' (Lk 18.12).

naxpankuntəwá·k·an IN 'gift' (Mt 23.18, 23.19 [2x]); xínkwi-naxpankuntəwá·k·an 'a big present' (1842:15.5).

naxpankuntəwá·k·ani·- II 'be a gift': naxpankuntəwá·k·anu 'it is a gift' (Jn 4.10; misunderstood).

naxpankunti·-: see naxpanko·m-.

naxpa·wsi·- AI+O 'live with O2, possess O2': ehaləmá·kami·k=č pəma·wsəwá·k·an naxpá·wsu 'he will have eternal life' (Jn 5.24); naxpá·wsi·kw pí·lsi·t manót·u 'possess the holy spirit (you pl.)' (Jn 20.22; KJV "receive ye [him]"); naxpa·wsíhti·t 'what they lived with'(?) (⟨nanpawsetet⟩ 1834a:18.2 [em., passage and form unclear]); šúkw=č nɔxpá·wsi·n pe·ma·wsó·wi·k ɔ·x·é·e·k 'but he shall live with the living light' (Jn 8.12; KJV "shall have the light of life").

náxpəne P 'even' (1834a:21.33; Mk 8.4, Jn 6.7, Jn 11.4), 'also' (OA); (with negative) (Lk 4.27, Mt 5.19, Mk 2.2, Lk 10.4, 14.24).

náxpi P 'with' (with an instrumental oblique complement [cf. Gr. §3.7c]): 'with' (Mk 5.26, Jn 17.5, 17.11), 'having' (Mt 6.24); "by [God]" (Mk 5.7).
- náxpi PV 'with O2' (né·xpi; Gr. 5.129aa) (Mt 23.23).
- né·xpi (Mt 13.14 [2x], 1834a:21.33).

naxpi·k·i·- (ne·xpi·k·i·-, |naxpīkī-|) AI+O 'be born with O2': nɔxpí·k·i·n kok·e·p·ínkɔ·n 'he was born (being) blind' (Jn 9.19, 9.20; Gr. 4.40r).
- ne·xpi·k·i·-: ne·xpi·k·í·li·t 'who (obv.) was born (being) blind' (Jn 9.32).

naxpo·x·we·- (|-ōxwē-| 'walk'; Gr. 4.61b) AI+O 'go having O2': nó·x təlsəwá·k·an mpéči-naxpó·x·we·n 'I come with my father's power' (Jn 5.43); nɔxpó·x·we·n=č 'he must take it with him' (Mt 16.24).

-nax·ó·ha: see xó·ha.

-nax·o·he·xka·l-: see xo·he·xka·l-*.

na·či·h- TA — na·či·t- TI(2) 'have to do with, concern oneself with, mess with, bother'.
- na·či·h- (TA): nna·čí·ha 'I bother him' (OA); káči na·či·hié·k·ač 'don't have anything to do with him (you sg.)' (Mt 27.19); káči na·či·hié·k·e·kw 'don't disturb it (a tree [anim.]) (you pl.)' (1834b:16.4, 1842:7.4); na·čihkóneč 'may he concern himself with you (sg)' (Mt 16.22; Gr. 4.114h); kéku=ksí wə́nči-na·číhkɔn 'why does it concern you?' (Jn 2.4).
- na·či·t- (TI): nna·čí·to·n 'I bother it' (OA); máta na·či·tó·wane nə́ni məne·ó·k·an 'if you (sg.) don't mess with drink' (1842:20.2); máta na·či·tuhtí·t·e 'if they do not mess with it' (1842:21.5); ní·=č máta háši nna·či·tó·wən 'I'll never mess with it' (1842:21.6); máta háši kəna·či·tó·wən '(that you) never mess with it (1842:20.2). ▸ Cf. ⟨Natschiton⟩ 'to engage in, take care of' (B&A 91).

na·či·taw- TA+O 'mess with O2 of': káči na·či·tawié·k·ač wi·t·a·wsó·mat wí·k·i·t 'do not mess with your neighbor's house (you sg.)' (1842:12.7).

na·hɔke·- AI 'follow after' (|nāwahkē-|; Gr. 2.38l, 5.102c): na·hɔ́ke· 'he followed (after)' (Jn 18.15). ▸ Cf. na·ɔl- TA 'follow'.

-na·ka·l-: see nhaka·l-.

-na·ka·t·-: see nhaka·l-.

-na·ka·t·amwe·ɔ·k·an-: see nhaka·t·amwe·ɔ́·k·an.

na·k·a·é·k·e P 'after a while' (Jn 5.14, Mk 6.25, Jn 9.4, etc.; LB).

na·k·é·i P 'for a while' (Lk 18.4, Mk 15.44 [KJV "any while," RSV "sometime"]). ▸ Cf. na·k·é·e 'for a while' (WL); ⟨Nakewi⟩ 'a little while' (B&A 90); Mun ná·ke·, ná·ke·w 'for a while'.

na·l- TA — na·t·- TI(1b) 'go to get' (Gr. 3.20d, 5.12b).
- na·l- (TA): ə́nta-péči-ná·lənt 'when they were come for' (OA); nná·la=á· ná xáskwi·m. 'I could go after Corn Person.' (V; Gr. 5.12b); nɔ·lawwá·ɔ 'they fetched him' (1834b:30.5).

▪ na·t- (TI): wə́nči-=á· .. máta -pi·p·éči- mpí -na·t·əmó·wa 'so that I would never come here to get water' (Jn 4.15); nná·t·əm tə́ntay 'I'm going after fire' (WL; Gr. 4.38b); pwéči- mpí -ná·t·əmən 'she came to get water (sbd.)' (Jn 4.7); káči lahápa kéku na·t·ínkhi·č 'let him not take the time to go and get things' (Mt 24.17).

na·ɔl- TA 'follow': ná·ɔl 'follow them (you sg.)' (1842:16.2); ná·ɔli·l 'follow me (you sg.)' (Jn 21.19, 21.22; Gr. 2.38l); na·ɔlí·t·eč 'let him follow me' (Jn 12.26); é·li- máta -na·ɔluk·ó·wenk 'because he did not follow us (exc.)' (Lk 9.49; Gr. 4.97o); kɔ́č=háč máta káski- yúkwe -na·ɔləló·wan 'why can't I follow you (sg.) now?' (Jn 13.37; Gr. 4.97u); na·ɔlólenk 'when we followed you' (Mt 19.27); wé·mi awé·n nɔ·ɔlá·ɔ 'everyone follows him' (Jn 12.19); nɔ·ɔlawwá·ɔ 'they follow him' (Jn 10.4); wəna·ɔlawwá·ɔ 'they followed him' (Mk 1.36, Mt 9.27; Gr. 2.56d); tá=á· wəna·ɔla·iwwá·ɔ 'they will not follow him' (Jn 10.5); nna·ɔlúk·o·k 'they follow me' (Jn 10.27; Gr. 2.27f); wəna·ɔlúk·u 'it (obv.) is following her' (Mt 21.5); tə́li-na·ɔluk·o·né·ɔ 'that he (obv.) was following them' (Jn 21.20).

na·ɔli·kxa·l-(?) TA 'follow after': máta .. †na·ɔli·kxa·lí·t·e 'if he does not follow after me' (Mt 10.38; KJV "followeth after").

♦ If an error for *na·ɔli·xka·l-, cf. xo·he·xka·l- 'leave all alone'.

na·pənal- TA 'confront, seize': nkát·a-na·pənála 'I'm going to go over and get after him' (OA); málahši=háč kehkəmó·tke·s kəna·pənaláhəmɔ 'did you (pl.) come out as if to seize a thief?' (Mt 26.55-56&; KJV "come out .. against"). ▸ Cf. ⟨Napenallan⟩ 'seize, take prisoner' (B&A 91); "have it out with" and "raise cain with .. (used in joking manner)" (LTD).

†na·ptáləm 'Nephthalim' (Mt 4.15).

ná·ta P 'in your direction' (Mt 12.38), '(to) where you are' (Lk 16.26, 1834b:22.9), ná·ta wə́nči 'from where you are' (Lk 16.26); ní· ná·ta ntá 'I go to you' (Jn 17.11). ▸ Opposed to: wə́ntax.

na·te·ləm- TA — na·te·lənt- TI(1a) 'think about, take thought for' (final pair: Gr. 5.12i).

▪ na·te·ləm- (TA): cf. ⟨natelëm-⟩ 'think about' (LTD).

▪ na·te·lənt- (TI): káči na·te·ləntánkhe·kw 'don't be concerned with it (you pl.)' (1842:17.1); kéku wə́nči-na·te·ləntame·kw 'why do you (pl.) take thought for it?' (Mt 6.28). ♦ Short /t/ is assumed because these presumably have the initial |nāht-| of na·či·h- 'bother'.

na·t·-: see na·l- — na·t·-.

na·t·ən- TA — TI(1b) 'take (to oneself), accept'.

▪ na·t·ən- (TA): kə́nč=á· .. na·t·əná·t·e 'unless he takes him' (Jn 6.44; KJV "draw him"); nɔ·t·əná·p·ani wi·k·i·má·č·i 'he accepted his wife' (Mt 1.24; KJV "took unto him").

†nčátan 'the Jordan (River)' (Lk 4.1, Jn 1.28); †nčátanink 'in (etc.) the Jordan' (Mt 3.6, 3.13, Jn 3.26, Mt 4.15, 4.25, Jn 10.40, Mt 19.1).

▪ †nčataní·i PN '(of) the Jordan' (Lk 3.3, Mt 3.5).

nčá·n 'John' (Jn 1.6, 1.15, Lk 1.13, etc.); nčá·nal (obv.) (Lk 3.15, Mt 3.13, Jn 1.19, etc.); nčá·na (obv.) (Mt 4.18-19, 21, Mk 6.20, etc.); nčá·na 'John (abs.)' (Acts 1.5); nčá·nink 'to John' (Jn 3.26).

†nčéliku 'Jericho' (Mt 20.30&); †nčelikó·wink 'Jericho (loc.)' (Lk 19.1, Mk 10.46), earlier †čelikó·wunk (Lk 10.30).

†nčeli·máya 'Jeremiah' (Mt 2.17); †nčeli·mayás·a (abs.) (Mt 27.9), †čeli·mayás·a (Mt 16.14).

†nčé·kəp 'Jacob' (1842:10.4, 13.1, 14.4); †nče·kə́pa (obv.) (⟨Nhrkwpu⟩ Mt 8.11); †nče·kə́pa (abs.) (⟨Nhrkupu⟩ Jn 4.5, 4.6, 4.12, etc.). ♦ Note: the spelling with ⟨wp⟩ points to /ə́p/.

nčím 'Jim', i.e., 'James' (Mt 4.21, Lk 6.14, 6.15, etc.); nčíma (obv.) (Mt 4.18-19&).

nčími 'Jimmy' (B: Title Page); i.e., James Conner.

†nči·ló·sələm 'Jerusalem' (Lk 2.41, Mt 3.5, Mt 5.35, etc.); †nči·lo·sələmink 'to, in Jerusalem' (Lk 2.22, 2.25, 2.38, Mt 2.1, etc.); íka .. †nči·ló·sələm 'to Jerusalem' (Lk 2.41); lí †nči·ló·sələm 'to Jerusalem'; táli †nči·ló·sələm 'in Jerusalem' (Lk 24.18): ⟨Nhelwsrlum(-)⟩ (Mt 2.1, Mk 10.32), ⟨Nhelwsulum(-)⟩ 52x.
 ♦ The spelling reflects a nineteenth-century English pronunciation with a long "e" (/iy/) in the first syllable.

†nči·lo·sələmí·ɔk 'the people of Jerusalem' (Jn 1.19, 7.25).

nčí·sas 'Jesus' (WS; Lk 1.31, Mt 1.21, Lk 2.52, etc.; Gr. 2.79f); nčí·sas kəláist 'Jesus Christ' (Jn 1.17, Mk 1.1); nči·sás·al (obv.) (Lk 2.27, Jn 1.29, 1.37, etc.), nči·sás·a (Jn 5.16, Lk 5.8, etc.); nči·sás·ink 'to Jesus' (Jn 1.42, 3.2, Lk 7.3, 8.35, etc.).
 ▪ nči·sástət (dim.) 'young Jesus' (Lk 2.43).
 ♦ Note: the spelling ⟨Hesus⟩ (1834b) is most likely for /nčí·sas/.

nčó· AN 'Jew' (Jn 4.9, 18.35); nčó·wak (Jn 2.6, 2.18, 3.25, 4.9, etc.); nčó·wa 'Jews (obv.)' (Jn 5.15, 8.31, 9.22, 11.33, etc.); nčó·wink 'among, (from) the Jews' (Jn 3.1, 4.22, 11.54); lí nčo·wi·ké·i P+P 'to, among the Jews' (Jn 18.38, Lk 23.5, Mt 28.15; Gr. 6.9g).
 ▪ nčo·wí·i PN 'Jewish' (Mt 2.2, Jn 2.13, Mt 24.16, etc.).
 ▪ PV: nčo·wí·i-sa·k·i·ma·iáne 'if you are the king of the Jews' (Lk 23.37).

†nčó·səs 'Joses' (Mt 13.55).

†nčo·taí·i PN 'of Juda': †nčo·taí·i-o·t·é·nay 'a town of Juda' (⟨Nhwtue⟩ Lk 1.39).
 ▸ Cf. †nčo·ti·í·i.

†nčó·tas 'Judas' (Lk 6.16, Mt 13.55, Jn 14.22); nčó·tas †iská·liat 'Judas Iscariot' (⟨Nhwtus Iskaliut⟩ Lk 6.16, Mt 10.4, Jn 6.71); †nčó·tas-iská·liɔt (⟨Iskaliot⟩ Jn 12.4); †nčó·tas-iska·liát·a (obv.) (⟨Iskaleutu⟩ Jn 13.2, 13.26); see also †iská·liat (⟨Iskrliut⟩). †ləpías-nčó·tas 'Lebbaeus Judas' (Mt 10.3).

†nčo·tí·a 'Judaea' (⟨Nhwteu⟩ Lk 2.4, Mt 2.1, 2.5, etc.); nčo·tí·yunk 'Judaea (loc.)' (⟨Nhwteuf⟩ Lk 1.5, 1.65, Jn 4.3, etc., 8x in pp. 6-63; later ⟨Nhwtebf⟩ Jn 7.3, ⟨Nhwtewf⟩ Jn 7.1, 11.7). †nčo·tí·ink táli 'in Judaea' (⟨Nhuteiftali⟩ Lk 3.1 [p. 17]). ♦ Note: the earliest spellings of the locative (on pp. 6-63) were evidently influenced by the spelling of 'Judea' as ⟨Nhwteu⟩, and in one case by the common locative -ink (⟨-if⟩), but no Unami locative ends in /-ank/, and the form was later spelled as if having /-unk/.

†nčo·ti·í·č·i·k 'Judaeans' (⟨Nhwteethek⟩ Mt 3.5).

†nčo·ti·í·i PN 'of Judaea': †nčo·ti·í·i-hák·ink 'in Judaea' (⟨Nhwtee vakif⟩ Jn 3.22; ⟨Nhwtei vakif⟩ Mt 19.1).

nčó·t·ie: see nčú below.

†nčo·wá·na 'Joanna' (⟨Nhwanu⟩ Lk 8.3). ▸ Cf. †nčɔ·é·ni.

nčo·wi·xsi·- AI 'speak Hebrew': nčo·wí·xsi·n 'it was in the Jews' language' (Jn 19.20).

†nčɔ·é·ni 'Joanna' (⟨Nhornc⟩ Lk 24.9-10). The spelling may reflect a dialectal English pronunciation with /-iy/ for "-a" (misprinted with ⟨-c⟩ for ⟨-e⟩); cf. †ani 'Anna'.
 ▸ Cf. †nčo·wá·na.

nčó·na 'Jonah' (Mt 16.17).

†nčɔ·nas 'Jonas' (Jn 1.42, 21.16); †nčɔ·nás·a (Mt 12.39, 12.40, 12.42, 16.4).

nčó·səp 'Joseph' (⟨Nhoscp⟩ 1842:13.1, 13.2; ⟨Nhosup⟩ 1842:15.2); nčɔ·sə́p·a 'Joseph (obv.)' (⟨Nhosipu⟩ Jn 6.42; ⟨Nhosupu⟩ 1842:14.3, 15.5, 17.1, 18.2); nčɔ·sə́p·ink 'to Joseph's place' (⟨Nhosupif⟩ 1842:17.1).

†nčɔ́·si 'Josey (i.e., Joseph)' (Lk 1.27, Mt 1.18, 1.20, Lk 2.4, 2.32, etc.); †nčɔ́·si (obv.) (Lk 2.43); †nčɔ́·sial (obv.) (Lk 2.16, Mt 2.19); nčɔ́·sia (obv.) (⟨Nhosiu⟩ Jn 4.5).

nčú (nčó·t·ie; Gr. 4.11f) 'my friend' (voc.; male to male) (Lk 11.5, 14.10, Jn 12.21); also apparent nčúh ⟨nhwv⟩ (Jn 12.21; 1834b 8:9, 1842:21.6).
• nčó·t·ie 'my friend (male to male)' (Mt 22.12, 26.50; Gr. 5.50a) ~ nčó·t·i (1834a: Cover); nčo·t·ié·sto·kw 'my friends' (voc.) (Mt 20.13; Gr. 4.11m).
♦ The vocative of ní·t·i·s 'my male friend (of a male)'.
=néh P 'possibly?' (indicates a skeptical question; Gr. 5.24n): awé·n=néh .. 'Who would ..?' (Jn 6.60, Mk 10.26); tá=néh=á·m=ét wə́nči-káski- nə -lé·w 'How could that possibly be?' (Jn 3.9)..
nehəla·l-: see nihəla·l-.
nehəlá·ləwe·t 'the Lord, the master' (Lk 1.17, 1.28, 1.32, Mt 1.20, etc.); nehəla·ləwé·li·t (obv.) (Lk 2.24), nehəla·ləwe·lí·č·i (obv.) (Lk 22.61, Mk 16.10&, Jn 20.20).
• (lexicalized participle) nehəla·ləwé·t·ink 'to the Lord' (Lk 1.16).
nehənaɔnke·s (Gr. 5.5d, 5.66c,f) AN 'horse' (1834a:14); nehənaɔnké·s·ak 'horses' (Lk 2.7); nehənaɔnké·s·al 'horse (obv.)' (1834a:14), nehənaɔnké·s·a (Lk 2.16).
▸ Cf. Northern Unami (Moraviantown) nehnawánke·s 'horse' (EJ; Goddard 2010:8).
nehəne·w-: see ne·w-.
nehəni·k·a·na·pto·né·t·əp: see ni·k·a·na·pto·ne·-.
nehəni·k·a·ní·i PV: see ni·k·a·ní·i.
nehəní·p·ai·t: see ni·p·ai·-.
nehəno·t·°: see no·t·əm-.
néke P '(at) the time' (Mk 5.19, Lk 13.1, etc.; Gr. 2.72f); misprinted ⟨ckc⟩ (Mt 25.34). ♦ ná-néke 'that same (time)' (this ná does not require sbd.): ná-néke kí·škwi·k 'that same day' (Jn 19.14); ná ɔ́·k néke kí·škwi·k 'that same day also' (Mk 16.12); ná-néke pí·ske·k 'that same evening' (Jn 20.19; uncertain in Jn 13.30 [KJV "and it was night"]); ná-néke ləkhíkwi 'at that same time' (Lk 13.1, Jn 11.51, Mt 26.3). ▸ See also under ná (3) P PRES and nána (2) P PRES.
♦ Later form: níke.
nenhiləwe·-: see nhiləwe·-.
nenhiləwe·t-: see nhiləwe·t-.
nentəl- TA+O 'show O2 to' ('cause to see O2, make see O2'; Gr. 5.87e): wənéntəla·n hók·ay 'he showed himself to him' (Mt 2.19); wənentəlúk·o·n 'he (obv.) showed it to him' (Gr. 2.45c; taken from Lk 1.11, but the /wə-/ must be an erroneous revision, and the text should be emended to tə́nta-nentəlúk·o·n 'showed (himself) to him there').
nentsi·taw- (|nēntəsīhtaw-|; Gr. 5.104m) TA 'appear to': mé·či .. nentsi·taɔ́·t·e 'after he had appeared to them' (Acts 1.3); é·li-nentsi·tá·k·uk 'how he (obv.) had appeared to her' (Mk 16.11); wənentsi·taɔ́·ɔ 'he appeared to them' (Jn 21.1); wənentsi·taɔ́·p·ani 'he appeared to them' (Mk 16.12); wənentsí·taɔ·n 'that he had appeared to them (sbd.)' (Jn 21.14).
▸ Cf. ⟨nentsítawi⟩ 'appear to me' (Z. 12). ♦ From unattested *nentsi·- AI 'show oneself, make oneself be seen' (Gr. 5.104m), from |nēntəl-| TA+O 'cause to see O2, show O2 to' (Gr. 5.87e).
†nésəlat: see násəlat.
newwe·- AI 'see people': néwwe· 'he saw people' (Mk 12.41; Gr. 3.11a).
né· P 'too' (Mt 5.32, Lk 14.14). ♦ With emphatic pronouns (Gr. 4.13).
ne·í·nxke (|-īnaxkē|; Gr. 2.30d, 5.31p) P 'forty' (⟨nrenxkc⟩ Mk 1.13, Acts 1.3, 1842:9.4); ne·í·nxke ɔ́·k kwə́t·a·š forty-six (⟨nrentxki⟩ Jn 2.20).
né·k, né·k°: see ná (2).
ne·ka·t·ánki·k: see nhaka·l- — nhaka·t·-.

né·k·a (né·k·əma; Gr. 3.10) 'he, she, etc.' (3s emph): né·k·a 'he' (Jn 1.8, 1.10, 2.12), 'himself' (Jn 5.45, Mt 5.35), 'as for him' (Mt 4.18-19&); né·k·a=tá (Jn 1.27); né·k·a=č ná 'it is *he* that will' (*lit.*, 'that one himself will') (Jn 14.26), 'his' (Jn 14.24).
- né·k·əma (Gr. 4.13) (Lk 1.9, Jn 4.12, 5.19, etc.); né·k·əma=tá (Jn 12.44).
- ne·k·əmá·ɔ 'they, themselves' (Jn 4.45, Mt 12.27, Lk 16.28, etc.), wə́nči ne·k·əmá·ɔ 'because of them' (Jn 17.19). Later variants are given in Gr. §3.6.

né·l, ne·l° (1): see ná, nə́.

ne·l° (2): fusion of nə́ and e·l° (Gr. 4.60); for conjunct forms ('while watching, etc.'), see l°.

né·ləma P 'not yet, before'.
- ♦ 'not yet' (1) with indep. neg.: né·ləma ankəló·wi 'he is not yet dead' (Jn 4.49). (2) with é·li PV in ch. conj.: é·li- né·ləma -tpəskwihəlá·k·əp 'as the time had not yet come' (Jn 8.20).
- ♦ 'before' (1) with ch. conj. (negative where distinguished): né·ləma ne·t·o·xtaɔ́·ɔt 'before you ask him' (Mt 6.8); né·ləma mayá·i íka pé·a·t 'before he had gotten all the way there' (Lk 15.20); né·ləma nə́ é·le·k 'before it happened' (Jn 11.35, Jn 14.29). (2) with ch. subj. (negative where distinguished): né·ləma .. wənči·mkó·wane 'before he called you' (Jn 1.48); né·ləma é·ləmi-haté·k·e hák·i 'before the world began' (Jn 17.24); né·ləma pe·s·əntpé·k·e hák·i 'before the earth was flooded' (Mt 24.38).

né·li (1) (in ch. conj. verbs; Gr. 5.128p) PV 'while' (Lk 1.8, 1.51, Mt 2.13, 3.16, etc.).

né·li (2) 'to there, yonder' (⟨Nrli⟩ Mk 6.33, Mt 7.13 [complement of á·l 'go!']). ♦ The occasioanl spelling ⟨nali⟩ (Mk 9.42, Lk 17.2) is probably also best read as /né·li/; cf. Mun né·lak 'over there', the equivalent of Mass ⟨na⟩ 'there' (/nā/) + PEA *ərakwi 'in {such} direction'.

né·li (3) 'that (obv.)', 'those (obv.)', 'those (inan.)': see ná, nə́.

ne·lkí·kwi-: see ləkhíkwi.

ne·lo·wá·wsi·t: see nalo·wa·wsi·-.

ne·m-: see ne·w- — ne·m-.

†né·man 'Naaman' (Lk 4.27).

nema- AI 'see': á·la-né·ma 'he can't see' (LB); wə́nči-nemá·an 'so that you (sg.) can see' (Jn 9.10); wə́nči-né·ma·t 'so that he saw' (Mt 12.22); nemá·č·i·k 'who see' (Jn 9.39); máta nemá·č·i·k 'who do not see' (Jn 9.39); wə́ski-nema·lí·č·i 'the newly seeing one (obv.)' (Jn 9.15); máta=háč nemá·i 'does he not see?' (Mk 8.18; Gr. 4.81e); nne·máhəna 'we (exc.) see' (Jn 9.41; Gr. 4.21g); ná nné·ma·n 'then I saw' (Jn 9.15); təli- ke·k·e·p·inkó·č·i·k -ne·ma·né·ɔ 'that the blind see' (Lk 7.22). ♦ Ostensible -nemhíti·t 'they see it' (⟨nrmvetet⟩ in Lk 4.18) is an error for -nemáhti·t 'they see'.

ne·mwe·ha·l- TA 'make see' (Gr. 5.83c): é·li-nemwe·há·lkɔn 'because he made you (sg.) see' (Jn 9.17); lí-nemwe·há·la·n 'that he had been made to see' (Jn 9.18).

ne·ɔ́·pxki (Gr. 2.30d) P 'four hundred' (Lk 16.6).

né·pe (Gr. 4.13) P 'I also, me also' (⟨nrpc⟩ Lk 2.48, Jn 5.17, Mt 10.32, etc. [20x, pp. 17-217]; ⟨nrpi⟩ Mt 2.8, Mt 10.40 [2x, pp. 15, 62]).
- né·pəna (V, ME; Gr. 4.13) P 'we also, us also' (Lk 3.14, Lk 23.39).

né·skɔ P 'before; not yet' (< ní + |ēskwa|).
- PV (in ch. conj.): né·skɔ-čhɔ·pwi·nxkéhti·t 'before they washed their hands' (Mk 7.5); né·skɔ-ála-hát·e·k 'before it ends' (⟨rlu⟩ Lk 21.9), e·lkí·kwi-=č -ála-hát·e·k 'when it shall cease to exist' (Mt 13.39); né·skɔ-=č wémi -ankəlíhti·t 'before they all (shall) die' (Lk 21.32); né·skɔ-=č ní·š·ən -kənčí·mwi·t típa·s 'before the rooster ('chicken') crows twice' (Mk 14.30).
- P (with ch. conj.): né·skɔ ke·š·i·lənčé·li·t 'before they (obv.) washed their hands' (Mk 7.2); né·skɔ nə́ é·le·k 'before it happens' (Jn 13.19);

é·li- .. né·skɔ -mi·lá·wənt 'for he had not yet been given it' (Jn 7.39), né·skɔ pəntaɔ́·wənt 'before he is heard' (Jn 7.51); né·skɔ xínkwi-mi·tsahtí·yunk 'before the big feast' (Jn 12.1).
• P (with ch. subj.): né·skɔ e·p·í·k·we 'before he was' (Jn 8.58).
• P (with ind. ind. neg.): né·skɔ ntəpskwilahtá·i 'my time has not yet come' (Jn 7.6); after é·li PV (Jn 7.30).

né·tami: see hítami.

ne·ta·e·khí·k·e·s 'Good-Writer' (1834b:1.2, 6.6). ▶ Cf. hita·e·khi·k·e- above.

†ne·tá·nəl 'Nathaniel' (⟨Nrtanil⟩ Jn 1.46 1.48, 1.49) ~ †natá·nəl (⟨Nutanul⟩ Jn 21.2); †ne·tá·nəla (⟨Nrtanilu⟩ Jn 1.45, 1.47).

ne·t·ia·s·í·č·i·k: see ntia·s·i·-.

ne·w- (nihəne·w- [Rih+], nehəne·w- [Rih+; IC], |nēw-|) — ne·m- (~ nen-) TI(3) 'see' (Gr. 3.20k, 5.4k).

▪ ne·w- (TA): né·e· lə́nəwa 'he saw a man' (Mt 9.9&; Gr. 2.24c); é·li-né·ɔ·t 'because he saw him' (Lk 15.27); é·li- tá·á· -ne·ɔ́hti·t 'because they will not see him' (Jn 14.17); ne·ɔ́·t·e 'when he saw him, them' (Lk 1.12, 2.26, Mt 3.7, etc.; Gr. 2.15b, 2.30a); ne·í·t·e 'if he sees me' (Jn 14.9; Gr. 2.30a); né·tami-ne·ɔ·li·tpáni 'those (obv.) that had first seen him (obv.)' (Mk 16.14; Gr. 4.76q); ne·ɔ́hti·t 'the one (obv.) they see' (Mt 18.10; Gr. 4.65m); ne·ɔ́hti·t·əp '[the star (obv.)] they had seen' (Mt 2.9; Gr. 4.76o); máta awé·n né·ɔ·t 'who (obv.) no one sees' (Mt 6.6); wénči-=č .. máta -ne·ykó·we·kw 'so that he won't see you (pl.)' (Mk 13.36; Gr. 4.97q); é·li-né·ian 'because you (sg.) see me' (Jn 20.29); é·li- .. máta čí·č -ne·í·yunk 'because I will not be seen any more' (Jn 16.10; Gr. 4.97t); lə́nəwak nné·ɔ 'I see men' (Mk 8.24; Gr. 4.24e); nné·ɔ=č 'I will see him' (Lk 23.8; Gr. 4.24f); takó· awé·ni ne·é·i 'he saw no one' (Jn 8.10; Gr. 4.83c); nne·ɔ́həna·p lə́nu 'we (exc.) saw a man' (Lk 9.49; Gr. 4.69b); ne·é·ɔk skinnúwa 'they saw a young man' (Mk 16.5; Gr. 4.24b); wəne·ɔwwá·p·ani·l né·l mi·məntə́t·al 'they saw the baby' (Mt 2.11; Gr. 4.69l); tá·á· čí·č kəne·i·húmɔ 'you (pl.) won't see me again' (Mt 23.39; Gr. 4.89e); kəne·wəlúhump 'I saw you (sg.)' (Jn 1.48; Gr. 2.53e, 4.69z); kəne·wəlúhəna·p 'we saw you' (Mt 25.38, 25.44; Gr. 4.69dd); ktə́li-ne·i·né·ɔ, 'that you (pl.) see me' (Jn 6.36; Gr. 4.50b).

• nihəne·w- (Gr. 5.41k): ká·xane nnihəne·ɔ́·wəna 'haven't we long known them [conjoined obviatives]?' (Jn 6.42); ɔ́·k=háč kənihəné·ɔ 'and have you (sg.) seen (him)?' (Jn 8.57).

• nehəne·w-: nehəne·ɔ́·č·i·k 'ones that used to see him' (Jn 9.8); nehəne·ɔ·tpáni·k 'his acquaintances' (lit., 'those who had regularly seen him') (Lk 23.49&).

▪ ne·m- (TI): é·li-né·ma 'for I have seen (it)' (Lk 2.30); ne·má·ne 'if I see (it) (Jn 20.25); éntxi-ne·mhíti·t 'as many as see thɔm (inan.)' (Lk 10.23, Gr. 4.67(4)y); né·ləma ne·mhiti·t 'before they see it' (Mt 16.28); kéku=tá nné·m 'I saw something' (1842:22.6; Gr. 4.38d); máta=č pəma·wsəwá·k·an ne·mó·wi 'he will not see life' (Jn 3.36; Gr. 4.91g); né·mo·k tə́ntay 'they saw a fire' (Jn 21.9; cf. Gr. 4.38s); wəne·məné·ɔ 'they saw it' (⟨nrmunro⟩ Mt 4.16); wəné·məne·p 'he saw it' (Jn 8.56; Gr. 4.70g); tá·á· kɔ́ski-ne·mó·wən 'he would not be able to see it' (Jn 3.3; Gr. 4.93h, 6.6i); nné·məne·n 'to see it' (lit., 'that we [exc.] see it') (Lk 17.22; cf. Gr. 4.49m); tə́li-=á· kéku -né·məli·n 'if he (obv.) could see anything' (lit., 'that he would see anything') (Mk 8.23); nkát·a-ne·mhúməna kéku 'We'd like to see something' (Mt 12.38; Gr. 4.38m); kəne·məné·na·p 'we (inc.) saw it' (Jn 1.14; Gr. 4.70k); wəne·məné·ɔ·p 'they saw it' (Jn 1.39; Gr. 4.70m).

• nen- (cf. Gr. 2.44): wə́nči-=č wé·mi awé·n -nénk 'so that everyone shall see it' (Lk 3.6); nénkəp 'the one who saw it' (Jn 19.35; Gr. 4.78k); éntxi-=á· -nénki·k 'everyone that saw it' (Lk 14.29; Gr. 4.67y); nénke 'when he saw it' (Lk 5.20; Gr. 2.44c).

♦ For ostensible -ne·mhíti·t (Lk 4.18), see ne·ma·-, end.

▪ ne·wti·- AI (recip.) 'see each other': ne·wtúwak 'they saw each other' (OA; ⟨nrxtwk⟩ 1834a:19.17; Gr. 5.110f).

né·wa P 'four' (Lk 2.37, Jn 4.35, Lk 5.18&, Jn 6.19, Mt 18.28; Gr. 2.15e).

ne·wennaɔhkən- TI(1b) 'make into four parts': wəne·wennaɔhkənəməné·ɔ 'they made four parts of it' (Jn 19.23).

né·wən P 'four times' (Mk 8.20); né·wən=hánkw nə́ txí 'four times that amount' (Lk 19.8); ahpá·mi=ét né·wən télən txá·pxki 'maybe about four thousand (*lit.*, four times ten hundred)' (Mt 15.38; Gr. 6.1j); né·wən ki·škwí·k·e 'on the fourth day' (1834b:15.10).

né·xpi: see náxpi.

†né·yən 'Nain' (Lk 7.11).

ne·ykwəs·i·- (ni·ne·ykwəs·i·- [Rī+], |nēwəkwəsī-|; Gr. 4.67t) AI — ne·ykɔt·- II 'appear, be seen' (Gr. 2.35a; Gr. 5.10m, 5.107d).

▪ ne·ykwəs·i·- (AI): énta-=č -ne·ykwə́s·ian 'where you will be seen' (Mt 6.18; Gr. 4.67(3)t); énta- máta -ne·ykwə́s·i·t 'where he can't be seen' (Mt 24.26); e·lkí·kwi- .. -ápi-ne·ykwə́s·i·t 'at the time when he has appeared' (Lk 17.30); máta ne·ykwə́s·i·t 'who is unseen' (Mt 6.4); e·lkí·kwi-ne·ykwəs·í·t·əp 'the time when it (anim.) had appeared' (Mt 2.7); máta čí·č təmí·ki ne·ykwəs·í·wəne·p 'he was no longer often seen' (Jn 11.54).

• ni·ne·ykwəs·i·-: máta ni·ne·ykwə́s·i·t 'who is never seen' (Mt 6.18).

▪ ne·ykɔt·- (II): né·ykɔt 'it is evident' (Lk 11.48), 'is visible' (Lk 12.2), wə́li-=č -né·ykɔt 'it shall be properly seen' (Mt 10.26); wénči-=č -né·ykɔ penkhɔké·e·k 'so that dry land will be visible' (1842:6.5); énta-ne·ykɔ́t·ək 'where it is seen' (Mt 6.4); máta ne·ykɔ́t·o·kw 'that is not visible' (Lk 11.44; Gr. 2.46a).

ne·yo·k·wənak·at- II 'be four days': mé·či ne·yo·k·wənák·at 'it had already been four days' (Jn 11.17, 11.39; Gr. 2.32f).

nə́ (ní, né·l; nə́ni, né·li; níke; Gr. 4.16b) 'the, that, it, those'.

• nə́ 'the, that (inan.)' (⟨nc⟩, ⟨nu⟩ Jn 1.1, 1.7, Lk 3.17, etc.), nə́=ké=x é·li- .. 'Well, in fact it was because ..' (Jn 11.13); 'there' (Jn 3.23, Lk 10.34, 17.12), nə́ táli P (Lk 15.14, Jn 12.2, Mt 13.58; Gr. 3.13(3)a); nə́ táli- PV (Jn 18.2).

• ní 'that (inan.)' (⟨ni⟩ Mt 9.28, Mt 12.33).

• né·l 'the (pl.), those (inan.)' (Lk 1.23, Jn 6.11, Mt. 6.32, etc.): né·l kéku 'those things' (Mt 6.32); né·l mahčí·kwi-skí·kɔ 'those weeds' (Mt 13.27, 13.29, etc.).

♦ nə́ni (weakly emphatic or more definite) 'that (inan.)': nə́ni 'that' (predominantly ⟨nuni⟩ Jn 1.9, Lk 1.20, 1.61, etc.; also ⟨nini⟩ Jn 1.8 2x; ⟨ncni⟩ Lk 2.9, Mt 6.34, Mt 7.14, etc.; ⟨nani⟩ Lk 1.25, 1.69, Mt 3.15, 14.2, Jn 1.33, etc.); nə́ni ɔ·ka·š·a·ɔ́·k·an 'what is circumcision' (Jn 7.22; construed as indefinite); nə́ni=č 'that is (how it) will be ..' (⟨nunih⟩ Lk 6.38); 'that (place), there' (Lk 2.9, 3.17); nə́n 'that' (1834a:22.43 [|-i| elided]).

• né·li 'those (inan. pl.)': né·li a·pto·nák·ana 'those words' (Jn 14.25).

♦ níke 'that' (abs. inan. sg.): níke mpíe 'the water (abs.)' (Gr. 3.9g); also 'then' (younger form of néke) (Gr. 2.72f).

nəkáhke 'those (abs.)': see ná.

-nəkahtᵒ: see nkal- — nkat·-.

-nəkalᵒ: see nkal- — nkat·-.

nəkhikwíti (Gr. 2.76e) P 'a short distance from here' (Lk 19.30&).

nəmí·s 'my older sister' (Lk 10.40); mwí·s·a 'her older sister' (Lk 10.39, Jn 11.28; Gr. 3.7a).

nəmó·t·ay 'my stomach, belly' (Gr. 4.6b); kəmó·t·ay 'your belly' (1842:8.1); ní mmó·t·ay 'his stomach, belly' (ME; Gr. 2.58p); mmó·t·enk 'in her belly' (1834b:23.13; V ⟨m-⟩ 'at his belly'); mmo·t·ayəwá·ink 'in their stomachs' (Mk 7.19).

nəmux·ó·məs 'my grandfather'; nəmux·o·msəná·na 'our grandfather (abs.)' (i.e., Abraham) (Jn 8.53; Gr. 4.8c); kəmux·o·msəná·na 'our ancestor (abs.)' (Lk 1.73); kəmux·o·msəna·nínka 'our ancestors (abs.)' (Lk 1.55, 1.72, Mt 23.30, 1842:20.4; Gr. 4.8e).

nənaw- TA — nən- TI(1a) 'recognize, know'.
- nənaw- (TA): é·li-nənaóhti·t 'how they recognized him' (Lk 24.35; Gr. 2.67j); nnənaó·ɔk nəmekí·s·əmak 'I know my sheep' (Jn 10.14); máta nnənaó·i·p 'I did not know him' (Jn 1.33; Gr. 6.6f); wənənaó·ɔ 'he recognized him' (Jn 18.15); máta wənənaɔ·í·ɔ 'she did not recognize him' (Jn 20.14); máta wənənaɔ·iwwá·ɔ 'they did not recognize him' (Lk 24.16); nnəná·k·o·k 'they know me' (Jn 10.14; Gr. 2.22b); máta wənəna·k·o·wí·ɔ 'they did not recognize him' (Jn .21.4); kənənaíhəmɔ 'you (pl.) know who I am' (Jn 7.28); ná wi·xkaóči wənənaɔ·né·ɔ 'then suddenly they recognized him' (Lk 24.31).
- nən- (TI): kéku=háč wénči- máta -nənamó·we·kw yúkwe ké·t·a-lé·k 'why do you (pl.) not recognize what is going to happen now?' (Lk 12.56); kənənaməné·ɔ=hánkw e·li·ná·k·ɔ 'you (pl.) recognize what it is like' (Lk 12.56).

nə́ni: see nə́.

nənk·wə́ti P 'one by one' (⟨nun kwti⟩ Jn 8.9; ⟨nanvkwti⟩ Mk 14.19, Mt 20.13), 'one each' (Mt 20.13); nənk·wə́ti awé·n 'one person here and there' (⟨Nunkwti⟩ 1842:10.1).
▶ Cf. ne·nk·wə́ti 'one by one' (LTD ND); nənk·wəthiksúwak si·p·əwá·s·ak 'the plums are just beginning to ripen (a few are ripe)' ([nənⁿkwʊt-] ME).

nənk·wət·ennaɔhki·x·ən- II 'be one here and one there': nənk·wət·ennaɔhki·x·ínkeč mpí 'let the water be (*lit.*) one here and one there' (⟨nun kw tr-|naov ke xif chi⟩ 1842:6.5).

nəno·staw- TA — nəno·st- (ne·no·st-, |nənōsət-|) TI(1a) 'understand'.
- nəno·staw- (TA): takó· wənəno·sta·k·o·wí·ɔ 'they (obv.) did not understand him (prox.)' (Jn 10.6); ná wənəno·staɔ·né·ɔ 'then they understood him' (Mt 16.12).
- nəno·st- (TI): nəno·stámo·kw 'understand it (you pl.)' (Mt 24.32; KJV "learn"); mái-nəno·stámo·kw 'go and understand it' (Mt 9.13; KJV "go ye and learn"); nəno·stánkeč 'let him understand it' (Mt 24.15); nəno·stánke 'when he understands it' (Mt 13.23; Gr. 2.67j); máta nəno·stamó·k·we 'if he does not understand it' (Mt 13.19; Gr. 2.46c, 4.99d); takó· nnəno·stamó·wən 'I don't understand it' (Lk 22.56-57&); tá=á· kənəno·stamo·wəné·ɔ 'you (pl.) will not understand it' (Mt 13.14; ⟨-amunro⟩, probably for ⟨-amwnro⟩).
• ne·no·st-: mé·či ne·no·stamihtí·t·e 'after they had understood it' (Lk 20.16; Gr. 4.62d).

nə́pe·h P (exclamation) 'Alright' (Mt 25.34; KJV "Come" [exhorting action]).

nə́škinkw IN 'my eye' (Gr. 5.13e); kə́škinkw 'your eye' (Mt 5.29, 6.22 [anim.], 6.23 [anim.], 18.9 2x), 'your face' (Mt 6.17); kəškínkɔ 'your eyes' (Jn 9.26, Mt 18.9); wə́škinkw '(his) eye, an eye' (Mt 5.38 [2x], 6.22), 'his face' (Mt 17.2); kəškinkəwá·ɔ 'your (pl.) eyes' (Mt 13.16); wəškinkəwá·ɔ 'their eyes' (Mt 9.30, Lk 10.23); wəškinkwí·li·t 'his, their (obv.) eyes' (Mt 9.29, Mk 8.23, Mt 20.34), 'his face' (Mt 18.10, 26.67, Lk 22.64); nəškínkunk 'on my eyes' (Jn 9.11, 9.15, 9.30); kəškínkunk 'in your eye' (Lk 6.41, 6.42); wəškínkunk 'in his eye(s)' (Lk 6.42, Jn 9.6, 9.14). ■ Exceptionally animate (personified, with AI verb): Mt 6.22, 6.23.

nhaka·l- (-na·ka·l-, ne·ká·l-, ninhaka·l [Rih+], nenhaka·l- [Rih+; IC], |nahkāl-|) TA — nhaka·t- (-na·ka·t-, ne·ka·t-, nənhaka·t- [Rə+], |nahkāt-|) TI(1a) 'use, rely on, depend on, trust' (Gr. 5.59h, cf. 5.12d).

■ nhaka·l- (TA): nhaká·lo· ke·tanət·ó·wi·t 'have faith in God (you pl.)' (Mk 11.22, Jn 14.1); nhaká·li 'believe in me' (Mk 5.36); nhaká·li·kw 'trust in me (you pl.)' (Jn 14.1); kwáč=háč nhaká·lian 'why do you rely on me?' (Mt 3.14; Gr. 4.60d); nhaka·lkúk·e 'if they (obv.) need his help' (Lk 18.7; KJV "cry unto him"); é·li-nhakállan 'what I need you to do' (Mk 10.35); tóləmi-nhaka·t·amənép·ani 'he set about putting them to use' (Mt 25.16; Gr. 4.70h).
• -na·ka·l-: kəna·ká·la=háč 'do you (sg.) believe in him?' (Jn 9.35 [KJV "believe on"]); nɔ·ka·láp·ani 'he trusted in him' (Mt 27.43); takó· ní· nna·ka·lkó·wi 'he does not trust in *me*' (Mt 10.37 [2x], 10.38; Gr. 4.85b); kəna·ká·ləl 'I believe in you' (Jn 9.38, Mk 9.24); kəna·kállən 'to believe in you (sbd.)' (*lit.*, 'that I believe in you') (Mk 9.24).
• ne·ká·l-: ne·ká·li·t 'who relies on me' (Jn 7.38); ostensible ne·ka·lí·t·e 'when he believed in me (ch. subj.)' (⟨nrkaletc⟩ Mk 9.23) is emended to nhaka·lí·t·e 'if he believes in me'.
• ninhaka·l-: ninhaka·lá·ɔk 'they were used' (1834a:19.12).
• nenhaka·l-: nenhaka·lé·k·əp 'who you rely on' (Jn 5.45); nenhaka·láč·i·k 'that you (sg.) use' (1834b:20.17).
■ nhaka·t- (TI): nhaká·t·amo·kw 'rely on it (you pl.)' (Jn 12.36; Gr. 4.106e).
• -na·ka·t-: kəna·ká·t·amən 'you (sg.) rely on them' (Lk 12.19); nɔ·ka·t·amǝné·p 'he had put faith in it' (Mt 27.57&).
• ne·ka·t-: ne·ka·t·ánkəp 'what he relied on' (Lk 11.22; Gr. 4.78g); kéku ne·ká·t·ame·kw 'what you (pl.) have faith in' (Mt 9.29); kéku=á· ne·ká·t·amink 'things that would be made use of' (Jn 13.29); ne·ka·t·ánki·k ahɔ·p·e·ó·k·an 'those who depend on wealth' (Mk 10.24).
• nənhaka·t-: e·ləmo·k·wənák·a=á· wənənhaka·t·amǝné·ɔ 'and they could rely on them forever' (1834a:24.60).
nhaka·t·amwe·ó·k·an (-na·ka·t·amwe·ɔ·k·an-; Gr. 5.59h) IN 'faith' (Mt 9.22, Lk 17.5, 18.8); ləkhíkwi-xínkwi-nhaka·t·amwe·ó·k·an 'such a great faith' (Lk 7.9).
• -na·ka·t·amwe·ɔ·k·an-: kəna·ka·t·amwe·ó·k·an 'your faith' (Lk 7.50, Mt 14.31, 15.28, etc.); kəna·ka·t·amwe·ɔ·k·anúwa 'your (pl.) faith' (Mt 17.20, Lk 17.6, 18.42&).
▶ Implying nhaka·t·ama·-* AI 'have faith'.
nhaka·t·a·s·i·- II 'be used': nhaka·t·á·s·u 'it is used' (1834a:16).
nhake·e·lənt- (TI(1a)) TI-O 'be hopeful': nhake·e·lə́nta 'be hopeful (you sg.)' (⟨nvakrl-⟩ Mt 9.2, ⟨nvakrrl-⟩ Mt 9.22); nhake·e·lə́ntamo·kw 'be hopeful (you pl.)' (⟨nvakril-⟩ Mt 5.12 [misprint]; ⟨nvakrrl-⟩ Mk 10.49, Jn 16.33); nhake·e·lə́ntamo·p 'he was hopeful' (⟨nvakrl-⟩ Lk 18.13).
nhake·e·ləntaməwá·k·an IN 'hope' (⟨nvakrl-⟩ Lk 2.25), ⟨Nhakewelendamoagan⟩ (B&A 95).
nhake·wsəwá·k·an (-na·ke·wsəwa·k·an-) IN 'faith' (Mt 23.23).
• -na·ke·wsəwa·k·an-: kəna·ke·wsəwa·k·anúwa 'your (pl.) faith' (Lk 12.28).
nhake·wsi·- AI 'have faith': é·li- .. máta -nhake·wsíe·kw (or -nhake·wsí·e·kw, if the negative inflection was distinct) 'because you (pl.) have no faith' (Mt 17.20); nhake·wsié·k·we 'if you (pl.) have faith' (Mk 21.21, Lk 21.19); ktankíti-nhake·wsíhəmɔ 'you (pl.) have little faith' (Mt 8.26).
♦ náxpi-nhake·wsi·- 'seek (medical) help (?) using (*lit.*, with) O2': wé·mi kéku éntxi-wəlá·ta·kw nɔ́xpi-nhaké·wsi·n 'she sought help using everything she had' (Mk 5.26; KJV "had spent all that she had," "upon physicians").
nhák·ay (|-hakay|) IN 'I, me, myself' (*lit.*, 'my body', |nə-hakay|) (Lk 1.19, Mk 14.42, Lk 22.61, etc.; Gr. 2.8, 2.62h, 4.14, 4.15a,b,c, etc.); nhák·ay AN 'myself' (Jn 17.19), 'I' (equated with AI participle; Lk 5.8, 7.8); khák·ay IN 'you' (Jn 1.19, 1.21, 1.22; Gr. 2.63h), 'your body' (Mt 6.22, 6.23); hók·ay IN 'him, himself' (Lk 1.11, 1.80, 2.34, etc.), 'body' (Mt 6.22); hókaya AN 'his body (obv.)' (Mt 6.27), 'herself (obv.)' (Lk 2.22); nhak·ayəná·nak AN 'we' (Lk 17.10);

khak·ayúwa 'yourselves' (Mk 9.50, Lk 16.15, Lk 23.28; Gr. 4.15j), 'you (pl.)' (Jn 15.8), 'your body' (Lk 12.4); nhák·enk 'in me' (Lk 1.38, Jn 14.30), 'on me' (Jn 12.7&), 'of me' (Jn 13.8), wənči nhák·enk 'concerning me' (Jn 5.46; Gr. 4.15e, 6.9m); khák·enk 'from you' (Lk 1.35, Mt 2.6), 'on your body' (Mt 6.25); hók·enk 'in, on him, her' (Jn 1.4, Lk 1.41, etc.); hák·i hók·enk wənči 'from the body of the earth' (Mk 4.28); nhak·ayə́na 'ourselves' (Gr. 4.15i); nhak·ayəná·nink 'to us, on us' (Lk 10.11, Mt 27.25); khak·ayúwa IN 'you (pl.)' (Jn 10.26, 15.8, 15.14), 'yourselves' (Mk 9.50, Lk 16.15, 17.14, 21.34), 'your (pl.) bodies' (Lk 12.4); khak·ayəwá·ink 'upon you (pl.)' (Mt 23.35, 23.36), 'in you' (Jn 14.17), 'to you' (Jn 15.26, Lk 24.49); hɔk·ayúwa IN 'themselves' (Mt 2.11, Mk 3.11, Jn 18.28), 'their bodies' construed as singular with má·ɔt 'is one' (Mt 19.5 [sbd.], 19.6 [ind.]); hɔk·ayəwá·ink 'in, to them' (Mt 13.14, 21.45&), lí hɔk·ayəwá·unk 'for them' (Lk 7.30); hɔk·aí·li·t 'his (obv.) life' (Jn 1.7), hɔk·aí·li·t wənči 'from him (obv.)' (Jn 13.3, 13.321; KJV "in him") .

nhíka·t 'my leg' (OA; Gr. 5.21e); nhiká·t·a 'my legs' (V); hwiká·t·ink 'on his legs' (Mk 5.4 [2x]), 'by his feet' (Mt 22.13).

nhil- (-nihəl- [~ -nil-], nehəl- [~ nel-], ninhil- [Rih+], nenhil- [Rih+; IC], |nəhl-|) TA — nhit- (-ni·t-, |nəht-|) TI(2) 'kill' (Gr. 5.4f).

▪ nhil- (TA): aesə́s·a=č nhíle·w 'he shall kill an animal' (1834b:21.11); nhíle· wi·s·i·lí·č·i wehšəmwi·t·ə́t·a 'he killed a fat calf' (Lk 15.27); máta nhile·í·ɔk 'they did not kill any' (Jn 21.3; Gr. 4.24e); nhíl 'kill him, her, it (anim.), or them' (Gr. 3.7c); nhilá·t·amo·kw 'let's kill him (you pl.)' (Lk 20.14&; Gr. 4.104cc); nhilát·e 'if you (sg.) kill him, her, it (anim.), or them' (Gr. 3.7b); wé·mi éntxi-nhílənt 'all that were killed' (Lk 11.50); tə́li-=á· -nhíla·n 'in order to kill him' (Mk 6.19, Mk 9.22; Gr. 4.50p); tə́li-=č -nhila·né·ɔ 'for them to kill him (*lit.*, that they would kill him)' (Mk 9.31, Jn 11.53).

• -nihəl- (~ -nil-; Gr. §2.5): nníhəla 'I killed him' (V, ME; Gr. 2.5i, 2.10b); wənihəlawwá·ɔ 'they killed them' (Mt 22.6); kənihəláwwa·p 'you (pl.) killed him' (Lk 11.51; Gr. 4.69j); nnílko·k 'they killed me' (V, ME; Gr. 2.5i, 2.16d); ne·k·əmá·ɔ=č kənilkəwá·ok 'and *they* will kill you (pl.)' (Mt 24.9).

• nehəl- (~ nel-; Gr. §2.5): nehəla·tpáni 'those he had killed' (Lk 13.1); nehəla·tpáni·k '(those) that killed them' (Mt 23.31); nehəlé·k·əp 'who you (pl.) killed' (Mt 23.35; Gr. 4.76n); nélkɔn=á· 'that would kill you' (1834b:12.10, 1842:22.4, 24.1).

• ninhil-: po·kwé·s·[a] n[i]nhíle· 'it kills mice (obv.)' (1834a:14).

• nenhil-: nenhílat 'you (sg.) who killed them' (Mt 23.37); nenhíla·t 'who kills them' (with a vocative noun; Lk 13.34).

▪ nhit- (TI): ké·ski-=á· šúkw -nhíta·kw khak·ayúwa 'one who would only be able to kill your (pl.) body' (Lk 12.4).

• -ni·t-: nní·to·n 'I killed it' (V; Gr. 5.4f).

▪ nhilti·- AI (recip.) 'kill each other' (also as a passive: Gr §5.8m): nhiltúwak 'they killed each other' (Gr. 5.110b); ehə́nta-nhíltink 'in the place of execution' (Mt 15.4, Lk 22.33; Gr. 5.113e).

nhiləwe·- (nehələwe·-, nenhiləwe·- [Rih+; IC], |nəhləwē·-|; Gr. 5.42j, 5.101c) AI 'kill people': nhíləwe·p 'he had murdered someone' (Mk 15.7); káči nhiləwé·han 'do not kill (you sg.)' (Mt 5.21, 19.18, 1842:12.3); tə́li-=á· -nhíləwe·n 'that he would kill' (Jn 10.10); é·li- .. -nhiləwé·t·əp 'because he had been a murderer' (Lk 23.25).

• nehələwe·-: nehələwe·lí·č·i 'murderers (obv.)' (Mt 22.7); nehələwehtí·t·e 'after they did the killing' (Lk 11.48).

• nenhiləweˑ-: nenhíləweˑt 'murderer' (Jn 10.1); nenhiləwéˑčˑiˑk 'murderers' (Mt 10.28); nenhiləweˑlíˑčˑi 'executioner (obv.)' (Mk 6.27).

nhiləweˑt-* (nenhiləweˑt- [Rih+; IC], |nəhləwēht-| [cf. Gr. 5.77, as if 'cause to kill people']) TI(2) 'use O1 to kill people': nenhiləweˑtúnki 'deadly weapons' (Mk 14.43&).

nhiltəwáˑkˑan (Gr. 5.114f) IN 'murder, killing' (Mt 15.19, Lk 9.31).

nhit-: see nhil- — nhit-.

nhitamaw- (-niˑtamaw-, |nəhtamaw-| Gr. 5.95h) TA+O 'kill O2 for': kəniˑtamáɔ wiˑsˑiˑlíˑčˑi wehšəmwiˑtˑətˑa 'you (sg.) killed a fat calf (obv.) for him' (Lk 15.30).

nhítaɔk 'my ear' (Gr. 3.5j); hwitaɔkˑa 'his ears' (Mk 7.35); hwitaɔkˑíˑliˑt 'his (obv.) ears' (Mk 7.33, Jn 18.10, etc.); khitaɔkˑəwáˑɔ 'your (pl.) ears' (Mt 13.16); nhitaɔkˑink '(to) my ears' (Lk 1.44); khitaɔkˑəwáˑink 'in your ears' (Mt 10.27); hwitaɔkˑəwáˑink 'in their ears' (Mt 13.15).

nhúpxkɔn 'my back' (usually for "side" in B): nhúpxkɔnink 'into my back' (Jn 20.27; KJV "side"); húpxkɔn 'his back' (Jn 20.20; KJV "side"); húpxkɔnink 'in his back' (Jn 19.34, 20.25; KJV "side"); hupxkɔníˑliˑt wənči 'behind him (obv.)' (lit., 'from his (obv.) back') (Mk 5.27). ▸ Cf. úpxkɔn 'his back' (V, OA, LB); núpxkɔn 'my back' (OA, WS), núpxkɔnink 'on my back' (OA), úpxkɔnink 'on his back' (ME. FE), upxkɔnətˑətˑink 'on its little back' (ME).

ní: see nə́.

nihəláči (Gr. 2.73i, 4.15a,c) P 'one's own, on one's own, oneself' (Lk 2.3, Jn 5.20, 5.26 [2x], 5.30, etc.); áhi-nihəláči 'completely on his own' (Mk 1.27).

♦ takóˑ níˑ nihəláči 'it is not my own' (Jn 7.16), '[you] are not my own' (Jn 14.10).

nihəlaˑl- (nehəlaˑl-, |nīhlāl-|) TA — nihəlaˑt- (nehəlaˑt-, |nīhlāt-|) TI(1a) 'own, be master of, be lord of, have the say over' (cf. Gr. 5.12d).

■ nihəlaˑl- (TA): mátɑ=áˑ nihəlaˑléˑi enkələlíˑčˑi 'he would not be a lord of dead people' (Lk 20.38&); nnihəlaˑláˑɔk 'they are mine' (Jn 17.10); kənihəlaˑláˑpˑaniˑk 'they were yours' (Jn 17.6; Gr. 4.69g); təli-=č -nihəláˑlaˑn 'to be master of them' (lit., 'that he be master of them') (Lk 12.44).

• nehəlaˑl- (with TH.1): wéˑmi nehəlaˑlákˑiˑk 'all that are mine' (Jn 17.10; Gr. 4.64t); nehəlaˑláčˑiˑk 'the ones that are yours' (Jn 17.10); nehəlaˑláˑčˑi 'those (obv.) whose master he was' (Jn 13.1).

• nehəlaˑl- (with TH.2): nehəláˑlkɔn 'your (sg.) Lord' (lit., who rules you') (Mt 4.7, 4.10, Mk 5.19, etc.; Gr. 4.64k); nehəlaˑlkúkˑi 'his master (obv.)' (Mt 18.25, 18.32, 18.34, etc.), 'his lord (obv.)' (Mk 12.26 3x); nehəláˑlkɔnkw 'our Lord' (p. [3]; Lk 1.15, 4.18, etc.); nehəlaˑlkɔ́nkwi 'our Lord (obv.)' (Jn 6.23, 20.2). nehəláˑlkweˑkw 'who is your (pl.) master' (Mt 23.10, 24.43, Jn 13.14); nehəlaˑlkwihtíˑčˑi 'their master (obv.)' (Mt 15.27, 18.31, etc.); nehəlaˑlkwíhtiˑt 'their Lord (obv.)' (Lk 1.6; cf. Gr. 4.65lmn).

• nehəlaˑl- (with TH.3): nehəláˑlian 'my Lord' (lit., 'you who rule me') (Lk 2.29, Jn 5.7, Lk 5.8, etc.); nehəláˑliˑt 'my Lord' (Lk 1.25, Mt 14.28, Lk 12.45, etc.); nehəlaˑliˑlíˑčˑi 'my lord (obv.)' (Mk 12.36); nehəláˑlienk 'Master (voc.)' (lit., 'you who rule us') (Mt 13.51, Lk 9.54, 12.41, etc.).

■ nehəláˑlkɔnkw 'our Lord' (as a lexicalized participle): nehəlaˑlkɔnkwíˑi PN 'of our lord, of the Lord' (Lk 1.9, 1.11; Gr. 5.123g).

■ nihəlaˑt- (TI): máiˑnihəláˑtˑamoˑkw 'go and take possession of it (you pl.)!' (Mt 25.34); kéˑtˑa-nihəláˑtˑank 'the one who is going to own it ("the heir")' (Lk 20.14&; Gr. 4.64n); wéˑmi kéku nnihəláˑtˑamən 'I am lord over everything' (Mt 11.27; Gr. 4.39b); takóˑ niˑlóˑna nnihəlaˑtˑamóˑwəneˑn 'we don't have the say over it' (Jn 18.31; Gr. 4.93i).

• nihəla·t- (partciple without IC): nihəlá·t·ank 'the lord of it' (Mt 12.8), 'who has it' (Jn 19.24); nihəlá·t·aman 'you who are lord of it' (Mt 11.25).
• nehəla·t-: nehəla·t·amá·nəp 'that I had' (Jn 17.5; Gr. 4.78a); nehəlá·t·aman 'you who are lord of them, the owner of it' (⟨Nrvl-⟩ Lk 10.21, Mt 25.11); nehəlá·t·aman 'what is yours' (Mt 25.25); nehəlá·t·ank 'what was his, that he owns (owned)' (Jn 1.11, Mt 13.44, 13.46, etc.), 'the one in charge of it, the manager of it, the one in control of it' (Mt 9.38, Lk 10.2, Acts 1.7).
▪ nihəla·t- TI-O 'have possessions': xínkwi-nihəlá·t·amo·p 'he owned a great deal' (Mt 19.22&; KJV "had great possessions").

nihəla·lkwəsi·- AI 'be owned' (Gr. 5.107e): é·li-nihəla·lkwəs·íhti·t 'because they are not free to act' (*lit.*, 'they are owned') (Mt 19.12).

nihəla·t·ama·- AI 'be free, control oneself, have authority' — nihəla·t·amwe·yo·wi·- II 'be autonomous' (Gr. 5.76l).
▪ nihəla·t·ama·- (AI): mé·či nihəlá·t·ama· 'he is now his own man' (Jn 9.21, 9.23); kənihəlá·t·ama=á· 'you (sg.) would be free' (Jn 8.36); é·li- málahši -nihəlá·t·ama·t 'as if he had authority' (Mt 7.29); wə́nči-=č -nihəla·t·amáhti·t 'so that they would be free' (Lk 4.18).
▪ nihəla·t·amwe·yo·wi·- (II): nihəla·t·amwe·yó·u 'it is free, autonomous' (Jn 3.8, with ⟨-rw⟩ for ⟨-rbw⟩ /-e·yó·u/; see note; 1834b:24.3).

nihəla·t·amwe·ha·l- (|nīhlātamwēhāl-|; Gr. 5.82a(2)) TA 'make free': nə́ wəla·məwe·ó·k·an kənihəla·t·amwe·ha·lko·né·ɔ=č 'the truth shall make you (pl.) free' (Jn 8.32).

nihəla·t·amwe·hɔ·l- (|nīhlātamwēwəhāl-|; Gr. 5.82a(1)) TA 'make free': nihəla·t·amwe·hɔ·lkóne 'if he makes you (sg.) free' (Jn 8.36).

nihəla·t·amwe·ó·k·an (Gr. 5.59j) IN 'freedom' (Lk 2.38; KJV "redemption"); kənihəla·t·amwe·ɔ·k·anə́na 'our (inc.) autonomy' (Jn 11.48; KJV "our .. nation").

nihəla·t·amwe·whe·- (|nīhlātamwēwəhē-|; Gr. 5.79d) AI+O 'set O2 free, redeem O2': ké·t·a-nihəla·t·amwé·whe·t ni·thake·wəná·na 'who is going to set our nation free' (Lk 24.21); é·li- .. nihəla·t·amwe·whé·təp wtənna·p·é·yəmal 'for he has redeemed his people' (⟨mwrt⟩ for ⟨mwrwvrt⟩; Lk 1.68).

nihəlá·wsu(?) 'working by himself(?)' (1834a:15).

nihəní·š·a P 'two each' (Lk 10.1, 1834b:18.6, 1842:9.2).

nihəní·š·a·š P 'seven each' (1842:9.2).

†nikɔtí·mas 'Nicodemus' (Jn 3.1, 3.4, 3.9, 7.50, 19.39); †niketí·mas 'Nicodemus' (⟨Nikctemus⟩ 1834b:23.9).

-nil-; see nhil-.

†ninipe·i·yúnka (abs. pl.) 'the ancient Ninevites' (Mt 12.41).

nink·əmé·i: see nkəmé·i.

nipahte·- II 'stand': nípahte· 'it stands' (Mt 3.10). ▶ Cf. Mun ní·păte·w 'it stands' (dict.).

níši (WL, OA, AD; Gr. 2.75b, 5.27f, 5.129cc) PV 'two (together)' (Lk 17.35); níši-kɔhɔ·k·é·ɔk 'they (two) pound corn in a mortar together' (Lk 17.35). ♦ ní·š·a (⟨neju⟩ Mt 2.16) is an error for níši PV.

ní· (Gr. 3.10) 'I, me, myself' (Jn 3.28, 4.9, 4.14 [2x], etc.); ntə́li- ní· -lə́s·i·n 'that I am me' (Jn 8.24, 28).

ni·k·a·n° (|nīkān-|) 'ahead' (Gr. §5.2a).

ni·k·a·nalo·ka·lkwəs·i- AI 'be sent ahead': nni·k·a·nalo·ka·lkwə́s·i 'I was sent ahead' (Jn 3.28). Derived from ni·k·a·nalo·ka·l-* TA 'send ahead' (cf. Gr. 5.107).

ni·k·a·na·pto·na·t- TI(1a) 'prophesy about': ni·k·a·na·pto·na·t·ankpána 'who (abs.) prophesied about it' (Mt 15.7; Gr. 4.78l).

ni·k·a·na·pto·ne·- AI(+O) 'prophesy (O2)': nehəni·k·a·na·pto·né·t·əp 'his prophecy' (*lit.*, 'what he used to prophesy') (Mt 13.14).

ni·k·á·ni PV 'ahead': ni·k·á·ni·ét lí-wí·t·e·w. 'He must be going on ahead with others.' (Lk 2.44).

ni·k·a·ni·- AI 'go ahead, go before': áləmi-ni·k·á·ni· 'he goes on ahead' (Jn 10.4); nčí·sas ni·k·á·ni·p 'Jesus went in the lead' (Mk 10.32&); ni·k·a·ní·č·i·k 'the ones in the lead' (Lk 18.39); nni·k·á·ni·č 'I shall go in the lead' (Mk 14.28); táli-=á· -ni·k·a·ní·li·n 'to go ahead' (*lit.*, 'that they (obv.) go ahead') (Mk 6.45).

ni·k·a·ní·i P 'ahead, ahead of time' (Lk 9.52, 19.4, Mt 20.16, Jn 12.7&, Jn 12.41, etc.); ni·k·a·ní·i=č ahpúwak 'they shall be in front, first' (Lk 13.30, Mk 10.31, 20.16, etc.); ni·k·a·ní·i e·p·í·č·i·k 'the first' (Mk 20.16); wwə́nči- ni·k·a·ní·i -wəntamə́ne·p 'by way of prophesying (that ..)' (Jn 11.51; P or PV).

• PV ni·k·a·ní·i (nehəni·k·a·ní·i [Rih+; IC]) 'ahead of time, in front': ni·k·a·ní·i-=tá -wé·wsi·t 'He's a prophet.' (Mk 6.15); kəni·k·a·ní·i-wwa·tələləné·ɔ 'I let you know (about him) ahead of time' (Lk 12.5); káči ni·k·a·ní·i-pəna·eləntánkhe·kw 'don't think about it ahead of time' (Lk 12.11).

• nehəni·k·a·ní·i (in all cases with we·wsi·- AI 'know' in participles meaning 'prophet'; Gr. 4.75v, 6.22bc): see we·wsi·-.

ni·k·a·ni·tam- TA 'go before, go ahead of' (Gr. 5.92a): nni·k·a·ní·tama 'I went ahead of him, I passed him' (OA); wé·mi éntxi-ni·k·a·ni·tamí·č·i·k 'all those that came before me' (Jn 10.8); é·li-ni·k·a·ni·tamí·t·əp 'as he was before me' (Jn 1.30); kəni·k·a·ní·tama=č 'you will go before [the Lord]' (⟨-unh⟩ Lk 1.76 [em.]; see note); wəni·k·a·ni·tamá·ɔl=č 'he will go before him' (Lk 1.17); kəni·k·a·ni·tamúk·o·n 'to go ahead of you (sg.)' (*lit.*, 'that he go ahead of you') (Mk 1.2, Lk 7.27).

ni·k·a·ni·taw- TA 'go before' (Gr. 5.91b): kəni·k·a·ni·tá·k·əwa 'he is going ahead of you (pl.)' (Mt 28.7); wəni·k·a·ni·ta·k·əwá·ɔl '[the star] went before them' (⟨nek-⟩ Mt 2.9 [em.]).

ni·k·a·ni·x·i·n- AI 'be first, be a leader': é·li-ni·k·a·ní·x·ink wehi·húnke·s 'as he was the head priest' (Jn 11.51), mayá·i-ni·k·a·ní·x·ink 'the true leader' (Jn 14.30), nál=ná ni·k·a·ní·x·ink wé·mi entxíhti·t móni mehəma·e·nínki·k 'he was the leader among all the tax-collectors' (Lk 19.2; Gr. 3.15b); awé·n káhta-ni·k·a·ni·x·ínke 'if anyone desires to be first' (Mk 9.35); ni·k·a·ni·x·ínki·k 'head [priests]' (Jn 12.10, Mt 21.15, etc.).

ní·l 'my head' (OA; Jn 13.9; Gr. 4.7c); kí·l 'your head' (1842:8.1), 'your hair' (Mt 6.17); wí·l 'his head' (V; Mt 8.20, Mk 6.24, 6.25, etc.), 'head' (V); wí·la 'heads' (V); kí·link 'your head (loc.)' (Mt 5.36); wi·lí·li·t 'his (obv.) head' (Mk 12.4&); wi·lí·li·t 'on his (obv.) head' (Mt 26.67, 27.30), wi·lí·li·t 'on their (obv.) heads' (Mk 10.16); íka .. wi·lí·li·t 'on his (obv.) head' (Mk 14.3); ki·ləwá·unk 'on your (pl.) heads' (Mt 10.30) ~ ki·ləwá·ink (Lk 12.7, Lk 21.18; Gr. 2.28b).

ní·lanu 'my tongue' (OA; Lk 16.24); wí·lanu 'his tongue' (OA, ME; Lk 1.64, Mk 7.35), wí·lanu '(a) tongue' (ME); wi·lanəwí·li·t 'on his (obv.) tongue' (Mk 7.33); ní·lanunk 'on my tongue' (1834b:30.7).

ni·ló·na (Gr. 3.10) 'we (exc.)' (Jn 3.11, 4.22).

ní·mat (-i·maht-, -i·mahtəs-) 'my brother (of a male)'; kí·mat 'your brother' (Mt 5.23, 5.24).

• -i·maht-: ni·mahtə́t·o·kw 'my brothers!' (voc.) (1834b:8.12; Gr. 4.11o); kí·mahtak 'your brothers' (Mt 5.47); wí·mahtal 'his brother' (Lk 3.1, Jn 1.40, 1.41, etc.), 'his brothers' (Mk 10.30), wí·mahta (Lk 3.19-20, Mt 5.22, etc.); wi·mahtí·nay 'his brothers' (Mt 12.46,

1842:13.2; Gr. 4.12e), wi·mahtí·na 'his brothers' (1842:13.2, 17.1); wi·mahtínka 'his late brother' (Mt 22.24&); ki·mahtəwá·ɔk 'your (pl.) brothers' (Mt 18.35, Lk 21.16); wi·mahtəwá·ɔ 'their "brethren"' (1 Cor 15.6), ní·š·a wi·mahtəwá·ɔ 'their two brothers' (Mt 20.24).
  • -i·mahtəs-: ní·mahtəs 'my brother (of a male)' (V; Mt 18.21); ni·mahtə́s·ak 'my brothers' (Mt 12.50, Lk 16.28, Mt 28.10); ni·mahtə́sto·kw 'My brothers!' (1834b:46.1; Gr. 4.11o); kí·mahtəs (Lk 6.41, 6.42 [2x], Mk 6.18, etc.); ki·mahtə́s·ak 'your brothers' (Lk 14.12, 22.32); wi·mahtə́s·a 'his brothers' (Lk 14.26); ki·mahtə́s·əwa 'your (pl.) brother' (1842:17.1); ni·mahtəs·i·ké·i P 'to my brothers' (Jn 20.17).
ni·ma·- AI(+O) 'take food along': ní·ma· 'he takes his lunch, took a lunch' (LB; Gr. 5.10a); é·li- .. -a·yáhi-ní·ma·t mi·č·əwá·k·an 'as he already has food with him' (Mt 10.10).
ni·núči: see núči.
ni·nutahpi·-: see nutahpi·-.
ni·p·ai- (nehəni·p·ai- [Rih+; IC]) AI 'stand ({smwh})': ní·p·o· 'he stands' (ME), íka ní·p·o· 'he stood there' (Lk 19.8, 19.33&); ní·p·o·p 'he was standing' (Jn 1.35, Lk 6.8, Jn 7.37, etc.); ni·p·ó·wak 'they were standing' (Mt 12.46, Lk 23.10, etc.); nní·p·ai 'I stand' (Lk 1.19); ní·p·ai·t 'who was standing' (Jn 18.22, 20.14, 1842:7.4); íka ni·p·ai·lí·č·i 'standing there (obv.)' (Lk 19.24, Jn 19.26); ni·p·aié·k·we 'when you (pl.) stand' (Mk 11.25); ni·p·aí·č·i·k '(ones) standing' (Mt 16.28, Jn 11.42, 12.29, etc.); íka le·lá·i mái-ní·p·ai·l 'go stand in the middle (you sg.)' (Lk 6.8).
  • nehəni·p·ai·-: nehəní·p·ai·t 'candlestick' (*lit.*, 'where it [a candle, anim.] usually stands') (Mt 5.15).
ni·p·al- TA — nipaht- TI(2) 'make stand ({smwh})' (Gr. 5.78k).
  ▪ ni·p·al- (TA): nní·p·ala 'I stood him up' (OA); wə́nči-=č -ní·p·ala·t 'so that he would make him stand' (Lk 2.22; 'he' for expected 'they'); ná .. wəní·p·ala·n pa·tamwe·i·k·á·ɔnink xkwi·t·á·k·e 'then he .. stood him on the roof of the temple' (Mt 4.5).
  ▪ nipaht- (TI): nnípahto·n 'I stood it up' (OA; Gr. 5.78k).
ní·p·ən IN 'summer' (FW, AD; Lk 21.30).
  ▪ ni·p·əní·i P 'in summer' (1834a:16).
ní·p·i·t 'my tooth' (V, LTD ND); wí·p·i·t 'a tooth' (Mt 5.38 [2x]); ki·p·i·t·əwá·ɔ 'your (pl.) teeth' (Lk 13.28); wi·p·i·t·əwá·ɔ 'their teeth' (Mt 8.12, 13.42, 13.50, 24.51).
ni·skᵒ (|nīsk-|) 'dirty' (Gr. §5.2a).
ni·skam- TA 'defile by mouth': kót·a-ni·skamá·ɔ hókaya 'he wants to defile himself (by drinking)' (1834b:11.12).
ni·skanət·ó·wi·t 'unclean spirit' (Mk 1.26). ▸ Cf. ní·ski-manə́t·u 'unclean spirit' (Mk 5.8), etc.
ni·skankəl- AI 'have a nasty disease: ni·skankələ́k·əp 'who had the nasty disease' (Mt 8.2; Gr. 6.24a); a·yáhi-ni·skankələ́k·əp 'who had previously had the nasty disease' (Mt 26.6); ni·skankələ́k·i·k 'those with the nasty disease' (Lk 4.27, Mt 10.8, Lk 7.22); ni·skankələ·lí·č·i 'ones (obv.) with the nasty disease' (Lk 17.12). ♦ Evidently coined for 'have leprosy'.
ni·skankələwá·k·an IN 'nasty disease': wəni·skankələwá·k·an 'his nasty disease' (Mt 8.3).
ni·ska·wsəwá·k·an IN 'foul behavior': ni·ska·wsəwá·k·anink 'in foul behavior' (Lk 15.30).
ni·ska·wsi·- AI 'live foully': ni·ska·wsí·č·i·k xkwé·ɔk 'degenerate women' (Mt 21.31, 21.32).
ni·skha·l- TA 'defile': ni·skhá·lkwe·kw 'that would defile you (pl.)' (Mt 15.11); wəni·skhá·lko·n 'it defiles him' (Mt 15.18); wəni·skha·lkó·na awé·n 'they (inan.) defile a person' (Mt 15.20; Gr. 4.27z); kəni·skha·lko·né·ɔ 'it defiles you (pl.)' (Mt 15.11); tá=á· wəni·skha·lko·wəné·ɔ 'they (inan.) will not defile them' (Mk 7.18; Gr. 4.85v).

ní·ski PN 'unclean' (Mk 5.8, Mt 12.43, Mk 1.27, etc.); 'foul': áhi-ní·ski-kéku 'a very foul thing' (Lk 11.39; Gr. §5.9c).
- ní·ski PV 'unclean' (Gr. 5.130a): ní·ski-manət·ó·wi·t 'one who had an unclean spirit' (Mk 1.23), etc. (see manət·o·wi·-).

ni·ski·na·kwsi·- AI — ni·ski·na·k·ɔt- II 'be, look foul, filthy' (Gr. 5.108b).
- ni·ski·na·kwsi·- (AI): ni·ski·ná·kwsi·t 'the foul one' (Mt 24.15).
- ni·ski·na·k·ɔt- (II): ni·ski·ná·k·ɔt 'it looks filthy' (Mt 23.27); ni·ski·ná·k·ɔ kéku 'filthy things' (Mt 23.25).

ni·ski·t- TI(2) 'defile': ni·ski·tuhtí·t·e hɔk·ayúwa 'if they defiled themselves' (Jn 18.28).

ni·sksi- AI 'be dirty': énta- máta=č ní·sksi·kw 'where it (anim.) will not be dirty' (1834a:15 [em.]).

ni·skto·nhe·- AI 'talk loud, nasty, dirty': é·li-=á· tá·mse xé·li awé·n -ni·sktó·nhe·t 'because there would maybe be an uproar from many people' (Mt 26.5); tá=á· ɔ́·k čí·č nni·skto·nhé·e 'I will also never again talk dirty' (1834a:13). ▸ Cf. ni·sktó·nhe· 'he's talking crazy' (OA), 'he talks dirty' (LB); ⟨Nisktonhen⟩ "to be noisy, to talk nasty" (B&A 98); ⟨nisktonhewagan⟩ "noise; tumult; uproar" (Z. 130, 206, 214), "dirty talk" (LTD).

ni·šháke AN 'two nations' (1834a:19.18).

ní·š·a P 'two' (Lk 2.24, Jn 1.35, 2.6, Mt 4.21, Lk 6.13, etc.); ke·k·e·p·inkɔ́·č·i·k ní·š·a lənəwak 'two blind men' (Mt 20.30&; Gr. 6.2i). ♦ Note: ní·š·a (⟨neju⟩ Mt 2.16) is an error for níši PV.

ni·š·á·pxki P 'two hundred' (1834b:13.4).

ní·š·a·š P 'seven' (Lk 2.36, Lk 8.2, Mt 12.45, Jn 6.7, etc.; ⟨nejaj⟩ 16x + 1x in 1834b, ⟨nejvaj⟩ 4x in Mt 18.21-22).

ni·š·ən P 'twice' (Lk 18.12); ní·š·ən télən 'two times ten' (Mk 5.13).

ni·š·i·- AI — ni·š·ən- II 'be two'.
- ni·š·i·- (AI): ní·š·əwak 'there are two of them' (WP); ni·š·i·ló·p·ani 'they (obv.) were two' (1834b:28.3); ni·š·ihtí·t·e=č lənəwak 'if there are two men' (Jn 8.17; Gr. 4.63c); tá=á· čí·č ni·š·i·í·ɔk 'they will no longer be two' (Mt 19.6); ni·š·í·lu e·le·khamaɔ́·č·i '.. who had two debtors' (lit., 'his debtors (obv.) were two' (Lk 7.41).
- ni·š·ən- (II): ni·š·ínki 'which are two' (Lk 3.11). Emended: ni·š·ínke 'if there are two'.

ni·š·i·k·a·p·ai·- AI 'stand as two' (Gr. 5.11b): ni·š·i·k·a·p·ó·wak 'the two of them were standing together' (Lk 24.4).
▸ Cf. li·k·a·p·ai·- (above); ɔ·ka·i·k·a·p·ó·wak 'they are standing in a circle' (OA).

ni·š·í·nxke (|-īnaxkē|; Gr. 5.31p) P 'twenty' (Jn 6.7, Lk 14.31).

ni·š·i·tkwihəla- AI 'kneel down': ni·š·i·tkwíhəle· 'he knelt down' (Mt 26.39); ná tɔ́ləmi-ni·š·i·tkwihəla·né·ɔ 'then they began kneeling down' (Mt 27.29).

ni·š·i·tkwi·taw- TA 'kneel down to': ni·š·i·tkwí·to· 'kneel down to him (you pl.)' (1842:14.3); káči ni·š·i·tkwi·tawié·k·ač 'don't kneel down to them (you sg.)' (1842:11.1); wəni·š·i·tkwi·taɔ́·p·ani 'he knelt before him' (Mt 8.2, Mk 10.17&); wəni·š·i·tkwi·taɔwwá·ɔ nčɔ·səp·a 'they knelt down to Joseph' (1842:15.5).

ni·š·o·k·wənak·at- (|-ōkwən-| 'day'; Gr. 5.31s) II 'be two days': ni·š·o·k·wənak·at 'it is two days, it was two days ago' (OA); čí·č ni·š·o·k·wənakháke 'in two more days' (Mt 26.2), ni·š·o·k·wənakháke 'after two days' (Jn 4.43).

ni·š·ó·k·wəni (Gr. 5.31s) P 'for two days' (Jn 4.40, 11.6).

ni·š·o·x·we·- (|-ōxwē-| 'walk'; Gr. 4.61b) AI 'go as two': ni·š·o·x·we·é·k·we 'when you two go together' (Lk 12.58).

-ni·tamaw-: see nhitamaw-.

-ní·tami: see hítami.
-ni·tamunšá·k·an- AN 'firstborn child'; wəni·tamunšá·k·ana 'her firstborn child' (Lk 2.7).
-ni·ta·: see híta·.
-ni·ta·t-: see hita·t-.
ni·tháke 'my fellow tribesman' (LB); ni·thake·wəná·na 'our nation (*lit.*, our fellow-countrymen) (obv.)' (Lk 24.21); ki·thaké·ɔk 'your own nation' (Jn 18.35; KJV "Thine own nation").
ní·tkuxkw 'my sister (of a woman)' (OA, ME); wi·tkúxkɔ 'her sister' (⟨wetkwxkov⟩ Jn 19.25; Gr. 5.72h). ▸ Cf. Mun ní·tkoxkw; ⟨nĩtgochk⟩ 'my sister', ⟨Wĩtgóchquall⟩ 'her sister' (Z. 174).
ní·t·i·s 'my (male) friend (of a male)' (Lk 11.6); ni·t·í·s·ak 'my friends' (Jn 15.14, 15.15); kí·t·i·s 'your friend' (1834a: Cover); ki·t·í·s·ak 'your friends' (Lk 14.12); wi·t·í·s·al '(his) friend' (Jn 3.29), wi·t·í·s·a 'his friend' (Lk 7.6), 'his friends' (Lk 7.34, 15.6, etc.); ni·t·i·s·əná·nak 'our friends' (Lk 24.24); ki·t·í·s·əna 'our friend' (Jn 11.11); ki·t·i·s·əwá·ɔk 'your (pl.) friends' (Lk 21.16); wi·t·i·s·əwá·ɔ 'their friends' (Lk 5.7); lí ki·t·i·s·i·ké·i P+P 'to your friends' (Mk 5.19; Gr. 4.10c). ♦ The corresponding vocative is: nčú 'my friend (voc.)'.
nkáhe·s 'my mother' (Mt 12.48, 12.49); nkahé·s·a 'my late mother' (V; Gr. 4.8a); kkáhe·s 'your mother' (Mt 12.47, Jn 19.27, 1842:12.2; Gr. 2.64i); kɔhé·s·al 'his mother' (Lk 1.60, Mt 2.11, etc.); kɔhé·s·a 'his, her mother' (Lk 1.43, 2.48, Jn 2.1, etc.; Gr. 2.55o); kɔhe·s·ínka 'his or her late mother' (V; Gr. 4.8b); kɔhe·s·í·li·t 'his (obv.) mother' (Mt 2.21); kkahé·s·əwa 'your (pl.) mother' (Mt 15.4); íka .. kɔhé·s·ink 'to her mother' (Mk 6.24); lá·mahte kɔhé·s·ink 'in his mother's womb' (Jn 3.4). ♦ The vocative is suppletive (Gr. 4.11c).
nkal- (-nək·al-, |nəkal-|) TA — nkat·- (-nəkaht-, |nəkat-|) TI(1b) 'leave, leave behind'.
 ▪ nkal- (TA): nkalá·t·amo·kw 'let's leave her behind (you pl.)' (ME; Gr. 2.67f); wənči-nkála·t 'by which he divorces her' (Mt 5.31); nkalá·t·e wi·č·e·ɔ́·č·i 'if he divorces his wife' (Mt 5.32; Gr. 2.67e); kɔ́č=háč nkálian 'why have you abandoned me?' (Mk 15.34; Gr. 4.60c); nčí·sas nkála·p 'Jesus was left' (Jn 8.9; Gr. 4.69m).
 • -nək·al-: wənək·alá·ɔ 'he left them' (Mt 21.17&, Mt 26.44; Gr. 2.67e), 'he outran him' (Jn 20.4; KJV "did outrun"); ná wənək·ala·n 'then he left them' (Mt 16.4); wənək·alúk·o·n pɔ·lsəwá·k·an 'his illness left him' (Jn 4.52; Gr. 4.27y).
 ▪ nkat·- (TI): máta nkat·ínke wé·mi 'if he does not leave behind everything' (Lk 14.33), awé·n=č nkat·ínke wi·k·í·č·i 'if anyone shall leave his houses' (Mk 10.29); mé·či nkat·əmánkwe yó·ni pe·mhakamí·k·e·k 'after we leave this earth' (1834b:48.3).
 • -nəkaht-: nnəkahtə́mən yú entalá·wsink 'I leave the world' (Jn 16.28); ná šá·e wənəkahtə́mən pɔ·lsəwá·k·an 'then she immediately left behind her disease' (Mk 1.31); wé·mi kéku nnəkahtəmə́ne·n 'we left everything' (Mt 19.27; Gr. 4.39p).
†nkápənal AN 'governor' (⟨fopunul⟩ Lk 23.4; Mt 27.14, 27.15, 27.21, 27.27, 28.14; pp. 200-213); †nkapənála (obv.) (Mt 27.2, 27.11; pp. 198-200). ▸ Cf. earlier: †kápənəl, †kapənəli·-.
nkatši·mwi·- (-nəkahtəš·i·mwi·-) AI 'flee', AI+O 'flee leaving behind O2': nkatší·mu 'he ran away abandoning (things, people)' (OA; Gr. 2.70b).
 • -nəkahtəš·i·mwi·-: wənəkahtəš·í·mwi·n nɔ́ či·t·anahémpəs 'he fled leaving behind the thick cloth' (Mk 14.52).
nkat·əmaw- (-nəkahtəmaw-; Gr. 5.94g) TA+O 'leave O2 behind for': wəlankuntəwá·k·an kənəkahtəmo·lhúmɔ 'I leave behind peace for you (pl.)' (Jn 14.27).
†nka·lalᵒ 'Galilee': see also †nkélali·, †keləlí·yunk, etc.
†nka·lalí·i PN '(of) Galilee': †nka·lalí·i-mənəp·é·k·unk 'by the sea of Galilee' (Mt 4.18, Mk 7.31); †nka·lalí·i-hák·ink 'land of Galilee' (Lk 4.31);†nka·lalí·i-lə́nəwak 'Men of Galilee' (Acts 1.11).

†nka·lali·i·- AI 'be Galilean': †nka·lalí·i·t=háč ɔ́·k ké·pe 'Are you also a Galilean?' (⟨Faluleet⟩ Jn 7.52); †nka·lali·í·č·i·k 'the Galileans' (⟨Falulethek⟩ Jn 4.45, p. 31); wé·mi †nka·lali·í·č·i·k 'all the Galileans' (⟨Faluleehek⟩wé. 122); é·li-†nka·lalí·ian 'as you are a Galilean' (⟨rli Faluleeu⟩ Lk 22.59-60& [would mean 'as I am a Galilean'], for ⟨-eeun⟩).

†nka·lalí·yunk: see †nkélali·.

†nka·talí·ns·ak 'Gadarenes' (Lk 8.37).

†nkélali· 'Galilee' (⟨Fclule⟩ Jn 7.1; p. 90) ~ †nké·lali· (⟨Frlule⟩ Lk 23.6; p. 201); nkelalí·yunk '(to) Galilee' (Lk 1.26, 2.4, etc.; pp. 7-19).
- ▪ †nka·lalí·yunk (loc.) (Lk 3.1, Jn 1.43, etc.; pp. 17-219).

nkelántink: see kelántink.

†nké·pələl 'Gabriel' (Lk 1.19); †nke·pəlɔ́lal (obv.) (Lk 1.26).

nkəli·ki·xsi·- AI 'speak Greek': nkəli·kí·xsi·n 'it was in Greek' (Jn 19.20).

nkəlí·ksak 'Greeks' (Jn 12.20).

nkəmé·i P 'always' (B ⟨fumri⟩ Mk 5.5, etc. [8x pp. 53-179]; ⟨kumri⟩ 1834b:44.2, Jn 7.6 [1x p. 90]; ⟨kumr⟩ 1834b:9.11 3x, Mt 6.25, 6.31, Lk 6.45 3x; 5x pp. 45-48).
- • nink·əmé·i 'always (habitually)' (⟨nenkumri⟩ Jn 11.42; Gr. 5.41m).
- ► Cf. nkəmé·e 'always' (V, OA, ME); nink·əmé·e (OA, AD) 'always'.

nki·skaw- (-nak·i·skaw-) TA 'meet': nkí·skae· 'he met (them)' (Lk 17.12; Gr. 4.24c); énta-nki·skaɔ́·t·əp 'where she had met him' (Jn 11.30).
- • -nak·i·skaw-: wənak·i·skaɔ́·ɔl 'he met them' (Jn 4.51); nɔk·i·skaɔwwá·ɔ 'they met him' (Mt 28.9); nɔk·í·skaɔ·n 'to meet him' (*lit.*, 'that he meet him') (Lk 14.31).

nkó·l IN 'gold' (Mt 2.11, 10.9, 23.16, 23.17 [2x]). ► Cf. nko·lí·i PN '(of) gold' (LB).

†nkɔma·lɔí·ɔk 'the people of Gomorrha' (⟨Fomaloeuk⟩ Mt 10.15).

nkɔ́·tsa 'goats (obv.)' (Mt 25.33); wɔ́nči nkɔ·tsi·ké·i P+P 'from goats' (Mt 25.32).

nkwəntá·k·an 'my throat' (Gr. 5.57a); kkwənta·k·anəwá·ɔl 'your throats' (1834b:12.7).

nkwɔ́ti PP 'all, the whole time of' (Gr. 5.133d): nkwɔ́ti-kí·škwe 'all day long' (Lk 2.44).

nkwí·s 'my son' (Mt 2.15, Lk 2.48, Mt 3.17, etc.); kkwí·s 'your son' (Jn 4.51, 1842:11.4); kkwí·s·al 'his, her son' (Lk 1.32, 1.35, Mt 1.20, etc.), kkwí·s·a (Jn 5.23, 5.27, Mk 3.11, etc.; Gr. 2.9c, 2.58n); kkwí·s·í·na 'his sons' (1834b:18.10, 1842:15.1; cf. Gr. §4.2g); nkwí·s·əna 'our son' (Jn 9.20); kkwí·s·əwa 'your (pl.) son' (Jn 9.19); kkwi·s·əwá·ɔl (1834b:17.7), kkwi·s·əwá·ɔ 'their sons' (Mt 20.20&).

nnáxk 'my hand' (V), 'my arm and hand' (OA); nnáxkal 'my hands' (Jn 13.9), nnáxka (Lk 24.39, Jn 20.27); kənáxk 'your (sg.) hand' (Mt 18.8 [2x]); kənáxka 'your (sg.) hands' (Mt 18.8); kənáxkink 'in your hands' (Lk 23.46); wənáxk 'his hand' (Lk 6.8, 6.10, 22.21, Jn 12.38; Gr. 2.56c); nɔ́xkal 'his hands' (Jn 11.44; Gr. 2.56c); wənáxka 'his hands' (Lk 24.40), 'hands' (Mk 14.58 2x); wənáxkink 'into his hands, by (*lit.*, on) his hands' (Jn 3.35, 20.25; Mt 22.13), wənáxkink wɔ́nči 'with his arm' (Lk 1.51), wənáxkink wɔ́nči PV 'by his hand (Lk 1.66); wənaxkí·li·t 'his, her (obv.) hand' (Mk 1.31, Mk 5.41, etc.; Gr. 2.56b); wənaxkəwá·ink 'in their hands' (Lk 6.1; Gr. 2.56c).

nní·č·a·n 'my child' (Jn 4.49, Lk 9.38); kəní·č·a·n 'your child' (Mt 7.11); kəni·č·á·nak 'your children' (Lk 19.44, 1834b:20.17); wəni·č·á·nal 'his, her children' (Mt 2.18, Mk 10.30, 1842:10.6); wəni·č·á·na 'his, her child, children' (Mt 7.9, 18.25, Lk 13.34, etc.; Gr. 2.57f); wəni·č·a·ní·li·t 'her (obv.) foal' (Mt 21.7&, 21.5); aha·nhúkwi nni·č·a·nəná·nak 'the succeeding generations of our children' (Mt 27.25); kəni·č·a·nəwá·ɔk 'your (pl.) children' (Mt 12.27, Lk 11.13, 23.28); wəni·č·a·nəwá·ɔ 'their children' (Mt 17.25, 17.26).

▪ kəni·č·a·nəwa·i·ké·i P 'on your and their descendants' (1842:8.1); wəni·č·a·ni·ké·i P 'on his children' (1842:11.1).
▪ wəni·č·a·nt·ə́t·a (dim.) 'her young one' (Lk 19.30&).

nó·čkwe P 'frivolously, in vain, for nothing, freely' (⟨nwhqc⟩ 10x B, 3x B 1842; ⟨nwhqi⟩ 4x B 1834b, 1x B; Gr. 5.129dd; ⟨nwhi⟩ 1x): 'frivolously, for no reason' (⟨nwhiqc⟩ Lk 3.14; ⟨nwhqc⟩ Mt 5.22, Mt 12.36, 1842:11.2), 'for nothing' (⟨nwhi⟩ Lk 6.35), 'for no reason' (⟨nwhqc⟩ Mt 5.22, 5.33), 'pointlessly' (Mt 6.7); nó·čkwe=á· 'it would be pointless' (Jn 13.10); nó·čkwe mahtak·əní·ma· 'he was unjustly accused' (1842:13.5); málahši nó·čkwe 'like so much foolish talk' (Lk 24.11; KJV "as idle tales").
▪ PV: nó·čkwe 'freely' (⟨nwhi⟩ Mt 10.8); kənó·čkwe-milləné·ɔ 'I gave it to you freely' (⟨knwhi⟩ Mt 10.8). ► Zeisberger (1821: sect. 36, p. 57) has /nó·čkwe/ ⟨nutschque⟩ in Mt 10.8.

no·čkwe·h- TA 'hit unprovoked': wəno·čkwe·hawwá·ɔ 'they hit him unprovoked' (Lk 22.63; KJV "smote him").

no·č·i·skóntae·t 'door-keeper' (Jn 10.3, Lk 22.56-57&); no·č·i·skɔntae·lí·č·i (obv.) (Mk 13.34, Jn 18.16).

no·lhant- AI 'be lazy': káči no·lhántkan 'don't be lazy' (OA; Gr. §4.12b, 4.110e); no·lhántək 'who is lazy' (Mt 25.26; in a vocative); yó·ki·k no·lhántki·k 'these lazy ones' (1834a:17).

nó·mhəmp: see wum-.

no·ná·k·an IN 'breast' (ND); no·ná·k·ana 'breasts' (Lk 11.27; Gr. 4.78d).

no·na·t- TI(1a) 'nurse from': no·na·t·amánəp 'which (sg. for pl.) you nursed from' (⟨nwnatamunrp⟩ Lk 11.27 [s.b. ⟨-nup⟩]; Gr. 4.78d).

no·ne·- AI '(baby to) nurse': no·né·č·i·k 'nursing infants' (Mt 21.16), ⟨Nonetschik⟩ 'sucking babes' (B&A 100).

no·t·amensəwí·i PN '(of) fisherman' (Gr. 5.125c): wəno·t·amensəwí·i-hémpəs 'his fisherman's shirt' (⟨wunwtamcnswe⟩ Jn 21.7; KJV "his fisher's coat").

no·t·amensi·- AI 'fish': nəmái-no·t·aménsi·n 'I'm going fishing (sbd.).' (Jn 21.3; Gr. 4.52a).
♦ Apparently originally 'fish with a spear'; cf. ⟨nutamensin⟩ "to spearfish" (Zeisberger 2016:66).

nó·t·e·s IN 'knapsack' (Mt 10.10; KJV "scrip"). ► Cf. mənó·t·e·s, mɔnií·i-nó·t·e·s.

no·t·əm- (nehəno·t·əm- [Rih+; IC]) TA — no·t·ənt- (nehəno·t·ənt- [Rih+; IC]) TI(1a) 'watch, guard' (Gr. 5.12h).
▪ no·t·əm- (TA): nó·t·əma·t '(one) who watches over them' (Jn 10.16); no·t·əmá·č·i·k 'ones watching them, shepherds' (Lk 2.8, 2.15); no·t·əmánči·k 'the flock' (lit., 'ones watched over') (Mk 14.27); ktə́li--č -nó·t·əma·n 'that you watch over them' (Jn 17.15).
• nehəno·t·əm-: nehənó·t·əma·t (mekí·s·a) 'shepherd' (lit., 'one who watches (sheep) customarily') (Jn 10.11 [2x], Mt 25.32, Mk 14.27); pl. nehəno·t·əmá·č·i·k (Lk 2.20).
▪ no·t·ənt- (TI): ⟨Nutindam⟩ 'watch a place' (B&A 102); no·t·əntánki·k 'guards' (Mt 28.4); no·t·əntankpáni·k 'those who had been guards' (Mt 28.11); no·t·əntaməlí·č·i=č 'ones (obv.) who would guard it' (Mt 27.66); tə́li-no·t·ə́ntamən 'that he is keeping a close watch on it' (1842:22.1).
• nehəno·t·ənt-: nehəno·t·əntánki·k 'guards for it' (Mt 27.65).

no·t·əma·l- TA 'guard': ɔ́·k=č kəno·t·əmá·lko·k 'and they shall guard you' (Lk 19.43).

no·t·əntamaw- TA+O 'watch O2 for': ktə́li-no·t·əntamá·k·o·n 'it watches for you' (1834b:8.13).

no·t·i·k·e·- AI 'stay home' (with PV wə́li 'watch over the house', lit., 'stay home well, alertly'): wi·šíki-wə́li-no·t·í·k·e·t 'the one working hard at watching the house' (Lk 12.42; Gr.5.129rr); wé·li-no·t·i·k·ehtí·t·e 'when they were watching the house' (Lk 12.37).

nó·we 'Noah' (⟨Noc⟩ 1842:8.3, 8.5, 8.6, 9.3) ~ †nó·wa (⟨Nou⟩ 1834b:18.1, 18.4 [2x]); yó·li †nó·wa (obv.) (⟨bli Nou⟩ 1834b:18.5); †no·wé·s·a 'Noah (obv.)' (⟨Nocsu⟩ 1842:8.7); †no·wé·s·a (abs.) (⟨Norsu⟩ Lk 17.26, 17.27, Mt 24.37, 24.38). ♦ Note KJV "Noe".

nó·x (núxa· [voc.]) 'my father' (Lk 2.49, Jn 2.16, etc.; Gr. 4.7d); nó·x·ɔ 'my father (obv.)' (Mt 18.10); kó·x 'your (sg.) father' (Lk 2.48, Mt 5.45, 5.48, etc.); ó·x·ɔl 'his father' (Jn 1.18, Lk 1.59, etc.); ó·x·ɔ 'his or her father' (⟨wxo⟩ Mk 5.40, Mk 10.46, Mt 15.4, Mt 10.35, 37, etc.; ⟨wxov⟩ Mt 19.5, as if /ó·x·ɔ[h]/); o·x·únka 'his late father' (Mt 2.22); no·x·əná·na 'our ancient father' (Jn 4.12, 8.39, Mk 11.10); no·x·əna·nínka 'our forefathers' (Jn 4.20, 6.31); kó·x·əna 'our (inc.) father' (Jn 4.21, Mt 23.9); kó·x·əwa 'your (pl.) father' (Mt 5.48, Mt 10.20, 10.29, etc.); ko·x·əwá·ɔ 'your father (obv.)' (Mk 5.16); ko·x·əwá·ɔ 'your father of old' (Jn 8.56; Gr. 4.8f); ko·x·əwá·ɔk 'your fathers' (1842:19.3); ko·x·əwa·únka 'your forefathers' (Jn 6.49, 6.58, 7.22, Lk 11.48; Gr. 4.8g); o·x·əwá·ɔ 'their father' (Mt 4.21, 13.43, Mt 27.32&); o·x·əwa·únka 'their fathers (abs.)' (Lk 6.26; Gr. 4.8h); nó·x·ink 'my father (loc.), (at) my father's' (Lk 15.18, Jn 8.38, 16.10, 20.17 [B 12x]), nó·x·unk (1834b:28.12); lí ó·x·unk 'to his father' (Jn 13.1); íka íka no·x·əná·nink 'with our father' (*lit.*, 'at our father's') (1842:15.2); ko·x·əwá·unk 'at your (pl.) father's (or fathers')' (Jn 8.38); lí .. ko·x·əwá·ink 'to your (pl.) father' (Jn 20.17); o·x·əwá·ink 'at their father's' (1842:17.1).
- • núxa· 'O father' (Mt 11.25, 11.26, etc.; Gr. 2.78c); nuxá·t·i 'father' (voc.) (Gr. 4.11h).

nó·x·wi·s 'my grandchild' (ME, ND; Gr. 2.41e); o·x·wí·s·al 'his descendants' (1834b:17.10); o·x·wi·s·əwá·ɔl '(their) grandchildren' (1834b:20.10) a·nhúkwi .. o·x·wi·s·əwá·ɔl '(their) great-grandchildren' (1834b:20.10).

†nsá·yən 'Zion' (Mt 21.5).

nsí·t·al (pl.) 'my feet' (Lk 7.44, Jn 13.9), nsí·t·a (Lk 7.44, 7.46, etc.); ksí·t 'your foot' (Mt 18.8 [2x]); ksí·t·al 'your (sg.) feet' (Mt 4.6); wsí·t·al 'his feet' (Jn 11.44); ksi·t·əná·nal 'our feet' (emending ⟨nsetunanul⟩ Lk 1.79; Gr. 4.4); nsí·t·ink 'on my feet' (Lk 7.45); e·k·wí·i ksí·t·ink 'under your (sg.) feet' (Mk 12.36); wsí·t·ink 'at his feet' (Lk 7.38 [2x], Mt 15.30); wsi·t·í·li·t 'his, their (obv.) feet' (Lk 17.16, Jn 11.2, 11.32, etc.); ksi·t·əwá·ink 'on your (pl.) feet' (Mt 10.14); wə́nči wsi·t·əwá·ink 'with their feet' (Mt 7.6).

nsúk·wi·s 'my mother-in-law' (LTD ND, ME); wsuk·wí·s·a 'her mother-in-law' (Mt 10.35, Lk 12.53).

ntáləmuns 'my animal' (ntáləmo·ns 'my dog' OA; Gr. §2.1c); ktaləmúnsak 'your (sg.) animals' (1834b:20.17, 1842:11.4); tɔləmúnsal 'his animals' (Jn 4.12, Mt 12.11), tɔləmúnsa 'his animal' (Lk 13.15, 14.5, 1842:12.7); nihəláči tɔləmúnsink 'on his own animal' (Lk 10.34).

†ntánəla 'Daniel (abs.)' (Mt 24.15).

ntaɔ·p·am- (-nat·aɔ·p·am-; Gr. 5.12l) TA 'look for': ná nɔt·aɔ·p·ama·né·ɔ 'then they looked around for him' (Jn 11.56).

ntaɔ·p·əwi·k·á·ɔn 'watchtower': ehalo·ka·lənti·i-ntaɔ·p·əwi·k·á·ɔn 'watchtower of the messenger' (Lk 13.4).

ntaɔ·p·i·- AI 'keep watch': máta=háč kkáski- íli kwə́ti-á·wəlink -sháki-ntaɔ·p·i·húmɔ 'could you (pl.) not even keep watch for one hour?' (Mk 14.37).

ntá·ktəl AN 'doctor' (Lk 4.23); nta·ktə́la (obv.) (Mt 9.12).

ntá·nəs 'my daughter' (Mk 5.23, Mt 9.22, 15.22; Gr. 2.62b); ktá·nəs 'your (sg.) daughter' (Mk 5.35, 1842:11.4).
- • -ta·n-: tɔ́·nal 'his daughter' (Lk 2.36), tɔ́·na 'his, her daughter' (Mt 10.37, Mk 6.22, Mt 15.28, etc.); †nči·lo·sələm tɔ·ní·na '(O) Daughters of Jerusalem' (Lk 23.28; Gr. 4.12d); tɔ·nəwá·a 'their daughter' (OA).

nté· AN 'my heart' (|nətēh|; Gr. 2.11a, 3.4n, 4.7a); kté· 'your heart' (⟨ktri⟩ Mt 6.21); wté·hal 'his heart' (1834b:31.10), wté·ha (Lk 6.45); wté· '(a) heart' (1834b:41.3), wté·hal 'heart(s) (obv.)' (1834b:16.2), wəski-wté·hal 'a new heart' (1834b:48.7); wté·hak 'hearts' (Gr. 4.7a); ktehəná·nak 'our hearts' (Lk 24.32); ktéhəwa 'your (pl.) heart (sg.)' (Mk 8.17, Lk 12.34), for 'your hearts'; ktehəwá·ɔ 'your hearts (obv.)' (Lk 16.15); ktehəwá·ɔk 'your hearts' (Mt 19.8); wtehəwá·ɔl 'their hearts' (Lk 4.18); wte·hí·li·t 'their (obv.) hearts' (1834b:17.6); nté·hink 'in my heart' (Lk 1.47, Jn 12.27); kté·hink 'in your heart' (Lk 2.25, 10.27, Mk 12.30); wté·hink 'in, to his heart' (Mt 5.28, Lk 6.45 [2x], etc.); ktehəwá·ink 'in your hearts' (Mt 23.28, Jn 14.1, etc.) ~ ktehəwá·unk (Lk 24.25); wtehəwá·ink 'in their hearts' (Lk 3.15, Jn 12.40).

†nté·pit 'David' (Lk 1.27, Mt 9.27, 12.23); †nte·pít·al (Lk 1.32, 1.68); †nte·pít·a (abs.) (Mt 1.20, Lk 2.4, etc.); †nte·pit·ínka (abs. obv.) (Lk 2.4).

ntəlankó·ma 'my relative': awé·n=háč ntəlankó·ma 'who is my kinsman?' (Lk 10.29; KJV "who is my neighbour?"); ntəlanko·má·wto·kw 'my kinsmen (voc.)' (Lk 12.4; KJV "my friends"; Gr. 4.11n); təlanko·má·ɔ '(was) a kinsman (obv.) of him (prox.) (who ..)' (Lk 1.27, 10.36; KJV "(was) neighbour unto him"). ▸ See lanko·m- TA; with |-āw| NF (Gr. 5.63b).

ntia·s·i·- (ne·t·ia·s·í·-): ntiá·s·u 'it (animal) is grazing' (ND, LB).
• ne·t·ia·s·i·-: ne·t·ia·s·í·č·i·k '(ones) that were feeding' (Mk 5.11).

ntíte 'I think': see líte.

nti·t·e·he·ɔ́·k·an 'my will'; kti·t·e·he·ɔ́·k·an 'your will' (Mt 6.10, Lk 11.2); wti·t·e·he·ɔ́·k·an 'his will' (Jn 6.38, 6.39, 6.40).

ntó·lhay 'my breast, chest' (V, OA, LB); wtó·lhay 'his chest' (Lk 18.13; OA, ME); wto·lhé·yunk 'his chest (loc.)' (Jn 13.23, 13.25); wto·lhaí·li·t 'in his (obv.) breast' (Jn 1.18); wto·lháyəwa 'their chests' (Lk 23.48).

nto·m- (-nat·o·m-, ne·t·o·m-) TA 'summon, call': ntó·m 'call them (you sg.)' (Mt 20.8); ntəli-=á· -ntó·ma·n 'so that I would summon them' (Mt 9.13); təli-ntó·ma·n 'he proceeded to call them to come' (Mk 9.35).
• -nat·o·m-: nɔt·o·má·ɔ 'he called him, them' (Jn 10.3, 18.33, Mt 27.47); nɔt·o·má·p·ani 'he called for her' (Lk 13.12); ná nɔt·ó·ma·n 'then he called him over' (Lk 15.26).
• ne·t·o·m-: ne·t·o·má·t·e 'after he called them' (Mt 10.1, 15.10).

ntó·n 'my mouth' (Gr. 4.7b); któ·n 'your mouth' (Lk 19.22; Gr. 2.63b); kto·nəwá·ink 'your (pl.) mouths (loc.)' (Mt 15.11 [2x], Lk 21.15); wtó·n 'his mouth' (1834a:12; Gr. 2.57a); wtó·nink 'his mouth (loc.)' (Lk 4.22, 6.46, Mt 15.18); wto·nəwá·ink 'their mouths (loc.)' (⟨°aif⟩ Lk 1.70, Mt 15.8, Mk 7.18) ~ wto·nəwá·unk 'their mouths (loc.)' (⟨°awf⟩ Mt 21.16).

nto·naw- (-nat·o·naw-) TA — nto·n- (nat·o·n-, nc·t·o·n-) TI(1a) 'search for' (Gr. 5.12z).
▪ nto·naw- (TA): lápi ntó·naw 'look for more of them (you sg.)' (Lk 14.23); wəli-ntó·no· ná mi·məntət 'search carefully for the baby (you pl.)' (Mt 2.8; Gr. 4.104w); wə́nči-nto·naíe·kw '(for which reason) you (pl.) looked for me' (Lk 2.49); ktəli-nto·naɔ·né·ɔ 'that you (pl.) are looking for him' (Mt 28.5&, 1834b:37.4).
• -nat·o·naw-: wənat·o·naɔwwá·ɔl 'they looked for him' (Lk 2.45; Gr. 4.24l); nɔt·o·naɔwwá·p·ani 'they were looking for him' (Jn 6.24); kənat·o·naíhəmɔ=č 'you (pl.) will seek me' (Jn 7.34, 7.36, 8.21, 13.33); ná nčó·wak nɔt·o·naɔ·né·ɔ 'then the Jews looked for him' (Jn 7.11).
▪ nto·n- (TI): ntó·na 'seek it (you sg.)' (Mt 7.7); ntó·namo·kw 'seek it (you pl.)' (Lk 11.9, 12.31); káči nto·nánkhe·kw 'don't seek it (you pl.)' (Lk 12.29); ntó·namo·k kəlo·ne·ɔ́·k·ana 'they searched for lies' (Mt 26.59); é·li- máta -nto·namó·wa 'for I do not seek it' (Jn 5.30; Gr. 4.99a); nto·nánke 'if he seeks it' (Mt 7.8, 10.39, Lk 17.33; Gr. 2.67h).

- -nat·o·n-: kéku=háč kənat·ó·nam 'what are you looking for?' (Jn 4.27; Gr. 4.38f); kéku kənat·o·namúhəmɔ 'what are you (pl.) seeking?' (Jn 1.38; Gr. 4.38n); takó· nnat·o·namó·wən 'I do not seek it' (Jn 8.50); nɔt·ó·namən 'he seeks it' (Jn 7.18).
- ne·t·o·n-: ne·t·o·nánke kéku 'when he looked for things' (Mt 13.45); ne·t·ó·name·kw 'you (pl.) who seek it' (Jn 5.44, Mt 12.39).

nto·p·ali- AI 'go to war': káhta-nto·p·alí·t·e 'if he wanted to go to war' (Lk 14.31).
▸ Cf. ⟨n'dopallo⟩ 'he is gone to war' (Z. 220); but ntóp·alu 'he's going hunting, looking for meat' (OA, ND).

nto·t·əmaw- (-nat·o·t·əmaw-, ne·t·o·t·əmaw-) TA(+O) 'ask (about O2)': ntót·əmaw né·k 'ask those (you sg.)' (Jn 18.21); nto·t·əmo·lé·k·we 'if I ask you (pl.)' (Lk 22.68; Gr. 2.67h); ó·li-nto·t·əmaɔ́·p·ani·l 'he carefully asked them' (Mt 2.7).
- -nat·o·t·əmaw-: nɔt·o·t·əmaɔ́·ɔ 'he asked him, them' (Mk 15.4, Lk 23.9, 23.20; Gr. 2.67h); máta čí·č awé·n wwínki- kéku -nto·t·əmaɔ·í·p·ani 'no one cared to ask him anything anymore' (Mt 22.46&); kənat·o·t·əmaɔ́wwa=á· 'you (pl.) should ask him' (Jn 9.21); nɔt·o·t·əmaɔwwá·ɔ 'they asked him, them' (Jn 8.7, 9.19, Acts 1.6); kéku kənat·o·t·əmo·lhúmɔ 'I ask you (pl.) one thing' (Mt 21.24); ná nɔt·o·t·əmáɔ·n 'then he asked him, them' (Jn 4.52, Mk 8.23, etc.).
- ne·t·o·t·əmaw-: kéku=háč ne·t·o·t·əmáe·kw 'what are you (pl.) asking them about?' (Mk 9.16).
  ▪ nto·t·əma·ɔhti- AI(+O) (recip.): nto·t·əma·ɔhtóp·ani·k 'they asked each other' (Mk 1.27, 9.10); kənat·o·t·əma·ɔhti·né·ɔ=háč 'are you (pl.) asking each other about it?' (Jn 16.19); ná tɔ́ləmi- nihəláči -nto·t·əma·ɔhti·né·ɔ 'then they began to ask each *other*' (Lk 22.23).

nto·t·əma·ɔhtəwá·k·an IN 'judgement' (Mt 5.21; Gr. 5.115e). ▸ Cf. ⟨ndotemawachtoágan⟩ "examen" (Z. 69; i.e., examination).

nto·xtaw- (-nat·o·xtaw-, ne·t·o·xtaw-) TA+O 'ask O1 a question, ask O1 (for, about) O2': kkwí·ta-nto·xtaɔ·né·ɔ 'they feared to ask him about it' (Mk 9.32; Gr. 5.128j); nto·xtá·kwke 'if he (obv.) asks him for (something)' (⟨ntwxtaqkc⟩ Mt 7.10).
- -nat·o·xtaw-: nɔt·o·xtaɔ́·ɔ 'he asked him, them' (Mt 16.13, Mk 9.33, Mk 10.17&); tá=á· kéku kənat·o·xtai·húmɔ 'you (pl.) will ask me nothing' (Jn 16.23); kwət·ennáɔhki kéku kənat·o·xto·lhúmɔ 'I ask you (pl.) one thing' (Lk 6.9; Gr. 2.22d); ná nɔt·o·xtáɔ·n 'then he asked him, them' (Jn 5.12, Mk 8.5).
- ne·t·o·xtaw-: né·ləma ne·t·o·xtaɔ́·ɔt 'before you (sg.) ask him for it' (Mt 6.8; Gr. 4.97b).

nto·x·əm- TA — nto·xt- (-nat·o·xt-) TI(2) 'ask for'.
  ▪ nto·x·əm- (TA): nto·x·əmo·mó·e 'ask for [a good man] (you pl.)' (Mt 10.11).
  ▪ nto·xt- (TI): nto·xtá·k·we 'if he asks for it' (Lk 11.11, 11.12; Gr. 2.67h).
- -nat·o·xt-: ná wé·na kənat·ó·xto·n 'then you still ask' ([+ complement] Mk 5.31); ná nɔt·ó·xto·n 'then she asked for it' (Mk 6.25).

ntuxkwé·yəmak: see xkwé·.

núči (ni·núči; Gr. 2.73k, 5.28g, 5.129ee) P 'since, starting from' (Lk 2.2, Jn 5.5, Lk 13.7); lápi .. núči .. (with participle) 'before' (Mt 2.9); lɔ·k·wəní·i núči mi·kəmɔ·s·í·č·i·k 'who began working in the evening' (Mt 20.9).
- ni·núči (Gr. 2.73j, 5.43f) P 'in, at, from the beginning; long before' (Lk 1.70; Mt 5.16 [KJV "before" misunderstood]); ní· ni·núči 'I was from the beginning(?)' (Jn 8.58; KJV "before [Abraham] was, I am"); ⟨Ninutschi⟩ 'at the beginning, before now' (B&A 97).
  ▪ PV (Jn 2.17 [ms. note has /ni·núči/], Mt 4.17); tə́ta e·lkí·kwi-núči- nə́ -ləs·í·li·t? 'For how long has he (obv.) been like that?' (Mk 9.21); télən ɔ́·k ní·š·a kahtən núči-mhukwí·ne·p 'she had had the bloody flux for twelve years' (Lk 8.43).

- niˑnúči PV: niˑnúči 'forever' (Lk 2.48), '(for) long' (Lk 22.15).

nuhəl- (|nōhl-| < |nōn-| + |-l|; Gr. 2.50b) TA 'nurse (at the breast)': máta háši awéˑni nuhəláˑčˑiˑk 'those who never nursed anyone' (Lk 23.29).

nuhəlaˑɔhsiˑ- TA 'nurse (a baby)': nuhəláˑɔhsu "she is taking care of a nursing baby" (LB); nuhəlaˑɔhsíˑčˑiˑk 'those who are nursing' (⟨nwvlasehek⟩ Mt 24.19; KJV "them that give suck").

-nukwtennaɔhkəsˑiˑ-: see kwətˑennaɔhkəsˑiˑ-.

nunšeˑ- AI 'give birth': wtə́li-=č -núnšeˑn 'for her to give birth' (Lk 1.57, 2.6; Gr. 2.61b).

nunšeˑw-* AN 'one giving birth' (but probably only possessed): wənunšéˑyəma 'his child-bearer' (Mt 20.20&).

nuntaeˑlənsiˑ- AI 'be humble (in mind)': awéˑn=č máta miˑməntə́tˑink ləkhíkwi-nuntaeˑlənsíˑtˑe 'if someone is not as humble as a little child' (Lk 18.17; Gr. 3.15a); nnuntaeˑlə́nsiˑn 'I feel unworthy (to do it)' (⟨nontyilinsen⟩ Lk 3.16, ⟨nontyrlinsen⟩ Jn 1.27).

▸ Cf. ⟨Nundajélensĭn⟩ 'bashful' (Z. 19; B&A 101 [A. "not feel equal to"]); Mun noˑntayeˑlə́nsəw 'he thinks himself inferior' (dict.).

nuntaeˑlənt- TI(1a) 'think little of': wənuntaeˑlə́ntaməné·ɔ 'they think little of it' (Jn 12.43).

nuntáˑi P 'less, lowly, worse' (Lk 1.48, 1.52, Jn 2.9, Mt. 11.11), PV (1834a); aləwíˑi .. nuntáˑi 'more .. less,' i.e., 'more .. than' (Mt 9.13); tɔləweˑlə́ntamən píˑskeˑk nuntáˑi ɔˑxˑéˑeˑk 'they preferred darkness more than light' (Jn 3.19). ▸ Cf. ⟨Nundawi⟩ 'less' (B&A 101); cf. Mun nóˑntaˑ 'less' (CH, dict.), noˑntaˑwíˑxən 'there is not enough of it' (dict.).

nuntaˑiˑnaˑkˑɔt- II 'be, seem inferior': nuntaˑiˑnáˑkˑɔ lehələmátahpink 'lesser seat' (⟨nwntae nako⟩ Lk 14.9, 14.10; KJV "lowest room").

nuntehəlaˑ- AI(+O) 'lack, be without': táˑmse=áˑ péxu nnuntehəláhəna 'maybe we (excl.) would soon run out' (Mt 25.9); kənuntehəláhəmɔˑp=háč kéku 'did you (pl.) lack anything?' (Lk 22.35); nuntehəláˑtˑe wáin 'when there was no wine for her' (Jn 2.3).

nutahpiˑ- (niˑnutahpiˑ- [Rī+]) AI 'be from the beginning': íka nútahpu 'he's been there from the start' (OA); ná náˑnéke wənutahpíˑneˑp kiˑšˑeˑləmúweˑt 'at that time God existed from the beginning' (⟨Nunu ncki⟩; Jn 1.2).

- niˑnutahpiˑ-: éˑli-niˑnutahpíˑtˑəp 'since he existed from the beginning' (Jn 1.15); ⟨Ninutachpin⟩ 'to be from the beginning' (B&A 97).

nuxkweˑkˑánkan 'my neck' (OA, ME), uxkweˑkˑánkan 'his neck' (OA, ND, LTD ND); uxkweˑkˑánkanink 'his neck (loc.)' (Mk 9.42, Lk 17.2; Gr. 3.13(7)e; LTD ND).

oˑ

óˑ (1) P 'Oh' (exclamation) (Mt 6.30, 11.25, 14.31, etc.), óˑ (Lk 19.42; not in KJV).

óˑ (2) P 'O' (vocative marker) (Mt 9.27, 15.22, 15.28, Lk 13.34, 18.37, Jn 17.5, etc.; KJV "O"). Probably not idiomatic, and perhaps this was intended for óˑ (1) in at least some cases.

-oˑkwenniˑ- AI 'wear around neck': noˑkwénniˑn 'I put it around my neck' (OA); oˑkwénniˑn 'he was wearing it around his neck' (1834a:19.13).

-oˑlahkəniˑm°: see wəlakˑəniˑm-.

oˑlépən AN 'onion' (FW; Gr. 3.1j); oˑlépənak (1834a:17).

-oˑləwalheˑ-: see wəluwalaheˑ-*.

-oꞏlhateꞏnaməwaꞏkꞏan: see wəlaꞏteꞏnaməwáꞏkꞏan.
-oꞏlhateꞏnamiꞏ-: see wəlaꞏteꞏnamiꞏ-.
-oꞏlsətꞏamweꞏɔꞏkꞏan-: see wələstamweꞏɔ́ꞏkꞏan.
-oꞏsksiꞏ-: see wəsksiꞏ-.
-oꞏtkihhwiꞏ-: see wtəkꞏiahwiꞏ-*.
-oꞏtx-: see tɔx·-.
-oꞏtꞏeꞏk°: see wteꞏkaw-.

oꞏtꞏeꞏnaiꞏkꞏeꞏ- (uhoꞏtꞏeꞏnaiꞏkꞏeꞏ- [Rvh+]) AI 'dwell in town': ɔꞏkáꞏi éꞏli-uhoꞏtꞏeꞏnaiꞏkꞏéꞏčꞏiꞏk 'those who lived in the villages around there' (⟨wvwtrnyekrthek⟩ Mk 6.6). ♦ Note: the reduplication presumably has /uh-/ rather than /oꞏh-/.

oꞏtꞏéꞏnay (Gr. 5.52c) IN 'town' (Mt 5.14, Mk 1.38, Jn 11.54); oꞏtꞏéꞏnaya 'towns' (Mt 11.1, Lk 10.1); oꞏtꞏéꞏnink 'in, to a town' (Lk 1.26, Mt 4.5, etc.; Gr. 4.9d), wənči oꞏtꞏéꞏnink 'out of the city' (Jn 19.17; Gr. 6.9j); †nasəlatꞏíꞏi-oꞏtꞏéꞏnink '(from) the city of Nazareth' (Lk 2.4, Mt 3.13), ahpɔꞏníꞏi-oꞏtꞏéꞏnink 'Bread Town' (Jn 7.42); wənči wéꞏmi oꞏtꞏeꞏnaiꞏkéꞏi P+P+P 'out of all the towns' (Mk 6.33; Gr. 4.10d); wtoꞏtꞏéꞏnay 'his city' (Mt 5.35); wtoꞏtꞏéꞏnink 'to his city' (Lk 2.3, 2.4, Mt 2.23, Jn 1.44); táli ntoꞏtꞏeꞏnayənáꞏnink 'in our towns' (Lk 13.26); ktoꞏtꞏeꞏnayəwáꞏink 'in your town' (Lk 10.11); woꞏtꞏeꞏnayəwáꞏunk 'to their city' (Lk 2.39) ~ wtoꞏtꞏeꞏnayəwáꞏink 'to their towns' (Mt 10.5, 10.23); wtoꞏtꞏeꞏnaíꞏliꞏt 'their (obv.) town' (Mt 22.7).

▪ oꞏtꞏeꞏneꞏtꞏə́tꞏink (dim. loc.) 'to a village' (⟨wtrnrtutif⟩ Lk 17.12, Lk 19.30&; ⟨wtrnututif⟩ Lk 24.13, 24.28); íka .. †sameꞏlíꞏi-oꞏtꞏeꞏneꞏtꞏə́tꞏink 'at a village of Samaria' (⟨wtrnrtitif⟩ Lk 9.52).

oꞏtꞏeꞏnayapꞏiꞏ- AI 'be a town-dweller': oꞏtꞏeꞏnayapꞏiꞏlíꞏčꞏi 'town-dweller (obv.)' (Lk 15.15: KJV "a citizen of that country").

oꞏx° 'father': see nóꞏx.

ɔ

ɔhčiꞏpꞏiꞏsꞏiꞏ- (wewčiꞏpꞏiꞏsꞏiꞏ-) AI 'have a convulsion': ɔhčiꞏpꞏiꞏsꞏu 'he has a convulsion, a seizure' (LB).

• wewčiꞏpꞏiꞏsꞏiꞏ-: wewčiꞏpꞏiꞏsꞏíꞏčꞏiꞏk 'those that had fits' (Mt 4.24).

♦ For /ɔhč-/ as the pronunciation of |wàwəč-|, cf. nɔhčiꞏčəwéhəla 'I have spasms in my calves' (OA; Gr. 5.34g).

ɔhčú IN 'hill, mountain' (OA, FW); yóꞏni ɔhčú 'this (inan.) mountain' (Mt 17.20; object of |əl-| TA 'say {so} to'; Goddard 2019: 98); ɔhčúwal 'hills' (Lk 3.5); ɔhčúnk 'in, on (the) hill(s), mountain(s)' (Lk 1.39, Mt 2.18, etc.); lí ɔhčuwiꞏkéꞏi P+P 'into the mountains' (Mt 18.12).

▪ ɔhčú AN 'mountain': wáni ɔhčú 'this (anim.) mountain' (Mt 21.21; object of |əl-| TA 'say {so} to'): ɔhčúwak 'hills' (Lk 23.30); amánki-ɔhčúwa 'the mountains (obv.)' (Lk 23.30).

▸ Cf. Mun wăčəw 'mountain' (CH, JA), pl. wăčəwal 'hills' (JP); ⟨wachtschù⟩ 'mountain' (Z. 2014:151).

ɔhələm° (|wāhləm-|) 'far away' (Gr. §5.2a).

ɔhələmapꞏiꞏ- (|wāhləmapī-|) AI 'be far away': máta ɔhələmapꞏíꞏtꞏe 'when he was not far' (Lk 7.6); néꞏli-ɔhələmapꞏíꞏliꞏt 'while he (obv.) is far off' (Lk 14.32); ɔhələmapꞏiꞏlíꞏtꞏe wtehəwáꞏɔ 'their hearts are far away' (Mt 15.8); takóꞏ kɔhələmapꞏíꞏi 'you (sg.) are not far' (Mk 12.34).

ɔ́hələmi P 'at a distance, far away' (Mk 5.6, 8.3, Lk 10.33, etc.).

- ɔhələmíči (dim.) 'some distance away' (Lk 17.12; Gr. 2.76f).

ɔhələmi·k·e·- AI 'live far way': ɔhələmi·k·é·č·i·k 'those living far away' (Lk 2.32).

ɔhɔ·m(x)kwi·k·i·-(?) AI 'be lame': ɔhɔ·m(x)kwi·k·í·č·i·k(?) 'the lame' (⟨ovomvqekethek⟩ Jn 5.3; KJV "halt"). ▸ Shape uncertain; ⟨v⟩ could be /x/ or an indication of partial voicelessness.

ɔhší·x·ay 'nest' (ND, FW; Gr. 4.9b, 5.71n): ɔhší·x·enk 'in nests' (1834b:26.7; cf. Gr. 4.9b).

ɔhši·x·ayo·wi·- II 'be a nest': ɔhši·x·ayó·wi·k šó·k·əl 'a honeycomb' (*lit.*, 'sugar that is a nest') (Lk 24.42; "honeycomb").

ɔlé·kw IN 'chaff' (Lk 3.17), 'dandruff' (LB).

†ɔlipí·i PN '(of) olive(s)' (Jn 8.1, Lk 19.37, etc.): †ɔlipí·i-ɔhčúnk 'the mount of Olives' (loc.).
  ▪ †ɔlipí·i P (Lk 21.37).

ɔnaxkwí·i P 'at the tip' (Mt 24.32).

ɔnko·m- (ɔɔnko·m- [Ra+], |wankōm-|) TA 'greet, bid farewell': káči awé·n ɔnko·mié·k·e·kw 'greet no one (you pl.)' (Lk 10.4); mɔ́i-ɔnko·mawwá·ɔ 'they were going to greet him' (Mk 9.15); nɔnkó·mukw 'he shakes hands with me' (LB); kɔnkó·məl 'I greet you' (Mt 26.49); kɔnko·məlúhəna 'we greet you' (Mt 27.29); tɔ́nta-ɔnko·má·ne·p 'she greeted her there' (Lk 1.40).
  - ɔɔnko·m-: kɔɔnko·məlúhəmɔ 'I greet you all' (Mt 28.9, Jn 20.19, 20.21, 20.26).

ɔnko·mkwəs·əwá·k·an IN 'greeting' (Lk 1.29, 1.44).

ɔnko·mkwəs·i·- (ɔɔnko·mkwəs·i·- [Ra+]) AI 'be greeted': wínki-ɔɔnko·mkwə́s·əwak 'they always like to be greeted' (Lk 20.46).

ɔnkunsəwá·k·an*: see wɔnkunsəwá·k·an.

ɔnkunsi·- AI 'give greetings': ɔnkunsi·mɔ́·e 'give greetings (you pl.)' (Mt 10.12; KJV "salute it [the house]").

ɔpahkwi·- (ɔɔpahkwi·- [Ra+]) AI 'dress in white': ɔɔpahkúwak 'they were dressed in white' (Acts 1.10).

ɔpahsəní·i PN 'of white stone' (Lk 7.37, Mt 26.7&; KJV "alabaster"; Gr. 5.122g).

ɔwčuh°: see čuh°.

ɔwəl° (|wawəl-|) 'good, fine (plural)' (cf. Gr. 2.17c).

ɔwəlahkɔn- TA 'dress in beautiful clothes': máta tilləkhíkwi-ɔwəlahkɔnk·ó·wəne·p 'he was never clothed as beautifully by it' (Mt 6.29).

ɔwəlahkwi·- (we·wəlahkwi·-) AI 'be dressed up': ɔwə́lahku 'he is dressed up, is well dressed' (LTD LB); ɔwə́lahko·p 'he dressed in fine clothing' (Lk 16.19 [em. ⟨-q⟩]); takó· tilləkhíkwi-ɔwəlahkwí·wəne·p 'he was never dressed so well' (Lk 12.27).
  - we·wəlahkwi·-: lə́nu we·wə́lahkwi·t 'a man wearing fine clothes' (Lk 7.25); the accent is generalized from the stem without IC.

ɔwəla·mhitaw-: see wəla·mhitaw-.

ɔwiákski P 'promiscuously' (1842:12.4). ▸ Cf. wiak- 'abundantly, plenty'.

ɔwisahki·h- TA 'mock, make fun of; torment': mé·či kíši-ɔwisahki·hahtí·t·e 'after they had mocked him' (Mt 27.31&); wɔwisahki·hawwá·ɔ 'they mocked him' (Lk 23.11, Mt 27.29), 'they tormented them' (Mt 22.6); ɔ́·k=č kɔwisahkihkəwá·ɔk 'and they will torment you' (Lk 21.12; KJV "persecute you"); ná=č ɔwisahkí·ha·n 'then he shall be mocked (sbd.)' (Lk 18.32; Gr. 5.36m).

ɔwši·ləntamwe·hɔ·ltó·p·ani·k: see wši·ləntamwe·hɔ·l-.

ɔxpahəla·- AI 'come to one's senses, regain consciousness, return to a normal mental state' (LTD): ɔxpáhəla "come to your right mind" (LB); mé·či ɔxpahəlá·t·e 'after he came to his senses' (Lk 15.17). ▸ Cf. Mun waxpáhle·w 'he woke up' (EJo).

ɔ·

†ɔ·e·lənt- (TI(1a)) TI-O 'be convinced' (with neg. 'doubt'): †ɔ·e·ləntamo·kw 'be convinced (you pl.)' (Jn 7.24); káči †ɔ·e·ləntamó·he·kw 'do not be convinced (you pl.)' (Jn 7.24; KJV "judge"); takó· †ɔ·e·ləntamó·wi 'he doubted' (Mk 15.44); máta †ɔ·e·ləntamo·wí·p·ani·k 'they doubted' (Mt 28.17); ná=č †nɔ·e·ləntamáne·n 'then we will be convinced' (Jn 14.8).

†ɔ·e·ləntamawá·k·an IN 'conviction' (Jn 7.24).

ɔ·í·k·an IN 'backbone' (1834a:12, ME); ɔ·wí·k·an 'his backbone' (|ɔ·ʷi·| OA, ME).

ɔ́·k P 'and, also, or': 'and' (Jn 1.9, 1.14, 1.16, Lk 1.7, etc.), 'along with' (Mk 10.46); ɔ́·k tá·mse 'or else' (Lk 16.13; KJV "or else"); 'or' (with negative) (Mt 17.21, Jn 16.3).

ɔ·ka·º (|wāhkā-|), ɔ·ke·º (|wāhkē-|) 'around, in a (whole or partial) circle' (Gr. §5.2a).

ɔ·ká·i P 'around' (Lk 1.65, 2.9, Jn 5.2, Mk 6.6, 9.14, etc.); lí ɔ·ká·i 'around the edge' (Mk 2.21).

ɔ·ka·me·nxkh- TI(1a) 'make a fence around': wɔ·ka·me·nxkhámən 'and he made a fence around them (sbd.)' (Mt 21.33).

ɔ·ka·š- TA 'circumcise': pi·laéčəč=á· ɔ·ka·š·únte 'if a boy would be circumcised ..' (Jn 7.23); ɔ·ka·š·á·ne·p 'he was circumcised' (Lk 2.21); kɔ·ka·š·áwwa 'you (pl.) circumcise him' (Jn 7.22); mói-ɔ·ka·š·awwá·ɔl 'they were going to circumcise him' (Lk 1.59).

ɔ·ka·š·a·ɔ́·k·an N 'the (practice of) circumcision' (Jn 7.22).

ɔ·ka·x·we·- AI+O 'walk around': wɔ·ka·x·wé·na 'he walked around him' (Lk 10.31).

ɔ·ke·kaw- TA — ɔ·ke·k- TI(1a) 'surround'.

▪ ɔ·ke·kaw- (TA): é·li- xé·li awé·n -ɔ·ké·kaɔ·t 'since many people surrounded him' (Lk 19.3); wɔ·ke·kaɔwwá·ɔ 'they came around him' (Jn 10.24); kɔ·ke·ká·k·o·k 'they surround you' (Lk 19.43); kəmhɔkw wɔ·ke·ka·k·o·né·ɔ 'a cloud surrounded them (sbd.)' (Lk 9.34).

▪ ɔ·ke·k- (TI): énta-=á· -ɔ·ke·kamíhti·t e·ləwé·li·t 'where they would circumscribe what he (obv.) said' (Mt 22.15; KJV "how they might entangle him in his talk"); táli-ɔ·ke·kaməné·ɔ †nči·ló·sələm 'that they are surrounding Jerusalem' (Lk 21.20).

ɔ·k(·)º (|wāk-|) 'bend'.

ɔ·khake·- AI 'be stooped, bent over': áhi-ɔ·kháke·p 'she was severely bent over' (Lk 13.11).

ɔ·khake·x·ən- II 'be a crooked road': énta-ɔ·khaké·x·ink 'the crooked roads' (Lk 3.5).

ɔ́·k·wəs (V, FW; Gr. 5.48d) AN 'fox' (Lk 13.32); ɔ́·kwsak 'foxes' (Mt 8.20, 1834b:26.7).

ɔ·lº (|wāl-|) 'hole, concave' (Gr. §5.2a).

ɔ·lahkat·- (|wālakat-|) II 'be a hole': ɔ́·lahkat 'it is a hole' (OA; Gr. 2.7d).

ɔ́·lakw IN 'hole', 'cave' (V, OA, ME); lí ɔ́·lahkunk 'into a pit' (Lk 14.5; Gr. 6.9h).

†ɔ·lhánti 'grave': wɔ·lhántink 'in his grave' (⟨waluntif⟩ 1834b:14.9). Cf. Munsee wa·lhá·ntəy 'cellar, storage pit'; wa·lha·ntəyámənk 'in his tomb' (Halfmoon 1852:15).

ɔ·lhe·- AI 'dig a hole': ɔ́·lhe·w 'he digs a hole' (V; Gr. 5.70e); ná=nə́ la·mamé·nxke tə́nta-ɔ́·lhe·n 'inside that fence he dug a hole ' (Mt 21.33).

ɔ́·lpe·kw (-ɔ·lpe·k·əm-) IN 'well' (⟨olprq⟩ Jn 4.11, ⟨wolprq⟩ Jn 4.12); ɔ·lpé·k·unk (⟨walprkwf⟩ Jn 4.6). Note: the spellings with ⟨w-⟩ were influenced by the possessed form, which occurs first.

• -ɔ·lpe·k·əm-: wɔ·lpé·k·əm 'his well' (⟨walprkum⟩ Jn 4.6).

†ɔ·ɔhšé·i P: 'bits and pieces(?)' (⟨oojri⟩ 1842:19.4; ⟨ojri⟩ 1834b:4.2). ▶ Cf. ɔhše·- in ⟨òhshèxahko⟩ 'woodchips' (LTD), sg. ⟨ɔhšáxakw⟩ (V; presumably incorrectly constructed from the plural, for expected ɔhšé·x·akw 'chip') (with |-axakw| 'wood').

ɔ́·ɔl IN 'egg' (OA, LB; Lk 11.12).

ɔ·phémpəs 'white cloth': ɔ·phémpsink 'in a white cloth' (⟨opvcmsif⟩ 1834b:36.3).

ɔ·psi·- (|wāpəsī-|; |wawāpəsī-| [Ra+], we·ɔ·psi·-) AI — ɔ·p·e·- II 'be white'.
- ɔ·psi·- (AI): ɔ́·psu 'he is white' (LB; Gr. 2.15h).
- we·ɔ·psi·-: we·ɔ́·psi·t 'white person' (1842:23.5, 23.6, 23.7); yó·l we·ɔ·psi·lí·č·i 'this white person (obv.)' (1834a:19.17). ♦ Presumably back-formed from the regularly reduplicated plural we·ɔ·psí·č·i·k; Heckewelder (1819:130) has the representative singular ⟨Wapsid Lenape⟩ "white people".
- ɔ·p·e·- (II): ɔ́·p·e· 'it's white' (AD); ɔ·p·é·ɔ málahši kó·n 'they were white like snow' (1834b:37.1).

ɔ·p·aláne AN 'bald eagle': ɔ·p·alané·ɔk 'bald eagles' (Lk 17.37, Mt 24.28; KJV "eagles").
▶ Cf. ⟨woapaláñe⟩ "bald Eagle" (Z. 63); ɔ·p·alánie 'bald eagle' (LTD ND).

ɔ·p·an- (|wāpan|; Gr. 5.10o, 5.17g) II 'be day, dawn': ɔ́·p·an 'it was dawn' (Mk 6.48); mé·či ɔ·p·ánke 'the next day' (Lk 6.13), 'after dawn' (Jn 21.4: KJV "when the morning was now come"), sé·ki-ɔ́·p·ank 'during the morning' (Mt 27.19); lápi ɔ·p·ánke 'the next day' (Jn 1.29, 6.22), íkali ɔ·p·ánke kwət·i kí·škwe 'one day later' (Lk 13.32); énta- lápi -ɔ́·p·ank 'the next day' (V).

ɔ́·p·askw IN 'corn husks' (Gr. 2.4b); ɔ́·pskɔl 'husks' (1834b:28.9).

ɔ·p·a·lo·kwé·p·ia·s 'White-Hat(-Wearer)' (1834a:1). Presumably a nickname of Blanchard.

ɔ·p·əle·x·i·n- AI — ɔ·p·əle·x·ən- II 'shine, shine white'.
- ɔ·p·əle·x·i·n- (AI): ɔ·p·əle·x·í·no·k 'they were shiny-white' (Jn 20.12).
- ɔ·p·əle·x·ən- (II): é·k·wi·t ləkhíkwi-ɔ·p·əlé·x·ən kó·nink 'his clothing shone as white as snow' (Mt 28.3); xkwíči wə́nči-ɔ·p·əlé·x·ənu 'they are solid white on the outside' (Mt 23.27); ɔ·p·əlé·x·ink '(which was) shiny-white' (Mk 16.5).

ɔ·p·ihəla·- II 'turn white': mé·či álǝmi-ɔ·p·ihəlé·ɔ 'they have already turned white' (Jn 4.35).

ɔ·p·i·t- TI(2) 'make white': é·li- máta·á́ -káski- náxpəne kwət·i mí·laxk -ɔ·p·i·tó·wan 'as you would not be able to make even one hair white' (Mt 5.36; Gr. 4.99h).

ɔ·s·° (1) (|wās-|) 'light' (Gr. §5.2a).

ɔ·s·° (2) 'across, on the other side' (historically /awas·-/, so the /ɔ·/ is not subject to shortening): ɔ·s·í·i P 'on the other side' (V, OA, ME; 1834b:39.3); ɔ·sahtáne P 'over the hill' (OA).

ɔ·s·áhkame P '(to, in) heaven' (Lk 2.13, 2.15, Mt 3.17, Jn 3.12, etc.): ⟨osavkumi⟩ 2x (pp. 12-13), ⟨osavkumc⟩ 9x, ⟨osavkamc⟩ 60x. ♦ When effectively used as a PN (Mt 5.3, 5.10, 5.19 2x, 5.20, 8.11; pp. 39-50), perhaps to be emended to ɔ·s·ahkame·í·i PN. ♦ A partly naturalized loan from Mun awasáhkame·(w), *lit.*, 'on the other side of the sky'; cf. ɔ·shákame (LTD ND).

ɔ·s·ahkame·í·i PN 'of heaven' (Gr. 5.124b): ɔ·s·ahkame·í·i-sa·k·i·ma·ɔ́·k·an 'kingdom of heaven' (Mt 3.2, etc.), (loc.) ɔ·s·ahkame·í·i-sa·k·i·ma·ɔ́·k·anink (Mt 13.52, etc.); mayá·i-ɔ·s·ahkame·í·i-ahpó·n 'the true bread of heaven' (Jn 6.32); ɔ·s·ahkame·í·i-ehalo·ká·lənt 'angel (*lit.*, 'heavenly messenger') (Jn 12.29).
- ɔ·s·ahkame·í·i P (Gr. 5.126b): sa·k·i·ma·ɔ́·k·an ɔ·s·ahkame·í·i 'the kingdom of heaven' (Mt 4.17); nó·x ɔ·s·ahkame·í·i 'my father in heaven' (Mt 7.21), ɔ·s·ahkame·í·i ná nó·x 'my heavenly father' (Mt 18.35).

ɔ·s·əle·- II 'be a light': ɔ́·s·əle· 'there is a light' (OA); wə́nči- wé·mi -wə́li-ɔ́·s·əle·k 'so that it gives a nice light everywhere' (Mt 5.15).

ɔ·s·əle·ní·k·an AN 'candle, lamp, lantern': ɔ·s·əle·ní·k·an ' lantern' (Jn 5.35); ɔ·s·əle·ní·k·ana 'candle(s) (obv.)' (Mt 5.15, Lk 15.8, Mk 14.43&); ɔ·s·əle·ní·k·ana 'lamps (obv.)' (Mt 25.3); nɔ·s·əle·ni·k·anəná·nak 'our lamps' (Mt 25.8); wɔ·s·əle·ni·k·anəwá·ɔ 'their lamps' (Mt 25.1, 25.7).

▪ ɔ·s·əle·nı́·k·an IN 'light; wick': kwe·šhaté·i·k ɔ·s·əle·nı́·k·an 'smoking wick' (Mt 12.20; KJV "smoking flax," the wick of an oil lamp); kɔ·s·əle·ni·k·anúwa 'your (pl.) light' (Mt 5.16).

♦ The Munsee cognate wa·sŏle·nı́·kan AN 'light, lamp' was recorded by Wolley (1902:63) in 1678-1680 as ⟨Woss-ra-neck⟩ 'white-pine candle' (i.e., ⟨-neek⟩, with voiceless final syllable).

ɔ·s·əle·x·i·n- AI 'shine' — ɔ·s·əle·x·ən- II 'shine, be bright'.

▪ ɔ·s·əle·x·i·n- (AI): ná=č né·k šaxahka·wsí·č·i·k wɔ·s·əle·x·i·nəné·ɔ 'then the righteous shall shine' (Mt 13.43).

▪ ɔ·s·əle·x·ən- (II): ɔ·s·əlé·x·ənu 'they shone' (Lk 24.4).

ɔ·tae·i·- II 'bloom': ɔ·taé·yu 'it blooms' (Mk 4.28; ME, LTD ND).

ó·tae·s IN (AN) 'flower'; ɔ·taé·s·al 'flowers' (Mt 6.28, then construed as animate), ɔ·taé·s·a (Lk 12.27, construed as inanimate).

▸ Cf. ⟨Woa ta wes⟩ 'a flower' (SB2:41), ⟨Woa ta wes sall⟩ 'flowers' (SB2:70).

♦ Later animate: ó·tae·s AN 'flower' (OA, ME, FW, AP, LTD ND), ɔ·taé·s·ak (V, OA, ME, FW, LB, LTD).

ɔ·wəlankunsi·-: see wəlankunsi·-.

ɔ·wié·i P 'later on' (Lk 18.4), ⟨ɔ·wiyé·⟩ (V; presumably for ɔ·wié·e); 'by and by' (Jn 13.7, KJV "hereafter"; Jn 13.36, KJV "afterwards").

ɔ·wtámi PV 'being slow in, to' (Gr. 5.27g, 5.129ff): é·li·ɔ·wtámi-pəna·eləntamíhti·t 'as they were slow in thought' (Mk 6.52). ▸ Cf. ɔ·wtámsu 'is slow, delays' (LTD LB); these forms are from |wətamī| with |Rā+| and narrowed meaning; cf. wé·t·ami (with IC) below.

ɔ·x·e(·)º (|wāxē-|) 'light, shine' (Gr. §5.2a).

ɔ·x·ehəla·- II 'shine': ɔ·x·éhəle· 'it shines' (Mt 24.27); ehələkhíkwi·=hánkw .. yú -táli·ɔ·x·éhəla·k 'as brightly as it shines here' (Lk 17.24).

ɔ·x·e·e·- (|wāxēyē-|) II 'be light, be lit, be illuminated': ɔ·x·é·e· 'it is lit' (Mt 6.22 [2x]); tá=á· ɔ·x·e·é·i 'there will be no light' (Mt 24.29); é·li·ɔ·x·é·e·k 'because it is light' (Jn 11.9); énta·ɔ·x·é·e·k 'light' (*lit.*, 'where it was light') (Jn 3.20).

▪ ɔ·x·é·e·k (-ɔ·x·e·e·k·əm-) IN 'light' (a lexicalized II participle) (Jn 1.5, 1.7, 1.8, 1.9, 3.20, etc.); AN: ɔ·x·é·e·k tɔmi·mánsəma 'the children of light' (Lk 16.8).

• -ɔ·x·e·e·k·əm-: kɔ·x·e·é·k·əm 'your light' (Mt 6.23).

ɔ·x·e·e·k·ami·- AI 'have light' (Gr. 5.117d): wénči·=č -ɔ·x·e·e·k·amíe·kw 'so that you (pl.) shall have light' (Jn 12.36).

ɔ·x·e·kamaw- TA 'give light to, shine a light for': ɔ·x·e·kamáɔ·t 'which shines a light for them' (Jn 1.9); wénči·ɔ·x·e·kamáɔ·t 'by which he gave light to them' (Lk 1.79); énta·ɔ·x·e·kamá·k·we·kw wənči 'in the light he cast on you (pl.)' (Jn 5.35).

ɔ·x·e·kaw- TA 'give light to' — ɔ·x·e·k- TI(1a) 'light up'.

▪ ɔ·x·e·kaw- (TA): ɔ·x·e·kaɔ́·ɔk=č 'they will be given light' (Lk 2.32); yó·ni pí·ske·k máta wɔ·x·e·ka·k·ó·wəne·p 'the darkness did not give light to them' (Jn 1.5 [inverse object must be sentient]; cf. KJV "the darkness comprehended it not," RSV "has not overcome it").

▪ ɔ·x·e·k- (TI): ki·ló·wa ɔ·x·é·kame·kw entalá·wsink 'you (pl.) are what lights up the world' (Mt 5.14; *lit.*, 'you (are) you who light (it)'); yúh nɔ·x·é·kamən entalá·wsink 'I light this world' (Jn 8.12); ná=ní ɔ·x·é·e·k wɔ·x·é·kamən énta-pí·ske·k 'that was the light that lit up the darkness' (Jn 1.5).

p

pahk° (|pak-|) 'hit' (Gr. §5.2a).

pahkam- (-pak·am-, pəpahkam- [Rə̀+]) TA 'hit, hit with (thrown object), throw (object) at' — pahkant- (-pak·ant-) TI 'strike' (Gr. 3.20a, 5.12k).

▪ pahkam- (TA): pahkám 'hit him, them (you sg.)' (Gr. 2.62a); ahsə́n=č pahkáma· 'she is to have stones (*lit.*, a stone) thrown at her' (Jn 8.5); awé·n=háč ktə́li-pahkámko·n 'who is it that hit you (sg.)?' (Lk 22.64; Gr. 4.50s).

• -pak·am-: hítami=č ahsə́n kpák·ama 'you (sg.) should be the first to throw a stone at her' (Jn 8.7); pɔk·amá·ɔ 'he struck him' (Jn 18.22); pɔ́k·ama·n 'he struck him with it' (Jn 18.10; Gr. 3.14c).

• pəpahkam- TA 'beat', TA+O 'throw O2 at': áhi=č pəpahkáma· he shall be severely beaten' (Lk 12.47); ehalo·ka·lə́nči·k a·yáhi-pəpahkámat ahsə́na 'you (sg.) who formerly threw stones at messengers' (Mt 23.37); ehalo·ka·lə́nči a·yáhi-pəpahkáma·t ahsə́na 'who formerly threw stones at messengers' (with a vocative noun; Lk 13.34); áləmi-pəpahkamá·t·e 'if he starts beating (them)' (Mt 24.49); pupahkamawwá·ɔ 'they beat him' (Lk 10.30, Lk 20.10&, etc.), ahsə́na pupahkamawwá·ɔ 'they threw stones at him' (Mk 12.4&); pupahkama·né·ɔ wi·lí·li·t 'they struck him on the head with it' (Mt 27.30).

▪ -pak·ant- (TI): pɔk·ántamən wtó·lhay 'he struck his chest' (Lk 18.13); pɔk·antamə·né·ɔ wto·lháyəwa 'they struck their chests' (Lk 23.48).

pahkánči (-pak·ánči, pe·k·ánči; Gr. 5.129gg) PV 'perfectly, completely, fully': pahkánči-lə́s·i·kw 'be perfect (you pl.)' (Mt 5.48); pahkánči-lé·p 'it came true' (Mt 2.15; cf. Mt 2.17), mé·či pahkánči-lé·w 'it has now been fulfilled' (Jn 3.29), 'it has come true' (Lk 4.21), pahkánči=č lé·w 'it shall come true' (Lk 1.45); wə́nči-pahkánči-lé·k .. e·ləwé·t·əp 'so that it would happen exactly as he said (Mt 1.22); wénči-=č -pahkánči-wəle·lə́ntame·kw 'what will make you (pl.) utterly joyful' (Jn 16.24).

• -pak·ánči: é·li né·skɔ mpak·ánči-tpəskwilahtá·i 'as my time has not yet fully come' (Jn 7.8).

• pe·k·ánči: pe·k·ánči-ləs·í·t·e wé·mi 'when he completed everything' (Lk 2.39), pe·k·ánči-ma·ehúnte sɔ́·čəlak 'after the whole band of soldiers was assembled' (Mt 27.27).

▪ pahkánči P: kxántki pahkánči 'eventually completely' (Jn 8.9).

pahkanči·xt- (-pak·anči·xt-) TI(2) 'complete': pahkančí·xto·kw 'complete them (you pl.)' (Mt 23.32); ntə́li-=á· -pahkančí·xto·n '(that I would) fulfill it' (Mt 5.17).

• -pak·anči·xt-: pɔk·ančí·xto·n nehəni·k·a·na·pto·né·t·əp 'he fulfills his prophecy' (Mt 13.14).

pahkante·nhe·- AI 'pay off a debt': kə́nč pahkante·nhé·ane 'until you (sg.) paid completely' (Mt 5.26, Lk 12.59); sháki pahkante·nhé·t·e 'until he completely paid off his debt' (Mt 18.34).

pahkanthate·- II 'be fulfilled': wénči-=č no·le·ləntaməwá·k·an .. -pahkantháte·k 'so that my joy will be fulfilled' (Jn 17.13).

pahki·l- (-pak·i·l-, pe·k·i·l-) TA — pahki·t- (-pak·i·t-, pe·k·i·t-) TI(2) 'throw down, throw away, cast aside, discard; send away, divorce' (Gr. 5.12c).

▪ pahki·l- (TA): awé·n pahki·lá·t·e wi·č·e·ɔ́·č·i 'if anyone divorces his wife' (Lk 16.18); pahki·lí·t·e 'when I am dismissed' (Lk 16.4); ɔ́·k=á· máta kkáski-pahki·la·íwwa 'and you (pl.) would not be able to discard them' (Jn 10.35).

• -pak·i·l-: kɔ́na pɔk·i·lá·ɔ wi·č·e·ɔ́·č·i 'he is free to divorce his wife' (Mt 19.7); pɔk·i·lawwá·ɔ 'they discarded them' (Mt 13.48); pɔk·í·la·n wi·č·e·ɔ́·č·i 'that he divorce his wife (sbd.)' (Mt 19.3).

- pe·k·i·l-: pe·k·í·lənt 'who was divorced' (Lk 16.18, Mt 19.9).
▪ pahki·t- (TI): nə́ni=á· wə́nči- .. -pahki·t·unk 'that's why .. it should be thrown away' (Mt 18.8); tépi-=á· šúkw -pahkí·t·o·n 'it would only be fit to be thrown away' (Lk 14.35).
- -pak·i·t-: kpak·í·t·o·n=č 'you must throw it away' (Mt 5.29, 5.30, 18.9); pɔk·í·t·o·n=č 'he will discard it' (Jn 15.2); ná pɔk·i·t·o·né·ɔ e·k·wíhti·t 'then they threw down their garments' (Mk 10.50).
- pe·k·i·t-: pe·k·i·t·úhti·t 'that they cast aside' (Lk 20.17).
▪ pahki·lti- AI (recip.) 'divorce each other': pahki·ltúwak 'they got divorced' (LB).

pahki·lkwəs·i- AI 'be rejected, be thrown out': ɔ́·k=č pahki·lkwə́s·u 'and he shall be rejected' (Lk 17.25).

pahki·t·a·s·i- II 'be wasted': nə́ni mɔ́ni éntxi-pahki·t·á·s·i·k 'that is how much money was wasted' (1834b:13.4).

pahki·t·a·t·amaw- (-pak·i·t·a·t·amaw-) TA(+O) 'forgive, forgive for O2': pahki·t·á·t·amaw 'forgive them (you sg.)' (Lk 23.34); pahki·t·a·t·amɔ́·me 'forgive him (you sg.)' (Lk 17.3, 17.4; Gr. 4.116f); pahki·t·a·t·amáɔ·n=č 'it ('sins', sg.) will be forgiven them' (Jn 20.23); tá=á· pahki·t·a·t·amaɔ́·wən 'it will not be forgiven them' (Jn 20.23); pahki·t·a·t·amo·mɔ́·e 'forgive them (you pl.)' (Mk 11.25; Gr. 4.116h); pahki·t·a·t·amaɔ́t·e 'if you (sg.) forgive them (for it)' (Mt 6.14, Lk 6.37); máta pahki·t·a·t·amaɔ·ɔ́t·e awé·n 'if you (sg.) do not forgive someone for it' (Mt 6.15; Gr. 4.97c).
- -pak·i·t·a·t·amaw-: ké·pe=č kpak·i·t·a·t·amá·k·e 'you (sg.) too will be forgiven' (Lk 6.37); mé·či mpak·i·t·a·t·amáɔ·n 'I have forgiven her' (Lk 7.47 [2x]); kpak·i·t·a·t·amá·k·o·n=č kčana·wsəwá·k·an 'he will forgive your misdeeds for you' (Mt 6.14); kpak·i·t·a·t·amó·lənə·p wé·mi nə́ ktəle·khamwe·ɔ́·k·an 'I forgave you (sg.) all of your debt' (Mt 18.32; Gr. 4.71j).

pahki·t·a·t·ama·ohtəwá·k·an (Gr. 5.114i) IN 'forgiveness' (Lk 1.77).

pahki·t·a·t·ama·s·i- (-pak·i·t·a·t·ama·s·i-, pe·k·i·t·a·t·ama·s·i-; Gr. 5.103c) AI+O 'forgive': awé·n=háč=á· káski-pahki·t·a·t·amá·s·u mahta·wsəwá·k·an 'who would be able to forgive sin?' (Mk 2.7).
- -pak·i·t·a·t·ama·s·i-: pɔk·i·t·a·t·amá·s·i·n mahta·wsəwá·k·an 'that he forgive sins (sbd.)' (Mk 2.10).
- pe·k·i·t·a·t·ama·s·i-: pe·k·i·t·a·t·amá·s·i·t mahta·wsəwá·k·an 'who forgives sins' (Lk 7.49).

pahki·t·e·ləntamaw- TA+O 'forgive for O2, forgive O2 for': pahki·t·e·ləntamaí·ne·n nčana·wsəwa·k·anə́na 'forgive our misdeeds for us' (Mt 6.12, Lk 11.4).

pahki·t·e·lənta·s·i- II 'be forgiven' (Gr. 5.105m): mahta·wsəwá·k·an káski-=č -pahki·t·e·ləntá·s·u 'sin will be able to be forgiven' (Mt 12.31).

-pahɔthitehəmaw-: see phɔthitehəmaw-.

pahs° (|pas-|) 'split' (Gr. §5.2a); irregular reduplication pe·pahs°.

pahsa·e·- II 'be a hollow, a valley': pahsá·e· 'there's a hollow' (FW); pahsá·e·k 'valley' (ND; for ə́nta-pahsá·e·k); éntxi-pahsá·e·k 'every valley' (⟨pasyrk⟩ Lk 3.5).

pahsən- (-pas·ən-) TI(1b) 'divide in half, tear in two': ntə́li-=á· -pahsə́nəmən 'that I divide it (in two)' (⟨pasinamun⟩ Lk 12.14).
- -pas·ən-: mpas·ə́nəmən 'I tore it in two' (LB).

pahsənəmaw- (pe·pahsənəmaw- [|Rēh+| REP, irreg.]) TA+O 'divide O2 for': ná pwe·pahsənəmáɔ·n 'then he divided it up for them' (Lk 15.12).

pahsihəla·- (pe·pahsihəla·- [|Rēh+| REP, irreg.]) AI 'be divided, separated': pe·pahsihəlé·ok=č 'they will be divided from each other' (Lk 12.52; ⟨-oh⟩ for ⟨-okh⟩);
tə́li-=č -pe·pahsihəla·né·ɔ 'so that they will be divided from each other' (Lk 12.51).

pahsí·i P 'half' (⟨pase⟩ Mk 6.23, ⟨pavse⟩ Lk 12.13, ⟨pavsei⟩ Lk 19.8).
pahsi·k·ihəla·- II 'split into halves': hémpəs pahsi·k·íhəle· 'the cloth split in two lengthwise' (⟨pasekevlr⟩ Mt 27.51).
pahsuk·wi·- (-paskwi·-, |pasəkwī-|) AI 'get up, stand up, arise': pahsúk·wi· 'he got up' (⟨paswqe⟩ Mt 9.19, Jn 13.4); pahsúk·wi·p 'he stood up' (⟨paswkwep⟩ Lk 4.16, Jn 11.29); pahsuk·wí·ɔk 'they got up' (Mk 10.50), 'they rise up' (Mt 24.11); pahsúk·wi·l 'get up (you sg.)' (⟨Paswqel⟩ Jn 5.8, ⟨paswkwel⟩ Lk 6.8); pahsúk·wi·kw 'get up (you pl.)' (⟨pavswqeq⟩ Mk 10.49, Jn 14.31; ⟨Paswqeq⟩ Mk 14.42); pahsuk·wí·t·e 'when he gets up' (⟨pavswqetc⟩ Lk 13.25).
 • -paskwi·-: ná póskwi·n 'then he got up' (Lk 5.28, 10.25, 15.20, etc.); ná pɔskwi·né·ɔ 'then they stood up' (Lk 4.29, 24.33).
pahsuwe·- (-pas·əwe·-) AI(+O) 'deny': pahsúwe· 'he denied it' (Lk 22.56-57&); máta pahsəwé·i·p 'he did not deny (that ..)' (⟨paswrep⟩ Jn 1.20); kə́nč naxə́n kíši-pahsəwé·ane nhák·ay 'until you (sg.) have denied me three times' (⟨keji pavswranc⟩ Jn 13.38, Lk 22.34); awé·n máta pahsəwé·k·we nhák·ay 'if anyone does not deny me' (⟨paswrqc⟩ Mt 10.32; Gr. 4.95l).
 • -pas·əwe·-: né·pe=č mpás·əwe·n hók·ay 'I will deny him' (⟨np-⟩ Mt 10.33); naxə́n=č kpás·əwe·n nhák·ay 'you will deny me three times' (Mk 14.30); tá=á· mpas·əwé·wən 'I will not deny him' (⟨np-⟩ Mt 10.32). ► Cf. Mun păsə́we·w 'denies'; LTD 'not tell the truth'.
†páilat 'Pilate' (Lk 3.1, Jn 18.29, 18.31, etc.); †pailát·a (Lk 13.1), "Pontius" †pailát·a (Mt 27.2); †pailát·ink 'to Pilate' (Lk 23.11, Mt 27.62).
páint (~ páent; -paintəm-) IN 'cup': páint (OA), páent (FF); paíntal 'cups' (Mk 7.4), paínta (LB); nə́ paíntink 'in the cup' (Jn 18.11; for 'from the cup'), paéntink (FF); kpaintəwá·ɔ 'your (pl.) cups' (Mt 23.25).
 • -paintəm-: kpaíntəm 'your cup' (Mt 23.26); pɔíntəm 'his cup' (1842:16.2); kpaintəməwá·ɔ 'your (pl.) cups' (Lk 11.39). ► Cf. páint AN (ME). ♦ A loanword from English *pint*.
pai·teh- (-pawhiteh-, |pawəhteh-|; Gr. 5.18h) TI(1a) 'thresh, brush off': pai·téha 'dust it off (you sg.)' (ME); énta-pai·téhank 'where he threshes it' (Lk 3.17).
 • -pawhiteh-: mpawhitehəmáne·n 'we shake it off' (Lk 10.11).
pai·te·xt- TI(2) 'knock off (dust)': pai·te·xto·mó·e púnkw 'knock the dust off (from your feet) (you pl.)' (Mt 10.14; Gr. 4.116n).
pak°, pak·° (|pàk-|) 'flat' (Gr. §5.2a).
pákahsən IN 'flat stone'; pakahsə́na 'flat stones' (1842:10.6).
pakče·e·- II 'be flat': ní·š·a pakče·é·k·i ahsə́nal 'two flat stones' (1834b:19.13).
pakhake·e·- (|pàkahkēyē-|) II 'be flat land': énta-pakhaké·e·k 'the plain' (Lk 6.17).
paksk- (pɔpaksk- [Rə̀+]; cf. Gr. 5.12y) TI(1a) 'flatten (by foot)': pupakskámən=č kí·l 'he shall flatten your head' (1842:8.1).
pak·ələnče·x·i·n- AI 'use the palm of the hand (in striking)': pak·ələnčé·x·i·n 'using the palm of his hand' (Jn 18.22); pak·ələnče·x·í·no·k 'using the palms of their hands' (Mk 14.65).
palalo·ka·s·i·- (pe·lalo·ka·s·i·-, pihpalalo·ka·s·i·- [Rih+], pehpalalo·ka·s·i·- [Rih+; IC]) AI 'be a criminal': é·li-palalo·ka·s·í·t·əp 'because he had been a criminal' (Lk 23.25); tə́li-palalo·ká·s·i·n 'that he was a criminal' (Mt 27.16).
 • pe·lalo·ka·s·i·-: ní·š·a pe·lalo·ka·s·i·tpáni·k 'two criminals' (⟨-ke-⟩; Lk 23.32).
 • pihpalalo·ka·s·i·-: wé·mi éntxi-pihpalalo·ka·s·i·li·č·i 'all who were criminals (obv.)' (Mt 13.41).
 • pehpalalo·ka·s·i·-: pehpalalo·ká·s·i·t 'criminal' (Lk 23.39; Gr. 5.65c); pehpalalo·ka·s·i·li·tpáni 'who (obv.) had been criminals' (Lk 23.33&; Gr. 4.75u).

- pehpalalo·ká·s·i·t (lexicalized participle): pehpalalo·ka·s·i·t·i·ké·i P 'among the criminals' (Mk 15.28; Gr. 4.10g, 5.65c).
palap·i·-* (-palahpi·-) AI+O 'be innocent of, escape (an event)': mpálahpi·n 'I am innocent of it' (Mt 27.24); kpalahpi·né·ɔ 'that you (pl.) escape it' (Lk 21.36).
  ▸ Cf. ⟨pallachpîn⟩ 'innocent' (Z. 103), with the stem generalized from prefixed forms.
palé·naxk P 'five' (Lk 1.24, 3.1, Jn 4.18, 5.2, Lk 16.28, etc.).
palí P 'away': palí á·l 'Get away!' (⟨Pali al⟩; Mt 4.10); allegro prevocalic form of /palí·i/.
palihəwe·- AI 'destroy (people)': tóli-=á· -palíhəwe·n '(that he would) destroy (people)' (Jn 10.10; cf. Gr. 5.101).
pali·h- (pe·li·h-; pehpali·h- [Rih+; IC]) TA — pali·t- (pe·li·t-) TI(2) 'destroy' (Gr. 5.12a).
  - pali·h- (TA): tá=á· téxi kéku kpalihko·húmɔ 'nothing at all will destroy you (pl.)' (Lk 10.19; Gr. 4.85a); kəmái-pali·híhəna 'you come and destroy us' (Mk 1.24); tá=á· pɔlihko·wəné·ɔ 'it will not cause them to perish' (Mk 16.18).
  • pe·li·h-: pe·líhkɔn 'which destroys you (sg.)' (1842:22.6); pe·lihkɔ́nkwi·k 'those that destroy us' (Lk 1.71).
  • pehpali·h-: pehpalíhkuk wé·mi awé·n 'what destroys everyone' (⟨pepalexkwk⟩ 1834a:21.36).
  - pali·t- (TI): palí·to·kw yó·ni pa·tamwe·i·k·á·ɔn 'destroy this temple (you pl.)' (Jn 2.19); kpali·to·né·ɔ 'you (pl.) destroy it' (Mt 15.6); mpalí·to·n=č yú pa·tamwe·i·k·á·ɔn 'I shall destroy this temple' (Mk 14.58); tóləmi-pali·tó·nal yó·li skí·kɔl 'it begins to destroy this grass' (1834a:17; Gr. 3.22c); énta-=á· máta mo·x·wé·s·ak -pali·túhti·t 'where insects would not destroy them' (Mt 6.20); ké·t·a-palí·taɔn 'you (sg.) who were going to destroy it' (Mk 15.29); mé·či wé·mi pali·tá·k·we 'after he had squandered everything' (Lk 15.14; no IC).
  • pe·li·t-: pe·lí·ta·kw 'the one who squandered it' (Lk 15.30).
palí·i P (Gr. 5.29f) 'away, elsewhere, in or to another place' (Lk 1.25, Mt 2.12, Lk 4.13, etc.). ♦ (apparently with a complement) palí·i ennínke .. yú entala·wsí·č·i·k 'when he removed it from mankind' (Lk 1.25). ♦ (idiom) palí·i lé·- 'be destroyed': lí·=č xɔləníti palí·i -lé· 'that it very soon will be destroyed' (Lk 21.20 [KJV "the desolation thereof is nigh"]); áhi-palí·i lé· 'it was utterly destroyed' (Mt 7.27); wénči-=hánkw máta palí·i -lé·k 'so that it is not destroyed' (Mt 24.43); takó· palí·i lé·i nɔ́ anshí·k·an 'the net was not destroyed' (Jn 21.11); tá=á· kwə́t·i .. palí·i lé·i. 'not one .. will be destroyed' (Lk 21.18 [KJV "shall not perish"]).
pali·íči P 'a little to one side, a little ways away' (Lk 22.56-57&, Jn 20.7); 'in a little different place' (OA).
pali·taw- TA+O 'destroy O2 of': wénči-=á· máta -pali·tá·k·uk 'so that he (a thief, obv.) will not break into it (his house)' (Lk 12.39; KJV "he would .. not have suffered his house to be broken through"); tá=háč=á· wwə́nči-káski- awé·n .. -palí·taɔn təlač·e·s·əwá·k·an 'how would anyone be able to .. destroy his [the owner's] possessions?' (Mt 12.29); pɔli·ta·k·o·né·ɔ e·li·xsíhti·t 'he destroyed their language' (1842:9.9).
pampi·hɔ·s·i·- II 'be cleared': ná kə́nč áləmi-pampi·hɔ́·s·u 'then it is cleared' (1834a:16).
  ▸ Cf. pampi·(w)- 'bald, hairless'.
panke·íti (Gr. 2.76g) P 'a little piece' (Lk 5.36).
pankpe·xt- TI(2) 'put a drop of water on': pankpe·xtá·k·we ní·lanunk 'if he would put a drop of water on my tongue' (1834b:30.7).
paɔle·t- TI1(a) 'winnow' ó·li-=č -paɔlé·tamən 'he will thoroughly winnow (the wheat)' (Lk 3.17).
paɔle·tí·k·an IN 'winnowing basket' (Lk 3.17; KJV "fan," for winnowing). ▸ Cf. Mun pawalehtí·kan 'fanning mill' (Goddard 2019: 102).
-paskwi·-: see pahsuk·wi·-.

pawən- TA 'sift': mpawə́nəmən 'I sifted it' (V, ME; Gr. 2.69d); né·k·a wpɔwə́nəmən 'she sifted it' (ME; Gr. 2.58h); któli-=á· -pawə́nk·o·n 'so that he can sift you' (Lk 22.31; Gr. 2.69d).

pawəna·s·i·- II 'be sifted': ehələkhíkwi-wóli-pawəná·s·i·k 'at the times when it is well sifted' (Lk 22.31).

-pawhiteh-: see pai·teh-.

paxkən- (pəpxkən- [Rə̀+]) TA — TI(1b) 'break (something stringlike, bonds), take by breaking off from the place of attachment (i.e., pick [fruit, corn, wheat])'.

▪ paxkən- (TA): mpaxkəná·ɔk 'I pick them (anim., e.g. apples)' (OA).

• pəpxkən-: pupxkəná·p·ani so·so·k·ahəlá·s·a 'he would break apart the chains' (Mk 5.4).

▪ paxkən- (TI): mpaxkənə́mən 'I pick it (e.g., corn)' (OA).

• pəpxkən-: tóləmi-pəpxkənəməné·ɔ nə́ hwí·t 'they began plucking the wheat' (Lk 6.1); ɔ́·k .. pupxkənə́mən 'and he would break them (iron constraints) (sbd.)' (Mk 5.4).

-paxkši·k·an-: see kší·k·an.

payaxkhí·k·an (Gr. 5.56e) IN 'gun' (1834a:18.12); payaxkhí·k·anal 'guns' (1834a:19.14).

pa·- (pe·a·-, pihpa·- [Rih+], pehpa·- [Rih+; IC], pi·p·a·- [Rī+]; Gr. 5.3b, 5.43a, 5.77c) AI — pe·ye·i·- (~ pe·e·i·-: Gr. 2.31i, §5.8d) II 'come'.

▪ pa·- (AI): pé·w 'he came' (Jn 4.47; Gr. 4.21c), pé·w=č 'he was going to come' (Jn 11.27); íka pé· 'she came to him' (Mk 5.27; Gr. 2.10c); tá=á· šá·e pé·i 'he won't come right away' (Lk 12.45, Mt 24.48; Gr. 2.12b); pé·ɔk 'they came' (Jn 4.27, Mt 8.11, etc.; Gr. 4.21o);   pá·l 'come (you sg.)' (Jn 4.49, Mt 5.24); pá·kw 'come (you pl.)' (Mt 22.4); káči pa·í·henk 'may we (exc.) not come' (Mt 6.13, Lk 11.4; Gr. §4.12b); pahtí·t·eč 'let them come' (Mt 22.3; Gr. 4.114b); pa·á·ne 'when I came (would come) back' (Lk 19.23; Gr. 4.63o); ní·=á· máta pa·á·p·ane 'if *I* had not come' (Jn 15.22; Gr. 4.74a); mpá 'I come' (⟨mpu⟩ Jn 10.10; ⟨mpav⟩ Jn 1.31, Jn 14.3, 14.28); pé·p·ani·k 'they came' (Mt 2.1, Jn 1.39, 3.23, etc.; Gr. 3.6e); alɔ́·t ná=nə núnči-pá·n 'yet that is the very reason why I came' (Jn 12.27; Gr. 4.42b); kéku=háč .. kúnči-pá? 'why have you come?' (⟨pav⟩ Mt 26.50); tə́li-=č íka -pá·n 'that he come there' (Jn 4.47; Gr. 4.50a); kúnči-=háč -pá·n ..? 'did you come because of it?' (Mk 1.24; with independent indicative clause as complement); wwə́nči-pá·ne·p 'he came because of it' (Jn 1.7; Gr. 2.20c); pá·t·e 'when he comes' (Jn 4.25, etc.), 'if he comes' (Jn 5.43), 'when he came' (Jn 4.54, Mt 16.13 [without IC]); pe·á·t·e 'when he came' (⟨preatc⟩ Lk 17.12); éntxən- .. -pá·t·e 'every time he came' (Lk 13.22).

• pe·a·-: pe·á·a 'when I came' (⟨Preau⟩ Jn 12.46); šé· ná pé·a·t 'here he comes' (⟨prat⟩ Mt 25.6; Gr. 4.64b); né·ləma mayá·i íka pé·a·t 'before he had gotten all the way there' (⟨prat⟩ Lk 15.20); pé·a·t '(who is) coming' (⟨prcat⟩ Mt 21.5); íka pe·á·t·e 'when he got there' (⟨preatc⟩ Mk 11.13&); íka pe·ahtí·t·e 'when they got there' (⟨pravtetc⟩ Lk 2.16, 7.4, Mk 5.15, etc.; Gr. 4.62e); né·ləma íka pe·áhti·kw 'before they got there' (1834b:37.8; Gr. 4.94).

• pihpa·-: pihpé·ɔk 'they frequently came' (LB).

• pehpa·-: ɔ·s·áhkame péhpa·t 'one who has been to heaven' (Jn 3.13; perfective semelfactive [Gr. 5.41hijk]); pehpáhti·t 'where the Jews come' (Jn 18.20).

• pi·p·a·-: mé·či pí·p·e·p 'he has already come' (Mk 9.13); čínke=ét=tá kpi·p·á·həmp 'when did you (sg.) come here?' (Jn 6.25).

♦ Note: ⟨pr⟩ (Mt 5.1; as if pé· 'he came'), should presumably be emended to ⟨rp⟩ (é·p 'he went to'; KJV "he went up").

▪ pe·ye·i·- (~ pe·e·i·- II; ⟨prer-⟩ 7x, ⟨prr-⟩ 3x): pe·yé·yu 'it comes' (Lk 19.9; Gr. 3.19b); pe·e·í·k·eč ksa·k·i·ma·ɔ́·k·an 'may your kingdom come' (Mt 6.10); pe·e·í·k·e 'when it comes'

(Mk 2.20) ~ pe·ye·í·k·e (Lk 17.20, 22.18; Gr. 2.31i); pe·ye·í·k·e=č ki·škwí·k·i 'when the days come' (Lk 17.22, Lk 23.29).

pa·kánke AN 'locust [cicada]' (ND); pa·kanké·ɔ 'locusts (obv.)' (⟨pakufr,⟩ Mt 3.4).

pa·la·p·i·k·ɔaehəla·- AI 'have neck droop': ná tólǝmi-pa·la·p·i·k·ɔaéhǝla·n 'then his neck began to droop' (⟨tolumi pulapekoarvlan⟩ Jn 19.30). ♦ For initial /pa·la·p·-/ (with post-radical -a·p·-), cf. Mun pa·la·pehlal- TA, pa·la·pehlat- TI(2) 'hang over'.

†pa·ləsí·i 'a Pharisee' (⟨Paluse⟩ Jn 7.48, Lk 11.37, 11.38; ⟨Palase⟩ 1x; ⟨Palisee⟩ Lk 7.36 [2x], 7.37, 7.39); †pa·ləsi·í·ɔ 'Pharisees (obv.)' (⟨Paluseu⟩ Mt 3.7, Lk 14.3); †pa·ləsi·i·yúnka (abs. pl.) (Lk 15.2: 'elsewhere the Pharisees'); pa·ləsi·í·ɔk 'Pharisees' (⟨Paliseuk⟩ Mt 12.2, Lk 6.7; ⟨Paliseeuk⟩ Lk 6.11, Mt 12.24, 12.38; ⟨Paluseuk⟩ Mt 5.20, Lk 5.17, 5.21, etc.; ⟨Palrseuk⟩ Jn 4.1); ⟨Paluseok⟩ Mk 7.1, 7.3, 7.5, Mt 16.5, Jn 7.32, etc.).
• †pa·ləsi·i·ké·i P 'to, among the Pharisees' (Jn 9.13, Mk 14.43&).
▪ pa·ləsi·í·i PN 'of Pharisee' (⟨Palusee⟩ Jn 1.24, 3.1; ⟨Palusei⟩ Mk 8.15; etc.): †pa·ləsi·í·i-pá·ste·k 'the yeast of the Pharisees' (⟨Palusei⟩ Lk 12.1); ná †pa·ləsí·i-lə́nu 'the Pharisee' (⟨Paluse linw⟩ Lk 18.11); etc.

pa·lsəwá·k·an IN 'sickness' (Jn 11.4); kpa·lsəwa·k·anə́na 'our illnesses' (Mt 8.17); pɔ·lsəwá·k·an 'his, her sickness' (Jn 4.52, Mk 1.31); pɔ·lsəwa·k·anúwa 'their diseases' (Lk 5.15); wə́nči kpa·lsəwá·k·anink 'from your sickness' (Lk 13.12).

pa·lsi·- AI 'be sick': pá·lsu 'he is sick' (V, OA; Jn 11.3); pá·lso·p 'he was sick' (Jn 11.1); pa·lsí·ləwal 'he (obv.) was sick' (Jn 4.46; Gr. 4.21e); mpa·lsí·həmp 'I was sick' (Mt 25.36, 25.42; Gr. 4.68a); tǝ́li-pa·lsí·li·n 'that he (obv.) was sick' (Jn 11.6); tǝ́li- xɔ́nsa -pa·lsi·lí·ne·p '(it was the one) whose older brother was sick' (Jn 11.2, *lit.*, 'that her ..'); é·li-pá·lsi·t 'as she was sick' (Mk 1.30; Gr. 4.61f); pa·lsí·t·əp 'who had been sick' (Lk 7.10; Gr. 4.75e); pa·lsí·č·i·k 'unhealthy people, the sick' (Jn 5.3, Mt 9.12; Gr. 2.47a); pa·lsi·lí·č·i 'sick (obv.)' (Lk 4.18, Mt 4.24, etc.).

pa·lso·ha·l- TA 'make sick': pɔ·lso·há·lko·n=hánkw 'it makes them sick' (1834a:20.27).

pa·mí·i PN '(of) palm' (Jn 12.13).

pa·pa·k·i·taw- TA 'cry out to' (cf. Gr. 5.38a): pɔ·pa·k·i·taɔwwá·ɔ 'they cried out to him' (Mt 9.27). ▸ Cf. pa·pa·k·alúhu 'he gives the war-whoop' (OA; cf. alúhu 'he chokes').

pa·pa·x·ihəla·- II 'split into pieces': ɔ́·k ahsə́na pa·pa·x·ihəlé·ɔ 'and rocks split in pieces' (Mt 27.51).

pa·pəwe·lənt- TI(1a) 'make light of': pɔ·pəwe·ləntaməné·ɔ 'they made light of it' (Mt 22.5).
▸ Cf. pá·pu 'he, she is playing, played' (FW).

pa·ste·- (pehpa·ste·- [Rih+; IC]) II 'rise (of flour, etc.)' (Gr. 2.7b): pá·ste· '(bread) rises' (Lk 13.21), pa·sté·ɔ 'they (batches of flour) rise' (Mt 13.33; KJV "was leavened").
• pá·ste·k 'that has risen' (Mk 14.12); (in compounds) 'yeast' (Mk 8.15, Mt 16.11, 16.12, Lk 12.1).
• pehpa·ste·-: pehpá·ste·k 'yeast' (Mt 13.33, Lk 13.21).

pa·t- (TI(1a)) TI-O 'pray': mái-pá·tam 'he went to pray' (Lk 6.12); pá·tamo·kw 'pray (you pl.)' (Mt 26.41); é·li-=á· -wi·šíki-pá·tamank 'how one should work hard at praying' (Lk 18.1); pa·tamé·k·we 'when you (pl.) pray' (Lk 11.2). ♦ More commonly pa·tama·- AI (see below); for the TI(1a)-O, cf. Mass ⟨peatam8k⟩ 'they pray' (Goddard and Bragdon 1988: 692).

pa·tahəwe·ɔ́·k·an (Gr. 5.59g) IN 'victory': pa·tahəwe·ɔ́·k·anink 'to victory' (Mt 12.20).

pa·tahi·lsi·- AI 'win out, gain': pa·tahi·lsúwak 'they won out' (Lk 23.23).
▸ Cf. pa·tuhwí·lsu 'he killed game' (OA); Mun ⟨Pachtachwilsin⟩ /pahtahwi·lsi·-/ AI "to gain by working" (B&A [A.] 109).

pa·tamaw- (pehpa·tamaw- [Rih+; IC]) TA 'pray to': ná=nə́ wə́nči-pá·tamo· 'therefore pray to him (you pl.)' (Lk 10.2); pa·tamáɔt 'who you (sg.) pray to' (Jn 4.22); pa·tamáɔ́·č·i·k 'the ones who pray to him' (Jn 4.23); né·l .. pa·tamá·k·uk=č 'the one who (obv.) will pray to him (prox.)' (Jn 4.23; Gr. 4.65n); tá=á· nkáski- yúkwe -pa·tamaɔ́·i 'I wouldn't be able to pray to him now' (Mt 26.53); pé·x·o·t=á· .. máta pa·tamaɔ́·e·kw 'soon you will not pray to him' (Jn 4.21; apparently ch. conj.); pɔ·tamaɔ́·ɔ 'he prayed to him' (Lk 6.12); nó·čkwe=á· mpa·tamá·k·o·k 'they would pray to me in vain' (Mt 15.9); ná pɔ·tamaɔ·né·ɔ 'then they prayed to him' (Lk 24.52).
- pehpa·tamaw-: pehpa·tamáɔ·t ke·tanət·o·wi·lí·č·i 'one who prays to God' (Jn 9.31).

pa·tama·- (|pāhtamā-|; Gr. 4.42q, 5.104a) AI 'pray': pá·tama· 'he prayed' (Mt 26.39; Gr. 2.24a); pá·tama·p 'he prayed' (Lk 5.16, 18.11; Gr. 4.68b); kóčəmink táli-pa·tamá·p·ani·k 'they were praying outside' (Lk 1.10; Gr. 6.7f); sé·ki-mái-pa·tamá·a 'while I go and pray' (Mt 26.36); né·li-pa·tamá·t·əp 'while he was praying' (Mt 3.16; Gr. 4.73b); é·li-pa·tamá·e·kw 'how you (pl.) pray' (Mt 23.15; Gr. 2.31b); kə́nč áhi-pa·tama·é·k·we 'unless you (pl.) pray hard' (Mt 17.21; Gr. 4.63k); ké·t·a-wíči-pa·tamá·č·i·k '(ones) who desired to join in the prayer' (Jn 12.20; Gr. 4.64r); ná=nə tə́nta-pá·tama·n 'there he prayed' (Lk 9.29; Gr. 2.60c, 4.42q).

pa·tamɔ·t- TI(1a) 'pray to' (|pāhtamwē-| [< |pāhtamā-| AI; Gr. §5.6h] + |-ht| TI [cf. Gr. 5.91a]): kéku pa·tamɔ́·tank 'things that he prayed to' (1842:10.3); kéku=á· pa·tamɔ́·tame·kw 'anything that you (pl.) would pray to' (1842:10.10).

pa·tamwe·i·k·á·ɔn (Gr. 5.54e) IN 'temple' (Jn 2.19, 2.20, 2.21, etc.), 'a house of prayer' (Mt 21.13&); pa·tamwe·i·k·á·ɔnink 'to, in the temple' (Lk 2.27, 2.37, 2.46, Mt 4.5, etc.).
- Literally, 'praying house'.
- pa·tamwe·i·k·a·ɔní·i PN '(of) temple' (Jn 2.17).

pa·tamwe·lx- (|pāhtamwēlax-|; Gr. 5.98) TA 'pray for, on behalf of': pa·tamwe·lxó·me 'pray for him (you sg.)' (Mt 5.44); né·li-pa·tamwé·lxa·t 'as he prayed for them' (Lk 24.51); mpa·tamwe·lxá·ɔk 'I pray for them' (Jn 17.9); takó· mpa·tamwe·lxa·í·ɔk 'I do not pray for them' (Jn 17.9; Gr. 4.83g); pɔ·tamwe·lxá·ɔ 'he prayed for them' (Lk 24.50); kpa·tamwé·lxəl 'I have prayed for you (sg.)' (Lk 22.32); ná pɔ·tamwe·lxá·ne·p 'then he prayed for them' (Mk 10.16).

pa·tamwe·ɔ́·k·an (Gr. 5.58k) IN 'prayer' (Mt 23.16, 26.3, Mk 14.43&); kpa·tamwe·ɔ́·k·an 'your prayer' (Lk 1.13).

pa·ta·h- (|pāhtāh-|) TA 'overpower, defeat': pa·ta·hiáni 'if you (sg.) defeat me' (ME; Gr. 4.63f); ɔ́·k=č máta háši mahtant·o·wí·i-pəna·eləntaməwá·k·an pɔ·tahko·wəné·ɔ 'and the devil's schemes shall never conquer them' (Mt 16.18).

†pa·tá·lamo·s 'Bartholomew' (Lk 6.14).

pa·ta·t- (|pāhtāht-|; Gr. 4.39i) TI(2) 'earn': pa·tá·to· 'it earned (it)' (Lk 19.16, 19.18; Gr. 3.22b); wə́nči-=á· -pa·tá·taɔ 'by which I would earn it' (Mt 19.16&); éntxi-pa·tá·taɔn 'the amount you earned' (Lk 19.23); éntxi-pa·ta·túhti·t 'how much they earned' (Lk 19.15); ehə́nta- mɔ́ni -pa·tá·tunk 'where money is earned' (Mt 25.27); palé·naxk (~ ní·š·a) íka núnči-pa·tá·tu 'I have earned five (~ two) from them' (Mt 25.20, 25.22; Gr. 5.128x); pɔ·tá·to·n=č mé·x·e·k tə́ntay 'he shall earn the great fire' (Mt 5.22; Gr. 4.39i); tə́li- máta kéku -pa·ta·tó·wən 'that he gained nothing' (Mt 27.24).

pa·xhakwe·- II 'be noon': pa·xhákwe· 'it is noon, noontime' (Jn 4.52, Jn 19.14); pa·xhakwé·k·e 'at noon' (Mt 20.5, Mk 15.33&).

pa·xsi·- AI 'be split in two pieces': pá·xsu 'he is split in two pieces' (Gr. 5.10k).

pa·xša·kó·k·an IN 'sawmill' (1834a:15).

pa·xša·s·i·- II 'be split off by cutting': álǝmi-pa·xšá·s·u si·k·á·xkɔ 'the boards began to be split off' (1834a:16).

péči P '(to come) here' (Lk 1.26); 'until' (Lk 1.20, Jn 5.17, Mt 13.30, Lk 17.8); 'as far as' (Jn 18.15); yúkwe péči 'up to now' (Jn 16.24); íka péči 'up to then' (Jn 13.1); nǝ́ wǝnči íka péči ankǝlǝwá·k·anink 'by which to go to death' (Mt 7.13).

■ péči (pi·p·éči [Rī+]; Gr. 2.74i, 5.128q) PV 'come and, come to; extending or facing this way': péči-wwa·tǝli·mɔ́·e 'come and let me know' (Mt 2.8); pwéči- mpí -ná·t·ǝmǝn 'she came to get water' (Jn 4.7); pwéči- (⟨prhi⟩ Jn 9.7, ⟨pchi⟩ 1x, ⟨pwchi⟩ 2x); pwéči- (omitted) (Lk 2.9); mpéči-naxpó·x·we·n 'I come with it' (Jn 5.43); íka .. péči-mǝkǝní·x·ink o·t·é·nay 'to the next town' (Mk 1.38); kpéči-lúkw 'he sends you this message [as follows]' (Mk 14.14); etc.

• pi·p·éči: wǝnči-=á· .. máta -pi·p·éči- mpí -na·t·ǝmó·wa 'so that I would .. never come here to get water' (Jn 4.15).

pehǝwe·- (|pēhǝwē-|; Gr. 2.5h, 5.101d) AI 'wait (for people)': péhǝwe·w 'he is waiting' (V; Gr. 2.5h); pehǝwé·č·i·k 'who were waiting' (Lk 3.15).

pehkwǝs·i·- AI 'be expected': kí·=háč pehkwǝs·ian 'are *you* the one expected to come?' (Lk 7.19, 7.20); pehkwǝs·i·t 'the one expected' (Lk 7.19); tǝ́li-pehkwǝs·i·n 'that is expected' (Lk 7.20).

♦ Cf. pe·h- TA 'wait for, expect' (see Gr. 5.107).

pehpalalo·ka·s·i·-: see palalo·ka·s·i·-.

pehpá·ste·k: see pa·ste·-.

péhpa·t: see pa·-.

pehpa·xhákwe·k 'the south' (⟨pcpaxaqrk⟩ Lk 12.55); assuming this is 'where noon is'.

penk(w)° (|pēnkw-|) 'dry (not wet)' (Gr. §5.2a, Gr. 5.10j).

penkhɔke·- II 'be dry land': énta-penkhɔ́ke·k 'dry land' (Mt 12.43; KJV "dry places").

■ penkhɔke·e- II 'be an area of dry land': penkhɔké·e·k 'the dry land' (1842:6.5).

†petapé·li 'Bethabara' (Jn 1.28).

†pétǝni 'Bethany' (Jn 11.1, 11.18, Lk 19.29&, etc.); †petǝní·yunk 'to Bethany' (⟨Pctunebf⟩ Jn 12.1, ⟨Pctuneuf⟩ Mt 21.17&).

†petsé·iti, †pi·tse·ité·ink: see †mpetsáite.

†petsé·te· 'Bethesda' (Jn 5.2).

péxu P (Gr. 2.73, 5.23j) FUT, 'soon' (Lk 13.31, Mt 25.9), pé·w=č péxu 'he will be coming' (Jn 11.56); péxu pi·ské·k·e 'tonight' (Lk 12.20). ♦ The later form xú is purely a future marker.

• pexulǝníti 'very soon' (⟨Pcvolineti⟩ 1834a:15; ⟨Pcxolineti⟩ 1834b:47.11).

▶ See also xulǝníti.

pé· PV (with IC) '(is) engaged in': pé-ahkɔ·ná·č·i·k namé·s·a 'who were fishing with a net' (Mt 4.18); tǝ́ta pé-wi·k·íhti·t 'whatever houses they were living in' (1834a:18.2). ♦ A reduced form of *pé·mi (from |pǝm-| with IC; see pǝm°).

pe·č·ihǝla·- AI — II 'come flying or rushing, come (as a voice, a spirit, time, a boat), reach'.

■ pe·č·ihǝla·- (AI): pe·č·íhǝla·t 'he flew down' (Jn 1.32); tǝ́li- hɔ́k·enk -pe·č·ihǝlá·li·n 'coming to him' (*lit.*, that [the spirit (obv.)] came to him') (Mt 3.16).

■ pe·č·ihǝla·- (II): ná a·pto·ná·k·an pe·č·íhǝle·p 'then a voice came' (Mt 3.17); pe·č·íhǝle·=č 'the time will come' (Jn 4.23); mé·či pe·č·ihǝlá·k·e múx·o·l 'after the boat came' (Lk 5.7).

pe·č·inkwehǝla·- AI 'take a look': ni·k·a·ní·i=hánkw pe·č·inkwéhǝle· 'he first takes a look' (1834b:8.10, 1842:21.7). ▶ LTD: pe·č·inkwéhǝle· kí·š·o·x 'here comes the sun'.

pe·e·i·-: see pa·-.

pe·h- TA — pe·t- TI(2) 'wait for, expect' (Gr. 5.12a, 5.77c).

■ pe·h- (TA): pé·hi·l 'be patient with me' (*lit.*, 'wait for me') (Mt 18.26, 18.29);

né·li- máta -pé·ha·t 'when he is not expecting him' (Lk 12.46, Mt 24.50); né·li-=č máta -pe·há·e·kw 'while you (pl.) do not expect him' (Mt 24.44); pe·hahtí·t·e 'when they wait for him' (Lk 12.36); pe·há·č·i·k 'who were waiting for him' (Lk 1.21); pe·hə́ntəp 'who was expected' (Mt 11.14); pwe·hawwá·p·ani 'they waited for him' (Lk 8.40); kpé·hukw 'he is waiting for you' (Mk 1.37); kpehəlúhəmɔ 'I waited for you (pl.)' (Gr. 2.5h).

▪ pe·t- (TI): pé·to·kw 'wait for it (you pl.)' (Acts 1.4); pe·túhti·t 'that they were waiting for' (Lk 2.28); pe·tá·k·wi·k 'those who wait for it' (Mt 25.1); pwe·to·né·ɔ 'they waited for it' (Jn 5.3).

pe·k·ánči: see pahkánči.

pe·lihᵒ: see pali·h-.

pe·má·p·ani·k (ppl. of pəma·p·ani·- II) 'heaven' (Lk 21.33), '(of) the air' (Mt 6.26).

pe·mhakamí·k·e·k (ppl. of |pəmahkamīkē-| II) 'the world, the earth' (Lk 4.5, Mt 5.5, etc.).

pe·mi·khátink (oblique ppl. of indef. form of |pəmīkē-| AI 'dwell along' + |-ahtī| coll. [Gr. §5.8c]) 'the country' (Mt 2.18, Lk 3.3); refers to the inhabited countryside.
  ▸ Cf. e·li·khátink (s.v. li·k·e·-).

pe·mi·k·é·č·i·k (ppl. of |pəmīkē-| AI) 'those living (somewhere)' (Lk 1.65, Mk 6.54).

pe·mí·te·k (lexicalized participle of pəmi·te·-* II): loc. pe·mi·t·é·k·ink 'in the grease' (Jn 13.26; presumably [no word in KJV]). ▸ Cf. Mes pemite·wi 'oil, lard'.

†pé·nəwel 'Phanuel' (Lk 2.36).

pe·pahsᵒ-: see pahsᵒ.

pé·škunk P 'nine' (Lk 17.17); pé·škunk txí·nxke ɔ́·k pé·škunk 'ninety-nine' (Mt 18.12, etc.).

pe·š·əw- (|pēšəw-|) TA — pe·t- TI(2) 'bring' (Gr. 3.20j, 5.12q).

▪ pe·š·əw- (TA): pé·š·əw 'bring them (you sg.)' (Lk 14.21, Jn 21.10; Gr. 2.10g, 4.104c), káhta-pe·š·əw (Lk 14.23); pé·š·o· 'bring him (you pl.)' (Lk 15.23; Gr. 4.104x), káhta-pé·š·o· (1842:17.3); íka pe·š·ó·k·one 'if he takes you (sg.) there' (Lk 12.58; Gr. 2.19d); ɔ́·k=č né·k mpe·š·əwá·ok 'I shall bring them also' (Jn 10.16); pwe·š·əwawwá·p·ani 'they brought him' (⟨prj-⟩ Lk 2.22; Gr. 4.69k); ná pe·š·əwa·né·ɔ·p 'then they were brought' (Mk 1.32; Gr. 4.72f); pe·š·əwa·línki 'one (obv.) who was brought' (Mt 18.24).

▪ pe·t- (TI): íka pé·t·o· mpí·s·o·n 'he brought medicine there' (Jn 19.39; Gr. 4.38i); pe·t·aóne kəmi·ltəwá·k·an 'if you (sg.) bring your gift' (Mt 5.23); wəlankuntəwá·k·an=ét mpé·t·u 'I am bringing peace' (Mt 10.34; Gr. 4.38c); pwé·t·o·n 'he brought it' (Mk 6.28; Gr. 2.55d).

pe·t- (TI with short /t/): see pe·h- — pe·t-.

pe·t(·)ᵒ (|pēt-|) 'coming (this way)' (Gr. §5.2a).

pe·thakhɔn- (|pētahkwahan-|) II 'be thunder': pe·thákhɔn 'there was thunder' (Jn 12.29).

pe·t·- (TI with long /t·/): see pe·š·əw- — pe·t·-.

pe·t·alo·ka·l- TA 'send (here)' (Gr. 5.17a): pe·t·alo·ká·lak=č 'who I will send' (Jn 15.26); pe·t·alo·ká·la·t 'the one that he sent' (Jn 3.34); pe·t·alo·ka·la·tpáni 'one (obv.) that he (prox.) has sent here' (Jn 6.29; Gr. 4.76l); pe·t·alo·ka·lkwénki·k 'those that sent us' (Jn 1.22); ná pe·t·alo·ká·li·t 'the one that sent me' (Jn 7.16; Gr. 3.15d); pe·t·alo·ka·lí·t·əp 'the one who sent me here' (Jn 1.33, 4.34, etc.; Gr. 4.77a); pe·t·alo·ka·li·lí·č·i 'the one (obv.) who sent me' (Jn 5.24 [em.]; Mt 10.40, Lk 10.16, etc.; Gr. 4.65c); pwe·t·alo·ka·lá·ɔ=č 'he shall send them' (Mt 13.41); mpe·t·alo·ká·lke 'I was sent here' (Lk 1.19; Gr. 4.29a).

pe·t·alo·ke·mwi·- AI 'send a message': íka pe·t·alo·ke·mwí·lu 'she (obv.) sent him a message' (Mt 27.19).

pe·t·aw- TA+O 'bring O2 to' (Gr. 5.95g): pé·t·aɔ· ke·k·e·p·inkɔ·lí·č·i lə́nəwa 'there was brought to him a blind man' (Mk 8.22); pe·t·aɔ́·na 'they (obv.) were brought to him' (Mt 4.24);

pe·t·o·lé·k·we 'if I bring him to you (pl.)' (Lk 22.5); kpe·t·o·lhúmɔ·p wəla·č·i·məwá·k·an 'I have brought you (pl.) good news' (Lk 2.10; Gr. 4.69bb); mpe·t·a·k·o·né·ɔ khák·ay 'they brought you (sg.) to me' (Jn 18.35; Gr. 4.15g, 4.41e); kpe·t·o·ləné·ɔ 'I bring him to you (pl.)' (Jn 19.4).

pe·t·a·č·i·mwi·- AI 'report (hither)' (Gr. 5.17c): pe·t·a·č·í·mu=č 'he must report it' (Jn 11.57).

pe·t·a·he·- AI+O 'throw (hither)': tépi=á· ahsə́n -pe·t·á·henk ləkhíkwi 'the distance that a stone could be thrown' (Mt 26.39).

pe·t·a·kwi·x·ən- II 'be a flood, be rising floodwaters': pe·t·a·kwí·x·əno·p 'a flood came' (Mt 7.27&, Lk 17.27), 'the water rose' (Mt 24.39).

pe·t·a·p·an- II 'be dawn, be the break of day' (Gr. 5.17g): mé·či áləmi-pe·t·á·p·an 'dawn was already breaking' (Mk 16.2&, 1834b:36.8); pe·t·á·p·ano·p 'it dawned' (Mt 4.16); né·ləma pe·t·a·p·anó·wi·p 'dawn had not yet come' (Mk 1.35); pe·t·á·p·ank 'the dawn' (Lk 1.78); mé·či pe·t·a·p·ánke 'after daybreak' (1842:16.2).

pe·t·a·s·i·- II 'be brought': é·li- ɔ·x·é·e·k -pe·t·á·s·i·k 'because light was brought' (1834b:25.2).

pe·t·a·wsi·- AI 'live until {smthg}': pe·t·a·wsiáne 'when you (sg.) come (*lit.*, live) to them' (1834b:20.14); ktə́li=č íka -pe·t·a·wsí·ne·n 'that we will live until' (1842:19.1).

pe·t·ehəla·- II '(sound) comes': pe·t·ehəlá·k·e 'when the sound of it came' (Lk 1.44).
  ▸ Cf. pe·t·é·wtəm 'he comes weeping' (LTD).

pe·t·əna·kwsi·- AI 'work until': †thakaé·t·u=č íka pe·t·əna·kwsúwak 'they will perform their tasks for a short time up until [their lives end]' (1834b:15.1).

pe·t·o·x·we·i·- II 'come': pe·t·o·x·wé·i·k=č 'that will come' (⟨prtwxrekh⟩ Mt 3.7; Gr. 5.76k).

pe·x·ó·č·i P 'very near' (1834a:19.17). ▸ Cf. ⟨pechotschi⟩ 'very near' (B&A 110).

pe·x·o·č·ihəla·- II 'come near': kéhəla pe·x·o·č·íhəle· 'the time is very near' (Lk 21.8); nčo·wí·i-ló·wi·n pe·x·o·č·íhəle·p 'the time for the Jews' Passover was near' (Jn 11.55); é·li-pe·x·o·č·íhəla·k ɔ·s·ahkame·í·i-sa·k·i·ma·ó·k·an 'the kingdom of heaven comes near' (Mt 3.2).

pe·x·o·č·i·k·a·l- TA 'live near': pe·x·o·č·i·k·a·lkúk·i 'her neighbors (obv.)' (Lk 1.58).

pe·x·o·shikaw- TA 'come near': pe·x·o·shikaí·č·i·k 'who come near me' (Mt 15.8); nčí·sas pwe·x·o·shikaɔ́·ɔ 'Jesus approached them' (Lk 24.15, Mt 28.18); tóləmi-pe·x·o·shikaɔ·né·ɔ·p 'they began to come near him' (Lk 15.1); kpe·x·o·shika·k·o·né·ɔ '(it) has come near you (pl.)' (Lk 11.20, 10.9, 10.11; Gr. 2.49a).

pé·x·o·t P 'soon': pé·x·o·t=á· .. máta pa·tamaɔ́·e·kw 'soon you will not pray to him' (Jn 4.21).
  ▸ Cf. Mun pé·xo·t 'nearly, just about'; ⟨péchot⟩ 'nearly; soon' (Z. 2014:116 [Munsee]).

pe·x·o·thate·-: see pe·x·utahpi·-.

pe·x·o·t·at- (or pe·x·o·t·ət-) II 'be close': ánči-pe·x·ó·t·at 'it is closer' (1842:19.2).

pe·x·utahpi·- AI — pe·x·o·thate·- II 'be near'.
  ▪ pe·x·utahpi·- AI: pe·x·útahpu 'he is near at hand' (Mk 14.42).
  ▪ pe·x·o·thate·- II: lí- ke·tanət·ó·wi·t sɔ·k·i·ma·ó·k·an -áhi-pe·x·o·tháte· 'that God's kingdom is very near' (Lk 21.31).

pe·ye·i·- (~ pe·e·i·-): see pa·-.

pəkwəna·s·i·-(?): áləmi-[pəkwən]á·s·u 'it begins to be (??)' (⟨puqunasw⟩ 1834a:16). ♦ Form, meaning, and context all uncertain.

†pəlaktələməwá·ɔ (but presumably /pwəl-/) 'their phylacteries' (⟨puluktulumwao⟩ Mt 23.5).

pəlali·k·á·xkwtət (dim.) 'little splinter' (Lk 6.42). ▸ Cf. Mun pə̄lalí·ka·xkw 'splinter' (APh, RS).

pələphitehw- (-pəlpi·tehw- TA 'slay'; |-əhtehw-|; Gr. 5.18h): mpəlpi·téhɔ=č 'I shall slay him' (Mk 14.27); mpəlpi·téhɔ 'I killed him (with one blow)' (OA).

pəmᵒ (|pəm-|) 'along, continuing, by' (Gr. §5.2a). ▸ Cf. ahpa·mᵒ < |(p)apām-| (Gr. 5.88d, 5.129b).

pəma·wsəwá·k·an (Gr. 3.5l) IN 'life' (Jn 3.15, 3.16, 3.36 [2x], etc.); pəma·wsəwá·k·anink 'in, to life' (Jn 4.14, 5.24, 5.29, etc.).

pəma·wsi·- AI 'live': ehaləmá·kami·k=č pəmá·wsu 'he will live forever' (Jn 6.51, 6.58); pe·má·wsi·t 'who is living' (Jn 6.57, Lk 24.5); é·li- né·k·a -wə́nči-pəmá·wsink 'as people are alive because of him' (Lk 20.38); tá=á· awé·n wwə́nči-pəma·wsí·wən 'a person will not live from it' (Lk 12.15).

pəma·wso·ha·l- (|pəmāwəsōhāl-|; Gr. 4.43b) TA 'give life to, save the life of': wénči-=č -pəma·wso·ha·lkwíhti·t yú entala·wsí·č·i·k 'so that it shall save the lives of the people of this world' (Jn 6.51); ná ó·k nə́ né·pe ntəlkí·kwi-=č -pəma·wso·há·la·n 'That is also the time when I, too, shall give life to (anyone who ..)' (Jn 6.57; Gr. 4.43b); ntə́li-pəma·wso·há·lko·n 'he gave me life' (Jn 6.57).

pəma·wso·ha·ləwe·- (pe·ma·wso·ha·ləwe·-) AI — pəma·wso·ha·ləwe·yo·wi·- II 'give life (to people)' (Gr. 5.76h).

  ▪ pe·ma·wso·ha·ləwe·- (AI): pe·ma·wso·há·ləwe·t 'the giver of life' (Mt 26.63).
  ▪ pəma·wso·ha·ləwe·yo·wi·- (II): mənt·uwwá·k·an=á· pəma·wso·ha·ləwe·yó·u 'his spiritual power would give life' (Jn 6.63).

pəma·wso·wi·- (pe·ma·wso·wi·-) AI — II 'be living, be a living one'.

  ▪ pe·ma·wso·wi·- (AI): pe·ma·wsó·wi·t ke·tanət·ó·wi·t 'the living God' (Jn 6.69, Mt 16.16).
  ▸ Cf. pe·má·wsi·t (see pəma·wsi·-).
  ▪ pəma·wso·wi·- (II): pəma·wsó·wi·k 'living [water, bread, etc.]' (Jn 4.10, 4.11, 6.35, 6.68).
  • pe·ma·wso·wi·-: pe·ma·wsó·wi·k 'living [water, bread, etc.]' (Jn 6.48, 7.38, 8.12; Gr. 2.30h).

pəməč·ehəlal- TA 'drive (in a wagon, etc.)': ná lí-pəməč·éhəlala·n 'and he was then driven (in it)' (1842:14.3).

pəməskaw- TA 'pass, go past': †pəməskaé·ɔk lə́nəwa 'they passed a man' (⟨pumeskarok⟩ Mt 27.32&). ▸ Cf. pəməska·-. Possibly this is pəmi·skaw- (as written); cf. nki·skaw- TA 'meet'.

pəməska·- (-pəmska·-, pe·mska·-, ahpa·mska·- [Ra+], -pəp·a·mska·- [Ra+; Gr. 5.34q], pep·a·mska·- [Ra+; IC]; Gr. 5.11f) AI 'walk': pəmə́ske· 'he or she walked' (Mk 5.42, Mt 14.29, ⟨prmwskr⟩ Mk 6.48, ⟨prmisr⟩ Mt 14.26 [em.]); íka pəməské·ɔk 'they came by there' (1842:13.4); pəmə́ska·l 'walk (you sg.)' (Jn 5.8, 5.11, 5.12, Mk 2.9); wə́nči-=č -pəmə́ska·t 'so that he can walk' (Jn 11.44; Gr. 3.6f); máta kí·kski-pəmə́ska·t 'one never able to walk' (Mt 15.31; Gr. 5.128); né·li-pəməskáhti·t 'as they walk' (Mk 8.3; Gr. 3.6f).

  • -pəmska·-: pwə́mska·n 'he went by (there, here)' (AP; ⟨pwmskan⟩ Lk 10.32, 18.37; Gr. 2.55e); ná–yu šúkw púmska·n 'he only walked by here' (OA; Gr. 2.59e); ná palí·i pwəmska·né·ɔ·p 'then they went a different way' (Mt 2.12).
  • pe·mska·-: pe·mská·t·e 'when he walked by' (Mt 4.18); íka pe·mskahtí·t·e 'when they passed by the place' (Mk 11.20).
  • ahpa·mska·- AI 'walk about': ahpá·mske·p 'he had walked around' (Jn 10.23); ahpa·mské·ɔk 'they are walking about' (Mk 8.24); né·li- pa·tamwe·i·k·á·ɔnink -ahpá·mska·t 'while he was walking in the temple' (Mk 11.27&).
  • -pəp·a·mska·-: mpəp·á·mska 'I was walking around' (OA; Gr. 5.34q); ná nə́ni nčí·sas pup·a·mská·ne·p 'then that is where Jesus walked around' (Jn 7.1).
  • pep·a·mska·-: pep·a·mská·t·e 'when he was walking around' (Jn 11.54); pep·a·mská·č·i·k 'those that passed by' (Mt 27.39; Gr. 3.6g).

pəməske·t-* (-pəmske·t-; cf. 5.91a) TI(2) 'go on': kəmó·t·ay=č kpəmské·to·n 'you shall go on your belly' (1842:8.1).

pəmət·o·nha·l- (-pəmto·nha·l-) TA 'preach to' — TI pəmət·o·nha·t- (-pəmto·nha·t-, pəp·a·mto·nha·t- [Ra+]; Gr. 5.88d) 'preach about'. ♦ Note: /pwəmt-/ is always ⟨pumt⟩ (5x).
- pəmət·o·nha·l- (TA): é·li-pəmət·o·nha·lá·t·əp 'as he had preached to them' (Mt 7.29); tóləmi-pəmət·o·nhá·la·n 'he began preaching to them' (Lk 5.3).
- -pəmto·nha·l-: pwəmto·nha·lá·p·ani 'he preached to them' (⟨pumt-⟩ Lk 4.31, Mt 13.54); ná pwəmto·nhá·la·n 'then he preached to them' (Mk 2.2).
- pəmət·o·nha·t- (TI): pəmət·o·nhá·t·amo·kw 'preach (you pl.)' (Mt 10.27).
- -pəmto·nha·t-: pwəmto·nha·t·amóne·p wé·lhik a·pto·ná·k·an 'he preached the gospel' (Mt 4.23, 9.35); máta=háč mpəmto·nha·t·amo·wəné·na·p 'haven't we preached about it?' (Mt 7.22).
- -pəp·a·mto·nha·t-: pup·a·mto·nha·t·amóne·p čhɔ·pwənəntəwá·k·an 'he preached about baptism' (Lk 3.3).

pəmət·o·nha·t·amaw- (-pəmto·nha·t·amaw-; Gr. 5.94d) TA+O 'preach O2 to': ntəli-=č -pəmət·o·nha·t·amáɔ·n wé·lhik a·pto·ná·k·an ke·t·əmá·ksi·t 'to preach the gospel to the poor' (*lit.*, 'that I preach ..') (Lk 4.18).

pəmət·o·nhe·- AI "preach" ('talk' OA; 'speak well' LTD): pəmət·ó·nhe·p 'he preached' (Lk 4.15, Mk 1.39, Mt 11.1, etc.); wé·mi lí-pəmət·o·nhé·p·ani·k 'they preached everywhere' (Mk 16.20); pəmət·ó·nhe·kw 'preach (you pl.)' (Mt 10.7); pe·mto·nhé·t·əp 'who preached' (Lk 24.19).

pəminni·- (pihpəminni·- [Rih+], |pəmīlənī-|) AI 'stay, remain': pəmínnu 'he stays' (1834a:14); á·pči té·kəna pəmínno·p 'he always stayed in the wilderness' (Lk 1.80); máta háši wəla·məwe·ó·k·anink pəminní·i 'he never dwelt in the truth' (Jn 8.44); ná=nə́ pwəminni·né·ɔ 'and they stayed there' (Jn 10.40; Gr. 4.42u).
- pihpəminni·-: pihpəminnó·p·ani·k 'they always stayed (there)' (Mt 8.28); íka kpihpəminníhəmɔ 'you (pl.) have stayed there' (1834b:46.2).

†pəminno·he·- AI+O 'make stay': palí·i=á· kpəminno·he·n khák·ay 'you (sg.) should make yourself stay away' (⟨kpenwvrn⟩ 1834b:14.2 [em.]).

pəmi·k·e·-: see pe·mi·khátink and pe·mi·k·é·č·i·k.

pəmi·k·i·- AI 'grow': pəmí·k·o·p 'he grew' (Lk 1.80).

pəmi·nehi·k·e·- AI 'quarrel': tá=á· pəmi·nehi·k·é·i 'he will not quarrel' (Mt 12.19; KJV "strive," RSV "wrangle").

pəmi·neho·t·i·- AI (recip.; Gr. 5.110i) 'argue with each other': pəmi·nehó·t·əwak 'they're quarreling' (OA); áhi-pəmi·nehó·t·əwak 'they argued greatly' (Jn 7.12).
- pəmi·neho·thati·- AI (with |-ahtī| coll. [Gr. §5.8c]) 'all argue with each other': pəmi·neho·thátəwak 'they all argued with each other' (Lk 22.24).

pəmuxɔht- (pe·muxɔht-) TI(2) 'take along': pumúxɔhto·n "he carries it around" (LTD ND).
- pe·muxɔht-: si·skəwə́nčunk mpí pe·múxɔhta·kw 'who is taking a clay vessel of water somewhere' (Mk 14.13).

pənae·ləm- TA 'think about': mpənaé·ləma 'I think about him, study about him' (LB); pənaé·ləmɔ· 'think of them (you pl.)' (Lk 12.24); né·li- máta -pənaé·ləma·t 'when he was not thinking of him' (Lk 12.46, Mt 24.50); pwənae·ləmá·p·ani 'he has thought about them' (Lk 7.16; KJV "visited"); pwənae·ləmawwá·p·ani 'they thought about him' (Lk 3.15); kəmáči-=háč -pənae·ləmíhəmɔ 'do you (pl.) think ill of me?' (Mt 20.15).
▸ Cf. pəna·elənt- (TI, TI-O).

pənáh (1) (and often pəná) P 'see' (Lk 1.44, 2.34, etc.), 'consider' (Mt 12.12), 'Behold' (Lk 13.35), 'Look how' (Jn 7.26). In origin the imperatve singular of pən- TI(1a) 'look at' (see

pənaw-). Translations include: 'why, here ..' (Mt 9.32), 'Here, ..' (Mt 10.16), 'Now, ..' (Mk 1.2, Lk 7.37), 'well, here ..' (Mt 12.46), 'Well, ..' (Mt 20.16), '.. and see' (Jn 11.34).
- ♦ yúkwe pənáh 'Now, ..' (Lk 1.20, 1.48, Mt 7.23), 'Now consider ..' (Jn 9.31), 'And here ..' (Mt 8.2).
- ♦ ná pənáh 'Then here ..' (Lk 2.9, KJV "And, lo, .."; Lk 5.18&, KJV "And behold, .."), 'Well, then ..' (Mt 13.57).
- ♦ šé· pənáh 'See here how ..' (Mt 15.6), 'See, ..' (Mt 17.26).

pənáh (2) P 'even' (V, OA; Mt 23.23, Lk 11.51, 23.5, 23.15): pənáh wáni 'Even this (man)' (Lk 19.9).

pənanihi·- AI+O 'throw down': táli-=č -pənaníhi·n 'to throw (them) down' (*lit.*, 'that he throw down') (Lk 2.34).

pənas·i·- AI 'descend, go or come down (a hill)': pənás·i· 'he's going downhill' (1842:21.4); mé·či pənas·í·t·e 'after he came down' (Mt 8.1); mé·či pənas·ihtí·t·e 'after they had come down' (Mk 9.9); ná íka wwə́nči-pənas·i·né·ɔ 'then they came down from there' (Lk 6.17).

pənaw- (pe·naw-) TA — pən- TI(1a) 'look at' (Gr. 5.4i).
- ▪ pənaw- (TA): pənáw 'Look at him (you sg.)' (Lk 2.48, Jn 1.46, Mt 21.5, etc.; Gr. 2.36c); pənó· 'look at him (you pl.)' (Jn 1.36, Lk 7.34, Jn 19.14, etc.; Gr. 4.104v); pənái·kw 'look at me (you pl.)' (Lk 24.39; Gr. 4.105k); pənaɔ́·t·e xkwé·ɔ 'if he looks at a woman' (Mt 5.28); é·li-pənaɔ́·t·əp 'for he has seen them' (Lk 1.68); pwənaɔ́·ɔ 'he looked at him' (Lk 6.20, 10.32, 22.61); pwənaɔ́·p·ani 'he looked at him' (Mk 10.21); pwənaɔwwá·ɔ=č 'they shall look at him' (Jn 19.37); mɔ́i-pənáɔ·n 'he went to look at it (anim.)' (Lk 13.6); kpənaɔ·né·ɔ '(that) you (pl.) look at him' (Lk 9.38).
- • pe·naw-: nči·sás·a pe·naɔhtí·t·e 'when they looked at Jesus' (Jn 19.33); pe·naí·t·e 'when he looked at me' (Lk 1.25; Gr. 4.62a).
- ▪ pən- (TI): pəná 'look at it (you sg.)' (OA, ME, LTD ND; Jn 11.34; Gr. 4.106a); pənámo·kw 'look at it, them (you pl.)' (Mt 6.28, 24.1); kéku=háč mé·i-pənáme·kw 'what did you (pl.) go to see?' (Lk 7.25); kó·li-=č -pənámən 'you (sg.) must look at it well' (Jn 7.52); wé·mi kéku pwə́namən 'he looked at everything' (Mk 11.11); mɔ́i-pənamə́né·ɔ 'they came to see (it)' (Mt 8.34&), táli-=á· -pənamə́né·ɔ 'to see it (*lit.*, that they would see it)' (Mk 16.2&).
- ▪ pəna·ɔhti·- AI (recip.) 'look at each other': ná .. pwəna·ɔhti·né·ɔ 'then they looked at each other' (Jn 13.22).

pəna·elənt- (pi·p·əna·elənt- [Rī+], pihpəna·elənt- [Rih+]) TI(1a) 'think about, study', TI-O 'think, understand'.
- ▪ pəna·elənt- (TI): pəna·elə́ntamo·kw ɔ·taé·s·a 'think about the flowers (you pl.)' (Lk 12.27); pəna·elə́ntamo·kw 'take care of it (you pl.)' (perhaps 'make it your concern') (Mt 27.24; KJV "see ye to it"); káči pəna·eləntánkhan 'do not think about it (you sg.)' (Mt 6.34); káči pəna·eləntánkhe·kw 'do not think about it (you pl.)' (Mt 6.25, Mt 10.19, etc.); pe·na·elə́ntánke 'when he considered it' (Lk 18.4); pwəna·elə́ntamən 'he thought about it' (Mt 21.29); pəna·elə́nta wenta·wsían 'study what to live by (you sg.)' (1842:12.8); skínnu wínki- .. kéku -pəna·eləntánke 'if a young man likes to study things' (1842:19.4).
- • pi·p·əna·elənt-: máta .. kéku pi·p·əna·eləntamó·wi 'he never studies things ..' (1842:19.4).
- • pihpəna·elənt-: šúkw=č ɔ·ɔhšé·i kéku pihpəna·elə́ntam 'except that he will always be studying bits and pieces(?) of things' (1834b:4.2).
- ▪ pəna·elənt- (TI-O): pəna·elə́ntam 'he is thinking' (LB), 1s mpəna·elə́ntam (LTD), 2s kpəna·elə́ntam (LB); né·li-pəna·eləntamíhti·t 'as they reflected' (Lk 1.51); ná

pwəna·eləntaməné·ɔ 'then they considered it' (Mt 21.25); ná tóləmi-pəna·eləntaməné·ɔ 'they began to reflect' (Lk 5.21). ▸ Cf. pənae·ləm-.

pəna·eləntaməwá·k·an IN 'thinking' (ME; Gr. 5.58n), 'understanding' (1834b:5.3); mahčí·kwi-pəna·eləntaməwá·k·an 'evil thinking' (Mt 15.19); mahtant·o·wí·i-pəna·eləntaməwá·k·an 'the devil's schemes' (Mt 16.18); məsəč·é·i wónči kpəna·eləntaməwá·k·anink 'with all your understanding' (Lk 10.27); pwəna·eləntaməwá·k·an 'his thought(s)' (Jn 8.44); pwəna·eləntaməwa·k·aní·li·t 'his (obv.) thought(s)' (Jn 13.2), 'their (obv.) understanding' (Lk 24.45); nihəláči pwəna·eləntaməwa·k·anúwa 'their own thoughts' (Jn 8.9).

pəna·elənta·s·i·- II 'be thought about': kíši-pəna·elənta·s·í·k·e 'after it had been studied' (1834a:22.41); pəna·elənta·s·í·k·i 'thoughts' (1834a:22.43).

pəna·kčehəl- AI 'jump down': pəna·kčéhəli 'jump down (you sg.)' (Mt 4.6; Gr. 3.13(7)a).

pəna·s·i·- (pe·na·s·i·-; Gr. 5.103a) AI 'look on': téxi šúkw pəná·s·əwak 'they did nothing but look on' (Lk 23.35); pəna·s·ó·p·ani·k 'they had looked on' (Lk 23.55&).

• pe·na·s·i·-: wé·mi pe·na·s·í·č·i·k 'all those who were looking on' (Lk 23.48).

pənčᵒ: see pəntᵒ 'enter'.

pənčihəla·- AI — II 'enter into, fall into'.

▪ pənčihəla·- (AI): íkali pənčihəlé·ɔk 'they entered into them' (Mk 5.13); pənčihəla·lí·t·e lí ó·lahkunk tələmúnsa 'if his animal falls into a pit' (Lk 14.5).

▪ pənčihəla·- (II): lí wto·nəwá·ink .. pənčíhəla·k 'what enters their mouths' (Mk 7.18).

pənčilahso·l- TA+O 'put O2 on': nihəláči ehahkwí·li·t pwənčilahso·la·né·ɔ 'they put his own clothes on him' (Mt 27.31). ▸ Cf. pənčílahsu 'he gets or got dressed' (ME, LB).

pənči·- AI 'enter (not through a door)' (Gr. 5.10d): aləwí·i á·p·əwi- kéməl -pónči· 'it is easier for a camel to enter' (Mt 19.24); máta íkali pənčí·i 'he did not go in there' (Jn 20.5); mahtánt·u íkali pónči·p 'the devil entered him' (Jn 13.27); pənčí·ɔk 'they go in' (Mt 12.45, Lk 24.3); káči čí·č íkali pənčí·han 'don't ever go in him again (you sg.)' (Mk 9.25); wénči- .. íkali -pənčíhti·t '(a rule) by which they entered there' (1842:9.2); mé·či wé·mi pənčihtí·t·e 'after they had all gone in' (1842:9.3); ntóli-=č íkali -pənčí·ne·n 'in order for us to enter into them' (Mk 5.12; KJV "that we may enter into them").

pənči·nxke·- AI 'stick hand or finger in': pənčí·nxke· hwitaɔk·í·li·t 'he put his fingers into his (obv.) ears' (Mk 7.33); pənčí·nxke lí nhupxkónink 'stick your hand into my side (you sg.)' (Jn 20.27); máta íkali pənči·nxke·ó·ne 'if I do not stick my hand in there' (Jn 20.25 [2x]; Gr. 4.95e).

pənən- TA 'lower, let down': ná íka tóli-pənəna·né·ɔ 'then they let him down in there' (Lk 5.19).

pənihəla·- (pe·nihəla·-) AI — II 'fall' (Gr. 3.18f, 5.11n).

▪ pənihəla·- (AI): pəníhəle·w 'he falls off' (V; Gr. 2.5f), pəníhəle· 'he fell' (Acts 1.18); tá=á· pənihəlé·i 'he will not fall' (Mt 10.29); ó·k=č pənihəlé·ɔk alánkɔk 'and the stars will fall' (Mt 24.29); tóli-pəníhəla·n 'that he fell' (Lk 10.18).

▪ pənihəla·- (II): ná .. pəníhəle· 'then they (inan.) fell' (OA; Gr. 4.49j); pəníhəla·k 'what falls' (Mt 15.27); pe·níhəla·k 'what fell' (1834b:30.3).

pəni·- AI (with péči PV) 'come down': péči-pəní· wónči ɔ·s·áhkame 'he came down from heaven' (Mt 28.2); péči-pəní·t '(who is) coming down' (Mk 14.62).

pəntᵒ (pənčᵒ): |pənt-| 'enter' (Gr. §5.2a).

pəntahsəná·k·an (Gr. 5.55g) IN 'tobacco bag' (Lk 10.4 [KJV "scrip"]; ME), 'tobacco pouch, bandoleer bag' (LTD FW).

pəntama·- AI 'hear, understand': é·li-póntama·t 'how he understood' (Lk 2.47);

é·li-wə́li-pəntamá·e·kw 'for you (pl.) can hear well' (Mt 13.16); máta=háč pəntamá·i 'does he not hear?' (Mk 8.18; Gr. 4.81f); tə́li-=č máta -pəntama·wəné·ɔ 'that they will not hear' (Mt 13.15).

pəntanihi·- AI+O 'throw in': ná mɔ́i-pəntaníhi·n ehə́nta-kpahó·t·ink 'then he went and threw him into prison' (Mt 18.30).

pəntaw- (pentaw-) TA — pənt- (-pi·p·ənt- [Rī+]) TI(1) 'hear, listen to, understand' (Gr. 3.20f, 5.4j).

▪ pəntaw- (TA): mpəntaɔ́·wəna·p 'we (exc.) heard him' (Mk 14.58; Gr. 4.69i); pəntaɔ́·t·əp 'who heard him (obv.)' (Jn 1.40; Gr. 4.76g); pəntaɔhtí·t·e 'when they heard him ..' (Lk 2.33, Mt 2.9, Jn 4.41, Jn 20.3); wé·mi éntxi-pəntaɔ́·č·i·k 'everyone who hears him' (Jn 6.45; Gr. 4.67(4)x); wé·mi éntxi-pəntá·k·uk 'all (obv.) that heard him' (Lk 2.47; Gr. 4.67(4)x); pə́ntai·kw 'hear from me (you pl.)' (Mt 13.18); énta-=á· -pə́ntaink 'where people would hear me' (Jn 18.20); máta kpəntai·húmɔ 'you didn't hear me' (Jn 9.27; Gr. 4.89b); ktə́li-pə́ntai·n 'that you listen to me' (Jn 11.41; Gr. 4.50k); pwəntaɔwwá·ɔl 'they listen to him' (⟨punawaul⟩ Jn 3.29 [em.]).

• pentaw-: pentaɔ́·t·e 'when he heard him' (⟨pcntaotc⟩ Mk 6.20).

▪ pənt- (TI): pə́ntamo·kw 'listen to it (you pl.)' (Lk 18.6, Mk 12.29); pəntánkeč 'let him hear it' (Mt 11.15, 13.9, etc.; Gr. 4.114m); pəntánke 'when he or she heard it' (Lk 1.41, Mt 2.3, + 27x; ⟨punufc⟩ Mk 5.27 [em.]; Gr. 2.44a); pəntamihtí·t·e 'when they heard it' (⟨pant-⟩ Mk 6.29), or pent- (em. to ⟨pcnt-⟩); éntxi-pəntánkəp 'everything she had heard' (Lk 2.19; Gr. 4.78h); é·li- .. -pəntamíhti·t 'in hearing it' (*lit.*, as they hear it') (Mt 13.13); kéku pwəntaməné·ɔ 'for them to hear things (sbd.)' (⟨pwnt-⟩ Mt 13.15); máta pwəntamo·wəné·ɔ 'they did not understand (it)' (⟨punt-⟩ Lk 2.50; ⟨pwnt-⟩ Lk 10.24); takó· háši awé·n pwəntamó·wən 'no one ever heard it' (⟨pwunt-⟩ Jn 9.32; Gr. 4.93e); pwəntaməlí·ne·p 'they (obv.) heard it' (Mk 11.14&; Gr. 4.70i); mpəntaməné·na·p 'we (exc.) have heard [from the law]' (Jn 12.34; Gr. 4.70j); tə́li-pəntaməné·ɔ·p 'that they had heard it' (Jn 4.1; Gr. 4.73j).

• -pi·p·ənt-: máta háši mpi·p·əntamó·u 'I have never heard it' (1834a:21.34).

▪ pənta·ɔhti·- AI (recip.) 'understand each other': é·li- máta -pənta·ɔhtíhti·t 'because they could not understand each other' (1834b:19.5, 1842:9.9).

♦ Normally does not show IC (like pənt- 'into' < PA *pi·nt-); but see pentaɔ́·t·e (Mk 6.20).

pənta·kwsi·- AI — pənta·k·ɔt- (|pəntākwat-|; Gr. 2.15c) II 'be heard' (Gr. 5.107f).

▪ pənta·kwsi·- (AI): pəntá·kwsu 'he is heard' (LTD ND; Gr. 5.107f).

▪ pənta·k·ɔt- (II): pəntá·k·ɔt 'it is heard' (OA; Mt 3.3, 28.15), 'the news of it was heard' (Mt 9.26); pəntákɔhto·p 'it was heard' (Mt 2.19, Mk 1.1, Lk 4.14, Mk 1.28, etc.; Gr. 6.5); takó· ní· wə́nči- nə́ -pəntakɔhtó·wi 'I was not the reason that was heard' (Jn 12.30); pəntá·khɔk 'the sound' (Jn 1.23); pənta·khɔ́ke 'when it was heard about' (Lk 1.65).

pənta·s·i·- AI 'hear, listen' (Gr. 5.103b) — II 'be heard' (5.105g).

▪ pənta·s·i·- (AI): pənta·s·í·č·i·k 'who were listening' (Jn 9.40).

▪ pənta·s·i·- (II): pəntá·s·u=tá 'it has been heard' (Lk 1.13).

pənuntəl- (pe·nuntəl-; Gr. 5.87f) TA+O 'cause to see O2, show O2 to': mái-pənúntəl khák·ay 'go and show yourself' (Mt 8.4); mái-pənúntəlo· khak·ayúwa 'go show yourselves' (Lk 17.14; Gr. 4.15k); wə́nči-=č .. -pənuntəlíenk khák·ay 'in order to show yourself to us' (Jn 14.22); xé·li wəlaehɔ·s·əwá·k·an kpənuntələlhúmɔ 'I have shown you many good deeds' (Jn 10.32; Gr. 2.5n, 4.33); pwənúntəla·n 'he shows it to him, them' (Lk 1.50, Jn 5.20 [2x], etc.; Gr. 2.59g); kwí·n kpənuntələlə́ne·p 'long have I shown it to you (sg.)' (Lk 10.15; Gr. 4.71i); ná

pwənuntəla·né·ɔ 'then they showed it to him' (Mt 22.19; Gr. 2.59g); ktə́li-=č -pənuntəla·né·ɔ 'for you (pl.) to testify about it to them' (Mt 10.18).
 • pe·nuntəl-: pe·nuntəlá·t·e †isəlólal hók·ay 'when he showed himself to Israel' (Lk 1.80); pe·nuntəlíenk 'that (which) you show us' (Jn 2.18).

pənunthike·- (pe·nunthike·-; Gr. 5.102e) AI+O 'show, manifest, reveal, bear witness, testify about O2 (to people)': kéku pənunthiké·ɔk 'they (will) show people things' (Mt 24.23); pənunthike·á·ne nhák·ay 'if I testify about myself' (Jn 5.31); nčá·n pənunthiké·t·əp 'which John had testifed about' (Jn 5.36); wtə́li-=č -pənunthíke·n kwət·əma·k·e·ləntəwá·k·an 'that he would show his mercy' (Lk 1.72).
 • pe·nunthike·-: pe·nunthiké·an 'that you are revealing' (Jn 6.30); pe·nunthíke·t təlač·e·s·əwá·k·ana 'who shows his possessions' (Mt 13.52); pe·nunthiké·t·e wtaləwí·i·ləs·əwá·k·an 'when he showed his power' (Jn 2.11).

pənunthike·ó·k·an IN 'testimony' (Jn 5.36); mpənunthike·ɔ·k·anə́na 'our testimony' (Jn 3.11).

pəpahkam- TA 'throw at, beat': see pahkam-.

pəphake·íti: see pháke.

pəphake·n°: see phake·n-.

pəpxkawən- TA 'fold, close': pupxkawəná·ne·p 'he closed [the book]' (Lk 4.20).

pəpxkawəna·s·i·- II 'be folded': pəpxkawəná·s·u 'it is all folded up' (Jn 20.7).
 ▸ Cf. Mun paxkawən- TA, TI(1b) 'fold'.

pəpxkən-: see paxkən-.

-pəp·á·mi: see ahpá·mi.

-pəp·a·mska·-: see pəməska·-.

-pəp·a·mxkwsi·- AI 'crawl around ({smwh})': ná=nə pup·á·mxkwsi·n 'there he crawled around' (Mk 9.20). ▸ Cf. pəmúxkwsu 'he's crawling', 1s mpə́mxkwsi (AD).

pəp·uhhiteh- ([Rə̀+]; |-əhteh-|, Gr. 5.18h) TI(1a) 'knock on (the door)': pəp·uhhitéha 'knock on it (you sg.)' (Mt 7.7); pəp·uhhitéhamo·kw 'knock on it (you pl.)' (Lk 11.9); pəp·uhhitehánke 'if he knocks on it' (Mt 7.8); pəp·uhhitehəməlí·t·e 'when he (obv.) knocks on it' (Lk 12.36); éntxi-pəp·uhhitehánki·k 'all who knock on it' (Lk 11.10); ná=č ktáləmi-pəp·uhhitehəmə né·ɔ kpáho·n 'then you (pl.) will start knocking on the door' (Lk 13.25).

phak° (|pahk-|) 'part, piece' (cf. Gr. 4.51d).

pháke (phaké·i, pəphake·íti [Rə̀+], dim.; Gr. 2.76h) P 'part, piece (of)'; kwə́t·i pháke 'one part' (Mt 5.29, 5.30, 27.3); xí·nxke pháke móni 'thirty pieces of money' (Lk 22.5; KJV "thirty pieces of silver"); ni·š·a pháke móni 'two pieces of money' (WL "First Money").
 • phaké·i †mhakahte·p·o·s·ínki namé·s·a 'a piece of a roasted fish (obv.)' (Lk 24.42).
 • pəphake·íti P 'little pieces' (Jn 6.7, 6.12).

phake·n- (pəphake·n- [Rə̀+], |pahkēn-|) TI(1b) 'break (by hand)': énta- ahpó·n -phake·nəməlí·t·e 'when he (obv.) broke the bread' (Lk 24.35).
 • pəphake·n-: puphaké·nəman 'he tore pieces off them' (Jn 6.11, Mt 26.26, Lk 24.30); pəphake·nəmá·ne 'when I broke them in pieces' (Mk 8.19).

phakwehəla- (-pa·kwehəla·-) AI 'run away': phakwéhəle· 'he ran off', 1s mpa·kwéhəla (ME); phakwehəla·lí·t·e 'if he (obv.) runs away' (Lk 15.4).

phɔkče·x·i·n- AI 'fall breaking open': phɔkčé·x·i·n 'his body burst open when he landed' (Acts 1.18).

phɔkhakeha·s·i·- (pwe·khakeha·s·i·-, |pwahkahkehāsī-|; Gr. 5.105b) AI 'be buried ({smwh})': phɔkhakehá·s·u 'he was buried' (1834b:30.5); é·li-=č -phɔkhakehá·s·ia 'the way I shall be buried' (Jn 12.7&).

- pwe·khakeha·s·i·-: pwe·khakeha·s·íhti·t 'where they are buried, their graves' (Lk 11.47, Mt 23.29 [2x]).

phɔkhakehw- (-pɔ·khakehw-, |pwahkahkehw-|) TA — phɔkhakeh- (-pɔ·khakeh-, |pwahkahkeh-|) TI(1a) 'bury, stick in the ground'.
- phɔkhakehw- (TA): phɔkhakého· 'he was buried' (Lk 16.22; Gr. 5.19b.2); lí-phɔkhakého·n 'that he had been buried' (Jn 11.17); nəmái-phɔkhakého·n 'that I go and bury him (sbd.)' (Mt 8.21).
  - -pɔ·khakehw-: lé·ləm ehankələk·i·k ppɔ·khakehɔ·né·ɔ enkələlí·č·i 'let the dead bury the dead' (Mt 8.22; Gr. 4.49d).
- phɔkhakeh- (TI): pé·-phɔkhakéhank 'what he is planting in the ground' (ME); nəmái-phɔkhakehəméne·p kəmoní·yəm 'I went and buried your coin' (Mt 25.25).
  - -pɔ·khakeh-: ppɔ·khakehəméné·ɔ 'they buried it' (Mt 14.12).
- phɔkhakehɔ·t·i·- (pwe·khakehɔ·t·i·-, |pwahkahkehōtī-|) AI (recip.) 'bury each other': pwe·khakehɔ·t·ihtí·t·e 'when they bury each other' (Jn 19.40; Gr. 4.62l).

phɔkhama·- (-pɔ·khama·-) AI+O 'break up O2 for oneself' (middle-reflexive: cf. Gr. 5.104d): ppɔ·khama·né·ɔ 'they broke it up' (Lk 6.1).
▸ Cf. phɔkh- (-pɔ·kh-, |pwahkah-|; Gr. 5.6g) TI(1a) 'break open. apart'.

phɔkhiteh- TI(a) (-pɔ·khiteh-, |pwahkəhteh-|; Gr. 5.18h): mpɔ·khitéhəmən 'I hit it so as to break it' (AD, ND); ppɔ·khitéhəmən nɔ́ hákhakw 'she broke the bottle' (Mk 14.3; Gr. 4.39h).

phɔthitehəmaw- (-pahɔthitehəmaw-, |pahwàtəhtehamaw-|; Gr. 5.94a) TA+O 'strike O2 off of with a blow, chop O2 off of': phɔthitehəmáɔ·t hwitaɔk·í·li·t 'the one (obv.) whose ear he (prox.) chopped off' (Lk 22.59-60&; no IC, no /-i/ obv.).
- -pahɔthitehəmaw-: pɔhɔthitehəmáɔ·n 'he struck it off of him with a blow' (Jn 18.10).

phwən- (pəphwən- [Rə̀+]) TI(1b) 'pull up, pull out: phwənəmé·k·we 'when you (pl.) pull them up' (Mt 13.29).
- pəphwən-: kóna=háč=á· nəmái-pəphwənəméne·n 'would it be alright if we went and pulled them up?' (Mt 13.28).

phwəna·s·i·- II 'be pulled up' (Gr. 5.105t): wé·mi=č phwəná·s·u 'everything shall be pulled up' (Mt 15.13).

†pílap 'Philip' (1834b:41.6, etc.); †piláp·al (1834b:41.12).

†pílaps 'Philip' (Jn 1.44, 1.45, 1.48, etc.); †pilápsal (Lk 3.1, Jn 1.43), †pilápsa (Lk 3.19-20, Mk 6.17, Jn 6.5).

píši P 'indeed', emphatic *do, did, is* (etc.) (Jn 3.8, Mt 22.8, 26.60); píši=k ktá 'yes, indeed, in fact' (Lk 7.26); píši=á· 'yes, you would' (1842:22.1); 'it is so' (LB; Gr. 2.73n).

pi·ihəla·- AI, II 'stay behind': pi·íhəle·p 'he stayed behind' (Lk 2.43). ▸ Cf. Mun pi·wíhle·w II 'be left over' (dict.).

pi·i·ne·- AI 'be left (after the rest have died)': takó·=tá kwə́t·i awé·n pi·i·né·i 'not one person survives' (1834b:43.3). For the meaning, cf. pi·ihəla·- AI, II and ši·k·wi·ne·- AI.

pi·k(·)º (|pīk-|) 'to pieces' (Gr. 5.1f, §5.2a).

pi·kš- TI(1b) 'cut up': énta-=á· mo·x·wé·s·ak -pi·kšəmíhti·t 'where insects would cut them up' (Mt 6.19).

pi·k·ən- TI(1b) 'crumble, tear up': pwi·k·ənəmóna 'he tore them into small pieces' (Mk 8.6; Gr. 2.55b).

pi·lº (|pīl-|) (1) 'different' (Gr. §5.2a).

pi·lº (|pīl-|) (2) 'clean' (Gr. §5.2a).

pi·laéčəč (WL recording, ME, LB, LTD ND; Gr. 2.77d) AN 'boy' (Lk 1.31, Mt 1.23, Jn 7.22, 7.23); pi·laečə́č·al (obv.) (Lk 1.36, Mt 1.21); pi·laečə́č·ak 'boys' (LB).
- ♦ Incorrect in Goddard (2010:8).

pi·laečəč·i- AI 'be a boy': pi·laečə́č·i·t '(who is a) boy' (Lk 2.23); nkát·a-wə́li-pi·laečə́č·i 'I want to be a good boy' (1834a:13).

pi·laehɔ·s·əwá·k·an IN 'purification' (Jn 3.25).

pi·laehɔ·s·i- AI 'perform act(s) of purification': mái-pi·laehɔ·s·ó·p·ani·k 'they went to perform acts of purification' (Jn 11.55); ehə́nta-pi·laehɔ·s·íhti·t 'where they performed acts of purification' (Jn 2.6).

†pi·lakayás·a 'Barachias' (⟨Pelukyusu⟩ Mt 23.35). ♦ Perhaps for ⟨Pclukyusu⟩; cf. Berechiah (1 Chronicles 3.20).

pi·la·wsəwá·k·an IN 'holiness'; pi·la·wsəwá·k·anink 'in holiness' (Lk 1.75).

pi·la·wsi- AI 'be holy': tə́li- .. -pi·la·wsí·li·n 'that he (obv.) was holy' (Mk 6.20); tə́li-=á· ɔ́·k ne·k·əmá·ɔ -káski-pi·la·wsi·né·ɔ 'so that they would also be able to become holy' (Jn 17.19).

pi·la·wso·ha·l- TA 'make holy': nihəláči mpi·la·wso·há·la nhák·ay 'I make my own self holy' (Jn 17.19).

pi·la·wso·he·- AI+O 'make O2 holy': pi·la·wsó·he·l 'make them holy (you sg.)' (Jn 17.17).

pi·lən- TA — TI(1b) 'clean by hand' (Gr. 3.20g).
- pi·lən- (TA): mpí·lən 'I cleaned him by hand' (Gr. 3.20g).
- pi·lən- (TI): mpi·lənə́mən 'I cleaned it by hand' (Gr. 3.20g).

pi·lət-: see pi·lsi·- — pi·lət-.

pí·lhik: see pi·lsi·-.

pí·li (1) (pi·pí·li; Gr. 5.38b) P 'different'; pí·li kéku 'different things' (Lk 3.18); pí·li awé·n 'someone else' (Jn 5.32, 5.43); pí·li awé·ni·k 'other people' (Jn 4.38, Lk 8.3); lí pí·li mux·ó·link 'in another boat' (Lk 5.7).
- pi·pí·li '(all) different, different from each other' (1842:10.1).

pí·li (2) PV 'pure' (1834b:8.7, 14.2).

pi·li·h- TA — pi·li·t- TI(2) 'clean' (Gr. 3.20h).
- pi·li·h- (TA): pi·lí·hɔ 'cleanse them (you pl.)' (Mt 10.8); pi·li·hə́nči·k 'that were made clean' (Lk 17.17); kɔ́t·a-pi·li·há·a 'he wants to clean it (a book [anim.])' (1834a:15); kkáski-=á· -pi·lí·hi 'you could make me clean' (Mt 8.2); tə́li-=č -pi·lí·ha·n hɔ́kaya mé·li 'for Mary to purify herself' (Lk 2.22).
- pi·li·t- (TI): pi·lí·to·l 'clean it (you sg.)' (Mt 23.26; Gr. 4.106m); pwi·li·tó·na 'he prunes them' (Jn 15.2; KJV "purgeth," RSV "prunes"); ó·li-=č -pi·lí·to·n 'he will thoroughly clean it' (Lk 3.17); kpi·li·to·né·ɔ .. kpaintəməwá·ɔ 'you (pl.) clean your cups' (Lk 11.39).

pi·li·t·e·ha·- AI 'have a pure heart': pi·li·t·e·há·či·k 'those with pure hearts' (Mt 5.8).

pi·lsi·- AI — pi·lət- II 'be clean, pure, holy' (Gr. 5.10m).
- pi·lsi·- (AI): é·li- məsəč·é·i -pí·lsi·t 'as he is clean all over' (Jn 13.10); kpi·lsíhəmɔ 'you (pl.) are clean' (Jn 13.10, 15.3); takó· wé·mi kpi·lsi·húmɔ 'you are not all clean' (Jn 13.11); ktə́li-=č -pí·lsi·n 'for you to be clean' (Mt 8.3; Gr. 4.50l); ná pwi·lsi·né·ɔ 'then they became clean' (Lk 17.14); pi·lsían núxa· 'Holy father (voc.)' (Jn 17.11); wé·li-pí·lsi·t 'the holy one' (Lk 1.49), pí·lsi·t či·čankw 'the Holy Spirit' (Lk 1.41); pí·lsí·li·t či·čánkɔl (obv.) (Lk 1.67), pi·lsí·li·t či·čánkɔ (Lk 2.25 [em.], 2.26, etc.; Gr. 4.65l), pí·lsí·li·t či·čánkunk 'in the holy spirit' (Lk 3.16); pí·lsí·č·i·k 'the clean ones' (1842:9.2); máta pi·lsí·č·i·k 'the unclean ones' (1842:9.2); pi·lsi·lí·č·i manət·ó·wa 'the Holy Spirit (obv.)' (Mt 12.32, Lk 11.13, 12.10).

♦ -pi·lsí·t·əm- ((lexicalized participle as possessed theme): pwi·lsí·t·əma 'his holy one' (Mk 1.24).

▪ pi·lət- (~ pi·lt-) (II): pí·lət 'it is clean' (Lk 11.41), lí-pí·lət 'for it to be holy' (1842:11.4); pí·ltək 'pure' (Mt 27.4), énta-áhi-pí·ltək 'in the very holy place' (Mt 24.15), wénči-=č xkwíči ɔ́·k -wənči-pí·ltək 'so that they will also be clean on the outside' (Mt 23.26).

• pí·lhik (cf. Gr. 2.48a) 'holy, pure' (Lk 1.35, Mt 4.5, 12.4); wəli-pí·lhik 'what is really holy' (Mt 7.6); wénči-pí·lhik 'because of which it is holy' (Mt 23.19).

pi·me·ləm- TA 'think deceitful': máta=háč=á· kúnči-pi·me·ləmí·wən 'wouldn't you think me deceitful because of it?' (1842:22.3, 22.4).

pi·məna·te·- AI 'make thread' — pi·məna·te·yo·wi·- II 'spin' (cf. Gr. 5.76f,g, etc.).

▪ pi·məna·te·- (AI): takó· pi·məna·te·í·ɔk 'they do not make thread' (Mt 6.28).

▪ pi·məna·te·yo·wi·- (II): máta pi·məna·te·yo·wi·í·ɔ 'they (flowers [inan.]) do not spin thread' (Lk 12.27).

▸ Cf. pi·məná·ta·n 'thread' (OA), ⟨pimenátan⟩ (Z. 197); Mun pi·mə̆náhta·n.

pi·ɔnta·si·- II 'be left uneaten' (Gr. 5.105.l): ké·x·a=háč tankhá·k·anink pi·ɔntá·s·o·p 'in how many baskets were there uneaten leftovers?' (Mk 8.19, 8.20); pi·ɔntá·s·i·k 'what was left' (Jn 6.12, Mt 15.37, Lk 16.21).

pi·pí·li: see pí·li.

pi·p·i·naw- TA — pi·p·i·n- TI(1a) 'choose, select'.

▪ pi·p·i·naw- (TA): pi·p·í·nae· télən ɔ́·k ní·š·a lə́nəwa 'he selected twelve men' (1834b:23.4); pi·p·í·naɔk 'whom I chose' (Mt 12.18); pi·p·i·naɔ́k·i·k 'those whom I have chosen' (Jn 13.18); pi·p·i·naɔ́·t·e 'if he chose him' (Mt 27.42); pi·p·i·naɔ́·č·i 'those he chooses' (Lk 18.7, Mt 24.31); pi·p·i·núnči·k 'the ones chosen' (Mt 20.16, 24.23); é·li-pi·p·i·nó·le·kw yú wə́nči 'because I selected you (pl.) from it' (Jn 15.19); takó· ki·ló·wa kpi·p·i·nai·húmɔ 'you (pl.) did not choose me' (Jn 15.16); kpi·p·i·no·lhúmɔ 'I chose you (pl.)' (Jn 15.16; Gr. 4.33); máta=háč ki·ló·wa kpi·p·i·no·lo·húmɔ·p 'have I not chosen *you* (pl.)?' (Jn 6.70).

▪ pi·p·i·n- (TI): tə́li-pi·p·i·naməli·n 'that they (obv.) were selecting them' (Lk 14.7).

pi·ska·kwihəla·- II 'get dark (outside)': pi·ska·kwíhəle· 'it was getting dark' (ME), 'it got dark' (⟨peskutqcvlr⟩ Mk 15.33& [em.]).

▸ Cf. ⟨Pisgáquihilleu⟩ "[it is] Dim" (Z. 56), "Gloomy" (Z. 84). ♦ The text of Mk 15.33& has here ⟨peskutqcvlr⟩ (misprinted for ⟨peskuntqcvlr⟩), which also appears a second time in this verse with the correct meaning of pi·skəntkwéhəle· (see below).

pi·ske·- II 'be dark' (Gr. 5.10c): pexuləníti pí·ske·w 'soon it will be dark' (1834a:15), kwiá·kwi pí·ske· 'it was still dark' (Mk 16.2&); ná-nćkc pí·ske·k 'that same evening' (Jn 20.19); énta-pí·ske·k 'in the dark' (Lk 1.79; KJV "in darkness"); énta-áhi-pí·ske·k 'into utter darkness' (Mt 8.12, Mt 22.13, 25.30; KJV "into outer darkness"); mé·či pi·ské·k·e 'after night had fallen' (Mk 6.47).

♦ pí·ske·k (lexicalized participle): 'darkness' (Jn 1.5, 3.19, Lk 22.53); pi·ské·k·ink 'in the darkness' (Mt 4.16, Jn 8.12).

pi·ske·e·- II 'be a dark place': pi·ské·e· 'it is a dark place' (Mt 6.23 [2x]).

pi·ske·nami·- AI 'be overtaken by night' (cf. Gr. 5.117): wə́nči-=č máta -pi·ske·namíe·kw 'so that you (pl.) are not overtaken by the dark' (Jn 12.35; or -pi·ske·namí·e·kw if the negative inflection was distinct).

pi·ske·wəní·i P 'at night' (Lk 2.8, Mt 2.14, Jn 3.2, etc.), 'by night' (Mk 4.27).

pi·skəntkwehəla·- AI 'go dark': pi·skəntkwéhəle· kí·š·o·x 'the sun went dark' (⟨peskutqcvlr⟩ Mk 15.33& [with ⟨ut⟩ for ⟨unt⟩]); pi·skəntkwehəlé·ɔk=č ki·š·ó·x·ɔk 'the sun and moon will go dark' (⟨Peskuntqrvlrokh⟩ Mt 24.29). ♦ Note: the first occurrence of ⟨peskutqcvlr⟩ in Mk 15.33& (also with ⟨ut⟩ for ⟨unt⟩) is taken to be an error for pi·ska·kwíhəle· 'it got dark (outside)' and is emended in the text; see pi·ska·kwihəla·-.

pi·skəntkwe·e·- II 'be a dark place': áhi-xínkwi-pi·skəntkwé·e· 'it is an extremely dark place inside' (Mt 6.23).

pi·tai·x·ən- II 'be an (additional) layer': tá=á· náxpəne ktás·ənəm pi·tai·x·ənó·wi 'not even (one) stone of yours will lie upon another' (Lk 19.44). ▸ Cf. Mun pihtawí·xən 'it's an extra layer'.

pi·tawənte·- II 'have or be an additional room': xé·li pi·tawə́nte· 'it has many rooms' (Jn 14.2).

pi·te·wto·ne·- AI 'foam at mouth': pi·te·wtó·ne· 'he foams at the mouth' (Mk 9.18, Mk 9.20).

†pí·təl 'Peter' (Jn 1.44, Mk 5.37, Mt 16.22, etc.); †pí·təla (obv.) (Mt 16.23, 17.1, 17.24, etc.).

pi·wən- TA 'leave behind': má·wsu pí·wəna· 'one (will) be left behind' (Mt 24.40 [2x]).
▸ Cf. Mun pí·wŏne·w TA, pí·wŏnəm TI 'has (s.o., it) left over, has unused' (dict.).

pkuwh-* (-puk·uwh-, |pəkə̀wah-|) TI(1a) 'seal (up)': ppuk·uwhamənéɔ nə́ ahsə́n 'they sealed the stone' (Mt 27.66). ▸ Cf. pkú 'pitch; gum' (ND, LB); Mun pkə́w.

pkwᵒ (|pəkw-|) 'hole (through)' (Gr. §5.2a).

pkwəs·i·- AI 'have a hole': é·škanš énta-pkwə́s·i·t 'the eye of a needle' (Mt 19.24).

po·kwᵒ (|pōhkw-|) 'break (sticklike in two; metaphorical)' (Gr. §5.2a).

pó·kwe·s AN 'mouse' (LTD ND, LB; ⟨pwqes⟩ or ⟨pwqcs⟩ 1834a:12); po·kwé·s[a] n[i]nhíle· 'it kills mice (obv.)' (1834a:14); po·kwé·s·ak 'mice' (1834a:14).

po·kwən- TI1(b) 'break': ppo·kwənə́mən 'he broke it (as, a stick)' (ME); ppo·kwənə́mən wi·k·inke·ó·k·an 'he breaks the marriage' (Mt 5.32 [2x]; cf. Gr. 2.58c); káči po·kwənínkhan wi·k·inke·ó·k·an 'do not break apart a marriage (you sg.)' (Mt 5.27).

po·kwihəla·- II 'break': ná=nə́ wə́nči-po·kwíhəle· 'and because of that it broke' (Lk 5.6).

po·kwilaht- TI(2) 'snap in two': máta=č kə́t·a-po·kwilahto·néɔ 'they will not try to snap it in two' (Mt 12.20); é·li- máta šúkw -po·kwílahto·kw 'since he not only broke it (metaphorically)' (Jn 5.18; Gr. 4.99k).

po·kwkaxkɔnehw- (po·po·kwkaxkɔnehw- [Rv+]; Gr. 5.21f) TA 'break the leg of' (redup.: 'legs'): tə́li-=á· -po·po·kwkaxkɔnehɔ·néɔ 'that they should break their (obv.) legs' (Jn 19.31); ná máta ppo·po·kwkaxkɔneho·wənéɔ 'then they did not break his legs' (Jn 19.33).

po·l- (|pōl-|; Gr. 5.4c) TA 'escape from': po·lkúk·i 'that (obv.) escaped from him' (Mt 18.12, Lk 15.4); máta po·lkó·k·wi 'those (obv.) that did not escape from him' (Mt 18.13); áləmi-po·lkúk·e· 'if he (obv.) goes and escapes from him' (Mt 18.12); po·lí·t·əp 'that escaped from me' (Lk 15.6).

po·nᵒ (|pōn-|) 'cease' (Gr. §5.2a).

po·ne·ləm- TA 'forsake' — po·ne·lənt- TI "forgive", 'stop thinking about' (LTD).

■ po·ne·ləm- (TA): kwáč=háč po·ne·ləmían? 'why did you (sg.) forsake me?' (1834b:35.5); nə́ni=č wwə́nči- lə́nu -po·né·ləma·n ó·x·ɔ ó·k kɔhé·s·a 'for that reason a man will forsake his father and mother' (Mt 19.5).

■ po·ne·lənt- (TI): ppo·ne·lə́ntamən[=č] kəmat·a·wsəwá·k·an 'he [shall] forgive your sin' (1834b:32.10).

po·ne·ləntamaw- TA+O 'forgive O2 for': ppo·ne·ləntamá·k·o·n entxe·kháma·t 'he (obv.) forgave him what he owed' (Mt 18.27).

po·nən- TA 'release': á·pči=hánkw .. pó·nəne· kwə́t·i ke·pha·s·i·lí·č·i 'he would always release one prisoner' (Mt 27.15); po·nənát·e wá lə́nu 'if you (sg.) release this man' (Jn 19.12); ppo·nənúk·u 'he (obv.) released him' (Mt 18.27); tá=á· kpo·nəni·húmɔ 'you (pl.) won't release me' (Lk 22.68); ná=č kə́nč mpóˑnənaˑn 'then I'll release him' (Lk 23.16, 23.22); ná kə́nč ppoˑnənanéˑɔ 'and *then* they let him go' (Lk 10.30).

poˑniˑh- TA — poˑniˑt- TI(2) 'leave alone'.
- poˑniˑh- (TA): póˑniˑw (OA, ND), poˑníˑhaw (OA) 'leave him alone (you sg.)!' (Gr. 2.11c); kiˑmíˑi=č mpoˑníˑha 'I shall leave her alone in secret' (Mt 1.19; Gr. 6.5b).
- poˑniˑt- (TI): kwə́la kpoˑníˑtoˑn 'I wish you (sg.) would leave it alone' (1842:20.3, 21.2); ppoˑnitoˑnéˑɔ=á· mɔtaˑwsəwaˑkˑanúwa 'they would cease their sins' (1834b:31.5).

poˑniˑm- TA — poˑnoˑt- TI(1b) 'stop talking about'.
- poˑniˑm- (TA): wénči=č -poˑníˑmiˑt 'so that he will stop talking about me' (Lk 18.3; Gr. 4.67(2)p); ná ppoˑnimanéˑɔ 'then they left him alone' (Mt 22.22).
- poˑnoˑt- (TI): nə́ni wwə́nči- máta -poˑnoˑtˑəmówən 'that is why he didn't stop talking about it' (1834a:23.53).

poˑsˑiˑ- AI 'get in a boat': pósˑu ~ pósˑiˑw 3s (Gr. 2.24f); muxˑóˑlink líˑpóˑsˑoˑp 'he went aboard a boat' (Mk 8.13; Gr. 3.13(1)b); muxˑóˑlink líˑpoˑsˑíˑɔk 'they got into a boat' (Jn 21.3; Gr. 6.7a); poˑsˑóˑpˑaniˑk 'they were getting on board' (Jn 6.22); poˑsˑíˑte lí muxˑóˑlink 'when he entered the boat' (Mt 24.38); ná .. muxˑóˑlink təli-póˑsˑiˑn 'then he got into a boat' (Lk 5.3).
▸ Later speakers used this verb for any vehicle; cf. Mun póˑsiˑw 'gets into a boat or wheeled vehicle' (RH, APh).

póˑšiˑs AN 'cat' (ME, LTD ND, LB; ⟨pwjes⟩ 1834a:12, 14; Gr. 2.79i), xínkwi-póˑšiˑs 'big cat' (1834a:14). ▸ Also póˑšˑiˑs 'cat' (OA).
▸ A loanword from Munsee póˑšiˑs (JH, Munceytown), beside usual Munsee póˑšiˑš.

poˑtaˑčˑíˑkˑan IN 'whistle' (FW, LTD WT; Gr. 5.56f); 'trumpet' (Mt 6.2); memmánkəweˑk poˑtaˑčˑíˑkˑan 'trumpet' (*lit.*, 'loud-sounding whistle') (Mt 24.31).

poˑtaˑl- TA — poˑtaˑt- TI(1a) 'blow at, on'.
- poˑtaˑl- (TA): mpoˑtˑáˑla 'I blow on it (anim.)' (Gr. 5.12d).
- poˑtaˑt- (TI): poˑtaˑt- TI(1a) 'blow (a trumpet)': káči hítami poˑtaˑtˑánkhan 'don't first blow a trumpet' (Mt 6.2); mpoˑtˑáˑtˑamən 'I blow on it' (ND; Gr. 5.12d).

poˑtáˑlaˑs AN 'skin bag (for liquids)' (LB; Lk 5.37); poˑtaˑláˑsˑa (obv.) (Lk 5.37); xúwi-poˑtaˑláˑsˑink 'in an old skin bag' (Lk 5.37); wə́ski-poˑtaˑláˑsˑink 'in a new skin bag' (Lk 5.38). ♦ LTD: 'bag for storing grease (made from the entire skin of an animal)'.

pɔkˑiˑº: see pahkiˑº.

póˑi PV 'be unable, be not possible' (also with negative) (Gr. 5.128r): póˑi-ləsˑiéˑkˑwe 'if you (pl.) are unable to do (it)' (Lk 12.26); éˑli- .. máta -póˑi- kéku -ləsˑiˑt 'since nothing is impossible for him to do' (Lk 1.37); táˑ=áˑ kéku kpóˑi-ləsˑiˑhúmɔ. 'Nothing would be impossible for you to do.' Mt 17.20).

pɔˑiˑ- AI 'be pregnant': póˑu 'she is pregnant' (Lk 1.36, Mt 1.23); áləmi-póˑoˑp 'she became pregnant' (Lk 1.24; Gr. 5.128b); éˑli-póˑiˑt 'because she is pregnant' (Mt 1.20); kpóˑi=č 'you will be pregnant' (Lk 1.31); təli-póˑiˑn 'that she was pregnant' (Mt 1.18).
▸ Cf. ⟨Pōawĩn⟩ 'Schwanger seÿn' (Z. 20), ⟨Pōawi⟩ "Big with child" (Z. 23).

-pɔkhiteh-: see phɔkhiteh-.

pɔˑɔleˑ- AI 'struggle with a burden': pɔˑɔléˑɔk 'they struggle with burdens' (⟨poolrok⟩ Lk 11.46).
♦ Shape and gloss based on cognates: Cree pwaˑwateˑw 'is overloaded, heavily burdened'; Men puawanɛw 'he cannot manage his pack; his load is too heavy for him'; Oj pwaˑwaneˑ 'carries a heavy burden on his back' (Hewson 1993:168, no. 2842).

ppukˑuwhamənéˑɔ: see pkuwh-*.

psakhwiteha·s·i- AI 'be crucified': énta-psakhwitehá·s·ian 'your cross' (*lit.*, 'where you are crucified' (Mt 27.40); wíči-psakhwitehá·s·i·t 'who was crucified with him' (Lk 23.39).

psakhwitehw- (-pəsahkwi·tehw-, |pəsakwəhtehw-|; Gr. 5.18h) TA 'crucify' — psakhwiteh- TI(1a) 'nail (to something)'.

■ psakhwitehw- (TA): psakhwitéhɔw 'crucify him (you sg.)' (Mk 15.13 [2x], Jn 19.15); psakhwitého· 'crucify him (you pl.)' (Jn 19.6 [3x]); a·lə́nte psakhwitehɔ́·p·ani·k 'some have been crucified' (Mt 23.34); énta-káhta-psakhwitehɔ́hti·t 'where they intended to crucify him' (Mt 27.31); énta-psakhwitéhunt 'where he was crucified' (Jn 19.41; Gr. 2.23e); psakhwitehúntəp 'who was crucified' (Mt 28.5&); tə́li-psakhwitehɔ·né·ɔ 'for them to crucify him' (Lk 18.32).

• -pəsahkwi·tehw-: mpəsahkwi·téhɔ=č=háč 'shall I crucify him?' (Jn 19.15); kpəsahkwi·tehó·lən 'that I crucify you' (Jn 19.10).

■ psakhwiteh- (TI): énta-=č -psakhwitehəmíhti·t nɔ́xkal ɔ́·k wsí·t·al hítkunk 'where they were to nail his hands and feet to a tree' (1834b:35.2).

psak·wº (|pəsakw-|) 'adhere, (be) up against' (Gr. §5.2a).

psak·wi·- AI 'adhere' (Gr. 5.11n): nə́ni=č wwə́nči- lə́nu .. -xkwé·yunk -lí-psák·wi·n 'for that reason a man will .. adhere to a woman' (Mt 19.5).

psak·wihəla·- (pesahkwihəla·-; Gr. 5.11n) II 'stick to (with loc. oblique)': púnkw .. pesahkwíhəla·k nhak·ayəná·nink 'the dust that sticks to us' (Lk 10.11).

psak·wi·xt- (-pəsahkwi·xt-) TI(2) 'affix': se·kantpe·x·í·nəli·t pwəsahkwí·xto·n 'he affixed it above his (obv.) head' (Jn 19.19).

psənthikaw- TA 'cover': psənthikaí·ne·n 'cover us (with yourselves)' (Lk 23.30).

psəntpat·- (-pəs·əntpat·-) TI(2) 'flood': tá=á· čí·č mpəs·əntpat·ó·wən yú pe·mhakamí·k·e·k 'I will never flood this earth again' (1842:9.7).

psəntpe·- (pe·s·əntpe·-) II 'flood': ná ílli wé·mi énta-amánkahtink psə́ntpe· 'then even all the large hills were under water' (1842:9.4); psəntpé·k·eč yú hák·i 'let this earth be flooded' (1842:8.6).

• pe·s·əntpe·-: né·ləma pe·s·əntpé·k·e hák·i 'before the earth was flooded' (Mt 24.38).

ptahw- TA — ptah- (-pəth-, |pətah-|) TI 'catch (as, a fish)'.

■ ptahw- (TA): xahé·li ptáhwe· namé·s·a 'he caught a great many fish' (Lk 5.6); sɔ́·mi xé·li ptahwé·ɔk 'they had caught so many' (Jn 21.6).

■ -pəth- (TI): takó· kéku mpəthamo·húmənə 'we caught nothing' (Lk 5.5; Gr. 2.43f, 4.91h).

▸ Cf. Mun ptáhe·w TA 'he caught (one fish, some fish)' (APh, VJ).

-puk·uwh-: see pkuwh-.

punkhwitehw- (|-əhtehw-|; Gr. 5.18h) TA 'grind to dust': ppunkhwitehó·k·o·n=č 'it will grind them (indef.) to dust' (Lk 20.18).

púnkw IN 'ashes, dust', later also 'gunpowder' (V, ME, LTD ND, LB): 'dust' (Mt 10.14, Lk 10.11, 1842:8.1); púnkunk 'in ashes' (Lk 10.13).

púnt* (-puntəm-) IN 'pound' (currency): kpúntəm 'your pound' (Lk 19.16, 19.18, 19.20).

púntink P 'pound(s)' (a unit of weight or currency), construed as IN; kwə́t·i púntink 'one pound' (Lk 11.42, 19.24, Mt 26.7&); télən púntink 'ten pounds' (Lk 11.42, 19.13, etc.); púntink 'pounds' (other amounts) (Lk 19.18, Jn 19.39).

puphake·nº: see phake·n-.

pupxkən-: see pəpxkən-.

pup·á·mi: see ahpá·mi.

pup·a·mto·nha·t·-: see pəmət·o·nha·l-.

†púšəlink: see †mpúšəlink.

pwe·khakeha·s·i°: see phɔkhake·ha·s·i·-.

pxankhwi·k·e·- AI(+O) 'patch (with)': takó· awé·n xuwa·khuk·wí·ɔnink tankíti wəskahkwí·ɔn pxankhwi·k·é·i 'no one puts a patch of a little bit of new cloth on an old coat' (Mk 2.21).
  ▶ Cf. Mun pxankhwí·ke·w 'patch things' (dict.).

s

sahka·kwən- (-sak·a·kwən-) TA 'lead': káski-=háč =á· ke·k·e·p·ínkɔ·t -sahká·kwəne· ke·k·e·p·inkɔ·lí·č·i 'can a blind person lead a blind person?' (Lk 6.39).
  • -sak·a·kwən-: sɔk·a·kwəná·ɔ 'he led him away' (Mk 8.23); ksak·a·kwənúk·əwa=č 'he will lead you (pl.)' (Jn 16.13; Gr. 4.27p).

†sáikəl 'Sychar' (Jn 4.5).

†sáili·n 'Cyrene' (Mt 27.32&).

†sailí·nas 'Cyrenius' (Lk 2.2).

†sáiman 'Simon' (Jn 1.42, Mt 4.18, Lk 5.5, etc.); †sáiman-pí·təl 'Simon Peter' (Jn 1.40, Lk 5.8. Lk 6.14, etc.); †sáiman-pí·təla (obv.) (Jn 13.6, 20.2); †sáimanal (obv.) (Jn 1.40, Lk 5.10); †sáimana (Lk 5.4, 7.44, Jn 12.4).

†sáitan 'Sidon' (Mk 3.8, Mt 11.22, Mk 7.31); †sáitanink 'in Sidon' (Lk 4.26, Mt 11.21, etc.).
  ▪ †saitanínka 'the people of Sidon (abs.)' (Lk 10.13).

sak·we·lənt- TI(1a) 'be troubled about', TI-O 'worry, be distressed'.
  ▪ sak·we·lənt- (TI): sak·we·lə́ntaman 'what you (sg.) are troubled about' (Mt 6.34).
  ▪ sak·we·lənt- (TI-O): sak·we·lə́ntam 'he was distressed' (Jn 11.33, 21.17); áhi-sak·we·lə́ntamo·k 'they were very distressed' (Mk 6.50, 1842:17.1); káči sak·we·ləntamó·han 'don't worry (you sg.)' (ND; Gr. 4.112c); káči sak·we·ləntánkhe·kw 'don't be distressed (you pl.)' (Lk 21.9&, Mk 13.11, etc.); nsak·we·lə́ntam 'I am distressed' (Jn 12.27); nə́ni wwə́nči-áhi-sak·we·lə́ntamən 'he was therefore very upset' (1842:14.1).

sak·we·ləntaməwá·k·an IN 'suffering' (Mt 16.24).

sak·wi·h- TA 'torment, bother': káči sak·wi·hí·han 'don't bother me (you sg.)' (Lk 11.7; KJV "trouble"; Gr. 4.111o); ksak·wihkəwá·ɔk=č 'they will torment you' (Jn 16.23, 16.33; KJV "have tribulation").

sak·wi·laehtəwá·k·an (Gr. 5.114j) IN 'persecution(s)' (Mt 13.21, KJV "tribulation or persecution"; ⟨sukwelaentwakun⟩ Mk 10.30 with ⟨cnt⟩ for ⟨cvt⟩, KJV "persecutions"); sak·wi·laehtəwá·k·ana 'persecutions' (Lk 21.11&).

sak·wi·lae·h- TA 'torment': ó·k=č a·lə́nte sak·wi·lae·há·ɔk 'and some will be tormented' (Lk 11.49; KJV "persecute"); kóč=háč sak·wi·laé·he·kw 'why do you (pl.) torment her?' (Mt 26.10; KJV "trouble"); nsak·wi·laé·hukw=á· 'she would torment me' (Lk 18.5; KJV "weary me").

†salapte·í·i-o·t·é·nink 'in the city of Sarepta' (Lk 4.26).

salaxkihəla·- AI 'be startled': salaxkíhəle·p 'he was agitated' (Lk 1.12, Mt 2.3); salaxkihəlé·ɔk 'they were agitated' (Mt 21.10; KJV "moved"); kóč=háč salaxkihəlá·e·kw 'Why are you (pl.) agitated?' (Lk 24.38; KJV "troubled").

sala·məwá·k·an (Gr. 5.58h) IN 'weeping' (Mt 2.18).

sala·mwi·- (səsala·mwi·- [Rə̂+]; Gr. 5.36b) AI 'cry out': salá·məwak 'they cried out' (Mk 5.38; Gr. 4.21l); énta-=č -salá·mwink 'where there shall be loud weeping' (Mt 22.13); é·li ksala·mwíhəmɔ=č 'for you shall cry out' (Lk 6.25).
- səsala·mwi·-: səsalá·məwak 'they screamed' (LTD ND; Gr. 5.36b); ná=č wé·mi entxa·ké·i·t yú entalá·wsi·t wsəsalá·mwi·n 'then all nations in the world will cry out' (Mt 24.30; KJV "mourn").

same·liáxkwe 'Samaritan woman' (⟨Sumrlie uxqr⟩ Jn 4.7, 4.9 [2x]; apparently ⟨ie u⟩ (= [iya]) is for /iá/, as the retention of /a/ shows that the preceding vowel is short).

†same·líí·- AI 'be a Samaritan': †same·líí·č·i·k 'Samaritans' (Jn 4.9).

†same·líí·i (~ †same·lí·i) PN 'of Samaria': †same·líí·i (Jn 4.5, Lk 10.33, Lk 17.16) ~ †same·lí·i (Lk 9.52).
- ♦ (prenoun as particle) †samelí·i khák·ay 'that you are a Samaritan' (Jn 8.48).
- ▪ †same·líí·yunk P 'Samaria (loc.)' (Lk 17.11); †same·lí·ink 'through Samaria' (Jn 4.4); †same·lí·yunk 'in Samaria' (Acts 1.8; Gr. 2.32c).

†same·líí·ɔk 'Samaritans' (⟨Sumrlieuk⟩ Jn 4.40, Mt 10.5; ⟨Sumrleuk⟩ Jn 4.39).

sap·e·- (səs·ap·e·- [Rə̂+]) II 'be a spot': énta-sap·é·t·i·k 'a little spot' (Lk 6.41; Gr. 5.73p).
- səs·ap·e·-: səs·áp·e· 'it is spotted, speckled' (LB; Gr. 5.36r).

-sa·kᵒ; see shakᵒ.

†sa·kaláyas 'Zacharias' (Lk 1.5, 1.12, 1.13, 1.18, 1.21, etc.); †sa·kalayás·al (obv.) (Lk 1.21, 1.40, 1.67), †sa·kalayás·a (Lk 11.51, Mt 23.35).

sa·khanihi·- AI+O 'throw out': ná .. sɔ·khanihi·né·ɔ 'then they threw him out' (Mt 21.39&); sɔ·khanihi·ne·ɔ́·i 'they threw him out' (Lk 20.12).

sa·khəskaw- TA 'cast out': ná sa·khə́skaɔ·n 'then he was expelled' (⟨sakvcskaon⟩ Jn 9.34; KJV "cast .. out"); lí-sa·khə́skaɔ·n 'that he was expelled' (Jn 9.35).

†sa·kí·as 'Zacchaeus' (Lk 19.2, 19.5, 19.8).

sa·kskihəla·- II 'sprout, come up': áləmi- skí·kw -sa·kskíhəle· 'grass is beginning to come up' (1834a:14).

sa·k·i·- AI — sa·k·ən- II 'sprout, grow'.
- ▪ sa·k·i·- (AI): sa·k·ihtí·t·eč hítko·k ɔ́·k skí·kɔ 'let trees and grass grow' (1842:6.5).
- ▪ sa·k·ən- (II): á·p·əwi-sá·k·ən 'it easily sprouted' (Mt 13.5); takó· káski-sa·k·ənó·wi 'it was not able to sprout' (1834b:27.1); wənči-sá·k·ink 'the reason why it sprouted') (Mk 4.27); mé·či sa·k·ínke nə́ hwí·t 'after the wheat had come up' (Mt 13.26).

sa·k·í·ma (-sa·k·i·ma·yəm-; Gr. 2.36f) AN 'king, prince, chief' (Mt 2.3, 2.6, Lk 3.19-20, Jn 12.31, etc.); sa·k·i·má·ɔk 'kings, princes' (Mt 17.25, 20.25, Lk 22. 25); sa·k·i·má·ɔl (obv.) (Mt 2.9), sa·k·i·má·ɔ (Lk 14.31); sa·k·i·ma·únka 'ancient kings' (Lk 10.24); sa·k·i·má·unk 'at the king's' (Lk 7.25; Gr. 2.28a); sa·k·i·ma·i·ké·i P 'among kings' (Mk 13.9; Gr. 2.36f, 4.10e); mahtant·o·wí·i-sa·k·í·ma 'Chief of the Devils' (Mt 10.25).
- -sa·k·i·ma·yəm-: ksa·k·i·má·yəm 'your (sg.) king' (Mt 21.5; Gr. 2.33a); ksa·k·i·ma·yəmúwa 'your (pl.) king' (Jn 19.14, 19.15); sɔ·k·i·má·yəma 'his chief' (V).
- ▪ sa·k·i·ma·í·i (Gr. 5.122h) PN 'king' (Mt 12.24; KJV "prince of"); sa·k·i·ma·í·i- .. -mahtánt·u 'the king of devils' (1834b:23.6).

sa·k·i·ma·- AI 'be a king': sa·k·i·má·t·e 'when he was king' (Lk 1.5, Mt 2.1, Lk 3.1), †isələlí·i-sa·k·i·má·t·e 'if he is the King of Israel' (Mt 27.42); təli- †a·či·lé·yas -sa·k·í·ma·n 'that Archelaus was king' (Mt 2.22).

sa·k·i·ma·i·- (|sākīmāwī-|; Gr. 5.67c) AI 'be a king': nčo·wí·i-sa·k·i·ma·iáne 'if you are the king of the Jews' (Lk 23.37; Gr. 2.36f).

saˑkˑiˑmaˑɔmiˑmə́nsak 'king's children' (Mt 8.12).

saˑkˑiˑmaˑɔ́ˑkˑan (Gr. 5.58s) IN 'kingdom' (Lk 4.5, Mt 6.13, Mk 3.24, etc.); saˑkˑiˑmaˑɔ́ˑkˑanak 'kingdoms' (Mt 24.7 [anim.]); saˑkˑiˑmaˑɔ́ˑkˑanink 'in the kingdom' (Mt 2.5, 5.19 [2x], 8.11); nsaˑkˑiˑmaˑɔ́ˑkˑan 'my kingdom' (Mk 6.23, Jn 18.36 [3x]); ksaˑkˑiˑmaˑɔ́ˑkˑan 'your kingdom' (Mt 6.10, Lk 11.2); wsaˑkˑiˑmaˑɔ́ˑkˑan 'his kingdom' (Lk 1.32, Jn 3.3, 3.5, etc.; Gr. 2.56b), sɔˑkˑiˑmaˑɔ́ˑkˑan (Lk 12.31, etc.; ⟨sokemokun⟩ Lk 10.11); íka wsaˑkˑiˑmaˑɔ́ˑkˑan 'on his kingdom' (⟨wsavkamaokun⟩ Mt 13.43 [em.]; correct without -ink LOC?); nsaˑkˑiˑmaˑɔ́ˑkˑanink 'in my kingdom' (Lk 22.30); sɔˑkˑiˑmaˑɔ́ˑkˑanink 'in his kingdom' (Lk 7.28, 9.62, 13.28, 13.29, etc.). ▸ For the animate use, see Goddard (2019: 98).

▪ saˑkˑiˑmaˑɔˑkˑaníˑi PN 'of the kingdom': ɔˑsˑahkaméˑi-saˑkˑiˑmaˑɔˑkˑaníˑi-tunkšeˑkɔ́ˑkˑan 'heavenly kingdom key' (Mt 16.19). ♦ (prenoun as particle) wéˑlhik aˑptoˑnáˑkˑan saˑkˑiˑmaˑɔˑkˑaníˑi 'the good word of the kingdom' (Mt 4.23).

saˑkˑiˑmaˑwheˑ- AI+O 'make O2 king': saˑkˑiˑmaˑwhéˑtˑe hɔ́kaya 'if he makes him king' (Jn 19.12; Gr. 2.28a); líˑkáhta-saˑkˑiˑmáˑwheˑn 'that there was a desire to make him king' (Jn 6.15).

saˑkˑiˑmáˑxkwe AN 'queen'; 'female chief' (LTD); saˑkˑiˑmaˑxkwéˑɔ 'queen (obv.)' (Mt 12.42).

†saˑlamána 'Solomon (abs.)' (Mt 6.29, Mt 12.42 [2x], Jn 10.23, Lk 12.27).

saˑpˑəlehəlaˑ- (saˑsaˑpˑəlehəlaˑ- [Rā+], |sāpəlēhlā-|) II 'be lightning flashing': málahši saˑpˑəléhəlaˑk 'like lightning' (1834b:37.1).

• saˑsaˑpˑəlehəlaˑ-: málahši saˑsaˑpˑəléhəleˑ 'as if there were lightning' (Lk 10.18); saˑsaˑpˑəléhəlaˑk 'lightning' (Lk 17.24); saˑsaˑpˑəléhəláˑkˑe 'when lightning flashes' (Mt 24.27).

♦ saˑsaˑpˑəléhəlaˑk 'lightning' (lexicalized participle): saˑsaˑpˑəléhəláˑkˑink liˑnáˑkwsu 'his expression was like lightning' (Mt 28.3).

saˑpˑəleˑeˑ- II 'be shiny, be bright': kéhəla wə́li-saˑpˑəléˑeˑ 'it's really shiny' (ME); wə́škinkw ləkhíkwi-saˑpˑəléˑeˑ kiˑšˑóˑxˑink 'his face was as bright as the sun' (Mt 17.2).

▸ Cf. sáˑpˑəleˑ 'it shines' (LB).

†saˑtamíˑɔk 'the people of Sodom' (Mt 10.15); †saˑtamiˑyúnka (abs.) (Lk 10.12). †sáˑtamink 'in Sodom' (Mt 11.23), wə́nči †sáˑtamink '(from) Sodom' (Lk 17.29).

†saˑtasíˑɔk 'Sadducees'; †saˑtasíˑɔk 'Sadducees' (Mt 16.1); †saˑtasíˑɔ (obv.) (Mt 3.7); †saˑtasíˑsˑa (obv.) (Mt 22.34).

se° (|sē-|) 'scatter' (Gr. 5.39a). ▸ Cf. ahse° above.

sehəlaˑ- (ahsehəlaˑ- [Ra+ used with plural subjects]) II 'scatter': séhəleˑw 'it scattered' (1834b:26.12): éˑli-séhəlaˑk 'which fell to {smwh}' (1834b:27.6).

• ahsehəlaˑ-: ahsehəléˑɔk 'they scatter' (Mk 14.27), ⟨achsehelléwak⟩ "they are scattered" (Z. 165); ktə́li-=č -ahsehəlaˑnéˑɔ 'you (pl.) will scatter' (Jn 16.32); éˑli-ahsehəláhtiˑt 'as they scattered' (Mt 9.36).

sehsiˑskəwahóˑsheˑs (Gr. 5.42d) AN 'clay-pot-maker, potter' (Mt 27.10).

séns P 'cent': kwə́tˑi séns 'one cent' (⟨scns⟩ Mk 12.42; misprinted ⟨sens⟩ Mt 10.29; KJV "a farthing" 2x); níˑšˑa séns 'two cents' (Lk 12.6; KJV "two farthings").

▸ Also séˑns [sẽˑs]; LB): télən séns 'ten cents; a dime'.

†sépati 'Zebedee' (Mt 10.2, Jn 21.2); †séˑpatiˑs (Mt 20.20&); †seˑpatíˑsˑa (abs.) (Mt 26.37). †sépələn 'Zabulon' (Mt 4.15).

seˑkaloˑxˑəlink(??) 'saw blade' (1834a:15).

seˑkantpéˑxˑink 'above his head' (Mt 22.20); seˑkantpeˑxˑíˑnəliˑt 'above his (obv.) head' (Jn 19.19). ▸ Cf. ⟨segantpéchünk⟩ "over head" (Z. 2).

sé·ki: see sháki.

se·ksí·t·ank 'a foot (measure)' (Mt 6.27, Lk 12.25; Gr. 3.13(6)d).

se·k·i·- AI 'multiply': áləmi-se·k·i·ló·p·ani 'they (obv.) began to multiply' (1834b:19.12, 1842:10.6). ♦ Assuming this is |sē-| 'disperse' + |-(ī)kī| AI 'grow'.

†sé·ləm 'Salim' (Jn 3.23).

†sé·lɔ·m 'Salome' (Mk 16.1).

se·nihi·- AI(+O) 'sow (seed)' (⟨srnrv-⟩ 1x, ⟨srniv-⟩ 1x, ⟨srnev-⟩ 9x; Gr. 5.39a): mái-se·níhi·p 'he went to sow' (Mt 13.3); se·níhi·t 'a sower' (Mt 13.3); né·li-se·níhi·t 'as he sowed' (Mt 13.4); se·nihí·lu mahčí·kwi-xkáni·m 'he (obv.) sowed bad seed' (Mt 13.25); náni se·nihí·t wé·ltək xkáni·m 'the one who sowed the good seed' (Mt 13.37); se·níhi·t 'the sower' (⟨srnivet⟩ Mt 13.39); se·nihí·č·i·k 'those that sow it' (⟨srnrvethek⟩ Jn 4.36); máta=háč kse·nihí·i wé·ltək xkáni·m 'didn't you (sg.) sow good seed?' (Mt 13.27).

†sé·pati·s, †se·patí·s·a: see †sépati.

se·s·e·k·ayehw- (B ⟨srsrkycv-⟩ 5x, ⟨acv⟩ 2x, ⟨aecv⟩ 1x) TA 'whip': hu kse·s·e·k·ayého·l 'I'm really going to whip you' (ME); tə́li-=č .. -se·s·e·k·ayehɔ·né·ɔ 'for them to whip him' (Lk 18.32; cf. Lk 18.33); kíši-se·s·e·k·ayehɔ́·t·e 'after he whipped him' (Mk 15.15); se·s·e·k·ayehɔ́·p·ani·k 'they have been whipped' (⟨srsrkaecvopanek⟩ Mt 23.34); wse·s·e·k·ayehɔwwá·ɔ 'they whipped him' (Mk 12.4&); ɔ́·k=č ehə́nta-ma·éhəlank ktə́nta-se·s·e·k·ayeho·k·éhəmɔ 'And you will be whipped in the synagogues.' (Mk 13.9).
  ▸ Cf. ⟨Sesegauwehícan⟩ 'whip' (Z 229); Mun se·xe·kawi·h- TA.

se·x·we·- (ahse·x·we·- [Ra+ used with plural subjects], -t-as·e·x·we·-) AI 'scatter, disperse': ɔ́·k áləmi-sé·x·we· 'and they began to scatter' (1834b:43.1); ná áləmi-sé·x·we·n 'then people began to disperse' (1834b:19.6).
  • ahse·x·we·- (-t-as·e·x·we·-) AI 'scatter, go to scattered places': áləmi-ahse·x·wé·ɔk 'they began to disperse' (1842:9.9); ahse·x·wé·č·i·k 'the ones who scattered' (Jn 7.35 [em.; ⟨vusrxwrthek⟩ for ⟨uvs°⟩]).
  • -t-as·e·x·we·-: nána tɔs·e·x·we·né·ɔ 'then they scattered' (1834b:41.5).

sək(·)° (|sə́k-|) 'black' (Gr. §5.2a).

səkahkəmhɔkɔt- II 'be dark clouds': səkahkəmhɔ́kɔt 'the clouds are dark' (1834a:13).

səkahkóle·s 'African' (1834b:41.7, 42.1, etc; Gr. 5.50j). ▸ Cf. ⟨Sachachquallees⟩ 'Negro' (Z. 129 [with a different initial if not miswritten]). Note: sək- 'black' + *ahkóle·s 'European', attested as ⟨Akoores⟩ 'Swede' (Campanius 1696:140).

sə́kahsən IN 'iron, iron thing, wire' (LB); səkahsə́na 'irons, iron fetters' (Mk 5.4 [2x]; Gr. 3.14a).

səkahsəno·wi·- II 'be of iron': kéku səkahsənó·wi·k 'things of iron' (1834a:18.12).

səkahtehw- (səsəkahtehw- [Rə+]) TA 'whip': ɔ́·k=á· ktɔ́li-səsəkahtehó·k·o·n 'and then they would whip you (sg.)' (⟨sisukavtrvwkwn⟩ Mt 10.17).
  ▸ Cf. se·sekahtehw-: nse·sekahtého 'I whipped him repeatedly' (LB); ⟨sëkahteh[w]-⟩ (LTD).

sə́ki PN 'black' (Gr. 5.120f).

sək·i·t- TI(2) 'make black: é·li- máta=á· -káski- náxpəne kwə́t·i mí·laxk .. -sək·i·tó·wan 'as you would not be able to make even one hair .. black' (Mt 5.36).

sələk·a·khw- (|sələk-āhkw-ah-|; Gr. 5.18g) TI(1a) 'press': énta-=č -sələk·á·khɔnk wísahki·m 'a place where he would press grapes' (Mt 21.23; KJV "a winepress"). ▸ Cf. sələkte·- 'fry', Mun sə̄ləsk- 'squeeze'; for the semantic range of the initial, cf. Mes si·- in 'to fry' and 'to milk'.

səsala·mwi·-: see sala·mwi·-.

səs·ukhɔ·l-: see sukhɔ·l-.

shak° ~ -sa·k° (|sahk-|) '{so far, so long}' (Gr. 3.13(6)).

shakahpi·- (-sa·kahpi·-) AI 'stay {smwh} (until ..)': ná=č nə́ ksá·kahpi·n 'that's where you (sg.) must stay (until ..)' (Mt 2.13).

shaka·wsi·- (se·ka·wsi·-) AI 'live {so long}': íka péči se·ka·wsían 'as long as you (sg.) live' (1842:8.1).

shakhake·- (se·khake·-, |sahkahkē-|; Gr. 3.13(6)c) AI 'be away {so long}': se·khaké·a 'for as long as I am away' (Lk 19.13; Gr. 4.67(5)aa); se·kháke·t 'while she was gone' (Jn 4.31).

sháki (-sá·ki, sé·ki, sisháki [Rih+], |sahkī|; Gr. 3.13(6), 5.28h, 5.128s) PV '{so far}, {so long}' (Lk 1.24, Mt 20.12, Mk 14.37); (with sbj.) 'until' (Mk 12.36).
- -sá·ki (Lk 13.33, Mt 10.11, Jn 10.24, etc.).
- sé·ki PV 'as long as, while, since' (Lk 1.10, 1.23, etc.); sé·ki-péči-təmi·k·é·a 'from the time I came in' (Lk 7.45); sé·ki-á·mwi·t 'since he had risen (from the dead)' (Jn 21.14).
- sisháki PV: máta=háč télən ɔ́·k ní·š·a á·wəlink sisháki-ki·škwí·i 'isn't it always day for twelve hours?' (Jn 11.9).
- sháki P 'as far as, until, up to, for (such time)': yúkwe sháki 'until now' (Jn 2.10, 17.4; Gr. 3.13(6)a); kwə́t·i máilink sháki 'for a mile' (Mt 5.41); sháki ní·š·a 'for two (miles)' (Mt 5.41); sháki †pétani 'as far as Bethany' (Lk 24.50); kwə́t·i á·wəlink sháki (PV) 'for one hour' (Mk 14.37); naxo·k·wənakháke sháki 'for three days (starting now)' (Mt 27.64); (with sbd.) le·lá·i tə́nta·n sháki 'until it (sun) stood halfway (down)' (Mk 15.33); sháki níši-kahtənamí·č·i·k 'ones up to the age of two' (Mt 2.16); sháki nə́ kí·škwi·k 'up until the day' (Mt 26.29).

shaki·h- TA 'make {so long}': awé·n=háč ki·ló·wa kɔ́ski-ánči-shaki·há·ɔ hɔ́kaya 'who of you (pl.) can lengthen his body?' (Mt 6.27).

shɔpᵒ (|swahp-|) 'close (circular opening)' (Gr. 5.13e.2).

shɔpinkwe·x·i·n- (|swahpīnkwēīxīn-|; Gr. 5.22b.2) AI 'have the eyes closed': shɔpinkwe·x·í·no·k 'they have their eyes closed' (Mt 13.15).

sía·kw IN 'whip' (Jn 2.15).

†sília 'Syria' (Lk 2.2); †silií·yunk (Mt 4.24).
- †silií·i PN 'of Syria, Syrian': †silií·i-lə́nu 'a Syrian man' (Lk 4.27).

†símian 'Simeon' (Lk 2.25, 2.34).

sinki·k·amí·k·a 'the corner of a house' (Mk 12.10; KJV "the head of the corner").
▸ Cf. ⟨Singigamika⟩ "corner of a house" (B&A 132).

†sisəlí·yunk †pilápai 'Caesarea Philippi (loc.)' (Mt 16.13).

si·khai·- AI 'be salt': ksi·khaíhəmɔ 'you (pl.) are salt' (Mt 5.13).

sí·khay IN 'salt' (Mk 9.50, Lk 14.34); íka sí·khenk 'in the salt' (OA).

si·khe·hɔ·s·i·- AI — II 'be salted'.
- si·khe·hɔ·s·i·- (AI): wsi·khe·hɔ·s·i·né·ɔ=č tə́ntay 'they shall be salted with fire' (Mk 9.49).
- si·khe·hɔ·s·i·- (II): wi·hunke·ɔ́·k·an ehələkhíkwi-si·khe·hɔ́·s·i·k 'whenever a sacrifice is salted' (Mk 9.49).

si·khe·ɔ́·k·an IN 'saltiness' (Mt 5.13, Mk 9.50, Lk 14.34).

si·khe·yo·wi·- II 'be salty' (Gr. 5.68g): tá=háč=á· wə́nči- lápi -si·khe·yó·u 'what would make it be salty again?' (⟨sekrww⟩ Mt 5.13); tá=háč=á· wə́nči-si·khe·yó·u 'what would make it be salty?' (lit., 'from what would it be salty') (⟨sekvrbw⟩ Mk 9.50); si·khe·yo·wí·k·eč khak·ayúwa 'let yourselves be salty' (Mk 9.50).

si·k·a·xkhwe·- AI 'make boards': si·k·á·xkhwe· 'makes boards' (1834a:13).

sí·k·a·xkw IN 'board; trunk, coffin' (OA, ME, LB, 1834a:12); si·k·á·xkɔ 'boards' (LB; 1834a:15).
- si·k·á·xkwtət (dim.) 'box' (Lk 7.37).

▸ Cf. Mun păsí·ka·xkw 'board'.

si·k·ɔn- II 'be spring': áləmi-sí·k·ɔn 'spring has begun' (1834a:14); si·k·ɔ́nke 'in the spring' (1834a:14).

si·k·ɔní·i P 'in spring' (1834a:16). ♦ wə́ski-si·k·ɔní·i 'in the new spring' (1834a:16).

†si·lɔ́·tu 'Zelotes' (⟨Selotw⟩ Lk 6.15). ♦ Perhaps a misprint for ⟨Selotes⟩.

si·ma·kɔ́·nal 'cornstalks' (obv. or inan. pl.) (⟨semakonul⟩ 1834b:44.3). Cf. ⟨simáquon⟩ (Z. 46), pl. ⟨-all⟩; si·p·á·kɔ·n AN 'cornstalk' (LTD ND, ME), si·p·a·kɔ́·nak (pl.) (OA, ME).

sí·p·u IN 'river' (V, OA, ME, FW); sí·p·əwa 'rivers' (OA, ME; ⟨sepw⟩ Jn 7.38 [em.]); †nčataní·i-sí·p·unk '(along) the Jordan River' (Lk 3.3, Mt 3.5; Gr. 2.19h).

†sí·sal 'Caesar' (Lk 2.1, 20.22, Mt 22.21 [2x], etc.); †sí·sala (obv.) (Jn 19.12).

si·skəwáho·s AN 'clay pot' (ND, LB); si·skəwahó·s·ak 'clay vessels' (Jn 2.6, Mk 7.4).

si·skəwə́nču* 'clay bowl(?)' (cf. Gr. 5.9i); si·skəwə́nčunk '(in) a clay vessel' (Lk 22.10; KJV "pitcher").

si·sko·he·- AI+O 'make clay (moistened dirt)': si·skó·he· 'he makes clay' (Gr. 5.70g); si·skó·he·p 'he made clay' (Jn 9.11, 9.14); wwə́nči-si·skó·he·n 'he made clay from (it)' (Jn 9.6).

sí·sku IN 'mud' (V, OA, ME, ND; Gr. 5.68h, 5.70g), 'clay' (Jn 9.6).

▪ si·skəwí·i PN '(of) clay' (Mt 27.7; Gr. 5.122i).

skapº (|səkàp-|) 'wet' (Gr. §5.2a).

skappal- (|səkàpəpal-|; Gr. 5.78f) TA 'wet': šəwá·p·unk tə́nta-skappalá·ɔ 'he wet it (anim.) in vinegar' (⟨skuppalao⟩ Mt 27.48). ♦ B does not normally write geminates, and ⟨pp⟩ for /pp/ is found only here; cf. ktə́li-skappat·aí·ne·n 'that you wet it for us' (ME; Gr. 5.95e).

skapsi·- (-səkapsi-) AI 'be wet': skápsu 'he's wet', nsəkápsi 'I'm wet' (OA; Gr. 2.70c).

skát·e·- II 'it burns': áləmi-skát·e· 'it starts burning' (Lk 12.49). ▸ Cf. ⟨skàte⟩ 'it (an open fire) is lit' (LTD); ⟨Skattek⟩ "burning, ardent, fervent, zealous, hot" (B&A 133).

skinnəwi·- (-o·skinnəwi·-, we·skinnəwi·-, |(wə)skīlənəwī-|; Gr. 5.67e) AI 'be a young man': né·li-skinnúwie·kw 'while you (pl.) are young men' (1834b:4.1, 1842:19.2).

• -o·skinnəwi·-: ko·skinnəwíhəmɔ 'you (pl.) are young men' (1834b:3.9).

• we·skinnəwi·-: we·skinnəwiáne 'when you (sg.) were a young man' (Jn 21.18; Gr. 2.36g, 5.67e).

skínnu (-o·skinno·yəm-, |(wə)skīlənəw-|; Gr. 2.26b, 5.14l) AN 'young man' (Lk 7.14, Mk 10.17&, etc.); skinnúwak 'young men' (Mk 14.51); skinnúwa 'a young man (obv.)' (Mk 16.5); skinnúwto·kw 'boys (voc.)' (⟨sken-|wvtwq⟩ 1842:18.4).

• -o·skinno·yəm-: no·skinno·yəməná·na·k 'our (exc.) young men' (ME; Gr. 2.33e).

▪ skinnó·t·ət (dim.) 'a young fellow' (Jn 6.9), 'young man' (1842:14.2).

skí·kw IN 'grass' (⟨skek⟩ 1834a:14; V), 'a blade of grass; a weed; hay' (LB); mahčí·kwi-skí·kw 'weed(s)' (*lit.*, 'bad grass') (Mt 13.36); skí·kɔl 'grass' (1834a:14, 16), skí·kɔ (Lk 12.28, 1842:6.5), 'grasses' (Mt 13.32), mahčí·kwi-skí·kɔ 'weeds' (Mt 13.27, 13.30), wə́nči skí·kɔ 'with (i.e., using) grass' (Mt 6.30), winkánki skí·kɔ 'sweet-tasting herbs' (Lk 11.42); winki·ma·khóki skí·kɔ 'sweet-smelling herbs' (Mt 23.23).

skí·xkwe (-o·ski·xkwe·yəm-, |wəskīxkwēw-|; Gr. 2.10a, 2.68f, 5.1c, 5.14k) AN 'young woman' (Lk 1.27); ski·xkwé·ɔk 'young women' (Mt 25.7, 25.11); ski·xkwé·ɔ 'the girl (obv.)' (Mk 6.22, 6.28); ski·xkwe·yúnka 'young women of old' (Mt 25.1).

• -o·ski·xkwe·yəm-: o·ski·xkwé·yəma 'one of his unmarried young women' (Lk 22.56-57&; Gr. 2.33b).

skóntay (-t-əskɔnte·yəm-; Gr. 2.68c) IN 'door, doorway, gate' (AD, OA, LB; Mt 7.13, 7.14, Jn 10.7, etc.); skóntenk (loc.) (⟨skontif⟩ Mt 7.13, ⟨skontrf⟩ Mk 1.33; LTD ND), tahčé·k skóntenk 'in the narrow door' (⟨skontrf⟩ Lk 13.24); skɔnté·yunk (loc.) (LTD ND).
- -t-əskɔnte·yəm-: wtəskɔnté·yəmink 'at his door' (Lk 16.20; Gr. 2.33c, 2.68c).
▸ And see next.

skónte P 'at the door' (⟨skontc⟩ Jn 18.16, Mk 11.4; ⟨skontr⟩ Jn 10.1, 10.2; ⟨skuntr⟩ Mk 2.2); wənči skónte 'by (i.e., through) the door' (Jn 10.1), skónte wənči (Jn 10.2); kí·xki skónte 'near the door' (Mk 2.2, Mk 11.4&).

skɔnte·amé·naxk IN 'gate' (LTD ND); kí·xki .. skɔnte·amé·nxkink 'near the gate in the wall' (Lk 7.12). ▸ Cf. mé·naxk above.

so·k(·)º (|sōk-|) 'pour, spill' (Gr. 5.11h).

so·kh- TI(1a) 'spill, pour out': wso·khámən 'she poured it' (Jn 12.7&; Gr. 2.57b, 2.63e).

so·khamaw- TA+O 'pour O2 for' (Gr. 5.94c): ná wé·mi íka wso·khamáɔ·n wi·lí·li·t 'then she poured all of it on his head' (Mk 14.3).

so·k·ahəla·- II 'spill, (of blood) be shed': ó·k=á· so·k·áhəle· 'and it would spill' (Lk 5.37); so·k·áhəla·k 'which was shed' (Mt 26.28); é·li-so·k·ahəlá·k·əp 'the way it has been shed' (Mt 23.35).

so·k·əla·n (si·s·o·k·əla·n- [Rī+]; Gr. 5.11h, 5.44e) II 'rain': káhta-só·k·əla·n 'it's going to rain' (Lk 12.54).
- si·s·o·k·əla·n-: máta si·s·o·k·əla·nó·wi·p 'it never rained' (Lk 4.25); máta si·s·o·k·əla·nó·k·we 'if it never rains' (1834a:14).

so·k·əla·nhe·- AI 'make rain': so·k·əlá·nhe· 'he makes rain' (Mt 5.45).

so·k·əla·nihəla·- II 'fall as rain': so·k·əla·níhəle·p tɔ́ntay ó·k wi·s·á·e·k ahsɔ́n 'it rained fire and yellow stone' (Lk 17.29; KJV "it rained fire and brimstone").

so·m- TA 'sue': nsó·ma 'I sued him' (LB); awé·n so·mkóne 'if someone sues you' (Mt 5.40).

so·psi·- AI 'be naked': nso·psí·həmp 'I was naked' (Mt 25.36, 25.43; Gr. 2.53b); é·li só·psu 'as he was naked' (Jn 21.7); ktəli-só·psi·n 'that you (sg.) were naked' (Mt 25.44).

so·pši·mwi·- AI 'flee naked': áləmi-so·pší·mu 'he ran away naked' (Mk 14.52).

†so·sána 'Susanna' (Lk 8.3).

so·so·k·áhəla·s AN 'chain': so·so·k·ahəlá·s·a 'chains (obv.)' (Mk 5.4); so·so·k·ahəlá·s·a 'with chains (instrumental oblique)' (Mk 5.3, 5.4). ▸ Cf. so·k·áhəla·s AN 'chain', obv. so·k·ahəlá·s·a (LB); so·k·áhəlas IN 'chain': ⟨Sogahellasall⟩ 'chains' (Zeisberger 1806:92).

sɔ́·čəl (-sɔ·čələm-) AN 'soldier' (AD; Jn 19.34); sɔ́·čəlak (OA, LB; Lk 7.8, Jn 18.12, Jn 18.12, etc.); né·li·l sɔ́·čəlal 'those soldiers (obv.)' (1834b:38.2); sɔ́·čəla 'soldiers (obv.)' (Lk 3.14, Mt 28.12).
- -sɔ·čələm-: wsɔ·čəláma 'his soldiers' (Lk 14.31 [2x], Mt 27.27); sɔ·čələməwá·ɔ 'their soldiers' (Mk 14.43&).

sɔ·k·i·ma·yəm-* (-o·s·a·k·i·ma·yəm-, |wəsākīmāwəm-|; Gr. 5.72f) TA 'have as king': ó·k=č o·s·a·k·i·ma·yəmúk·o·l †isəlálal 'Israel (obv.) will have him as king' (Lk 1.33).
▸ Cf. sɔ·k·i·má·yəma 'his chief' (V): see sa·k·í·ma.

sɔ·k·i·ma·yəmi·- (-o·s·a·k·i·ma·yəmi·-, we·sa·k·i·ma·yəmi·-, |wəsākīmāwəmī-|; Gr. 5.72f) AI 'have a king'.
- -o·s·a·k·i·ma·yəmi·-: takó· pí·li no·s·a·k·i·ma·yəmi·húməna 'we (exc.) have no other king' (Jn 19.15; Gr. 4.81j).
- we·sa·k·i·ma·yəmi·-: we·sa·k·i·ma·yəmíhti·t=č 'who will be their king' (Mt 2.6).
▸ See sɔ·k·i·ma·yəm-* TA.

só·mi (Gr. 5.129hh) P 'too, too much, very much, absolutely' (Lk 1.18, 1.20, 5.9, Mk 3.9, Mt 13.22, Lk 18.5, 20.16, Mt 22.8, Lk 21.23, Mt 26.38, Lk 22.44, Jn 21.6).
  ▪ só·mi PV (Lk 1.15, Jn 5.13, Mt 7.14, 28.8&, Lk 24.41). These are not provably preverbs, but só·mi PV is attested later: ko·s·á·mi-ča·kəná·kwsi 'you made too much noise' (ME).
spankwehəle·ó·k·ane P 'the blink of an eye, an instant': kwə́t·i spankwehəle·ó·k·ane ləkhíkwi 'in one instant of time' (⟨spufwruliokunc⟩ Lk 4.5 [em.]; KJV "a moment of time"). ♦ The spelling must be a misprint for ⟨*spufwrvlrokunc⟩; cf. spankwe·ó·k·an 'the blink of an eye' (LB) (⟨spanquewoácan⟩ 'wink; moment' [Z. 232]); spánkwe· 'he blinked his eye (once)' (OA, LB; Gr. 2.70e); /spankwéhəle·/ 'he blinked his eye' (LTD).
spihəla·- II 'go up': ahpá·mi le·lá·i lí-spíhəle· 'the sun goes about halfway up' (Mt 20.3; KJV "about the third hour").
spínkw IN 'tear (from the eye)' (LB); nsəp·ínkɔ 'my tears' (AD); wsəp·ínkɔ 'her tears' (Lk 7.38, 7.44).
sukhɔ·l- (səs·ukhɔ·l- [Rə̀+]) TA 'spit on': mé·či kíši-sukhɔ·lá·t·e wəškinkwí·li·t 'after he had spit on his eyes (*lit.*, spit on him in his eyes)' (Mk 8.23); wsukhɔ·lá·ɔ wi·lanəwí·li·t 'he spat on his tongue' (Mk 7.33).
  • səs·ukhɔ·l-: ná=č .. səs·ukhɔ́·la·n 'then he shall be spat upon' (Lk 18.32); wsəs·ukhɔ·lawwá·ɔ 'they spat on him' (Mt 27.30); ná wsəs·ukhɔ·la·né·ɔ 'then they all spat on him' (Mt 26.67).
  ♦ Note: for the /s·/, see next.
suk·w- (səs·uk·w- [Rə̀+]) AI 'spit': súkw 'he spat' (OA, FW); hák·ink lí-súk·o·p 'he spat on the ground' (Jn 9.6; Gr. 3.13(1)a).
  • səs·ukw-: sə́s·ukw 'he is spitting' (OA).
suk·wi·ná·k·an IN 'spit, spittle' (ND); wsuk·wi·ná·k·an 'his spit' (Jn 9.6).
sunso·ksi·- AI — sunso·kte·- II 'be withered'.
  ▪ sunso·ksi·- (AI): sunso·ksí·č·i·k 'withered people' (Jn 5.3; KJV "withered").
  ▪ sunso·kte·- (II): wtənne·há·ɔn sunsó·kte· 'his right hand was withered' (Lk 6.6); sunso·kté·li·k wənáxk 'one whose hand was withered' (Lk 6.8; Gr. 4.64c).

š

=š: see =č.
-šahwe·ləmwi·-: see šhwe·ləmwi·-.
šame·- II 'be greasy': áhi wé·ltək šé·me·k mpí·s·o·n 'very fine ointment' (*lit.*, 'very good greasy medicine') (Mt 26.7&), mpi·s·ó·na ɔ́·k šé·me·k 'medicines and ointment' (Lk 23.56).
  ▸ Cf. šé·me·k 'castor oil' (LB), šé·me·kw (V).
šamən- (še·mən-) TA — TI(1b) 'anoint'.
  ▪ šamən- (TA): nšámənukw 'she anointed me' (Jn 12.7&).
  • še·mən-: še·mənáhti·t=á· 'which they would rub him with' (Mk 16.1).
  ▪ šamən- (TI): šɔmənəmə́na nsí·t·a 'she anointed my feet' (Lk 7.46; Gr. 2.55p).
-šamhukwe·n- TA 'anoint the head of': takó· kšamhukwe·ní·i 'you (sg.) did not anoint my head' (Lk 7.46). ▸ Stem: |šam-əhkwē-(ə)n-|, with |-əhkwē-| 'head, hair' (Gr. 5.13f).
šaɔla·mwi·- AI 'starve': šaɔlá·mu 'he starved to death' (LB); nšaɔlá·mwi 'I am starving' (ND; Lk 15.17).

šaɔnkəl- AI 'be infirm': šaɔnkələk·i·k 'ones who were infirm' (Mt 15.31; KJV "maimed"); šaɔnkələlí·č·i (obv.) (Mt 15.30; KJV "maimed"). ◆ Initial change in ⟨Schewongellikik⟩ "the lame" (B&A 128); stem: |šaw-ankəl-|, with |-ankəl| 'die, be diseased' (Gr. 5.17b).

šaɔp·ən- TI(1b) 'bend (a reed)': šɔɔp·ənəmən 'he bent it' (Mt 12.20; KJV "bruised," i.e., 'broke').

šaɔp·ihəla·- II 'bend': íkali šaɔp·ihəlé·ɔ 'they bent over towards it' (1842:13.2).

šaɔ́sksi·- AI 'wither, wilt' — šaɔskte·- II 'wilt'.

▪ šaɔ́sksi·- (AI): šaɔ́sksu=č 'he will wither' (Jn 15.6); ná hít·ukw šá·e šaɔ́skso·p 'then the tree immediately withered away' (Mt 21.19).

▪ šaɔskte·- (II): šaɔ́skte· 'it wilted' (Mt 13.6 [2x]), áləmi-šaɔ́skte· 'it began to wither' (1834b:26.14).

šawº (|šaw-|) 'weak' (Gr. §5.2a). Also in the preceding words with šaɔº.

šawəs·əwá·k·an IN 'weakness'; kšawsəwa·k·anóna 'our infirmities' (Mt 8.17).

šawəs·i·- (-šawsi·-) AI — šawəs·o·wi·- II 'be weak, infirm'.

▪ šawəs·i·- (AI): šawə́s·əwak=á· 'they would become weak' (Mk 8.3); é·li-šawəs·íhti·t 'as they were infirm' (Mt 9.36; KJV "they fainted").

• -šawsi·-: kšawsíhəna 'we are weak (1834b: back cover 9).

▪ šawəs·o·wi·- (II; assuming this is regularly formed, as in Gr. 5.76abcde): wahtuhé·p·i šawəs·ó·u 'the body is weak' (⟨jawusw⟩ Mt 26.41, presumably with ⟨-w⟩ for ⟨-ww⟩).

šaxahkº (|šāxak-|) 'straight' (Gr. §5.2a).

šaxahkankwe·p·i·- (šəšaxahkankwe·p·i·- [Rə+]) AI 'sit in a row': šəšaxahkankwé·p·əwak 'they sat in rows' (Mk 6.40; KJV "they sat down in ranks").

šaxahka·č·i·mwi·- AI 'tell the truth': šaxahka·č·í·mo·p 'he told the truth' (Jn 1.20).

šaxahka·p·e·i·- AI 'be righteous': šaxahka·p·e·yó·p·ani·k 'they were righteous' (Lk 1.6); šaxahka·p·é·ian núxa· 'O righteous father' (Jn 17.25); šaxahka·p·e·í·č·i·k 'righteous men' (Lk 20.20).

šaxahka·p·e·ɔ́·k·an IN 'righteousness' (lit., 'uprightness'); šaxahka·p·e·ɔ́·k·anink 'in righteousness' (⟨prok⟩ Lk 1.75).

šaxahka·wsəwá·k·an IN 'righteousness' (lit., 'upright living') (Mt 3.15, Jn 5.27, Mt 5.6, etc.); wšaxahka·wsəwá·k·an 'his righteousness' (Mt 6.33); kšaxahka·wsəwa·k·anúwa 'your (pl.) righteousness' (Mt 5.20).

šaxahka·wsi·- AI 'be upright, be righteous': wəli-šaxahká·wsu 'he was good and righteous' (Mt 27.57&; KJV "a good and just man"); šaxahká·wso·p 'he lived an upright life' (Lk 2.25); šaxahká·wsi·t 'good, righteous' (Mt 27.19); šaxahka·wsi·lí·č·i·k 'the righteous (obv.)' (s.b. -lí·č·i; Lk 1.17); šaxahka·wsi·tpáni·k 'those who had been righteous' (Lk 14.14, Mt 23.35); šaxahka·wsí·č·i·k 'the righteous' (Mt 9.13, 12.7, etc.); énta-šaxahká·wsink 'where the righteous are', lit., 'where one is (or people are) righteous' (Mt 5.45, 13.49); énta- máta -šaxahká·wsink 'where the unrighteous are' (Mt 5.45); šaxahka·wsi·tpanínka 'righteous ones (abs.)' (Mt 13.17, 23.29; Gr. 4.75o); təli-šaxahka·ws·í·li·n 'that he (obv.) was righteous' (Mk 6.20).

šáxahke·- II 'be righteous': šáxahke·k 'honest' (Jn 7.24; KJV "righteous").

▸ Cf. ⟨Schachachgeu⟩ "straight; right, exact, correct," ⟨Schachachgek⟩ "just so" (B&A 125).

šaxahkəna·s·i·- II 'be made straight' (Gr. 5.105u): wé·mi=č šaxahkəná·s·u 'all shall be made straight' (Lk 3.5).

šáxahki P 'certainly' (1834b:9.1, 9.6, 9.8; 1842:22.3); šáxahki=á· 'it would certainly be true (that)' (Lk 11.20). ▸ Cf. ⟨Schachachki⟩ "certain, certainly true, surely" (B&A 125).

- šaxahkí·i P 'certain' (1834a:20.20).

šaxahki·t- TI(2) 'make straight': šaxahkí·to·l 'make it straight' (Mt 3.3).

šá·e P 'immediately' (Lk 1.44, 1.64, Jn 4.28, Lk̯ 4.14, etc.; ⟨jai⟩ 31x [pp. 9-87], but ⟨jac⟩ 37x [pp. 35-218]); ná šá·e 'and promptly' (with ind. ind.) (Lk 20.30).
- šá·e núči 'right from the start' (Jn 15.27). ▸ Cf. Mah ⟨scháwa⟩, Ill ⟨cha8e⟩; ⟨scháwi⟩ 'immediately' (Z. 100) is presumably Mun šá·wi (EJ).

ša·e·s·i·- AI 'make haste': ša·é·s·i·kw 'make haste (you pl.)' (1834b:40.9, 1842:17.3).
▸ Cf. šá·e 'immediately'; ⟨Schauwessin⟩ 'to make haste' (B&A 126).

ša·khantí·k·an IN 'scabbard' (V); kša·khantí·k·anink 'into your scabbard' (⟨kjakvuntekunif⟩ Mt 26.52; KJV "sheath").

ša·khuk·wí·ɔn IN 'coat' (⟨jakvwqeun⟩ Lk 23.11; 1842:13.1, 14.4); kša·khuk·wí·ɔn 'your coat' (⟨kjakvoqeun⟩ Mt 5.40); ní·š·a ša·khuk·wí·ɔna 'two coats' (⟨jakvoqeonu⟩ Mt 10.10); šɔ·khuk·wí·ɔna 'his coats' (emending ⟨jakvoqeunu⟩ Lk 3.11); šɔ·khuk·wi·ɔnəwá·ɔ 'their coats' (⟨jokvwqeunwao⟩ Mt 23.5). ♦ In B the 8 exx. of the noun and 3 exx. of the derived noun final are spelled with ⟨kvoq⟩ (as if /khɔk·w/) 3x, and with ⟨kvwq⟩ (as if /khuk·w/) 8x; they have ⟨eon⟩ (as if /i·ɔn/) 4x, and ⟨eun⟩ (as if /i·an/ or possibly /i·ɔn/) 7x; in the phonemic text these variations have been normalized to ša·khuk·wí·ɔn (-a·khuk·wí·ɔn NF).
▸ Cf. Zeisberger (1776:54) ⟨Schakhocquiwan⟩ "a Coat".
▸ See also: wša·khuk·wi·ɔni·-, xinkɔ·khuk·wí·ɔn, xuwa·khuk·wí·ɔn.

ša·ɔné·yunk P (Gr. 5.26f) 'in, to the south' (Mt 12.42, Lk 13.29, 1834b:44.9).

ša·p·wələnčeho·l- TA 'put a ring on': ša·p·wələnčehó·lo· 'put a ring on his finger (you pl.)' (Lk 15.22).

ša·p·wələnčého·n IN 'ring' (1834b:29.1; LTD LB).

†ša·wanó·unk 'at Shawanoe' (⟨Jawanouf⟩ B: Title Page; phonemics conjectured).

šéh (⟨Jcv⟩) P '(well) look!' (Jn 7.20; in an explanation). ▸ Cf. ⟨Sche!⟩ 'see there; lo!' (B&A 127).

šehəlal- TA 'hang': wšehəlalá·ɔ hókaya 'he hanged himself' (Mt 27.5; Gr. 4.15m); ké·t·a-šehəlalúkwki 'those that wanted to hang him' (1834b:35.1).

šehəla·- (|šēhlā-|) AI 'hang': takó· kɔt·a·t·amo·wəné·ɔ wšehəlá·li·n 'they did not want for them (obv.) to be hanging up' (Jn 19.31; Gr. 4.49b).

šehši·k·wí·ta·s AN 'robber' (Gr. 5.42e). ▸ Cf. ši·k·wi·taw-.

šenk⁰ 'lie, lay'.

šenki·x·əm- TA 'lay down': ó·k=č kšenki·x·əmúk·o·k 'and they shall lay you down' (Lk 19.44); wšenki·x·əma·né·ɔ énta- nehənaɔnké·s·ak -xámənt 'they laid him in a manger' (Lk 2.7).

šenki·x·i·n- AI — šenki·x·ən- II 'lie ({smwh})' (Gr. 3.18a, 5.11m).
- šenki·x·i·n- (AI): šenki·x·í·no·p 'she was lying down' (Mk 1.30); šenkí·x·ink 'who was lying (there)' (Mk 5.40, Lk 10.33 [both prox. for obv.]); šenki·x·ínkəp 'the place where he lay' (Mt 28.6; Gr. 4.75k); tɔ́li-šenki·x·í·nəli·n 'lying there' (*lit.*, 'that he [obv.] was lying there') (Jn 5.6; Gr. 4.50e); [tɔ́li-]šenki·x·i·nəné·ɔ (⟨jifexenru⟩ '([them] to be) lying there' (Lk 2.16); wšenki·x·i·nəné·ɔ 'they lay there' (⟨wjifexenunrw⟩ Jn 5.3).
- šenki·x·ən- (II): šenki·x·ínki '(which were) lying there' (Jn 20.5, 20.6); tɔ́ta šenki·x·ínke 'if it is lying somewhere' (Lk 17.37, Mt 24.28).

šé· P PRES (Gr. 6.10j, etc. §6.5d): šé· 'Listen' (Mt 24.26), 'Alright' (1842:14.3); šé·, nču 'Look, my friend' (1842:12.8).
♦ šé· 'Here is ..': šé· méhəlamunt=č nhák·ay wənáxk 'Here is the hand of the one who will sell me out' (Lk 22.21; KJV "behold"); šé· wá lənu 'Here is the man' (Jn 19.5; KJV "Behold the man"; Gr. 6.10.l); šé· yó·l ní·š·a amankanší·k·ana 'Here are two swords' (Lk 22.38; Gr. 6.10q).

♦ šé· pənáh 'see!': šé· pənáh kpali·to·né·ɔ 'See here how you destroy it' (Mt 15.6); šé· pənáh, wəni·č·a·nəwá·ɔ máta 'See, not their children' (⟨jr punu⟩ Mt 17.26).
♦ šé·=láh: 'Here now' or 'Look at you!' (Jn 5.14; KJV "Behold").
♦ šé· yúh: 'it is this (as follows)' (Mk 12.31; Gr. 6.10j).

šé·me·k: see šame·-.

še·p·á·e 'early this morning' (LB; Lk 24.22). ▸ Cf. ⟨schepaje⟩ "this morn early" (Z. 63).

šé·t·o·n IN 'lip' (LTD ND), 'lips' (OA); wšé·t·o·n 'his lip; the lip' (V); wše·t·o·nəwɔ́·ɔ 'their (pl.) lips' (V; Gr. 4.4); wše·t·o·nəwá·ink 'with their lips' (Mt 15.8).

šəmúč P 'what's more' (⟨jwmwh⟩ Jn 7.27).
▸ Cf. šəmúč ɔ́·k "and also" (OA), ⟨cəmu′tc‛⟩ "also" (Speck 1937:108).

šəšəwanahkwi·- (with |Rə̀+| REP) AI 'speak English': šəšəwánahku 'he's speaking English' (OA); énta-šəšəwánahkwink 'in English' (B: Title Page; cf. Gr. 5.36d). ▸ Cf. šəwánakw.

šəw° (-šuw°, |šəw-|) 'sour' (Gr. §5.2a).

šəwah- (-šuhh-) TI(1a) 'salt': šəwáha 'salt it (you sg.)' (OA; Gr. 2.38g).
• -šuhh-: nšuhhómən 'I salt it' (ME; Gr. 2.38g).

šəwan- II 'be salty': tá=háč=á· wə́nči-šəwán 'what would make it be salty?' (*lit.*, 'from what would it be salty?') (Lk 14.34).

šəwánakw AN 'white person' (1834b:12.8, OA; Gr. 5.67h); pl. šəwánahkɔk (1834b:12.8, OA, ME, LTD ND, LB), šəwánahko·k (V, OA); obv. šəwánahkɔl (1834b:44.10).

šəwá·p·u IN 'vinegar' (Mt 27.34, Lk 23.36, Jn 19.29); šəwá·p·unk 'in vinegar' (Mt 27.48).

šh(w)° (|šahw-|) 'weak, faint' (cf. Gr. 588i; Mun šahw- 'slow').

šhɔmant- TI-O 'feel weakness': thakíti máta kéku šhɔmantamo·wí·ɔk 'they did not feel any brief weakness' (1834b:17.2).

šhɔt·- II 'be weak': hwitaɔk·əwá·ink šhɔ́t 'there is a weakess in their ears' (Mt 13.15); šhɔ́t ktehəwá·unk 'there is a weakness (or faintness) in your hearts' (Lk 24.25; KJV "you are .. slow of heart [to believe]").

šhwe·ləmɔ·t·- (|šahwēləmwāt-|; Gr. 5.88i) TI(1a) 'have doubts about': káči šhwe·ləmɔ·t·ánkhe·kw 'don't be doubtful about it (you pl.)' (Lk 12.29).

šhwe·ləmwi·- (-šahwe·ləmwi·-) AI 'have doubts': kéku wə́nči-šhwe·ləmwían 'why do you (sg.) doubt?' (Mt 14.31); šhwe·ləmwí·t·e 'if he has doubts' (Lk 14.32); máta šhwe·ləmwí·t·e 'if he does not have doubts' (Mk 11.23); máta šhwe·ləmwié·k·we (or -i·é·k·we) 'if you (pl.) do not have doubts' (Mt 21.21); wé·mi entxíe·kw yúkwe=č te·phúkwi·k kšahwe·ləmwíhəmɔ 'this night all of you will lose your will' (Mk 14.27; KJV "be offended"; RSV "fall away" = desert, turn your backs, apostasize).

šhwi·laɔ·- (-šahwi·laɔ·-) AI 'be faint-hearted': šhwí·lae· 'he is faint-hearted' (OA); wə́nči- .. takó· -šhwi·laɔ́hti·t 'so they would not lose heart' (Mk 6.26).
• -šahwi·laɔ·-: nšahwí·laɔ 'I am cowardly' (V); kšahwí·laɔ "you have no heart to tell anyone anything" (OA).
▸ Cf. ⟨schwílawe⟩ 'faint hearted' (Z. 71).

ší= P 'or' (always followed by =tá P FOC or an interrogative enclitic).
♦ ší=tá 'or' (Jn 1.13 [2x], 2.6, 3.8, 4.27, etc.; Lk 3.14).
♦ ší=háč 'or (what?)' (Mt 16.26).
♦ ší=néh 'or (was it?)' (Jn 9.2).

šihəla·- (-t-əš·ihəla·-, |əšīhlā-|) AI — II 'run, rush to {smwh}'.

- šihəla·- (AI): íka šíhəle· 'he ran there' (Mk 5.6, Mt 27.48; Gr. 3.13(1)f); íka šíhəle·p 'he ran up to him' (Mk 10.17&); íka šihəlé·ɔk kwəškwəš·i·ké·i 'they rushed to the hogs' (Mk 5.13); íka šihəlé·ɔk mahči·k·amí·k·unk 'they ran to the tomb' (Jn 20.3).
  - -t-əš·ihəla·-: ná ni·k·a·ní·i təš·íhəla·n 'then he ran on ahead' (Lk 19.4); íka təš·ihəlá·li·n 'he (obv.) rushed to him' (1834b:28.15).
- šihəla·- (II): palí·i šíhəle·=č 'it will overflow' (Lk 6.38; KJV "running over").

šíhkanč: see ší·kanč.

šinkayəw- TA 'be unwilling to receive': wšinkayó·k·o·n 'it was unwilling to receive him' (Jn 1.11).

šinka·l- TA — šinka·t·- TI(1a) 'hate, be an enemy of'.
- šinka·l- (TA): šinka·lá·t·e 'if he hates him' (Mt 6.24); šinka·la·tpáni·k 'his (obv.) enemies' (Lk 13.17); ná aləwí·i wšinka·la·né·ɔ 'then they hated him more' (1842:13.5); nšinká·lukw 'he is my enemy' (Jn 6.70; Gr. 2.27a); nšinká·lko·k 'they hate me' (Jn 7.7, Jn 15.25; Gr. 2.27a); nšinka·lko·ná·nak 'they hate us (exc.)' (Jn 15.24; Gr. 4.27m); takó· kkáski-šinka·lko·wí·ɔk 'they cannot hate you (sg.)' (Jn 7.7; Gr. 4.85e); šinká·lkɔn 'your adversary (*lit.*, one who dislikes you)' (Mt 5.25 [2x]. 5.43, etc.); šinka·lkwé·k·wi·k (pl.) 'those that hate you (pl.)' (Lk 6.35); šinka·lké·ankw 'our enemy' (Lk 1.71, 1.74; Gr. 3.17c, 4.64o); šinka·lí·č·i·k 'the enemies of mine' (Lk 19.27).
- šinka·t·- (TI): šinká·t·ank 'who hates it' (Jn 12.25); wšinká·t·amən 'he hates it' (Jn 3.20, Lk 16.15; Gr. 2.57c).
- šinka·lti·- AI (recip.; Gr. 5.110a) 'hate each other': ó·k=č šinka·ltúwak 'and they will hate each other' (Mt 24.10); íkali wə́nči-šinka·ltó·p·ani·k. 'They had been enemies before.' (Lk 23.12).

šinka·ltəwá·k·an IN 'hatred' (1842:8.1); wšinka·ltəwá·k·an 'his hatred' (Jn 3.36; Gr. 5.116c).

šínki (šihšinki [Rih+], šehšínki [Rih+; IC]; Gr. 5.128t) PV 'be unwilling, refuse' (Mt 10.14 [2x], etc.):

kšínki- wə́ntax -áhəmɔ 'you are unwilling to come here' (Jn 5.40); šínki-kələsta·k·wé·k·we 'if he refuses to listen to you' (Mt 18.17).
- šihšínki: šihšínki-mi·kəmɔ·s·í·t·e 'if he habitually hates to work' (1834a:17).
- šehšínki-mi·kəmɔ·s·í·č·i·k 'ones that hate to work' (1834a:17).

šinki·naw- TA 'hate': šinki·na·k·wé·k·we 'if [mankind] hates you' (Lk 6.22).
▸ Cf. Mun ši·nki·nawá·wak 'they were hated' (JA).

ši·e·ləm- TA 'grieve for': tóhi-ši·e·ləmawwá·ɔ 'they grieved very much for him' (Lk 23.27); kši·e·ləməlhúməna 'we grieved for you' (Lk 7.32; Gr. 2.43e, 4.33).

ši·e·lənt- (TI(1a)) TI-O 'be sorry, be sad': ši·e·lə́ntam 'he felt sorry' (Mt 27.3), áhi-ši·e·lə́ntam 'he was truly very upset' (Mk 6.26); áhi-ši·e·lə́ntamo·p 'he was very upset' (Mt 19.22&); ši·e·lə́ntamo·k 'they felt sorry' (Mt 18.31; KJV "were very sorry"); ši·e·lə́ntamo·kw 'be sorry (you pl.)' (1834b:39.7, 40.8); ši·e·lə́ntank 'who is sorry' (Lk 3.3); ši·e·lə́ntánke 'if he is sorry' (Lk 17.3); ši·e·lə́ntánki·k 'those that grieve' (Mt 5.4); ktáhi-=č -ši·e·ləntamúhəmɔ 'you (pl.) will be very sad' (Jn 16.20); nši·e·lə́ntamən 'that I am sorry' (Lk 17.4); tɔ́li-áhi-ši·e·ləntamə́li·n 'that he (obv.) was very upset' (Lk 18.24).

ši·e·ləntaməwá·k·an IN 'sorrow' (Mt 2.18, 24.8, Jn 16.6; Gr. 5.58m); kši·e·ləntaməwa·k·anúwa 'your (pl.) sadness' (Jn 16.20).

ši·e·ləntaməwí·i PV 'sorrowfully' (Lk 2.48; Gr. 5.132a).

ši·e·ləntaməwi·t·e·ha·- AI 'have a repentant heart': wə́nči-=č awé·n .. -ši·e·ləntaməwi·t·é·ha·t 'by which anyone will have a repentant heart' (Lk 3.3).

ší·kanč P 'only, totally': ší·kanč wenčí·k·ink ó·x·unk 'which comes entirely from his father' (Jn 1.14); ná=nə́ ší·kanč kɔ·x·e·é·k·əm 'that's all for your light' (Mt 6.23); nə́ ší·kanč tə́li-má·wsi·n we·k·wí·s·ink 'the only one is the Son' (Jn 1.18); tákta ší·kanč 'come what may' (1842:15.5).
  ▶ Cf. ⟨schigántschi⟩ 'entirely, totally, wholly' (Z. 67, 202, 230).
  ▪ šíhkanč P 'all, entire' (OA, ME): ná=nə́ tə́lsi·n šíhkanč 'she did the best (she could)' (⟨jevkunh⟩ Mk 14.8); šíhkanč éntxi-wəntá·wsi·t 'the entire amount that she lives on' (Mk 12.44&); tə́ta šíhkanč 'come what may' (LTD). ▶ Cf. Mun šíhka·nč 'very' (RH, APh, RS, EJo).
ší·ki (Gr. 5.120g) PN 'good' (Mt 7.17, 1834a:20.25, 1842:14.3).
  ▶ Cf. ⟨pschiki⟩, ⟨pschíki⟩ "fine, nice, pretty" (Z. 74, 129, 148).
  ▶ Cf. Mun pšíhki 'fine, good' (EJ), pšíhkə (APh, RS).
  ▪ P: ší·ki=á·=máh 'it would have been good, better' (Lk 19.42, Mk 14.21).
ši·k·o·xkpeh- TI(1a) 'strain, filter': kši·k·o·xkpehəməné·ɔ 'you (pl.) strain it' (Mt 23.24).
ši·k·ɔnt- TI(1a) 'leave uneaten': ši·k·ɔntamíhti·t 'what they left uneaten' (1834b:28.9).
  ▶ Cf. Mes ši·kwatamwa 'leaves it uneaten'.
ši·k·wi·ne·- AI — ši·k·wi·ne·yo·wi·- II 'be orphaned'.
  ▪ ši·k·wi·ne·- (AI): ši·k·wí·ne· 'he was an orphan' (LTD FW). ▶ Cf. Mun ši·kwi·né·wak 'they are orphans' (APh).
  ▪ ši·k·wi·ne·yo·wi·- (II): ši·k·wi·ne·yó·wi·k 'the inheritance' (*lit.*, 'what was orphaned') (Lk 12.13).
ši·k·wi·taw- TA+O 'rob of O2, steal O2 from': ši·k·wi·taɔ́·t·am 'let's take it away from him [used with a plural addressee]' (Lk 20.14&; Gr. 4.104bb).
ši·ɔmalsi·- AI 'feel grief and pain': wə́nči-ši·ɔmalsían 'it's why you feel grief and pain' (1834b:9.11). ▶ Cf. ⟨Schiwamallsin⟩ "to feel grief and pain" (B&A 130).
ši·ph- TI(1a) 'spread out (grain to dry, etc.)': máta háši ši·phamó·wa 'what I never spread out' (Mt 25.26; Gr. 4.99b); máta háši ši·phamó·wan 'what you (sg.) never spread out' (Mt 25.24; KJV "strawed"; Gr. 4.99c).
ši·p·i·nxke·- AI 'hold out one's hand': ši·p·í·nxke· 'hold out your hand (you sg.)' (Lk 6.10); kši·p·í·nxke=č 'you (sg.) will stretch out your hands' (Jn 21.18).
škwi·skh- TI(1a) 'crush, mash' (|šəkwísk-ah-|): škwí·skha 'crush it, mash it (you sg.)' (LB).
škwi·skhite·x·i·n- AI 'be smashed (by landing hard)' (|šəkwīsk-əhtēxīn-|): škwi·skhité·x·i·n 'he is smashed to pieces (by the fall)' (Lk 20.18).
šó·k·əl IN 'sugar' (FW); a·məwe·í·i-šó·k·əl 'honey' (*lit.*, 'bee sugar') (Mt 3.4; FF).
  ▶ A loanword from Mun šó·kəl, from Dutch *suiker* (Goddard 1974:157).
šo·k·əli·po·k·ɔt- II 'taste sweet': kéku (..) šo·k·əli·pó·k·ɔ 'something sweet' (Jn 6.31, 6.49, Mt 7.16), šo·k·əli·pó·k·ɔ 'sweet fruit' (Lk 13.6).
šɔ° (|wəšay-|) '(at the) edge of' (Gr. 5.31m.2).
šɔí·i P 'at the edge' (B ⟨joei⟩ 2x): šɔí·i o·t·é·nink 'at the edge of the city' (Jn 19.20); kɔ́čəmink šɔí·i skɔ́nte 'outside beside the door' (Jn 18.16).
šɔi·xkanáe P 'at, by the side of the road' (⟨joexkunai⟩ Mt 13.4; ⟨joexkunac⟩ Mt 13.19, etc. [the last 3x]). ▶ With |-īxkanawē| PF 'road' (Gr. 5.31r).
šɔ́ype P 'at the edge of the water, on the shore' (⟨joyvpc⟩ 1834b:43.9; |wəšayəpē|). Cf. later šɔ̆hpe (Gr. 5.31m.2; V, OA); Mun wšáyə̆pe (CS), wšáype (dict.).
†šte·tó·wi·- II 'be a state': lí·=á· †-šte·tó·u me·xke·ɔhkə́s·i·t wə́nči '(for it) to be a state for the Indians' (⟨Jtrtww⟩ 1834b:45.1).
†šte·t° 'state': †šte·tsal 'states' (1834b:45.4); †šte·tink 'state (loc.)' (1834b:46.8 [2x]).

šuhəmaw- TA+O 'rub O2 on': mpí·s·o·n íka ehəli-šuhəmaɔ́·t·əp wsi·t·í·li·t 'that had rubbed medicine on his (obv.) feet' (Jn 11.2); ná ɔ́·k íka tə́li-šuhəmáɔ·n mpí·s·o·n 'and then she also smeared them with the medicine' (Lk 7.38); íka ntə́li-šuhəmá·k·o·n nəškínkunk 'he rubbed it on my eyes' (Jn 9.11). ▸ Note: the person smeared is the O1, and the bodypart is an oblique.

-šuhh-: see šəwah-.

šúkw P 'but, only' (Jn 1.5, 1.10, 1.13, etc.); 'and just' (Lk 1.22), 'but only' (Jn 17.9); ikalísi .. šúkw '(not) more than (*lit.*, (not) more .. but only)' (Lk 3.13); ahpɔ́·n šúkw 'bread alone' (Mt 4.4).

t

tá (1): tá P WH (content-question interrogative, used with =háč Q; usually treated as a definite object or oblique).

♦ tá=háč (with no verb or relative root) 'where?': tá=háč ná? 'where is he?' (Jn 7.11); tá=háč nəkáhke pé·škunk? 'where are the (absent) nine?' (Lk 17.17). Without =háč: tá=tá .. nə́ e·li·ná·k·ɔ 'what kind is that?' (Lk 1.29; *lit.*, 'what is that kind?').

♦ tá=háč (+ ná, nə́ 'that (anim., inan.)', etc.) 'which? what one?': tá=háč ná lə́nu 'which (is the) man?' (1834b:10.9); tá=háč nə́ aləwí·i á·p·əwat 'which is easier? (Mk 2.9; KJV "Whether is it easier .."); tá=háč nə́ aləwí·i lé· 'which is greater?' (Mt 23.19, 23.27); tá=háč nə́ wé·lhik 'what good thing?' (Mt 19.16, etc.); tá=háč=ét e·li·ná·kwsi·t 'which one (do you think)..?' (*lit.*, 'one of which kind?'; Mt 21.31); tá=háč e·li·ná·k·ɔ 'which ones?' (Mt 19.18); tá=háč e·li·ná·k·ɔ a·pto·ná·k·an 'which commandment?' (Mt 22.36); tá=háč né·l e·li·ná·k·ɔ 'which ones (inan.)?' (Jn 10.32).

♦ tá=háč (+ |əl-| '{so}'; Gr 3.13(1)) 'what?; in what way?' (Lk 1.66, Jn 2.18, etc.): tá=háč=á·ntə́lsi·n 'what should I do?' (Lk 10.25); tá=háč tənnə́mən 'what did he do?' (Jn 9.26); tá=háč lé·w 'what happened?' (Jn 9.10; cf. Jn 9.15, Lk 1.43); tá=háč li·ná·k·ɔt 'what kind is it?' (Jn 6.30).

♦ tá=háč (with virtual |əl-| 'to {smwh}'; Gr 3.13(2)): tá=háč ktá? 'Where are you going?' (Jn 16.5); tá=háč ktá·n? 'Where are you going? Where did you go?' (ME).

♦ tá=háč (+ |tal-| '{smwh}'; Gr. 3.13(3)) 'where?': tá=háč ktihə́nta- nə́ -ləs·i·n? 'Where do you do that?' (Mt 14.14).

♦ tá=háč (+ virtual |tal-| '{smwh}'; Gr. 3.13 (4)) 'where?': tá=háč kəwí·k·i·n? 'where do 'you live?' (Jn 1.38; Gr. 4.42f); tá=háč ktáhəla·n? 'Where have you (sg.) put him?' (Jn 11.34).

♦ tá=háč (+ (|tax-| '{so many}, {so much}'; Gr. 3.13(5)) 'how much? how many?': tá=háč txí ahpɔ́·na hát·e·? 'How many loaves of bread are there?' (Mk 6.38); tá=háč ktəntxe·khamáɔ·n 'how much do you owe him?' (Lk 16.5).

♦ tá=háč (+ |sahk-| '{so far}, {so long}'; Gr. 3.13(6)) 'how far? how long?': tá=háč ksá·ki-witahpi·mələné·ɔ. 'How long will I be with you (pl.)?' (Gr. 3.13(6)).

♦ tá=háč (+ |wənt-| 'from {smwh}'; Gr. 3.13(7)) 'for what (reason)? how? from where? from which?': tá=háč kúntən 'where do you get it from?' (Jn 4.11); tá=č=háč wə́nči-káski- nə́ -lé·w? 'How will that be possible?' (Lk 1.34); tá=háč kunčí·ai 'Where are you from?' (Jn 19.9); tá=háč nə́ wənčí·ayu né·l 'where did those (inan.) come from?' (Mt 13.27); also (Lk 2.48, Jn 1.47, etc.).

tá (2) P 'not' (optionally replaces máta 'not' before =á· 'would, etc.'): tá=á· 'will not, would not' (e.g., ⟨Ta⟩ Jn 11.4; ⟨ta⟩ Mt 12.19, Lk 17.21; ⟨taa⟩ Lk 19.42, Jn 16.23); tá=á·. 'No.' (responding to a yes-no question containing =á·; Mt 13.29); tá=á· á·pči 'it will not always be' (Mk 14.7); after é·li- PV 'because' (Jn 14.17 [2x]). ▸ Cf. ⟨Ta am⟩ 'not at all' (B&A 134), presumably wrongly glossed.

=tá (3) P FOC (marker of weak focus, Gr. 5.24o): nəwínki-=á·-tá -wəntánkələn khák·ay 'I will willingly die for you' (Jn 13.37); ná=tá íkali té·kəna tóp·i·n 'he's out in the desert' (Mt 24.26); ná=tá wənčí·ayu 'that's where it's from' (Mk 11.33&); takó·=tá kki·ɔləlo·húmɔ 'I didn't cheat you' (Mt 20.13).

♦ In substantive sentences: ní·=tá 'it's me, etc.' (Jn 1.23, 9.9, 18.5, etc.; KJV "I am he"); máta=xán=tá 'he was not' (Jn 1.18), 'it is not' (Jn 4.42); i·láyas=tá 'he is Elias' (Mk 6.15); nčí·sas=tá 'it was Jesus' (Jn 5.15); ni·k·a·ní·i-=tá -wé·wsi·t 'he is a prophet' (Mk 6.15; Gr 6.10b).

=tá (4) P '{smwh}' (like táli P, after yú): yú=tá 'there (anaphoric)' (1834b:45.9); yú=tá we·mhíti·t 'where they had been' (ME). ♦ wé·mi=yú=tá 'everywhere': see wé·mi.

tahče·- II 'be narrow': tahčé·k '(which is) narrow' (Lk 13.24; participle without IC), énta-tahčé·k 'into a narrow place' (Mt 6.6).

tahči·kaw- (-tačhikaw-) TA 'crowd against': é·li-tahči·kaóhti·t 'because they crowded up against him' (Lk 5.1); wənči-=á· máta só·mi -tahči·ká·k·uk 'so that they would not crowd up against him too much' (Mk 3.9); wwə́nči- pa·lsi·lí·č·i -tahči·ká·k·o·n 'therefore the sick crowded up to him' (Mk 3.10).

• -tačhikaw-: ntačhiká·k·o·k "they crowded me up" (ME); tɔčhikaɔwwá·ɔ 'they crowded up to him, them' (Lk 8.42, Mk 3.20); ktačhiká·k·e 'you are crowded, pressed by the crowd' (Mk 5.31).

tahči·ka·s·i·- II 'be oppressed, beset (lit., crowded against)' (Gr. 5.105j): tahči·ká·s·u 'it has been oppressed' (Mt 11.12; KJV "suffereth violence").

tahkóč·i·- (-takɔhči·-, |takwačī-|; Gr. 2.3g, 5.11p) AI 'be cold': tahkóč·u 'he is cold' (1834a:15); wə́nči- máta -tahkɔč·íhti·t 'so that they don't get cold' (1834a:17).

• -takɔhči·-: ntákɔhči 'I'm cold' (V; Gr. 2.3g, 5.11p).

tahkɔhɔ·khw- (apparently |takwahāhkwah-|) TI(1a) 'grind': tóləmi-tahkɔhɔ·khómən(?) 'he begins to grind it' (1834a:15). ▸ Cf. kɔhó·k·an (|(ta)kwahākan|) 'mortar' (Gr. 2.6c).

tahkɔp·o·hal- (tekɔhpo·ha·l-, |takwapōhāl-|; Gr. 4.63q, 5.81f) TA 'unite in marriage'.

• tekɔhpo·ha·l- (in a lexicalized participle; cf. Gr 5.65de): tekɔhpo·há·lənt '(the one) being married' (Jn 3.29 [3x] "the bridegroom"); tekɔhpo·ha·lénči (obv.) (Jn 2.9).

▪ tahkɔp·o·ha·lti·- (tekɔhpo·ha·lti·-) AI (recip.; Gr. 5.113d) 'be united in marriage'; (with an indefinite subject effectively) 'there is a wedding': tahkɔp·o·ha·ltí·ne·p 'there was a wedding' (Jn 2.1); énta-tahkɔp·o·há·ltink 'to or at the wedding' (Jn 2.2, Mt 22.4, etc.), yú énta-káhta-tahkɔp·o·há·ltink 'to this wedding' (Mt 22.3), íkali .. énta-káhta-tahkɔp·o·há·ltink 'to where the wedding was going to take place' (Mt 25.10).

• tekɔhpo·ha·lti·-: tekɔhpo·ha·ltínke 'at a wedding (lit., when there is a wedding)' (Mt 22.11).

▪ tahkɔp·o·ha·ltəwí·i PN 'of wedding' (Mt 22.12; Gr. 5.125d).

tahkɔ·č·i·mo·lsi·- AI 'deliberate together': ná tóləmi-tahkɔ·č·i·mo·lsi·né·ɔ 'then they began to deliberate together' (1834b:19.3).

tahkɔ·ké·x·ən- II 'be paths together': énta-tahkɔ·ké·x·ink 'where paths came together' (Mk 11.4&).

tahkɔ·k·əní·i P 'in fall' (ME; ⟨takokunc⟩ 1834a:16, with ⟨-c⟩ for ⟨-e⟩ [as in PN]).

■ tahkɔ·k·əní·i PN 'of fall, fall-time' (⟨takokune⟩ 1834a:17).
tahkɔ·k·i·- (|takwākī-|) II 'be fall': tahkɔ́·k·u 'it is fall' (OA; 1834a:16; Gr. 2.24e).
tahkwəna·s·i·- II 'be mixed' (Gr. 5.105v): tahkwəná·s·əwa 'they are mixed together' (Jn 19.39).
tahkwí·i P 'together' (Jn 4.36, Mt 12.45, Jn 9.22, etc.; Gr. 5.29g). ▸ Cf. ⟨tachquìwi⟩ (Z. 201).
tahkwi·p·wi·- (te·k·wi·p·wi·-) AI 'eat together, feast': é·li-tahkwi·p·wínke 'when that feast was held' (Mt 27.15); két·a-tahkwi·p·wí·č·i·k 'who (pl.) wanted to take part in the feast' (Jn 12.12); tə́li-=č -tahkwi·p·wi·né·ɔ 'to have the feast' (*lit.*, 'that they have a feast') (Jn 19.14).
 • te·k·wi·p·wi·-: te·k·wi·p·wi·lí·č·i 'the feast-goers (obv.)' (Mt 27.15).
tahkwi·xt- (te·k·wi·xt-) TI(2) 'join together'.
 • te·k·wi·xt-: kéku ke·tanət·ó·wi·t te·k·wí·xta·kw 'what God has joined together' (Mt 19.6).
tahpantəwá·k·an (-tap·antəwa·k·an-; Gr. 5.114k) IN 'commandment(s)' (Mk 12.29, 12.30, Jn 13.34); xínkwi-tahpantəwá·k·an 'the great commandment' (Mk 12.30); tahpantəwá·k·ana 'commandments' (Mt 22.40).
 • -tap·antəwa·k·an-: ntap·antəwá·k·an 'my commandments' (Jn 14.15, 14.21; Gr. 5.116f).
 ▸ Cf. tahpa·m- TA: ə́nta-píči-mái-tahpá·mienk 'when you brought us the gospel' (ME).
tahpa·l- (-tap·a·l-, te·p·a·l-, |tapāl-|) TA 'take care of, be merciful to': kəní·ta·-tahpa·lawwá·ɔk kəni·č·a·nəwá·ɔk 'you're (pl.) good at taking care of your children' (Lk 11.13; KJV "give good gifts unto").
 • -tap·a·l-: tɔp·a·lawwá·p·ani 'they took care of him' (Lk 8.3).
 • te·p·a·l-: te·p·a·la·tpáni·k '(those) who had tended to his needs' (Lk 23.49&); é·li-=č -tahpá·lənt 'for people will be merciful to them' (Mt 5.7; KJV "they shall obtain mercy").
tahpa·ləwe·- (tetahpa·ləwe·- [Rih+; IC]) AI 'be merciful to people': tetahpa·ləwé·č·i·k 'those that are merciful' (Mt 5.7).
-tahwən-: see thwən-.
†taipí·las 'Tiberius (Ceasar)' (Lk 3.1); †taipi·liás·ink 'from Tiberias (the town)' (Jn 6.23).
†taipi·lias·í·i PN 'of Tiberias': táli †taipi·lias·í·i-mənəp·é·k·unk 'at the "sea" ('lake') of Tiberias' (Jn 21.1).
ták P: in ták .. -tá, a resolution of tákta (see below) in the idiom ták=ét=tá téxi 'I have no idea at all' (Jn 9.29). ▸ See also taktá·ni.
takó· (Gr. 5.23k) P 'not' (Jn 1.10, Lk 1.8, Mt 1.19, etc.).
 ♦ takó· háši awé·n 'no one ever' (Jn 1.18).
 ♦ takó· 'No' (Lk 22.35); takó·, takó· 'It is not so!' (Mt 5.37).
 ▸ Later akó· and kó·.
tákɔ·k (OA, ME, LB; cf. Gr. 2.72i) 'another' (Jn 4.37), 'the other one' (Mt 5.39, Jn 20.4); takó·ki·k 'others' (OA, ME, LB; Mk 4.36, Mt 26.8, etc.); takó·ki 'the other, another (obv.)' (Mt 6.24, Mt 8.21, Lk 16.7, etc.).
tákta P 'whatever, wherever' (Mt 12.34, Jn 12.6); tákta awé·n 'whoever, anyone' (Mt 5.28, Mk 9.42); tákta kéku 'whatever' (Mt 4.23, Mk 6.22, Mt 16.19 [2x]), 'anything' (Jn 14.13, 14.14).
 ♦ tákta ší·kanč 'come what may' (1842:15.5). ▸ See also: ták.
taktá·ni 'I don't know' (ME; ⟨tuk tani⟩ Jn 9.12).
talankələn- 'die {smwh}': tə́li-=á· nə́ -talánkələn 'so that he would die there' (1834b:35.2).
talaxhakiá·k·an IN 'plow' (OA; Lk 9.62; Gr. 5.55e).
talaxhakia·s·i·- AI 'be plowed': talaxhakiá·s·u 'it is plowed' (1834a:16).
talaxhakie·- (-talxa·kie·-) AI 'plow' (Gr. 5.19b.1): talaxhákie·w 'he plows' (1834a:14); talaxhakie·lí·t·e 'if he (obv.) plows' (Lk 17.7).

- -talxa·kie·-: ntalxa·kie 'I'm plowing' (OA).

tala·č·i·mo·lsi·- (ehəntala·č·i·mo·lsi·- [Rih+; IC]) AI hold a council {smwh}':
ehəntala·č·i·mó·lsink 'where councils were held' (Mt 27.27).

tala·lahkat·- (|talālakat-|) II 'be a hole': é·li- .. -xínkwi-talá·lahka 'for there is a big hole' (Mt 7.13).

tala·wsi·- (-t-əntala·wsi·-, entala·wsi·-) AI 'live {smwh}': íka=č talá·wsu 'he shall live (where ..)' (Jn 12.25); ktəli-=č -ála- yú -tala·wsí·ne·n 'for us to cease living here' (1842:19.1).

- -t-əntala·wsi·-: šúkw nəni hák·i .. təntalá·wsi·n e·ləmo·k·wənák·a 'but that land .. is where he lives forever' (1834a:22.48).

- entala·wsi·-: entalá·wsi·t 'where he lives' (V); yú entalá·wsi·t 'mankind, people' (*lit.*, 'the one who lives here [on earth])' (Lk 2.14, Jn 2.25, etc.); yó·ni entalá·wsi·t 'the world, mankind' (Jn 3.19, 5.34. Lk 6.22); yú entala·wsí·č·i·k 'mankind, people, the people of this world' (Jn 1.4 [KJV "men"], Jn 7.7 [KJV "the world"]; Lk 1.25, 3.27, Mk 9.31); yú entala·wsi·lí·č·i 'mankind (obv.)' (Lk 2.52, Jn 1.29, 3.17, Mt 23.4); nəni entala·wsi·lí·č·i 'those that live there' (Jn 3.17); yó·ni entala·wsi·lí·č·i·k (as obv.) (s.b. -lí·č·i; Jn 3.16); entalá·wsink 'the world (*lit.*, where people live)' (Jn 3.17, 8.12, Mk 5.14); yú entalá·wsink 'this world' (Mk 10.34, Jn 7.4, Jn 8.23, 9.5), 'the earth' (1842:11.4); yú táli entalá·wsink 'in this world' (Mt 12.32, Lk 12.8, 12.9, 17.25, 18.8, etc.), yó·ni táli entalá·wsink (Mt 16.19); táli entalá·wsink 'in the world' (Jn 14.30, 16.21, Mt 5.13, Lk 12.51, Jn 17.13); lí entalá·wsink 'in, into the world' (Jn 17.15, Jn 17.18); éntxi- yú -tala·wsi·lí·č·i 'all mankind (obv.)' (Jn 1.9).

tale·khama·- (entale·khama·-) AI+O 'owe (money)': entale·kháma·t 'what he owes' (1834b:45.10).

tale·kha·s·i·- (entale·kha·s·i·-, |(-ən)talēkahāsī-|; Gr. 3.13(4)d) AI — II 'be written {smwh}'.

- tale·kha·s·i·- (AI): íka tale·khá·s·u '(anim.) is drawn there' (ME).
- tale·kha·s·i·- (II): máta=háč ktəle·khi·k·anəwá·ink tale·kha·s·í·i 'isn't it written in your law?' (Jn 10.34).
- entale·khá·s·i·k 'where it was written' (Lk 4.17; Gr. 4.67(3)r), palí·i entale·khá·s·i·k 'what is written in another place' (Jn 19.37).

tale·lənsi·- (entale·lənsi·-) AI 'want to be {smwh}': entale·lə́nsi·t 'where he wants to be' (1834a:22.41 [em.]; ⟨cnta lrlinsek⟩ for ⟨cnta lrlinset⟩).

táli PV: (-t-ə́nta, -t-ihə́nta [Rih+], énta [IC], ehə́nta [Rih+; IC], |(-ən)tal-|; Gr. 2.74k, §4.6b, 4.61def, 5.41s, 5.128u) PV '{smwh}'.

- táli '{smwh}' (Jn 1.28, Jn 5.39, Mk 4.38, Mt. 10.23, etc.): kóčəmink táli-pa·tamá·p·ani·k 'they were praying outside' (Lk 1.10); ná-ní táli-pahkánči-lé·p 'that was where it came true' (Mt 2.17); nə́ táli-məša·t·amáne 'if you remember there (that ..)' (Mt 5.23); mái-=ét íka -táli-ləpákw 'she must be going to weep there' (Jn 11.31).
- -t-ə́nta (Lk 1.11, 1.40, 2.7, Jn 3.23, etc.): ná=č nə́ ntə́nta-ne·yko·né·ɔ. 'That's where they will see me.' (Mt 28.10); wté·hink tə́nta-po·kwənə́mən 'he breaks it in his heart' (Mt 5.28), tə́nta-ne·ɔ·né·ɔ lə́nəwa 'they saw there the man' (Lk 8.35).
- -t-ihə́nta: tihə́nta-wi·nəwe·né·ɔ '.. and they would beg there' (Mk 10.46); tá=háč ktihə́nta- nə́ -lə́s·i·n 'where do you do that?' (Mk 14.14).
- énta (1) 'where' (Lk 2.7 [2x], 2.12, Mt 2.4, etc.); énta-pakhaké·e·k '(to) the plain' (*lit.*, 'where the land is flat') (Lk 6.17); énta-=č -ahhaphiká·s·i·k 'where it will be trampled on' (Mt 5.13); énta-pí·ske·k 'the darkness' (*lit.*, 'where it was dark') (Jn 1.5); énta-nihəlá·t·ank '(to) what was his' (*lit.*, 'where he owned it') (Jn 1.11); énta-le·khí·k·e·t 'a place to write' (*lit.*, 'where he wrote') (Lk 1.63; perhaps for énta-=á· 'where he would ..').

- ehə́nta 'where (repeatedly)': ehə́nta-wi·nəwé·ankw 'where we always beg' (Jn 9.8); ehə́nta-ma·éhəlank 'synagogue' (*lit.*, 'where people always gather') (Jn 9.22, etc.); ehə́nta-nhíltink 'the place of execution' (Mt 15.4, Lk 22.33); ehə́nta-a·č·i·mo·lsíhti·t 'where they had their councils' (Lk 22.66).
- énta (2) (in a changed conjunct or changed subjunctive verb; Gr. 5.128e) 'when' (Lk 1.20, Mt 1.20, etc.).
- táli PN '{smwh}': nə́ táli-ke·kayə́mhe·t 'a ruler there' (Lk 7.2).
- táli P '{smwh}' (Lk 1.5, 1.8, 1.51, 1.75, 2.2, etc.): nə́ táli 'there' (Jn 3.23); wtehəwá·ink táli 'in their hearts' (Lk 1.51); e·linkwé·x·ink táli 'before him' (Lk 1.75); táli ɔ·s·áhkame 'in heaven' (Mt 5.12); táli mahtánt·unk 'in Hell' (Mt 10.28); táli wí·k·i·t 'in his house' (Lk 5.29); nə́ táli xinkwi·k·á·ɔnink 'in the house of worship' (Lk 1.8).
- ♦ The younger form of énta (1) and énta (2) is ə́nta (OA, ME, ND).
- ► See also énta P.

tamak·i·taw- TA 'bow to' (with a prefix; cf. Gr. 2.70fgh): tɔmak·i·tá·k·u 'they (obv.) bowed down to him' (1842:13.3); ní·=háč·á· ɔ́·k kkáhe·s ɔ́·k kxánsak ktamak·i·to·lhúmǝna 'do I and your mother and your brothers bow down to you?' (1842:13.4). ► Cf. Mun tamak- 'bend'.

támas 'Thomas' (Lk 6.15, Mt 10.3, Jn 11.16, etc.); †tamás·a (obv.) (Jn 20.27).

tank- (|tank-|) 'small' (Gr. §5.2a). ► Note: not in tankam- 'stab' (see next).

tankam- TA 'stab, pierce': tankamahtí·č·i 'the one (obv.) they pierced' (Jn 19.37); tɔnkamá·ɔ 'he pierced him' (⟨tafamao⟩ Jn 19.34), tɔnkamá·ɔl (⟨tufamal⟩1834b:35.3).

tankamí·k·an IN 'sword' (Lk 2.35, Mt 10.34), 'spear' (Jn 19.34).

tankami·məntə́t·ak AN (dim. pl.) 'little children' (Jn 13.33 [as a vocative]; Gr. 5.14c).

tankamux·ó·ltət IN (dim.) 'small boat': tankamux·o·ltə́t·ink 'in small boats' (Mk 4.36).

tanke·ləmukwsi·- AI 'be thought little of': tanke·ləmúkwsu=č 'he shall be thought little of' (Lk 14.11, Mt 23.12); é·li- .. -tanke·ləmúkwsi·t 'for he is thought little of' (Lk 18.13).

tanke·lənsi·- (tenke·lənsi·-; Gr. 5.104f) AI 'be humble, be meek': tanke·lə́nsu 'he is humble' (Mt 21.5); awé·n tanke·lənsí·t·e 'if anyone is humble' (Lk 14.11); tanke·lənsí·č·i·k 'those that think little of themselves, meek ones' (Mt 5.5, Mt 18.14); ntanke·lə́nsi 'I am meek' (Mt 11.29).
- tenke·lənsi·-: tenke·lənsí·č·i·k 'meek ones' (Mt 18.10); tenke·lənsi·lí·č·i 'humble ones (obv.)' (Mk 9.42, Lk 17.2).

tanke·lənt- TI(1a) 'think little of': šúkw=č awé·n tanke·ləntánke hók·ay 'but if anyone thinks little of themself' (Mt 23.12); tɔnke·lə́ntamən=č hók·ay 'he must think little of himself' (Mt 16.24); tanke·lə́ntank hók·ay 'who thinks little of himself' (Lk 18.13).

tankhake·x·ənti·- II 'be a small road': tankhake·x·ə́ntu 'the road is small' (Mt 7.14).

tankhá·k·an IN 'basket' (ME, ND, LB); tankhá·k·ana 'baskets' (LTD ND; Jn 6.13); tankhá·k·anink 'in the baskets' (Mk 8.19, 8.20).

tankíti (LTD ND, LB, BS; Gr. 2.76i) P 'a little' (Mk 2.21, Lk 18.34), 'even a little' (Lk 11.46, Jn 16.29); tankíti kéku 'the little bit of a thing' (Lk 6.42); nə́ni tankíti 'that small thing' (Lk 19.17).
- tankíti (Gr. 5.129ii) PV: ktankíti-nhake·wsíhəmɔ 'you (pl.) have little faith' (Mt 8.26).

tanki·na·kwsi·- AI — tanki·na·k·ɔt- II 'appear small'.
- tanki·na·kwsi·-: tanki·ná·kwsu 'he looks small' (LB).
- tanki·na·k·ɔt-: tanki·ná·k·ɔ kéku 'the small sort of thing' (Lk 12.26).

tanksi·si·- (tenksi·si·-) AI 'be small' (ME /s/): tenksí·si·t 'the younger or youngest sibling' (Lk 15.13); tanksí·si·t 'the younger' (1834b:28.4); tenksi·sí·t·əp 'the younger one (of two brothers)' (Lk 15.12); tenksi·sí·t·a (obv.) (1842:15.4); tenksi·si·lí·č·i 'the younger one (obv.)'

(Mt 21.30); tenksi·sí·č·i·k 'the smallest ones' (Mt 25.40, 25.45; KJV "least"); məkə́ni tenksi·sí·č·i·k 'smallest ones' (Mt 25.45; KJV "the least"); tenksi·sí·t·ink 'like the most junior' (Lk 22.26).

tankti·t·i·- (tenkti·t·i·-) AI — tanke·t·i·- (ahtanke·t·i·- [Ra+]) II 'be small' (Gr. 5.73o).
- tankti·t·i·- (AI): áhi-tanktí·t·u 'he is the least' (*lit.*, 'very small') (Mt 5.19); takó· ktankti·t·í·i 'you are not small' (Mt 2.6).
- tenkti·t·i·-: tenkti·t·iá·ne núči 'since I was little' (Mt 19.20; Gr. 4.62g).
- tanke·t·i·- (II): tanké·t·u 'it is small' (Mt 7.14, Mt 14.31, Lk 12.28); tanké·t·i·k '(which is) small, the least of, the smallest' (Mt 5.19, 7.13, Mt 13.32).
- ahtanke·t·i·-: a·lə́nte ahtanké·t·əwal 'some are small' (1834a:15).

taɔnkəl- (te·ɔnkəl-) AI — taɔnkən- II 'be lost' (Gr. 5.17b).
- taɔnkəl- (AI): taɔ́nkəlo·p 'he was lost' (Lk 15.24); takó· kwə́t·i taɔnkəló·wi 'not one was lost' (Jn 17.12); či·mí·i=á· taɔnkələ́k·e 'if he would be permanently lost' (Mt 18.14); wénči-=č .. máta -taɔnkəlíhti·t 'so that they will not be lost' (⟨taful-⟩ Jn 3.16 [see textual note]); ná taɔ́nkələn 'then he died' (⟨taufalin⟩1834b:17.10).
- te·ɔnkəl-: te·ɔnkələ́k·əp 'who was lost' (Lk 15.32); te·ɔnkələ́k·i·k '(who are) lost' (Mt 10.6, 15.24); te·ɔnkələ́lí·č·i 'the ones (obv.) that are lost' (Mt 18.11, Lk 19.10).
- taɔnkən- (II): šúkw=á· taɔnkínke nə́ si·khe·ɔ́·k·an 'but if the saltiness is lost' (Mk 9.50); wə́nči-=č máta kéku -taɔ́nkəno·kw 'so that nothing will be lost' (Jn 6.12; Gr. 4.95t).

taɔ·lahkat·- II 'be an open hole, be space': taɔ́·lahkat 'there is room' (Lk 14.22); lí-taɔ́·lahkat 'that a hole opens' (Jn 1.51).

taɔ·lahkənəmaw- TA+O 'open a hole for': ɔ́·k .. hɔ́kunk taɔ·lahkənəmáɔ·n 'and then .. a hole in heaven was opened to him' (Mt 3.16).

†táyal 'Tyre' (Mk 3.8, Mt 11.22, Mk 7.31); †táyalink (loc.) (Mt 11.21, Mk 7.24).
- †tayalínka 'people of Tyre (abs.)' (Lk 10.13).

ta·- (tənta·-, -t-ənta·-, enta·-) II 'the sun is {smwh}' (irregular) (in expressions for time of day).
- tənta·-: šúkw mé·či áləmi- hukwé·yunk -təntá·k·e 'but after the sun got high in the sky' (Mt 13.6; s.b. é·ləmi-?).
- -t-ənta·-: le·lá·i tə́nta·n sháki 'until the sun stood halfway down' (Mk 15.33&).
- enta·-: mé·či le·lá·i entá·k·e 'when the sun was halfway' (Mk 15.34); le·lá·i entá·k·e lápi 'when the sun was halfway (down) again' (Mt 20.5).
▸ An AI ('(sun) to be {smwh}') partly restructured as an II.

tá·mse (ta·tá·mse) P 'sometimes, perhaps' (Jn 5.4, Mt 5.40, Mt 10.17, etc.); ná tá·mse 'then at some point' (Lk 16.22, Mk 10.32&, Jn 12.9); (with -á· 'would') 'might' (Mt 7.6).
- ta·tá·mse 'sometimes, at times' (Mt 5.25, Lk 16.21).

tá·ni P 'where is?' (always with an interrogative particle, except in 1834a:12): tá·ni=háč ná kó·x 'where is your father?' (Jn 8.19); tá·ni=č=háč táli 'where will it be?' (Lk 17.37).
▸ tá·ni is the equivalent of tá (1) 'where?' in some verbless sentences.

ta·níka (interrogative demonstrative pronoun; Gr. 4.17) 'where is he (etc.)?' (always with an interrogative particle): ta·níka=háč? 'Where is he (abs.)?' (Jn 9.12).
♦ ta·nikáhke=háč yukáhke 'where are they (abs.)?' (Jn 8.10).

tá·ɔni (Gr. 5.25h) P 'even, even though' (Mk 5.3, 6.23, 7.36, Jn 7.22, 7.23, etc.).

ta·tá·mse: see tá·mse.

ta·txənti·- II 'be not much': ta·txə́ntu 'there is not much of it' (Mt 6.30).

ta·txíti (Gr. 2.76j) P 'a little' (⟨tatxiti⟩ Lk 16.10, Mt 25.23; ⟨tutxiti⟩ Mt 25.21); 'a few': ta·txíti me·xkánki·k 'there are not many that find it' (⟨tatxiti⟩ Mt 7.14). Cf. i·yəntxíti.

ta·txi·t·i·- AI 'be few': hwə́ska áhi mé·či ta·txí·t·u '(the Lenape [representative singular]) has become very few' (1834a:19.17); wə́nči-áhi-ta·txí·t·i·t 'why he [the Indian (representative singular)] is very few' (1834a.21.37); ta·txí·t·əwak 'they are few, scarce' (Mt 9.37, Lk 10.2, Mt 20.16, etc.);· ta·txí·t·ie·kw 'you (pl.) few' (Lk 12.32); ta·txi·t·í·č·i·k 'being few' (1834b:42.12).

ta·xkinkwe·- AI 'open one's eyes, have one's eyes open': ta·xkínkwe·kw 'open your (pl.) eyes (and see)' (Lk 18.42&; KJV "receive your sight"); ná .. tə·xkinkwe·né·ə 'then their eyes were opened' (Mt 20.34; KJV "their eyes received sight").

ta·xkinkwe·n- TA 'open the eyes of (the blind)': ta·xkinkwe·ní·ne·n 'open our eyes' (Mt 20.33); káski-=háč=á· .. -ta·xkinkwé·ne· ke·k·e·p·inkə·lí·č·i? 'would he be able to open the eyes of a blind person?' (Jn 10.21); a·yáhi-ta·xkinkwé·na·t 'who previously opened the eyes of [blind people]' (Jn 11.37). ▸ Cf. Mun ta·xkše·nkwe·n- 'pull the eye of down, hold the eye of open' (dict.), with postradical |-əše·-| 'opening, rim'.

tá·x·an (-mət·a·x·an-, |mətāxan-|; Gr. 2.6b, 2.68e) IN 'piece of wood' (Lk 6.41, 1834a:15); xínkwi-tá·x·an 'a large piece of wood' (Lk 6.42).
 • -mət·a·x·an-: nəmət·á·x·an 'my (piece of) wood' (V, OA, ME; Gr. 2.6b).

tehtəməš·ínki·k: see təməš·-.

tehwənə́nči·k 'the captives': see thwən-.

tekəhpo·ha·l-: see tahkəp·o·hal-.

télən P 'ten'; télən ó·k ní·š·a 'twelve' (Lk 2.42, Lk 6.13, Lk 8.42, etc.); télən ó·k palé·naxk 'fifteen' (Lk 3.1); télən ó·k xá·š 'eighteen' (Lk 13.4, 13.11, 13.16).
 ▪ télən PN 'ten'; télən-o·t·é·nink 'in Ten-City' (Mt 4.25, Mk 5.20, 7.31; KJV "Decapolis").

tépi (Gr. 5.128v) P 'enough' (Mt 6.11, Jn 6.7); tépi=tá 'it's enough' (Lk 22.38); mé·či tépi 'it's enough' (Mt 26.45, Lk 22.51).
 ▪ PV 'be able, be ready, be enough, be fit, be worthy': 'can rightly' (Mk 15.7, Jn 8.48), 'be able' (Acts 1.7); tépi=á· -təmšá·s·u 'it would be ready to harvest' (Jn 4.35); ntépi=č -nhílko·n 'enough that it will kill me' (*lit.*, 'it will succeed in ..') (Mt 26.38); tépi=á· šúkw -pahkí·to·n 'it would only be fit to be thrown away' (Lk 14.35); ntépi-lə́s·i·n 'that I am worthy' (Lk 7.7); wtépi-pəna·elə́ntamən '(it) thinks enough about it' (⟨tcpi⟩ Mt 6.34); é·li- máta -tépi-lə́s·í·ə 'for I am not worthy' (Lk 7.6).
 ♦ Expected /wtépi-/ is ⟨wtcpi⟩ (Mt 3.9), ⟨vwtcpi⟩ (Lk 9.62), ⟨vwtrpi⟩ (Jn 11.37), ⟨tcpi⟩ (Mt 6.34, Mt 10.25 2x); expected /ktépi-/ is ⟨ktcpi⟩ (Jn 8.48, Lk 15.32), ⟨ktrpi⟩ (Mk 10.38 2x, Jn 16.12), ⟨trpi⟩ (Acts 1.7).
 ▪ tihtépi P 'the appropriate amount each time' (Lk 10.7).

tetahpa·ləwé·č·i·k: see tahpa·ləwe·-.

tethwə́nəwe·s AN 'policeman' (LB; Mt 5.25); tethwənəwé·s·ink 'to the police' (Lk 12.11).
 ▸ Agent noun (cf. Gr. 5.66) from thwə́nəwe·- AI 'arrest people' (with [Rih+; IC]; cf. thwən-).

téxi P 'utterly' (Gr. 2.73o): 'altogether' (Mt 19.10); téxi šúkw 'utterly' (Jn 9.34; KJV "altogether"), 'nothing but' (Jn 10.10, Lk 12.19, Lk 20.26, Mt 22.16, Lk 23.35, Mt 23.28); (w. neg.): '(not) at all' (Mt 5.34, Jn 9.29).

texnaki·° (⟨tcxnaki⟩ 1834a:24.64); form and meaning uncertain.

te·he·-: see the·-.

té·ka P: té·ka=tá 'beware! watch out!' (LTD LB; Mk 8.15, Mt 16.11, 18.10, Mk 13.23).

té·kəna P 'in (into) the wilderness' (Lk 1.80, Lk 5.16, etc.; 14x); té·kəna lí 'to the wilderness' (Lk 4.1); té·kəna táli 'in the wilderness' (Lk 3.2, Mt 3.3, Jn 1.23, Jn 3.14, etc.). ▸ Cf. /té·kəne/ (OA, ME); ⟨tékene⟩ 'the woods' (Z. 234).

te·pháte·- II '(so much of it) could be held': ní·š·a ší=tá naxá kelántink te·pháte· 'two or three gallons could be held (in each)' (Jn 2.6).

te·phúkwi·k: see tpo·kwi·-.

te·psəwá·k·an IN 'fitness' (OA); wte·psəwá·k·an 'his abundance (or completeness)' (Jn 1.16; KJV "fulness").

te·psi·- AI+O 'be full of O2': wte·psi·né·p·ani 'he was full of it (obv.)' (Lk 1.67; Gr. 4.71a).

te·p·e·lənt- TI(-O) 'be satisfied (with)': te·p·e·ləntamihtí·t·e 'after they have had enough' (Jn 2.10); te·p·e·lə́ntamo·kw e·le·nha·k·é·e·kw 'be satisfied with what you (pl.) are paid' (Lk 3.14).

te·p·ihəla·- II 'be enough': te·p·íhəle· 'it is enough' (Mt 6.34).

te·t·aí·i P 'between' (Lk 11.51, Lk 16.26, Mt 23.35; ⟨tr ta e⟩ 1842:8.1); táli pa·tamwe·i·k·á·ɔnink ɔ́·k ehə́nta-winki·ma·khwiksəmá·t·əp te·t·aí·i 'between the temple and his incense altar' (Mt 23.35), táli ehə́nta-winki·ma·khwiksəmá·t·əp ɔ́·k pa·tamwe·i·k·á·ɔnink te·t·aí·i 'between his incense altar and the temple' (Lk 11.51).
▸ Cf. Mun té·tawi· 'between' (EJo, RS).

te·x·əla·n- II 'rain excessively(?)': téxi máta te·x·əla·nó·u 'it is by no means raining too much [for ducks]' (1834a:14).

te·x·əní·k·an IN 'litter' (Lk 5.19); te·x·əní·k·anink 'on a litter' (Lk 5.18&, Lk 7.14).

-tək·awsi·-: see tkawsi·-.

-tək·awsi·tam-: see tkawsi·tam-.

təlanko·má·ɔ: see ntəlankó·ma.

†təle·kanitə́s·ink (loc.): ahpá·mi †təle·kanitə́s·ink 'around Trachonitis' (Lk 3.1).

tə́li (stranded PV): see lí.

təlo·hí·k·an 'his forefinger' (Jn 8.6, Lk 16.24).

təlsəwá·k·an, təlsəwa·k·aní·li·t: see ləs·əwá·k·an.

təmahí·k·an IN 'axe' (ME, FE, LTD ND; ⟨tamrvekun⟩ Mt 3.10; ⟨tumivekun⟩ 1834a:18.12 [2x], ⟨tumrvekun⟩ 1834a:19.13); təmahí·k·anal 'axes' (⟨tumivekunul⟩ 1834a:19.14).

təmá·k·an (-mət·əma·k·an-; Gr. 2.68d, 5.55f) IN 'road' (Mk 1.2, Mt 7.14, Lk 7.27); təmá·k·anink 'in the streets' (Mt 12.19), 'to the road' (Mk 10.17&); təma·k·ani·ké·i P 'to the streets and roads' (Mt 22.9, 22.10).
• -mət·əma·k·an-: mwət·əmá·k·an 'his way, path' (Lk 1.76, Mt 3.3); kəmət·əmá·k·anink 'on your path' (1834b:8.13); mwət·əma·k·anəwá·ink 'into their streets' (Lk 10.10).

tə́me AN 'a wolf' (Mt 7.15, Jn 10.12; Gr. §1.3), pl. təmé·ɔk.
▪ təme·i·ké·i P 'among wolves' (Lk 10.3).
♦ In Oklahoma, commonly 'coyote'.

təme·i·ke·- II 'be (an abundance of) wolves': énta-təme·í·ke·k 'among wolves' (Mt 10.16).

təməš- (~ təmš-; -təmš-, te·mš-, tehtəməš- [Rih+; IC]; Gr. 5.42b) TI(1b) 'reap'.
• təməš-: ntə́li-təmə́š·əmən 'that I reap it' (Lk 19.22, Mt 25.26).
• təmš-: kəmái-təmšəməné·ɔ hwí·t 'you (pl.) went to reap the wheat' (Jn 4.38).
• -təmš-: ktəmšə́mən 'you reap it' (Lk 19.21, Mt 25.24); wtəmšə́mən 'he reaps it' (Jn 4.37).
• te·mš-: né·k te·mšínki·k hwí·t 'those who reap the wheat' (Jn 4.36 [2x]).
• tehtəməš-: tehtəməš·ínki·k 'ones that reap it, reapers' (Mt 13.30, 13.39).
♦ TI and II with |təməš-|: ⟨tumj-⟩ 6x, ⟨tomsj-⟩ 2x, ⟨tumusj-⟩ 1x, ⟨tumij-⟩ 2x.

təməš·a·s·i·- (~ təmša·s·i·-) II 'be cut off, be harvested' (Gr. 5.105r).
• təməš·a·s·i·- 'be cut off': nə́ni=á· wə́nči- .. -təməš·á·s·i·k 'that's why .. it should be cut off' (Mt 18.8).

- təmšaꞏsꞏiꞏ- 'be harvested': təmšáꞏsꞏu 'it is harvested' (Jn 4.35 [2x], Mk 4.29); eꞏlkíꞏkwi-təmšáꞏsꞏiꞏk 'the time when it is reaped' (Mt 13.30 [2x], 13.39).

†təmíꞏas 'Timaeus' (Mk 10.46).

təmíꞏki (tihtəmíꞏki) P 'often' (Mk 9.22, Mk 7.3, Lk 13.34, etc.).
- tihtəmíꞏki 'often' (Mk 5.4, Mt 9.14, Jn 18.2). ▸ Cf. təmiꞏkíti 'every little while' (OA).

təmiꞏkꞏal- TA — təmikaht- TI(2) 'bring in (to a house)' (Gr. 5.78e).
- təmiꞏkꞏal- (TA): təmiꞏkꞏaláꞏɔ †píꞏtəla 'he brought Peter in' (Jn 18.16); ktəmiꞏkꞏalíhəmɔꞏp 'you (pl.) took me in' (Mt 25.35); takóꞏ ktəmiꞏkꞏaliꞏhúmɔꞏp 'you (pl.) did not bring me inside' (Mt 25.43); ktəmiꞏkꞏalǝlhúmənaꞏp 'we brought you inside' (Mt 25.38; Gr. 4.69ee).
- təmikaht- (TI): mpéči-təmíkahtoꞏn 'I brought it in' (OA; Gr. 578e).

təmiꞏkꞏam- (-təmiꞏkꞏam- ~ -mətꞏəmiꞏkꞏam-; Gr. 5.89b) TA 'go to (the home of)': wtəmiꞏkꞏamáꞏɔ †pailátꞏa 'he entered where Pilate was' (Lk 23.52&); wtəmiꞏkꞏamáꞏpꞏani †saꞏkalayásꞏal 'she went into Zacharias's house' (Lk 1.40); ná šáꞏe wtəmiꞏkꞏamaꞏn saꞏkꞏiꞏmáꞏɔ 'then she immediately came in to the king' (⟨tum-⟩ Mk 6.25).
- -mətꞏəmiꞏkꞏam-: mwətꞏəmiꞏkꞏamáꞏpꞏani 'he came in to where she was' (Lk 1.28).

təmiꞏkꞏeꞏ- (teꞏmiꞏkꞏeꞏ-) AI 'enter' (usually with loc. comp.): íkali təmíꞏkꞏeꞏ †nčiꞏloꞏsəlɔ́mink 'he went into Jerusalem' (Mt 27.53); takóꞏ wínki-təmiꞏkꞏéꞏi 'he was unwilling to go in' (Lk 15.28); íkali təmiꞏkꞏéꞏɔk 'they went in there' (Jn 18.1); ntəmíꞏkꞏeꞏn wíꞏkꞏian 'I came into your house' (Lk 7.44); təmíꞏkꞏeꞏl 'enter (you sg.)' (Mt 25.21, 25.23); káči íkali təmiꞏkꞏehtíꞏhiꞏč 'let them not enter it' (Lk 21.21; Gr. 4.110i); séꞏki-péči-təmiꞏkꞏéꞏa 'from the time I came in' (Lk 7.45); ktəmíꞏkꞏeꞏn 'for you (sg.) to enter' (⟨tumekn⟩ Mt 18.9 [k- asumed from context]); táꞏáꞏ téxi ktəmiꞏkꞏeꞏwənéꞏɔ 'you (pl.) will not at all enter' (Mt 5.20); ktə́liꞏáꞏ -káski-təmíꞏkꞏeꞏn 'for you to come in' (*lit.*, 'to be able to come in') (Lk 7.6; Gr. 4.50j); tə́liꞏáꞏ .. íkali -təmíꞏkꞏeꞏn 'that he would enter (it)' (⟨tumekri⟩ Lk 24.26 [em.]).
- teꞏmiꞏkꞏeꞏ-: teꞏmíꞏkꞏeꞏt 'who enters' (Jn 10.2); teꞏmiꞏkꞏehtíꞏte 'when they came in' (Mt 2.11).

təmpihpéꞏkꞏa 'Missouri River' (AP); énta-təmpihpéꞏkꞏa (⟨cnta Tumpeprqu⟩ 1834a:22.42); weꞏtꞏəmpihpéꞏkꞏa (⟨Wrtumpeprku⟩ 1834b:44.4).
▸ Lexicalized participles of |(wə)təmpīwəpēkat-| II 'have brainy water', an obvious reference to the turbidity of the stream.

tə́ntay (|təntay|, |təntēw-|) IN 'fire' (Mk 9.44, 9.48, 9.49, etc.); təntéꞏyunk 'in the fire' (Mt 3.10, Lk 3.16, 3.17, etc.; Gr. 2.28c).

təntaꞏ-: see taꞏ-.

tənteꞏiꞏkꞏáꞏɔn IN 'furnace'; tənteꞏiꞏkꞏáꞏɔnink 'into a furnace' (Mt 13.42, 13.50; KJV "furnace of fire"). ♦ *Lit.*, 'fire structure'.

tənteꞏwhe- AI 'make a fire' (Gr. 5.70h): təntéꞏwheꞏ 'he's making fire' (OA), tənteꞏwhéꞏɔk 'they made a fire' (Jn 18.18&); ntəntéꞏwhe 'I made a fire' (OA).

təp(ꞏ)° (|təp-|) 'around, circling' (Gr. §5.2a).

təpčéh- TI(1a) 'roll': xínkwi-ahsə́n íkali təpčéhəmoꞏk 'they rolled a large stone there' (Jn 19.42&).

təpčéhəlaꞏs (~ tətꞏəpčehəl°) AN 'wagon' (V, OA, LTD ND; Gr. §2.4 end, 3.2t, 5.66c); təpčehəláꞏsꞏak 'wagons' (1842:17.1); təpčehəláꞏsꞏa 'wagons (obv.)' (1842:18.2); šíꞏki-təpčehəláꞏsꞏink 'in a chariot (*lit.*, fine wagon)' (1842:14.3).
- tətꞏəpčehəláꞏsꞏink 'in a wagon' (1834b:41.7, 41.10).

təpꞏənaꞏsꞏi- II 'be turned, twisted': təpꞏənáꞏsꞏu 'it was twisted (together)' (Jn 2.15).

təpꞏihəlaꞏ- II 'turn': təpꞏíhəleꞏ 'it turns' (1834a:15); təpꞏihəléꞏɔl 'they turn around' (1834a:15).

tətá (~ tə́ta) P 'wherever, whatever, whenever, etc.' (depending on context): 'wherever' (Lk 4.30, Mt 8.19, Mk 6.55, etc.), 'wherever (it is that), where (it may be that)' (Jn 8.14 2x, 8.21, 11.57, 12.35; Mk 9.18, etc.), 'anywhere, any place (where)' (Lk 19.21, 19.22; Mt 8.20, 23.6; Mk 14.9), 'somewhere' (Lk 17.31, 17.37; Mt 24.28); tə́ta táli 'someplace' (Mt 18.15); tə́ta e·li·ná·kwsi·t 'what kind he may be' (Lk 9.55); tə́ta=č éntxi- .. -ankhítaɔn 'whatever amount .. you lose' (Lk 10.35); tə́ta e·lkí·kwi-núči- nə́ -ləs·í·li·t 'since when (beginning at whatever time) he had been like that' (Mk 9.21).

▶ Note: usually seems to be tətá in OA and ME texts, but OA has tə́ta táli 'someplace (or other)' and tə́ta=á· 'whatever (might be)'. In some cases the accent is conjectural.

təto·xkən-: see to·xkən-.

tətpahw-: see tpahw-.

tətpi·taw- (|tə̀təpīhtaw-|; Gr. 5.91c) TA 'make signs to': wtətpi·tá·k·u 'he (obv.) signed to him' (Lk 1.63); wtətpi·ta·k·əwá·ɔ 'he (obv.) made signs to them' (Lk 1.22; Gr. 2.61f, 4.27r); ná .. tətpí·taɔ·n 'then he gestured to him' (Jn 13.24; Gr. 2.60h); ná wtətpi·taɔ·né·ɔ 'then they made signs to him, them' (Lk 1.62, 5.7).

▪ tət·ətpi·ta·ɔhti·- AI (recip.): tət·ətpi·ta·ɔhtúwak 'they made signs to each other' (1834a:18.11).

tət·antahko·kwehəla·- AI 'shake the head': tət·antahko·kwehəlé·ɔk '(they were) shaking their heads' (Mk 15.29; KJV "wagging their heads").

†thakaé·t·u P 'in a short time, a short time later' (⟨tvakartw⟩ Lk 13.19, 1842:9.8, 19.2; ⟨ta ky r to⟩ 1834b:3.9; ⟨ta ky r tw⟩ 1834b:6.1).

thakíti P '(for, in) a little while' (Jn 5.35, Mt 13.21, Jn 7.33, 12.35, etc.; Gr. 2.76k).

thakɔ·kwti·t·i·- (te·kɔ·kwti·t·i·-) AI 'be short': é·li-thakɔ·kwtí·t·i·t 'since he was short' (Lk 19.3).

• te·kɔ·kwtí·t·i·t 'the short one' (ME).

thakwi·t- TI(2) 'shorten': nehəlá·ləwe·t=á·=máh máta thakwi·ta·kpáne né·l ki·škúwa 'if the lord had not shortened those days' (Mt 24.22; non-negative); wwə́nči- né·l ki·škúwa -thakwí·to·n 'because of (them), he shortened those days' (Mt 24.22).

tha·khwik- TI(1a) 'cast (as) a shadow': tha·khwíkamən 'there is a shadow' (OA, LB); énta-tha·khwikamíhti·t '(in) their shadow' (1834b:44.3); ə́nta-tha·khwíkaman 'your shadow' (OA).

tha·khwikamaw- (te·ha·khwikamaw-) TA 'cast a shadow on': né·k te·ha·khwikama·khwíti·t 'when it cast a shadow over them' (Lk 1.79; Gr. §2.12b).

tha·kɔt- II 'be shadow': énta-thá·kɔ 'in the shadow' (*lit.*, 'where there is shadow') (Mt 4.16).

the·- (te·he·-, |tahē-|) II 'be cold': áhi thé·w 'it's very cold' (1834a:13); é·li-thé·k 'as it was cold' (Jn 18.18&).

• te·he·-: té·he·k 'the cold' (1834a:15).

thɔm- (-tahəm-, |tahwam-|) TA — thɔnt- (-tahɔnt-, |tahwant-|) TI(1a) 'bite'.

▪ thɔm- (TA): thɔ́m 'bite him!' (V; Gr. 2.29c).

• -tahəm-: ntáhəmukw 'he bit me' (OA, ME, LB; Gr. 2.29c).

▪ thɔnt- (TI): né·tami-thɔ́ntank 'the first one that bites it' (Mt 17.27).

• -tahɔnt-: ntahɔ́ntamən 'I bit it' (ME; Gr. 2.29c), tɔhɔ́ntamən 'he bit it' (OA).

thupahtaw- (|tahəpataw-|; Gr. 5.95f) TA+O 'cool O2 for': thupahtaí·t·eč 'let him cool it for me' (⟨tvwpavtaetch⟩ Lk 16.24).

♦ For thup°, cf. thúp·e·kw 'well' (ME, LTD OA and ME); ntahpé·k·əm (|nə-tahəpēkw-əm|) 'my well' (ME), tɔhpé·k·əm 'his well' (OA, ME; Gr. 2.55n).

thwən- (-tahwən-, tehwən-, -tithwən- [Rih+], |tahwən-|) TA 'seize, grab, arrest': thwə́na· 'she was arrested' (Jn 8.4; Gr. 2.10d, 4.24m); é·li- só·mi xé·li namé·s·a -thwənáhti·t 'as they had caught very many fish' (Lk 5.9); énta-mái-thwə́nie·kw 'when you (pl.) came to arrest me' (Mt 26.55-56&; Gr. 4.61f); ná kót·a-thwəna·né·ɔ 'then they wanted to arrest him' (Jn 7.30).

• -tahwən-: má·wsu=č šúkw ntáhwəna 'I will detain only one' (1842:15.3); ktahwənáwwa 'you (pl.) seize him' (Mk 14.44; =č FUT missing?); tɔhwənawwá·ɔ 'they seized him' (Mt 22.6, 26.50, etc.); namé·s·ak tɔhwənuk·o·né·ɔ 'it (a net) caught fish' (Mt 13.47; Gr. 4.27cc).

• tehwən-: tehwənə́nči·k 'the captives' (Lk 4.18); tehwənúkwki 'those (obv.) that seized him' (Mt 26.55-56&).

• -tithwən-: lə́nu=č ktithwə́na 'you will be catching men' (Lk 5.10). ▸ See also: tethwə́nəwe·s.

thwəna·s·i·- II 'be taken': nə́ni thwəná·s·u 'that is taken' (⟨tvona-|sw⟩ 1834b:12.1).

tihtəmí·ki: see təmí·ki.

tillǝkhíkwi: see lǝkhíkwi.

típa·s AN 'chicken' (Gr. 2.79k, 5.14j), 'hen' (Lk 13.34, Mt 23.37), 'rooster' (Jn 13.38, Lk 22.34, etc.); tipá·s·ak (Mk 13.35). ▸ A loanword adapted from Swedish (Gr. 2.79k; Goddard 1974:157).

ti·la·yəm°: see í·la.

ti·t·e·ha·-: see li·t·e·ha·-.

tkawsi·- (-tək·awəs·i·-, |təkàwəsī-| [and later |təkàwəsī-|]) AI 'be gentle': tkáwsu 'he is gentle' (V, ME, AD; Gr. 5.92b; Z. 82, 85, 123, 128, 227 'gentle, good-natured, mild, well-minded').

• -tək·awəs·i·-: ntək·awə́s·i 'I am gentle' (Mt 11.29; KJV "meek").

▸ Cf. 1s ntək·áwsi (V), ntə́kawsi (ME).

tkawsi·tam- (-tək·awsi·tam-, |təkàwəsīhtam-|; Gr. 5.92b) TA 'be well-minded towards': ktək·awsí·tamukw 'he is well-minded towards you (sg.)' (Lk 1.30; KJV "thou hast found favor with (him)").

tkawso·ke·- AI+O 'make gentle, tame': takó· awé·n kóski-tkawso·ké·wəna 'no one was able to make him be gentle' (Mk 5.4).

tko·wi·- II 'be or have waves': énta-tkó·wi·k 'the waves' (Mk 4.39& [KJV "the raging of the water"], Lk 21.25 [KJV "the waves"]). ▸ Cf. tkó·wi·k 'wave of water' (V [preverb missing]); Mun me·nki-tko·wí·ke 'when there were great waves' (CH).

tkú 'waves' (Mk 4.37). ▸ Assuming inan. sg. used as collective plural (like ké·kw 'wampum').

▸ Cf. Mun tkó·wak 'waves' (NP [F.T. Siebert, Jr.]), or perhaps tkə́wak (: Unami *tkúwak).

to·kən- TA 'wake up' (V): nəmái-tó·kəna 'I go to wake him up' (Jn 11.11); mói-to·kənúk·u 'they (obv.) went and woke him (prox.) up' (Mt 8.25).

to·kihəla·- AI 'wake up' (V, OA, ME; Gr. 5.11n): to·kihəlá·t·e 'when he woke up' (Mt 1.24); mé·či to·kihəlahtí·t·e 'after they woke up' (Lk 9.32).

to·ki·- AI 'be awake': tó·ki· 'he is wake' (Mk 4.27).

▸ Cf. Mun tóhki·w 'he is awake' (RS), tóhki· (MR); tóhki·l 'wake up (you sg.)' (CH).

to·xkam- TA 'tear apart by biting': ná=á· .. kəmái-to·xkamúk·o·n 'then they would go and tear you apart (sbd.)' (Mt 7.6; KJV "rend").

to·xkən- (təto·xkən- [Rə+]) TA — TI(1b) 'tear (by hand)', 'tear up' (LTD).

■ to·xkən- (TA): mé·či .. to·xkəná·t·e 'after he had torn him' (Mk 1.26); wto·xkəná·ɔ 'he (a spirit) tears him' (Mk 9.18), tóhi-to·xkəná·ɔ 'he tore him greatly' (Mk 9.26); ná .. wtó·xkəna·n 'then (the spirit) tore him' (Mk 9.20).

• təto·xkən- (or possibly tət·o·xkən-): aésəs wtəto·xkəná·ɔ 'an animal tore him to pieces' (1842:14.4).

▪ toˑxkən- (TI): ntoˑxkənə́mən 'I tore it' (AD), wtoˑxkənə́mən 'he tore it' (Mt 26.65).
toˑxkhikaw- TA 'tear (as, by body)': nə́=áˑ wáin toˑxkhikaɔ́ˑɔ poˑtˑaˑláˑsˑa 'the wine would tear the skin bag' (Lk 5.37; Gr. 3.22a).
toˑxkihəla·- II 'tear': toˑxkihəléˑɔ 'they (the clothing) would tear' (Mk 2.21).
toˑxkšéˑxˑən- II 'be a gap': teˑtˑaíˑi .. xínkwi-táli-toˑxkšéˑxˑən 'there is a wide gap between' (⟨toxjrxun⟩ 1834b:31.2).
tɔkˑaneˑ- II 'be mild weather': wəli-tɔ́kˑaneˑw 'it's warming up nicely' (1834a:14), tɔ́kˑaneˑ 'it is mild weather' (Mt 16.2); méˑči tɔkˑanékˑe 'after the weather is warm' (1834a:16).
▸ Cf. Mun wtákaneˑw 'be warm out, be mild out' (dict.).
tɔkˑihəla·- II 'become tender': tɔkˑihəléˑɔ 'they (inan.) become tender' (Mt 24.32).
tɔləmunsi·- (weˑtˑaləmunsi·-, |wətaləmōnsī-|; Gr. 5.71d) AI+O 'have (as) an animal': tɔləmunsíˑtˑe 'if he has them (sheep)' (Mt 18.12, Lk 15.4).
• weˑtˑaləmunsi·-: weˑtˑaləmúnsiˑt 'the owner (of it)' (Lk 19.33&); weˑtˑaləmúnsiˑt mekíˑsˑa 'the owner of the sheep' (Jn 10.12).
tɔloˑkaˑkˑanəm- (-oˑtˑaloˑkaˑkˑanəm-, weˑtˑaloˑkaˑkˑanəm-, |wətalōhkākanəm-|; Gr. 5.71k) TA 'have as servant': takóˑ háši awéˑn noˑtˑaloˑkaˑkˑanəmkoˑwíˑwəna 'we have never been the servants of anyone' (lit., 'no one ever had us as servants') (Jn 8.33; Gr. 4.85j); nál nə́ oˑtˑaloˑkaˑkˑanə́mkoˑn 'that is what he is the servant of' (Jn 8.34).
• weˑtˑaloˑkaˑkˑanəm-: weˑtˑaloˑkaˑkˑanə́mkuk 'one who is his (obv.) servant' (Lk 1.38); weˑtˑaloˑkaˑkˑanəmkúkˑi 'the one (obv.) whose servant he was' (Mk 18.27; KJV "the lord of that servant").
tɔloˑkaˑkˑani·- (-oˑtˑaloˑkaˑkˑani·-, |wətalōhkākanī-|; Gr. 5.71k) AI(+O) 'have (O2 as) a servant or slave': tɔloˑkaˑkˑaníˑtˑe 'if he has a servant' (Lk 17.7); tɔloˑkáˑkˑaniˑn=č 'he must be a servant', lit., 'he must be had as a servant' (Mt 20.26); tɔloˑkaˑkˑanínak 'they will be slaves' (1842:16.2); kəmáˑwəni-=č -tɔloˑkaˑkˑaniˑnéˑɔ 'you (pl.) must all have him as your servant' (Mk 10.44).
• -oˑtˑaloˑkaˑkˑani·-: níˑ=áˑ koˑtˑaloˑkáˑkˑaniˑn nhákˑay '*I should be your slave*' (1842:17.1).
tɔlskweˑkamənéˑɔ: see alaskweˑkˑ-*.
tɔmiˑmənsəm- (-oˑtˑamiˑmənsəm-, |wətamīmənsəm-|; Gr. 5.72e, 6.6a) TA 'have as a child': koˑtˑamiˑmə́nsəmukw=č 'you will be the child of him' (Lk 6.35); ktə́li-=áˑ -tɔmiˑmənsəmúkˑoˑn kóˑx 'so that you (sg.) may be the child of your father' (Mt 5.45).
tɔmiˑmənsəmi·- (-oˑtˑamiˑmənsəmi·-, |wətamīmənsəmī-|; Gr. 5.71p) AI(+O) 'have (O2 as) a child': takóˑ tɔmiˑmənsəmiˑíˑɔk 'they had no children' (Lk 1.7; Gr. 4.81q, 6.6a); táˑ=áˑ nkáski-tɔmiˑmənsəmíˑwən 'he would not be able to be my pupil' (lit., 'I would not be able to have him as a child') (Lk 14.26, 14.27, 14.33); ktə́li-tɔmiˑmə́nsəmiˑn 'that they are your (sg.) children (sbd.)' (Mt 11.25).
• -oˑtˑamiˑmənsəmi·- (əˑns): noˑtˑamiˑmə́ˑnsəmi 'I have children' (OA; Gr. 5.71p, cf. §2.1c).
tɔpíči(?): see ahpíči*(?).
tɔpˑóˑnəm: see ahpóˑn.
tɔpˑɔˑnəmi·- (|wətapwānəmī-|) AI 'have bread': éˑli- máta -tɔpˑɔˑnəmíeˑkw 'because you (pl.) have no bread' (Mk 8.17; or -tɔpˑɔˑnəmíˑeˑkw, if the negative inflection was distinct).
†tošˑáˑskamən: see †ašaˑskˑ-(?).
tɔxˑ- (-oˑtx-, weˑtx-, |wətax-|) TA 'come to, visit': tɔ́xˑiˑkw 'come to me (you pl.)' (Mt 11.28; Gr. 4.105m); tɔxˑíˑtˑe 'if he comes to me' (Jn 6.35, 6.37, 7.37; Gr. 2.19c); nəmái-tɔ́xˑa 'I go to him' (Jn 16.5); móˑi-tɔxkóˑpˑaniˑl 'they (obv.) went to visit him' (Mt 3.5; Gr. 4.69r);

enkələlí·t·əp tóxko·k 'one who had died (obv.) comes to them' (Lk 16.31; Gr. 4.27g, cf. 4.27h); wi·š·a·s·əwá·k·an tóxko·k 'fear came over them' (Lk 7.16; Gr. 4.27h); ktə́li-=á· -tóx·ələn '(that I) come to you' (Lk 7.7).

• -o·tx-: o·txá·ɔ †sáiman-pí·tə·la 'she came to Simon-Peter' (Jn 20.2; Gr. 2.19c); no·txá·wəna=č 'we will come to him' (Jn 14.23; Gr. 4.24i); o·txawwá·ɔ 'they came to him, them' (Mt 9.28, Mk 6.30, Mt 17.24, etc.); no·txúk·o·k 'they come to me' (Jn 6.37; Gr. 2.19c, 2.65d, 4.27i); o·txúk·u 'he, they (obv.) came to him (prox.)' (Mt 2.13, 8.19, 13.10, etc.; Gr. 4.27k); wi·š·a·s·əwá·k·an tóxko·p 'fear came over him' (Lk 5.9; Gr. 4.69o).

• we·tx-: we·txá·t·əp 'who had come to him' (Jn 7.50); we·txa·tpáni·k 'who (pl.) had come to visit her' (Jn 11.31, 11.45; Gr. 4.64w); we·txúkwki '(obv.) who came to him' (Lk 6.17); we·txukhwití·t·əp 'those to whom it came' (Jn 10.35; Gr. 4.76aa).

tɔx·i·pi·lá·ɔ: see xi·pi·l-.

tɔ·ki·i- AI 'have land' (-o·thaki·i·-, |wətahkīwī-|): tɔ·kí·yu 'he has land' (OA; Gr. 2.32b).

• -o·thaki·i·-: no·thakí·i 'I have land' (OA; Gr. 2.32b).

tó·nal: see ntá·nəs.

tpahw- (tətpahw- [Rə+]; Gr. 4.104m) TA 'point to, at': ná tə́li-tpáhɔ·n 'and with that he pointed to them' (Mt 12.49).

• tətpahw-: tətpáhɔw 'point at him (you sg.)' (OA); ntətpáhɔ 'I point at him' (V; Gr. 5.12r).

tpəskwe·ləm- (-təpskwe·ləm-) TA 'consider equal': ktalo·ka·k·ani·ké·i=č ktəpskwé·ləmi. 'You shall consider me equal to your servants.' (1834b:28.14); ktəpskwé·ləma·n 'you (sg.) consider them equal (sbd.)' (Mt 20.12).

tpəskwe·lənsi- (-təpskwe·lənsi·-) AI 'consider oneself equal': é·li- kí·.. -tpəskwe·lə́nsian ke·tanət·o·wí·t·ink 'because you consider *yourself* equal to God' (Jn 10.33).

• -təpskwe·lənsi·-: nihəláči wtəpskwe·lə́nsi·n ki·š·e·ləməwé·t·ink 'he thinks of himself as equal to God' (Jn 5.18; with ⟨tup-⟩ for wtəp-).

tpə́skwi (Gr. 5.25i, 5.129jj) P 'like, equally, correspondingly, opposite' (Jn 5.19, 5.26, Lk 14.33), 'likewise' (Lk 6.26, Mt 18.14); nə́ni tpə́skwi lé· 'it is like that' (Lk 14.33); nə́ tpə́skwi 'at the same time' (Lk 7.21); nə́ni=č tpə́skwi lé· 'that is what it will be like' (Mt 24.27); nə́ni tpə́skwi lə́s·i·l 'also do like that' (Mt 5.33); nə́ni tpə́skwi 'like that' (Mt 23.28), nə́ni tpə́skwi lé· 'it is like that' (Lk 14.3); tpə́skwi ká·mink †nčátan 'on the opposite side of Jordan' (Jn 1.28); tpə́skwi hukwé·yunk 'right above' (Mt 2.9).

▪ PV: tpə́skwi-lé· 'it is like ..' (Mt 22.2).

▪ tpəskwí·i P 'directly' (Mk 12.41; Gr. 5.29h).

tpəskwihəla·- II 'be the time': tpəskwíhəle·=č 'the time will come' (Jn 5.25, 5.28, Lk 21.6, Jn 13.1, etc.); tpəskwíhəla·k 'the time (for something to happen)' (Mt 26.39; KJV "the hour"), é·li- mé·či -tpəskwíhəla·k 'for the time has come' (Mk 4.29), éši-tpəskwíhəla·k 'whenever it is the right time' (Lk 12.42, Mt 24.45); né·ləma tpəskwíhəla·k 'before the time comes' (Mt 8.29, Jn 12.27, Jn 13.1); é·li- né·ləma -tpəskwihəlá·k·əp 'as his time had not yet come' (Jn 8.20); mé·či tpəskwihəlá·k·e 'after the time had come' (Lk 2.22, 14.17, etc.), énta-tpəskwihəlá·k·e 'when it was the time' (Jn 10.22); éntxən-tpəskwíhəla·k 'every time (that ..)' (Mt 21.41&).

tpəskwilahta·- (-təpskwilahta·-, |təpəskwīhlatā-|) AI 'one's time has come, it is one's time': mé·či ntəpskwílahta 'my time has now come' (Mk 14.14); né·ləma=tá ntəpskwilahtá·i. 'It is not yet time for me.' (Jn 2.4; KJV "mine hour is not yet come"; Gr. 4.81b), é·li né·skɔ mpak·ánči-tpəskwilahtá·i 'as my time has not fully come' (Jn 7.8); ktəpskwilahtáhəmɔ 'it is your (pl.) time' (Jn 7.6, Lk 22.53), yúkwe ktəpskwilahtáhəmɔ 'now your (pl.) time has come'

(Lk 22.53; KJV "this is your hour"); tpəskwílahta·p 'the time was completed for her ..' (Lk 2.6); ná wtəpskwilahtá·ne·p 'then her time had come' (Lk 1.57).

tpó·kw P 'night' in: kwə́ni-tpó·kw 'all night' (Lk 5.5, 6.12, Mk 5.5); kwə́ni-kí·š·ukw ɔ́·k kwə́ni-tpó·kw '(all) day and (all) night' (Lk 2.37, Lk 18.7).

▪ tpó·kwe P 'night': kwə́ti-tpó·kwe 'all night' (Jn 21.3; LB).

▪ tpó·kəwe P '(so many) nights': náxi-tpó·kəwe 'for three nights' (⟨nuxi tpwkwc⟩ Mt 12.40 [2x]). ▸ Cf. tpó·kəwe P 'last night' (Gr. 5.23l; OA).

▪ tpo·kwəní·i P 'night' in: lá·i-tpo·kwəní·i 'at midnight' (Mk 13.35).

tpo·kwi·- II 'be night': lá·i-tpó·ku 'it is midnight' (Lk 12.38), ahkɔ́·ni-tpó·ku 'the nights are long' (OA); nə́ni=č te·phúkwi·k 'on that (future) night' (Lk 17.34); mayá·i yúkwe te·phúkwi·k 'this very night' (Mk 14.30); lá·i-tpo·kwí·k·e 'at midnight' (Lk 11.5, Mt 25.6).

túhɔn (|təhwan|) IN 'branch' (V, LB; Gr. 2.29e).

▪ tuhənət·ət IN (dim.) 'little branch' (Jn15.6); wisahki·munšií·i-tuhənə́t·ət 'branch of the vine' (Jn 15.4); tuhənət·ə́t·a 'branches' (Mt 21.8, 24.32, Jn 15.2 [2x], 15.5), pa·mí·i-tuhənət·ə́t·a 'palm branches' (Jn 12.13); tuhənət·ə́t·ink 'on the little branches' (⟨twvuntitif⟩ Mt 13.32).

tukɔhtən- (|təkwatən-|) II 'be a round hill': énta-túkɔhtink 'Round Hill' (Jn 19.13; Gr. 5.11i).

tuk·ɔme·nxkha·s·i·- II 'be fenced around': táli énta-tuk·ɔme·nxkhá·s·i·k 'in the garden' (*lit.*, 'place encircled by a fence') (Lk 22.59-60&).

tunkᵒ (|tōnk-|) 'open' (Gr. §5.2a; often with |-əšē-| 'opening, rim' Gr. 5.13g).

tunkšehəla·- II 'open': ná .. tunkšehəlé·lu 'then they (obv.) opened' (Mt 9.30); ná šá·e tunkšehəlé·ɔ 'then immediately they opened' (Mk 7.35); tunkšehəlá·k·eč 'let them open' (Mk 7.34; Gr. 4.114f).

tunkšelaht- TI(2) 'open': tɔ́ləmi-tunkšélahto·n 'he began to open it' (1834a:15).

tunkše·h- TA 'open': túnkše·(h) 'open it (anim.) (you sg.)' (1834a: Cover).

tunkše·kɔ́·k·an AN 'key' (OA, LTD LB); ɔ·s·ahkamé·i-sa·k·i·ma·ɔ·k·aní·i-tunkše·kɔ́·k·an 'the heavenly-kingdom key' (Mt 16.19); ləpwe·ɔ·k·aní·i-tunkše·kɔ́·k·an 'the key of knowledge' (Lk 11.52 [object of TA]).

tunkše·n- TI(1b) 'open' (Gr. 5.13g): tunkšé·ni 'open it (you sg.)' (ME; Gr. 4.106d); tunkšé·nəmo·kw 'open it (you pl.)' (ME; Gr. 4.106g); énta-=á· .. -tunkše·nəmíhti·t 'where they would open them' (Mt 6.19); ɔ́·k=á· énta- máta .. -tunkše·nəmíhti·t 'and where they would not open them' (Mt 6.30); wtunkše·nəməné·ɔ 'they opened a hole in it' (Mk 2.4).

tunkše·nəmaw- (|tōnkəšēnəmaw-|; Gr. 5.94h) TA+O 'open O2 for': tunkše·nəmaí·ne·n 'open the door for us' (Lk 13.25, Mt 25.11); wtunkše·nəmáɔ·n 'he opens it for him' (Jn 10.3); ná tunkše·nəmáɔ·n pwəna·eləntaməwa·k·aní·li·t 'then he opened their (obv.) understanding' (Lk 24.45, with ⟨t-⟩ for /wt-/); tunkše·nəmáɔ·n=č 'it shall be opened for them' (Mt 7.8).

tunkto·ne·- AI 'open one's mouth': ná .. wtunkto·né·ne·p 'then his mouth opened' (Lk 1.64).

tunkto·ne·n- TA 'open the mouth of': ktunkto·né·na=č 'you (sg.) must open its mouth' (Mt 17.27).

txa·ke·i·-* (entxa·ke·i·- [IC]) AI 'be {so many} nations': wé·mi entxa·ké·i·t (sg. form) 'all nations' (Lk 2.1, 2.3 ⟨-krt⟩; Mt 21.13&, 24.14, etc. ⟨-kret⟩); wé·mi yó·ki·k entxa·ke·íhti·t 'all these nations' (⟨cntxakctet⟩ 1834b:39.12); télən ɔ́·k ní·š·a entxa·ke·í·č·i·k 'the twelve tribes' (Mt 19.28, Lk 22.30); entxa·ke·i·lí·č·i 'all nations (obv.)' (⟨cntxakrlehi⟩ Lk 1.50).

♦ (lexicalized participle): télən ɔ́·k kwə́t·a·š txa·ke·i·t·i·ké·i wə́nči 'from sixteen nations' (1834b:39.11 [em.]; see Gr. 4.10). ♦ Note: forms with apparent /entxa·ke(·)-/ are found only in B 1834b and in the early pages of B (3x, pp. 10 and 12); forms with /entxa·ke·í·-/ are found later in B (7x, pp. 139-220).

txa·kɔt-* (entxa·kɔt-) II 'be {so many} (sticklike things)': wé·mi entxá·kɔ mí·laxk 'all the number of hairs (*lit.*, hair [sg.])' (Lk 12.7).

txa·pto·na·l- (entxa·pto·na·l-) TA 'speak {so much} to': entxa·pto·ná·lənt 'talks addressed to them' (1834b:3.1).

txa·pto·ne·-* (entxa·pto·ne·-) AI 'utter {so much}': wtɔ·pto·nák·an entxa·ptó·ne·t náni ki·š·e·ləmúwe·t 'every word that God utters' (Mt 4.4).

txá·pxki P '{so many} hundred' (with numbers above four): palé·naxk txá·pxki 'five hundred' (Lk 7.41); xá·š txá·pxki 'eight hundred' (Lk 16.6, 16.7); télən txá·pxki 'a thousand' (Lk 16.7); ní·š·ən télən txá·pxki 'two thousand' (1842:8.3); palé·naxk-txə́n télən-txá·pxki 'Five-Thousand' (*lit.*, 'five times ten hundred') (Mk 5.9); télən txə́n télən txá·pxki 'ten thousand' (Mt 18.24, Lk 14.31); ni·š·í·nxke txə́n télən txá·pxki 'twenty thousand' (Lk 14.31).

txa·pxksi·- AI 'be {so many} hundred': ní·š·ən télən txa·pxksúwak 'there were two thousand of them' (*lit.*, 'two times ten hundred') (Mk 5.13).

txennaɔhkəs·i·-* (entxennaɔhkəs·i·-, |(-ən)taxēlənawakəsī-|) AI 'be of {so many} kinds': wé·mi entxennaɔhkə́s·i·t aésəs 'every kind of animal' (1842:8.1); wé·mi entxennaɔhkəs·í·č·i·k aesə́s·ak 'creatures of every kind' (Mt 13.47, 1842:9.2).

txennáɔhki (1) P '{so many} kinds, sets': palé·naxk txennáɔhki a·ksə́nak 'five teams of oxen' (Lk 14.19). ▸ See also entxennáɔhki (1).

txennáɔhki* (2) (entxennáɔhki [IC]) PV '{so many} kinds': wé·mi entxennáɔhki-lankələ́k·i·k 'people with all sorts of diseases' (Mk 1.32); wé·mi entxennáɔhki-lankələlí·č·i 'ones (obv.) with all kinds of afflictions' (Mt 4.24); wé·mi entxennáɔhki- .. máta -hakí·he·t 'every kind of thing he did not plant' (Mt 15.13).

txe·khamaw-* (-t-əntxe·khamaw-, entxe·khamaw-, |(-ən)taxēkahamaw-|) TA 'owe {so much} O2 to': tá=háč .. ktəntxe·khamáɔ·n 'how much do you owe him?' (Lk 16.5, 16.7).
 • entxe·khamaw-: entxe·khamák·uk 'how much they (obv.) owed him' (Mt 18.23).

txe·khama·-* (entxe·khama·-, |(-ən)taxēkahamā-|) AI 'owe {so much}': entxe·kháma·t 'what he owed' (Mt 18.27; Gr. 4.67(4)v).

txə́n P '{so many} times': tá=č=háč txə́n 'how many times?' (Mt 18.21); palé·naxk-txə́n télən-txá·pxki 'Five-Thousand' (*lit.*, 'five times ten hundred') (Mk 5.9).

txə́n (éntxən [IC]; Gr. 5.128f) PV '{so many} times': éntxən 'as many times as, every time that': éntxən-kahtínk 'every year' (Lk 2.41); éntxən- o·t·é·nink -pá·t·e 'every time he came to a town' (Lk 13.22); éntxən-tpəskwíhəla·k 'anytime (it was time that)' (Mt 21.41&).

txí (-t-ə́ntxi, éntxi [IC], |(-ən)taxī|; Gr. 3.13(5), 5.128w, 5.129kk) PV '{so many}, {so much}' (Lk 1.24, 3.23, Mt 25.27).
 • -t-ə́ntxi: (Mt 20.10; Gr. 6.7g).
 • éntxi PV 'as many, as much' (with sg. or pl.): wé·mi entxi-luwé·t·əp 'everything he had said' (Lk 2.39); éntxi-=č awé·n -wé·t·ənink xinkɔnší·k·an 'as many people as shall take up the sword' (Mt 26.52; Gr. 5.128w); wé·mi éntxi- xkwé·yunk -wə́nči-ki·š·í·k·i·t 'of all .. who have been born of women' (Lk 7.28); éntxi-mi·liáni·k 'as many as you gave me' (Jn 17.9; Gr. 5.128).
 ▪ PP (Gr. 5.133g): ní·š·a·š txí-kahtəné·i 'for seven years' (Lk 2.36); ní·š·a·š txí-kí·škwe 'in seven days' (Lk 18.12).
 ▪ P '{such} amount': nə́ txí 'that amount, that many' (Lk 19.8, Jn 21.11); nə́ni txí 'the amount' (Mk 10.30); ná=ní txí 'that same amount' (Lk 6.34); mé·či, ná=ni txí. 'That's all.' (OA, ME); tá=háč txí 'how many?' (Mk 6.38); aləwí·i txí 'more, a greater amount' (Lk 10.35, Mk 12.43, Mk 25.27); kwət·ennáɔhki txí 'the same amount' (Mt 20.10).

- ehə́ntxi P (Rih+; IC): wé·mi ehə́ntxi 'every one of them (in turn)' (Mt 25.15).

txihəla- II 'be all gone': lí-=á· kəna·ka·t·amwe·ó·k·an máta -txihəlé·i 'so that your faith would not dissipate' (Lk 22.32; KJV "fail not").

txi·- (-t-əntxi·-, entxi·-, |(-ən)taxī-|; Gr. 3.13(5)b) AI — txən- (entxən-) II 'be {so many}' (Gr. 5.10n).

▪ txi·- (AI): ní·š·a·š txí·nxke txúwak 'they were seventy in number' (Lk 10.1); télən ó·k ní·š·a txi·ló·p·ani kkwí·s·al 'he had twelve sons' (*lit.*, 'his sons were twelve') (1834b:19.11); palé·naxk txó·p·ani·k 'there have been five of them' (⟨txwpani⟩ Jn 4.18; echoes ⟨-pani⟩ in Jn 4.17); télən txə́n télən txá·pxki txi·lí·t·e 'if they (obv.) were ten thousand' (Lk 14.31); ə́nta-palé·naxk txə́n télən txá·pxki -txihtí·t·e 'when there were five thousand' (Mk 8.19).

• -t-əntxi·-: ní·, nuntá·i=č ntəntxíhəna 'I and mine shall be less' (*lit.*, 'we shall be less') (Jn 3.30).

• entxi·-: ə́ntxi·t 'every' (Lk 2.23); ni·š·í·nxke txə́n télən txá·pxki entxí·li·t wsɔ·čələ́ma 'one whose soldiers (obv.) numbered twenty thousand' (Lk 14.31; Gr. 4.64d); entxíenk awé·n 'any of us' (1842:16.2); wé·mi entxíe·kw 'all of you' (Jn 13.18, Mt 26.27, etc.); wé·mi entxi·tpáni·k 'all those who had been present' (Mt 7.28; Gr. 4.75n); wé·mi entxíhti·t 'among all' (Lk 19.2), entxíhti·t e·p·í·č·i·k 'everyone that was (there)' (Jn 4.53; Gr. 4.67(4)z).

▪ txən- (II): palé·naxk txə́nu 'they (inan.) are five' (Jn 5.2); kwət·á·pxki txə́nu 'they were a hundred (times)' (Mt 13.8).

• entxən-: wé·mi ə́ntxink 'all (of them) that there are' (Mt 13.32 [2x], etc.); ə́ntxink o·t·é·naya 'as many towns as there are' (Lk 10.1).

txí·nxke P '{so many} tens' (⟨txenxkc⟩ 6x, ⟨txenxki⟩ 1x, ⟨txentkc⟩ 1x, ⟨txenkc⟩ 3x, ⟨txentxkc⟩ 1x, ⟨txenk⟩ 1x; |-īnaxkē|, Gr. 5.31p): palé·naxk txí·nxke 'fifty' (Lk 7.41, Jn 8.57, 21.11); kwə́t·a·š txí·nxke 'sixty' (Mt 13.8); ní·š·a·š txí·nxke 'seventy' (Lk 10.1, 10.17); xá·š txí·nxke 'eighty' (Lk 2.37); pé·škunk txí·nxke 'ninety' (Mt 18.12, 18.13).

txo·k·wənak·at- II 'be {so many} days': télən ó·k ní·š·a txo·k·wənakháke 'in twelve days (from now)' (ME); mé·či xá·š entxo·k·wənakháke 'after it had been eight days' (Lk 2.21).

txó·k·wəni P '{so many} days' (OA; cf. Gr. 5.31s): ne·í·nxke txó·k·wəni 'forty days' (Mk 1.13, Acts 1.3, 1842:9.4); kwə́t·a·š txó·k·wəni 'six days' (Jn 12.1).

txo·nal- (-t-əntxo·nal-) TA 'make the number of {so}': aləwí·i təntxo·nalúk·o·n 'it made his numbers more' (1834a:20.23); also with nuntá·i 'less'.

u

-uhəl-: see hwil-.

uho·t·e·nai·k·e·-: see o·t·e·nai·k·e·-.

um-: see wum-.

-uxkwe·-: see xkwé·.

uxkwe·k·ánkan, uxkwe·k·ánkanink: see nuxkwe·k·ánkan.

w

wá (wáni, yó·kᵒ, yó·l, wáka, yukáhke; Gr. 3.6b, 4.16a) 'this, this one (anim.)'.
- wá 'this (anim.)' (Mt 2.9, Lk 3.15, 4.22, etc.); usually ⟨wu⟩, but also ⟨wuv⟩ (Mt 21.10).
- wáni 'this (anim.)' (Jn 1.15, Lk 2.34, Mt 3.3, 3.4, 3.17, etc.).
- yó·kᵒ 'these (anim.)' (Gr. 2.72c): yó·k (Jn 2.7, Mt 4.24, 8.12, etc.); yó·ki·k (1834a:13, 1834b:8.6).
- yó·l 'this, these (obv.)': 'this' (Mt 2.13, Jn 9.8, 1834a:14); 'these' (Jn 8.31, Mk 9.42).
- wáka (Gr. 2.72a) 'this (abs. anim.)' (Mt 27.54&).
- yukáhke 'these (abs. anim.)' (Jn 8.10).
▸ For the inan. forms, see yú.

wahtuhé·p·i: see ahtuhé·p·i.

wahtuhe·p·i·i·- (|-īwī |) II 'be flesh': wahtuhe·p·í·yu=hánkw (|-īwəw|) 'it is flesh' (⟨-iw⟩ Jn 3.6).

wáin IN 'wine' (Lk 1.15, Jn 2.3, 2.9, 2.10, 4.46, etc.).

wanə́š·i P 'I give thanks to you' (Jn 11.41), 'thank you' (Mt 11.25, Lk 18.11, Jn 11.41).

wani·- (-ɔni·- ~ -wani·- [Gr. 4.40a,b, etc.], wi·wani·- [Rī+], |wanī-|; Gr. 2.15g, 3.21a) AI+O 'forget': káči wani·he·kw 'don't forget it (you pl.)' (1842:18.6); wénči-=á· máta -wani·li·t 'so that they (obv.) would not forget it' (1842:10.6); tá=á· ma·wsí·lu wwaní·wəna ke·tanət·ó·wi·t 'God would not forget one' (Lk 12.6); máta wwaní·wəne·p 'he did not forget it' (1842:10.4); wwani·né·ɔ 'they forgot it' (Mk 8.14; Gr. 4.40h).
- -ɔni·-: nɔ́ni·n 'I forgot it' (OA, LB; Gr. 3.21a, 4.40a).
- wi·wani·-: wénči·=č máta -wi·wani·e·kw 'so that you will never forget it' (1834b:20.1).

wánkɔna: see nánkɔn.

wa·weši·tᵒ (⟨wawcjeton⟩ 1834a:19.13): [wāwešītōn] is not possible in Delaware and suggests nothing that is, but it would be exactly Southwestern Ojibwe owawezhitoon 'he decorates it' and might be the early Ottawa (Odawa) cognate of this, which could have been learned from the printer Jotham Meeker (for information on Meeker, see Blanchard and Conner 2021:v).

wča·tsi·- AI 'be hard': wča·tsúwak 'they are hard' (ME); é·li yó·k wtehəwá·ɔ áləmi-wča·tsí·lu 'for their hearts (obv.) become hard' (⟨wthahselw⟩ Mt 13.15 [possibly with /čs/]; KJV "is waxed gross" [= 'dense, thick, solid'], RSV "has grown dull"). ▸ Cf. wčá·če· II 'it is hard, not tender' (like overcooked meat or an insect bite) (ME).

wehe·məwa·l- (|wehwēməwāl-|, always with repetitive reduplication [Gr. 5.39c]) TA 'laugh at, make fun of': wehe·məwa·lɔ́nte 'if he is mocked' (Lk 14.27); wwehe·məwa·lá·ɔ 'he made fun of him' (Lk 23.39, 1834a:19.13); wwehe·məwa·lawwá·ɔ 'they mocked him' (Lk 14.29, Mt 27.39, etc.); ná wwehe·məwa·la·né·ɔ 'then they laughed at him' (Mk 5.40, Jn 9.28, Lk 16.14).

wehi·húnke·s AN 'priest' (Jn 11.49, 11.51); wehi·hunké·s·a 'priests (obv.)' (Mt 27.3); wehi·hunke·s·i·ké·i P 'to the priests' (Lk 22.4). ▸ Cf. wi·hunke·-.

wehí·khe·s AN 'carpenter' (Mt 13.55 [em.]; LB; cf. 5.42, 5.66). ▸ Cf. wi·khe·-.

wehi·nəwe·- see wi·nəwe·-.

wehi·penke·-: see wi·penke·-.

wehi·t·a·č·i·mo·lsi·-: see wi·t·a·č·i·mo·lsi·-.

wehšəmwi·s AN 'cow'; wehšəmwí·s·ak 'cattle' (1834a:14, 1834b:47.2); wehšəmwí·s·a 'cattle (obv.)' (Lk 17.7). ▸ Cf. ⟨weuchschúmmuĩs⟩ 'cow or ox' (Z. 34), implying /wewšə̆mwi·s/ (lit., 'one that has horns').
▪ wehšəmwí·t·ət (dim.) 'calf' (Lk 15.23); wehšəmwi·t·ə́t·a (obv.) (Lk 15.27, 15.30).

wehwəlankunso·ha·ləwe·-: see wəlankunso·ha·ləwe·-.

wehwəla·te·namo·ha·ləwe·-: see wəla·te·namo·ha·ləwe·-.
wehwəla·te·namo·há·ləwe·s AN 'comforter' (*lit.*, 'one who makes people happy'; Gr. 5.81c) (Jn 15.26, Jn 16.7); wehwəla·te·namo·ha·ləwé·s·a (obv.) (Jn 14.16; KJV "Comforter").
wenčahkənəmaw- TA+O 'make O2 ready for': wenčahkə́nəmaw é·a·t=č nehəlá·ləwe·t 'make ready the way that the Lord will go' (⟨wcnhavkinumu⟩ Jn 1.23).
wenčahki·- AI 'prepare': wenčahkúwak 'they prepared' (Jn 19.14, 19.31); ná šá·e wwénčahki·n 'then he immediately got ready' (1842:18.3).
wenčinke·- AI 'invite people': wenčínke·t 'the host' (Mt 9.15). ▸ Cf. wenči·m-.
wenči·ai·-: see wənči·ai·-.
wenči·m- TA — wenčo·t- TI(1b) 'call, summon, invite'.
- wenči·m- (TA): xé·li awé·ni wenčí·me·p 'he invited many people' (Lk 14.16; Gr. 4.69a); wenči·má·p·ani·k 'they were invited' (Jn 2.1; Gr. 4.69n); wenči·mó·me ke·t·əma·ksí·č·i·k 'invite the poor (you sg)' (Lk 14.13; Gr. 4.116d); wenči·makpáni·k 'the ones I invited' (Lk 14.24, Mt 22.3, etc.; Gr. 4.76c); é·li- tá=á· -káski- ne·k·əmá·ɔ né· a·šíte -wenči·mkó·wan 'because *they* would not be able to also invite *you* (sg.) in turn' (Lk 14.14; Gr. 4.97i); né·ləma .. wenči·mkó·wane 'before he called you (sg.)' (Jn 1.48; Gr. 4.97k); wwenči·má·p·ani 'he called him, them over' (Jn 2.9, Lk 7.19, etc.); kəwenčí·mukw 'he is calling for you (sg.)' (Lk 7.4, Jn 11.28, 1842:18.1; Gr. 4.27j).
- wenčo·t- (TI): máta=háč=á· nəwenčo·t·əmo·húmənatə́ntay lí ɔ·s·áhkame 'should we not summon fire from heaven?' (Lk 9.54; Gr. 4.91i).

wenk°: see wum-.
wewči·p·i·s·i·-: see ɔhči·p·i·si·-.
weyákski: see wiákski.
we·č·ilaht- (|wēčīhlat-|) TI(2) 'grab': wwe·č·ílahto·n 'he grabbed it' (Jn 21.7).
we·hitaɔk·i·-: see hwitaɔk·i·-.
we·hɔk·ai·-: see hɔk·ai·-.
we·hɔmaw- (|wēwahamaw-|) TA 'notify': mái-we·hómo· 'go notify them (you pl.)' (1834a:22.49); kəwe·hɔmá·k·əwa 'he lets you (pl.) know' (Jn 16.13).
we·itahkəno·t·əmaw- TA+O 'explain O2 to': né·li- .. -we·itahkəno·t·əma·k·ónkwe 'when he explained to us [the old texts]' (Lk 24.32); ná tɔ́ləmi-we·itahkəno·t·əmáɔ·n 'then he began to explain it to them' (Lk 24.27). ▸ See we·i·t·°.
we·i·č·i·xt- TI(2) 'explain': we·i·č·í·xto·l nɔ́ e·nunthake·ɔ́·k·an 'explain the parable (you sg.)' (Mt 13.36; KJV "Declare unto us"; RSV "Explain to us"); ké·ski-=á· -we·i·č·í·xta·kw e·la·š·í·mwian 'who would be able to explain your dream' (1842:14.2); we·i·č·i·xtá·k·əp e·la·š·í·mwia 'he explained my dream' (1842:14.2). ▸ See we·i·t·°.
we·i·k·i·-: see wwi·k·i·-.
we·i·mahti·°: see wwi·mahti·-.
we·i·t·° (we·it°, we·i·č·°) 'possible, probable, evident(ly)'. ▸ Cf. ⟨Wewitschi⟩ "perhaps" and ⟨Wewitschinaquot⟩ "it is likely; probable" (B&A 156).
we·i·t·e·lənt- TI(1a) 'think probable, expect': we·i·t·e·lə́ntam 'he thinks it probable' (1834a:22.47); áhi-we·i·t·e·ləntánke 'if he firmly expects' (Mk 11.23; KJV "believe"); áhi-we·i·t·e·ləntamé·k·we 'if you (pl.) firmly expect it' (Mk 11.24).
we·í·t·ət P 'I guess' (OA, ME): we·í·t·ət=ét 'I suppose' (Lk 7.43).
we·khwiksi·- AI 'burn up': énta-we·khwíksi·t 'where he had completely burned up' (WL); wə́nči-=á· -we·khwiksíhti·t 'so that they would be burned up' (Lk 9.54).
we·kw° (|wēhkw-|) 'completely (destroyed, etc.)' (Gr. §5.2a).

wé·kwi PV 'completely' (OA), "the last of" (1834a:21.48).
we·kwi·h- TA 'massacre, exterminate': we·kwi·há·ɔk 'They were all killed off.' (OA); wwe·kwi·hawwá·ɔ 'they killed every one' (Mt 22.7).
we·kwi·t- TI(1a) 'eat or drink all': wwe·kwi·taməné·ɔ 'they ate them all' (1834b:26.13); kə́nč we·kwi·tamá·ne 'unless I drink it up' (Mt 26.42); máta=č=háč nəwe·kwi·tamó·wən 'will I not drink it all?' (Jn 18.11).
we·k·wi·s·əmᵒ: see kkwi·s·əm-.
we·k·wí·s·i·t 'father': see kkwi·s·i·-.
we·la·k·əwé·k·e: see lɔ·k·əwe·-.
we·lhal-: see wəlahəl-.
wé·lhik: see wələs·i·-.
we·m-: see wum-.
we·mala·mwi·- AI 'shout all together': we·malá·məwak 'they all shouted' (Mk 15.13).
wé·mi (Gr. 5.25j, 5.129ll) P 'all' (Lk 1.6, 1.28, 1.50, 1.65, etc.); 'every' (Lk 1.70); wé·mi kéku 'everything' (Jn 1.3, 3.35, 4.25, etc.); wé·mi awé·n 'everyone' (Jn 1.7, Lk 2.10, 3.6, etc.); wé·mi awé·n 'everyone (obv.)' (presumably an error for wé·mi awé·ni; Jn 2.24, Jn 3.26, Mt 14.5); wé·mi pí·lsi·t 'every holy one' (Lk 1.70); wé·mi yó·ni 'all this' (Lk 1.20, Mt 1.22).
  ♦ (idiom): wé·mi=yú=tá 'everywhere' (1834b:41.3; V, OA): wé·mi=yú=tá .. e·lo·t·é·nai·k 'to all the towns' (Mt 9.35).
we·mihtəwá·k·an IN 'massacre(s)' (Gr. 5.114l): 'massacres' (Lk 21.11&).
  ▸ From we·mihti·- AI (recip.) 'be all killed'.
we·mi·h- TA 'kill all': we·mi·há·ɔk 'they have all been killed' (LB); ɔ́·k=č wwe·mi·há·ɔ 'and he will kill all those' (Mk 12.9), tóhi·=č -ktəmáki-we·mi·há·ɔ 'he will kill them all very miserably' (Mt 21.41&); wwe·mihko·né·ɔ·p 'it killed them all' (Lk 17.29; Gr. 4.69v).
wé·na P 'still, yet': ná wé·na 'while (in contrast), yet, (but) still' (Mt 9.14, Mk 5.31, Mt 20.12, Mt 23.23, 23.24, 23.25, 1834b:3,5, 1842:18.7); 'and then still' (Lk 6.46).
we·ni·č·a·ni·ᵒ: see wəni·č·a·ni·-.
we·ɔ·hᵒ: see wwa·h-.
we·ɔ·psi·-: see ɔ·psi·-.
we·skinnuwi·-: see skinnuwi·-.
we·thaki·há·k·ani·t 'the owner of the field' (Mt 13.27, 20.8, Mk 12.6&, Jn 20.15); we·thaki·ha·k·ani·lí·č·i (obv.) (Mt 20.11).
  ▸ Participle of |wətahkīhākanī-| AI 'have a field' (Gr. 5.71l).
we·txᵒ: see tɔx·-.
we·t·aləmúnsi·t 'owner (of an animal)': see tɔləmunsi·-.
wé·t·ami PV (with IC; |wətamī| Gr. 5.129mm) 'be busy with': wé·t·ami-mái-mhalamɔ·s·íhti·t 'while they were occupied with going to buy' (Mt 25.10). ▸ Cf. also ɔ·wtámi above.
we·t·á·nink 'daughter' (lit., 'who one is had as a daughter'; Gr. 5.71e) (Lk 12.53).
  ▸ Participle of |wətānī-| AI+O 'have (O2 as) a daughter'.
we·t·əmpihpé·k·a: see təmpihpé·k·a.
we·t·ən- TA — TI(Ib) 'pick up, take, accept, receive, take in, adopt (a practice)' (Gr. 5.8b).
  ▪ we·t·ən- (TA): wé·t·ən 'take him (you sg.)' (Mt 2.20); wé·t·əno· 'take him (you pl.)' (Jn 19.6); mahtáhəlaya wé·t·əne· 'he took the moss' (Mt 27.48); ɔ́·k=č xkó·k·a we·t·əné·ɔk 'and they shall pick up snakes' (Mk 16.18); wénči·=č .. -we·t·əníhti·t 'so that they will accept me' (Lk 16.4; KJV "receive me into their houses"); ktə́li-wé·t·əna·n '(for you) to take her (as a wife)' (Gr. 4.50h); ná wwe·t·əná·ne·p 'then he picked them up' (Mk 10.16).

- we·t·ən- (TI): wé·t·əni ktap·í·nay 'pick up your bed (you sg.)' (Jn 5.11, 5.12, Mk 2.11; Gr. 2.51b); máta káski-we·t·ənəmó·wi kéku 'he cannot receive anything' (Jn 3.27; Gr. 4.91e); takó· nəwe·t·ənəmó·wən 'I do not receive it' (Jn 5.41; Gr. 4.93b); ná nčí·sas wwe·t·ənəmən ahpó·na 'then Jesus took the loaves' (Jn 21.13; Gr. 2.57d, 4.49l); máta kəwe·t·ənəmo·wané·ɔ 'you (pl.) do not accept it' (Jn 3.11; Gr. 4.93l); wwe·t·ənəməne·ó·i né·l mónia 'they took those coins' (Mt 27.6; Gr. 4.39x); wwe·t·ənəməne·ó·p·ani 'they received them' (Jn 17.8; Gr. 4.70n).

we·t·əna·s·i·- II 'be taken': nən=á· we·t·əná·s·u 'that would be taken' (1834a:22.43).

we·t·ənəmaw- TA+O 'accept O2 from, take O2 from': we·t·ənəmá·k·ɔne 'if he takes it from you' (Mt 5.40); we·t·ənəma·k·é·e·kw 'who was taken from you (pl.)' (Acts 1.11); we·t·ənəmáɔ·n 'to take it from them (sbd.)' (Mt 15.26); máta awé·ni wwe·t·ənəma·k·ó·wən e·la·č·í·mwi·t 'no one (obv.) accepts (from him) his testimony' (Jn 3.32); sɔ·k·i·ma·ó·k·an=č ke·tanət·ó·wi·t kəwe·t·ənəma·k·e·né·ɔ 'God's kingdom will be taken from you (pl.)' (Mt 21.43).

we·t·o·t·e·nai·-: see wto·t·e·nai·-*.

we·t·ó·x·əmənt: see wto·x·əm-*.

we·t·ó·x·ink: see wto·x·i·-.

we·wsi·- AI 'know': wé·wsu 'he knows, he hears or has heard the news' (ME; Gr. 5.8a).

♦ we·wsi·- (with PV ni·k·a·ní·i, nehəni·k·a·ní·i [Rih+; IC]) 'be a prophet': ni·k·a·ní·i-=tá -wé·wsi·t 'he's a prophet' (Mk 6.15; Gr. 6.10b); nehəni·k·a·ní·i-wé·wsi·t 'prophet' (Lk 2.36, Jn 1.21, 4.19, 4.44, etc.); nehəni·k·a·ní·i-we·wsí·č·i·k 'prophets' (Lk 11.49, Mt 23.34); nehəni·k·a·ní·i-we·wsi·tpána 'prophet (abs.)' (Mt 2.17, 3.3, Jn 1.23, etc.); nehəni·k·a·ní·i-we·wsi·tpáni·k 'prophets of old' (Lk 24.25, 24.27); nehəni·k·a·ní·i-we·wsi·li·tpanínka 'prophets (abs. obv.)' (Mt 5.12; Gr. 4.75v).

♦ ⟨ni·k·a·niwéwsu⟩ 'he is a prophet' (V): probably for /ni·k·a·ní·i-wé·wsu/.

■ (verb of being back-formed from the participle of the compound verb, with IC retained): nehəni·k·a·ní·i-=á· -we·wsí·t·e 'if he is a prophet' (Lk 7.39); é·li-nehəni·k·a·ní·i-we·wsí·li·t 'as (he [obv.] is) a prophet' (Mt 10.41).

■ (lexicalized participle): wənehəni·k·a·ní·i-we·wsí·t·əmal 'his prophet' (Lk 1.76, with ⟨n-⟩).

■ (AI made on the lexicalized participle): nehəni·k·a·ní·i-we·wsi·t·i·- AI 'be a prophet': máta=x=á·.. náni nehəni·k·a·ní·i-we·wsi·t·í·ɔne 'if you are not that prophet' (Jn 1.25).

we·x·ánsi·t: see xɔnsi·-*.

wé·x·əmink: see xumi·-*.

we·x·i·s·əməs·í·č·i·k: see xwi·s·əməs·i·-*.

we·yhukɔ·m-(?) TA 'silence by argument, refute': wénči-=č .. tá=á· téxi †-we·yhukɔ·mkó·we·kw 'because of which they will not at all be able to refute you (pl.)' (Lk 21.15; KJV "gainsay nor resist," RSV "withstand or contradict"); tə́li-†we·yhukɔ·ma·n 'that he had refuted them' (Mt 22.34; KJV "put to silence," RSV "silenced").

wəl° (|wəl-|) 'good, well, nicely' (Gr. §5.2a).

wəlaehɔ·s·əwá·k·an IN 'good deed(s)' (Jn 10.32, 10.33).

wəlaehɔ·s·i·- AI 'do a good deed': wəlaehɔ·s·iá·ne 'if I do a good deed ..' (1834a:13).

wəlaehɔ·s·i·taw- TA 'act well towards': mɔ́i-wəlaehɔ·s·i·taɔwwá·ɔ 'they went and acted nicely towards him' (Lk 20.20).

wəláha P 'rather, better' (⟨wlava⟩ Mt 4.4, Jn 4.14, Mt 15.11, etc.); ki·ló·wa=á· wəláha '*you* should all the more' (⟨wlavu⟩ Jn 13.14, KJV "ye also ought to"); kí·=á· wəláha 'it should rather be *you*' (Mt 27.4; KJV "see thou to that"); nə́ni wəláha kəni·skha·lko·né·ɔ 'that is rather what defiles you' (Mt 15.11).

♦ wə́lah=á· 'rather let it be' (⟨wlava⟩ Lk 1.60).

▸ Cf. ⟨wuláha⟩ 'better' (Z. 23).
♦ Note: some occurrences of ⟨wlava⟩ may be for wə́lah=áˑ; later there was only kwə́lah=áˑ 'I wish ..' (OA, ME, LB, LTD ND).

wəlahəl- ([~ wəlal-], -oˑlhal-, weˑlhal-, |wəlahl-|; Gr. 3.5e) TA — wəlaˑt- (-oˑlhat-, weˑlhat-, |wəlaht-|) TI(2) 'have, keep'.

▪ wəlahəl- (TA): ɔ́ˑk kéˑxˑa wəlahəlépˑaniˑk nameˑtˑətˑal 'and they had a few small fish' (Mk 8.7); nčíˑsas méˑči wəlahəláˑtˑe piˑlsíˑliˑt čiˑčánkɔ 'after Jesus had the holy spirit' (Lk 4.1); wəlahəlánkwe 'if we (inc.) marry (lit., keep) him' (ME; Gr. 2.5e); awéˑn šínki-wəlalkwéˑkˑwe 'if someone is unwilling to put you (pl.) up' (lit., 'keep you') (Mt 10.14).

• -oˑlhal-: koˑlhaláhəmɔ=tá nehənoˑtˑəntánkiˑk 'you (pl.) have some guards for it' (Mt 27.65); koˑlhálǝl 'I keep you' (V; Gr. 4.33).

• weˑlhal-: weˑlhaláˑčˑiˑk '(ones) who have it (anim.)' (1834a:18.3).

▪ wəlaˑt- (TI): paléˑnaxk ahpɔ́ˑna wəláˑtoˑ 'he has five loaves' (Jn 6.9); wáin máta wəlatoˑwíˑɔk 'they have no wine' (Jn 2.3; Gr. 4.91.l); wéˑmi kéku éntxi-wəláˑtaɔ 'everything I have' (Lk 18.12); wəlaˑtáˑkˑwe 'if he has it' (Lk 22.36); máta wəlaˑtáˑkˑwe 'if he does not have it' (Lk 22.36); éntxi-wəláˑtaˑkw 'all that he has' (Lk 19.26); éntxi- awéˑn máta -wəláˑtaˑkw 'everyone that doesn't have any' (Lk 19.26); éˑli- máta -wəlaˑtóˑwankw ahpɔ́ˑn 'because we (inc.) have no bread' (Mk 8.16; Gr. 4.99m).

• -oˑlhat-: méˑči xéˑli lačˑeˑsˑəwáˑkˑan koˑlhátu 'you now have many possessions' (Lk 12.19); koˑlhátoˑn wéˑlhik wáin 'you kept the good wine' (Jn 6.68); éˑli oˑlhatóˑneˑp nɔ́ mpíˑsˑoˑn 'for she had kept the medicine' (Jn 12.7&).

• weˑlhat-: wéˑmi kéku weˑlhátaɔn 'everything you have' (Lk 11.41); weˑlhátaˑkw 'what he has' (Mt 18.25; Gr. 2.46d), wáni télən púntink weˑlhátaˑkw 'he is one who has ten pounds' (Lk 19.25); awéˑni máta weˑlhatóˑliˑkw 'someone (obv.) who has none' (Lk 3.11; Gr. 4.99l); weˑlhatáˑkˑwiˑk 'who (pl.) keep it' (Lk 11.28; Gr. 4.64z).

▪ wəlaltiˑ- AI (recip.) 'marry each other': wəlaltiénke 'if we (exc.) get married (to each other)' (ME; Gr. 2.5e).

wəlaiˑkˑaw- (|wəlawīkaw-|; Gr. 5.90c) TA 'arrange a place to stay for': kɔ́tˑa-wəlaiˑkˑaɔwwáˑɔ 'they intended to arrange a place for him to stay' (Lk 9.52; KJV "to make ready for him").

wəlaiˑkˑeˑ- AI 'be well settled': méˑči xeˑlháke kiši-wəlaiˑkˑéˑɔk 'now many tribes have settled well' (1834a:23.58).

wəláki (Gr. 2.73p, 5.25k) P 'just' (Mk 11.4&; KJV "even (as he had said)"); takóˑ wəláki 'I just didn't' (Lk 23.15); táˑ=aˑ wəláki 'I'm not going to do it' ([taˑ] OA).

wəlakšía (|wəlakəšəy-|) 'the intestines' (Acts 1.18); noˑlahkəšˑia 'my guts' (V).

wəlakˑeˑkinkeˑ- (-oˑlahkeˑkinkeˑ-) AI 'teach well': koˑlahkeˑkínke 'you (sg.) teach correctly' (Lk 20.21). ▸ Cf. ahkeˑkinkeˑ- 'teach', lakˑeˑkinkeˑ- 'teach {so}'.

wəlakˑəniˑm- (-oˑlahkəniˑm-) TA — wəlakˑənoˑtˑ-* (-oˑlahkənoˑtˑ-) TI 'speak well of, praise, worship' (cf. Gr. 5.12m).

▪ wəlakˑəniˑm- (TA): wəlakˑəniˑmiáne 'if you (sg.) would worship me' (Lk 4.7); tɔ́nta-wəlakˑəniˑmaˑnéˑɔ 'that they were praising him there' (Lk 24.53).

• -oˑlahkəniˑm-: oˑlahkəniˑmáˑpˑani 'he spoke well of him' (Lk 16.8).

▪ -oˑlahkənoˑtˑ- (TI): koˑlahkənoˑtˑəmənéˑɔ nihəláči khakˑayúwa 'you (pl.) speak well of yourselves' (Lk 16.15).

wəlakˑəniˑmkwəsˑəwáˑkˑan (-oˑlahkəniˑmkwəsˑəwaˑkˑan-) IN 'praise' (Mt 21.16): oˑlahkəniˑmkwəsˑəwaˑkˑanúwa 'their praise' (Lk 2.32).

wəlak·əni·mkwəs·i·- (-o·lahkəni·mkwəs·i·-) AI 'be praised': wəlak·əni·mkwə́s·i·n 'for one to be praised (sbd.)' (Jn 12.43).

wəlalo·ka·s·əwá·k·an (-o·lalo·ka·s·əwa·k·an-) IN 'good deeds': ko·lalo·ka·s·əwa·k·anúwa 'your (pl.) good deeds' (Mt 5.16).

wəlamalsəwá·k·an IN 'the happiness' (Mt 25.34; KJV "the kingdom"), 'good health' (1834b:3.2, 1842:18.5). ▸ Cf. ⟨wullamallessoágan⟩ 'bliss, health' (Z. 25, 91 [a Munsee form]).

wəlamalsi·- (-o·lamalsi·-, ɔ·wəlamalsi·- [Rā+]) AI 'be well': wəlamálsu 'he was well' (Lk 7.10); wəlamalsúwak 'they were whole and well' (Mt 14.36); awe·n wəlamalsí·t·e 'when someone is well' (Mt 9.12).

• -o·lamalsi·-: no·lamálsi=č 'I will be well' (Mk 5.28); ko·lamalsíhəmɔ 'you (pl.) are well' (1842:7.6).

• ɔ·wəlamalsi·- 'be healthy': aləwí·i ɔ·wəlamalsó·p·ani·k 'they were healthier' (1842:20.4); tá=á· háši kúnči-ɔ·wəlamalsí·wən 'you (sg.) will never be healthy from it' (1842:20.3); wénči-=č -ɔ·wəlamalsíe·kw yú táli 'the means by which you (pl.) will be well in this place' (1842:17.1).

wəlamalso·ha·l- (-o·lamalso·ha·l-) TA 'heal, make well': kəna·ka·t·amwe·ɔ́·k·an ko·lamalso·há·lko·n 'your (sg.) faith has made you well' (Lk 17.19).

wəlamalso·ke·- AI+O 'heal': sɔ́·ki- .. -wəlamalsó·ke·n pa·lsi·lí·č·i 'how long he healed the sick' (1834b:26.5).

wəlamant- TI(1a) 'feel good in': tɔ́hi-wəlamántamən məsé·i hók·ay 'she felt very good all over her body' (Mk 5.29).

wəlami·kəmɔ·s·əntamaw- TA 'do a good thing for' (*lit.*, 'do a good job for'): é·li-wəlami·kəmɔ·s·əntamái·t 'for she has done a good thing for me' (Mt 26.10; KJV "wrought a good work upon").

wəlana·ke·- (-o·lana·ke·-, |wəlanāhkē-|) AI 'make a pallet', AI+O 'spread O2 as a mat': wəlaná·ke· 'she made a pallet' (OA).

• -o·lana·ke·-: o·lana·ke·né·ɔ ehahkwihtí·č·i 'they spread their clothing on the ground' (Mt 21.8&; Gr. 4.40i); o·lana·ke·ne·ɔ́·i 'they spread them (inan.) on the ground' (Mt 21.8; Gr. 4.40l).

wəlanət·o·wi·- (we·lanət·o·wi·-) AI 'be a good spirit': we·lanət·o·wí·č·i·k 'good spirits' (1834b:30.5).

wəlanko·m- (-o·lanko·m-) TA 'be on good terms with, be at peace with or make peace with, acknowledge'; 'be good to, apologize to' (WL): wəlanko·mó·me naɔč·í·i 'be on good terms with him on the way' (Lk 12.58); wəlanko·mát·e 'if you (sg.) are on good terms with them' (Mt 5.47); wəlanko·mí·t·e 'if he acknowledges me' (Lk 12.8; KJV "shall confess me", RSV "acknowledges me"); tɔ́li=á· -wəlankó·mko·n 'so that he (obv.) would make peace with him' (Lk 14.32).

• -o·lanko·m-: no·lankó·ma 'I (will) acknowledge him' (Lk 12.8); o·lanko·má·ɔ 'he is friendly with them' (Lk 15.2); ná †símian o·lanko·má·ne·p 'then Simeon greeted them kindly' (Lk 2.34).

▪ wəlankunti·- AI (recip.; Gr. 5.110p) 'be at peace with each other': wəlankúntəwak 'they became reconciled as friends' (Lk 23.12); wəlankúnti·kw 'be at peace with each other (you pl.)' (Mk 9.50); ktɔ́li=á· -wəlankunti·né·ɔ 'so that you will be at peace' (Jn 16.33); wəlankuntí·t·e 'if they (representative sg.) are at peace with each other' (1834b:44.11).

wəlankunsəwá·k·an (-o·lankunsəwa·k·an-) IN 'friendship': ko·lankunsəwa·k·anúwa 'your friendship' (Mt 10.13, Lk 10.6 [2x]; KJV "your peace").

wəlankunsi·- (ɔ·wəlankunsi·- [Rā+], |wəlankōnsī-|) AI 'be friendly': wəlankó·nsu 'is friendly' (V; Gr. 5.104g).
  • ɔ·wəlankunsi·-: ɔ·wəlankunsihtí·t·e 'if they are friendly' (Lk 10.6).
wəlankunso·ha·l- TA 'make friendly' (Gr. 5.81d): wəlankunso·ha·lkwé·k·weč 'let it make you (pl.) be neighborly' (Lk 16.9; Gr. 4.114k).
wəlankunso·ha·ləwe·- (wehwəlankunso·ha·ləwe·-; Gr. 5.101f) AI 'make people friendly': wehwəlankunso·ha·ləwé·č·i·k 'peacemakers, those that make people be friends' (Mt 5.9).
wəlankuntəwá·k·an (-o·lankuntəwa·k·an-; Gr. 5.60f, 5.114m) IN 'peace' (⟨luf-⟩ Mt 10.34; ⟨wluf-⟩ Mt 10.34, Lk 7.50, Jn 14.27); wəlankuntəwá·k·anink 'to peace' (Lk 1.79).
  • -o·lankuntəwa·k·an-: no·lankuntəwá·k·an 'my peace' (Jn 14.27).
  ▸ From wəlankunti·- AI (recip.): see wəlanko·m-.
wəlankuntəwa·k·ani·- II 'be peace': wəlankuntəwá·k·anu=č 'there will be peace' (Lk 12.51); wəlankuntəwa·k·aní·k·eč 'let there be peace' (Lk 2.14, 10.5, 19.38).
wəlankunti·-: see wəlanko·m-.
wəlant·uwwá·k·an IN 'good power' (1834b:38.8).
wəlaskat- II 'be good grass': áhi-wəláskahto·p 'there was a lot of nice grass' (Jn 6.10; Gr. 2.15c).
wəla·č·i·məwá·k·an IN 'good news' (Lk 2.10).
wəla·məwe·- (-o·la·məwe·-, we·la·məwe·-, ɔwəla·məwe·- [Ra+]) AI 'tell the truth' — wəla·məwe·yo·wi·- II 'be a true utterance' (Gr. 5.76i).
  ▪ wəla·məwe·- (AI): wəlá·məwe· 'he tells the truth' (Jn 7.18, 7.28, etc.); wəlá·məwe·p 'he told the truth' (Jn 10.41); ktəli-wəlá·məwe·n 'that you (sg.) tell the truth' (Mt 22.16).
  • -o·la·məwe·-: ko·lá·məwe 'you (sg.) tell the truth' (Jn 4.17, 4.18, Lk 7.43, etc.; Gr. 2.19b); takó· ko·la·məwé·i 'you do not tell the truth' (Jn 8.13; Gr. 4.81d).
  • we·la·məwe·-: we·la·məwé·an ke·tanət·ó·wian 'you (sg.) .. the truthful god' (Jn 17.3).
  • ɔwəla·məwe·-: ɔwəlá·məwe·w 'he always told the truth' (Jn 1.15; Gr. 4.21c).
  ▪ wəla·məwe·yo·wi·- II 'be true': wəla·məwe·yó·u 'it (saying, word) is true' (Jn 4.37, 8.16).
wəla·məwé·i PV 'truly' (⟨wlamwri⟩ Jn 4.23). ▸ Perhaps should be: wəla·məwe·í·i P.
wəla·məwe·i·ná·k·ɔt- (wəla·məwe·i·ná·k·ɔ, wəla·məwe·i·nakoht-) II 'appear to be true': wəla·məwe·i·ná·k·ɔt 'it is seen to be true' (Jn 5.32); tá=á· wəla·məwe·i·nakohtó·wi 'it would not be seen to be true' (Jn 5.31); wənči-=č .. -wəla·məwe·i·ná·k·ɔ 'so that it shall be seen to be true' (Mt 18.16).
wəla·məwe·ó·k·an (-o·la·məwe·ɔ·k·an-; Gr. 5.58c) IN 'truth' (Jn 1.17, 4.24, 5.33, Jn 8.32, etc.); (AN) 'truth (personified)' (Mt 12.20); wəla·məwe·ó·k·anink 'in truth' (Jn 3.21, 4.23); wé·mi lí wəla·məwe·ó·k·anink 'to all truth' (Jn 16.13; Gr. 6.9i).
  • -o·la·məwe·ɔ·k·an-: ko·la·məwe·ó·k·an 'your (sg.) truth' (Jn 17.17).
wəla·məwe·ɔ·k·ani·- (we·la·məwe·ɔ·k·ani·- [IC]) AI 'be truth': we·la·məwe·ó·k·ani·t 'who is truth' (Jn 14.17).
wəla·məwe·ɔ·k·aní·i (Gr. 5.122j) PN 'of truth' (Jn 15.26, 16.13).
wəla·məwe·yó·u: see wəla·məwe·-.
wəla·mhitaw- (-o·la·mhitaw-, we·la·mhitaw-, |wəlāməhtaw-|) TA — wəla·mhit- (-o·la·mhit-, we·la·mhit-, |wəlāməht-|) TI(1a) 'believe' (Gr. 5.12aa).
  ▪ wəla·mhitaw- (TA): ktəli-=á· -wəla·mhitaɔ·né·ɔ·p 'so that you (pl.) would have believed him' (Mt 21.32); káči wəla·mhitawié·k·e·kw 'don't believe him, them (you pl.)' (Lk 17.23, Mt 24.23, 24.26; Gr. 2.36b, 4.111d); wəla·mhítai·l 'believe me (you sg.)' (Jn 4.21, 14.11; Gr. 2.36b); káči wəla·mhitaí·he·kw 'don't believe me (you pl.)' (Jn 10.37; Gr. 4.111u); kéku=háč wénči- máta -wəla·mhitaɔ·é·k·əp 'how come you (pl.) didn't believe him?' (Mt 21.25; Gr.

4.97f); é·li- máta -wəla·mhitaó·wənt 'because he was not believed' (Mt 13.58; Gr. 4.97h); wəla·mhitaí·t·e 'if he believes me' (Jn 11.26; Gr. 2.30b); máta=á· wəla·mhitaié·k·we 'if you (pl.) don't believe me' (Jn 10.38; or wəla·mhitai·é·k·we, if the negative inflection was distinct); kóč=háč=á· máta wəla·mhitaíe·kw? 'why would you not believe me?' (Jn 8.46; or wəla·mhitaí·e·kw, if the negative inflection was distinct); wə́nči-=č .. -wəla·mhitaíe·kw 'so that you (pl.) will be able to believe about me (that ..)' (Jn 10.38).

• -o·la·mhitaw-: wé·mi=á· awé·n o·la·mhitaó·ɔ 'everyone would believe him' (Jn 11.48); máta náxpəne xwi·s·əmə́s·a o·la·mhita·k·o·wí·ɔ 'not even his brothers believed him' (Jn 7.5; Gr. 4.85h); máta=á· ko·la·mhitai·húmɔ 'you (pl.) would not believe me' (Jn 3.12; Gr. 4.89c, 6.6h); ko·la·mhitai·né·ɔ 'that you (pl.) believe in me (sbd.)' (Jn 11.15; Gr. 4.49a).

• we·la·mhitaw-: we·la·mhítaɔ·t 'who believes him' (Jn 3.36, 7.48; Gr. 4.64i); awé·n we·la·mhítai·t 'anyone who believes in me' (Jn 11.25, 12.44); we·la·mhitaíe·kw 'you (pl.) that believe me' (Jn 8.31).

• ɔwəla·mhitaw-: wɔwəla·mhitaó·p·ani 'he was obedient to them (i.e., did what they said, made what they said be true)' (Lk 2.51; KJV "was subject unto them").

■ wəla·mhit- (TI, TI-O): wəla·mhíta 'believe it to be true (you sg.)' (Jn 20.27); wəla·mhítamo·kw ná laehɔ·s·əwá·k·an 'believe the deeds (you pl.)' (Jn 10.38); é·li- máta -wəla·mhítank 'as he does not believe it' (Jn 3.18); é·li- máta -wəla·mhitamə́li·t 'the fact that they (obv,) did not believe' (Mk 16.14); máta wəla·mhitánke 'if he does not believe' (Mk 16.16); máta wəla·mhitamo·wé·k·we 'if you (pl.) do not believe it' (Jn 5.47; Gr. 4.99e).

• -o·la·mhit-: ko·la·mhitaməné·ɔ '(for you) to believe (it)' (Lk 24.25); máta=háč ko·la·mhitamó·wən 'don't you (sg.) believe it?' (Jn 14.10; Gr. 4.93d); o·la·mhítamən 'he believed it' (Jn 4.50, 12.38, 20.8).

• we·la·mhit-: we·la·mhítank 'who believed' (Lk 1.45); we·la·mhitánki·k 'those who believed it' (Jn 2.23, 15.20 [2x]; Gr. 4.64x), máta we·la·mhitánki·k 'unbelievers' (Mk 9.19; with voc. 2p ppl.).

wəla·pto·na·l- (-o·la·pto·na·l-; Gr. 5.88a) TA 'say good things to or about': wəla·ptó·na·l 'say good words about him' (Mt 5.44); wénči-wəla·pto·nállan 'because I have good news to tell you (sg)' (Lk 1.19).

• -o·la·pto·na·l-: ko·la·pto·ná·la=č 'you (sg.) must make excuses to him' (Lk 14.18, 14.19); no·la·pto·na·lá·wəna=č 'we say nice words to persuade him' (Mt 28.14; Gr. 5.88a).

wəla·pto·ne·- (-o·la·pto·ne·-; Gr. 5.17d) AI 'say good words, speak well': wəla·pto·ne·á·ne 'if I have said good things' (Jn 18.23); é·li-wəla·ptó·ne·t 'at the good words he spoke' (lit., 'as he spoke good things') (Lk 4.22); e·lkí·kwi-wəla·pto·né·li·t 'how well he spoke' (Mk 12.34).

• -o·la·pto·ne·-: ko·la·ptó·ne 'you speak correctly' (Lk 20.21).

wəla·p·antama·- AI 'see properly': wə́nči-káski-wəla·p·antamá·li·t 'the ability (for them [obv.]) to see properly' (Lk 7.21); é·li-wəla·p·antamá·e·kw 'for you (pl.) can see well' (Mt 13.16).

wəla·p·ensi·- (-o·la·p·ensi·-, we·la·p·ensi·-) AI — wəla·p·enso·wi·- (|wəlāpēnsōwī-|) II 'be blessed' (Gr. 5.76e).

■ wəla·p·ensi·- (AI): wəla·p·énsu xkwé· 'blessed is the woman' (⟨lapcnsw⟩ Lk 1.45; ⟨l-⟩ for /wəl-/); wəla·p·énsəwak 'they are blessed' (Mt 5.3, 5.4, etc.; KJV "Blessed are they ..").

• -o·la·p·ensi·-: ko·la·p·énsi 'you (sg.) are blessed' (Mt 16.17); ko·la·p·ensíhəmɔ 'blessed are you (pl.)' (Lk 6.22).

• we·la·p·ensi·-: we·la·p·énsi·t '(one who is) blessed' (Lk 1.48, Lk 7.23, Mt 21.9&).

- wəla·p·enso·wi·- (II): wəla·p·ensó·u 'it is blessed' (⟨rlapcnsw⟩ Lk 1.42 [⟨r⟩ is a misprint]); wəla·p·ensó·u lá·mahte 'blessed is the womb' (⟨Wlapcnsw⟩ Lk 11.27); wəla·p·ensó·yəwa 'they (inan.) are blessed' (Mt 13.16, Lk 10.23; Gr. 2.34f).

wəla·p·enso·ha·l- (-o·la·p·enso·ha·l-, we·la·p·enso·ha·l-) TA — wəla·p·enso·ha·t- TI(1a) 'bless' (Gr. 5.81e).
- wəla·p·enso·ha·l- (TA): wəla·p·enso·ha·lkwénkeč 'may he bless us (exc.)' (Mk 11.10; Gr. 4.114j).
- -o·la·p·enso·ha·l-: no·la·p·enso·há·lukw 'he blesses me' (Lk 13.35, Mt 23.39).
- we·la·p·enso·ha·l-: we·la·p·enso·há·lkwe·kw nó·x 'you (pl.) who my father blessed' (Mt 25.34).
- wəla·p·enso·ha·t- (TI): nəni wwə́nči- ke·tanət·ó·wi·t -wəla·p·enso·há·t·amən ala·x·i·məwí·i-kí·škwi·k 'for that reason, God blessed the day of rest' (1842:12.1).

wəla·p·enso·ha·ləwe·- (we·la·p·enso·ha·ləwe·-) AI 'bless people': we·la·p·enso·há·ləwe·t 'the giver of blessings' (Mt 26.63).

wəla·p·ent- (-o·la·p·ent-, we·la·p·ent-) TI(1a) 'benefit from': aləwí·i=č ko·la·p·éntamən 'you will benefit more from it' (Mt 5.29, 5.30).
- we·la·p·ent-: wé·mi kékw we·la·p·éntamankw 'everything we make good use of' (1842:18.5).

wəla·p·entamo·ha·t- (-o·la·p·entamo·ha·t-; Gr. 5.87g) TI(1a) 'bless': o·la·p·entamo·há·t·amən 'he blessed it' (Mt 26.26).

wəla·tae·i·- II 'have beautiful blossoms': e·lkí·kwi- yó·l -wəla·taé·i·k 'as beautifully as their blossoms are' (Mt 6.29; KJV "like one of these" flowers).

wəla·ta·-* (wi·wəla·ta·- [Rī+], |wəlahtā-|; Gr. 5.104b) AI 'put up food (for oneself)': takó· wi·wəla·ta·í·ɔk 'they never put up food' (Mt 6.26; KJV "nor gather into barns"; Gr. 4.81o, 5.44j).

wəla·te·naməwá·k·an (Gr. 5.58f) IN 'happiness' (Jn 14.18, KJV "comfort-"; V, ME), ⟨wulatenamowôagan⟩ 'happiness' (Z. 91).
- -o·lhate·namawa·k·an-: no·lhate·namawá·k·an 'my joy' (Jn 15.11).

wəla·te·nami·- (-o·lhate·nami·-, wihwəla·te·nami·- [Rih+]) AI 'be happy, be joyful': wəla·té·namu 'he is happy' (V, ME, ND); wəla·te·namúwak=č 'they shall be in good spirits' (Mt 5.4); wénči-=č -pahkánči-wəla·te·namíe·kw 'in order that your (pl.) joy will be complete' (Jn 15.11).
- -o·lhate·nami·-: ko·lhaté·nami=č 'you (sg.) will be happy' (Lk 14.14); ko·lhate·namíhəmɔ=č 'you (pl.) will be happy' (Jn 13.17).
- wihwəla·te·nami·-: wihwəla·té·namu 'he is always in good spirits' (1834b: back cover 14).

wəla·te·namo·ha·ləwe·- (wehwəla·te·namo·ha·ləwe·- [Rih+; IC]) AI 'comfort people': wehwəla·te·namo·há·ləwe·t 'comforter' (Jn 14.26).

wəla·wsəwá·k·an IN 'salvation' (Lk 1.77), *lit.* 'the good life'.

wəla·wsi·- (we·la·wsi·-, |wəlāwəsī-|) AI 'live well, be good': wəlá·wsu=tá 'he is good' (1834b:20.13); énta-wəlá·wsink 'where the good are', *lit.*, 'where people (indef.) are good' (Mt 5.45).
- we·la·wsi·-: we·la·wsi·tpáni·k 'those that led good lives' (Jn 5.29; Gr. 4.75m).

wəla·wsəwi·na·kwsi·- (-o·la·wsəwi·na·kwsi·-) AI 'appear righteous': ko·la·wsəwi·na·kwsíhəmɔ 'you (pl.) appear to be righteous' (Mt 23.28).

wəla·wso·ha·l- (we·la·wso·ha·l-) TA 'save', i.e., 'deliver from sin and eternal damnation': we·la·wso·há·lkɔnkw 'that will be our salvation' (Lk 1.69).

wəlé P 'far away, out (on the water)' (Mk 6.47), 'over there' (Lk 17.21, Mt 24.23), wəlé (OA); wále táli (OA).

wəle·ləm- (-o·le·ləm-) TA 'like, think well of' — wəle·lənt- (-o·le·lənt-, wi·wəle·lənt- [Rī+]) TI(1a) 'think good', TI-O 'be glad, happy'.

▪ -o·le·ləm- (TA): o·le·ləmá·p·ani 'he thought well of him' (Mk 6.20); o·le·ləmuk·ó·p·ani wé·mi awé·ni 'he was well liked by everyone' (Lk 4.15).

▪ wəle·lənt- (TI): é·li-wəle·lə́ntama 'what pleases me' (Mk 14.36); é·li-wəle·lə́ntaman 'what pleases you' (Mk 14.36, Mt 26.42); é·li-wəle·lə́ntank '(in a way) that is pleasing to him' (Mt 22.16, Jn 21.19); ílli=č ní·š·a ki·ló·wa lí-wəle·ləntamé·k·we kéku 'if even two of you agree for something to be' (Mt 18.19); wé·mi tə́li-wəle·ləntaməné·ɔ 'they all agreed to do it' (1842:9.8).

▪ wəle·lənt- (TI-O): áhi-wəle·ləntam 'he is very glad' (Jn 3.29, Lk 23.8); wəle·lə́ntamo·p 'he was glad' (Jn 8.56 [2x], Lk 13.17; Gr. 4.70c); wəle·lə́ntamo·k 'they rejoice' (Lk 15.7, Jn 16.20); tá=háč ktə́li-wəle·lə́ntamən ntə́nta-wəli·tó·ne·n 'where are you pleased that we prepare it?' (Mk 14.12); wəle·lə́nta 'be happy (you sg.)' (Lk 12.19; Gr. 2.51a); é·li-wəle·lə́ntank 'because he was happy' (Lk 1.44); hók·enk núnči-wəle·lə́ntam 'I am pleased because of him' (Mt 3.17; Gr. 6.7c).

• -o·le·lənt-: no·le·lə́ntam 'I am glad' (Jn 11.15, 1842:18.4; Gr. 2.65a); ko·le·lə́ntam=č 'you (sg.) will be glad' (Lk 1.14; Gr. 4.38g); ko·le·ləntamúhəna 'we (inc.) are joyful' (Lk 15.23; Gr. 2.43c).

• wi·wəle·lənt-: máta wi·wəle·ləntaməlí·č·i 'those (obv.) who are never glad' (Lk 6.35).

wəle·ləme·lənt- (TI(1a)) TI-O 'be astonished': wəle·ləme·lə́ntamo·p 'he was astonished' (Lk 7.9); wəle·ləme·ləntamó·p·ani·k 'they were astonished' (Lk 1.21, 2.33, Jn 4.27, Lk 4.22).

wəlé·ləmi PV 'peculiar, wonderful': wəlé·ləmi-lé· 'it is odd' (Jn 9.30; KJV "marvellous"); we·lé·ləmi-ləs·i·tpána 'worker of wonders (abs.)' (⟨wrlrli⟩ Mt 21.26).

▶ Cf. wəlé·ləmi PN 'peculiar, strange' (LB); ⟨Wulelemi⟩ 'wonderful' (B&A 173).

wəle·ləmi·na·k·ɔt- II 'be peculiar': wəle·ləmi·ná·k·ɔ kéku kɔhɔ́·k·an 'a mill is a peculiar thing' (1834a:15).

wəle·ləmukwsəwá·k·an (-o·le·ləmukwsəwa·k·an-) 'high regard, honor': o·le·ləmukwsəwá·k·an 'his good reputation' (Mt 4.24; KJV "his fame").

wəle·ləmukwsi·- AI 'be well regarded': wəle·ləmukwsí·t·eč yú entalá·wsi·t 'let mankind be well regarded' (Lk 2.14); é·li-káhta-wəle·ləmukwsíe·kw 'because you (pl.) want to be well liked' (Mt 23.14).

wəle·lənsi·- AI 'think well of oneself': é·li-wəle·lə́nsi·t 'as he thought well of himself' (Lk 10.29).

wəle·ləntamaw- TA 'be pleased with': é·li-wəle·ləntamái·t 'that he is pleased with me' (Jn 8.29).

wəle·ləntamawá·k·an (-o·le·ləntamawa·k·an-) IN 'happiness' (1834b:25.9).

• -o·le·ləntamawa·k·an-: no·le·ləntamawá·k·an 'my joy' (Jn 3.29, Jn 17.13); ko·le·ləntamawa·k·anúwa 'your (pl.) joy' (Jn 16.22).

wəle·ləntaməwi·m-, in wiči-wəle·ləntaməwi·m- 'rejoice with': wiči-wəle·ləntaməwí·mi·kw 'rejoice with me' (Lk 15.6, Lk 15.9; Gr. 5.99h).

wəle·ləntaməwo·x·we·- AI 'go along rejoicing': áləmi-wəle·ləntaməwó·x·we· 'he was rejoicing as he went' (1834b:42.7); wəle·ləntaməwo·x·wé·ɔk 'they walked joyfully' (Lk 10.17).

wəle·lənta·s·i·- II 'be permitted, be acceptable' (Gr. 5.105n): lí-wəle·ləntá·s·u 'it is acceptable to do' (Mt 16.19; KJV " be loosed"). ♦ This is preceded in the verse by a use as a translation of KJV "be bound," presumably an error for the corresponding negative verb.

wəle·nhaw-* (-o·le·nhaw-) TA 'pay well': ko·le·nho·lhúmɔ=č 'I'll pay you (pl.) well' (Mt 20.4).

wəle·nha·ɔhtəwá·k·an IN 'good pay' (Mt 20.7).

wəlale·whe·- (-o·ləle·whe·-) AI+O 'adjust the flame on O2 (a lamp)': o·ləle·whe·ne·ɔ́·i wɔ·s·əle·ni·k·anəwá·ɔ 'they adjusted the flame on their lamps' (Mt 25.7).

wəlastamwe·ɔ́·k·an (-o·lsət·amwe·ɔ·k·an-) IN 'faith', ⟨wullestamoewōagan⟩ (Z. 71).
- -o·lsət·amwe·ɔ·k·an-: ko·lsət·amwe·ɔ·k·anúwa 'your (pl.) faith' (Mt 6.30).

wəlastaw- (-o·lsət·aw-, we·lsət·aw-) TA — wəlast- (we·lsət·-) TI(1a) 'listen to', TI-O 'believe'.
- wəlastaw- (TA): máta wəlastaɔ́·k·we 'if he does not listen to him' (Mt 15.6); wəlastae·kpáne 'if you (pl.) had listened to him' (Jn 5.46; Gr. 4.74f); ktə́li-=č -wəlastaɔ·né·ɔ 'for you (pl.) to listen to him' (Jn 6.29).
- -o·lsət·aw-: ko·lsə́t·aɔ 'you are his adherent' (Jn 9.28; KJV "Thou art his disciple"); o·lsət·aɔ́·ɔl 'he listens to him' (Mt 6.24); †mo·šə́š·a no·lsət·aɔ́·wəna 'we are adherents of Moses (abs.)' (Jn 9.28); máta ko·lsət·aɔ·íwwa 'you (pl.) do not believe him' (Jn 5.38); o·lsət·á·k·o·n 'and then they (inan.) obey him (sbd.)' (Lk 8.25&).
- wəlast- (TI): wəlastamé·k·we 'if you (pl.) believe them' (Mt 11.14).
- we·lsət·-: awé·ni máta we·lsət·aməlí·k·wi 'the ones (obv.) who did not believe it' (Jn 6.64; Gr. 4.99g).
- wəlast- (TI-O): wəlastámo·k 'they believed' (Jn 4.39); wé·mi éntxi-wəlastánki·k .. tɔ·pto·ná·k·an 'all those that believed his words' (1834b:40.10). ▶ Cf. ⟨Wulistammen⟩ 'believe' (B&A 175); Mun wŏlə́stam TI-O 'believes, becomes a believer (i.e., a Christian)'.

wələs·i·- (we·lsi·-, ɔwəlsi·- [Ra+]) AI — wələt·- (we·lt- ~ we·lh-, ɔwəlt- [Ra+], we·wəlt- [Ra+IC]; Gr. 2.48a) II 'be good' (Gr.3.18d, 5.10m).
- wələs·i·- (AI): wələs·u 'he or she is good, good-looking' (V, LB); wələs·əwak 'they are good' (LB); wələs·í·t·e hít·ukw 'if a tree is good' (Mt 12.33); máta wələs·i·í·ɔl 'they (obv.) are not good' (1834b:17.6).
- we·lsi·-: we·lsi·lí·č·i 'good ones (obv.)' (Mt 13.48, 22.10); máta we·lsi·lí·č·i 'bad ones (obv.)' (Mt 13.48, 22.10).
- ɔwəlsi·-: ɔwəlsúwak 'they are good-looking' (V; Gr. 5.34h).
- wələt·- (II): wələ́t 'it is good' (Mt 12.33, Lk 19.17, Mt 25.21, 25.23); aləwí·i-wələ́t 'it is better' (Lk 11.41); tá=á·.. wələt·ó·wi 'it would not be good' (Lk 14.35; Gr. 2.12d, 4.81x); wələ́t·əlu 'they (obv.) were fine' (1834b:30.2 [cf. Gr. 4.20 (end) and 4.21f]); wələ́t·ək=č 'that will be good' (Jn 6.27); énta-wələ́t·ək 'where it was good' (Mt 13.8, 13.23).
- we·lt-: wé·ltək '(which is) good' (Mt 13.24, 13.27, Lk 15.22, etc.); wé·ltək kéku 'something good' (Lk 13.8).
- we·lh- (Gr. 2.48a): wé·lhik '(what is) good' (Lk 1.53, Mt 3.10, Jn 1.46, Jn 2.10 2x, Lk 4.18, Mt 4.23, Mt 24.13, etc.). ♦ Lexicalized participle: wé·lhik '(the) good' (Lk 6.45, Mt 12.35); lí we·lhíkink 'towards the good' (Mt 24.13), 'in the good way' (1834b:47.13).
- ɔwəlt-: ɔwə́lto·l 'they (inan.) are good' (V, OA; Gr. 2.17c, 5.34h).
- we·wəlt-: we·wəltə́k·i 'good ones (inan.)' (Lk 14.7).

wə́li (-ó·li, wé·li; Gr. 2.74l, 5.129nn) PV 'carefully, thoroughly, well' (Mt 2.7, 2.8, Lk 3.17 [2x]); wə́li-pí·lhik 'what is really holy' (Mt 7.6).
- -ó·li (Mt 2.7, Lk 3.17, etc.).
- wé·li: wé·li-lə́s·i·t 'who did right' (Lk 12.42), wé·li-lə́s·i·t ntalo·ká·k·an 'my good servant' (Lk 19.17 [vocative]); wé·li-no·t·i·k·ehtí·t·e 'when they were carefully watching the house' (Lk 12.37).
- wə́li P 'right, in a good way': ki·ló·na wə́li 'for us it is right' (Lk 23.41); áhi-wə́li máta káhta-mi·tsí·ɔne 'when you (sg.) fast' (lit., 'when in a very good way you do not want to eat') (Mt 6.16, 6.17), wə́li máta káhta-mi·tsí·i 'he is fasting' (Mt 6.16).

wəli·h- (-o·li·h-) TA 'treat well, do well by, cure' — wəli·t- (-o·li·t-, we·li·t-) TI(2) 'make, fix'.
- ▪ wəli·h- (TA): wəlí·ho· 'treat them well (you pl.)' (Lk 6.35); takó· káski-wəli·há·i 'she could not be made well' (Lk 8.43; Gr. 4.83v).
- • -o·li·h-: aləwí·i ko·lihko·wíwwa 'he will treat you better' (Lk 12.28); ná mé·či ko·lí·ha·n 'then you (sg.) (will) have done well by him' (Mt 18.15).
- ▪ wəli·t- (TI): wəli·tó·me kí·l 'fix your hair (you sg.)' (Mt 6.17; Gr. 4.116m); wəli·tó·p·ani·k winki·ma·khóki mpi·s·ó·na 'they prepared sweet-smelling medicines' (Lk 23.56); nəmái-wəlí·to·n 'I go to make it' (Jn 14.2); tá=háč .. ntənta-wəli·tó·ne·n 'where (are you pleased that) we prepare it?' (Mk 14.12).
- • -o·li·t-: náni=č o·lí·to·n 'he will make that' (Mk 1.2); ko·li·to·né·ɔ 'you (pl.) fix them up' (Mt 23.29; KJV "ye build .. and garnish").
- • we·li·t-: we·li·tuhtí·t·əp 'that they had prepared' (Mk 16.2&).

wəli·k·e·- AI 'have a nice dwelling': we·lí·k·e·t 'who has a nice house' (Mt 13.52).

wəli·k·ən- II 'grow well': wəlí·k·ən 'it grows well' (Mk 4.27), ləkhíkwi-wəlí·k·ən '(how) they grow so beautifully (sbd.)' (Mt 6.28; cf. Lk 12.27); wənči máta káski-wəli·k·ənó·wi 'so that it cannot grow well' (Mt 13.22); e·lkí·kwi-wəlí·k·ink 'how beautifully they grow' (Lk 12.27); wəli·k·ínki '(grass, pl.) which grows nicely' (Mt 6.30, Lk 12.28).

wəli·laentəwá·k·an (-o·li·laentəwa·k·an-) IN 'comfort, comforting words': ko·li·laentəwa·k·anúwa 'your (pl.) comfort' (Lk 6.24; KJV "consolation"). ▸ Cf. ⟨wulilawendewoágan⟩ 'comfort' (Z. 39).

wəli·lae·h- (-o·li·lae·h-, we·li·lae·h-) TA 'make glad, make feel good, please':
énta- máta -wəli·lae·híe·kw 'in which you (pl.) do not please me' (Jn 8.26; or -í·e·kw, if the negative inflection was distinct).
- • -o·li·lae·h-: o·li·lae·há·ɔ 'he pleased him' (Jn 12.26, Mt 21.31); no·li·laéhko·p 'he has made me feel good' (Lk 1.47).
- • we·li·lae·h-: né·k we·li·lae·há·č·i·k 'the ones that please him' (1834b:25.4).

wəli·lae·m- TA 'please or comfort (with words)': é·li-káhta-wəli·laé·ma·t 'as he wanted to say something to please them' (Mk 15.15); kót·a-wəli·laé·mku 'he (obv.) wanted to appease him' (Lk 15.28).

wəli·naw- (-o·li·naw-) TA — wəli·n- (-o·li·n-) TI(1a) 'admire, like' (Gr. 5.12z).
- ▪ -o·li·naw- (TA): †hélat o·li·naó·p·ani 'Herod admired her' (Mk 6.22).
- ▪ wəli·n- (TI): é·li-áhi-wəlí·nank 'how he admires it a lot' (Mt 13.44).
- • -o·li·n-: no·lí·namən 'I admire it' (Mt 12.7); o·li·naməné·ɔ ləpwe·ó·k·an 'they admire wisdom' (Lk 7.35).

wəli·na·kwsəwá·k·an (-o·li·na·kwsəwa·k·an-) IN 'glorious appearance ': o·li·na·kwsəwá·k·an 'his glorious appearance' (Jn 1.14).

wəli·na·kwsi·- AI — wəli·na·k·ɔt- II 'look good'.
- ▪ wəli·na·kwsi·-: wəli·ná·kwsu 'he or she is good looking, looks good' (LB).
- ▪ wəli·na·k·ɔt- (wəli·nakɔht-) II: wəli·ná·k·ɔt 'it looks good' (LB); wəli·nákɔhtu 'they look nice' (OA; Mt 23.27).

wəli·t-: see wəli·h- — wəli·t-.

wəli·taw- TA+O 'make O2 good for, fix or prepare O2 for': énta-wəli·tá·k·ɔn kəškínkɔ 'when he fixed your eyes for you' (Jn 9.26); ktəli-=č -wəlí·taɔ·n 'for you to prepare it for him' (Lk 1.76).

wəli·ta·s·i·- II 'be made nice' (Gr. 5.106c): wəli·tá·s·u 'it is made nice' (Lk 3.5).

wəli·t·e·ha·- (we·li·t·e·ha·-) AI 'be good-hearted': áhi-wəli·t·é·he·w 'he was very good-hearted' (Jn 1.14); é·li- ní· -wəli·t·e·há·a 'because I am good-hearted' (Mt 20.15).

- we·li·t·e·ha·-: we·li·t·e·há·č·i·k 'those with good hearts' (1834b:43.5); we·li·t·e·ha·lí·č·i (1834b:26.1 [em.]).
  ▶ Cf. ná we·li·t·é·ha·t wíli pé·n 'the good-hearted William Penn' (ME).
wəli·t·e·he·ó·k·an (-o·li·t·e·he·ɔ·k·an-) IN 'good-heartedness' (Jn 1.17).
- -o·li·t·e·he·ɔ·k·an-: o·li·t·e·he·ó·k·an 'his good-heartedness' (Jn 1.16).
wəli·xsi·- AI 'speak well, clearly, plainly': wəlí·xsu 'he spoke plainly' (Mk 7.35).
wəli·xt-: see wəli·x·əm- — wəli·xt-.
wəli·xtaw- TA+O 'arrange O2 for': ná=č nə́ ktə́nta-wəli·xtaí·ne·n 'that's where you must make it ready for us' (Mk 14.15).
wəli·xta·s·i·- II 'be set up, in good order': wəli·xtá·s·u 'it is set up' (1834a:16); wəli·xtá·s·əwa 'they are stored' (1834a:16).
wəli·x·əm- (-o·li·x·əm-, we·li·x·əm-, |wəlīxəm-|) TA 'put away properly, *esp.*, lay (the deceased) to rest, bury' — wəli·xt- (-o·li·xt-) TI 'put in order, set up, arrange, put away, prepare' (Gr. 5.12g).
  ▪ wəli·x·əm- (TA): ná wəli·x·əma·né·ɔ 'then they (potatoes) are stored away safely' (1834a:17).
  - -o·li·x·əm-: no·lí·x·əma 'I buried him' (V; Gr. 5.12g).
  - we·li·x·əm-: we·li·x·əma·línke 'when he (obv.) was laid to rest' (Lk 23.55&; Gr. 4.62f).
  ▪ wəli·xt- (TI): wəlí·xto·l 'put it in order (you sg.)' (Lk 16.2), wəlí·xto·l mehəmí·č·ink 'prepare food (you sg.)' (Lk 17.8).
  - -o·li·xt-: no·lí·xto·n 'I put it away' (V; Gr. 5.12g).
wəli·x·ən- (we·li·x·ən-) II 'be in good order, right, lawful' (often negative): wəlí·x·ən 'it is lawful' (Mt 12.12), aləwí·i wəli·x·ən 'it is better' (Mt 18.8, 18.9, 25.9); tá=á· wəli·x·ənó·wi 'it would not be right' (Lk 5.3); takó· wəli·x·ənó·u 'it is not legal (or lawful)' (Jn 5.10, Mt 12.4, Mk 6.18; Gr. 2.12d); máta=háč wəli·x·ənó·wi? 'is it not right?' (Lk 13.16, Mt 20.15; Gr. 4.49f, 4.81z); wəlí·x·əno·p=á· 'it would have been the right thing' (Mt 23.23; Gr. 4.68f); énta- wé·mi kéku -wəlí·x·ink 'where everything is in good order' (Mk 14.15).
  - we·li·x·ən-: kéku we·lí·x·ink 'what is right' (Lk 12.57).
wəlo·x·we·- AI 'walk well': wəló·x·we·kw 'walk well (you pl.)' (Jn 12.35).
wəlúnkɔn AN 'wing' (V): kəlúnkɔnak 'your wings' (V; Gr. 3.4t), wəlúnkɔna 'his wings' (V [accent corrected]).
wəlunkɔnípahkɔ 'wing-leaves' (1834a:16); uncertain and unidentified.
wəlúnkwink 'under his arm' (1834b:35.3), 'in the fold of his robe' (Lk 16.22; 16.23; KJV "into (his) bosom"). ▶ Discussed in Goddard (2015:256 n. 61, 2019:102-103).
wəluwalahe·-* (-o·ləwalhe·-) AI+O 'bundle up O2': o·ləwálhe·n wé·mi kéku 'he bundled up everything' (Lk 15.13).
wə́nči (1) PV (-únči, wénči, wehə́nči [Rih+; IC]; Gr. 5.128x) 'from {smwh}, because of {smthg}, by (means of) {smthg}, about {smthg}': ɔ·s·áhkame wə́nči-mi·lɔ́nte 'if it is given to them from heaven' (Jn 3.27); hɔ́k·enk wə́nči-kčí·l 'come out of his body (you sg.)' (Mk 1.25); wwə́nči-káski-ktə́skaɔ·n 'because of it he is able to cast them out' (Mt 12.24); wwə́nči- ni·k·a·ní·i -wəntamə́ne·p 'thereby prophesying that ..' (*lit.*, 'he prophesied by it') (Jn 11.51); wənaxkəwá·ink=č wwə́nči-aspənúk·u 'they shall lift him up in their hands' (Mt 4.6); tá=háč=á· wwə́nči-káski- awé·n -ki·š·í·k·i·n 'how would someone be able to be born?' (Jn 3.4); wwə́nči-pənunthíke·n 'he gives testimony about it' (Jn 5.32; i.e., 'about me' [nhák·ay in Jn 5.31]); hɔ́k·enk wwə́nči-kčo·há·la·n yú entala·wsi·lí·č·i 'to save mankind by means of himself'

(Jn 3.17); nə́ni .. wə́nči- kanšaehɔ·s·əwá·k·an -pənunthíke·n hók·enk wə́nči 'that is why miracles are manifest from him' (Mt 14.2).

• -únči: tá=č=háč nə́ núnči-wwá·to·n 'what's the reason I will know that?' (Lk 1.18); hók·enk núnči-wəle·ləntam 'I am pleased because of him' (Mt 3.17); takó· nə́ni núnči-pá·wən 'I did not come because of that' (Mt 9.13; Gr. 3.13(7)c); tá=háč kúnči-wəla·mhitaməné·ɔ 'how can you believe?' (Jn 5.44). ♦ Idiom: wə́nči PV (attested for núnči- and kúnči-) + pa·- AI 'come in order to' (with ind. compement): núnči-pá·ne·n, nəmái-xinkɔhkəni·má·wəna. 'We come to worship him.' (Mt 2.2); kúnči-=háč -pá·n, kəmái-amax·ahi·laéhi ..? 'do you come in order to torment me?' (Mt 8.29).

♦ Note: /núnči-/ is misprinted as ⟨wunhi⟩ (⟨Wunhi⟩) for ⟨nwnhi⟩ (⟨Nwnhi⟩) in Mt 2.2, Mk 1.38, and Jn 16.15, and is spelled ⟨nwunhi⟩ in Mt 5.17 (possibly the later form /nəwə́nči); ⟨nwnhi⟩ is found 25x.

• wénči: wénči-kčihtí·t·əp 'who they had gone out of' (Lk 8.35); ləpwe·innúwak wénči-kčinkwéhəla·k wenči-aí·č·i·k 'wise men who were from the east' (Mt 2.1; Gr. 3.13(7)d); yú wáin mpínk wénči-manní·tunk 'the wine that had been made from water' (Jn 2.9; Gr. 3.13(7)b); wénči-=č -ki·š·əna·kwso·ké·tunt 'so that they will be made ready for him' (Lk 1.17); wénči-=č -wwáhkɔ 'so that it will be known' (Lk 2.35); wénči-wəla·pto·nállan 'in order that I tell you good news' (⟨wcnhi⟩ Lk 1.19); wénči-=č -lé·khunt 'by which they were to be enrolled' (Lk 2.1); wénči-ɔ·x·e·kamáɔ·t 'by which he gave light to them' (Lk 1.79).

• wə́nči (for wénči): Jn 1.7, 5.7, etc.; wə́nči-pahkánči-lé·k 'so that it would happen exactly' (Mt 1.22); wə́nči-kčinkwéhəla·t 'so that it (anim.) rises' (Mt 5.45)'; wə́nči-=č .. máta -wwáhkɔ 'so that .. it is not known' (Mt 6.4); wə́nči- hák·i -luwentá·s·i·k 'why the land is called (so)' (Mt 27.8); etc.

• wehə́nči: wehə́nči-ɔ́·p·ank '(in) the east' (*lit.*, 'the direction where dawn breaks') (V, FW); wehə́nči-kčinkwéhəla·k '(in) the east' (*lit.*, 'the direction of the sunrise') (Lk 13.29, Mt 24.27); wehə́nči-tpahí·k·e·t 'his index finger' (*lit.*, 'what he points at things with') (ME).

♦ Note: |wənt-| (wə́nči PV, P) is used instead of |tal-| with wténk 'behind' as a complement.

wə́nči (2) P 'from {smwh}, because of, about, by (means of), for {smthg}, in the direction of {smthg}': hók·enk wə́nči 'from him' (Mt 14.2); wə́nči ní· 'because of me' (Mk 13.9), ní· wə́nči 'for my sake' (Mt 16.25), 'by me' (Jn 14.6); wə́nči məsəč·é·i kté·hink 'with all your heart'; pəna·kčéhəli yú wə́nči 'jump down from here (you sg.)' (Mt 4.6; Gr. 3.13(7)a); néke ki·š·i·k·í·t·e wə́nči 'from the time he is born' (Lk 1.15); mɔt·a·wsəwa·k·anəwá·unk wə́nči 'from their sins' (Mt 1.21).

♦ With a non-locative form as complement: nə́ wə́nči 'from that' (= 'because of that, therefore') (Jn 8.24, Mt 18.23, etc.); wə́nči ankələwá·k·an 'from death' (Mk 6.16); wə́nči nči·sás·a 'because of Jesus (obv.)' (Jn 12.9); wə́nči šaxahka·wsəwá·k·an 'because of righteousness' (Mt 5.6; Gr. 6.9n); wə́nči né·l mi·məntə́t·al 'about the baby (obv.)' (Lk 2.17); wə́nči nhák·ay 'about me, regarding me' (Jn 5.37, Lk 22.37; Gr. 6.9m); wə́nči pí·lsi·t čí·čankw 'by the Holy Spirit (Mt 1.18); wə́nči čí·čankw ɔ́·k wəla·məwe·ɔ́·k·an 'by spirit and truth' (Jn 4.24; Gr. 6.9o); wə́nči wə́škinkw 'by the eye' (Mt 6.22); wə́nči wsəp·ínkɔ 'with her tears' (Lk 7.38); wə́nči wi·t·í·s·a 'for his or her friends' (Jn 15.13); hukwé·yunk wə́nči '[taken up] to heaven' (Lk 9.51).

♦ Followed by a conjunct verb with é·li- PV ('(it is) because ..'): wə́nči é·li- .. -pe·x·o·č·íhəla·k 'because (of how) it approaches' (Mt 4.17); wə́nči é·li-ne·ykwíhti·t 'because it's how they (obv.) see them' (Mt 6.5); wə́nči é·li- .. máta=á· -káski-pəntamó·we·kw 'it's because you cannot understand it' (Jn 8.43).

wənčihəla·- (wenčihəla·-) II 'come from {smwh}': wənčíhəle· 'it comes from' (Lk 6.45, 9.35), hók·enk wənčíhəle·p 'it came from him (his body)' (Lk 5.17); wənčihəlé·p·ani 'they came from [Tiberias, loc.]' (Jn 6.23; Gr. 4.68m); wenčíhəla·k 'where it comes from' (Jn 3.8); kéku wtó·nink wenčíhəla·k 'what issues from his mouth' (Mt 15.18; cf. Mt 15.11).

wənči·ai·- (-unči·ai·-, wenči·ai·-) AI — II 'be from {smwh}'.

▪ wənči·ai·- (AI): wənčí·ayu 'he comes from (there)' (Mt 10.36, Jn 7.41); wənčí·ai·t 'who comes from (there)' (Jn 1.46, 3.31 [3x], Jn 3.33, etc.); wənči·aí·č·i·k 'who came from (there)' (Lk 2.13 [s.b. obv.], Mt 3.5, etc.); é·li- máta -wənči·aíe·kw 'because you (pl.) are not from (it)' (Jn 15.19; or -wənči·aí·e·kw if the negative inflection was distinct); †sáiman †ké·nanink wənčí·ayo·p 'Simon (who came) from Canaa' (Mt 10.4; cf. the syntax of luwénsu '(who is) named').

• -unči·ai·-: ní· hukwé·yunk nunčí·ai 'I am from above' (Jn 8.23); tá=háč kunčí·ai 'where are you from?' (Jn 19.9); tá=á· nhák·enk kunči·aí·i 'you won't be part of me' (Jn 13.8; KJV "thou hast no part with me").

• wenči·ai·-: wenči·aía 'where I come from' (Jn 7.28); wenčí·ai·t 'where he comes from' (Jn 7.27); wenčí·aíe·kw 'where you're from' (Lk 13.25, 13.27); wenči·aí·č·i·k 'those who are from' (Jn 10.16, Mt 27.7, etc.).

▪ wənči·ai·- (II): ší·ki·hítkunk wínkank wənčí·ayu 'from a good tree comes good-tasting fruit' (Mt 7.17); palí·i wənčí·ayu 'it belongs to another pace' (Jn 18.36); wənčí·ai·k 'what comes from ..' (Lk 1.43, Mt 12.38, Jn 6.58, Mt 16.23); tépi·=á·=máh xé·li e·lá·ohti·k -wənčí·ayo·p 'a large amount would have come from it' (Mt 26.9); ; éntxi- máta .. -wənčí·ai·kw 'as many as it does not come from' (Mt 7.19; Gr. 4.95s).

• wenči·ai·-: wenčí·ai·k 'which comes from ..' (Jn 6.41, 6.50, etc.).

wənči·k·i·- (-unči·k·i·-, wenči·k·i·-) AI 'be born from {smwh}' — wənči·k·ən- (wenči·k·ən-) II 'grow from {smwh}, be from {smwh}'.

▪ wənči·k·i·- (AI): ntəli- ke·tanət·o·wí·t·ink -wənčí·k·i·n 'that I was born from God' (Jn 16.27); é·li- ke·tanət·o·wí·t·ink -wənčí·k·ia 'for I was born from God' (Jn 8.42).

• -unči·k·i·-: mahta·wsəwá·k·anink téxi šúkw kunčí·k·i 'you were utterly born in sin' (Jn 9.34); kwi·škaməwé·yunk kunčí·k·íhəmɔ 'you (pl.) are born from copperheads' (Mt 23.33).

• wenči·k·i·-: wenčí·k·i·t 'where he came from' (Jn 13.3); a·nhúkwi hók·enk wenčí·k·i·lí·č·i 'those (obv.) descended from him' (Lk 1.55).

▪ wənči·k·ən- (II): hók·enk xé·li kéku wənčí·k·ən 'many things grow from him or her' (Jn 15.5); ní wənčí·k·ink 'what grows from it' (Mt 12.33; no IC).

• wenči·k·ən-: wenčí·k·ink 'which comes or grows from {smwh}' (Jn 1.14, 3.6 [2x], Mt 12.33 [2x]); máta .. wenčí·k·ənokw 'from which it does not come' (Mt 3.10).

wənči·x·ən- II 'be from': ná=nə wənčí·x·ən 'that's the beginning' (OA); tə́ta wənčí·x·ink 'wherever it comes from' (1834a:18.5).

wəni·č·a·nəm- (we·ni·č·a·nəm-) TA 'have as a child': wəni·č·a·nəmuk·we·kwpáne=á· †e·pəliháma 'if you (pl.) had been children of Abraham (abs.)' (Jn 8.39; Gr. 4.74g).

• we·ni·č·a·nəm-: we·ni·č·a·nəmúk·we·kw 'you (pl.) who are their offspring' (Mt 3.7; Gr. 5.72a).

wəni·č·a·ni·- (we·ni·č·a·ni·-, wi·wəni·č·a·ni·- [Rī+]; Gr. 5.71a) AI(+O) 'have (O2 as) a child': wəni·č·á·nu=č khak·ayə́na. 'He will have us as his children.' (1834b:29.12); takó· wəni·č·a·ní·i·p 'he had no children' (Lk 20.29); takó· náxpəne kwə́t·i wəni·č·a·ní·p·ani·k 'they did not even have one child' (Lk 20.31); máta wəni·č·a·nihtí·t·e 'if they have no children' (Mt 22.24&); təli-=č -wəni·č·á·ni·n 'for her to have a child' (Jn 16.21).

- we·ni·č·a·ni·-: máta háši we·ni·č·á·ni·t 'who never had children' (Lk 23.29); we·ni·č·á·ni·t '(who is a or the) father, mother' (*lit.*, 'who has a child, children') (Mt 3.9, Jn 2.5, Lk 23.29; ⟨wrnehanul⟩ Jn 2.3); we·ni·č·a·ni·lí·č·i 'mother (or father) (obv.)' (*lit.*, 'who has a child') (Lk 2.34, 7.15, 9.42); lə́nu we·ni·č·á·nink (*lit.*, 'man who someone has as child'), used once for "the Son of man" (Jn 1.51)—see the note to the translation used otherwise: lə́nu we·k·wí·s·ink, under kkwi·s·i·-.
- wi·wəni·č·a·ni·-: é·li- takó· -wi·wəni·č·a·ní·t·əp 'as she had never had a child' (Lk 1.7; Gr. 5.44i).

wənt- (1) (-unt-, went-) TI(3) 'get from {smwh}' (Gr. 5.4g): é·li- tá=á· kéku -wəntó·wan 'because you won't get anything .. from it' (1842:20.3); tá=háč wwə́ntən yú ləpwe·ó·k·an 'where does he get this wisdom from?' (Mt 13.56); máta=á· təmí·ki tə́li- nalahí·i -wəntó·wən múx·o·l 'he would not often get a boat from upstream' (assuming ⟨nalauntwn⟩ for *⟨nalavewuntwn⟩ [or the like] 1834b:44.8).
- -unt-: tá=háč kúntən 'from where do you (sg.) get that?' (Jn 4.11; Gr. 2.50a); ná=ni núntəne·n 'that's where we got it' (OA; Gr. 2.65j, cf. Gr. 3.13(8)b); t=éč kuntəné·ɔ 'where'd you (pl.) get them?' (ER; Gr. 2.65k).
- went-: wentánki(?) (⟨wcntufi⟩ 1834a:24.62), intended for 'places where he gets it from', is presumably an error for expected wéntək 'where he got it from' (cf. Mun wé·ntək).
▸ See hwil- TA.

wənt- (2) TI(1a) 'name, mention' (with PV ni·k·a·ní·i 'prophesy'): wwə́nči- ni·k·a·ní·i -wəntamə́ne·p 'thereby prophesying (that ..)' (*lit.*, 'he prophesied by it') (Jn 11.51). ▸ See wihəl- TA. ▸ Cf. Mun wí·ntam 'names (it), mentions (it) by name'.

wəntahká·me P 'on this side of the water' (1834b:42.10). Cf. ⟨wëntahkame⟩ 'this side of the water' (LTD).
- wəntahká·mink 'on the side of (the river)' (1834a:42).

wə́ntahkwi P 'direction (toward {smwh})' (Lk 1.12; 1834b:8.4); nə́ wə́ntahkwi 'that way' (Mt 7.13); palí·i wə́ntahkwi lí-kwələp·i· 'he turned away' (Mt 16.23).

wəntahkwi·x·ən- (wentahkwi·x·ən-) II 'be on one side of {smwh}'.
- wentahkwi·x·ən-: nə́ íka wentahkwí·x·ink 'the next one to it (*lit.*, the one that is on one side of it)' (Mk 12.31). ▸ Cf. ⟨wundachquiechen japèwi⟩ "on the River Side" (Z. 173).

wəntalo·ka·l- (wentalo·ka·l-) TA 'send from {smwh}': wentalo·ká·link 'where I was sent from' (Jn 7.33; Gr. 4.67(2)g).

wəntalo·ka·lkwəsi·- AI 'be sent (as a messenger) from': ki·š·e·ləməwé·t·ink wəntalo·ka·lkwə́s·o·p 'he was sent from God' (Jn 1.6).

wəntamaw- (-wəntamaw- ~ -untamaw-; Gr. 2.19f, 5.97c) TA(+O) 'tell (about)': wəntamaí·ne·n 'tell us' (Lk 11.1; Gr. 2.19f); wəntamái·l=ksí 'so, explain to me (you sg.)' (1834b:8.2; Gr. 4.105f); é·li-wəntamaɔ́·t·əp 'how he told them' (Lk 11.1); wwəntamáɔ·n 'he told him (how ..)' (Jn 21.19; Gr. 2.20d, 2.66b); wwəntamaɔ́·ne·p 'he informed him about it' (Mt 2.22; Gr. 4.71d); takó· wəntamaɔ́·i 'he was not taught' (Jn 7.15; Gr. 2.12c).
- -untamaw-: nuntama·k·ó·ne·n=č wé·mi kéku 'he will tell us (exc.) about everything' (Jn 4.25); kuntamo·ləné·ɔ 'I tell you (pl.) it' (Mk 13.23, Jn 13.19; Gr. 2.19f, 2.65i).

wəntama·s·i·- (-untama·s·i·-; Gr. 5.103d) AI 'tell about, explain': wwəntamá·s·i·n 'he explains it' (Jn 12.33; KJV "signifying"); wəntamá·s·i·n 'it is taught' (Lk 16.16; KJV "is preached"); kéku=č e·ləwé·a ɔ́·k wəntamá·s·ia 'the things I was to say and explain' (Jn 12.49).
- -untama·s·i·-: ɔ́·k=č kuntama·s·i·né·ɔ nhák·ay 'and you (pl.) shall bear witness to me' (Acts 1.8).

wəntankəl- AI 'die for {smthg}': nəwínki-=á·=tá -wəntánkələn khák·ay 'I would willingly die for you' (Jn 13.37).

wə́ntax P 'to me, to here, to this point' (Jn 4.16, Mk 9.19, Lk 15.22, Lk 16.16, Lk 22.53, etc.): wə́ntax á·l 'come, come here (you sg.)' (Jn 1.46, Lk 7.8, Mt 9.18, etc.), wə́ntax á·kw (you pl.) (Jn 4.19, Lk 14.17, etc.). ▸ Opposed to: ná·ta.

wənta·me·- II 'derive from {smwh}, have {smwh} as source': wəntá·me· wé·mi khwitələt·əwá·k·ana 'that are the source of all the laws (sbd.)' (Mt 22.40).

wənta·pt- (|wəntāhpət-|; Gr. 5.12f) TI(2) 'tie from {smwh}': uxkwe·k·ánkanink wənta·ptúnke 'if it were tied from his neck' (Lk 17.2; Gr. 3.13(7)e); uxkwe·k·ánkanink wənta·ptunkpáne 'if it had been tied from his neck' (Mk 9.42); mux·ó·link wwənta·pto·né·ɔ 'they tied it from the boat' (Jn 21.8).

wənta·wsi·- (wenta·wsi·-) AI 'live from or on {smthg}': šíhkanč éntxi-wəntá·wsi·t 'the entire amount that she lives on' (Mk 12.44&).
  • wenta·wsi·-: wenta·wsiánəp 'what you (sg.) lived off' (Lk 15.30; Gr. 4.75d); wenta·wsíe·kw 'what you (pl.) live from' (Mt 6.25, Lk 12.22); wenta·wsíhti·t 'what they live on' (Mt 23.14).

wənte·ləm- TA 'be concerned about because of {smthg}': ná=nə .. wwənte·ləma·né·ɔ 'because of that they were concerned about him' (Jn 5.16; KJV "persecute"). ▸ Cf. ntáhi-wənte·lə́ntamən 'I worried a lot because of it' (WL).

wəntəna·s·i·- II 'be taken from {smwh}' (Gr. 5.105w): énta-šəšəwánahkwink wəntəná·s·u 'it was taken from English' (B: Title Page).

wənthita·k·ɔt- II 'be heard from {smwh}': hukwé·yunk wənthitá·k·ɔt 'it was heard from on high' (Jn 12.28).

wənto·x·we·- (-unto·x·we·-) AI 'go from or because of {smthg}': kéku=háč kuntó·x·we 'why did you (sg.) go?' (1834a:12).

wəntpehəla·- II 'flow out from {smwh}': íka wəntpéhəle· mhúkw ɔ́·k mpí 'blood and water flowed out from there' (Jn 19.34).

wəntxən- II 'blow from {smwh} (of wind)': mə́si-=hánkw -wə́ntxən. 'It blows from all over.' (1834b:24.3); lí- †pehpa·xhákwe·k -wə́ntxən 'that the wind blows from the south (sbd.)' (Lk 12.55).

wəskᵒ (|wəsk-|) 'new, young' (Gr. §5.2a).

wəskahkwí·ɔn IN 'new cloth' (⟨wwskaqeon⟩ Mk 2.21, ⟨wwskavqeon⟩ Lk 5.36).

wəskələna·p·e·i·- AI 'be a young person': né·li-wəskələna·p·é·ian 'when you (sg.) are a young person' (1834b:4.6, 4.7, 1842:19.7, 20.2).

wəskələna·p·é·ɔk 'young people' (1842:21.5).

wəskən-: see wəsksi·- — wəskən-.

wə́ski (Gr. 5.120h) PN 'new' (1834b:46.7; Lk 5.38, Mt 19.28, 26.28).
  ▪ wə́ski (wé·ski; Gr. 5.129oo) PV 'new(ly)'; 'anew' (Jn 3.3): né·l wə́ski-ne·ma·lí·č·i 'the newly seeing one' (Jn 9.15).
  • wé·ski: wé·ski-ki·š·í·k·i·t 'new-born one' (Mt 2.2).

wəsksi·- (-o·sksi·-) AI 'be young' — wəskən- II 'be new'.
  ▪ wəsksi·- (AI): né·li-wəsksían 'while you (sg.) are young' (1834b:4.9. 20.2, 1842:20.2); né·li-wə́sksi·t 'while he's young' (1834b:4.5, 19.5, 1842:19.5).
  • -o·sksi·-: wé·mi ko·sksíhəna 'we (inc.) are all young' (1834b:3.5, 1842:18.7).
  ▪ wəskən- (II): wə́skən 'it is new' (LB); wə́skink '(which is) new' (Mk 1.27, Lk 5.37, etc.); wəskínki 'new ones' (⟨wwskifc⟩ Mt 13.52).

wəsksi·taw- TA+O 'make O2 new for': ntə́li-=á· awé·ni -wəsksí·taɔ·n wəlehəle·x·e·ɔ́·k·an 'I came in order to renew people's lives' (1834b:24.12).

wəskši·lənt- (-o·skši·lənt-; TI(1a)) TI-O 'be newly married': no·skši·ləntam 'I'm newly married' (Lk 14.20).

wə́skxəm AN 'young animal' (LB; Gr. 5.9c); ⟨Wuskchum⟩ 'young creature' (B&A 176).
- wəskxə́mtət AN (dim.) 'colt' (Lk 19.33&); wəskxəmtə́t·a (obv.) (Mk 11.4&).

wə́ški IN 'whiskey' (LB; ⟨Vwijki⟩ 1842:22.6, ⟨Vwjki⟩ 23.3); wə́škink 'whiskey (loc.)' (⟨vwijkif⟩ 1842:23.4).
♦ Presumably ⟨v-⟩ /h-/ in the early spellings (⟨vwiski⟩ 1834b:7.4; ⟨vwiskiif⟩ 1834b:11.12) was only orthographic; similarly /s/ after the English spelling.

wəškinkwi·- (we·škinkwi·-, |wəškīnkwī-|; Gr. 5.21d) AI 'have eye(s)': we·škínkwi·t 'one with eyes' (Mk 8.18). ▸ Cf. nə́škinkw.

wiakhá́ki 'abundant things' (⟨weukuku⟩ 1834a:17).

wiáki (|wəyakī|; Gr. 2.74m, 5.27h, 5.129pp) PV 'plenty, abundantly' (Lk 15.17, Mt 25.29); ⟨Wiaki⟩ "enough and to spare, plenty" (B&A 156).
▸ Cf. Mun wŏyak- 'plenty, a lot, etc.' See also wiákski.

wiaksi·- AI 'have plenty': wiaksíe·kw 'you (pl.) who have plenty' (Lk 6.25).

†wiákski (weyákski [with IC]) PV 'promiscuously' (apparently |wəyak-ī| with intensifier |-ask-|): weyákski-wi·k·inké·č·i·k 'ones who are (sexually) promiscuous' (⟨wceukski⟩ Lk 18.11; KJV "adulterers"). ▸ Cf. ⟨wijagásxu⟩ "unruly" (Z. 213), ⟨Wijagaskau⟩ (read ⟨Wijagasksu⟩) "fickle" (B&A 157). ▸ Cf. Mun wŏyakask- 'nauseous' (a different narrowing of the meaning).

wiák·at II 'there is plenty of it' (1842:15.1). ▸ Cf. Mun wŏyákat 'it is abundant, there is plenty of it'.

wiak·i·h- TA 'make plenty for(?)': wé·mi kéku wwiak·íhko·n 'everything was plentiful for him' (1834b:31.7).

wiamxkahpi·- AI 'be (live) mixed together': énta-wiamxkahpíhti·t 'where they live mixed together' (Jn 7.35).

wiámxki P 'mixed' (|wəyamv̆xkī|; Gr. 2.65f): kéku áhi-wísahkank wiámxki 'mixed with something very bitter' (Mt 27.34). ▸ Cf. Mun wŏyamoxk- 'stir, shake up'.

wíči (1) (-íči PN + pronominal prefix; Gr. 2.74n, 5.120i) PN '(one's) fellow'.
• wíči (with |wə-| 3): wíči-alo·ká·k·ana 'his fellow servants' (Lk 12.45), kwə́t·i wíči-alo·ká·k·ana 'one of his fellow servants' (Mt 18.26).
• kíči (with |kə-| 2): kíči-xkwé·ɔk 'other women' (lit., 'your fellow women') (Lk 1.42); kíči alo·ká·k·an 'your fellow servant' (Mt 18.33). ▸ See next.

wíči (2) PV 'with the other one or others' (Gr. 5.99abcgh, 5.129qq): né·pe=č nəwíči- íka -ahpí 'I shall also be present, too' (Mt 18.20); wé·mi wíči-wəle·ləntamó·p·ani·k 'they were all happy along with her' (Lk 1.58; Gr. 5.99c); ná .. wwíči- íka -ahpi·né·ɔ 'then they were also sitting with him' (Mt 17.3); šé· ké·pe kəwíči-amax·ahi·laehkwə́s·i 'and here you (sg.), too, are in torment with him' (Lk 23.40).
♦ wíči PV + |-(ī)m| TA '(do so) with': wíči-wəle·ləntamə́wí·mi·kw 'rejoice with me (you pl.)' (Lk 15.6, 15.9); kəwíči-=č -a·mwi·mkúwa 'she will rise up along with you' (Mt 12.42; Gr. 5.99g).
- wíči P 'with him, her, or them; with the other one or others': ɔ́·k wíči †helat·í·i-lə́nəwak 'and with them Herod's men' (Mt 22.16,&); ɔ́·k wíči=č ehalo·ka·lə́nči·k 'and with him will be angels' (Mt 16.27); wənáxk wíči ehəntali·p·wínkink hát·e· 'his hand is on the table with the others' (Lk 22.21).

wihəl (~ wil-, |wīhl-|; Gr. 2.5j) TA 'name': káči nó·čkwe wihəlié·k·ač nehəlá·ləwe·t 'don't call the name of the Lord frivolously (you sg.)' (1842:11.2); nó·čkwe wihəlí·t·e 'if he names me frivolously' (1834b:20.12); nó·čkwe wilkúk·i 'who (obv.) names him frivolously' (1842:11.2). ▸ See wənt- (2) TI(1a).

wihínki: see wínki.

wihi·nəwe·-: see wi·nəwe·-.

wimpəne·m- TA 'die with': ktəli-=č -wimpəne·má·ne·n 'so that we shall die with him' (Jn 11.16); kəwimpəné·məl 'I die with you' (Mk 14.31). ▸ Cf. ⟨wimpànem-⟩ 'die with', ⟨wímpënem-⟩ 'be sympathetic to' (LTD); these are presumably the same word.

wink° (|wīnk-|) 'like' (Gr. §5.2a).

winkahpi·- AI 'like to stay': aləwí·i wwínkahpi·n 'that one would rather stay' (1834a:23.51).

winkan-: see wínkəl — winkan-.

winkayəw- TA 'be willing to have, receive': éntxi-winkayó·kwki 'all (obv.) who were willing to have him' (Jn 1.12); kəwinkayəwáwwa 'you (pl.) are willing to receive him' (Jn 5.43); máta kəwinkayəwi·húmɔ 'you (pl.) were not willing to receive me' (Jn 5.43).

winka·l- TA 'like' (B frequently "be welcoming to") — winka·t- TI(1a) 'like'; (cf. Gr. 5.12d).
- winka·l-: awé·n winka·lí·t·e 'if anyone is welcoming to me' (Mt 10.40); wwinka·lá·ɔ 'he is welcoming to him' (Mt 10.40); nəwinká·lukw 'he is also welcoming to me' (Mt 10.40); winka·lkúk·e 'if he (obv.) likes him' (Mt 27.43).
- winka·t-: é·li-winká·t·ame·kw kta·pahpi·né·ɔ 'for you (pl.) like to sit there' (Lk 11.43); aləwí·i nəwinká·t·am ktəma·k·e·ləntəwá·k·an 'I like mercy more' (Mt 9.13); ktəli-winka·t·aməné·ɔ 'that you (pl.) approve of it' (Lk 11.48).

winka·wsəwá·k·an IN 'paradise'; winka·wsəwá·k·anink 'in paradise' (Lk 23.43).

winka·wsi·- AI 'live joyfully: énta-winká·wsi·t 'where he is living joyfully' (Mt 25.21, 25.23).

winke·- AI 'like to': wínke·w 'he likes it' (1834a:13); winké·ok .. kəmo·tké·ok xáskwi·m 'they like to steal corn' (1834a:14). ♦ Dubious; these should presumably be wínki PV.

winke·ləm- TA 'accept on friendly terms, welcome': mái-winké·ləm 'go and get on good terms with him (you sg.)' (⟨ifrlum⟩ Mt 5.24); mɔ́i-winke·ləmúk·o·l 'and he went to reconcile himself to him' (⟨moifrlumwkwl⟩ 1834b: 29.9); máta winke·ləma·í·ɔk 'they are not accepted on friendly terms' (Jn 4.9); winke·ləmək·e·é·k·we 'if you (pl.) are welcomed' (Lk 10.8); máta winke·ləmək·e·é·k·we 'if you are not welcomed' (Lk 10.10); máta winké·ləmi·t 'who does not like me' (Mt 12.30); máta wwinke·ləma·iwwá·ɔ 'they did not welcome him' (Lk 9.53); nəwinke·ləmák·e 'I am welcomed' (Mt 18.5); ktəli- máta -winke·ləmuk·ó·wən 'that he is not on friendly terms with you' (Mt 5.23).

winke·ləmukwsi·- AI 'be welcomed': ɔ́·k=č awé·n winke·ləmúkwsu 'and someone shall be welcomed' (Mt 18.5).

winkəl- AI — winkan- II 'taste good' (Gr. 3.18e; 5.10g).
- winkəl- (AI): wínkəl AI 'it (anim.) tastes good' (V, ME, AD; Gr. 3.19e).
- winkan- (II): wínkan 'it tastes good' (V, ME, AD); wínkank 'good-tasting fruit' (Mt 7.17, 7.18, 7.19); winkánki skí·kɔ 'sweet-tasting herbs' (Lk 11.42).

winkəle·- II 'be blazing': yú táli énta-wínkəle·k 'in this blazing fire' (Lk 16.24).

wínkəp: see wum-.

winkhikaw-(?): kəwinkhíka·kw(?) 'you are beset(?), buffeted(?) by (it)' (1834b:31.1).

wínki (wihínki [Rih+], wehínki [Rih+; IC]; Gr. 5.128y) PV 'like to, be willing to':

wínki-=á· -ləs·iáne 'if you're willing to' (Mt 8.2); wwínki-ne·ɔwwá·p·ani 'they were glad to see him' (Lk 8.40); tá=á· awé·n wwínki-manni·tó·wən 'no one would be willing to make it' (1842:23.7); nəwínki-ánkəl 'I am willing to die' (Jn 10.17); etc.
- wihínki PV '(always) like to': wihínki-pa·tamá·ɔk 'they always like to pray' (Mt 6.5); nəwihínki-lúkw 'he always likes to say to me' (1842:24.1).
- wehínki: yó·ki·k wehínki-məné·č·i·k 'those who like to drink' (1834b:7.11-12).
- wínki P '(is) willing': ləna·p·e·ɔ́·k·an=hánkw píši wínki 'the soul is indeed willing' (Mt 26.41); máta wínki 'he was unwilling' (Lk 18.4).

winki·ma·khwiksa·s·i·- II 'be burned as incense' (Gr. 5.105q): énta-winki·ma·khwiksá·s·i·k 'altar' (Lk 1.11), nə́ ehə́nta-winki·ma·khwiksá·s·i·k kéku (Mt 23.19), ehə́nta- kéku -winki·ma·khwiksá·s·i·k (Mt 23.18, 23.20). ♦ Note: an altar is 'where incense is burned' or 'where things are burned as incense', *lit.*, 'where things are burned to smell sweet'.

winki·ma·khwiksəma·- (wihinki·ma·khwiksəma·- [Rih+]) AI 'burn one's incense' (*lit.*, 'burn to make it smell sweet for oneself'): ehə́nta-winki·ma·khwiksəmá·t·əp 'his incense altar' (*lit.*, 'the place where he used to burn to make it smell sweet for himself') (Lk 11.51, Mt 23.35); sé·ki- wi·k·əwáhəmink -táli-winki·ma·khwiksə́mank 'while the incense was burned in the building' (Lk 1.10).
- wihinki·ma·khwiksəma·-: tə́li-=č né·k·əma -wihinki·ma·khwiksə́ma·n 'that *he* was to be the one to (always) burn incense' (Lk 1.9).

winki·ma·k·ɔt- II 'smell sweet': nə́ winki·má·k·ɔ mpí·s·o·n 'that sweet-smelling medicine' (Jn 12.3); winki·ma·khɔ́ki kéku 'sweet smelling things' (⟨wefemakvwk⟩ Mt 2.11 [em.]; KJV "frankincense, and myrrh"); winki·ma·khɔ́ki (..) skí·kɔ 'sweet-smelling herbs' (Lk 11.42, Mt 23.23); winki·ma·khɔ́ki mpi·s·ó·na 'sweet-smelling medicines' (Lk 23.56).

winki·naht- TI(2) 'be fond of making use of': sé·ki- yó·ni -winkí·nahta·kw 'as long as he is fond of making use of this' (1834a:21.37).

winko·s·əməwá·k·an IN 'drunkenness' (1834b:14.10); lí winko·s·əməwá·k·anink 'toward drunkenness' (1842:21.4).

winko·s·əmwi·- AI 'be fond of drinking, be a dunkard': winkó·s·əmu 'he is a drunkard' (1842:23.5); kéhəla winko·s·əmwiáne 'if you (sg.) are very fond of drink' (1842:20.2); winkó·s·əmwi·t 'drunkard' (1842:21.2); ktə́li-=č -áhi-winkó·s·əmwi·n 'for you (sg.) to be very fond of drink' (1842:20.2); tə́li-winko·s·əmwi·né·ɔ 'that they are drunkards' (1842:23.5).

winko·x·we·- AI 'like to go' (Gr. 5.1e): winkó·x·we·w 'he likes to go' (Jn 3.21).

winksət·aw- TA — winksət·- TI(a) 'like to hear'.
- winksət·aw- (TA): wwinksət·aɔ́·p·ani 'they liked to hear him' (Mk 12.37).
- winksət·- (TI): máta winksət·ank 'who does not like hearing it' (Jn 12.48).

winkto·nha·l- TA 'talk with, converse': kwáč=háč winkto·nhá·lat 'why are you talking with her?' (Jn 4.27); é·li-winkto·nhá·la·t 'how he was having a conversation with her' (Jn 4.27).

wió·s (-o·ó·s·əm-, |wəyōs|) IN 'meat, flesh' (Mt 16.17, Lk 17.37, Mt 24.28); wió·s·ink '(from) flesh' (Jn 1.13, 1834b:24.1).
- -o·ó·s·əm-: no·ó·s·əm 'my flesh' (Jn 6.51; Gr. 2.31l); o·ó·s·əm 'his flesh' (Jn 6.52, 6.53, 6.63) ~ o·yó·s·əm 'his meat' (V; Gr. 2.34).

wio·s·o·wi·- AI — II 'be meaty, be flesh'.
- wio·s·o·wi·- (AI): manə́t·u takó· wio·s·o·wí·i 'the spirit does not have flesh' (Lk 24.39).
- wio·s·o·wi·- (II): wio·s·ó·u 'it is meaty, has meat on it' (LB; Gr. 5.68q); wio·s·ó·o·p 'it became flesh' (Jn 1.14).

wisahk° (|wīsak-|) 'bitter' (Gr. §5.2a).

wisahkamalsi·- AI 'be in pain' (3s 'he is in extreme pain' LTD); wisahkamalsi·lí·č·i 'ones (obv.) in pain' (Mt 4.24).

wisahkan- II 'be bitter': wísahkàn 'it is bitter, strong tasting' (FW, AP, LB); kéku áhi-wísahkank 'something very bitter' (Mt 27.34); wísahkank 'sweet flag (calamus)' (LB).
▶ Cf. ⟨Wisachgank⟩ 'rum, brandy' (B&A 162).

wísahki·m IN 'grape(s)' (Mt 7.16, Mt 21.33); ⟨wisachgim⟩ 'wild grapes' (B&A 162).

wisahki·mi·ná·p·u IN 'wine' (Lk 22.18, Mt 26.27, 26.29).

wisahki·múnši IN 'vine' (|-īmōnšəy|; cf. Gr. 5.9l); ní· wisahki·múnši 'I am the vine' (Jn 15.5); mayá·i-wisahki·múnši 'the true vine' (Jn 15.1); wisahki·múnšia 'grape vines' (Mt 21.33); wisahki·múnšink 'to the vine' (Jn 15.4).
▪ wisahki·munšií·i PN 'of the vine' (⟨Wesavkemwnjei⟩ Jn 15.4).

witᵒ: see wi·t·ᵒ.

witahki·m- TA 'count with the others': witahkí·ma· 'he was counted among them' (Mk 15.28).

witahki·mkwəs·i·- (|wītakīməkwəsī-|; Gr. 5.99e) AI 'be counted with the others': witahki·mkwə́s·u me·t·a·wsi·t·i·ké·i 'he was counted in among the sinners' (Lk 22.37).

witahpi·- AI 'be with': íka witahpúwak 'they were there among them' (Jn 12.20).

witahpi·m- (|wītapīm-|; Gr. 5.99m) TA 'live with': sé·ki-witahpi·mák·əp 'while I was with them' (Jn 17.12); é·li- we·t·ó·x·əmənt -witahpí·mi·t 'as the father is with me' (Jn 16.32); énta-witahpí·məle·kw 'when I am with you (pl.)' (Lk 22.27); kəwitahpi·məlúhəmɔ·p 'I was with you (pl.)' (Lk 22.53); tá=háč ksá·ki-witahpi·mələné·ɔ 'how long will I be with you (pl.)?' (Mk 9.19; Gr. 3.13(6)b); kəwitahpi·mko·né·na·p 'it lived with us' (Jn 1.14; Gr. 4.69u); máta=háč kəwitahpi·mko·wi·wəná·nak 'are they not with us?' (Mt 13.56; Gr. 4.85o).

wi·č·ᵒ (|wīt-|) 'with' (Gr. §5.8i).

wi·č·e·w- (ɔ·i·č·e·w- [Rā+]) TA 'accompany, marry': péči-wi·č·é·e· xé·li lənəwal 'he came with many men' (Mk 14.43&); wi·č·é·i·kw 'come with me (you pl.)' (Jn 1.39; Gr. 4.105l); wi·č·e·yó·me 'go with him (you sg.)' (Mt 18.16; Gr. 4.116e); wi·č·e·ɔ́·t·əp 'who had been the wife of (him)' (Mk 6.17); é·li- .. -wi·č·é·ie·kw 'as you (pl.) have been with me' (Jn 15.27; Gr. 2.36d); wi·č·e·ykúk·i 'who (obv.) were with him' (Lk 5.9, 9.32, 22.49, Mt 27.54&; Gr. 4.65f); nkəmé·i=č wi·č·é·ykuk 'who (obv.) would always be with him' (1834b:23.4; cf. Gr. 4.65n); wi·č·e·ykónəp 'the one who was with you (sg.)' (Jn 3.26; Gr. 4.76t); máta ki·š·e·ləməwe·lí·č·i wi·č·e·ykó·k·we 'if God (obv.) was not with him' (1834b:23.11, Jn 3.2; Gr. 4.97n); wwi·č·e·ykó·ne·p 'it was with him' (Jn 1.1; Gr. 4.69t); ná tólǝmi-wi·č·e·yko·né·ɔ·p 'then he (obv.) started off with them' (Lk 7.6; Gr. 4.72h); kəwi·č·e·wəlóne·n 'And we're going with you (sbd.).' (Jn 21.3; Gr. 4.52b). ♦ wi·č·é·ɔk 'my spouse' (Lk 1.18); wi·č·e·ɔ́·č·i·k 'his (obv.) companions' (Mt 21.11); wi·č·e·ɔ́·č·i 'his wife' (Lk 2.33, Mt 5.31, 5.32, etc.), 'her husband' (Mk 10.12); wi·č·e·é·k·wi·k 'your (pl.) wives' (1842:17.1); wi·č·e·ɔhtí·č·i 'their wives' (1834b:18.10, 1842:9.3).
• ɔ·i·č·e·w-: ɔ·i·č·e·ykúk·i 'who (obv.) were accompanying him' (1834b:33.10).
▪ wi·č·e·wti·- AI 'be married to each other': né·ləma .. wi·č·e·wti·í·p·ani·k 'they were not yet married' (⟨wethaoteepanek⟩ Mt 1.18; KJV "before they came together").
▶ Cf. ne·wti·-; the spelling with ⟨aot⟩ appears to be influenced by the reciprocals with /-a·ɔht/ regularly made from stems in |-aw| (Gr. 5.110jklm).

wi·č·əm- TA — TI(1a) wi·č·ənt- 'help' (Gr. 5.12h).
▪ wi·č·əm- (TA): wí·č·əmi·l 'help me (you sg.)' (Mt 15.25); wi·č·əmí·t·eč 'she should help me (lit., may she help me)' (Lk 10.40; Gr. 4.114l); wí·č·əma·t 'one that helped him' (Lk 16.3); wi·č·əma·tpáni·k 'those that helped him' (Mk 15.7); wi·č·əmukwpáni 'his helper' (lit., 'the one

(obv.) that helped him') (Lk 16.1; Gr. 4.76u); é·li- tá=á· čí·č -wi·č·əmí·ɔn 'as you will not be my helper any longer' (Lk 16.2); wí·č·əmi·t 'who helps me' (Jn 5.7); wwi·č·əmá·p·ani·l 'he helped him' (Lk 1.54); nál=ná nəwí·č·əmukw 'he is one who helps me' (Lk 9.50); kəwí·č·əmi 'you (sg.) help me' (Lk 17.8; Gr. 4.31); wwí·č·əma·n 'that he help him (sbd.)' (Mt 27.32&).
- wi·č·ənt- (TI): nəwi·č·əntamən 'I helped it' (ND; Gr. 5.12h).
- wi·č·ənti·- AI 'help one another' (wihi·č·ənti·- [Rih+]; recip.; Gr. §5.8m): šúkw máta wi·č·ənti·í·p·ani·k 'but they did not help each other' (1834b:43.2).
  • wihi·č·ənti·-: wihi·č·əntó·p·ani·k=máh 'they used to help each other' (1834b:42.14); nó·čkwe=á· wwihi·č·ənti·né·ɔ 'they would freely help each other' (1834b:42.12).

wi·č·i·k·e·m- TA 'dwell together with': kəwi·č·i·k·e·mkúwa awé·n 'someone lives among you (pl.)' (Jn 1.26; Gr. 4.27o).

wi·hunke·- (wehi·hunke·- [Rih+; IC]) AI(+O) 'offer O2, make a sacrifice, be a priest': wi·húnke·l kəmi·ltəwá·k·an 'offer your (sg.) gift' (Mt 5.24); wi·húnke 'make a sacrifice (you sg.)' (Mt 8.4); sé·ki-wi·húnke·t 'during the time when he was a priest' (Lk 1.23); né·li-wi·hunke·lí·t·əp 'while they (obv.) were sacrificing' (Lk 13.1); énta-wi·húnkenk '(to, at) the altar' (*lit.*, 'place of offering (a ritual meal)') (Mt 5.23, 5.24).
  • wehi·hunke·-: wehi·húnke·t 'priest' (*lit.*, 'one who customarily sacrifices') (Lk 1.15, Mt 8.4, Lk 10.31); wehi·hunké·č·i·k 'priests' (Mt 12.4, 12.5, Mt 16.21, etc.); wehi·hunke·tpáni·k 'priests' (Lk 3.2; KJV "high priests"); wehi·hunke·lí·č·i 'priests (obv.)' (Jn 1.19, Lk 23.13).
- Lexicalized participle: wehi·hunké·t·ink 'to the priests' (Jn 7.45).
▸ Cf. wehi·húnke·s AN 'priest'.
▸ Cf. wi·ho·m- TA 'serve a memorial feast to' (OA).

wi·hunke·ó·k·an IN 'sacrifice' (Mt 9.13, 12.7, Mk 9.49, 12.33). ▸ See wi·hunke·-.

wi·k(w)º (|wīhkw-|) 'end' (Gr. §5.2a).

wí·kənaskw IN 'reed' (⟨Wekunusq⟩ Lk 7.24, Mt 27.29, Mt 27.30; ⟨Wekonusq⟩ Mt 12.20); loc. wi·kənáskunk (⟨wekunuskwf⟩ Mt 27.48). ▸ Cf. ⟨wigenaskunk⟩ (Denke 2014:102, Jn 19.29); Mass ⟨wekinashq⟩, ⟨weekinasq⟩, etc. 'reed'; Narr ⟨Wékinash-quash⟩ sg., pl. (Williams 1936:96).

wi·kha·- AI 'build one's house': wi·khá·t·əp 'who built his house' (Mt 7.26). ♦ A middle-reflexive (cf. Gr. 5.104) derived from wi·khaw- TA 'build a house for' (kəwí·kho·l 'I build a house for you' [LB]), which is an applicative derived from wi·khe·- AI (Gr. 5.90d; see next).

wi·khe·- (|wīkahē-|; Gr. 5.90d) AI 'build (a house)': wí·khe· 'he built' (Lk 14.30), káhta-wí·khe· 'he wants to build a house' (Lk 6.47&); áləmi-wi·khé·t·e 'if he were to begin building' (Lk 14.28); wi·khé·č·i·k 'builders' (Lk 20.17).
- wi·khahti·- AI (coll.): wi·khahtó·p·ani·k 'they all built houses' (Lk 17.28).

wi·khɔkami·k·e·- (|-ahkamīk-| 'earth' + |-ē|; cf. Gr. 5.7b) II 'be the end of the earth': wi·khɔkamí·k·e·k 'the ends of the earth' (Mt 12.42); é·li-wi·khɔkamí·k·e·k 'to the ends of the earth' (Acts 1.8).

wi·kɔ·wsi·- AI 'have one's life end': tá=á·=tá wi·kɔ·wsí·i 'his life will not end' (Jn 6.50); wi·kɔ·wsúwak=č 'they will come to the end of their lives' (1834b:4.1, 1842:19.2); mé·či wi·kɔ·wsúnka 'their (abs.) lives have ended' (Jn 6.49); wi·kɔ·wsihtí·t·e 'when their lives end' (1842:19.3); ná wwi·kó·wsi·n 'then he came to the end of his life' (1842:10.5).

wi·kwe·- (wi·i·kwe·- [Rī+]) II 'end': takó· káhta-wi·kwé·i 'it is not going to end' (Mt 12.20; Gr. 4.81u); máta (..) wí·kwe·k 'that does not end' (Mk 10.30, Jn 17.2, 17.3); wi·kwé·k·e hák·i 'when the world ends' (Mt 13.49).

- wi·i·kwe·-: ɔ́·k=č wsa·k·i·ma·ɔ́·k·an máta wi·i·kwé·i 'and his kingdom shall never end' (Lk 1.33; Gr. 4.81v, 5.44k).
†wi·kwé·link 'outside (a house)' (Mt 12.46; KJV "without"). ♦ If this was specifically 'outside the door of the house' (which would be at the east end), it might have been extended from an original meaning 'at the end of the canoe': |wīhkwē-| 'end' + PA *-weθ- 'canoe' (Goddard 2019: 101).

wí·kwi PV 'end' (1834b:15.1).

wi·kwihəla·- AI 'be tired' (Gr. 5.11n): wi·kwíhəle· 'he was tired' (Jn 4.6; Gr. 2.7g).

wí·k·əwam (|wīkəwahm|; Gr. 2.5k) IN 'house, building' (Mt 7.25&, Mt 7.27&, Mk 3.25, etc.); wi·k·əwáhəmal 'houses' (Mk 10.30); amánki-wi·k·əwáhəma 'great-buildings' (Mt 13.2); wi·k·əwáhəmink 'in, to the building, house' (Lk 1.10, 1.21, Mt 5.15, etc.; Gr. 4.9c).

wi·k·inke·- (|wīkīnkē-|; Gr. 5.102h) AI 'marry or be married to someone': takó· nəwi·k·inké·i 'I am not married' (Jn 4.17 [2x]); wi·k·ínke·p 'she had been married' (Lk 2.36); weyákski-wi·k·inké·č·i·k 'ones who are promiscuous' (Lk 18.11; KJV "adulterers").

wi·k·inke·ɔ́·k·an (Gr. 5.59b) IN 'marriage' (Mt 5.27, 5.32 [2x]); máta ki·mí·i-wi·k·inke·ɔ́·k·an wə́nči 'not because of fornication' (Mt 19.9).

wi·k·inke·whé·- AI+O 'have a wedding for O2': ké·t·a-wi·k·inke·whé·t·e kkwí·s·al 'when he wanted to have a wedding for his son' (Mt 22.2). ♦ A causative of wi·k·inke·- AI 'marry someone' (cf. Gr. 5.79).

wi·k·i·- (wehi·k·i·- [Rih+, IC]) AI 'live {smwh}': ná=nə nəwí·k·i·n ə́nta-káhta-wí·k·ia· 'I live where I want to live' (OA); šé· yú nəwi·k·í·ne·n 'here's where we (exc.) live' (ME); ná=nə́ wwi·k·i·né·ɔ 'they live there' (Mt 12.45).

- Participle with the oblique complement as head: wí·k·ia 'my house' (*lit.*, 'where I live') (Lk 9.61, 14.23); wí·k·ian 'your house' (Lk 7.44, 19.5, Mk 14.14); wí·k·i·t 'his or her house' (Jn 2.16, Lk 6.47&, etc.); wi·k·í·li·t 'the house where he (obv.) lived' (Jn 1.39); wi·k·í·č·i 'his houses' (Mk 10.29); wi·k·ié·k·wi 'your (pl.) houses' (Lk 13.35, Mt 23.38); wi·k·ihtí·č·i 'their houses' (1834a:23.60); lí nihəláči wi·k·íhti·t 'to their own houses' (Jn 7.53).
- wehi·k·iénkəp 'where we (exc.) used to live' (V).

wi·k·i·m- TA 'be married to': wi·k·í·mat 'your wife' (Lk 1.13), 'your husband' (Jn 4.16, 4.18); wi·k·i·matpáni·k 'ones who were your (sg.) husbands' (Jn 4.18; Gr. 4.76f); wi·k·i·má·č·i 'his wife, her husband(s) (obv.)' (Lk 1.5, 1.24, Mt 1.18, Mt 1.24); takó· khiči·i kəwi·k·i·má·i 'you're not really married to him' (Jn 4.18; Gr. 4.83i); ktə́li-wé·t·əna·n, -wi·k·í·ma·n 'to take her to be your wife' (*lit.* 'to take her and marry her') (Mt 1.20).

wí·lanu: see ní·lanu.

wi·ne·- II 'snow' (Gr. 5.117e): kɔ́na=ét péxu wí·ne· 'I guess it's going to snow' (1834a:13).

wi·nəwam- TA 'ask, beg' (Gr. 5.89c): wi·nəwámo· 'ask him (you pl.)' (Mt 9.38); wi·nəwámi·l 'ask me (you sg.)' (Mk 6.22); nəwi·nəwáma=č 'I will ask him' (Jn 14.16; KJV "pray"); takó· kəwi·nəwaməló·wi 'I do not ask you (sg.)' (Jn 17.15; Gr. 2.12d, 4.89h); wwi·nəwama·né·ɔ 'And they asked him' (Mt 14.36, Mk 7.32).

wi·nəwe·- (wihi·nəwe·- [Rih+], wehi·nəwe·- [Rih+; IC]) AI(+O) 'ask (for O2)': wí·nəwe· 'he begged' (1834b:31.11); wí·nəwe·kw 'ask (you pl.)' (Lk 11.9, Jn 16.24), 'pray' (Mt 24.20); wi·nəwe·mɔ́·e wə́nči ní· 'ask through me (you pl.)' (Jn 16.26; Gr. 4.116b); wi·nəwé·ane=č 'if you (sg.) ask' (Mt 7.7); wé·mi ə́ntxi-wí·nəwe·t 'everyone that asks' (Mt 7.8); ehə́nta-wi·nəwé·ankw 'where we (inc.) always beg' (Jn 9.8); kéku wi·nəwe·é·k·we 'when you (pl.) pray for something' (Mt 18.19); ə́ntxi-wi·nəwé·č·i·k 'all who ask' (Lk 11.10); takó· háši kéku kəwi·nəwe·húmɔ 'you (pl.) have never asked for anything' (Jn 16.24).

- wihi·nəwe·-: nəwihí·nəwe·n 'that I beg (sbd.)' (Lk 16.3; Gr. 4.49q).
- wehi·nəwe·-: wehí·nəwe·t 'beggar' (Lk 16.20, 16.22).

wi·nəwe·lx- (|wīnəwēlax-|; Gr. 5.98) TA(+O) 'ask (for O2) on behalf of': nəwi·nəwé·lxa 'I beg for him' (OA); kəwi·nəwe·lxəlané·ɔ 'I ask for it *for* you (pl.)' (Jn 14.14).

wí·ɔhšo·n IN 'pack' (OA); nəwí·ɔhšo·n 'my pack' (Mt 11.30; KJV "my burden").

wi·penke·- (wehi·penke·- [Rih+; IC], |wīhpēnkē-|; Gr. 5.102i) AI 'sleep with someone' (with ki·mí·i P: 'secretly sleep with someone' = 'commit adultery'): káči ɔwiákski wi·penké·han 'do not sleep with others just any way (you sg.)' (1842:12.4); énta- ki·mí·i -wi·pénke·t '(when) committing adultery' (Jn 8.4); né·li- ki·mí·i -wi·penké·li·t 'while she (obv.) was committing adultery' (Jn 8.3).
- wehi·penke·-: wehi·penké·č·i·k 'fornicators' (Mt 16.4). ▸ Lexicalized participle: énta wehi·penke·t·i·ké·i P+P 'among the fornicators' (Mk 8.38).

wi·penke·ɔ́·k·an IN 'adultery' (*lit.*, 'sleeping with others'; Gr. 5.59c), 'fornication' (Mt 15.19); ki·mí·i-wi·penke·ɔ́·k·an 'unfaithfulness' (Mt 5.32); ki·mí·i-wi·penke·ɔ́·k·anink '(from) adultery' (Jn 8.41).

wi·pe·m- (|wīhpēm-|; Gr. 5.99n) TA 'sleep with': nəwi·pé·mko·k 'they are in bed with me' (Lk 11.7).
- wi·penti·- AI (recip.; Gr. 5.110r) 'sleep together': wi·péntəwak 'they sleep in the same bed' (Lk 17.34).

wi·po·m- TA 'eat with' (|wīhpōm-|; Gr. 5.99o): mái-wi·pó·mi 'come and eat with me (you sg.)' (Lk 11.37); wi·po·máč·i·k 'the ones you (sg.) are eating with' (Lk 14.10); wi·pó·ma·t 'who ate with him' (Lk 14.15); wi·po·ma·tpáni·k 'the ones who ate with him' (Jn 13.28); wi·po·má·č·i·k 'who ate with him' (Mk 6.22, 6.26), ké·t·a-wi·po·má·č·i·k '(his) guests' (*lit.*, 'ones expecting to eat with him') (Mt 22.10); wi·po·má·č·i 'those he ate with' (Lk 7.49, Lk 14.7); wi·pó·mie·kw 'you (pl.) who are eating with me' (Mk 14.18; Gr. 4.66d); wwi·po·má·ɔ 'he eats with them' (Lk 15.2); ná mɔx·ínkwi-wi·pó·mko·n 'then they (obv.) attended a great feast with him' (Mk 6.21).
- wi·punti·- AI (recip.; Gr. 5.113a) 'eat together': énta-wi·púntink 'at a feast, at the meal' (Mt 23.6, Lk 22.27).

wí·p·i·t: see ní·p·i·t.

wi·shwi 'gall' (1834b:35.5). ▸ Cf. ⟨Wīsmi⟩, ⟨Wiswi⟩ 'Gall' (Z. 81).

wi·s·a·(w)° (|wīsāw-|) 'yellow' (Gr. §5.2a).

wi·s·a·e·- II 'be yellow': wi·s·á·e· 'it is yellow' (ME); wi·s·á·e·k ahsə́n 'yellow stone' (Lk 17.29; KJV "brimstone"). ▸ Cf. ⟨Wisaweu⟩ '(it is) yellow' (B&A 162).

wi·s·a·ɔhsənhó·s·ak 'brass kettles' (Mk 7.4).

wi·s·i·- AI 'be fat': wí·s·i·t '(which is) fat' (Lk 15.23, 1834b:29.2); wi·s·i·lí·č·i (obv.) (Lk 15.27, 15.30).

wi·s·o·ke·- (|wīsōhkē-|; Gr. 5.85a) AI+O 'fatten (an animal)': wi·s·o·kénki·k 'fattened ones' (Mt 22.4; KJV "fatlings").

wi·šək° (|wīšə̱k-|; Gr. 2.74o) 'with maximum strength or effort'. ▸ Cf. wi·šíki.

wi·šəksəwá·k·an IN "zeal" (KJV), "the best physical effort" (LTD): pa·tamwe·i·k·a·ɔní·i-wi·šəksəwá·k·an 'the zeal of the temple' (Jn 2.17; KJV "the zeal of thine house").

wi·šəksi·- AI 'expend maximum effort, be forceful, work hard' — wi·šəkso·wi·- II 'be at its most powerful'.

- wi·šəksi·- (AI): wi·šə́ksi 'do your best (you sg.)' (LB; Mk 13.34); wi·šəksí·č·i·k 'violent ones, ones using force' (Mt 11.12: KJV "the violent" [i.e., the Romans]); ntə́nta-wi·šəksíhəna 'we worked hard (there)' (Mt 20.12). ▸ Cf. ⟨Wischixin⟩ 'to exert oneself, etc.' (B&A 162).
- wi·šəkso·wi·- (II): é·li-wi·šəksó·wi·k 'as it (his spiritual power) was at its most powerful' (Lk 4.14).

wi·šíki PV 'working hard at' (Gr. 2.74o, 5.27i, 5.129rr): wi·šíki-wə́li-no·t·í·k·e·t 'who works hard at watching the house' (Lk 12.42); kéhəla ke·x·ennáohki kəwi·šíki-lami·kəmɔ́·s·i 'you work hard at quite a few things' (Lk 10.41), é·li-=á· -wi·šíki-pá·tamank 'how one should work hard at praying' (Lk 18.1). ▸ Cf. ⟨Wischiki⟩ 'busily' (B&A 162).
- wi·šíki P (1834b:5.4).

wi·š·ahəla·- AI 'become frightened': wi·š·áhəle·p 'he became frightened' (Lk 1.12).

wi·š·a·s·əwá·k·an IN 'fear' (Lk 5.9, 7.16).

wi·š·a·s·i·- AI 'be afraid': wi·š·á·s·u 'he was afraid' (Jn 19.8); wi·š·á·s·o·p 'she was frightened' (Lk 1.29); wi·š·á·s·əwak 'they were afraid' (Lk 5.26, 9.34; Gr. 4.21k); wi·š·a·s·ó·p·ani·k 'they were afraid' (Mk 4.41&, Mk 10.32&); káči=tá wi·š·a·s·í·han 'don't be afraid (you sg.)' (Lk 1.13); káči wi·š·a·s·í·he·kw 'don't be afraid (you pl.)' (Lk 2.10, Mt 10.31, etc.); kéku wə́nči-wi·š·á·s·ie·kw 'why are you (pl.) afraid?' (Mt 8.26; Gr. 4.67(2)k).
- wi·š·a·shati·- AI (coll.): wénči-=č -wi·š·a·shátink 'that will cause terror' (Lk 21.11&); áhi-=č -wi·š·a·shátin 'there will be great terror' (Mt 24.21, Lk 21.25; Gr. 5.75j).

wi·t(·)° (wit-, |wīt-|) 'with' (Gr. §5.8i).

wi·thukwe·p·i·m- (|wītəhkwēpīm-|; Gr. 5.99k) TA 'sit with': wwi·thukwe·p·i·mawwá·ɔ=č 'they shall sit with them' (Mt 8.11).

wi·t·ae·m- TA 'stay with': wi·t·ae·mkóne 'if they are living with you (sg.)' (1842:11.4); sé·ki-wi·t·aé·məle·kw 'while I was living with you (pl.)' (Jn 14.25); nəwi·t·ae·má·wəna 'we will live with him' (Jn 14.23); sɔ́·ki-wi·t·ae·má·p·ani 'she stayed with her {so long}' (Lk 1.56); kəwi·t·aé·mi 'you are with me' (Lk 15.31).

wi·t·a·č·i·mo·lsi·- (wehi·t·a·č·i·mo·lsi·- [Rih+; IC]) AI 'hold council together'.
- wehi·t·a·č·i·mo·lsi·-: wehi·t·a·č·i·mó·lsi·t 'a member of the council' (Mt 27.57&); wehi·t·a·č·i·mo·lsí·č·i·k 'councillors' (Mt 27.20, 27.41). ▸ Cf. ⟨Witatschimolsin⟩ "to advise with, to hold council with" (B&A 163).

wi·t·a·henke·- AI 'help people': wi·t·a·henké·č·i·k 'helpers of the people' (Lk 22.25).

wi·t·a·he·m- TA 'help': wi·t·a·hé·mi·l 'help me (you sg.)' (Mk 9.24); nəwi·t·a·hé·ma·n 'I'll help her (sbd.)' (Lk 18.5); kkáski-wi·t·a·he·mawwá·ɔk 'you could help them' (Mk 14.7); wwi·t·a·he·má·ɔ 'he helps him' (Lk 18.8); máta=háč=ét ɔ́·k ketanət·ó·wi·t wwi·t·a·he·ma·í·ɔ 'Don't you think God also helps them' (Lk 18.7); wwi·t·a·he·má·p·ani 'he helped them' (Mk 16.20; Gr. 4.69h); tə́li-=á· awé·ni -wi·t·a·hé·ma·n 'to serve people' (Mt 20.28; KJV "to minister"). ▸ Cf. ⟨Witaheman⟩ "to assist somebody, to relieve some one" (B&A 163), ⟨witáheem⟩ "help him" (Z. 93).

wi·t·a·wso·m- (Gr. 5.99i) TA 'live with': sé·ki-wi·t·a·wsó·mat 'while you (sg.) are with him' (Mt 5.25), wi·t·a·wsó·mat 'your (sg.) neighbor' (Mk 12.31; KJV "thy neighbour"); wi·t·a·wso·má·č·i 'his neighbor' (Mk 12.33); é·li-wi·t·a·wso·mələ́·k·əp 'because I was living among you (pl.)' (Jn 16.4; Gr. 4.73g).

wi·t·e·- AI 'go along, accompany others': ni·k·á·ni=ét lí·wí·t·e·w 'he must be going on ahead with others' (Lk 2.44); wwi·t·e·li·n 'that he (obv.) go along (sbd.)' (1842:15.4).

wi·t·o·s·əmwi·m- (|wītōsəmwīm-|; Gr. 5.99l) TA 'drink with': wi·t·o·s·əmwi·má·t·e 'if he drinks with them' (Mt 24.49).

wi·to·te·nayahe·m- TA 'be a citizen with' (*lit.* 'make a town together with'; Gr. 5.70d, 5.99j): wi·to·te·nayahe·má·či·k 'his fellow townsmen' (Lk 19.14; KJV "his citizens"; Gr. 5.70d); wwi·to·te·nayahe·má·ɔ 'he treated him as a fellow citizen' (Jn 4.45).

wi·wələnčé·p·i IN 'hand-wrapping' (1834a:14).

wi·wəni·kaw- TA 'envelop'; kəwi·wəni·ká·k·o·n=č 'it shall envelop you' (Lk 1.35).

wi·wənthákami·kw (Gr. 5.33a) P 'since the world began' (Lk 11.50, Mt 23.35), 'since the beginning of the world' (Mt 13.35; KJV "from the foundation of the world").

wi·wəno·x·we·- AI+O 'travel around': kəwi·wəno·x·we·né·ɔ hák·i ɔ́·k mpí 'you (pl.) travel the circuit of land and sea' (Mt 23.15).

wi·wši·lənt-: see wši·lənt-.

wi·xkaɔ́či P 'suddenly, right away' (Lk 1.41, 2.13, Jn 4.27 [KJV "upon this"], etc.), 'unexpectedly' (Lk 12.46); ná wi·xkaɔ́či 'then at some point' (Lk 12.1; KJV "In the mean time").

wi·xko·l- TA 'take by surprise': wénči-=č nə kí·škwi·k máta -wi·xko·lkó·we·kw 'lest that day take you (pl.) by surprise' (Lk 21.34; Gr. 4.97r). ▸ Cf. Mun wí·xkwi· 'all of a sudden' (dict.).

wi·xkwehw- TA 'wrap': wwi·xkwehɔ·né·ɔ nə yá·e·k hémpəs 'they wrapped him in that piece of cloth' (Jn 19.40).

wi·xkwe·pt- TI(2) 'wrap and tie': nəwi·xkwe·ptó·ne·p 'I wrapped it up' (Lk 19.20).

wi·xkwe·ptaw- TA+O 'bind up O2 for': ná wwi·xkwe·ptáɔ·n ehalhitehɔ́·link 'then he bound up his (obv.) wounds for him' (Lk 10.34).

wi·xkwe·pti·k·e·- (|wīxkwēpətīkē-|; Gr. 5.100b) AI+O 'wrap and tie O2': wí·l čí·t·ane·k hémpəs wi·xkwe·ptí·k·e·n 'he had his head tied around with a thick cloth' (Jn 11.44; Gr. 3.14b); wi·xkwe·pti·k·énkəp wí·l 'what his head had been bound up with' (⟨-kif-⟩ Jn 20.7; Gr. 3.14e).

wi·xkwe·p·í·s·u 'he is wrapped with something tied on' (V "he is tied with something wrapped around").

wi·xkwe·x·əm- TA 'wrap up': énta-wi·xkwe·x·əmənt 'where he was wrapped up' (Lk 2.7, 2.12); é·li-wi·xkwe·x·əmə́ntəp 'as he had been wrapped up' (Jn 11.44); ɔ·phémpsink tə́nta-wi·xkwe·x·əmá·ɔl 'he wrapped him in a white cloth' (1834b:36.3).

wkº: see kkº.

wɔnkunsəwá·k·an 'her greeting' (⟨wafwnswakun⟩ Lk 1.41). ▸ Probably /wɔnk-/, but /wank-/ or /wwank-/ is also possible; see also ɔnko·mkwəs·əwá·k·an.

wɔš·i·x·ai·- (|wəwašīxayī-|; Gr. 5.71n) AI 'have a nest': wɔš·i·x·ayúwak 'they have nests' (Mt 8.20). ▸ Cf. ɔhší·x·ay 'nest' above.

wɔ·lɔhkwi·- AI 'have a hole' (|wəwālakwī-|; Gr. 5.71o): wɔ·lɔhkúwak 'they have holes' (Mt 8.20, 1834b:26.7).

wɔ·lpé·k·əm: see ɔ́·lpe·kw.

wsa·k·i·ma·yəm-: see sɔ·k·i·ma·yəm-.

wsa·k·i·ma·yəmi·-: see sɔ·k·i·ma·yəmi·-.

wsi·ka·- II 'be sunset': wsí·ka· 'the sun sets, it is sunset' (V; Gr. 2.24b, 5.10a); éhəli-wsí·ka·k 'west' (Lk 12.54, 13.29, Mt 24.27; V, OA, ME, LB); éhəli-wsí·ka·k wə́nči 'from the west' (Mt 8.11); mé·či wsi·ká·k·e 'after sunset' (Mk 1.32). ▸ Note: é·li-wsí·ka·k 'to the west' (ME) is also a possibility; éhəli-wsí·ka·kw (LTD ND) is presumably a recent form.

wsuk·wí·s·a: see nsúk·wi·s.

wša·khuk·wi·ɔni·- AI+O 'wear O2 as a coat': wša·khuk·wí·ɔno·p †kaməlí·i-mi·x·é·k·əna 'he wore a coat of camel hair' (⟨wjakvwqeunwp⟩ Mt 3.4; Gr. 2.67d). ▸ Cf. ša·khuk·wí·ɔn.

wše·t·o·nəwá·ink: see šé·t·o·n.

wšənt-: see wši·m- — wšənt-.
wši·ləm- (we·š·i·ləm-, |wəšīləm-|; Gr. §5.7f) TA 'have as father-in-law': é·li-wši·ləmá·t·əp †ke·ápas 'since he was the father-in-law of Caiaphas' (Jn 18.13; *lit.*, 'since Caiaphas had him as father-in-law').
- we·š·i·ləm-: we·š·i·ləmúk·ɔnkw 'one who has us (inc.) as parents-in-law' (⟨-ə́k·unk⟩ V "affinal kin").

wši·lənt- (wiwši·lənt- [Rih+], ɔwši·lənt- [Ra+], |wəšīlənt-|) TI-O 'get married': wši·lə́ntam 'he or she gets married' (ME); wši·lə́ntamo·p 'he got married' (Lk 20.29); tá=á· náxpəne káhta-wši·ləntamo·wí·ɔk 'they will not even want to marry' (Lk 20.35); wši·ləntamó·p·ani·k 'they married' (Lk 17.27); ké·t·a-wši·lə́ntank 'who was going to be married' (Mt 25.5, 25.6, 25.10; KJV "the bridegroom"); ké·t·a-wši·ləntamə́lí·č·i 'who (obv.) was going to be married' (Mt 25.1).
- wiwši·ləntam-: wiwši·lə́ntamən 'people marry' (Lk 20.34; Gr. 4.39y).
- ɔwši·ləntam-: ɔwši·ləntamó·p·ani·k 'they were marrying' (Mt 24.38).

wši·ləntamwe·ha·l- (ɔwši·ləntamwe·ha·l- [Ra+]) TA 'give in marriage'.
■ ɔwši·ləntamwe·ha·lti- (recip.): ɔwši·ləntamwe·ha·ltó·p·ani·k 'they gave each other in marriage' (⟨owvjeluntumwrvaltwpanek⟩ Mt 24.38; Gr. 5.82b(2)).

wši·ləntamwe·hɔ·l- (ɔwši·ləntamwe·hɔ·l- [Ra+]) TA 'give in marriage'.
■ ɔwši·ləntamwe·hɔ·lti- (recip.): ɔwši·ləntamwe·hɔ·ltó·p·ani·k 'they gave each other in marriage' (⟨ovjelintamwrvoltwpanek⟩ Lk 17.27; Gr. 5.82b(1)).

wši·m- (-o·š·i·m-) TA — wšənt- TI(1a) 'flee from' (cf. Gr. 5.12n).
■ -o·š·i·m- (TA): o·š·i·mawwá·ɔ=á· 'they would run away from him' (Jn 10.5).
■ wšənt- (TI): wšəntamo·kw 'flee from it (you pl.)' (⟨wjintamwq⟩ Mt 3.7).

wši·mwi·- AI 'flee': wší·mu 'he runs away' (Jn 10.13); wší·məwak 'they ran away' (Mk 16.8); tə́li-wší·mwi·n 'he would then run away' (Jn 10.12); ktə́li-=č máta lo·waní·i -wši·mwi·wəné·ɔ 'that you (pl.) do not flee in winter' (Mt 24.20).

wténk P 'behind' (Mk 9.35, Lk 13.30 [2x], Mt 20.8, etc.); wténk=č ahpúwak 'they shall be behind' (Mk 10.31, Mt 20.16); wténk e·p·í·č·i·k 'ones behind' (Mk 10.31); məkə́ni wténk 'last of all' (Mk 12.6, Mk 12.22); wténk wə́nči (PV; wénči with IC) 'last, after the others' (Mt 20.8, 20.12, 20.14), wténk wə́nči (P) 'after the others' (Mt 26.60); wténk úm 'he came behind' (⟨vwtcfwm⟩ Jn 18.15); wténk á·l 'get behind me (you sg.)' (Mt 16.23).

wtenka·lté·e 'in the stern of the boat' (⟨-ri⟩ s.b. ⟨-rc⟩; Mk 4.38). ▶ For analysis, see Goddard (2019: 101).

wté·: see nté· 'my heart'.

wte·hi·- AI 'have a heart': é·li-mahči-wte·híhti·t 'because they had wicked thoughts' (1834b:22.6); wtə́li-máhči-wte·hí·li·n 'that they (obv.) had bad hearts' (1834b:22.3).

wte·kaw- (-o·t·e·kaw-, we·t·e·kaw-) TA 'come after, follow': wté·kai·l 'follow me (you sg.)' (Lk 5.27); wté·kai·kw 'follow me (you pl.)' (Mt 4.18-19&); tɔ́ləmi-wte·kaɔ́·ɔ 'he began to follow him' (Mk 14.51).
- -o·t·e·kaw-: o·t·e·kaɔwwá·p·ani 'they followed him' (Jn 1.37); no·t·é·ka·kw 'he comes after me' (Jn 1.30; Gr. 2.22a); o·t·e·kaɔ́·ɔ 'he followed behind him' (Mt 27.32&, Lk 23.27); ko·t·e·kó·lən 'I'm going to follow you (sg.) (sbd.)' (Lk 9.57; Gr. 4.52c).
- we·t·e·kaw-: we·t·e·kaɔ·tpáni·k 'ones who followed him (obv.)' (Mt 4.25, Mk 2.15; Gr. 4.76k); we·t·é·kai·t 'the one who comes after me' (Jn 1.15, Lk 3.16, Jn 1.27).

wtək·iahwi·-* (-o·tkihhwi·-) AI+O 'carry O2 on shoulder': o·tkíhhwi·n(?) 'he carried it on his shoulder' (Jn 19.17, Mt 27.32&); o·tkihhwí·na(?) 'he puts it (obv.) on his shoulders' (Lk

15.5). ▸ An unprefixed shape wtək·iahwi·-* is likely, given ntək·iáhwi·n 'I carry it on my shoulder' (ME), which points to a variant tək·iáhwi·- (with tə- for wtə-). [ME also accepted apparent ntək·íhwi·n for this, which suggests that B's forms could have had o·tkihwi·-.] The original underlying form would have been |wətəkəy-ahwī-|, with |wətəkəy-| 'shoulder' (cf. ntək·i 'my shoulder', wtək·ia 'his shoulders' [OA]; Gr. 2.31f).

wtən- (-o·t·ən-) TI(1b) 'pull': tó·lai-wtənəməné·ɔ 'they were unable to pull it up' (Jn 21.6).
- -o·t·ən-: o·t·ənəmən nə́ anshí·k·an 'he pulled on the net' (Jn 21.11).

wtó·lhay: see ntó·lhay.

wto·t·e·nai·-* (we·t·o·t·e·nai·-, |wətōtēnayī-|; Gr. 5.71m) AI 'have a town': we·t·o·t·e·naí·č·i·k 'townspeople' (Jn 4.30, Mk 1.33, Lk 7.12, etc.); we·t·o·t·e·naí·li·t 'the people (obv.) of the towns' (Mt 11.20).

wto·x·əm-* (-o·t·o·x·əm-, we·t·o·x·əm-, |wətōxəm-|; Gr. 4.64l, 5.65e, 5.72c) TA 'have as father': no·t·ó·x·əma 'he is my father' (Jn 5.18); no·t·o·x·əmá·wəna 'we have him as our father' (Mt 3.9).
- we·t·o·x·əm-: we·t·ó·x·əmənt 'father' (*lit.*, 'one had as a father') (Jn 3.35, 4.23, [2x], etc.); we·t·o·x·əmə́lan 'Father of mine (voc.)' (Mk 14.36); we·t·o·x·əmə́lenk 'you who are our father' (Mt 6.9, Lk 11.2; Gr. 4.66b). ▸ Lexicalized participle: we·t·o·x·əmánči 'father (obv.)' (Jn 4.23, 6.46 [2x]); we·t·o·x·əmántink 'father (loc.)' (Jn 14.28, Jn 15.26, etc.).

wto·x·i·- (-o·t·o·x·i·-, we·t·o·x·i·-, |wətōxī-|; also written with /x·w/; Gr. 4.64f) AI 'have a father', AI+O 'have O2 as father': wtó·x·u 'he has a father' (V; Gr. 5.71j); kó· wto·x·í·i 'he has no father' (ME; Gr. 2.41d); ke·tanət·ó·wi·t=á· wto·x·ié·k·we 'if God is your (pl.) father' (Jn 8.42); ktəli-wto·x·wi·né·ɔ 'that you (pl.) are their offspring' (⟨ktuli vwtwxwenro⟩ Mt 23.31); təli- .. -wtó·x·wi·n 'that he has him as father' (⟨tcli .. toxwen⟩ 1834b:42.3).
- -o·t·o·x·i·-: kwə́t·i no·t·o·x·íhəna 'we have one father' (Jn 8.41, 1842:15.2).
- we·t·o·x·i·-: we·t·ó·x·ink 'father' (*lit.*, 'one had as father') (Jn 5.20, Mt 10.21, etc.); we·t·o·x·ínki (obv.) (Jn 14.9, 14.26).
▸ Lexicalized participle: we·t·o·x·ínkink 'the father (loc.)' (Jn 14.6).

wum- ~ um- (win-, mm-, -o·m-, we·m- [~ wen-], |wəm-|) AI 'come from {smwh}': e·li·khátink wúm 'he was coming from the country' (⟨owm⟩ Mt 27.32&); ntúwi wúm 'he came from Dewey' (OA); ɔ́hələmi wténk úm 'he kept far behind' (⟨vwtcfwm⟩ Jn 18.15); tá=héč úm? 'Where did he come from? Where has he been?' (LB).
- win-: é·li- wi·khɔkamí·k·e·k -wínkəp 'for she came from the ends of the earth' (Mt 12.42).
- mm- (Gr. 2.67): énta-mhalamá·ɔhtink mmó·k 'they come from the market' (Mk 7.4; Gr. 4.20), é·li- .. íka -mmá 'for I came from him' (Jn 8.42); təli- nčí·sas †nčo·tí·yunk -mmə́n 'that Jesus came from Judaea' (Jn 4.47; Gr. 2.67b).
- -o·m-: nó·mən 'I came from (there)' (1834a:12); ɔ·s·áhkame nó·mhəmp 'I came from heaven' (Jn 6.38; Gr. 2.53c); kó·mən 'you came from (there)' (1834a:12).
- we·m- (~ wen-): wé·ma 'where I came from' (Mt 12.44, Jn 8.14 [2x]); íka we·má·ne 'when I came from there' (Jn 9.11); naɔč·í·i yú we·mánkwe 'when we were on our way here' (Mk 9.33; KJV "by the way"); wénk 'where he came from' (Jn 9.30); íka wénke énta-xé·link 'when he came from the crowd' (Mk 7.17); nə́ni wénkəp 'who came from there' (Jn 3.13; Gr. 4.75j), ⟨Wengup⟩ 'whence he came' (B&A 154); wténk wénki·k '(those) coming behind' (Mt 21.9; KJV "that followed").

wwahkwəs·i·- (we·ɔhkwəs·i·-, |wəwāhəkwəsī-|) AI — wwahkɔt·- (wwáhkɔ, we·ɔhkɔt·-, |wəwāhəkwat-|) II 'be known' (Gr. 5.107g).

- wwahkwəs·i·- (AI): wwahkwə́s·u 'he is known' (Mt 12.33); wwahkwə́s·i·l 'make yourself known (you sg.)' (Jn 7.4); wə́nči-=č -wwahkwə́s·i·t 'by which he will be known' (Mt 24.30).
- we·ɔhkwəs·i·-: we·ɔhkwə́s·i·t '(who was) well-known' (Mt 27.16).
- wwahkɔt·- (II): ɔ́·k=č wé·mi kéku wwáhkɔt 'and everything shall be known' (Lk 12.2); wə́li-=č -wwáhkɔt 'it shall be properly known' (Mt 10.26); takó· wwahkɔt·ó·wi 'it is not known' (Lk 17.18); wénči-=á· -wwáhkɔ 'so that it would be known' (1842:9.7).
- we·ɔhkɔt·-: máta we·ɔhkɔ́t·o·kw 'what is unknown' (Lk 12.2).

wwa·h- (-o·wa·h-, we·ɔ·h-, |wəwāh-|) TA — wwa·t- (-o·wa·t-, we·ɔ·t-, |wəwāht-|) TI(2) 'know' (Gr. 5.12a).
- wwa·h- (TA): é·li-wə́li-wwá·ha·t 'as he well knew about them' (Jn 2.25); é·li- tá=á· -wwa·háhti·t 'because they will not know him' (Jn 14.17); mé·či nkíši-wwá·ha 'I have now come to know him' (Lk 23.14; KJV "having examined him"); tá=háč kúnči-wwá·hi·n 'how do you know me?' (Jn 1.48; Gr. 2.65h, 5.128x).
- -o·wa·h-: no·wa·há·ɔk 'I know them (anim.)' (Jn 13.18; Gr. 3.6h); ko·wa·háwwa 'you (pl.) know him' (Jn 14.17; Gr. 4.24j); ko·wahəlúhəmɔ 'I know (about you, pl.) that (you) ..' (Jn 5.42); ko·wahəlúhəna 'we know you' (Mk 1.24; Gr. 2.43d); máta no·wa·há·i lə́nu 'I know no man' (Lk 1.34; Gr. 4.83a, 6.6g), takó· no·wa·há·i 'I don't know him' (Jn 8.55, 9.25, etc.; Gr. 2.12a); máta o·wa·ha·í·ɔl 'he did not know him' (Jn 5.13; Gr. 4.83l); máta no·wa·ha·í·wəna 'we do not know him' (Jn 9.21; Gr. 2.30c); yú entala·wsí·č·i·k máta ko·wahko·wí·ɔk 'mankind does not know you (sg.)' (Jn 17.25; Gr. 4.85f); máta o·wahko·wí·ɔ 'they (obv.) did not know about him' (Jn 7.10; Gr. 4.85i); takó· ko·wahəlo·húmɔ 'I don't know you (pl.)' (Lk 13.25, 13.27; Gr. 4.89n).
- we·ɔ·h-: we·ɔ́·ha·t 'who knew them' (Lk 10.25; Gr. 4.64h); awé·n máta we·ɔ·há·e·kw 'someone you (pl.) do not know' (Jn 1.26, 7.28; Gr. 4.97e); we·ɔhkukpáni 'his acquaintances (obv.)' (Lk 2.44).
- wwa·t- (TI): é·li- máta -wwa·tó·wan 'because you (sg.) do not know it' (Lk 19.44, 19.28; Gr. 4.99j); káči awé·n wwa·tó·hi·č 'don't let anyone know about it' (Mt 9.30; Gr. 4.112i); é·li-wwá·ta·kw 'as he knew it' (Jn 6.6, 18.4); é·li- máta -wwá·ta·kw 'because he does not know it' (1834b:11.5); kɔ́t·a-wwa·tó·li·n e·lsíhti·t 'he (obv.) wanted to know what they had done' (Mt 25.19; Gr. 4.39o); tá=háč núnči-wwa·tó·ne·n 'how do we know it?' (Jn 14.5; Gr. 2.65g).
- -o·wa·t-: takó· téxi kéku ko·wa·to·húmɔ 'you (pl.) know nothing at all' (Jn 11.49; Gr. 4.91j); no·wá·to·n 'I know it' (Jn 4.25, 8.37, 9.25, etc.; Gr. 2.19a, 2.65c, 4.50c); máta o·wa·tó·wən 'he did not know it' (Jn 2.9, 12.35; Gr. 4.93f); o·wa·tó·ne·p 'he knew it' (Mk 2.8&; Gr. 4.70f); no·wa·tó·ne·n 'we (exc.) know it' (Jn 4.42, 6.69, etc.; Gr. 4.39s); takó· no·wa·tó·wəne·n 'we (exc.) do not know it' Jn 20.2; Gr. 4.93j); takó· ko·wa·tó·wəne·n 'we (inc.) don't know it' (Jn 16.18; Gr. 4.93k); máta o·wa·to·wəné·ɔ 'they do not know it' (Mt 24.39; Gr. 4.93o).
- we·ɔ·t-: máta háši awé·n we·ɔ́·ta·kw 'what no one has ever known' (Mt 13.35); we·ɔ·tá·k·we 'when he knew that' (Mt 2.16, Jn 4.1, Mt 12.15, etc.; Gr. 2.46e); máta we·ɔ·tó·we·kw 'what you (pl.) do not know about' (Jn 4.32; Gr. 4.99n); né·k máta we·ɔ·ta·kwpáni·k 'those that did not know about it' (Mt 25.3, 25.8).

wwa·t- TI(2): see wwa·h- — wwa·t-.

wwa·taw- TA+O 'know O2 about': wə́nči-=č -káski-wwa·taíe·kw 'so that you (pl.) will be able to know about me (that ..)' (Jn 10.38).

wwa·ta·s·i·-* (we·ɔ·ta·s·i·-; cf. Gr. 5.106) II 'be known': we·ɔ·ta·s·í·k·e 'after it was known' (Mk 1.45).

wwa·təl- (-o·wa·təl-, |wəwāhtəl-|; Gr. 5.87b) TA(+O) 'cause to know O2, let know O2, teach about O2': péči-wwa·təli·mɔ́·e 'come and let me know (you pl.)' (Mt 2.8; Gr. 4.116j); éntxi- nehəlá·ləwe·t -wwa·təlúk·ɔnkw 'everything the Lord made known to us' (Lk 2.15); é·li- nčá·n -péči-mái-wwa·təluk·wé·k·əp šaxahka·wsəwá·k·an 'for John came to teach you (pl.) about righteousness' (Mt 21.32; Gr. 4.73f); kəni·k·a·ní·i-wwa·tələləné·ɔ 'I let you (pl.) know ahead of time' (Lk 12.5).
  • -o·wa·təl-: o·wá·təla·n 'he let him know it' (Lk 22.4); ɔ́·k=xán ko·wa·tələk·e·né·ɔ 'see, you (pl.) have also been allowed to know it' (Mt 13.11).
wwa·thike·- (-o·wa·thike·-) AI+O 'make O2 known': ntɔ́li-=č -wwa·thíke·n wəla·məwe·ɔ́·k·an 'to make known the truth' (*lit.*, 'that I will make known') (Jn 18.37).
  • -o·wa·thike·-: ki·ló·wa=č ko·wa·thike·né·ɔ '*You* (pl.) shall bear witness to it' (Lk 24.48); o·wa·thike·né·ɔ 'they made it known' (Mk 7.36).
wwa·t- (TI(1a)) TI-O 'have sense': máta wwa·t·amó·u 'he's got no sense' (ME); takó· wwa·t·amó·wi 'he was unaware of himself' (Lk 9.33; KJV "not knowing"; Gr. 4.91d).
wwa·t·amwe·ɔ́·k·an (-o·wa·t·amwe·ɔ́·k·an-; Gr. 5.59k) IN 'wisdom': o·wa·t·amwe·ɔ́·k·an 'his wisdom' (Lk 11.49); wə́nči məsəč·é·i ko·wa·t·amwe·ɔ́·k·anink 'with all your mind' (Mk 12.30); wə́nči məsəč·é·i o·wa·t·amwe·ɔ́·k·anink 'with all his mind' (Mk 12.33; KJV "with all the understanding"). ▶ Note: derived from an unattested wwa·t·ama·-* AI; cf. ⟨wowoatam moágan⟩ 'wisdom' (Z. 233), from wwá·t·am TI-O.
wwi·k·i·- (we·i·k·i·- [IC], |wəwīkī-|; Gr. 5.71r) AI 'have a house': wwí·k·u 'he has a house' (ME); we·i·k·i·t 'house-owner' (Lk 12.39, 13.25, 14.21, 14.23, etc.), 'who has a house' (Mt 24.43); we·i·k·í·č·i·k 'house-owners' (Mt 10.25); we·i·k·i·lí·č·i (obv.) (Mt 10.25, Lk 10.35, Mt 23.21). ▶ Cf. wi·k·i·-.
wwi·mahti·- (we·i·mahti·-, |wəwīmatī-|; Gr. 571g) AI+O '(male to) have O2 as a brother'.
  • we·i·mahti·-: we·i·mahtí·t·əp 'one who had been his (obv.) brother' (Mt 22.24&); we·i·mahtí·č·i·k 'his (obv.) brothers' (1842:13.6).
  ▪ wwi·mahtənti·- (-o·wi·mahtənti·-, we·i·mahtənti·-, |wəwīmatəntī-|; Gr. 5.72g) AI (reciprocal) 'be brothers (to each other)': wénči-wwi·mahtə́ntiankw 'which makes us brothers' (1834b:47.6).
  • -o·wi·mahtənti·-: ko·wi·mahtəntíhəmɔ 'you (pl.) are brothers' (⟨-vmwv⟩ Mt 23.8).
  • we·i·mahtənti·-: we·i·mahtəntí·č·i·k 'brothers' (Mt 4.21; Gr. 4.64s); we·i·mahtənti·tpáni·k 'who were brothers' (Mt 22.25).
wwi·t·i·s·i·- (-o·wi·t·i·s·i·-, |wəwītīsī-|; Gr. 5.71f) AI(+O) 'have (O2) as a friend (both being male)': é·li-wwi·t·í·s·i·t 'because he is his friend' (Lk 11.8); tá·msc-á· ki·ló·wa awé·n wwi·t·i·s·í·t·e 'if one of you has a friend' (Lk 11.5).
  • -o·wi·t·i·s·i·-: no·wi·t·í·s·i 'I have a friend' (V); tá=á· ko·wi·t·i·s·í·wən 'you will not be his friend (*lit.*, have him as friend)' (Jn 19.12).
  ▶ Cf. ní·t·i·s.

X

=x (Gr. 5.24p) P 'in fact' (Jn 1.25); nə́=ke=x 'well, in fact it was ..' (Jn 11.13); é·li-=x 'It's because ..' (1834b:12.3, 1842:23.6).

xahe·l-: see xe·l-.

xahe·lá·pxki P 'many hundreds' (Mt 26.53).

xahe·lennáɔhki: see xe·lennáɔhki.

xahé·li: see xé·li.

xahinkɔ·m- TA 'fix eyes on': tɔ́hi-xahinkɔ·mawwá·ɔ 'they had their eyes fixed firmly on him' (Lk 4.20).

xale·t·ia·- (me·x·ale·t·ia·-, |(ma)xalētəyā-|; Gr. 5.118a) AI 'be greedy': xalé·t·ie· 'he is greedy' (WT; Gr. 5.118a) ~ xəlé·t·ie· (LB; Gr. 5.119a).
- me·x·ale·t·ia·-: me·x·alé·t·ia·t 'glutton' (⟨mrxulrteat⟩ Lk 7.34).
♦ The pronunciation with /əl/ used by women is presumably a euphemism (avoiding the objurgative infix /-ale·-/, *lit.* 'penis').

xam- (-t-ax·am-, e·x·am- [IC], ihxam- [Rih+], ehxam- [Rih+; IC], |axam-|) TA 'feed', TA+O 'feed O2 to, give O2 to to eat': xám 'feed them (you sg.)' (Jn 21.15, 21.16, 21.17); xámo· 'feed them (you pl.)' (Mt 14.16, 1842:16.1); xáma·n mwe·k·ané·ɔk 'to feed it to dogs (sbd.)' (Mt 15.26); xamá·t·e 'if he feeds them' (Lk 17.7 [for obviative on further obviative]); nkwí·la- kéku -xáma 'I have nothing to feed him' (Lk 11.6); énta-xámənt 'manger' (Lk 2.16), short for: énta- nehənaɔnké·s·ak -xámənt 'manger' (*lit.,* 'where horses were fed') (Lk 2.7, 2.12; Gr. 4.67(3)s).
- -t-ax·am-: tɔx·amá·ɔ 'he feeds them' (Mt 6.26); ktax·amíhəmɔ·p 'you fed me' (Mt 25.35; Gr. 4.69y); takó· ktax·ami·húmɔ·p 'you (pl.) did not feed me' (Mt 25.42).
- e·x·am-: tákta kéku e·x·amúk·we·kw 'whatever they give you (to eat and drink)' (Lk 10.7).
- ihxam-: táli-=á· -ihxáma·n kwəškwə́š·a 'that he have the job of feeding hogs' (⟨ixaman⟩ Lk 15.15); tihxamá·ɔ 'he (always) feeds them' (⟨texamao⟩ Lk 12.24).
- ehxam-: ehxáma·t 'what he was feeding to them' (Lk 15.16).

=xán (=xánne·) P 'however, although, but' (Gr. 5.24q) (Jn 1.8, 2.10, 5.6, 5.30, etc.).
- =xánne· (Jn 12.6, 1834a:2).

-xans-: see naxáns.

xántki-: see kxántki.

xaskwča·- (me·x·askwča·-) AI 'be big-bellied': me·x·askwča·-: /me·x·áskwča·t/ ⟨Mechasktschat⟩ 'thick bellied' (B&A 77); me·x·askwčá·č·i·k '(those) that are big with child' (Mt 24.19).
▸ Cf. Mun xwáskwče·w 'have a big belly, be pregnant' (dict.).

xáskwi·m (Gr. 3.5n, 5.9k) IN 'corn' (1834a:14).

xáx·a·kw (Gr. 3.1g) AN 'sycamore tree' (Lk 17.6); xax·á·kunk lí 'to a sycamore tree' (Lk 19.4).

xa·kwi·x·ən- II 'be a flood': xa·kwí·x·ən 'there was a flood' (Mt 7.25&), áhi-xínkwi-xa·kwí·x·ən 'there was a very great flood' (1834b:18.8).

xá·š P 'eight' (Lk 1.59, 2.21, 2.37, Jn 4.10, etc.); télən ɔ́·k xá·š 'eighteen' (Lk 13.4, 13.11, 13.16); xá·š txá·pxki '800' (Lk 16.6).

xa·whita·kwsi·- AI 'shout' (Gr. 5.109d): é·li- .. -xa·whita·kwsíhti·t 'that they were shouting' (Mt 21.15; KJV "crying"); táli- šúkw -wə́nči- ahaləwí·i -xa·whita·kwsí·li·n 'that they (obv.) only shouted all the more because of it' (Mt 27.24); ná .. tɔ́ləmi-xa·whita·kwsi·né·ɔ 'then they began shouting' (Mk 15.8; KJV "crying aloud").

xe·l- (me·x·e·l-, |(ma)xēl-|; ~ xahe·l-; Gr. 5.31j.3) AI — xe·lət- II 'be many' (Gr. 5.11k).

▪ xe·l- (AI): xé·lo·k 'there were many' (Lk 6.17, Mk 2.15), áhi-xé·lo·k 'there were a great many' (Mk 3.8); xe·ló·p·ani·k 'they were many' (Lk 1.21, 3.21, 5.29); é·li-xé·lenk 'for there are many of us (exc.)' (Mk 5.9; KJV "for we are many"); xe·lən 'people are many' (Gr. 4.20): sɔ́·mi xé·lən 'the crowd was too great' (Jn 5.13); énta-xé·link 'where the crowd was' (Mk 7.33), 'in a large crowd' (Jn 6.9).
• me·x·e·l-: me·x·é·lki·k 'the crowd, the multitudes' (Lk 3.10, 5.1, Mk 3.20, etc.); me·x·e·ləlí·č·i (obv.) (Mt 5.1, 15.10, 15.30, etc.).
• xahe·l-: xáhe·l kó·n 'there was a lot of snow' (V); xahé·lo·k 'there were many (of them)' (Mt 12.15); xahé·lən 'the crowd' (*lit.*, 'that there are many people') (Mk 5.31; Gr. 4.20).
▪ xe·lət- (~ xe·lt-): é·li xé·lət nɔ́ táli mpí 'as there was much water there' (Jn 3.23); é·li-=č -áhi-xé·ltək mahta·wsəwá·k·an 'because there will be much sinfulness' (Mt 24.12); xe·lták·e 'if they (inan.) are many' (Lk 12.15).
▪ xe·lti·- AI (dim.) 'be fairly many': ləná·p·e xé·ltu 'the Delaware was fairly numerous' (1834a:19.17).
xe·lami·mənse·- AI 'have many children': xe·lami·mənsé·ɔk 'they had many children' (1834b:17.8).
xe·la·pto·ne·- AI 'speak many words': káči nó·čkwe xe·la·pto·né·han 'don't pointlessly speak with many words (you sg.)' (Mt 6.7).
xe·lennáɔhki (~ xahe·lennáɔhki; Gr. 5.31j.3) P 'many kinds, etc.'.
• xe·lennáɔhki: 'many kinds' (Lk 3.18, Mt 7.22, Mk 7.4, etc.), 'many things' (Mt 13.3, Jn 8.26, Mk 9.12, etc.), 'various things' (Mk 6.20).
• xahe·lennáɔhki: xahe·lennáɔhki .. kéku 'many (different) things' (Mt 16.21).
xe·lháke AN (representative singular) 'many tribes'; xe·lháke nihəláči mɔnní·to·n 'many tribes made their own ..' (1834b:19.8, 1842:10.2). ▸ Cf. ni·tháke 'my fellow tribesmen'.
xé·li (~ xahé·li, məmxé·li, |(ma)xēl-|; Gr. 5.25l, 5.63g) P 'many, much' (Lk 1.10, 2.13, Mk 3.10, etc.; 110x); xé·li awé·n 'many people' (Lk 1.14, 2.35, 3.18, etc.), xé·li awé·ni (obv.) (Lk 2.34); xé·li awé·ni·k 'a lot of people' (OA).
♦ (verbless predicate): xé·li nɔ́ wɔ́ntahkwi e·á·č·i·k 'many are the ones that go that way' (Mt 7.13); xé·li sak·we·ləntaməwá·k·an 'there is much suffering' (Mt 16.24); also Mt 4.25, 20.16, 22.14, Lk 6.17.
▸ Cf. ⟨Macheli⟩ 'much, many' (B&A 68).
• xahé·li P 'many' (Lk 5.6, Mt 20.29, 21.9, Lk 23.27; 4x).
• məmxé·li P 'great numbers' (1834a:19.19).
xe·ló·k·wəni (for the final, cf. Gr. 5.31s) P 'for many days' (OA; Jn 2.12).
xe·lto·nhe·- AI 'speak a lot': wɔ́nči-xe·ltó·nhe·t 'why he speaks a lot' (Mt 6.7).
xé·s (xé·s·-, -t-ax·e·s·-; Gr. 3.4x, 5.5a, 5.14d) AN 'skin'; xé·s·ak 'pelts, hides' (V); xé·s·a 'skins (obv.)' (1834a:19.12).
• -t-ax·e·s·-: tɔx·e·s·əwá·ɔ 'their skins' (1834a:19.14).
xink(w)- ~ -max·ink(w)- (|(ma)xīnkw-|) 'big' (Gr. 5.7c).
xinkɔehɔ·s·əwá·k·an IN 'great deeds' (Lk 19.37; with wé·mi 'all').
xinkɔhkəni·m- (~ maxinkɔhkəni·m-, -max·inkɔhkəni·m-, |(ma)xīnkwakənīm-|; Gr. 2.68i, 5.7c) TA 'praise, glorify, worship': xinkɔhkə́ni·m kkwí·s 'glorify your son (you sg.)' (Jn 17.1); xinkɔhkəní·mi·l 'glorify me (you sg.)' (Jn 17.5); nəmái-xinkɔhkəni·má·wəna 'we came to worship him' (Mt 2.2).
• maxinkɔhkəni·m-: wénči-=č .. -maxinkɔhkəní·mak 'so that I can worship him' (Mt 2.8).

• -maxˑinkɔhkəniˑm-: kəmaxˑinkɔhkəníˑma=č 'you shall worship him' (Mt 4.10); mɔxˑinkɔhkəniˑmáˑɔl 'he praised him' (Lk 1.64); xinkɔhkəniˑmáˑɔ 'he praised him' (⟨xifoxkunemao⟩ Mt 27.54&), for expected mɔxˑinkɔhkəniˑmáˑɔ; mɔxˑinkɔhkəniˑmaˑnéˑɔ 'they praised him (sbd.)' (Mt 14.33, 15.31).

xinkɔhkəniˑmhaˑt- (-maxˑinkɔhkəniˑmhaˑt-, |(ma)xīnkwakənīmahāt-|; Gr. 5.86a) TI(1a) 'praise': xinkɔhkəniˑmháˑtˑa 'glorify it!' (Jn 12.28); ɔ́ˑk=č ntánči-xinkɔhkəniˑmháˑtˑamən 'and I shall glorify it over again' (Jn 12.28).

• -maxˑinkɔhkəniˑmhaˑt-: nəmaxˑinkɔhkəniˑmhaˑtˑaméneˑp 'I have glorified it' (Jn 12.28).

xinkɔhkəniˑmkɔt- II 'be praised': xinkɔhkəniˑmkɔ́tkeč 'may it be praised' (Mt 6.9, Lk 11.2; Gr. 4.114d).

xinkɔhkəniˑmkwəsˑəwáˑkˑan (-maxˑinkɔhkəniˑmkwəsˑəwaˑkˑan-) IN 'glory' (Jn 17.5, 17.22).

• -maxˑinkɔhkəniˑmkwəsˑəwaˑkˑan-: nəmaxˑinkɔhkəniˑmkwəsˑəwáˑkˑan 'my glory' (Jn 17.24).

xinkɔhkəniˑmkwəsˑəwaˑkˑani- II 'be praise': xinkɔhkəniˑmkwəsˑəwaˑkˑaníˑkˑeč 'let there be praise' (Lk 19.38; KJV "glory").

xinkɔhkəniˑmkwəsˑi- (~ maxinkɔhkᵒ, -maxˑinkɔhkəniˑmkwəsˑi-, |(ma)xīnkwakənīməkwəsī-|; Gr. 5.107i) AI 'be praised, glorified': xinkɔhkəniˑmkwə́sˑu 'he is glorified' (Jn 13.31 [2x]); méˑči xinkɔhkəniˑmkwəsˑítˑe 'after he was glorified' (Jn 12.16).

• maxinkɔhkəniˑmkwəsˑi-: maxinkɔhkəniˑmkwəsˑíˑtˑeč 'may he be praised' (Lk 1.68).

• -maxˑinkɔhkəniˑmkwəsˑi-: ná šáˑe mɔxˑinkɔhkəniˑmkwə́sˑiˑn 'then he is glorified immediately' (Jn 13.32).

xinkɔhkəniˑmkwəsˑoˑhaˑl- (-maxˑinkɔhkəniˑmkwəsˑoˑhaˑl-, |(ma)xīnkwakənīməkwəsōhāl-|; Gr. 5.81h) TA 'glorify' (*lit.*, 'cause to be talked about as great or honored'): néˑskɔ xinkɔhkəniˑmkwəsˑoˑhaˑláˑiˑp 'he had not yet been glorified' (Jn 7.39).

• -maxˑinkɔhkəniˑmkwəsˑoˑhaˑl-: nəmaxˑinkɔhkəniˑmkwəsˑoˑháˑlkoˑk 'they cause me to be glorified' (Jn 17.10).

xínkɔhsən IN 'large stone' (1834b:37.1).

xinkɔnšíˑkˑan (amankanšíˑkˑan- pl.; |(ma)xīnkw-anšīkan-| sg., |amank-anšīkan-| pl.; Gr. 5.9b) IN 'sword' (Lk 22.36, 22.49, Jn 18.10, Mt 26.52& [2x]), xinkɔˑnšíˑkˑan 'big knife' (V).

• amankanšíˑkˑan-: amankanšíˑkˑana 'swords' (Lk 22.38, Mk 14.43&, Mt 26.55-56&).

▸ Cf. xínkwi-kšíˑkˑan (Lk 21.24).

xinkɔˑkhukˑwíˑɔn (-maxˑinkɔˑkhukˑwiˑɔn-; Gr. 5.14o) IN 'great coat' (⟨xifokvwqeon⟩ Jn 19.23): máxkeˑk xinkɔˑkhukˑwíˑɔn 'a large red coat' (Mt 27.28, Jn 19.5).

• -maxˑinkɔˑkhukˑwiˑɔn-: nəmaxˑinkɔˑkhukˑwíˑɔn 'my large coat' (⟨numuxifokvwqeon⟩ Jn 19.24); kəmaxˑinkɔˑkhukˑwíˑɔn 'your greatcoat' (⟨kmuxifokvwkqeun⟩ Mt 5.40). ▸ Cf. šaˑkhukˑwíˑɔn.

xinkɔ́ˑltay IN 'large boat' (1834b:18.5, 1842:8.7).

xinkɔˑɔhtiˑ- (meˑxˑinkɔˑɔhtiˑ-) II 'be of great value': kéku meˑxˑinkɔ́ˑɔhtiˑk 'something of great value' (Mt 7.6).

xinkweˑ- (meˑxˑinkweˑ-) II 'be large': xínkweˑ 'it is big' (AD), aləwíˑi xínkweˑw 'it is more important' (1834b:7.12); éˑli-xínkweˑk 'for it is large' (Mt 7.13).

• meˑxˑinkweˑ-: aləwíˑi meˑxˑínkweˑk 'that is larger' (1834a:20.21).

xinkweˑksi- AI (?): xinkweˑksían '(that) you (sg.) —' (1834a:13).

xinkweˑləm- (-maxˑinkweˑləm-) TA 'honor, respect, glorify' (*lit.*, 'think highly of') — xinkweˑlənt- (-maxˑinkweˑlənt-) TI(1a) 'think highly of'.

▪ xinkwe·lәm- (TA): xinkwé·lәm kó·x ó·k kkáhe·s 'respect your father and your mother (you sg.)' (Mt 19.19); xinkwé·lәmo· 'respect them (you pl.)' (Mt 15.4); xinkwé·lәma· 'he is honored' (Jn 5.23); xinkwe·lәmihtí·t·e 'if they praise me' (Mt 15.8).

• -max·inkwe·lәm-: nәmax·inkwé·lәma nó·x 'I honor my father' (Jn 8.49); mɔx·inkwe·lәmawwá·ɔ 'they respect him' (Mk 12.6&); nәmax·inkwé·lәmukw 'he thinks highly of me' (Jn 8.54).

▪ xinkwe·lәnt- (TI): xinkwe·lә́ntank hɔ́k·ay 'who thinks highly of himself' (Lk 18.13); é·li tɔ́hi-xinkwe·lәntamәné·ɔ 'for they greatly revered it' (Jn 19.31).

• -max·inkwe·lәnt-: kәmax·inkwe·lә́ntam=č 'you (sg.) shall honor it' (1834b:20.14).

xinkwe·lәmukwsәwá·k·an (-max·inkwe·lәmukwsәwa·k·an-) IN 'glory, honor' (Jn 5.41, 5.44), 'fame' (Mk 15.10; Gr. 3.15b).

• -max·inkwe·lәmukwsәwa·k·an-: mɔx·inkwe·lәmukwsәwá·k·an 'his glory' (Jn 11.40, Mt 24.30, 25.31), 'their glory' (Lk 4.6; *i.e.*, of all the kingdoms, treated as anim. sg.); mɔx·inkwe·lәmukwsәwá·k·anink 'into his glory' (Lk 24.26).

xinkwe·lәmukwsi·- (me·x·inkwe·lәmukwsi·-; Gr. 5.107h) AI 'be well thought of, honored': xinkwe·lәmúkwsu=č 'he will be well thought of' (Lk 1.15, 1.32, 14.11, etc.); máta xinkwe·lәmukwsí·i 'he is not regarded highly' (Lk 4.24, Mt 13.57); énta-xinkwe·lәmukwsían 'where you are glorified' (Mk 10.37); xinkwe·lәmúkwsi·t 'one highly regarded' (Jn 4.46, 4.48, Lk 7.4, etc.); xinkwe·lәmukwsí·č·i·k 'noblemen' (Mt 20.25); xinkwe·lәmukwsi·tpána 'a nobleman (past)' (Lk 19.12); énta-xinkwe·lәmúkwsi·t 'in the place where he is glorified, in his place of honor' (Mt 25.31, Mt 27.19, Jn 19.13); é·li=á· awé·n -xinkwe·lәmúkwsi·t 'about who (*lit.*, how someone) would be regarded highly' (Mk 9.34; KJV "who should be the greatest"); tә́li=č .. -xinkwe·lәmúkwsi·n 'that he might be thought great' (Jn 11.4; KJV "glorified").

• me·x·inkwe·lәmukwsi·-: me·x·inkwe·lәmúkwsi·t 'Highly esteemed one' (as a vocative) (Lk 1.28), 'highly regarded one' (Mt. 9.23).

xinkwe·lәmuwahkәni·m- (-max·inkwe·lәmuwahkәni·m-) TA 'praise': mɔx·inkwe·lәmuwahkәni·mawwá·p·ani 'they praised him' (Lk 2.13).

xinkwe·lәnsәwá·k·an IN 'honor, glory' (Jn 5.44, Jn 7.18, Jn 8.50).

xinkwe·lәnsәwi·t- TI(2) 'make ostentatious': tɔ́nči-xinkwe·lәnsәwi·to·né·ɔ šɔ·khuk·wi·ɔnәwá·ɔ 'they make their coats more ostentatious (*lit.*, vain)' (Mt 23.5).

xinkwe·lәnsi·- AI 'think oneself great': ní·=á· nihәlá́či xinkwe·lәnsiá·ne 'if I think *myself* great' (Jn 8.54).

xinkwe·lәnta·s·i·- II 'be esteemed': xinkwe·lәnta·s·ó·p·ani 'they were greatly esteemed' (Mt 11.13).

xínkwi (~ maxínkwi, -max·ínkwi, me·x·ínkwi; Gr. 5.120j, 5.129ss) PV 'big, greatly' (Lk 2.42, Jn 2.13, 2.23, etc.); xínkwi-ɔ·x·é·e·k '(a) great light' (Mt 4.16).

• maxínkwi; 'in a major way' (Jn 18.30); maxínkwi-kí·škwi·k 'when there was a holiday (*lit.*, a great day)' (Lk 2.41).

• -max·ínkwi (Mk 12.27); tá=á· nәmax·ínkwi-lәs·í·i 'I would not be great '(Jn 8.54); ná mɔx·ínkwi-wi·pó·mko·n 'then they attended a great feast with him' (Mk 6.21).

• me·x·ínkwi 'mighty' (with lәs·i·- AI): me·x·ínkwi-lәs·i·t 'who is mighty' (Lk 1.49); me·x·ínkwi-lәs·í·li·t 'who (obv.) are mighty' (Lk 1.52); me·x·ínkwi-lәs·í·č·i·k 'those that do great things' (Lk 22.2).

▪ PN 'large, great' (Mt 5.12, 5.21, 5.35, Lk 6.42, Mt 7.13, etc.); (with a participle) xínkwi we·lé·lәmi-lәs·i·tpána 'a great worker of wonders (abs.)' (Mt 21.26).

▪ P 'great' (in a substantive or equational sentence): 'great is (etc.) ..' (Mt 9.37, Mt 15.28, Lk 10.2); nə́ni aləwí·i xínkwi 'it is the largest' (Mt 13.32).
xinkwi·k·á·ɔn IN 'Big House', the traditional tribal ceremonial structure (Gr. 5.7c); nə́ táli xinkwi·k·á·ɔnink 'in the house of worship' (Lk 1.8).
xinkwi·na·k·ɔt- (xinkwi·nakɔht-, me·x·inkwi·na·k·ɔt-) II 'appear great': tá=á· xinkwi·nakɔhtó·wi 'it will not appear to be great' (Lk 17.20); xinkwi·ná·k·ɔ kéku 'great things' (Lk 21.11&, Mt 24.23).
• me·x·inkwi·na·k·ɔt-: aləwí·i .. me·x·inkwi·ná·k·ɔ 'deeds (lit., sg.) of a greater kind' (Jn 5.20).
▶ Cf. ⟨Mechinquinaquot⟩ "it appears large, it looks great" (B&A 77).
xinkwi·t- (-max·inkwi·t-) TI(2) 'make big': mɔx·inkwi·to·né·ɔ 'they make them large' (Mt 23.5).
xinkwi·xsi·- AI 'shout in a loud voice: xinkwí·xsu 'he shouted in a loud voice' (1834b:35.5).
xí·nxke (|-īnaxkē|; Gr. 5.31p) P 'thirty' (Lk 3.23, Jn 5.5, Mt 13.8, 13.23, Jn 12.5, etc.).
xi·pi·l-* (-t-ax·i·pi·l-) TA 'treat with externally applied medicine': tɔx·i·pi·lá·ɔ pəmí ɔ́·k me·xkpé·k·a 'he treated him with oil and wine' (Lk 10.34).
▶ Cf. xi·pí·s·u 'he doctors himself' ('dresses his wound' [B&A 11]), 1s ntax·i·pí·s·i (ME); Mun wtaxihpí·si·n=č 'he will treat himself with it' (JA).
-xi·s·əməs-: see naxí·s·əməs.
xí·tkwe·- II 'be deep water': énta-xí·tkwe·k 'where it is deep' (Lk 5.4, Mk 9.42).
xkán (-o·xkan-) IN 'bone' (ME, 1834a:12); enkələk·í·i-xkána 'the bones of the dead' (Mt 23.27; Gr. 6.10c).
• -o·xkan-: no·xkanə́ma 'my bones' (WL, ME); kwə́t·i ó·xkanəm 'one bone of his' (Jn 19.36).
xkanántəp IN 'skull' (Gr. 5.9e); xkanántpink 'Skull Place' (lit., 'at the skull') (Jn 19.17, Mt 27.34).
xkáni·m IN 'seed' (Mt 13.4, Lk 8.11, Mt 13.19, etc.); mahčí·kwi-xkáni·m' bad seed' (Mt 13.25, 13.26, 13.38).
xkano·wi·- AI (II) 'be bony, have bones'.
• AI: manə́t·u takó·.. xkano·wí·i 'the spirit doesn't have bones' (Lk 24.39).
• II: xkanó·u 'it is bony' (ME; Gr. 5.68e).
xke·lí·x·ən IN 'rib' (⟨xrleuxun⟩ 1834b:16.1; OA, ME, FW, LTD).
xkəma·- AI+O 'plant': xkə́ma·p wisahki·múnšia 'he planted grapevines' (⟨xkumap⟩ Mt 21.33); xkəmá·t·e 'if he plants it' (⟨xkumatc⟩ Lk 13.19). ▶ Cf. xkə́mu 'he plants (seeds)' (FW, FF); ntáxkəmi·n 'I plant it' (ME, FW).
xkó·k (Gr. 5.14e) AN 'snake' (Mt 10.16); xkó·k·ak 'snakes' (Lk 10.19); xkó·k·al 'snake (obv.)' (Jn 3.14, Mt 7.10); xkó·k·a 'snake (obv.)' (Lk 11.11, 1842:8.1); xkó·k·ink 'snake (loc.)' (1834b:17.3, 1842:7.6).
xko·k·i·-* (-t-axko·k·i·-) AI 'be a snake': ktaxko·k·íhəmɔ 'you (pl.) are snakes' (Mt 23.33).
xkɔhka·- (-kɔxkahka·-, kwe·xkahka·-, |kwaxkakā-|; Gr. 2.68g) AI(+O) 'cross over (water)': xkɔ́hke· 'he crossed the water' (OA); mé·či xkɔhkahtí·t·e mənə́p·e·kw 'after they had crossed the sea' (Mk 5.1&).
• -kɔxkahka·-: ná kɔ́xkahka·n 'then he crossed over' (Jn 18.1).
• kwe·xkahka·-: mé·či lápi kwe·xkahká·t·e 'after he crossed again' (Mk 5.21).
xkwé· (-uxkwe·yəm-; |axkwēw-|, but |-t-əxkwēw-əm-|; Gr. 2.10e, 5.5h) AN 'woman' (Lk 1.45, 2.36, Jn 4.11, etc.); xkwé·ɔl 'a woman (obv.)' (Jn 4.27), xkwé·ɔ 'a woman' (Mt 5.28, Lk 7.48, 7.50, etc.); xkwé·ɔ 'the woman (abs.)' (Mk 12.22); xkwé·ɔk 'women' (Lk 8.2, Mt 14.21, 15.38, etc.); xkwé·yunk 'women (loc.)' (Lk 7.28, Mt 19.5; Gr. 2.32e).

• -t-uxkwe·yəm- ('sister of a man; womenfolk of a group'): ntuxkwé·yəmak 'my sisters' (Mt 12.50); wtuxkwé·yəmal 'his sisters' (Mk 10.30; Gr. 2.61g), wtuxkwé·yəma (Lk 14.26, Mk 10.29, Jn 11.1; cf. Gr. 2.60i); wtuxkwe·yəmí·na 'his sisters' (Mt 13.56; Gr. 4.12c); ntuxkwe·yəməná·nak 'our women' (Lk 24.22). ♦ Note: The first vowel of the stem is given as underlying |a| because it appears as /a/ in new formations (see same·liáxkwe), but it is |ə| in the possessed form, which has an archaic, specialized meaning.

xkwé·čəč 'girl' (AP, LB; Mk 5.39; KJV "damsel"); xkwe·čə́č·a (obv.) (Mk 5.41); xkwe·čə́č·ak 'girls' (ME, LB; 1834a:13). ♦ Note: an irregular diminutive of xkwé· 'woman' (Gr. 2.77e).

xkwe·i·- (e·xkwe·i·-, |axkwēwī-|) AI 'be a woman': wé·mi e·xkwé·ian '(of) all you who are women (representative singular)' (Lk 1.28; Gr. 4.66a).

xkwíči (Gr. 2.73q) P 'above, on top of' (Lk 11.44, Mk 14.62, Jn 19.42&, etc.); xkwíči wə́nči 'on the outside' (Lk 11.39, Mt 23.25, etc.); nə́ xkwíči 'the outside' (Lk 11.40).
  ▸ Cf. Mun wáxki·č, waxkí·či·, waxki·čí·wə 'on top'.

xkwitahsə́ne P 'on the rocks' (1834b:27.7).

xkwitahtə́ne (Gr. 5.31c.2) P 'at the top (of a hill or mountain)' (Mt 4.8).

xkwí·spe (Gr. 5.31m.1) P 'on the water' (Mk 4.68, Mt 14.26, 14.28, 14.29).

xkwi·thakamí·k·we (|waxkītahkamīkwē|; Gr. 5.31a) P 'on the earth' (Jn 1.10, 3.12, etc.).
  • xkwi·thakamí·k·i (1834a:21.36).

xkwi·t·á·k·e (Gr. 5.31e) P 'on the roof' (Mt 4.5, Mk 2.4&, Mt 10.27, etc.).

xó·ha P 'alone' (Mk 1.35, 2.7, Mt 12.4, Mk 10.44, Acts 1.7); 'except only' (Mt 12.39); šúkw †silií·i-lə́nu †né·man xó·ha 'except for a lone Syrian man .. Naaman' (Lk 4.27).
  ▪ -nax·ó·ha (|(-na)xōha|) PV 'alone': kí·=č kənax·ó·ha-ktəmá·ksi·n 'it is you alone that will be miserable' (1842:8.1).

xo·he·te·- II 'be abandoned' (of houses): wi·k·ié·k·wi=č xo·he·té·ɔ 'your houses will be abandoned' (Lk 13.35, Mt 23.38; KJV "left .. desolate").

xo·he·xka·l-* (-nax·o·he·xka·l-) TA 'leave all alone': máta we·t·ó·x·əmənt nnax·o·he·xka·lkó·wi 'the Father has not left me all alone' (Jn 8.29). ♦ Cf. na·oli·kxa·l-(?) TA 'follow after'.

xo·t·é·nay 'big town, city': nihəláči xo·t·e·nayəwá·unk táli 'in their own town' (⟨xotrnywauk⟩ 1834a:24.66). ▸ The lack of a possessive prefix is presumably not idiomatic.

xulə́níti P 'very soon' (⟨xwl°⟩ Lk 24.29; OA, Gr. 2.76m) ~ xɔlə́níti (⟨xolu°⟩ Lk 21.20; ⟨volineti⟩ 1834b:44.1). ▸ Cf. also xɔnníti V (WL); xuníti, xunníti "pretty soon" (OA). ♦ A shortened form of pexulə́níti 'soon'; see péxu.

xɔnsi·-* (we·x·ansi·- [IC], |wəxansī-|) AI(+O) 'have (O2 as) an older brother': we·x·ánsi·t '(the one who was) his (next) younger brother', lit. 'the one who had him as older brother' (Lk 20.30); we·x·ansí·t·əp 'who had been his younger sister' (Jn 11.39); pí·li we·x·ansí·t·əp 'another (one who had been his) younger brother' (Mk 12.21&). ▸ Cf. naxáns.

xúma: see naxə́m.

xumi·-* (we·x·əmi·- [IC], |wəxəmī-|) AI(+O) 'have (O2 as) a daughter-in-law': wé·x·əmink 'the (one who is had as a) daughter-in-law' (Lk 12.53). ▸ Cf. naxə́m 'my daughter-in-law'.

xuw° (|xə̀w-|) 'old' (Gr. 5.1c).

xuwa·khuk·wí·ɔn- IN 'old coat': xuwa·khuk·wí·ɔnink 'old coat (loc.)' (⟨xoakvwqeonif⟩ Mk 2.21). ▸ Cf. ša·khuk·wí·ɔn.

xuwa·kwi·- (|-āhkw|; Gr. 5.9d) AI 'be a dead (tree)': xuwa·kwi·lí·t·e 'when it (tree, obv.) is dead' (IC not marked; Lk 23.31); tə́li-xuwa·kwí·li·n 'that it (obv.) was dead' (Mk 11.20).
  ▸ Cf. xúwa·kw 'dead tree' (OA), "dry tree" (FW).

xuwe·- II 'be old': xúwe·k '(which is) old' (Lk 5.39 [3x]); xuwé·k·i 'old (pl.)' (Mt 13.52); tá=á·háši xuwé·k·i '(ones) that will never become old' (Lk 12.33).

xúwi (Gr. 5.120k) PN 'old' (Mt 5.17, 5.18, Lk 5.37, Mt 11.13, 12.5, etc.).

xuwskwe·e·- II 'be a place with old grass': énta-xuwskwé·e·k '(in) a place where there is old grass' (⟨cntu vawsqrrk⟩ 1834b:27.1; ⟨cntu vusqrak⟩ 1834b:27.8); é·li-xuwskwé·e·k 'because it was a place with old grass' (⟨rli vawsqrrk⟩ 1834b:27.1). Cf. ⟨chowasquall⟩ 'old dried grass' (Z. 61; cf. B&A 28), ⟨Mechowasquall⟩ 'old, dry grass' (B&A 78); Munsee xə̀wáskwal 'old grass, weeds'.

xwi·s·əmə́s·a: see naxí·s·əməs.

xwi·s·əməs·i·-* (we·x·i·s·əməs·i·- [IC], |wəxīsəməsī-|) AI(+O) 'have (O2 as) a younger brother or sister': we·x·i·s·əməs·í·č·i·k 'his (obv.) older brothers', *lit.* 'the ones who had him (obv.) as a younger brother' (1842:13.5, 1842:14.4). ▸ Cf. naxí·s·əməs (|-xīsəməs|; Gr. 2.62g).

y

yá·e·k IN 'cloth' (Mk 14.51); nə́ yá·e·k hémpəs 'that piece of cloth' (Jn 19.40).
▸ Note: 'yard goods, cloth; a yard (of length)' (LTD). ▸ Cf. yá·tink.

ya·k·á·ɔn (ND, LB) IN 'arbor' ("shade house" [Voegelin 1946:135]; "hut, shelter, bark house" [LTD]); ya·k·á·ɔna 'arbors' (Jn 5.2). In Oklahoma applied especially to a one-sided shelter used to provide outdoor shade.

ya·né·i P 'always' (Lk 10.40; KJV "was cumbered about much"). ▸ Cf. Mun ya·né·wi (⟨Yanewi⟩ "always" [B&A 178 < Z.]; ⟨jáneewi, jànéwi, janeewi⟩ [Zeisberger 2014: 52]), yá·ne·w (MH), yá·ne· "always, frequently, quite often" (APh).

ya·p·é·i (Gr. 5.30a) P 'on, to the shore' (Lk 5.11, Mt 13.1, 13.2, Mt 13.48, Jn 21.4); wə́nči ya·p·é·i 'from the shore' (Lk 5.3; Gr. 6.9p). ▸ Cf. ya·p·é·i· (LB), ya·p·e·í·i (ME); ⟨japèwi⟩ 'on the river side' (Z. 173).

yá·tink 'yard, yards' (of distance) (Jn 21.8).

yó·k: see wá.

yó·l (1): see wá.

yó·l (2): see yú.

yú (yó·ni, yó·lº; Gr. 3.6d, 4.16a) 'this (inan.); here'.
• yú 'this (inan.)': yú wáin 'this wine' (Jn 2.9); yú hák·i 'this earth' (Mt 6.30); yú lə́s·i·l 'do this (you sg.)' (Lk 7.8); šé· yú e·lá·t·əp 'this is what he said' (Jn 1.20; Gr. 6.10p); ná=yú wə́nči 'from then' (Lk 1.26).
• yó·ni 'this (inan.)': yó·ni pí·ske·k 'this darkness' (Jn 1.5).
• yó·lº 'these (inan.)': yó·l (Mt 3.9, Mt 4.3); yó·li skí·kɔl 'this grass (pl.)' (1834a:17).
▪ yú 'here' (Mt 4.6); yú ahpá·mi 'what's around here' (1842:15.2); ná=yú 'here' (Lk 9.33, 16.26, Mt 26.38, Lk 23.5, Jn 21.23); ná=yú tóp·i·n 'here there is one' (Mt 12.41, 12.42); ná=č yú kələmahtap·i·né·ɔ 'you (pl.) must sit here quietly' (Mt 26.36).

yúh (1) 'this (inan.); here' (⟨bv⟩ 1834b 14x, Jn 1.28, 5.7, 8.12, Mk 1.27); šé· yúh 'it is this' (Mk 12.31); nál yúh 'this is' (Mk 12.33); yúh lí. 'Move over here.' (Lk 14.9).
▸ An apparent variant of yú 'this; here'.

yúh (2) P 'well! alright' (V, OA); an utterance-initial exhortation or self-exhortation.

- yúh=tá 'Alright' (1834b 2x, Lk 2.15, 14.23, 15.18, 18.5, 23.16, 23.22, 23.24); 'Come on' (Lk 20.14&); 'You'd better' (Mt 27.64); 'Come and' (Mt 28.6; KJV "Come, ..").

yukáhke: see wá.

yúkwe P 'now' (Lk 1.48, 2.29, Mt 3.15, Jn 1.50, 4.18, etc.; Gr. 2.72e): 'Now (considering this, etc.), ..' (Lk 1.20, 4.7, 10.36); yúkwe mé·či 'now' (Lk 2.11); yúkwe péči 'until now' (Mt 11.12, 23.34); yúkwe .. sháki 'up to now' (Jn 14.9).

- Reinforcing yú, yó·ni 'this': yó·ni yúkwe 'this (just mentioned)' (Jn 11.51); yúkwe yó·ni 'this (just mentioned)' (Lk 18.9); yúkwe yó·ni 'this as follows' (Mk 1.1; Mk 4.26, Lk 9.44); yúkwe yú(h) 'this as follows' (Lk 2.12, Jn 1.28, Mk 13.9); yúkwe yó·ni 'this (here)' (Mk 1.1, Lk 22.15, Jn 9.39); yúkwe yú 'this (present)' (Jn 7.8, Mt 24.14), yúkwe yú táli 'here, in this place' (Mt 26.63).

Table of Gospel Locations

Verse	Page (2021)	Page (1837)	Chapter (1837)
Matthew			
Mt 1.18	14	8	4
Mt 1.19-25	14-16	9	4
Mt 2.1	33-34	14	9
Mt 2.2-2.13	34-37	15	9
Mt 2.13-2.20	37-39	16	9
Mt 2.15	39	16	9
Mt 2.21-2.23	40	16	9
Mt 3.2	44	18	11
Mt 3.3	45	18	11
Mt 3.4-3.9	44-46	18	11
Mt 3.9-3.10	47	19	11
Mt 3.13-3.14	50	19	12
Mt 3.14-3.17	50-51	20	12
Mt 4.1	52	20	13
Mt 4.3-4.8	52-53	20	13
Mt 4.10	54	21	13
Mt 4.11	54	21	13
Mt 4.12	102	35	23
Mt 4.14-4.16	107	37	23
Mt 4.17	108	37	23
Mt 4.18	108	37	24
Mt 4.18-19, 21	111	38	24
Mt 4.21	108	37	24
Mt 4.23	107	37	23
Mt 4.23-24	111-112	38	25
Mt 4.25	112	39	25
Mt 5.1	114	39	26
Mt 5.1	115	39	26
Mt 5.2-5.3	115	39	26
Mt 5.4-5.10	115-116	40	26
Mt 5.11-5.12	117	40	26
Mt 5.13-5.15	118-119	40	26
Mt 5.15-5.25	119-122	41	26
Mt 5.25-5.37	122-125	42	26
Mt 5.37-4.46	125-127	43	26
Mt 5.47	127-128	43	26
Mt 5.48	128	43	26
Mt 6.1-6.13	128-132	44	26
Mt 6.13-6.25	132-135	45	26
Mt 6.25-6.34	135-137	46	26

Verse	Page (2021)	Page (1837)	Chapter (1837)
Mt 6.38	138	79	45
Mt 7.1	138	46	26
Mt 7.2	138	46	26
Mt 7.6-7.13	140-142	47	26
Mt 7.13-7.20	142-143	48	26
Mt 7.21-7.24	144-145	48	26
Mt 7.24	See Lk 6.47&	——	——
Mt 7.25&	145-146	48	26
Mt 7.26	146	49	26
Mt 7.27&	146-147	49	26
Mt 7.28-7.29	147	49	26
Mt 8.1-8.4	147-1.48	49	27
Mt 8.7	150	50	28
Mt 8.11-8.13	151-152	50	28
Mt 8.16-8.17	156	52	30
Mt 8.18-8.22	157-158	52	31
Mt 8.24	See Mk 4.37&	——	——
Mt 8.25	159	52	31
Mt 8.26	159	52	31
Mt 8.26	See Mk 4.39&	——	——
Mt 8.28	160	53	32
Mt 8.28	See Mk 5.1&	——	——
Mt 8.29	162	53	32
Mt 8.32	163	54	32
Mt 8.33	See Lk 8.34&	——	——
Mt 8.34&	164	54	32
Mt 9.2	168	55	33
Mt 9.2	See Lk 5.18&	——	——
Mt 9.9	170-171	56	34
Mt 9.9&	171	56	34
Mt 9.12-14	172-173	56	34
Mt 9.15	173	56	34
Mt 9.18	175	57	35
Mt 9.19	176	57	35
Mt 9.22	178	58	35
Mt 9.23	179	58	35
Mt 9.26	180	58	35
Mt 9.27-9.30	180-181	58	36
Mt 9.31-9.34	181-182	59	36
Mt 9.35	182-183	59	37
Mt 9.36-9.38	183-184	59	37
Mt 10.1-10.2	184	59	37
Mt 10.3-10.17	184-187	60	37
Mt 10.18-10.31	188-191	61	37

Verse	Page (2021)	Page (1837)	Chapter (1837)
Mt 10.32-10.42	191-194	62	37
Mt 10.48	See Mt 20.31&	——	——
Mt 11.1	194	62	37
Mt 11.12-11.15	199-200	64	39
Mt 11.20-11.29	202-205	65	39
Mt 11.29-11.30	205	66	39
Mt 12.2-12.7	209-211	67	41
Mt 12.8	211	68	41
Mt 12.9	211	68	42
Mt 12.11-12.12	213	68	42
Mt 12.14-12.19	214-215	68	42
Mt 12.20-12.21	215	69	42
Mt 12.22-12.25	216-217	69	43
Mt 12.26-12.27	217-218	69	43
Mt 12.29	218	70	43
Mt 12.30-12.32	219-220	70	43
Mt 12.33-12.37	220-222	70	43
Mt 12.38-12.45	222-224	71	43
Mt 12.46-12.47	225	71	43
Mt 12.48-12.50	225-226	72	43
Mt 13.1-13.13	226-228	72	44
Mt 13.13-13.18	228-231	73	44
Mt 13.19-13.22	231-232	73	44
Mt 13.22-13.30	232-235	74	44
Mt 13.31-13.42	236-239	75	44
Mt 13.42-13.54	239-243	76	44
Mt 13.54-13.58	243-244	77	44
Mt 14.1-14.2	245	77	45
Mt 14.5	246	77	45
Mt 14.12	249	78	45
Mt 14.14-14.15	251	79	45
Mt 14.16	251	79	45
Mt 14.21	251	79	45
Mt 14.26	256	80	46
Mt 14.28-14.31	256-257	80	46
Mt 14.33-14.34	257-258	80	46
Mt 14.36	258	80	46
Mt 15.3-15.6	273-274	85	48
Mt 15.7-15.11	275	85	48
Mt 15.12-15.14	277-278	86	48
Mt 15.18-15.20	276-277	86	48
Mt 15.21	278	86	49
Mt 15.22-15.27	278-279	86	49
Mt 15.27-15.28	280	87	49

Table of Gospel Locations

Verse	Page (2021)	Page (1837)	Chapter (1837)
Mt 15.30-15.31	282-283	87	50
Mt 15.37-15.39	285	88	51
Mt 16.1-16.4	285-286	88	52
Mt 16.4	286	89	52
Mt 16.11-16.12	289	89	52
Mt 16.13-16.22	340-342	103	57
Mt 16.22-16.26	342-344	104	57
Mt 16.27-16.28	344-345	104	57
Mt 17.1	345	104	58
Mt 17.2-3	345-346	104	58
Mt 17.13	349	105	58
Mt 17.20-17.21	354-355	107	59
Mt 17.24-17.27	356-357	107	60
Mt 17.27	357	108	60
Mt 18.1-18.5	358-359	108	60
Mt 18.7	360-361	108	60
Mt 18.7-18.8	361	109	60
Mt 18.9	361-362	109	60
Mt 18.10-18.15	362-364	109	60
Mt 18.15-18.28	364-367	110	60
Mt 18.29-18.35	368-369	111	60
Mt 19.1	457	136	79
Mt 19.1-19.4	458	136	79
Mt 19.5-19.9	459-460	137	79
Mt 19.10-19.12	460-461	137	79
Mt 19.13	461-462	137	80
Mt 19.15	463	138	80
Mt 19.16&	463	138	81
Mt 19.17-19.18	463-464	138	81
Mt 19.18	464	138	81
Mt 19.19	465	138	81
Mt 19.19-19.20	465	138	81
Mt 19.20	See Mk 10.17&	——	——
Mt 19.21	465	138	81
Mt 19.22&	466	138	21
Mt 19.23	466	138	81
Mt 19.24-19.25	467	139	81
Mt 19.27-19.29	468-469	139	81
Mt 20.1	470	139	81
Mt 20.1-20.16	470-474	140	81
Mt 20.16	474	141	81
Mt 20.18-20.19	489	144	83
Mt 20.20	490	145	83
Mt 20.20&	490	145	83

Verse	Page (2021)	Page (1837)	Chapter (1837)
Mt 20.23	492	145	83
Mt 20.24	492	145	83
Mt 20.25-20.26	492-493	145	83
Mt 20.28	493	145	83
Mt 20.29	500	147	85
Mt 20.30	501	147	85
Mt 20.30	501	148	85
Mt 20.30&	500	147	85
Mt 20.31	See Mk 10.48&	——	——
Mt 20.31&	501	148	85
Mt 20.32&	501	148	85
Mt 20.32-34	502	148	85
Mt 21.2	See Lk 19.30&	——	——
Mt 21.4-21.5	512-513	151	87
Mt 21.6	509	150	87
Mt 21.7&	510	150	87
Mt 21.8	511	150	87
Mt 21.8&	511	150	87
Mt 21.9	511, 512	150	87
Mt 21.9&	511	151	87
Mt 21.10-12.12	516	152	88
Mt 21.13	529	155	91
Mt 21.13&	529	155	91
Mt 21.14-21.16	516-517	152	88
Mt 21.16&	527	155	91
Mt 21.17	526	154	90
Mt 21.17&	526	154	90
Mt 21.19	528	155	91
Mt 21.19	See Mk 11.13&	——	——
Mt 21.19&	527	155	91
Mt 21.20	530	155	92
Mt 21.20	530-531	156	92
Mt 21.21	531-532	156	92
Mt 21.23	See Mk 11.27&	——	——
Mt 21.24-21.26	534-536	156	93
Mt 21.26	535	157	93
Mt 21.28-21.32	536-538	157	94
Mt 21.33	539	158	95
Mt 21.34&	539	158	95
Mt 21.36	540	158	95
Mt 21.37	See Mk 12.6&	——	——
Mt 21.38	541	158	95
Mt 21.38	See Lk 20.14&	——	——
Mt 21.39&	542	158	95

Verse	Page (2021)	Page (1837)	Chapter (1837)
Mt 21.40-21.41	542	158	95
Mt 21.41&	542-543	158	95
Mt 21.42	543	158	95
Mt 21.43	544	159	95
Mt 21.45&	544-545	159	95
Mt 21.46&	545	159	95
Mt 22.1-22.10	545-548	159	96
Mt 22.10-22.14	548-549	160	96
Mt 22.15	549	160	97
Mt 22.16	550, 551	160	97
Mt 22.16&	550	160	97
Mt 22.16-22.17	551	160	97
Mt 22.18&	551-552	160	97
Mt 22.18-22.20	552	160	97
Mt 22.20-22.21	552-553	161	97
Mt 22.22	553	161	97
Mt 22.23&	553	161	98
Mt 22.24&	553-554	161	98
Mt 22.25	554	161	98
Mt 22.28	555	161	98
Mt 22.30&	556	161	98
Mt 22.32	See Lk 20.38&	——	——
Mt 22.33	557	162	98
Mt 22.34-22.35	557	162	99
Mt 22.35-22.36	558	162	99
Mt 22.40	559	162	99
Mt 22.41	560	163	99
Mt 22.41&	560	163	99
Mt 22.42	561	163	99
Mt 22.43	561	163	99
Mt 22.43	See Mk 12.36&	——	——
Mt 22.45-22.46	562	163	99
Mt 22.46&	562	163	99
Mt 23.1&	562	163	100
Mt 23.2-23.3	562-563	163	100
Mt 23.4-23.5	563	163	100
Mt 23.5	564	163	100
Mt 23.5-23.6	564	164	100
Mt 23.7-23.16	564-567	164	100
Mt 23.17-23.26	568-571	165	100
Mt 23.26-23.37	571-574	166	100
Mt 23.37-23.39	575	167	100
Mt 24.1	577	167	102
Mt 24.2	578	167	102

Verse	Page (2021)	Page (1837)	Chapter (1837)
Mt 24.3-24.5	579	168	102
Mt 24.6	580	168	102
Mt 24.7	580	168	102
Mt 24.7	See Lk 21.11&	——	——
Mt 24.8	581	168	102
Mt 24.9	582	168	102
Mt 24.9	See Lk 21.12&	——	——
Mt 24.10	581	168	102
Mt 24.10	583	169	102
Mt 24.11-24.14	584	169	102
Mt 24.15-24.16	585	169	102
Mt 24.17	585	169	102
Mt 24.19-24.21	586	169	102
Mt 24.21	586-587	170	102
Mt 24.22-24.23	587-588	170	102
Mt 24.26-24.29	589-590	170	102
Mt 24.29	590	170	102
Mt 24.30	591	170	102
Mt 24.30-24.31	591-592	171	102
Mt 24.32	592	171	102
Mt 24.36	594	171	102
Mt 24.37-24.40	595-596	171	102
Mt 24.40	596	172	102
Mt 24.43	596	172	102
Mt 24.43-24.51	597-599	172	102
Mt 25.1-25.15	600-604	173	103
Mt 25.15-25.30	604-608	174	103
Mt 25.30-25.43	608-612	175	103
Mt 25.43-25.46	612-613	176	103
Mt 26.1-5	613-614	176	103
Mt 26.6	503	148	86
Mt 26.7&	503	148	86
Mt 26.8-26.9	505	149	86
Mt 26.10	505	149	86
Mt 26.10	505-506	149	86
Mt 26.12	See Jn 12.7&	——	——
Mt 26.23	640	183	108
Mt 26.25-26.26	641	183	108
Mt 26.27	642	183	108
Mt 26.28	642	183	108
Mt 26.29-26.30	642-643	183	108
Mt 26.33	673	192	111
Mt 26.35	674	192	111
Mt 26.36	674	192	112

Table of Gospel Locations

Verse	Page (2021)	Page (1837)	Chapter (1837)
Mt 26.36-26.39	674-675	192	112
Mt 26.40	676	192	112
Mt 26.41	677	192	112
Mt 26.41-26.42	677	193	112
Mt 26.44	678	193	112
Mt 26.45	678-679	193	112
Mt 26.47	See Mk 14.43&	——	——
Mt 26.49-26.50	682	194	113
Mt 26.50	683	194	113
Mt 26.52&	684	194	113
Mt 26.53-26.54	684	194	113
Mt 26.55-56&	685	194	116
Mt 26.56	685-686	195	113
Mt 26.58	689	195	113
Mt 26.59-60	692	196	114
Mt 26.63	693	196	114
Mt 26.65	694	196	114
Mt 26.65-26.67	694	197	114
Mt 26.69-70	See Lk 22.56-57&	——	——
Mt 27.1	700	198	116
Mt 27.2	701	198	116
Mt 27.2&	701	198	116
Mt 27.3-27.5	701-702	199	117
Mt 27.6-27.10	703-704	199	117
Mt 27.11	706	200	119
Mt 27.14	708	200	119
Mt 27.15-27.16	712	201	120
Mt 27.17	713	202	120
Mt 27.19-27.21	714	202	120
Mt 27.22	715	202	120
Mt 27.24	716	202	121
Mt 27.24-27.25	716-717	203	121
Mt 27.27-27.30	717-718	203	121
Mt 27.30	718	203	121
Mt 27.31	723	204	123
Mt 27.31&	723	204	123
Mt 27.32&	724	250	123
Mt 27.34	725-726	205	123
Mt 27.36	728	206	124
Mt 27.39	729	206	124
Mt 27.40	730	206	124
Mt 27.41-27.43	730-731	206	124
Mt 27.45	See Mk 15.33&	——	——
Mt 27.47	734	207	125

Verse	Page (2021)	Page (1837)	Chapter (1837)
Mt 27.48-27.49	734-735	207	125
Mt 27.51-27.53	736	208	125
Mt 27.54&	736-737	208	125
Mt 27.55	See Lk 23.49&	——	——
Mt 27.57&	740-741	209	127
Mt 27.58	See Mk 15.45&	——	——
Mt 27.60	743	209	127
Mt 27.60	See Jn 19.42&	——	——
Mt 27.61	See Lk 23.55&	——	——
Mt 27.62-27.66	744-746	210	128
Mt 28.1	See Mk 16.2&	——	——
Mt 28.2-28.4	747-748	211	129
Mt 28.5&	250	211	129
Mt 28.6-28.7	250-251	211	129
Mt 28.8&	752	212	129
Mt 28.9-28.15	757-759	213	131
Mt 28.16	782	219	137
Mt 28.17	782	219	137
Mt 28.18	782	220	137
Mt 28.19	783	220	137
Mt 28.19&	783	220	137
Mt 28.19-28.20	783	220	137
Mark			
Mk 1.1-1.2	44	18	11
Mk 1.13	52	20	13
Mk 1.21-1.28	152-154	51	29
Mk 1.29-1.34	154-156	51	30
Mk 1.32	113	39	25
Mk 1.35-1.39	156-157	52	31
Mk 1.45	148	49	27
Mk 2.1-2.2	166-167	54	33
Mk 2.2	167	55	33
Mk 2.3	See Lk 5.18&	——	——
Mk 2.4	168	55	33
Mk 2.4&	168	55	33
Mk 2.6-2.7	169	55	33
Mk 2.8&	169	55	33
Mk 2.9-2.11	169-170	55	33
Mk 2.12&	170	55	33
Mk 2.14	171	56	34
Mk 2.15-2.16	171-172	56	34
Mk 2.19	173	56	34
Mk 2.20	173-174	56	34

Table of Gospel Locations

Verse	Page (2021)	Page (1837)	Chapter (1837)
Mk 2.21	174	56	34
Mk 2.27	211	67	41
Mk 3.7	112	39	25
Mk 3.8-3.10	112-113	39	25
Mk 3.11-3.12	113-114	39	25
Mk 3.20-3.21	215-216	69	43
Mk 3.23-3.26	217	69	43
Mk 3.29-3.30	220	70	43
Mk 4.26-4.28	235-236	74	44
Mk 4.29	236	75	44
Mk 4.36	158	52	31
Mk 4.37	158	52	31
Mk 4.37&	158	52	31
Mk 4.38	159	52	31
Mk 4.38	159	52	31
Mk 4.39	159	53	31
Mk 4.39&	159	52	31
Mk 4.41	160	53	31
Mk 4.41&	159	53	31
Mk 4.41	See Lk 8.25&	——	——
Mk 5.1&	160	53	32
Mk 5.3-5.7	160-162	53	32
Mk 5.7-5.12	162-163	53	32
Mk 5.12-5.13	163	54	32
Mk 5.13	163	54	32
Mk 5.15	164	54	32
Mk 5.15&	165	54	32
Mk 5.16	165	54	32
Mk 5.18-5.20	165-166	54	32
Mk 5.21	166	54	33
Mk 5.22-23	175	57	35
Mk 5.26	176	57	35
Mk 5.26-5.31	176-177	57	35
Mk 5.33	177	57	35
Mk 5.35-5.37	178-179	58	35
Mk 5.38-5.43	179-180	58	35
Mk 6.5-6.6	244	77	44
Mk 6.15-6.20	245-246	77	45
Mk 6.20	247	78	45
Mk 6.20-6.29	247-249	78	45
Mk 6.30-6.34	249-250	78	45
Mk 6.34	251	79	45
Mk 6.36	251	79	45
Mk 6.38	252	79	45

Verse	Page (2021)	Page (1837)	Chapter (1837)
Mk 6.40	253	79	45
Mk 6.42	253	79	45
Mk 6.45	254-255	80	46
Mk 6.47-6.48	255	80	46
Mk 6.48	256	80	46
Mk 6.49-6.50	256	80	46
Mk 6.51-6.52	257	80	46
Mk 6.54-6.55	258	80	46
Mk 7.1-7.2	272	84	48
Mk 7.3-7.5	272-273	85	48
Mk 7.13	274	85	48
Mk 7.16-7.17	275-276	85	48
Mk 7.17-7.20	276	86	48
Mk 7.24	278	86	49
Mk 7.30	280	87	49
Mk 7.31-7.36	280-282	87	50
Mk 8.1	283	87	51
Mk 8.1-8.7	283-284	88	51
Mk 8.13-8.20	286-289	89	52
Mk 8.22-8.25	289-290	89	52
Mk 8.26	290	90	52
Mk 8.38	344	104	57
Mk 9.9-9.10	347-348	105	58
Mk 9.11-9.13	348-349	105	58
Mk 9.14	349	105	59
Mk 9.15-9.17	350	106	59
Mk 9.18-9.27	350-353	106	59
Mk 9.28	354	107	59
Mk 9.30-9.32	355-356	107	60
Mk 9.33-9.35	358	108	60
Mk 9.39	360	108	60
Mk 9.41-9.42	360	108	60
Mk 9.44	361	109	60
Mk 9.48-9.50	362	109	60
Mk 10.1	458	136	79
Mk 10.10-10.12	460	137	79
Mk 10.13	See Lk 18.15&	——	——
Mk 10.14	462	137	80
Mk 10.14	462	137	80
Mk 10.16	463	138	80
Mk 10.17	See Mt 19.16&	——	——
Mk 10.17&	463	138	81
Mk 10.19	464	138	81
Mk 10.19	464	138	81

Verse	Page (2021)	Page (1837)	Chapter (1837)
Mk 10.21	465	138	81
Mk 10.23	466	138	81
Mk 10.24	466-467	139	81
Mk 10.26-10.27	467	139	81
Mk 10.27	468	139	81
Mk 10.30-10.31	469-470	139	81
Mk 10.32&	488	144	83
Mk 10.35	See Mt 20.20&	——	——
Mk 10.35-10.37	490-492	145	83
Mk 10.38-10.40	491-492	145	83
Mk 10.41	492	145	83
Mk 10.42	492	145	83
Mk 10.44	493	145	83
Mk 10.46	500	147	85
Mk 10.46	500	147	85
Mk 10.48&	501	148	85
Mk 10.49	See Mt 20.32&	——	——
Mk 10.49-10.50	502	148	85
Mk 10.52	See Lk 18.42&	——	——
Mk 11.1	508	150	87
Mk 11.1	See Lk 19.29&	——	——
Mk 11.3	508-509	150	87
Mk 11.4&	509	150	87
Mk 11.5	See Lk 19.33&	——	——
Mk 11.6	510	150	87
Mk 11.7-11.8	See Mt 21.8&	——	——
Mk 11.10	512	151	87
Mk 11.11	516	152	88
Mk 11.11	526	154	90
Mk 11.11	See Mt 27.17&	——	——
Mk 11.12	See Mt 21.16&	——	——
Mk 11.13&	527	155	91
Mk 11.14	527-528	155	91
Mk 11.14	See Mt 21.19&	——	——
Mk 11.15	528	155	91
Mk 11.15-11.16	528-529	155	91
Mk 11.17	See Mt 21.13&	——	——
Mk 11.18	529	155	91
Mk 11.18-11.19	530	155	91
Mk 11.20	530	155	92
Mk 11.21-11.23	531	156	92
Mk 11.23-11.26	532-533	156	92
Mk 11.27	533	156	93
Mk 11.27&	533	156	93

Verse	Page (2021)	Page (1837)	Chapter (1837)
Mk 11.28	533-534	156	93
Mk 11.30	534	156	93
Mk 11.33&	535-536	157	93
Mk 12.1	536	157	94
Mk 12.2	See Mt 21.34&	———	———
Mk 12.3	See Lk 20.10&	———	———
Mk 12.4&	540	158	95
Mk 12.5	540	158	95
Mk 12.6	541	158	95
Mk 12.6&	540-541	158	95
Mk 12.9	543	158	95
Mk 12.9	See Mt 21.41&	———	———
Mk 12.11	544	159	95
Mk 12.12	See Mt 21.45&	———	———
Mk 12.12	See Mt 21.46&	———	———
Mk 12.13	See Mt 22.16&	———	———
Mk 12.14	See Mt 22.16&	———	———
Mk 12.15	See Mt 22.18	———	———
Mk 12.18	See Mt 22.23	———	———
Mk 12.19	See Mt 22.24&	———	———
Mk 12.21&	554	161	98
Mk 12.22-12.23	554-555	161	98
Mk 12.24	555	161	98
Mk 12.25	See Mt 22.30&	———	———
Mk 12.26	556	161	98
Mk 12.27	557	162	98
Mk 12.28	557	162	99
Mk 12.29-12.31	558-559	162	99
Mk 12.32-12.33	559-560	162	99
Mk 12.33-12.34	560	163	99
Mk 12.34	See Mt 22.46&	———	———
Mk 12.35	561	163	99
Mk 12.35	See Mt 22.41-42&	———	———
Mk 12.36&	561	163	99
Mk 12.36-12.37	561-562	163	99
Mk 12.38	563	163	100
Mk 12.38&	563	163	100
Mk 12.41	576	167	101
Mk 12.42-12.43	576-577	167	101
Mk 12.44&	577	167	101
Mk 13.1-13.2	578	167	102
Mk 13.3-13.4	578-579	168	102
Mk 13.7	580	168	102
Mk 13.7	See Lk 21.9&	———	———

Table of Gospel Locations

Verse	Page (2021)	Page (1837)	Chapter (1837)
Mk 13.8	See Lk 21.11&	—	—
Mk 13.9	581-582	168	102
Mk 13.9	See Lk 21.13&	—	—
Mk 13.9&	581	168	102
Mk 13.11	582	168	102
Mk 13.12	583	169	102
Mk 13.15	586	169	102
Mk 13.23	588	170	102
Mk 13.27	592	171	102
Mk 13.34-13.35	597	172	102
Mk 13.35-13.37	599-600	172	102
Mk 14.3	504	148	86
Mk 14.3	See Mt 26.7&	—	—
Mk 14.5	505	149	86
Mk 14.6	505	149	86
Mk 14.7-14.8	506	149	86
Mk 14.8	See Jn 12.7&	—	—
Mk 14.9	506-507	149	86
Mk 14.12-14.13	624	179	106
Mk 14.14-14.16	625-626	179	106
Mk 14.17	638	182	108
Mk 14.18	639	183	108
Mk 14.19-14.20	640	183	108
Mk 14.21	640-641	183	108
Mk 14.23	642	183	108
Mk 14.27-14.28	672-673	192	111
Mk 14.30-14.31	673	192	111
Mk 14.36	676	192	112
Mk 14.37	676	192	112
Mk 14.40	676	193	112
Mk 14.42	679	193	112
Mk 14.43&	679-680	193	113
Mk 14.44	682	194	113
Mk 14.48-49	See Mt 26.55-56&	—	—
Mk 14.49	685	194	113
Mk 14.51-14.52	686	195	113
Mk 14.53	687	195	114
Mk 14.54	689	195	114
Mk 14.56	691	196	114
Mk 14.58-14.61	692-693	196	114
Mk 14.62	693	196	114
Mk 14.65	694-695	197	114
Mk 14.66-68	See Lk 22.56-57&	—	—
Mk 14.72	699	198	115

Verse	Page (2021)	Page (1837)	Chapter (1837)
Mk 15.3-15.4	708	200	119
Mk 15.7	712-713	201	120
Mk 15.8	713	202	120
Mk 15.9-15.10	713	202	120
Mk 15.12-15.13	715	202	120
Mk 15.14	716	202	120
Mk 15.15	717	203	121
Mk 15.20	See Mt 27.31&	———	———
Mk 15.21	See Mt 27.32&	———	———
Mk 15.28	726	205	123
Mk 15.29-15.30	729-730	206	124
Mk 15.33&	733	207	125
Mk 15.34	734	207	125
Mk 15.49	See Mt 27.54&	———	———
Mk 15.41	738	208	125
Mk 15.43	See Lk 23.52&	———	———
Mk 15.43	See Mt 27.57&	———	———
Mk 15.44	741	209	127
Mk 15.45&	741-742	209	127
Mk 15.46	742	209	127
Mk 15.47	See Lk 23.55&	———	———
Mk 16.1	746	210	129
Mk 16.2&	746-747	210	129
Mk 16.3-16.4	748	211	129
Mk 16.5	749	211	129
Mk 16.5&	750	211	129
Mk 16.6	See Mt 28.5&	———	———
Mk 16.8	748	211	129
Mk 16.8	See Mt 28.8&	———	———
Mk 16.9	754-755	212	130
Mk 16.10&	759	214	132
Mk 16.11	760	214	132
Mk 16.12	760-761	214	133
Mk 16.13	767	215	133
Mk 16.14	769	216	134
Mk 16.14	See Lk 24.36&	———	———
Mk 16.14	See Jn 20.19&	———	———
Mk 16.15	783	220	137
Mk 16.15	See Mt 28.19&	———	———
Mk 16.16-16.18	783-784	220	137
Mk 16.19&	788	221	138
Mk 16.20	789	221	138

Verse	Page (2021)	Page (1837)	Chapter (1837)
Luke			
Lk 1.5-1.13	5-7	6	2
Lk 1.13-1.25	7-11	7	2
Lk 1.26	11	7	3
Lk 1.27-1.38	11-14	8	3
Lk 1.39-1.46	16-18	9	5
Lk 1.47	18	10	5
Lk 1.47-1.63	18-21	10	6
Lk 1.63-1.79	21-24	11	6
Lk 1.79-1.80	24-25	12	6
Lk 2.1-2.13	25-27	12	7
Lk 2.13-2.21	28-29	13	7
Lk 2.22-2.25	29-30	13	8
Lk 2.26-2.39	30-33	14	8
Lk 2.41-2.52	40-43	17	10
Lk 3.1-3.2	43-44	17	11
Lk 3.2-3.3	44	18	11
Lk 3.5-3.6	45	18	11
Lk 3.10-3.18	47-49	19	11
Lk 3.19-20	101-102	35	23
Lk 3.21	50	19	12
Lk 3.23	51	20	12
Lk 4.1	51-52	20	13
Lk 4.2	52	20	13
Lk 4.5-4.7	53-54	21	13
Lk 4.13	54	21	13
Lk 4.14-4.15	102	35	23
Lk 4.16-4.27	102-106	36	23
Lk 4.27-4.32	106-107	37	23
Lk 4.41	156	51	30
Lk 5.1	108	37	24
Lk 5.3-5.4	109	37	24
Lk 5.4-5.10	109-111	38	24
Lk 5.11	111	38	24
Lk 5.15-5.16	148-149	49	27
Lk 5.17	113	39	25
Lk 5.17	167	55	33
Lk 5.18	168	55	33
Lk 5.18&	167	55	33
Lk 5.19	See Mk 2.4&	——	——
Lk 5.19	168	55	33
Lk 5.19-20	168	55	33
Lk 5.21	168-169	55	33

Verse	Page (2021)	Page (1837)	Chapter (1837)
Lk 5.22	See Mk 2.8&	——	——
Lk 5.25	See Mk 2.12&	——	——
Lk 5.25-5.26	170	55	33
Lk 5.27	See Mt 9.9&	——	——
Lk 5.27-5.29	171	56	34
Lk 5.30	172	56	34
Lk 5.33	173	56	34
Lk 5.36	174	56	34
Lk 5.36-5.37	174	56	34
Lk 5.37-5.39	174-175	57	34
Lk 6.1	209	67	41
Lk 6.6-6.9	211-213	68	42
Lk 6.10-6.11	213	68	42
Lk 6.12-6.17	114-115	39	26
Lk 6.20	115	39	26
Lk 6.22	116-117	40	26
Lk 6.24-6.26	117-118	40	26
Lk 6.32	127	43	26
Lk 6.34-6.35	128	43	26
Lk 6.37	138	46	26
Lk 6.38-6.39	138	46	26
Lk 6.39-6.42	138-140	47	26
Lk 6.45-6.46	144	48	26
Lk 6.47	145	48	26
Lk 6.47&	145	48	26
Lk 6.48	146	49	26
Lk 6.48	See Mt 7.25&	——	——
Lk 6.48	See Mt 7.25&	——	——
Lk 6.49	See Mt 7.27&	——	——
Lk 7.1-7.5	149-150	50	28
Lk 7.6-7.9	150-151	50	28
Lk 7.10	152	50	28
Lk 7.11	194	62	38
Lk 7.12-7.18	194-195	63	38
Lk 7.19-7.22	195-197	63	39
Lk 7.23-7.28	198-199	64	39
Lk 7.29-7.32	200-201	64	39
Lk 7.32-7.35	201-202	65	39
Lk 7.36-7.46	205-208	66	40
Lk 7.47-7.50	208-209	67	40
Lk 8.1-8.3	183	59	37
Lk 8.11	231	73	44
Lk 8.22	158	52	31
Lk 8.23	See Mk 4.37&	——	——

Verse	Page (2021)	Page (1837)	Chapter (1837)
Lk 8.24	See Mk 4.39&	——	——
Lk 8.25&	160	53	31
Lk 8.25	See Mk 4.41&	——	——
Lk 8.27	160	53	32
Lk 8.34&	164	54	32
Lk 8.35	164	54	32
Lk 8.35	See Mt 8.34&	——	——
Lk 8.35	See Mk 5.15&	——	——
Lk 8.37	165	54	32
Lk 8.40	166	54	33
Lk 8.42	142	57	35
Lk 8.42-8.43	176	57	35
Lk 8.46-8.47	177	57	35
Lk 8.47	178	57	35
Lk 9.29	345	104	58
Lk 9.30-9.36	346-347	105	58
Lk 9.36	348	105	58
Lk 9.37	349	105	59
Lk 9.38	350	106	59
Lk 9.42-9.43	353	106	59
Lk 9.43-45	353-354	107	59
Lk 9.49-9.50	359-360	108	60
Lk 9.51-9.56	369-371	111	61
Lk 9.57	371	112	61
Lk 9.61-9.62	371	112	61
Lk 10.1-10.11	371-374	112	62
Lk 10.12-10.13	374-375	113	62
Lk 10.15-10.23	375-377	113	62
Lk 10.24	378	114	62
Lk 10.25-10.35	378-381	114	63
Lk 10.36-10.37	381	115	63
Lk 10.38-10.42	381-383	115	64
Lk 11.1-11.4	383-384	115	65
Lk 11.5-11.13	384-386	116	65
Lk 11.20	218	69	43
Lk 11.21-11.22	218-219	70	43
Lk 11.27-11.28	224-225	71	43
Lk 11.37-11.40	386-387	116	66
Lk 11.41-11.51	387-391	117	66
Lk 11.52-11.54	391-392	118	66
Lk 12.1-12.9	392-395	118	67
Lk 12.10-12.24	395-398	119	67
Lk 12.24-12.37	398-402	120	67
Lk 12.38-12.52	402-406	121	67

Verse	Page (2021)	Page (1837)	Chapter (1837)
Lk 12.53-12.59	406-408	122	67
Lk 13.1-13.5	408-409	122	68
Lk 13.6-13.9	409-410	123	68
Lk 13.10-13.17	410-413	123	69
Lk 13.18-13.21	413-414	124	69
Lk 13.22-13.30	414-416	124	70
Lk 13.31-13.35	416-418	125	71
Lk 14.1-14.8	418-419	125	72
Lk 14.8-14.21	420-423	126	72
Lk 14.21-14.24	423-424	127	72
Lk 14.25-14.34	424-427	127	73
Lk 14.35	427	128	73
Lk 15.1-15.12	428-430	128	74
Lk 15.13-15.28	430-435	129	74
Lk 15.28-15.32	435-436	130	74
Lk 16.1-16.8	436-438	130	75
Lk 16.8-16.20	438-442	131	75
Lk 16.20-16.31	442-445	132	75
Lk 17.1-17.10	445-448	133	76
Lk 17.11-13	448	133	77
Lk 17.14-17.28	448-452	134	77
Lk 17.28-17.37	452-454	135	77
Lk 18.1-18.7	454-455	135	78
Lk 18.8-Lk 18.13	455-457	136	78
Lk 18.15&	462	137	80
Lk 18.16	462	137	80
Lk 18.17	462-463	138	80
Lk 18.18	See Mk 10.17&	—	—
Lk 18.22	465	138	81
Lk 18.23	See Mt 19.22&	—	—
Lk 18.24	466	138	81
Lk 18.27	467	139	81
Lk 18.29	469	139	81
Lk 18.31	488	144	83
Lk 18.31	See Mk 10.32&	—	—
Lk 18.32-33	489-490	144	83
Lk 18.34	490	145	83
Lk 18.35	See Mt 20.30&	—	—
Lk 18.36-37	500	147	85
Lk 18.38-18.39	501	148	85
Lk 18.40	502	148	85
Lk 18.42&	502	148	85
Lk 18.43	503	148	85
Lk 19.1	493	145	84

Verse	Page (2021)	Page (1837)	Chapter (1837)
Lk 19.2-19.17	493-497	146	84
Lk 19.18-19.27	497-500	147	84
Lk 19.29&	508	150	87
Lk 19.30	508	150	87
Lk 19.30&	508	150	87
Lk 19.32	See Mk 11.4&	——	——
Lk 19.33&	510	150	87
Lk 19.34	510	150	87
Lk 19.35	See Mt 21.7&	——	——
Lk 19.36	See Mt 21.8&	——	——
Lk 19.37	511	150	87
Lk 19.38	512	151	87
Lk 19.38	See Mt 21.9	——	——
Lk 19.39-19.44	514-515	151	88
Lk 19.44	515	152	88
Lk 19.47	529	155	91
Lk 19.48	529	155	91
Lk 19.48	530	155	91
Lk 20.1	See Mk 11.27&	——	——
Lk 20.6	535	157	93
Lk 20.7	See Mk 11.33&	——	——
Lk 20.8	See Mk 11.33&	——	——
Lk 20.9	539	158	95
Lk 20.10&	539	158	95
Lk 20.10	See Mt 21.34&	——	——
Lk 20.11	See Mk 12.4&	——	——
Lk 20.12	540	158	95
Lk 20.13	See Mk 12.6&	——	——
Lk 20.14	541	158	95
Lk 20.14&	541-542	158	95
Lk 20.15	See Mt 21.39&	——	——
Lk 20.16-20.17	543	158	95
Lk 20.17	543	158	95
Lk 20.18	543	159	95
Lk 20.19	See Mt 21.45&	——	——
Lk 20.19	See Mt 21.46&	——	——
Lk 20.20	550	160	97
Lk 20.20	See Mt 22.16&	——	——
Lk 20.21	551	160	97
Lk 20.21	See Mt 22.16&	——	——
Lk 20.22	551	160	97
Lk 20.23	See Mt 22.18&	——	——
Lk 20.26	553	161	97
Lk 20.27	See Mt 22.23&	——	——

Verse	Page (2021)	Page (1837)	Chapter (1837)
Lk 20.28	See Mt 22.24&	——	——
Lk 20.29	554	161	98
Lk 20.30	554	161	98
Lk 20.31	554	161	98
Lk 20.31	See Mk 12.21&	——	——
Lk 20.34-20.36	555-556	161	98
Lk 20.36	See Mt 22.30&	——	——
Lk 20.38	556	162	98
Lk 20.38&	556	162	98
Lk 20.39	557	162	98
Lk 20.45	See Mt 23.1&	——	——
Lk 20.46	564	164	100
Lk 20.46	See Mk 12.38&	——	——
Lk 21.1	576	167	101
Lk 21.2	576	167	101
Lk 21.4	577	167	101
Lk 21.4	See Mk 12.44&	——	——
Lk 21.5	577-578	167	102
Lk 21.6	578	167	102
Lk 21.8	579-580	168	102
Lk 21.9	580	168	102
Lk 21.9&	580	168	102
Lk 21.11&	580-581	168	102
Lk 21.12	581	168	102
Lk 21.12	See Mk 13.9&	——	——
Lk 21.12&	581	168	102
Lk 21.13&	582	168	102
Lk 21.15	582	168	102
Lk 21.15	582	169	102
Lk 21.16	583	169	102
Lk 21.18-21.19	583	169	102
Lk 21.20	584-585	169	102
Lk 21.21	585	169	102
Lk 21.22	586	169	102
Lk 21.23-21.24	587	170	102
Lk 21.25	590	170	102
Lk 21.25-21.26	590-591	170	102
Lk 21.28-21.29	592	171	102
Lk 21.30-21.33	593-594	171	102
Lk 21.34-21.35	594-595	171	102
Lk 21.36	596	172	102
Lk 21.37	530	155	91
Lk 21.38	528	155	91
Lk 22.2	614	176	103

Verse	Page (2021)	Page (1837)	Chapter (1837)
Lk 22.3	621	178	104
Lk 22.4-22.6	622-623	178	105
Lk 22.6	623	179	105
Lk 22.10	624-625	179	106
Lk 22.14-22.18	638-639	182	108
Lk 22.18	639	183	108
Lk 22.19	641	183	108
Lk 22.21	640	183	108
Lk 22.23	640	183	108
Lk 22.24-22.36	643-646	184	109
Lk 22.36-22.38	647	185	109
Lk 22.39	672	191	111
Lk 22.40	674	192	112
Lk 22.43-22.45	678	193	112
Lk 22.47	682	194	113
Lk 22.48	682-683	194	113
Lk 22.49	683	194	113
Lk 22.51	684	194	113
Lk 22.52-53	See Mt 26.55-56&	——	——
Lk 22.53	685	194	113
Lk 22.55	689	195	114
Lk 22.56-57&	695-696	197	115
Lk 22.61	699	197	115
Lk 22.63	694	197	114
Lk 22.64-22.65	695	197	114
Lk 22.66	699	198	116
Lk 22.66-22.71	700-701	198	116
Lk 23.1	701	198	116
Lk 23.2	705	200	119
Lk 23.5	709	200	119
Lk 23.5-23.12	709-711	201	119
Lk 23.13-23.16	711-712	201	120
Lk 23.18	714	202	120
Lk 23.20	715	202	120
Lk 23.22	715	202	120
Lk 23.23	716	202	120
Lk 23.24	717	203	121
Lk 23.25	717	203	121
Lk 23.26	See Mt 27.32&	——	——
Lk 23.27-23.33	724-725	205	123
Lk 23.33&	726	205	123
Lk 23.34	726	205	123
Lk 23.34	727	206	124
Lk 23.35	730	206	124

Verse	Page (2021)	Page (1837)	Chapter (1837)
Lk 23.36-23.37	731	206	124
Lk 23.39	731	206	124
Lk 23.39-23.43	731-732	207	124
Lk 23.44	See Mk 15.33&	——	——
Lk 23.46	735	207	125
Lk 23.47	See Mt 27.54&	——	——
Lk 23.48	737	208	125
Lk 23.49	738	208	125
Lk 23.49&	738	208	125
Lk 23.52&	741	209	127
Lk 23.54	See Jn 19.42&	——	——
Lk 23.55&	744	210	127
Lk 23.56	744	210	127
Lk 24.1	See Mk 16.2&	——	——
Lk 24.3-24.4	749	211	129
Lk 24.5	750	211	129
Lk 24.5	See Mk 16.5&	——	——
Lk 24.6-24.7	751	211	129
Lk 24.8	752	212	129
Lk 24.9-11	760	214	132
Lk 24.12	754	212	129
Lk 24.13-24.21	761-763	214	133
Lk 24.21-24.35	763-766	215	133
Lk 24.36&	767	216	134
Lk 24.37-24.40	768	216	134
Lk 24.41-24.43	769	216	134
Lk 24.44-24.47	770-771	216	134
Lk 24.48	771	217	134
Lk 24.49	785	220	138
Lk 24.50-24.51	787	221	138
Lk 24.51	See Mk 16.19&	——	——
Lk 24.52		221	138
Lk 24.53		221	138
John			
Jn 1.1-1.14	1-4	5	1
Jn 1.15-1.18	4-5	6	1
Jn 1.19-1.28	54-57	21	14
Jn 1.29-1.42	57-60	22	15
Jn 1.43-1.51	60-62	23	15
Jn 2.1-2.5	62-63	23	16
Jn 2.6-2.11	63-65	24	16
Jn 2.12-2.17	65-66	24	17
Jn 2.17-2.25	66-68	25	17

Verse	Page (2021)	Page (1837)	Chapter (1837)
Jn 3.1-3.4	68-69	25	18
Jn 3.5-3.18	70-73	26	18
Jn 3.18-21	73-74	27	18
Jn 3.22-3.30	74-76	27	19
Jn 3.31-3.36	76-78	28	19
Jn 4.1-4.9	78-79	28	20
Jn 4.9-4.23	80-83	29	20
Jn 4.23-4.38	83-86	30	20
Jn 4.39-4.42	86-87	31	20
Jn 4.43-4.52	87-89	31	21
Jn 4.52-4.54	90	32	21
Jn 5.1-5.10	90-92	32	22
Jn 5.11-5.23	93-95	33	22
Jn 5.24-5.36	96-99	34	22
Jn 5.37-5.47	99-101	35	22
Jn 6.5-6.7	251-252	79	45
Jn 6.8-6.10	252-253	79	45
Jn 6.10-6.11	253	79	45
Jn 6.12-6.13	253-254	79	45
Jn 6.14	254	79	45
Jn 6.15	255	80	46
Jn 6.19	255	80	46
Jn 6.22-Jn 6.31	258-262	81	47
Jn 6.32-6.45	262-265	82	47
Jn 6.45-6.58	265-269	83	47
Jn 6.59-6.71	269-272	84	47
Jn 7.1-7.16	290-294	90	53
Jn 7.17-7.31	294-297	91	53
Jn 7.31-7.46	298-301	92	53
Jn 7.47-7.53	301-302	93	53
Jn 8.1-8.10	303-305	93	54
Jn 8.10-8.23	305-309	94	54
Jn 8.24-8.39	309-313	95	54
Jn 8.39-8.52	313-317	96	54
Jn 8.52-8.59	317-319	97	54
Jn 9.1-9.7	319-320	97	55
Jn 9.7-9.21	320-325	98	55
Jn 9.21-9.36	325-328	99	55
Jn 9.37-9.41	328-329	100	55
Jn 10.1-10.11	329-332	100	55
Jn 10.11-10.21	332-335	101	55
Jn 10.22-10.24	335	101	56
Jn 10.25-10.39	336-339	102	56
Jn 10.40-Jn 10.42	339-340	103	56

Verse	Page (2021)	Page (1837)	Chapter (1837)
Jn 11.1-11.16	474-478	141	82
Jn 11.17	478	142	82
Jn 11.18-11.19	478	142	82
Jn 11.20-11.37	478-482	142	82
Jn 11.38-11.51	482-486	143	82
Jn 11.51-11.57	486-488	144	82
Jn 12.1-2	503	148	86
Jn 12.2	503	148	86
Jn 12.3	504	148	86
Jn 12.3	See Mt 26.7&	——	——
Jn 12.3-12.6	504-505	149	86
Jn 12.7&	506	149	86
Jn 12.9-12.11	507	149	86
Jn 12.12	See Lk 19.29&		
Jn 12.12-12.13	509	150	87
Jn 12.13	See Mt 21.9&		
Jn 12.16	513	151	87
Jn 12.17-12.19	513-514	151	88
Jn 12.20-12.26	518-519	152	89
Jn 12.26-12.39	519-523	153	89
Jn 12.40-12.43	523-524	154	89
Jn 12.44-12.50	524-526	154	90
Jn 13.1-13.4	614-616	176	104
Jn 13.4-13.20	616-619	177	104
Jn 13.20-13.27	620-621	178	104
Jn 13.27-13.30	621-622	178	104
Jn 13.31-13.35	626-627	179	107
Jn 13.36-13.38	628	180	107
Jn 14.1-14.11	628-631	180	107
Jn 14.11-14.24	631-636	181	107
Jn 14.25-14.31	636-638	182	107
Jn 15.1-15.10	647-650	185	110
Jn 15.11-15.24	650-653	186	110
Jn 15.24-15.27	654	187	110
Jn 16.1-16.13	655-657	187	110
Jn 16.13-16.23	657-661	188	110
Jn 16.24-16.33	661-664	189	110
Jn 17.1-17.3	664-665	189	110
Jn 17.4-17.16	665-669	190	110
Jn 17.16-17.26	669-672	191	110
Jn 18.1	672	191	111
Jn 18.1-18.2	674	192	112
Jn 18.3	See Mk 14.43&	——	——
Jn 18.4-18.7	680-681	193	113

Verse	Page (2021)	Page (1837)	Chapter (1837)
Jn 18.8-18.9	681-682	194	113
Jn 18.10	683-684	194	113
Jn 18.11	684	194	113
Jn 18.11	See Mt 26.52&	——	——
Jn 18.12-18.4	686-687	195	114
Jn 18.15-17	688	195	114
Jn 18.17	See Lk 22.56-57&	——	——
Jn 18.18	689	195	114
Jn 18.19-18.20	690	195	114
Jn 18.20-18.23	690-691	196	114
Jn 18.24	687	195	114
Jn 18.25	See Lk 22.58&	——	——
Jn 18.26-27	See Lk 22.59-60&	——	——
Jn 18.26-27	See Lk 22.59-60&	——	——
Jn 18.28	701	198	116
Jn 18.28	See Mt 27.2&	——	——
Jn 18.28-18.31	704-705	199	118
Jn 18.32	705	200	118
Jn 18.33	706	200	119
Jn 18.33-18.38	706-708	200	119
Jn 18.39	713	202	120
Jn 18.40	715	202	120
Jn 19.3	718	203	121
Jn 19.4-19.7	719-720	203	122
Jn 19.7-19.16	720-723	204	122
Jn 19.17	723	204	123
Jn 19.18	See Lk 23.33&	——	——
Jn 19.19-19.22	728-729	206	124
Jn 19.23-19.24	727	205	124
Jn 19.24	727-728	206	124
Jn 19.25-19.27	732-733	207	125
Jn 19.28-19.29	734	207	125
Jn 19.30	735	207	125
Jn 19.30	735	208	125
Jn 19.31-19.34	738-739	208	126
Jn 19.35-19.37	739-740	209	126
Jn 19.38	See Mk 15.45&	——	——
Jn 19.39-19.41	742-743	209	127
Jn 19.41	742-743	209	127
Jn 19.42&	743	209	127
Jn 20.2	748-749	211	129
Jn 20.3-20.10	752-754	212	129
Jn 20.11-20.13	755	212	130
Jn 20.13-20.17	756-757	213	130

Verse	Page (2021)	Page (1837)	Chapter (1837)
Jn 20.18	See Mk 16.10&	———	———
Jn 20.19	767	216	134
Jn 20.19&	767	216	134
Jn 20.20	768-769	216	134
Jn 20.21-20.25	771-772	217	134
Jn 20.26-20.29	772-773	217	135
Jn 21.1-21.2	774	217	136
Jn 21.3-21.15	774-778	218	136
Jn 21.15-21.23	778-781	219	136
Acts 1.3-1.4	784-785	220	138
Acts 1.5-1.6	785-786	220	138
Acts 1.7-1.9	786-787	221	138
Acts 1.9	787	221	138
Acts 1.10-1.11	788	221	138
Acts 1.12	789	221	138
Acts 1.18	702	199	117
1 Cor 11.25	642	183	108
1 Cor 15.5	760	214	132
1 Cor 15.6	782	219	137

www.ingramcontent.com/pod-product-compliance
Lightning Source LLC
Chambersburg PA
CBHW060418010526
44118CB00017B/2268